A VIEW OF VENICE

A View *of* Venice

Portrait *of a* Renaissance City

9 Kristin Love Huffman,
EDITOR

DUKE UNIVERSITY PRESS   *Durham and London*   2024

Cover art Jacopo de' Barbari, *View of Venice* (detail), ca. 1497–1500. Woodblock print on six sheets, 137.7 × 277.5 cm. The John R. Van Derlip Fund (2010.88), Minneapolis Institute of Art. Duke Digital Repository: 10.7924/G8MK69TH. Colorization created by Kristin Love Huffman, Ludovica Galeazzo, and Hannah Jacobs.

© 2024 DUKE UNIVERSITY PRESS

Printed in China on acid-free paper ∞

Project Editor: Liz Smith
Designed by A. Mattson Gallagher

Typeset in Arno Pro by A. Mattson Gallagher and Copperline Book Services

The author gratefully acknowledges support from the National Endowment of the Humanities–Mellon Foundation, which helped make this book possible.

Duke University Press gratefully acknowledges the Venetian Research Program at The Gladys Krieble Delmas Foundation; the Renaissance Society of America–Samuel H. Kress Foundation; the Trinity College of Arts & Sciences at Duke University; the Department of Art, Art History & Visual Studies at Duke University; and Furthermore: a program of the J. M. Kaplan Fund, which provided funds toward the publication of this book.

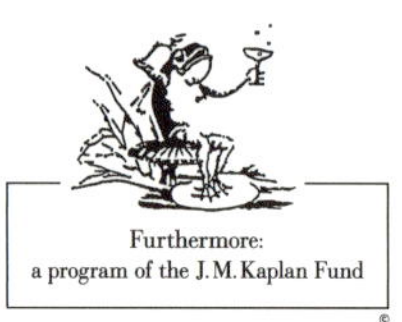

Library of Congress Cataloging-in-Publication Data

Names: Huffman, Kristin Love, editor.
Title: A view of Venice : portrait of a Renaissance city / Kristin Love Huffman.
Description: Durham : Duke University Press, 2024. | Includes bibliographical references and index.
Identifiers: LCCN 2023001611 (print)
LCCN 2023001612 (ebook)
ISBN 9781478019176 (paperback)
ISBN 9781478016533 (hardcover)
ISBN 9781478023807 (ebook)
Subjects: LCSH: Barbari, Jacopo de', active 15th century. Venetie MD. | Wood-engraving, Italian—Italy—Venice. | Art, Renaissance—Italy—Venice. | Architecture, Renaissance—Italy—Venice. | Venice (Italy)—Maps—Early works to 1800. | Venice (Italy)—Aerial views—Early works to 1800. | Venice (Italy)—Pictorial works—Early works to 1800. | Venice (Italy)—History. | BISAC: ART / History / Renaissance
Classification: LCC NE1300.8.I82 B345 2024 (print) | LCC NE1300.8.I82 (ebook) | DDC 769.92—dc23/eng/20230817
LC record available at https://lccn.loc.gov/2023001611
LC ebook record available at https://lccn.loc.gov/2023001612

CONTENTS

ILLUSTRATIONS

Illustrations

xii

ABBREVIATIONS

Libraries and Museums

Venetian Archival Terminology

Abbreviations

fol.
foglio (page or sheet)

inv.
inventario (inventory)

ms./mss.
manoscritto/manuscritti (manuscript/
manuscripts)

n.
numero (number)

proc.
processo (legal record)

prot.
protocollo (record)

qd.
quondam (formerly)

reg.
registro (register)

ACKNOWLEDGMENTS

The many multifaceted exchanges that occur over the life of a large-scale, collaborative publication invariably net unimaginable riches. The conception, development, and completion of this volume, with its complex network of authors, organizations, and now readers, is no exception. It is my hope that those who peruse its contents—text and images—intuit these dynamic and synergistic exchanges: a confluence of viewpoints and disciplinary methodologies among scholars made possible by the intersecting magnanimity of museums, institutions, and nonprofit granting foundations. It is also an aspiration that the collective volume and its individual essays express an overarching passion for Venice and the iconic image, more than five hundred years old, that forms its focus.

First, I would like to thank the authors of this volume, who not only contributed their scholarly expertise but also demonstrated indefatigable patience during the editing and review process, which largely occurred over the challenge of the COVID pandemic. The following authors also offered precious guidance at various moments: Karen-edis Barzman, Patricia Fortini Brown, Stanley Chojnacki, Tracy Cooper, Blake de Maria, Holly Hurlburt, and Mary Pardo. Cherished colleagues and students provided editorial and imagery assistance at the very moments when their talents were most needed: a special thanks to Dana Hogan for her insightful recommendations and invaluable contributions; to John Taormina, who read the volume from cover to cover; to Jehangir Malegam and Kristen Neuschel, who provided suggestions about the front matter; to Hannah Jacobs and former students Noah Michaud and Daphne Turan, who each made noteworthy interventions with the imagery; and to colleagues at Duke Libraries, especially Sean Aery and Will Sexton, for making the high-resolution image of the *View* available to the public in the Duke Digital Repository. The anonymous peer reviewers offered their own bird's-eye view—unparalleled perspectives and practical suggestions that helped the volume take its final shape. I am grateful to them for their time and commitment, especially noteworthy given they receive unnamed recognition.

Important museums and institutions deserve special acknowledgment for their facilitation of this in-depth study on the *View of Venice*. These include the Museo Correr (part of the Musei Civici di Venezia) and its director, Andrea Bellieni, and senior curator, Valeria Cafà. I remain grateful to the Minneapolis Institute of Art for the loan of the *View* for my exhibition in 2017 and to Rachel McGarry, who orchestrated its arrival at Duke University; a debt of gratitude to the Nasher Museum of Art and its then director, Sarah Schroth, who graciously hosted the exhibition and a scholarly symposium for our academic and broader community. Finally, I would like to thank the National Gallery of Art in Washington, D C, and colleagues there, namely Jonathan Bober, Michelle Facini, Ginger Hammer, Peter Lukehart, Steven Nelson, and Eve Straussman-Pflanzer, for their encouragement of this project and my work on Jacopo de' Barbari. Duke University, Trinity College of Arts and Sciences, the Department of Art, Art History & Visual Studies, and its Digital Art History & Visual Culture Research Lab (formerly Wired!) provided institutional infrastructure and initial financial support; in particular, I would like to thank Caroline Bruzelius, Sheila Dillon, Paul Jaskot, Neil McWilliam, and Gennifer Weisenfeld. *Visualizing Venice / Visualizing Cities* colleagues also played a role in early intellectual exchanges; they include Donatella Calabi, Ludovica Galeazzo, Andrea Giordano, Gianmario Giudarelli, Cosimo Monteleone, and Elena Svalduz. While I have greatly benefited from above-mentioned individuals and their various insights, any outstanding need for improvement with the book remains solely my own.

Finally, it bears underscoring that this publication would not have been possible without subventions from the foundations that generously awarded it based solely on its potential. These include the Furthermore Foundation, the Gladys Krieble Delmas Foundation, the National Endowment of the

Acknowledgments

Humanities–Mellon Foundation, and the Samuel H. Kress Foundation via the Renaissance Society of America. This volume has benefited greatly not only from their financial beneficence but also their trust and scholarly sponsorship; I hope that it elicits pride for their indispensable support. Last of all, I would like to thank Duke University Press, its governing board, the many editors and designers who assiduously contributed to the volume's production, in particular Liz Smith and A. Mattson Gallagher, and above all executive editor Courtney Berger for an unwavering commitment to its publication.

On a more personal note, I would like to acknowledge those individuals who offered steadfast encouragement—indispensable, even if largely invisible. Christiana and Bob Kernodle, Ayda Haddad, and Carol Magee loyally accompanied the highs and lows of realizing a complex publication. A good part of Henri and Simon Lanzoni's maturation into young adults paralleled the ripening of my research on the *View*, Jacopo de' Barbari, and this book. The awe-inspiring "sisters"—my mom Janet Huffman and aunts Barbara Holland, Cathy Van Dyke, and Terry Van Dyke—routinely expressed curiosity. And immeasurable thanks to Deanna Kashdan, my sister and confidante; during travel restrictions from the pandemic, our time together on the west coast of Florida reconfirmed my devotion to a city built in the middle of a brackish lagoon, an ecosystem not unlike that of our childhood. Finally, one person's presence, that of Allison Sherman, never lapsed despite her absence. This volume is dedicated in memory of her as an exceptional colleague and friend.

Story of the Edited Volume

Jacopo de' Barbari's *View of Venice*, first published in 1500 under the direction of the German merchant Anton Kolb, visually captured the Renaissance city as a moment suspended in time (plate 1). A monumental woodcut print, the *View* features Venice's urban fabric gracefully interwoven with its aqueous environment—a tessellation of over 120 small, interconnected islands. The siting of buildings and their orientation adapted to requisite aquatic access to, and movement throughout, the city. The woodcut's refinement draws attention to Venice's architecture and distinctive features: ornamented government spaces, churches with expansive gardens, palaces with frescoed façades, elaborately engineered bridges, boats that point to the city's maritime tradition. The printed cityscape presents an urban phenomenon that seemingly defies the imagination, even today.

A View of Venice: Portrait of a Renaissance City is the culmination of a collaborative, multidimensional digital humanities project related to the *View of Venice*. An exhibition at Duke University's Nasher Museum of Art in 2017, *A Portrait of Venice: Jacopo de' Barbari's* View *of 1500*, featured seven digital displays as companions to the extraordinary woodcut print prominently on view—a new installation prototype. The original work of art, with its meticulous description of the urban fabric and idiosyncratic details, inspired engaged looking. Layer upon layer of curated content contained within the interactive displays, visual and written, encouraged further exploration of the woodcut print. The touchscreens not only brought Venice and its history to life for a broad and varied public, but they also celebrated the print's extraordinary visual content and the context of its production. Innovative visualization tools and strategies were as important for the *View's* conception and dissemination as they have been for the realization of this project, including the exhibition and this edited volume.

The occasion of the Nasher exhibition provided an exceptional opportunity to convene a symposium with international, interdisciplinary scholars of early modern Venice. Many essays here expand on those early, engaging presentations and ongoing conversations. Additional essays solicited from specialists complement this content as related to two broad themes: the *View* as a printed cartographic and artistic phenomenon; and the woodcut as a reflection of Venice and Venetian life. In addition to the original woodcut, scholars had access to the high-resolution image produced for the exhibition: the largest, highest-quality version available for study (Duke Digital Repository image 10.7924/G8MK69TH). The ability to look in an optimized way resulted in novel discoveries. The Nasher exhibition also created an opportunity to form a collaboration between Duke University and the Musei Civici di Venezia, including the Correr Museum in Venice, home to the six wooden blocks (matrices) used to print the *View* and two of the twelve extant first-state woodcuts. This partnership permitted a team of colleagues from *Visualizing Venice*, an international consortium of art and architectural historians, architects, engineers, and visual and media specialists, along with the staff from the Correr Museum, to conduct light laser scans of the wooden matrices. An installation featuring newly designed content from the original exhibition and analyses of scanned data will be on display at the Correr alongside the wooden blocks and the woodcut print, a project realized by the authors of this prologue.

    This edited volume is intended for anyone with a curiosity about Venice—from individuals with a recently adopted interest to those with a long-standing passion for the city. In addition, it may attract those interested in European history, the Renaissance, urban studies, and art and architectural history. The essays present original material and engaging content as they demonstrate the relevance and intrigue of an image published over five hundred years ago. The volume also reflects the serendipitous opportunities, remarkable exchanges, new findings, and privileged understandings of its many contributors, all of whom continue to derive great pleasure from the wonders Venice offers.

June 2022

Plates

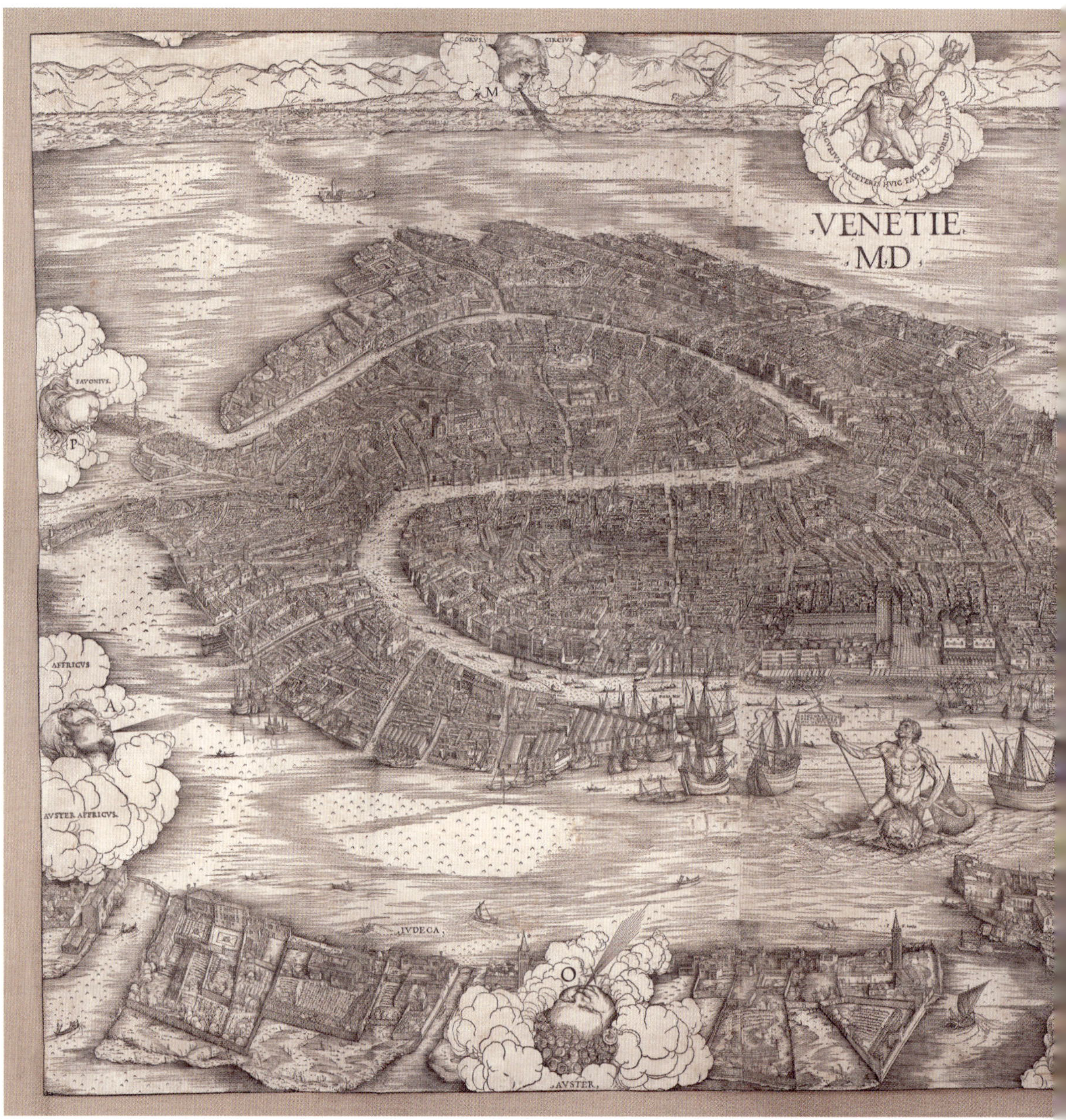

1

Jacopo de' Barbari, *View of Venice*, ca. 1497–1500. Woodblock print on six sheets, 137.7 × 277.5 cm. The John R. Van Derlip Fund (2010.88), Minneapolis Institute of Art.

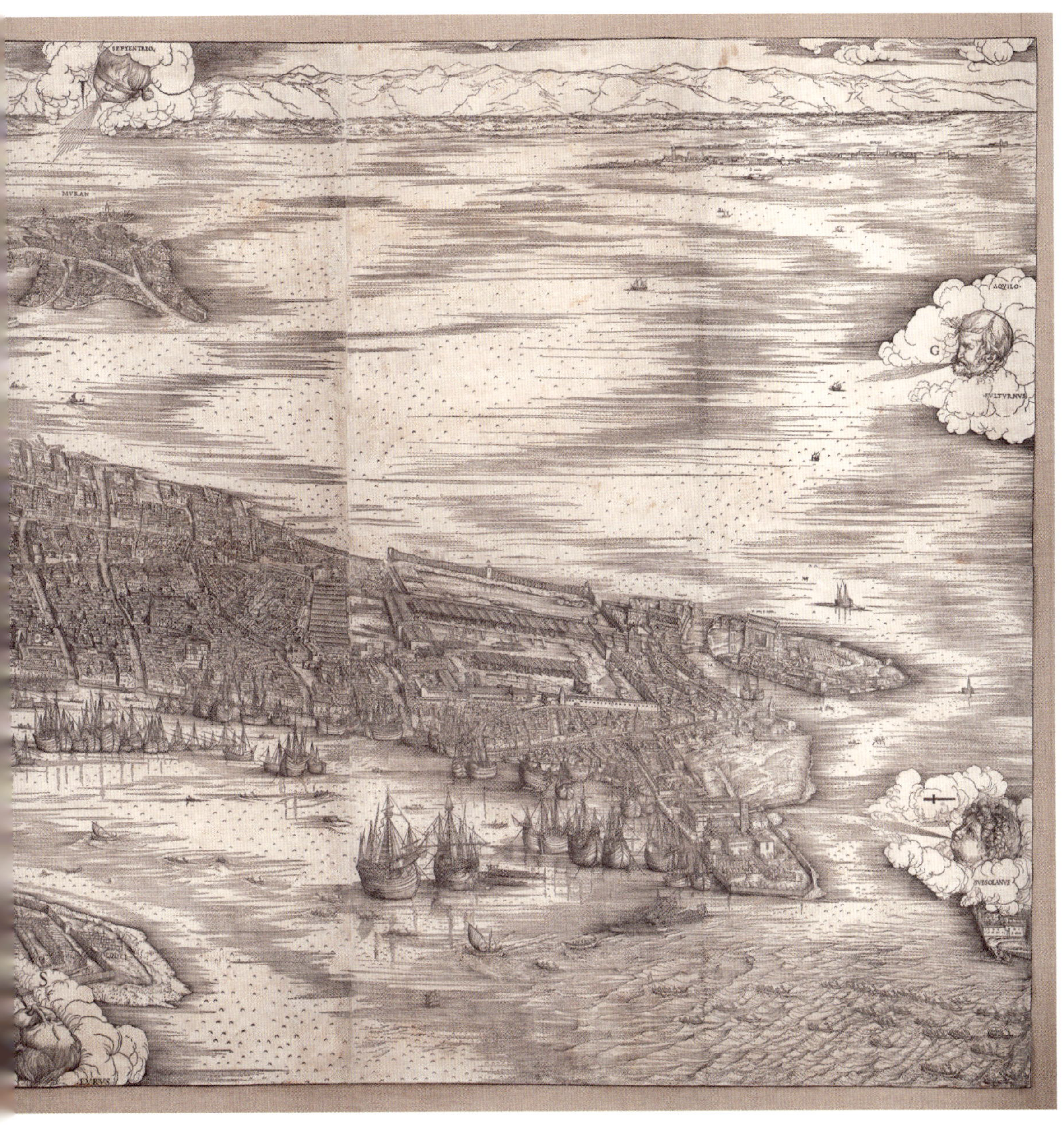

SEPTENTRIO
MVRAN
AQVILO
G
FVLTVRNVS
SVBSOLANVS
S
EVRVS

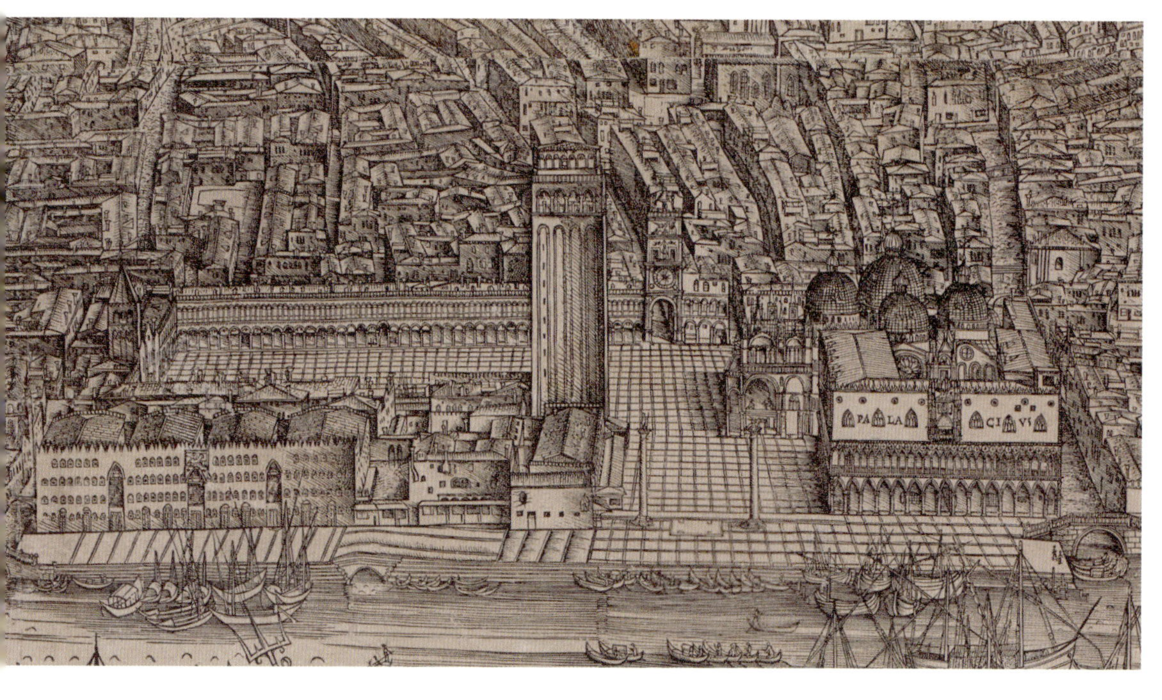

PA LA CI VS

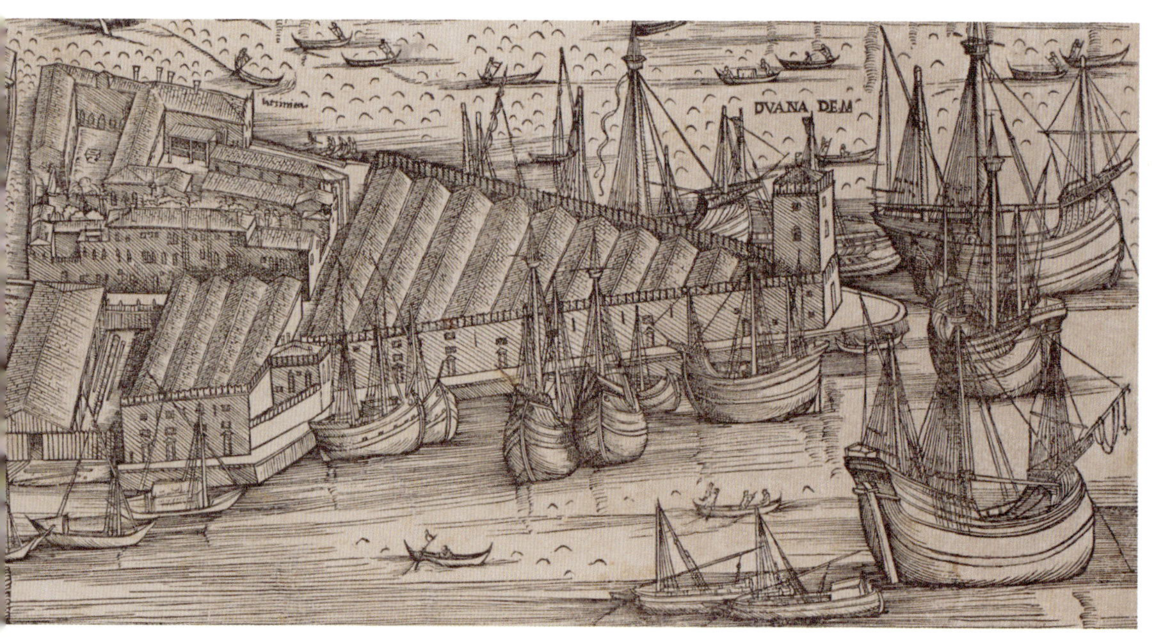

hrimin.
DVANA DE M

Detail of Piazza San Marco from
Jacopo de' Barbari, *View of Venice*,
ca. 1497–1500. Woodblock print on
six sheets, 137.7 × 277.5 cm. The
John R. Van Derlip Fund (2010.88),
Minneapolis Institute of Art.

Detail of the Customs House from
Jacopo de' Barbari, *View of Venice*,
ca. 1497–1500. Woodblock print on
six sheets, 137.7 × 277.5 cm. The
John R. Van Derlip Fund (2010.88),
Minneapolis Institute of Art.

Detail of the Rialto from Jacopo
de' Barbari, *View of Venice*, ca. 1497–
1500. Woodblock print on six sheets,
137.7 × 277.5 cm. The John R. Van
Derlip Fund (2010.88), Minneapolis
Institute of Art.

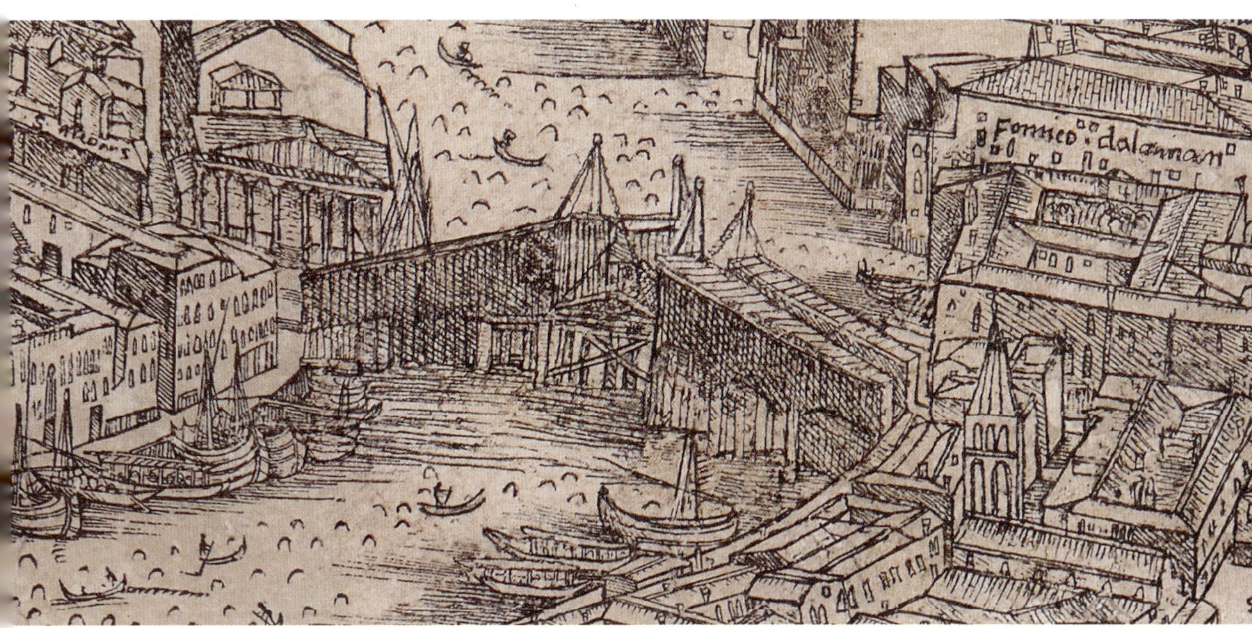

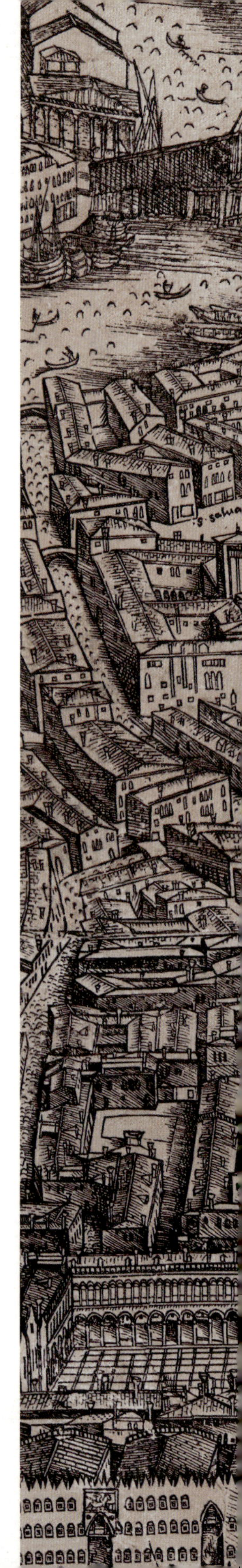

5

Detail of the Mercerie, highlighted, from Jacopo de' Barbari, *View of Venice*, ca. 1497–1500. Woodblock print on six sheets, 137.7 × 277.5 cm. The John R. Van Derlip Fund (2010.88), Minneapolis Institute of Art.

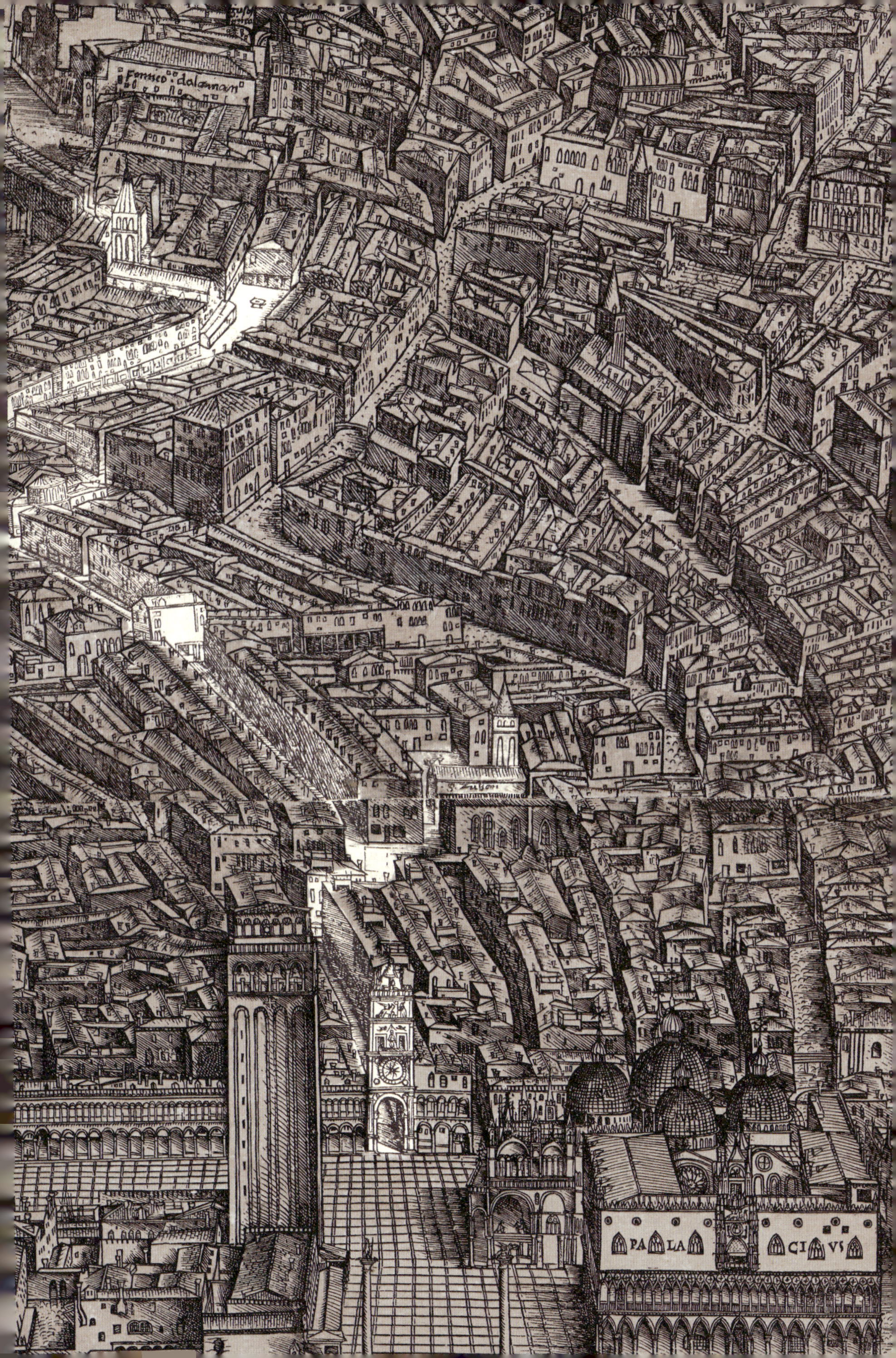

Fonteo dalamani
PA LA
CI VS

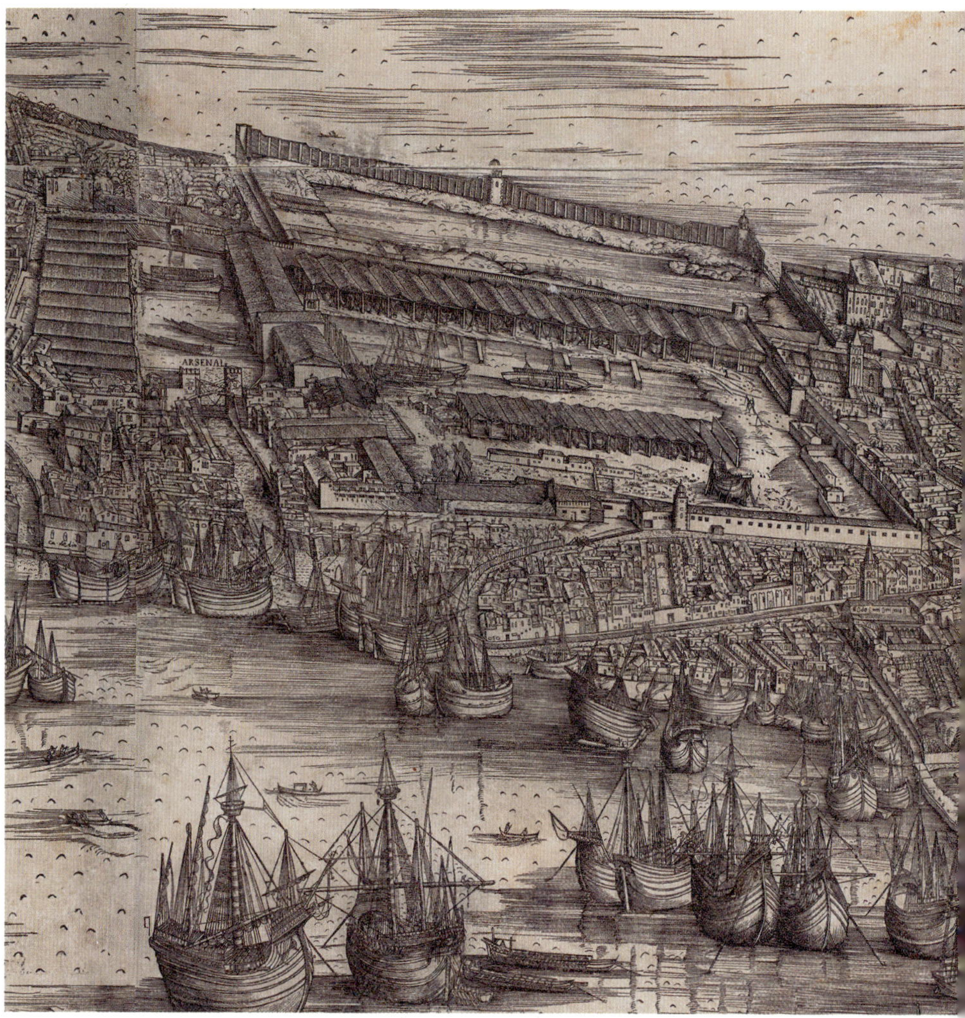

6

Detail of the Arsenal from Jacopo de' Barbari, *View of Venice*, ca. 1497–1500. Woodblock print on six sheets, 137.7 × 277.5 cm. The John R. Van Derlip Fund (2010.88), Minneapolis Institute of Art.

7 OPPOSITE

Details of Mercury (*above*) and Neptune (*below*) from Jacopo de' Barbari, *View of Venice*, ca. 1497–1500. Woodblock print on six sheets, 137.7 × 277.5 cm. The John R. Van Derlip Fund (2010.88), Minneapolis Institute of Art.

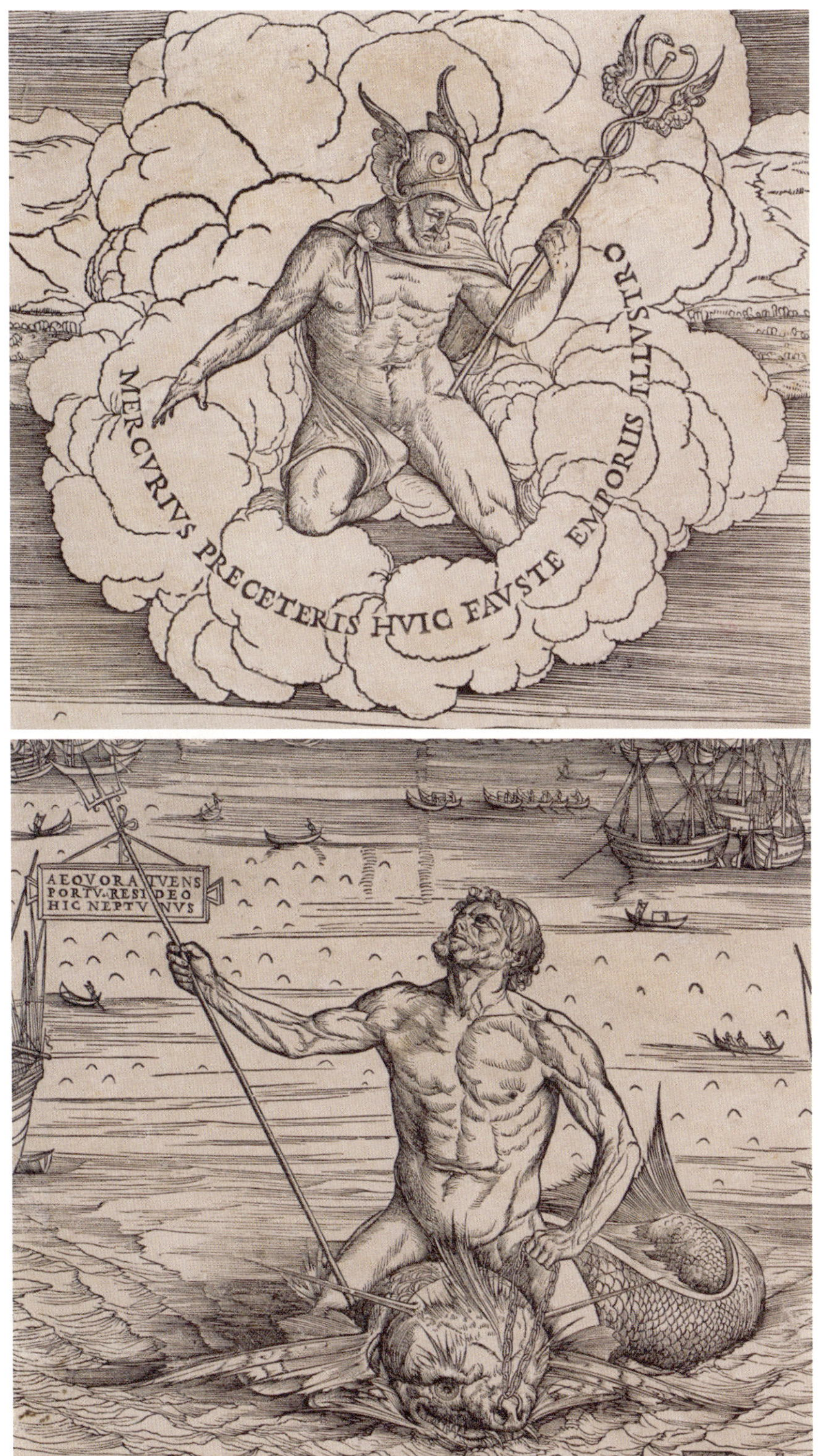
MERCVRIVS PRECETERIS HVIC FAVSTE EMPORIIS CRISATTI

AEQVORA TVENS
PORTV RESIDEO
HIC NEPTVNVS

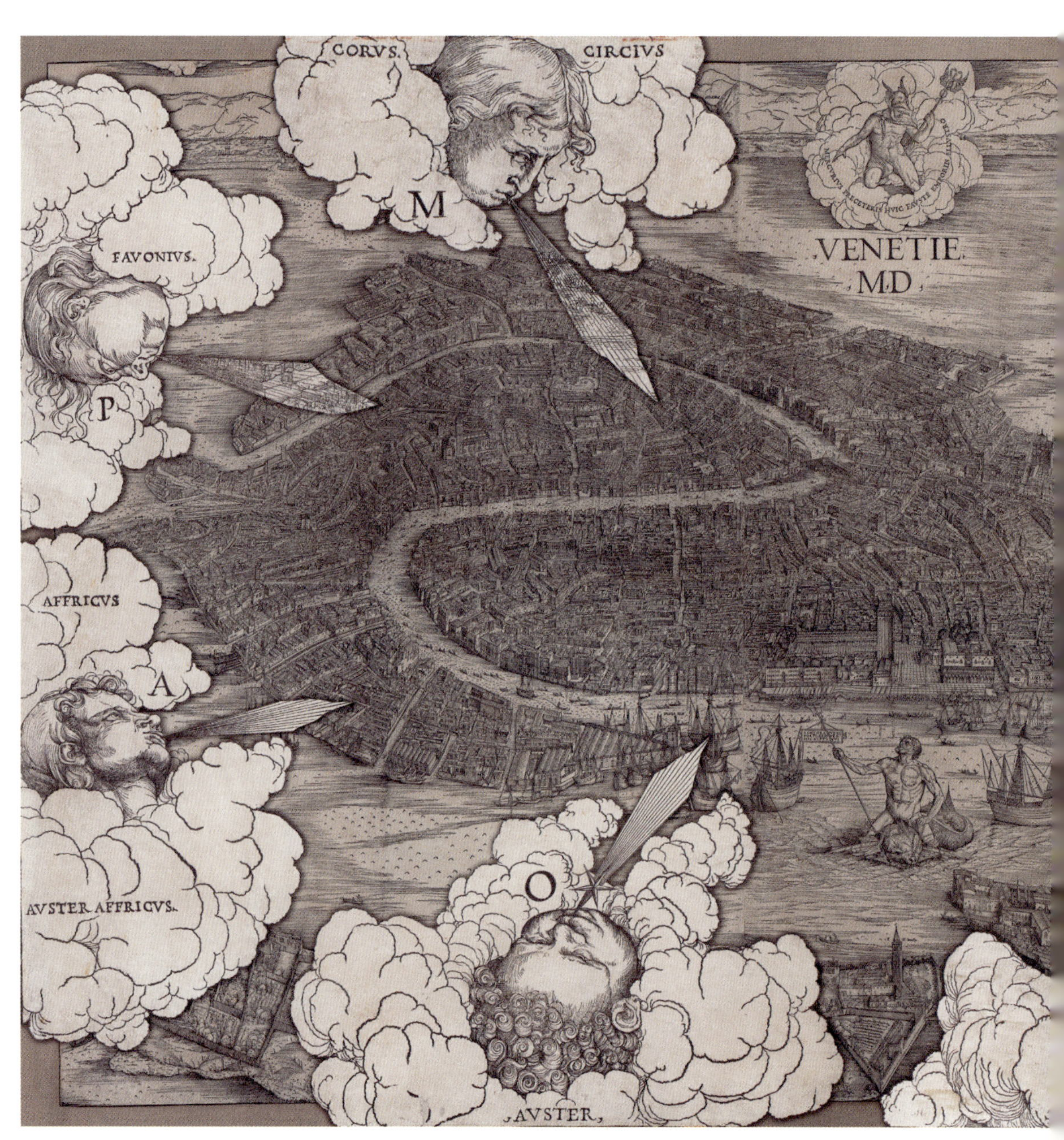

CORVS.
CIRCIVS
M
FAVONIVS.
P
VENETIE
M.D
AFFRICVS
A
AVSTER AFFRICVS.
O
AVSTER,

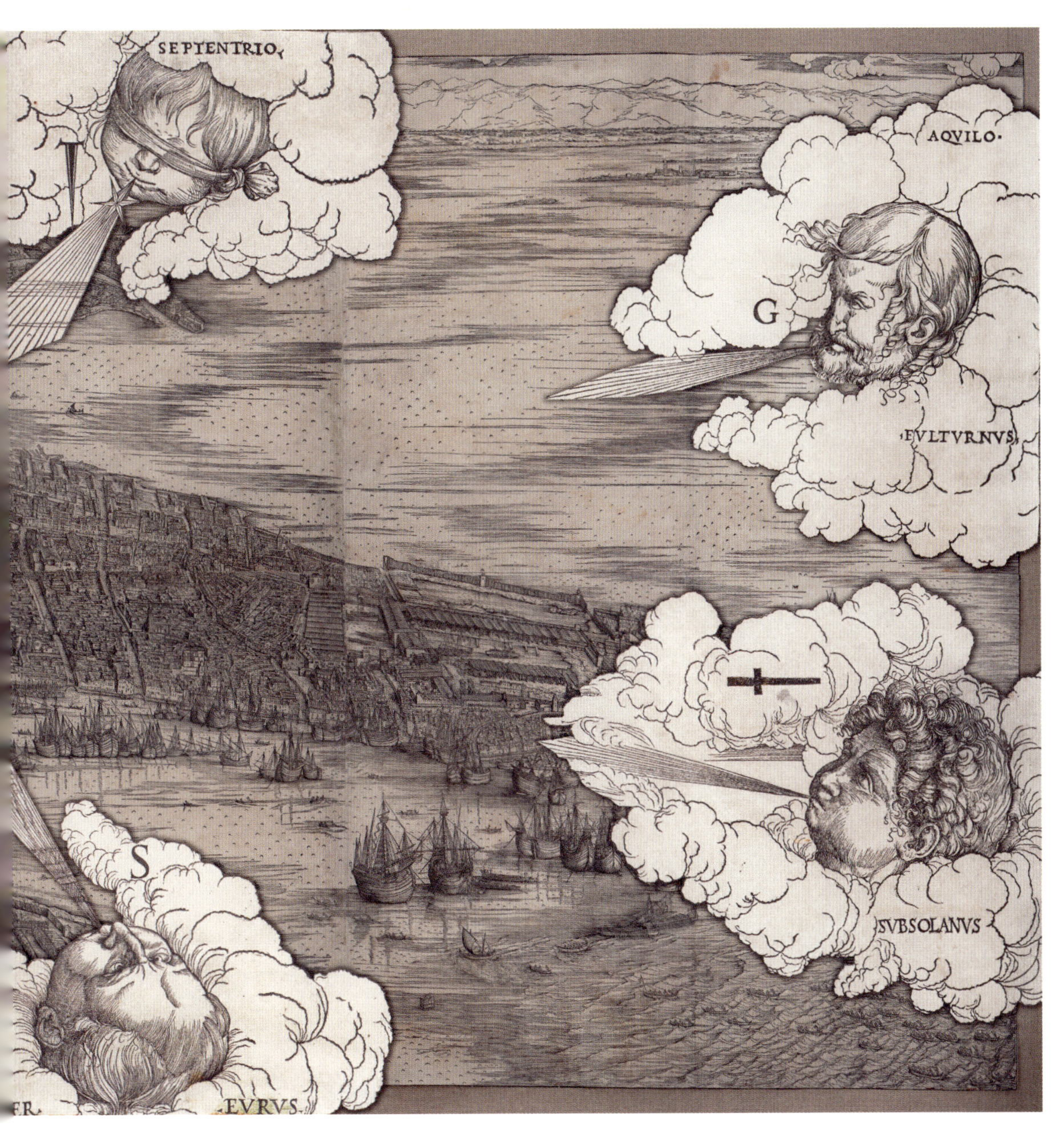
SEPTENTRIO.
AQVILO.
G
FVLTVRNVS.
S
SVBSOLANVS.
EVRVS.

Detail of the Winds, enlarged and
appearing clockwise from upper right:

SEPTENTRIO;

AQUILO—FVLTURNVS;

SVBSOLANVS;

EVRAVSTER—EVRVS;

AVSTER;

AFFRICVS—AVSTERAFFRICVS;

FAVONIVS;

CORVS—CIRCIVS.

Jacopo de' Barbari, *View of Venice*,
ca. 1497–1500. Woodblock print on
six sheets, 137.7 × 277.5 cm. The
John R. Van Derlip Fund (2010.88),
Minneapolis Institute of Art.

Kristin Love Huffman

Introduction

The *View* as an Urban Portrait

THE *VIEW OF VENICE*, ca. 1497–1500, is one of the greatest artistic and technological masterpieces of its time—a portrait of a distinctive Renaissance city (plate 1).[1] In unprecedented fashion, the woodcut print portrays Venice's unique morphology within an aqueous setting as it meticulously describes the city's urban fabric and idiosyncratic details. Additional pictorial elements promote the *View*'s message as a glorification of the Venetian state. The ancient gods, Mercury and Neptune, align to safeguard the city, while inscriptions accompanying them make clear their protection over the state's commercial interests and its maritime dominion (plate 7). The mountainous landscape that frames the top includes toponyms to indicate Venetian territorial possessions on the mainland and passageway to northern Europe. Personified winds, including the blindfolded Tramontane blowing down from the Alps and Apennines in the North, surround the periphery of this bird's-eye view like a map's compass rose (plate 8). Framing the lower border, islands such as those of the Giudecca and San Giorgio are tilted and magnified to reveal luxurious gardens otherwise hidden behind private villas and monastic complexes. A conspicuously labeled regatta on the lower right showcases the leisure activities that only the most thriving of Renaissance cities could afford. Venice is here jubilantly triumphant: visible evidence of its wealth and power recorded with timeless splendor.

Kristin Love
Huffman

Also known as *Venetie MD*, an emblematic title emblazoned at the top to signal a printing date at the turn of a demi-millennium, the iconic image celebrates Venice at the peak of its international authority. Yet the printed image is far more than a celebration of the city's mythical identity; it is also a manifesto of Renaissance thought. As an innovative print, it embodies the city's cultural status as a center for the production of knowledge, capitalizing on the new technology of the printing press to circulate and promote information (real and imagined) in written and visual terms. A groundbreaking scientific and artistic invention, the *View* was printed on six separate sheets of high-quality paper, the largest produced in Europe at the time, from six exquisitely carved, large-scale wooden blocks known as matrices. Its monumental composite dimensions (more than 1.35 by 2.75 meters), its complexities of production, and its groundbreaking scientific and artistic invention signal the scope of the project. Its elusive but well-connected artist, Jacopo de' Barbari (ca. 1460/70–1516), and its ambitious German sponsor, Anton Kolb (ca. 1471–1541), suggest a large-scale collaborative enterprise with an international agenda. Recognizing the *View*'s magnitude, novelty, and prowess, in October 1500 the Venetian state granted Kolb one of the earliest known copyright permissions for a printed image (see appendix 2).

The *View of Venice* assumes the general characteristics of a Renaissance portrait in its tension between perceived realism and idealization. Visual enhancements and optical alterations include a composite of multiple viewpoints that enliven and enrich a viewer's observations. De' Barbari manipulated the bird's-eye view to distinguish Venice's unique *forma urbis* and to emphasize site-specific locations, permitting more of the city to be seen. Piazza San Marco with the Ducal Palace, seat of Venetian governance on the square's eastern edge, appears almost straight on (plate 2). Not only did the architecture and its decorative detail in this principal civic space confirm the mythic identity of Venice, but it also flaunted Venetian confidence and awareness of its natural lagoon defenses. The two columns featuring the city's Christian patron saints, Saint Theodore and Saint Mark, boundary markers that signal the formal entrance into Venice, highlight the absence of traditional, fortified gates enclosing most other Renaissance city-states.

The Arsenal, a companion locus to the Ducal Palace for securing state secrets, is inclined so as to permit onlookers to peer over its walls (plate 6), otherwise not visible if rendered according to Renaissance codes of linear perspective. There, military ships for Venetian fleets and mercantile vessels intended for voyage to exotic places, such as Alexandria and Beirut, Flanders and India, were built with scientific acumen and noteworthy speed. While many ships were routinely anchored there, select vessels coming into the city would have first stopped at the Customs House, where taxes were paid on merchandise for trade carried deeper into the city by smaller barges (plate 3). Visibly moving up the Grand Canal, many of these smaller barges traveled to the Rialto Bridge, the only link across the Grand Canal connecting the city's two halves (*de ultra* and *de citra*) and the focal point of a densely concentrated commercial zone (plate 4). This location, also angled for better viewing, connects back to San Marco via an economic corridor of paved, interconnected streets lined with over three hundred shops, the Mercerie (plate 5). Its triumphal entryway from Piazza San Marco is framed by the Clocktower, a technological and artistic marvel of its own, realized in the same years as the *View*. In addition to the visual manipulation of vital administrative and commercial centers, optical enhancements recommence as the eye meanders into the city's interstices to follow the pathways of interconnecting and intersecting streets, squares, and canals.

The *View of Venice*, in capturing such intrinsic detail, has continued to incite awe and intrigue among scholars and the general public despite conundrums surrounding its production—the exact "how" and "why" it was made. This edited volume contributes new considerations and enhances understandings about Jacopo de' Barbari's and Anton Kolb's iconic woodcut impression of Venice and its many cultural facets. It also presents original scholarship and new archival evidence about Renaissance Venice. As the essays in this volume highlight, the epic portrait of Venice constitutes a cartographic exercise, a documentation of important places and spaces *and* a work of art that calls attention to its own artifice and technical expertise. At the same time, it celebrates a unique city. The *View* implicitly signals, as select essays maintain, the life of a vibrant Renaissance city, its regulatory patterns and governance (secular and ecclesiastic), and the intersecting networks of people who resided there and experienced it, natives and foreigners alike, much like Jacopo de' Barbari and Anton Kolb.

The volume is therefore divided into two parts. The first, centripetally conceived, contains essays that delineate the *View* as an advanced product of the artistic, humanist, and scientific culture of the Renaissance world. The essays that form the second part, more centrifugally conceived, relate to the urban systems and lived experiences of early modern Venice—its unique identity and idiosyncrasies, its social, political, and economic infrastructures, and its cosmopolitan residents. Using de' Barbari's image as a point of departure, each of the essays has been conceived as stand-alone even though interrelated themes weave throughout the two parts and across them.

The *View* as a Printed Cartographic and Artistic Visualization (Part I)

The essays in part I expand understandings of the scientific strategies as well as artistic and theoretical paradigms for interpreting the cooperative elements of this extraordinary and, at the time, incomparable representation of a city. The *View of Venice*, published as a set of six woodcuts to form a monumental composite image, shows that there was a receptive, culturally sophisticated market for innovative topographical prints. Its more than three-year realization highlights the woodcut as a product of technological advancements in printmaking and international collaboration. Part I contextualizes the *View*'s artistic genesis and offers insights into Jacopo de' Barbari, whose elusive career in Venice remains undocumented. De' Barbari's *View*—a visual record of Venice *and* a timeless view—gives full expression to the kaleidoscope of places that constitute the city and sheds light on its artistic communities. As the essays in this part make known, the world of Jacopo de' Barbari represents a moment of rich transnational cultural exchange—one that spurred artistic and scientific invention across the Alps, notably in Nuremberg: works on paper were the ideal vehicles for the circulation of imaginative expression.

Venice and Nuremberg, the native city of Anton Kolb, were two of the most vibrant cultural centers in the world. An important north–south land route across the Alps connected the cities, an axis that facilitated not only trade but also the steady flow of ideas. The circulation of the *Nuremberg Chronicle* (*Liber chronicarum*, 1493) exemplified this flow of knowledge.

4

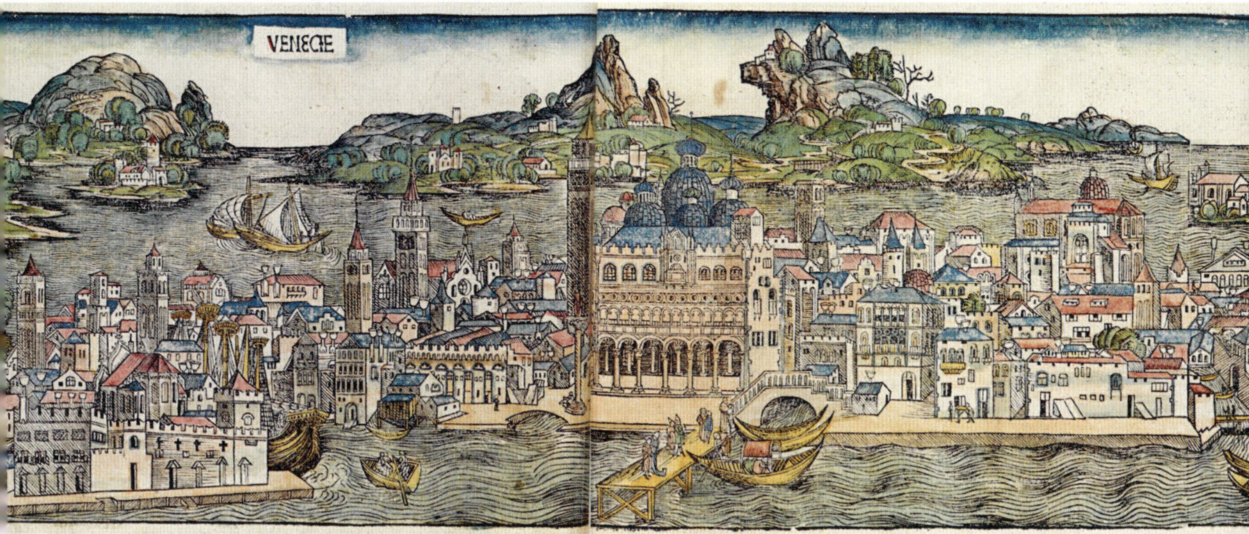

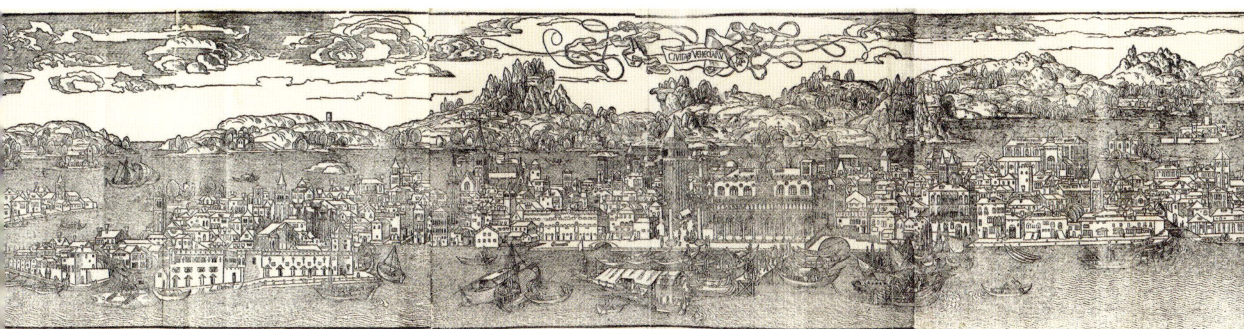

A masterpiece of early printing, the book was also the most extensively il-lustrated incunable (among the earliest books printed prior to 1501), a task undertaken by Michael Wolgemut (ca. 1434/37–1519). The illustrations included early city views in the form of profile renderings such as that of Venice (fig. I.1). Wolgemut's modestly scaled representation of Venice in the *Nuremberg Chronicle* derives from his understanding of Erhard Reuwich's *Civitas veneciarum* (fig. I.2) in *Peregrinatio in Terram Sanctam*, a book by Bernhard von Breydenbach, first published in Mainz in 1486. This woodcut image, a large-scale panoramic view of Venice, first established the type. Reu-wich's illustration, measuring around 30 by 163.5 centimeters and printed on four sheets that folded out from the book containing it, highlighted Venice as a port of passage for pilgrims en route to the Holy Land.

5

Karen-edis Barzman's essay opens part I, placing the *View* within the early history of city views, like Reuwich's, and of state-sponsored representations of Venetian territorial possessions. She has identified a pivotal year, 1460 (1459 *more veneto*[2]), and a government mandate that disclosed a desire by Venetian state officials to have informed geographic knowledge about the world and Venice's place in it. Barzman has discovered a treasure trove of state-commissioned maps of Venetian sites that constitute an early geographic archive, or analog GIS (geographic information system). These "eyewitness" visuals, often bird's-eye views, verified and supplemented the narrated accounts about the terrain and natural features of territories within the state's dominion. Such chorographic representations, or descriptive mapping, emerged as part of the ancient Ptolemaic tradition. In addition, understandings of Strabo's *Geography* (written ca. 7 BCE–17 CE), first translated into Latin in 1458 under the sponsorship of a Venetian patrician and government official, informed the labeling identifiers and units of measurement that became keys to reading these maps. Given this context, Barzman argues that the *View of Venice* and its seemingly ancillary features, such as the naming devices and winds, point to its mapping impulses.

Piero Falchetta furthers understandings of these maplike tendencies within the *View*. He first presents the historiography of the mapping debate among scholars regarding the *View*, leading readers to a consideration of Venice as a city of the world. He discusses the inclusion of the eight winds as a Ptolemaic convention to represent the world as a sphere and to help explain the distorted surfaces in the *View* that, according to him, scholars have misunderstood as indications of technological limitations. Rather, the application of this precept resulted in an invention—the first Ptolemaic perspective map of a city. Unsurprisingly, the mathematical plotting of fixed coordinates would have proven invaluable to a city that relied on seafaring trade and movement among maritime places. This value placed on mathematics as part of the scientific and artistic backdrop of fifteenth- and sixteenth-century Venice is outlined by Cosimo Monteleone in his essay. Indicating artists' access to known ancient mathematical treatises in the state's library, bequeathed to Venice in 1460 by Cardinal Bessarion (1403–72), along with contemporary manuscripts and printed books, he notes that the basic mapping of space would have used geometric models to translate measurable reality. Artists such as Leon Battista Alberti (1404–72), Piero della Francesca (ca. 1416/17–92), and de' Barbari's contemporary, Albrecht Dürer (1471–1528), codified these approaches in written and visual form.

Perspective and its geometric principles offered structure for divine perfection and cosmic order.

Directional order can also come through social networks as mapped within the *View*. Giorgio Tagliaferro offers a theoretical model for thinking about the *View* not merely as a topographical record but also as part of a lived experience, understood through the interconnections of spaces. He considers the movement of people and objects, focusing on the intrinsic qualities of a unique habitat. This would be important with respect to the artistic community and their interconnected professional and personal relationships. For painters, such as Giovanni Bellini (ca. 1431/36–1516) or Vincenzo Catena (ca. 1470/80–1531), the places where they resided, worked, and purchased materials necessary for their craft generated a series of social networks connected to place. In this, Tagliaferro offers a new way for art historians to think about the field, one that extends beyond technical or aesthetic questions.

Artists absorbed new trends via their circulation in Venice. A sense of shared community and exchange of ideas, even if not fully accounted for in surviving documents, is palpable in the interconnections of artistic communities. Although in Venice each craft organized and managed its own guild, collaborative projects would have brought artists and artisans together— painters with wooden frame makers, printmakers with artisans of paper, stone carvers with architects, and so forth. And while the guilds generally protected native Venetian artistic work from any perceived competition by foreign artists, at times, sojourns by those who traveled there and received occasional commissions within the city could also make an impact on the broader artistic community. Albrecht Dürer was one such artist, having apprenticed in Nuremberg with the illustrator of the *Nuremberg Chronicle*, Wolgemut, prior to making his first trip to Venice shortly after the book's publication in 1493. He, along with Jacopo de' Barbari, and their skills and knowledge, would have crossed the Alps via the Brenner Pass. Anna Christine Swartwood House points to the neglect of the margins in understanding the entirety of the *View*'s message, not just the urban form that tends to be the focus of scholarly considerations. In particular, the mountainous landscape that anchors the upper register of the *View* also functions as a mapping indicator, with named cities as guideposts that formed the trade route for the movement of people across the Brenner Pass, from Venice to the north. This was not only the route that people would have taken but also the guided path for the movement of objects and luxury goods, including printed materials—quite possibly the six sheets of the *View* and most certainly the *Nuremberg Chronicle*—to reach an export market abroad.

About sixty years before the *View*'s publication in 1500, the printing press was invented in Germany, and by the time early copies of the woodcut print were sold, Venice had become a leader in the industry. Immediately following the introduction of printing in Mainz, Germany, twelve other cultural and commercial centers established large book printing industries. While these urban centers each made contributions to book production, Venice stood as the leading manufacturer and trade center, qualitatively and quantitively. By 1500, the more than two hundred print shops were publishing the largest number of books of any European city. Subjects included philosophy, law, religion, classics, and science. The city's numerous foreign communities meant that texts were published in a variety of languages, some of which required the construction of new movable type for letters, such as Greek, Hebrew, and Arabic, distinctive from publications in Latin and the European vernaculars. Within these books of wide-ranging language and subject, printed text quickly aligned with woodcut imagery to illustrate content in novel ways and generate a growing artistic and aesthetic interest. Art and technology united to open new possibilities for the transmission of knowledge, written and visual.

Text and image about the Venetian state mutually reinforced one another. Monique O'Connell contextualizes the *View* as a part of the tradition in Venice of recording "truths" in written form. Humanist chronicles included the documentation of broader patterns of the Venetian past, such those written by Marcantonio Sabellico (1436–1506) and Bernardo Giustinian (1408–89), along with the diaries of Marin Sanudo (1466–1536) that detailed quotidian Venetian life, prosaic and extraordinary. These two literary approaches to documenting Venice's history—general praise and propaganda as well as detailed realism—are present in the *View*. O'Connell, however, leads us to a question that challenges traditional interpretations of the image: Was it a representation of the state at the peak of its prosperity or, rather, visual expression to occlude a watershed moment? In the years prior to the *View*'s publication, wars on two fronts, the eastern Mediterranean and the mainland, threatened Venetian hegemony, while the Portuguese's circumnavigation of the Cape of Good Hope endangered the Venetian economy, namely its monopoly over the lucrative spice trade. This, she indicates, had an impact on the city's culture of communication. Like the many ships represented in the *View*, vessels for maritime commerce and symbolic of

Venetian prosperity, the image itself functioned as a self-contained vessel of communication about Venice. It formed part of a network of political communication, written and visual, that asserted the state's persistent strength despite any political and economic challenges.

The print industry had primacy in the dissemination of hyperbolic messages about the Venetian state. Bronwen Wilson offers a consideration of the *View* as a tool for mapping the business of print. Venice—a crossroads of import and export for printing—was, as has been noted, the leading center of the industry around 1500. Wilson demonstrates how directional indicators, such as Neptune's trident, guide viewers now (and guided early modern visitors then) to the places, commercial printing establishments and presses, noteworthy for illustrated books and maps. The business of print benefited from transnational networks and international investments clustered near the Rialto, Piazza San Marco, and the axis that connected the two principal sites, the Mercerie. The Frezzaria, a street running just west of Piazza San Marco, had a concentration of immigrants and print shops at the beginning of the sixteenth century. Foreigners and printing often went together; many early recorded printers actively working in Venice were immigrants, primarily Germans, a community required by the Venetian state to reside in their warehouse near the Rialto Bridge, the Fondaco dei Tedeschi, the longtime residence of Anton Kolb.

While the German merchant Kolb likely orchestrated the production of the *View of Venice* as its financier, Jacopo de' Barbari as the artist would have coordinated the components necessary for its artistic realization. Without doubt it was an enormous, collaborative undertaking that legitimized the prints' high cost of three florins: a luxury good for a market with ready buyers. Yet beyond these two major players, documentary evidence has not yet come to light to reveal the names of the specialized labor force necessary to realize such an ambitious project. The woodcarvers, along with the surveyors, the artisans responsible for the specially commissioned, large-scale paper, the craftsmen who procured the pearwood and then pieced and primed the custom-made blocks for the woodcarvers, and, finally, the printmakers necessary for its publication and the print shop or perhaps multiple venues for its sale, still remain a scholarly enigma. De' Barbari would have interpreted and assembled the surveyor's records to design the urban portrait, and to the city's general forma urbis and the image's compositional arrangement, he would have added the mountainous background that anchors the upper sections; the winds to indicate directional orientation and

*Kristin Love
Huffman*

its mapping ancestry; the pagan gods to suggest divine protection; and many different types of water vessels to further characterize a city seemingly built atop water. The artist would then have passed along the overall image to woodcarvers responsible for extracting the detail in reverse into the six corresponding wooden blocks, the four corner impressions inverted (upper left sheet corresponding to upper right block, lower right sheet corresponding to the lower left block, and so forth).

Discussed by Valeria Cafà, the matrices, the sculptural artifacts used to print the *View*, and their exacting detail, indicate the effort and value of the three-year project. As works of art in their own right and not simply functional objects, they have maintained a history and presence within Venice, having been passed along as part of the collections of esteemed residents. These include the Tassis, a citizen family of Bergamese origins, who held state-appointed posts, and later the patrician Teodoro Correr (1750–1830), who bequeathed them to the city. The display strategies of Correr within his palazzo on the Grand Canal, namely the presentation of the wooden blocks next to the print and therefore visually connecting the two works of art, woodcut and matrices, continue today in the Correr Museum in Venice.

No official documentation of the *View*'s highly trained woodcarvers has yet come to light. Nor have any documents related to Jacopo de' Barbari's career in Venice. As the editor of this volume discusses, however, while de' Barbari has remained in the shadow of his contemporaries—Andrea Mantegna (1430/31–1506), Giovanni Bellini, and Albrecht Dürer, to note three with international acclaim—his invention in the graphic arts is noteworthy. This is especially recognizable with the woodcuts he created just prior to the publication of the *View* and the engravings and watercolor produced in the years immediately following. The objects and their analyses reveal information about his engagement in a visual repartee among contemporary printmakers regarding the medium's inherent potential for artistic invention. His adoption of Hermes's/Mercury's caduceus as his signature, featured in most attributed prints and select paintings, is one such example of his clever erudition. While scholars have maintained that the earliest of these signatures appears in the *View* through the noteworthy presence of Mercury, the woodcuts completed earlier already indicate his identification with the god.

Mary Pardo's essay places de' Barbari's realization of the *View* in the context of artistic representational strategies. She points out that the *"fan-*

tasia" or imaginative invention in the conception of distant landscape views by distinguished Venetian artists such as Giovanni Bellini formed part of an artistic tradition traceable to Jan van Eyck (ca. 1395–1441). Venetian connoisseurs had long appreciated northern artists, such as van Eyck, whose paintings hung within palaces in the Veneto. The artist's panoramic topographies within his paintings, including the one visualized in the Ca' d'Oro *Crucifixion*, offered models for portrait-like urban depictions and bird's-eye projections; the deliberate uptilting to visualize topographical detail is recognizable in the *View*. De' Barbari's illusionistic rendering of urban stereotomy, or descriptive geometry, indicates not only his sophisticated understanding of van Eykian visual strategies but also his place among celebrated contemporaries like Bellini, recognized by prestigious patrons for his *fantasia*.

Jacopo de' Barbari's northern clientele, eminent rulers and their courts, recognized the artist's theoretical understandings and capabilities. Before the *View of Venice* was officially published in late 1500, de' Barbari had already departed for the court of the Holy Roman Emperor in Nuremberg, the first Italian to receive this prestigious invitation and appointment as court artist. There, for a few years, de' Barbari and Dürer would have had opportunities to learn from each other, excelling in the arts of painting, woodblock prints, and engraving that, along with the artists' development of theoretical principles, affected artistic practice throughout northern Europe. De' Barbari was, as outlined by Rangsook Yoon, an urbane humanist who demonstrated an uncanny adaptability as he moved among prestigious courts in northern Europe. She indicates the ways he remained in demand with cultivated patrons and highlights his expansive awareness and international influence.

That the *View* persisted for over two hundred years as the quintessential image of Venice—a memory legacy of the city—further attests to its iconic status, cultural relevance, and graphic value. Subsequent representations of the city adopted the *View*'s visual strategies as *the* mode of visualizing Venice to the world until the eighteenth century. Not until 1729, when the printer Giuseppe Baroni (d. 1730) published Ludovico Ughi's plan of Venice, was the *View of Venice* superseded in printed form. Ughi's eighteenth-century map marked the transition to standard mathematically charted representations, geo-rectifiable within digital platforms, and, therefore, relatable to nineteenth-century modern cadasters and today's contemporary maps. Until then, the *View* was *the* view of Venice.

Kristin Love

Huffman

The *View* as a Reflection of Venice and Venetian Life (Part II)

The *View* visualized Venice's mythic identity on a monumental scale, a detailed description of a city built on water. The essays in part II highlight the many ways this iconic image represented (and presented for circulation) Venice in stately glory and as a world apart—an archipelago of many islands within an expansive lagoon. Seeming to defy natural physical laws, the city gracefully rose up and extended across its aqueous environment, a coexistence of man-made ingenuity within a mutually fortifying ecosystem. Sites highlighted within the woodcut call attention to documented "truths" about Venice's mythical qualities—not only as Queen of the Adriatic, suggesting sovereignty over a vast maritime domain, but also as the beauteous mythological goddess Venus, born of the sea. Another of these enchanting narratives was that the city's divine claims, both classical and Christian, meant that it remained untouched and unblemished by foreign attack for over one thousand years. Reality in this case supported mythology. The lagoon's waterways provided Venice with natural defenses: the channels were navigable almost exclusively by the city's savvy mariners, who understood their fluctuating depths according to the tides and winds.

The *View*, along with contemporary written chronicles and personal accounts, reinforced the notion of Venice as a city of marvel, miraculous and divine. In the woodcut print, hundreds of bridges connect a mosaic of islands defined by canals. While palatial architecture announced boundless riches, churches embedded within the city's dense urban fabric as parish posts and scattered around the periphery as larger complexes affirmed the notion of piety; this was reaffirmed by their great number and international reputation as repositories of sacred and highly venerated relics. The architecture in the zones around Piazza San Marco and the Rialto, principal sites of governance and commerce, promoted a distinctive civic identity and reflected the concordant sociopolitical infrastructure. The singularity of Venice recorded in the *View*, along with the specificity of its many exceptional details, served to underscore the power, wealth, and exceptionality of a harmonious Venetian state, otherwise known as La Serenissima (the most serene Republic).

The initial impression of a city built atop water seemingly subverts the realities of its practical and, at times, tedious urban expansion. Yet on closer observation, while the *View* visualized the city's inimitable forma urbis, the print's details reveal its highly sophisticated infrastructure and point to it as a product of man-made ingenuity. Much of the city's "land" had been re-claimed by filling in the water with collected debris and staking out a sub-terranean forest of timber pilings. The edifices sitting atop this constructed land have their own unique features. Buildings, typically three to four stories high, principally face out onto the canals, their main entryways accessed via water. The unique architectural features of Venice appear not only in the siting and design of larger structures, such as palaces and churches, but also in myriad details—idiosyncratic chimney pots to reduce flying cinders, a cistern network marked by wellheads to provide fresh water in a brackish lagoon, its many bell towers signaling a rhythmic, even if at times discor-dant, soundscape.

The essays in part II open with the systems and networks, the organiza-tion and provisioning necessary for a city that prided itself on its uniqueness and international status as an entrepôt—the invisible ingenuity necessary for a city built in a lagoon. Richard Goy introduces readers to the process of expansion and land reclamation, a dynamic phenomenon recognizable in the *View* on the western and eastern edges of the city, an evolving process over the Quattrocento. Urbanization remained a balance between public and private interests, secular and religious. Specifically with the construction of palaces, there is an investment in the city that displays patriotic pride. As Goy points out, Marin Sanudo, one of the city's great chroniclers, noted that palaces were built in "our mode," underscoring local identity, pride of place, and the unique building strategies necessary for construction. By the time de' Barbari's *View* was published in 1500, the overall form of the city and its networks of communication had been established. Land reclamation would not cease in an effort to ease congestion, notably along the northern rim of the city in the sixteenth century, but the general shape of the city's curvi-linear perimeter was complete. In this, as Goy shows, the print showcased the command of the Republic over its natural environment, and by exten-sion, its management implied measured control over the city's divine destiny.

Like palaces as embodiments of personal urbanistic interventions, the sculpted wellheads distributed within the city provided subsistence even as they functioned as loci for personal encounters. While the below-ground cistern network for collecting fresh water was largely hidden, the wellheads as markers for access to it were highly visible. Discussed by Patricia Fortini Brown, the more than fifty ornamental wellheads identified in the *View* marked the locations for access to fresh water, essential for quotidian life in a brackish lagoon. While practical and invaluable, close analysis reveals that the decorative style of wellheads mirrored the changing tastes in architecture and sculpture over time in Venice. As decorative markers, carved imagery indicated the history of a site, at times connoting a specific individual or corporation with coats of arms, or, more generally, the importance of place.

Kristin Love Huffman

The wellheads were not the only distinctive features that structured daily life; the many bell towers with architecturally unique belfries had the same effect. The more than one hundred bell towers scattered throughout Venice, all connected to churches, have, like the wellheads, been documented within the *View*. While the notion of piety is marked by Venice's many churches (and its foundational mythology), the bells in their towers, as examined by Jonathan Glixon, organized the life of the city. This daily framework included bell ringing for religious services to peals that marked the beginning and ending of the working day. This sonic environment structured the rhythm of everyday life—religious and civic—and occasionally signaled celebratory as well as catastrophic moments. With the exception of the coordinated workday bells at the Rialto church of San Giovanni Elemosinario and the Arsenal with those at the Campanile in Piazza San Marco, the independent determination of bell ringing, notably among the churches, generated a soundscape that resounded across the city from dawn until dusk—its asynchronous sonic vibrations effectively reverberating across spaces, given that water amplifies sound.

The essays within part II also highlight the visibility and invisibility of residents in Venice and the lives lived within its many walls. Four of the following essays place into relief the active, dynamic role select groups residing within the city—those typically perceived as located in the margins (figuratively or literally)—played within the political, economic, and religious life, and overall social vitality of early modern Venice. Saundra Weddle focuses on convents and the nuns who lived behind their enclosed walls— isolation that may have begun in the margins but, with urban growth, resulted in their embeddedness within Venice's urban fabric. She discusses two convents in close physical proximity, the Dominican nuns at Corpus Domini and the Augustinians at Santa Lucia, to show how growth over time led to a perception of encroachment; potential disruption to devotional life, such as with the sonic resonances of nearby bells; and financial repercussions due to the ownership rights and devotional attraction of sacred relics. She reminds readers that the *View* visually documented a historic moment prior to when church and civic authorities imposed rigorous convent reform, notably Counter-Reformation and post-Tridentine enclosure in the sixteenth century.

The tension between the enclosed life of monastic and conventual devotional practices and the practical contributions they made to sustain the city can also be understood through a close reading of the *View*. Ludovica Galeazzo highlights the functions of monastic and conventual complexes as connective, urban hubs. These complexes form a notable ring around the periphery of the city, occupying the margins that included more extensive properties. Within these sites, in addition to a built complex (church, cloisters, dormitories, outbuildings, and sometimes libraries and hospitals), religious communities cultivated sizable green spaces that contained medicinal plants, along with vineyards and edible fruits and vegetables. The economic connection to the outside world, however, did not end with the production and provisioning of plants, fruits, and vegetables to Venice's inhabitants; it also had an impact on sociocultural forces within the city. Larger complexes such as the Benedictine monastery of San Giorgio Maggiore, featured prominently in the lower border in the *View*, were important sites for hosting visitors to the city. Other complexes, through their enterprising nature, rented building spaces as storage facilities or leased landholdings to local industries such as cloth dyeing and sail manufacture. This dynamic interplay of religious institutions in service to their communities and the city as a whole illustrates the connective nature of the city's various residents.

Venice's inhabitants—men and women, natives and foreigners, patricians, the bourgeois citizen class, and general populace—while largely hidden within the *View* nonetheless reinforced state interests as they advanced their own. Holly Hurlburt argues for the reconsideration of women as integral to politics, visible with civic ritual and honorary processions throughout the city. She outlines specific ceremonial events in the last decade of the fifteenth century that involved female heads of state, such as Caterina Cornaro (1454–1510), queen of Cyprus, or leading consorts, such as Eleonora of Naples (1450–93), Duchess of Ferrara, and Beatrice Sforza (1475–97), Duchess of Milan. The patrician women of Venice who received these foreign female dignitaries dressed lavishly for such occasions and processed throughout civic spaces as living pageantry in visual demonstration of the city's wealth. Palaces also served as loci for political strategizing. A commingling of women and men at weddings and *ridotti*, rooms in palaces for pleasurable pastimes such as gambling, offered celebratory moments ripe for advancing political agendas. Public events within civic and semiprivate spaces reinscribed women not only as contributors of the state but also as necessary for its successful continuation.

In his essay, Stanley Chojnacki tracks residential variety among patrician families. While some families stayed in one parish for decades, others, such as the Vitturi family, moved around to reside in six different ones. Chojnacki traces the peripatetic movement of Cateruzza Vitturi within the city (and to Treviso, a Venetian mainland territory) to enact her loyalties and also protect her self-interests. While women typically had fewer choices than men, Cateruzza demonstrates the determination and maneuverings of a woman to mediate her interests within the socially constrained obligations of marital life. Married twice, her second union less fortunate than her first, Cateruzza nonetheless ended her circuit where she began, that is, taking up residence in the longtime parish of San Moisè, that of her first husband, Moisè Venier. The culmination of the protagonist's movement, enhanced with the fortuitous inheritance of properties from both marriages, points to the simultaneity and balance of female agency within societal expectations.

Visible wealth—in the form of architectural commissions lining the canals within the woodcut print or even the *View*'s tangible embodiment as a luxury good in its own right—bestows impressions of Venetian prosperity. Of the more than five hundred boats depicted, almost half were cargo or merchant ships, presenting a picture of Venice's robust position within the global market. By 1500, Venice had experienced a centuries-long history as sovereign of an Italian state, a powerful oligarchic Republic with expansive territorial and maritime possessions. Yet at this moment the Venetian state, more wide-reaching than the city's administrative epicenter alone, had reached its zenith. The maritime hegemony that had fueled its dramatic expansion was fatally undermined by the rising Ottoman Empire and European monarchies along with the accelerating expansion of trade routes outside the Mediterranean. Columbus's discovery of the Americas in 1492 led to the reconceptualization of a new world and a shift in the international market. By 1500, the Portuguese had already circumnavigated the Cape of Good Hope.

Nonetheless, market demands and the steady import/export of traded goods, including luxury items, formed one of the persistent features of early modern Venice's economic vibrancy. Networks of individuals and commodities reflected global markets. Giada Damen lends insight with her focus on

Domenico di Piero (1406–97), a jeweler and antiquarian who not only sold lavish merchandise, such as gems, in Venice and Damascus but also outfitted high-profile clientele, including the popes in Rome, the Medici in Florence, and the Este in Ferrara. A member of the citizen class, Domenico di Piero's wealth and status allowed him to contribute to the embellishment of the façades at the Scuola Grande di San Marco and his palace on the Grand Canal. Both of these late fifteenth-century structures, encrusted with expensive colored marbles and decorative sculptures, visibly reflected the trade this citizen-merchant practiced, the jewels he sold, his social standing, and the noteworthy prestige of his international clientele.

Discussed by Blake de Maria, this global network included the manufacture, trade, and retail of luxury goods in Venice, including items overlooked today, such as soap, alongside more commonly prized items, such as gems, which could hail from as far as Myanmar in Southeast Asia. The sale of luxury goods could be self-reflexive. Merchant families contributed not only to the decorative embellishment of the city via palatial architecture but also to the infrastructure necessary for growing and maintaining their commercial enterprises, such as the construction of row housing and rental units for workers. De Maria, in addition to noting the mutually beneficial enterprise of luxury trade, traces its concentration from the Rialto to Piazza San Marco: gemstones, textiles, paintings and their gilt frames. While the boutiques that lined the Mercerie had these lavish items for sale year-round, feast days and their festivals, such as that of the Sensa (Venetian for Ascension), resulted in the erection of ephemeral stalls in central locations to accommodate the throngs of visitors and their desire to make significant purchases.

Retail production and trade could also be highly specialized and localized. Julia A. DeLancey focuses inward on the movement of goods and materials via the waterways in Venice to consider coloring materials, in particular the manufacture and sale of lead white. She identifies clusters of activity, such as the series of buildings lining Campo San Bartolomeo near the Rialto Bridge, and the connection of coloring materials to the luxury goods of paintings, glass, and textiles displayed in this zone. Lead white produced in Venice, not only necessary for local goods, dominated the global market. This seemingly prosaic retail item made select individuals highly wealthy, including citizen-merchants who could compete with patrician standards of living. Despite social rigidity with a strictly fixed class system, an individual's economic prominence permitted mobility; economic fluidity allowed resourceful individuals to prosper in an otherwise hierarchically fixed state.

The *View*, while celebrating the wealth of Venice and the affluence of select patricians and merchant citizens, also subtly indicates the grittiness of a port city via unexpected details. In Piazza San Marco on the front façade of the Beccaria (butchery and meat market), the building to the left of the two entry columns and therefore front and center, de' Barbari visibly highlights a hole from which ruinous cracks radiate (plate 2). The building would soon be demolished as part of a larger architectural campaign to transform Piazza San Marco in both visual form and suitable function. This urban renewal, spearheaded under the direction of Doge Andrea Gritti (r. 1523–38) following the Wars of the League of Cambrai and Venice's political and economic losses, would effectively rearticulate the state's message of a Venice Triumphant, much as the *View* had done at the turn of the century.

Despite this curious detail at the Beccaria, the *View* generally represents the state's mythologized sociopolitical serenity, an ideological vision of Venetian society. Maartje van Gelder and Claire Judde de Larivière point to state strategies for maintaining social harmony, which at times masked the realities of unrest and civil discord centered on Piazza San Marco; these were also replicated in microcosmic territorial jurisdictions, such as the island of Murano. The state granary—a superstructure to the left of the Beccaria within Piazza San Marco—stands out as the largest edifice in Venice. Originally over 350 feet long and four stories high, it functioned as an administrative complex as well as storage facility to house grain and flour imported from near and far. The grain and flour for bread, basic sustenance for the majority of Venetians, and its availability, had a direct correlation with social harmony: feast ensured peace, while famine led to unrest. Government policy and management of essential needs, centrally controlled in Venice but also overseen in satellite Venetian territories, could either maintain or disrupt social cohesion. Murano, important to the glassmaking industry, offers a case study. While in close proximity to Venice proper, it functioned as an independent, yet interdependently governed dominion, like other Venetian territorial possessions including Padua and Bergamo, Cyprus and Crete. Murano had its own governance via a podestà (state appointed representative) who oversaw it. As the authors of this essay discuss, the Muranese podestà, like the state, was at times subjected to severe disapproval on the part of local citizens who effectively made clear their dissatisfaction.

Despite periodic moments of civic unrest, Venetians and foreigners alike contributed to the promotion of Venice as a mythical and marvelous city: a most serene Republic. Visits from the constant influx of merchants and pilgrims, not to mention international movement of Venetians to far-away lands, kept its reputation alive—unique in origins, visible wealth, and sociopolitical harmony. As noted in part I, while published historical chronicles, documented diaries, and pilgrim's accounts expressed this through the written word, the *View of Venice* visualized it. An important travel destination due to its prosperity and prominence as a commercial entrepôt and holy site, Venice was a model melting pot. Here, the city's native residents, foreign dignitaries conducting state affairs, merchants transacting business, and pilgrims passing en route to the Holy Land, rubbed elbow to elbow in densely trafficked zones such as Piazza San Marco and the Rialto. Venice stood at a crossroads of worldly encounters, including those who established residential communities, such as the Germans and Jews, together with foreigners traveling to and fro, far and wide—east, west, north, and south. Martina Massaro discusses the cosmopolitan nature of Venice and government tactics for welcoming (and containing) foreigners. Examining the case of Jewish residents who formed the first permanent foreign community in 1516, she discusses a series of mandates that led to the relocation of non-Venetians from guesthouses near Piazza San Marco to other sites in Venice. The concomitant shift of economic activity to cluster predominantly at the Rialto facilitated state control over foreign communities and provided steady sources of tax revenue to the city. As Massaro describes, the establishment of the three ghettos in Venice between 1516 and 1630 created a cosmopolitan microcosm within a cosmopolitan city. The end of the Venetian Republic and the subsequent opening of the Ghetto following Napoleon's occupation of Venice in 1797 led to the Jews' acquisition of property in Piazza San Marco and re-habitation there, recalling the historic hostelries that originally welcomed the city's immigrants to foreground a reversal of social and economic sway.

The volume concludes with Tracy E. Cooper's epilogue, in tandem with short entries of key sites in Venice and visible elements of the *View* in appendix 1. Cooper considers the importance of the woodcut print as an artifact that mediates past and present—visualization of the Renaissance city that permits rediscovery of a lost Venice. The *View* encourages close and slow looking, which in turn prompts comparative analyses and authorizes understandings and interpretations of Venice now and then. Enhanced abilities to "see" have been furthered by digital tools, such as the high-resolution image produced in conjunction with *A Portrait of Venice*, the exhibition from which this edited volume emerges. The woodcut's technological achievement in the late fifteenth century is amplified by the application of twenty-first-century digital technologies in this expansive project (see the prologue).

One of the woodcut's mesmerizing charms is that it entices onlookers to access it from any number of locations, the eyes moving across sites to rest periodically on curious details. The essays mirror this varied, richly complex, and dynamic approach to looking in their consideration of documented historic realities. Via its many scholarly contributions, the volume's examination of the sociopolitical and cultural context of early modern Venice, and its presentation of original insights about this iconic image, offer readers new content, varied perspectives, and tantalizing curiosities about a complex and distinctive Renaissance city and the portrait view that preserves its memory.

Kristin Love Huffman

NOTES

1 For select publications with content related to the *View*, see Jay A. Levenson, "Jacopo de' Barbari and Northern Art of the Early Sixteenth Century" (PhD diss., Columbia University, 1978), 278–81; Juergen Schulz, "Jacopo de' Barbari's View of Venice: Map Making, City Views, and Moralized Geography before the Year 1500," *Art Bulletin* 60, no. 3 (1978): 425–74; Piero Falchetta, "La misura dipinta: Rilettura tecnica e semantica della veduta di Venezia di Jacopo de' Barbari," *Ateneo Veneto* 178 (1991): 273–305; Martin Kemp, "Jacopo de' Barbari: *View of Venice*," in *Circa 1492: Art in the Age of Exploration*, exhib. cat, ed. Jay A. Levenson (Washington, DC: National Gallery of Art, 1991), 253–55; Deborah Howard, "Venice as a Dolphin: Further Investigations into Jacopo de' Barbari's *View*," *Artibus et Historiae* 18, no. 35 (1997): 101–11; Giselle Lambert, *Les premières gravures italienne: Quattrocento du cinquecento. Inventaire de la collection du Département des Estampes et de la Photographie* (Paris: Bibliotèque nationale de France, 1999), 331–33; Giandomenico Romanelli, Susanna Biadene, and Camillo Tonino, eds., *A volo d'uccello: Jacopo de' Barbari e le rappresentazioni di città nell'Europa del Rinascimento*, exhib. cat. (Venice: Arsenale, 1999); Corrado Balistreri-Trincanato and Dario Zanverdiani, *Jacopo de Barbari: Il racconto di una città*, 2 vols.

(Venice: Cetid, 2000); Gert Jan van der Sman, "De eeuw van Titiaan: Venetiaanse prenten uit de Renaissance," in *Le siècle de Titien: Gravures vénitiennes de la Renaissance* (Zwolle: Waanders Uitgevers, 2003), 40–41; Simone Ferrari, *Jacopo de' Barbari: Un protagonista del Rinascimento tra Venezia e Dürer* (Milan: B. Mondadori, 2006), 150–54; Vanna Bagarolo and Vladimiro Valerio, "Jacopo de' Barbari: Una nuova ipotesi indiziaria sulla genesi prospettica della veduta *Venetie MD*," in *Cartografi veneti: Mappe, uomini e istituzioni per l'immagine e il governo del territorio*, ed. Vladimiro Valerio (Padua: Editoriale Programma, 2007), 118–35; Beate Böckem, *Jacopo de' Barbari: Künstlerschaft und Hofkultur um 1500* (Cologne: Böhlau Verlag, 2016), 32–33, 39–50, 428–29; Kristin Love Huffman, "Jacopo de' Barbari's *View of Venice* (1500): 'Image Vehicles' and 'Pathways of Culture' Past and Present," *Mediterranea* 4 (2019): 165–214.

2 *More veneto* (m.v.) refers to dates that signal the Venetian calendar, with each new year beginning March 1.

I

The *View* as a Printed Cartographic and Artistic Visualization

Karen-edis Barzman

The *View of Venice* in a Genealogy of City Views and Government Mapping

THIS ESSAY PLACES Jacopo de' Barbari's *View of Venice* in a brief history of city views and locates its production in early phases of the systematic collection and visualization of geospatial data in government archives. This watershed in the history of cartography dates to the second half of the fifteenth century, when Venice conceived what we might call a geographic information system (GIS) to better manage its territories. It could hardly be coincidental that de' Barbari embarked on his unprecedented *View* at the moment when Venice was making its landholdings fully visible through pictures. We may never determine the method of its production, but features shared with maps in Venetian chanceries place it in the realm of the cartographic. It surely emerged from the same mapping impulses, which stemmed from circumstances particular to Venice at the time.

De' Barbari and City Views

Karen-edis Barzman

As Juergen Schulz aptly noted, the *View* is best described in superlatives— "the largest and most detailed," "the most influential," "a major work of art."[1] It took the pictorial representation of cities to new heights, presenting urban topography with unprecedented accuracy from a lofty plane. And it did so in a monumental format. There was nothing comparable for any city, even in antiquity. The marble *Plan of the City of Rome* (*Forma urbis romae*, third century) was colossal and more exacting but largely ichnographic, reducing built form to plan.[2] Thus, it does not qualify as a view, which approximates sight even when exceeding what the eye can take in at a glance.

Interest in the accurate rendering of urban topography (the appearance of cities and the relative location of their parts) emerged in the fifteenth century, from which the city view was born as a genre.[3] Of course, not all views were monumental or comprehensive in scope. Leon Battista Alberti's *Venice in Perspective*, ca. 1425, is a good example.[4] No longer extant, it probably resembled Filippo Brunelleschi's small panels of the Florentine Baptistry and Palazzo della Signoria, 1425, also lost, but renowned in their day.[5] As practical applications of optics in the picturing of urban form, Brunelleschi's paintings each featured a structure in unified space, as seen from a proximate vantage point near ground level. This fixed position was key, determining the size and placement of everything depicted as well as the ideal position of the viewer. Alberti later geometrized the technique in written form (*De pictura*, 1435) and likely employed aspects of it in his painting of Venice, which, according to Vasari, also featured a single structure (the church of San Marco).[6] Alberti's view of the city, then, would have been small as well as partial and low in perspective, replicating what the artist saw at the scene.

While still tied to the notion of embodied viewing, Pinturicchio's *Venice* from the 1480s was something else, elevated in perspective as well as large in size and sweeping in its visual field.[7] Frescoed in a loggia in the Vatican Belvedere, on the wall opposite the structure's arcade, it belonged to a series of cityscapes badly damaged today. Yet we know that Pinturicchio relied on atmospheric effects rather than Brunelleschi's or Alberti's method of perspective to create the illusion of Venice in the distance, as if seen from the loggia itself. Significant here is the loggia's position on a hilltop, which justified the altitude of what was still putatively a grounded view. De' Barbari's woodcut was different in this regard. Despite a fusion of perspectives, it gives the impression of a fixed bird's-eye view from a height unattainable at that time and place, belying any plausible location for the spectator.

Similar in this regard was Erhard Reuwich's woodcut of Venice in Bernhard von Breydenbach's *Peregrinatio in Terram Sanctam* (Mainz, 1486; fig. I.2), although the imagined viewing altitude is lower than de' Barbari's.[8] Reuwich's *Venice* falls somewhere between a bird's-eye view and the panoramic, making contemporary prints of Venice appear small and gestural in comparison. Yet it elides much of the city on either side of the Grand Canal, at least partly because of its foldout format, which was Reuwich's innovation for the book. Reuwich extended his view across four sheets of paper measuring approximately 30 by 163.5 centimeters when pasted side by side (the height dictated by the book itself). This horizontal format left no option but to compress the city, which appears as a strip dominated by façades on the Bacino (Basin of St. Mark) and south-facing *fondamente* (quays).[9] Although Reuwich spent three weeks in Venice in the 1480s and clearly viewed the city from multiple points, he was likely unaware of its "dolphin" footprint, which de' Barbari introduced to the world of print.[10] Free from the constraints of the book, de' Barbari would choose a less elongated format while presenting the city from a higher elevation and tipping it toward the viewer, thereby accommodating its distinctive outline (distortions notwithstanding) while reducing overlap of built form.[11]

Precedents for such strategies are found in the work of Francesco Rosselli, a miniaturist and engraver with a successful print shop in Florence—the earliest to be documented selling maps.[12] Like Reuwich, Rosselli produced city views more than ten years prior to de' Barbari's *View of Venice*.[13] Although Rosselli did not represent Venice itself, he and Reuwich had something else in common—both used inscriptions to identify structures and peripheral locations in their prints, a practice that did not belong to the pictorial arts. As David Friedman suggests, Rosselli may have intended these prints as examples of chorography.[14] Described by Ptolemy in the second century as the counterpoint to geography or global mapping, chorography focused on discrete locations (examples of which also came from Rosselli's shop).[15] More on Ptolemy below, but here we should note that the reduction necessary to represent sites around the globe limited geography to the largest features (first and foremost, major cities), while sacrificing detail for user-friendly size. By contrast, chorography operated on a much larger scale—the larger the mapping scale, the smaller the area covered on the ground, allowing for more detail.

Regardless of Rosselli's intentions, we can affirm that his inscriptions *as text* lie in a plane and thus sit in tension with the features they identify. That said, they are small and few in number and do not compromise what remained city views. Rosselli's works were unrivaled in print, both in accuracy and size, his *Florence* measuring approximately 58 by 134 centimeters, and his *Rome* 87 by 176 centimeters. Yet de' Barbari's *View of Venice*, at approximately 135 by 275 centimeters, exceeded these dimensions, not to mention the genre of the view itself, combining place-names with other features increasingly associated with the cartographic.

De' Barbari's *View* and Mapping in Venice

Here we should note that cartography in early modern Venice went far beyond commercial production, involving the state as never before. To date, no archival evidence links de' Barbari's woodcut with government initiatives. When the sponsor, Anton Kolb, petitioned the Venetian Collegio for privileges and protections regarding the *View*, the print was ready for sale.[16] Some scholars have underscored its potential to compromise state security,[17] and in fact, its production required access to restricted sites (e.g., the Arsenal), whose operations were guarded secrets. Still, while nothing has surfaced to document state interventions, it is instructive to situate the print in terms of the government's concurrent efforts to compile a geodatabase in the form of a picture archive.

A thriving entrepôt and engine of global trade, Venice also functioned as a metropole (*dominante*) with dominions in northeastern Italy (the Venetian *terraferma*) and a string of maritime provinces with strategic port cities in the Mediterranean (the Venetian *stato da mar*). These holdings had a sprawling footprint that brought administrative challenges, given Venice's centralized decision-making about places many officeholders in the metropole had never seen. To provide a baseline of shareable information, the Council of Ten, Venice's most powerful governing body, issued the following decree in February 1460 (1459 *more veneto*):

As concerning cities, fortresses and provinces, which by the grace of
God are subject to our rule, there is no one in our government who,
when there is deliberation concerning those places, is able to give *specific information about their site, breadth and length, and borders, and
which dominions are nearby.* …

Whence, it should be undertaken to have in our chancery or in
our council room, in [a] true picture [*in vera pictura*], the representation and copy of all our cities, lands, fortresses, provinces, and regions,
in order that whoever wanting to consult and advise about the aforementioned [places] might have true and specific knowledge according
to sight and not according to someone's opinion.

Let it be enacted that by the authority of this council it should be
written and sent to the Rectors of our cities, lands, and fortresses that,
having had *good and right counsel from citizens local to the place and from
others practiced and knowledgeable about the city or its surroundings, they
have drawn the land, place, and its district with indications of the winds and
east and west,* fortresses, rivers, plane, and *distance from place to place,
and places near to us and their distance,* and they should diligently have
the methodically rendered drawing examined by learned and experienced [men] to see if it is well and rightly depicted. And once done they
must each send the picture to our government.[18] (Emphasis added)

Implicitly rejecting the prevailing practice of recording and transmit-
ting geographic data via text, the Ten affirmed the power of images to re-
move the subjective from discussions of place.[19] They stipulated drawing
as the medium for their pictures, which were to orient viewers with respect
to "the winds" (cardinal points) and provide quantified data about places
and distances between them while remaining "true" to sight. They also required input from locals and experts' review of the drawings prior to final
submission.

The combination of these practices had no precedent in government.
Why they occurred first in Venice is complicated to explain. The decree
was drafted shortly after the Peace of Lodi in 1454, which permitted Venice to consolidate its *terraferma* as far west as Bergamo and Brescia. At the
time, then, Venetian territories were more expansive than ever before. It
was also before the Ottoman-Venetian wars, the first five of which eroded
its *stato da mar*.[20] But size is insufficient as an explanation. Larger empires existed throughout history, many with pictures in their own archives.

Yet none had made a concerted turn to visualization in the management of territory.

The rise of the paper industry in Europe was surely a factor, facilitating the practice of drawing on inexpensive, portable supports. Other considerations include the development of humanism in Italy and its impact on art theory and practice as well as on governance. Consider that in 1459 the Council of Ten included Jacopo Antonio Marcello, a Venetian with vast military and political experience and a profound commitment to humanist inquiry.[21] Like other elites with a similar bent, Marcello was an avid reader of Ptolemy, whose *Geography* had started circulating in Latin manuscripts earlier in the century.[22] This text provided instructions for mapping places around the world that were so far apart as not to be visible or easily accessible one from the other. To determine their relative locations, Ptolemy codified a set of mathematical procedures. He combined timed observations of the heavens from fixed locations with geometric calculations, establishing coordinates of latitude and longitude for each site on a gridded model of the earth as a sphere. These coordinates could then be transferred or "projected" from the gridded sphere to a gridded plane in a method of mapping that sidestepped measurement on the ground, where contingencies interfere with mathematical precision. This precision, we should note, concerned not linear measure (on which, see below) but, rather, angles measured in degrees from the theoretical core of the earth—a highly abstract method of calculation.

The significance Marcello attached to Ptolemy's *Geography* prompted his gift of an elaborate manuscript copy to Rene d'Anjou, deposed king of Naples and personal friend, in 1457.[23] His engagement with geography, however, went beyond Ptolemy. In 1455 he financed the first Latin translation of Strabo's *Geography* (first century CE), completed in 1458.

Strabo intended his work for statesmen and those conducting commercial affairs who benefited, he argued, from detailed information about place. And, indeed, Strabo made much of his extensive travels when claiming authority.[24] In addition to positional data, he provided direct observation and historical narrative as the basis of a *descriptive* geography, commenting on economic and (geo)political opportunities afforded by resources around the world, from waterways and harbors facilitating trade to mountains providing natural boundaries. Such concerns, which called for site specificity, were shared by officials managing Venice's territories.

As with Ptolemy, Marcello played a role in circulating Strabo, presenting Rene d'Anjou with a manuscript copy of the translation in 1459 as yet another gift.[25] Before this, Strabo had only been available in Greek manuscripts, which limited readership, even among humanists. This Latin translation of Strabo was the first to enter print (1469); the first print edition of Ptolemy appeared six years later (1475). Thus, Marcello belonged to an exclusive group of Strabo literati and an only marginally larger Ptolemy readership in 1459, when his presence on the Ten likely informed the council's embrace of visualization for the state's new geodatabase, directional orientation for accuracy in location (key for Ptolemy), and the involvement of provincial subjects to verify local details (in the tradition of Strabo).

Worth asking at this juncture is whether mapping as then practiced could deliver what the Ten envisioned. The answer is that something new was required. By the mid-fifteenth century, cartography had a long history with diverse traditions, but most had sacrificed locational and topographic accuracy to other demands. In medieval Europe, precedence was given to "moralizing" imperatives both religious and secular in nature. Fra Mauro's monumental *mappamundi*, a planispheric map of the world (parchment on wood, approximately 196 centimeters in diameter) is a good example of this enduring tradition in fifteenth-century Venice.[26] The erudite monk behind its production still included "Earthly Paradise," even if in a corner of the work's square frame. And while he added places unknown in antiquity, he deduced their locations from unscientific travel accounts and positioned them on his map without a grid, notwithstanding his knowledge of latitude and longitude. The sole surviving copy was completed in Venice in 1460, the year the Ten issued its decree, which likewise did not call for the use of coordinates. Of course, the decree concerned large-scale mapping, more in keeping with chorography, where the grid did not come into play. But chorography also excluded measured data, which were requisite for the Ten's drawings, thus eliminating them from this category of geospatial visualization.

The Ten's picture archive is no longer intact, and the history of its dispersion is currently unknown. But we may infer things about it from maps that ended up in a "miscellaneous" collection after the fall of the Venetian Republic in 1797 (fig. 1.1), and from maps commissioned by Venetian magistrates overseeing land reclamation, forest resources, and the like, best documented from the sixteenth century on. These officials stored their collections in their own chanceries in the Ducal Palace, a sprawling information environment behind the scenes where wear and tear compromised the works' long-term preservation and functionality. By the time the overseers of Venetian fortresses (*Provveditori alle fortezze*) catalogued their collection in the mid-eighteenth century, deterioration was a serious problem. The inventory lists 26 drawings bound together in book form, 299 bundled in nineteen separate rolls and noted in "good condition," and 124 in four other rolls, "of little consequence because torn or mutilated." It also listed 184 poly-chrome reliefs of fortresses and surrounding terrain, "ninety-six acceptably preserved, the remaining eighty-eight of little consequence, either in bad condition from overuse or mutilated [and] a good number of fragments, all unusable."[27] These *modelli*, made of more durable materials than the drawings, also suffered from extensive handling and neglect.

Maps were also made for Venetian officials in the provinces and sent to the metropole in dispatches (*dispacci*) with timely information regarding matters from disintegrating infrastructure to border disputes (figs. 1.2–1.3). Addressed to the Senate, the dispatches often glossed the drawings, which were generally archived with them as inserts. A drawing labeled *Appearance of the Fortress of Novigrad* (1620), still bound in a seventeenth-century volume (*filza*) with its accompanying documentation, is a good example (fig. 1.2). Others were kept with their dispatches as loose documents in file folders (*buste*). Many are now curated separately due to their fragility and may only be viewed as digital files (fig. 1.3).

Taken together, these examples make clear that Venice's archival drawings comprised a new modality of representation, with text and graphic calculating devices layered over carefully observed and scaled features of topography in aerial views. In terms of their making, it merits noting that Venice's territories were relatively small, with many sites in the same view-shed or visible by moving from one site to the other at ground level or from successive towers and peaks in the terrain. This permitted embedded procedures for determining quantitative data, with state-funded engineers adapting sighting instruments for surveying to carry out their fieldwork, including the addition of lodestones with needles and pivot pins for orientation on the ground.[28]

In site drawings the engineers typically presented constructed form in detail and in three dimensions—from the bird's-eye point of view, as seen in the drawing of Novigrad (fig. 1.2). These were the only drawings that could be construed as chorographic, given the absence of quantified spatial data. In more sweeping views including large swaths of countryside, they employed the "god trick" of all-seeing vision from even higher elevations

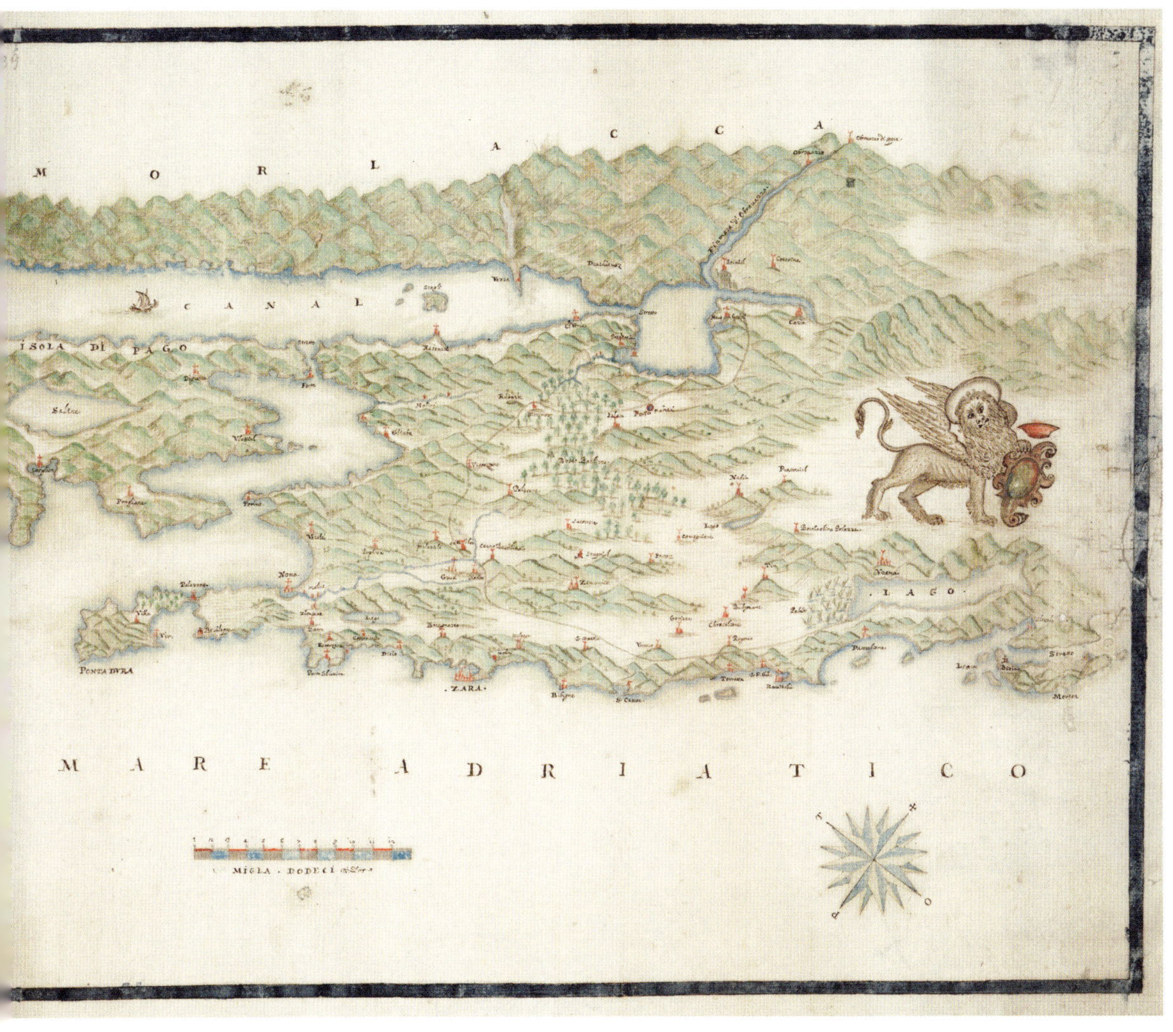

(figs. 1.1 and 1.3).[29] Regardless of scale, their works must have qualified as "true pictures," with hatching, cross-hatching, and graduated earth tones used for terrain, added by way of ink wash or watercolor. Yet most combined overhead views (particularly for bodies of water) with other features seen from acute angles while using the horizon to indicate limits of sovereignty rather than sight.

With the image field in place, other elements are presented as if *above*, including place-names in the local vernacular (unlike those on contemporary print maps, with largely classicizing toponyms) and legends in Italian

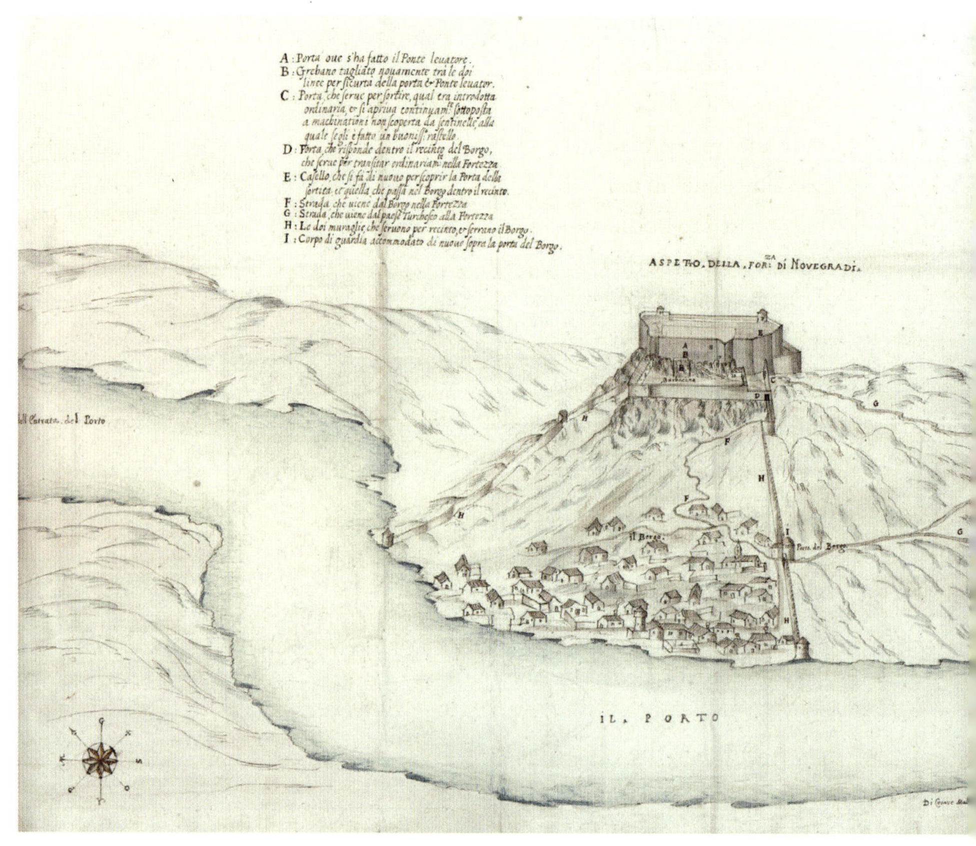

A : Porta oue s'ha fatto il Ponte leuatore.
B : Grebano tagliàto nouamente trà le doi linee per sicurtà della porta & Ponte leuator.
C : Porta, che serue per sortire, qual era introdotta ordinaria, et si apriua continuam.te sottoposta a machinationi non scoperta da sentinelle, alla quale se gli è fatto un buoniss. rastello.
D : Porta, che risponde dentro il recinto del Borgo, che serue per transitar ordinariam.te nella Fortezza
E : Casello, che si fa di nuouo per scoprir la Porta della sortita, et quella che passa nel Borgo dentro il recinto.
F : Strada, che uiene dal Borgo nella Fortezza
G : Strada, che uiene dal paese Turchesco alla Fortezza
H : Le doi muraglie, che seruono per recinto, er serrano il Borgo.
I : Corpo di guardia accommodato di nuouo sopra la porta del Borgo.
ASPETTO DELLA FOR:ZA DI NOVEGRADI
dell Cauata del Porto
il Borgo
Porta del Borgo
IL PORTO

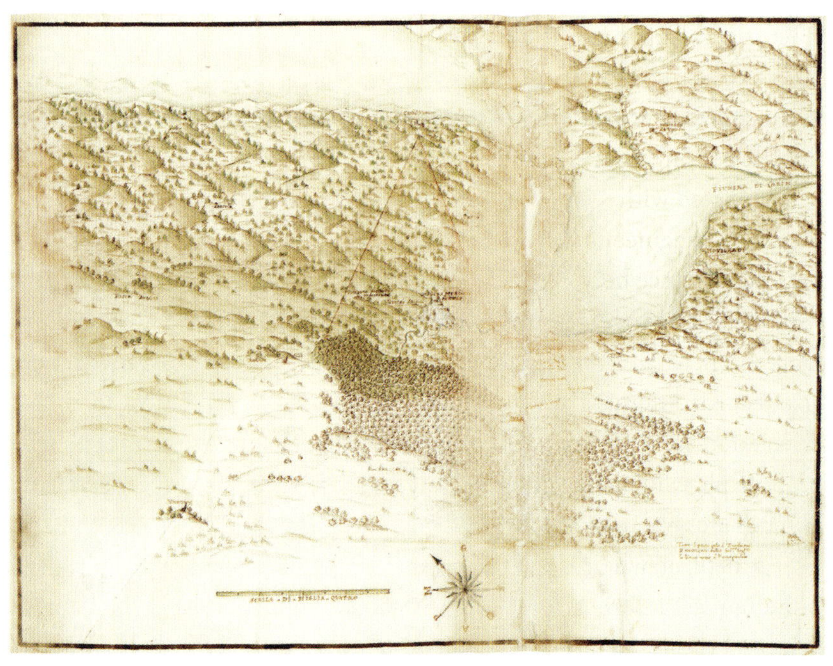

FIVMERA DI SANTO
SCALA DI MIGLIA QVATRO

(often in Venetian dialect), which may be taken as coplanar. Additional features include a four-, eight-, or sixteen-point compass rose with abbreviations of wind names from the lingua franca of Mediterranean maritime trade and a scale bar to gauge distance with the Venetian mile (*miglio*), a linear value equal to one thousand strides (*passi*) or five thousand feet (*piedi*), thus, rooted to bodies in transit (figs. 1.1 and 1.3).[30] These devices were often rendered in three dimensions but in a size wholly incommensurate with the topographic field below, which was necessary for them to be functional. Thus, they occupy their own superimposed registers of representation.

In the late sixteenth century, curved lines started to appear as graphic indicators of negotiated borders in contested regions (fig. 1.1), and in the seventeenth century, color coding and polygons were used to draw the eye to specific areas of concern.[31] Such features abound in drawings of the more volatile borderlands that Venice repeatedly mapped, prime among them the edge of the northern part of Venetian Dalmatia (present-day Croatia) that was shared with Ottoman Bosnia. User instructions regarding these features appear in the dispatches but also often on the maps, as in the unframed key on the lower right of the example from 1605 (fig. 1.3): "All the land [in] yellow is Turkish, the remaining [land belongs to] the Most Serene Signoria, [and] the red lines [indicate the area of] usurpation [by Ottoman subjects from neighboring Bosnia]" (Tutto il paese zalo è Turchesco, il rimanente della ser:ma Sig.ria, le linee rosse è l'usurpacion). While the yellow has faded, the red lines are clearly visible and, in their particular configuration, suggest triangulation (fig. 1.3)—a field technique using the known distance between two sites as a baseline to establish distance to a third. By measuring the interior angles on either side of the baseline, all three sites could then be connected with straight lines to generate the geometric form. For some reason, the engineer did not draw the triangle's base here, but its length and thus the distance between the sites at either end could easily be calculated with the scale bar and a jointed compass or straight edge, as could the distances from each to the site at the top vertex. Relevant distances were often also recorded numerically in the dispatches, but such drawings permitted calculations to be made independently.[32]

While evidence suggests occasional tracing from prototypes, most of Venice's archival maps were drawn freehand, a time-consuming practice in the age of print, when base maps with predetermined datasets (landmasses, mountain ridges, waterways, the littoral; cities, towns, fortresses; roads, bridges, etc.) could have been cheaply reproduced. Shifting borders or new

1.2

Appearance of the Fortress of Novigrad (*Aspetto della fortez[z]a di Novegradi*), site drawing with unframed legend, enclosed with a dispatch dated June 5, 1620. 57 × 44 cm. Archivio di Stato di Venezia, Provveditori da Terra e da Mar, filza 60, disegno 2.

1.3

Map of Novigrad and the arable land, hills, and waterways in its jurisdiction, enclosed with a dispatch dated October 10, 1605. 156 × 43 cm. Archivio di Stato di Venezia, Provveditori da Terra e da Mar, filza 419, disegno.

structures could have been added by hand as needed. Multiple prints already on the market could have been adapted for this purpose, at least for regional views of Dalmatia. But such a practice was not employed.

In any case, over time map layouts became increasingly complex with the addition of flaps by the seventeenth century to provide before-and-after views for proposed construction and/or to illustrate damage resulting from war. Even before this literal form of layering, the virtual nesting of features made the experience of maps more dynamic and interactive, comprising a radical departure from classical and medieval cartography and requiring a new set of user skills.

De' Barbari's *View of Venice* shared some of these nested features, including text and directional indicators, even if these indicators appeared as wind heads drawn from the classical tradition of world mapping. Together with the figures of Mercury and Neptune, these interface tools clutter the surface of the *View* and to some degree compromise its mimetic effects. Yet it is clear that verisimilitude was as much an imperative for de' Barbari and Kolb as it was for the Venetian government in its mapping initiative. In fact, Kolb referred to the *View* in his copyright petition as *vero des[e]gno* or "true design,"[33] which aligned it in key respects with the "true pictures" commissioned by the state. In Venice, as nowhere else, the time was ripe for the congruence of public and private interests in the evolving field of cartography. And this could be nowhere more apparent than in the publication of de' Barbari's print.

NOTES

1 Juergen Schulz, "The Printed Plans and Panoramic Views of Venice (1486–1797)," *Saggi e memorie di storia dell'arte* 7 (1970): 17.

2 Tina Najbjerb, "The Severan Marble Plan of Rome (Forma Urbis Romae)," Stanford Digital Forma Urbis Romae Project, accessed June 23, 2020, http://formaurbis.stanford.edu/docs/FURmap.html.

3 Lucia Nuti, "The Perspective Plan in the Sixteenth Century: The Invention of a Representational Language," *Art Bulletin* 76, no. 1 (1994): 105–28; David Friedman, "'Fiorenza': Geography and Representation in the Fifteenth Century

Karen-edis Barzman

City View," *Zeitschrift für Kunstgeschichte* 64 (2001): 56; Schulz, "The Printed Plans and Panoramic Views of Venice," 18.

4 Nuti, "The Perspective Plan," 109.

5 Norris Kelly Smith, "The Lost *Tavolette*," chap. 1 of *Here I Stand: Perspective from Another Point of View* (New York: Columbia University Press, 1994).

6 "Figurò [Alberti] una Vinegia in prospettiva e San Marco…," in Giorgio Vasari, *Le vite de' più eccellenti pittori scultori e architettori*, ed. Gaetano Milanesi (Florence: Sansoni, 1878–85), 2:547.

7 Juergen Schulz, "Pinturicchio and the Revival of Antiquity," *Journal of the Warburg and Courtauld Institutes* 25, no. 1/2 (1962): 39–40.

8 Elizabeth Ross, *Picturing Experience in the Early Printed Book: Breydenbach's "Peregrinatio" from Venice to Jerusalem* (University Park: Pennsylvania State University Press, 2014).

9 Nuti, "The Perspective Plan," 110.

10 On its earlier appearance in drawings, see Schulz, "The Printed Plans and Panoramic Views of Venice," 16.

11 On the *View*'s distortions, see Juergen Schulz, "Jacopo de' Barbari's View of Venice: Map Making, City Views, and Moralized Geography before the Year 1500," *Art Bulletin* 60, no. 3 (1978): 425–74; and Deborah Howard, "Venice as a Dolphin: Further Investigations into Jacopo de' Barbari's *View*," *Artibus et Historiae* 18, no. 35 (1997): 101–11.

12 On the inventory in Rosselli's shop, see Arthur M. Hind, *Early Italian Engraving: A Critical Catalogue with Complete Reproduction of All the Prints Described* (London: B. Quaritch, 1938), 1:304–8.

13 Friedman, "'Fiorenza,'" 56; and Jessica Maier, "Francesco Rosselli's Lost View of Rome: An Urban Icon and Its Progeny," *Art Bulletin* 94, no. 3 (2012): 394–411, both with citations to earlier scholarship.

14 Friedman, "'Fiorenza,'" 61.

15 On Rosselli's cartographic output, see Roberto Almagià, "On the Cartographic Work of Francesco Rosselli," *Imago Mundi* 8, no. 1 (1951): 27–34; and Suzanne Boorsch, "The Case for Francesco Rosselli as the Engraver of Berlinghieri's *Geographia*," *Imago Mundi* 56, no. 2 (2004): 152–69.

16 For an abstract of the petition (itself no longer extant), see appendix 2 in this volume.

17 David Landau and Peter Parshall, *The Renaissance Print, 1470–1550* (New Haven, CT: Yale University Press, 1994), 43; Howard, "Venice as a Dolphin," 102.

18 Archivio di Stato di Venezia (ASVe), Misti Consiglio dei Dieci 1454–59, Registro 15, fol. 197. The original Latin follows:

> 1459 [1460 m.v.] 27 febbraio. Cum de civitatibus castellis et provinciis

*Karen-edis
Barzman*

quae nostro Dominio per Dei gratiam subiectae sunt nemo est in regimine nostro qui, quando de illis locis consullitur, sciat dare particularem informationem de situ eorum, de latitudine et longitudine e de confinis, et que dominia vicina sunt et qui passus . . . , unde pro omni bono respectu providendum est habere in Cancelleria nostra aut Camera Consilii nostri Decem *in vera pictura* formam et esemplum omnium civitatim terrarium castellorum provinciarum et locorum nostrorum, ut quicunque volens consulere et providere super predictis habeat veram et particularem noticiam *ad oculum* et non ad opinionem alicuius. Vadit pars quod auctoritate hujus consilii scribatur et mandetur omnibus Rectoribus civitatum terrarum et castellorum nostrorum quod habito bono et vero consilio a civibus terre et ab aliis practicis et intelligentibus civitatis aut loci sui, designari faciat terram locum et districtum suum per signa ventorum et orientis et ponentis, castella, flumina, planiciem et distantiam de loco ad locum et loca vicina nobis et distantiam eorum, et illarum designationem ordinate depictam faciant diligenter a doctis et praticis examinari, si bene et recte depicta est; et hoc facto, illam picturam mittere debeant nostro Dominio.

For a summary of the scholarship, see Karen-edis Barzman, "Cartographic Line

and the 'Paper Management' of the Early Modern State: A Case Study of Venetian Dalmatia," *Mapline* 122 (2014): 10n4.

19 See Nuti, "The Perspective Plan," 106, on the humanist-informed articulation of the primacy of sight among the senses and the superiority of visual over textual representation, due in part to its presumed immediacy.

20 The seven Ottoman-Venetian Wars occurred in 1463–79 (Venetian loss of Negroponte); 1499–1503 (loss of strongholds in the Morea); 1537–40 (major losses in the Aegean); 1570–73 (Cyprus lost); 1645–69 (Crete lost); and 1684–99 and 1714–18, with Venetian gains in the Morea and Dalmatia.

21 Michael Mallett, *The Military Organization of a Renaissance State: Venice, 1400–1617* (Cambridge: Cambridge University Press, 1984), 203–4; Margaret King, "An Inconsolable Father and His Humanist Consolers: Jacopo Antonio Marcello, Venetian Nobleman, Patron and Man of Letters," in *Supplementum Festivum: Studies in Honor of Paul Oskar Kristeller*, ed. James Hankins (Binghamton, NY: Binghamton University Press, 1987), 221–46.

22 Patrick Gautier Dalché, "The Reception of Ptolemy's *Geography* (End of the Fourteenth to Beginning of the Sixteenth Century)," in *Cartography in the European Renaissance*, vol. 3 of *History of Cartography*, ed. David Woodward (Chicago: University of Chicago Press,

1987), 324; John Larner, "The Church and the Quattrocento Renaissance in Geography," *Renaissance Studies* 12, no. 1 (1998): 26–39.

23 King, "An Inconsolable Father," 228.

24 Daniela Dueck, "The Geographical Narrative of Strabo of Amasia," in *Geography and Ethnography: Perceptions of the World in Pre-modern Societies*, ed. Kurt A. Raaflaub and Richard J. A. Talbert (Oxford: Wiley-Blackwell, 2010), 236–51, 238.

25 Millard Meiss, "Strabo's Geography in Albi," chap. 2 of *Andrea Mantegna as Illuminator* (New York: Columbia University Press, 1957).

26 Piero Falchetta, *Fra Mauro's World Map with a Commentary and Translations of the Inscriptions* (Turnhout: Brepols, 2006).

27 ASVe, Provveditori alle fortezze, 11 (dated 1759, unpaginated), 2v, 30r.

28 For descriptions of such instruments in Italian, see Cosimo Bartoli, *Del modo di misurare* (Venice, 1564).

29 On "the god trick," see Donna Haraway, "Situated Knowledges: The Science Question in Feminism and the Privilege of Partial Perspective," *Feminist Studies* 14, no. 3 (1988): 575–99.

30 Ronald Edward Zupko, *Italian Weights and Measures from the Middle Ages to the Nineteenth Century* (Philadelphia: American Philosophical Society, 1981), 153.

31 James R. Akerman, "The Structuring of Political Territory in Early Printed Atlases," *Imago Mundi* 47 (1995): 138–54; Barzman, "Cartographic Line."

32 For details of some of the maps shown here and for additional examples from the Venetian archive, see Karen-edis Barzman, *The Limits of Identity: Early Modern Venice, Dalmatia, and the Representation of Difference* (Leiden: Brill, 2017), plates 5, 6, 11, 12, 13, 43, 44, and accompanying text. See also Barzman, Kristijan Juran, and Josip Faričić, "Cartography in the Service of the Venetian State: An Early Sixteenth-Century Map of Central and Northern Dalmatia by an Unknown Draftsman," *Geoadria* 24, no. 2 (2019): 93–139.

33 See Nuti, "The Perspective Plan," 107–8, on terms used to affirm the "truthfulness" of city views.

Piero Falchetta

A City as a World

Jacopo de' Barbari's *View* in 1500

2 THE YEAR 1962 MARKED THE BEGINNING of the modern debate on whether Jacopo de' Barbari's *View of Venice* is, or is not, a map. That year, Giuseppe Mazzariol and Terisio Pignatti published a one-to-one reproduction of a first-state print of the *View* accompanied by two short but innovative studies on de' Barbari and his representation of Venice.[1] In his essay within the 1962 volume, Pignatti insists on the hypothesis that the *View* was composed according to purely cartographic principles and methods.

Since that time, the battleground of scholars engaged in the study of this masterwork has often been dominated by two conflicting theories, though it seems difficult to trace a line that demarcates a clear separation between them. On one side, there are supporters of a theory that read the image as the result of an artistic work whose aim was to celebrate the power and the splendor of Venice. Rejecting the hypothesis of a cartographic origin of the map, in the concluding hypothesis of his deep investigation of de' Barbari's *View* published in 1978, Juergen Schulz stated that its purpose was most likely celebratory.[2] This shift marked a decided turn from a long scholarly trajectory originating from Schulz's early proposal that the *View* was most likely the result of a "scientific" program.[3] It is important to note that the role of artistic invention was strengthened in opposition to the role of cartographic procedures available at that time, possibly employed by Jacopo de' Barbari and his team of collaborators.

A similar "artistic" key of interpretation of the nature and the meaning of the *View* has been adopted by other historians interested not only in unveiling the method and procedures de' Barbari used but also in deciphering the ideology embedded in his work. In their writings they seem inclined to consider the *View*'s ultimate significance as a rhetorical glorification of Venice. In addition to Schulz, the scholars Giorgio Bellavitis, Giandomenico Romanelli, and Deborah Howard contributed to this line of reasoning; in particular, Howard developed an ideological meaning of the *View* and concluded that the notable compression within the left upper and lower sheets was deliberate to support a specific iconographic purpose—to present Venice visually as a dolphin.[4] In fact, the lack of documents related to the method followed by de' Barbari and his collaborators has led historians to base their analyses and interpretations mainly on the consideration of this specific issue: What was the impetus and reason for the perspectival distortions on the map, especially in the western part of the city?

Schulz and others have regarded those distortions as the direct consequence of unsystematic procedures possibly adopted by the author and his assistants, but they have also been considered the result of a "deliberate manipulation" intended to give the city allegoric imagery (Howard) or to exalt the strategic importance and power of the Venetian Arsenal (Bellavitis and Romanelli). On the other side of the debate, the cartographic theorists assert that those distortions were produced by the inadequacy of the tools and techniques employed in surveying the urban space, in measuring distances and bearings, and in transforming the rough geometric data into the drawing of Venice.

Schulz and others have plotted a grid of parallels and meridians over de' Barbari's *View* and have transferred that grid onto a present-day map of Venice. The experiment revealed that the space represented is not a flat surface but rather a curved space. In particular, Schulz suggested the joining of a panorama that reflects convexly bowed parallels across most of the image with those concavely bowed in the far distance, resembling something of a curved horizon, in attaining a broad panoramic image.[5] His opinion was that convexity and concavity are errors that reflect a wrong order of composition and were simply accidental. But this point has been disputed first by me, by Martin Kemp, and more recently by Vanna Bagarolo and Vladimiro Valerio.[6] The sophisticated technical analysis carried out on de' Barbari's *View of Venice*—analysis that took its cues from previous investigations—attempted to demonstrate from indirect evidence that those distortions were not introduced by accident or as an "artistic" choice by the author but rather that they are the result of a geometric process and, in particular, the projection of perspective onto a cylindrical surface.[7]

The overview of the different theories and hypotheses summarized here reveals that up to this point much scholarly discussion of the *View* has been largely centered on technical features (either specific ones or as a counterpoint to them), and in particular on the specific effects of the distortions, most likely produced by inadequate instruments and the process of converting the surveyed urban fabric into a drawing taken from an artificially elevated viewpoint. The aim of this summary of the scholarly debate is to set up what has been the crux of the dialogue about how and why the *View* was composed in an effort to recenter the whole question about the distortions from an entirely different point of view.

The *View* is surrounded by eight heads that are personifications of the principal winds or main directional coordinates, in accordance with the tradition of the medieval *computus* (a method for the calculation of the calendar date of Easter) and the cartographic practice of portolan charts and atlases produced in select Mediterranean cities, especially Venice, from the early fourteenth century onward. Five of these heads are portrayed in a standard way as putti blowing their own wind (plate 1). They are SVBSOLANVS (eastern wind, accompanied by the usual symbol of the cross), AVSTER / O[stro] (southern wind), AFFRICVS / AVSTERAF-FRICVS A[frico] (southwestern wind), FAVONIVS / P[onente] (western wind), and CORVS / CIRCIVS / M[aestro] (northwestern wind). The wind AQUILO / FVLTURNVS / G[reco] (northeastern wind) is a portrait of a bearded, middle-aged man—a proposed self-portrait of Jacopo de' Barbari—and the wind EVRAVSTER / EVRVS S[cirocco] (southeastern wind) is a proposed portrait of Anton Kolb (see also plate 8).[8] The northern wind

SEPTENTRIO / T[ramontana] is depicted as a blindfolded putto, a very uncommon—and possibly unprecedented—representation. The meaning of this allegorical figure in that specific position is not clear, but it is possible to associate it with the goodwill existing—or at least hoped for—between Venice and northern people, possibly for Anton Kolb and his relationship to the Serenissima.[9] The personification of goodwill as a blindfolded putto was described by Cesare Ripa in his treatise *Iconologia overo Descrittione dell'imagini universali cavate dall'antichità et da altri luoghi* (1593) as "un giovane nudo, allegro . . . con una benda agli occhi" (a young nude, cheerful . . . with a blindfold over his eyes).[10] It is important to note that for the first time there is a crown of winds blowing on a portrait of a city—no other examples are known prior to de' Barbari's *View*. Is their presence simply a decorative element, or it is possible to argue that they have a more specific function as an essential component of this work?

Heads and winds surrounding geographical space are often depicted on world maps, especially on Ptolemaic world maps composed from the mid-fifteenth century onward, both manuscript and printed. While it is uncertain whether manuscript maps with winds circulated in Venice in de' Barbari's time, Ptolemy's *Geography* was published in several printed editions during the second half of the fifteenth century, some of which bear world maps with winds. Among them there are Ptolemy's edition printed in Bologna by Domenico de Lapis (1477); the editions printed in Rome and Augsburg (around 1480); the Florentine edition by Francesco Berlinghieri (1482); and the world map by Johann Schnitzner from Armszheim for the edition printed in Ulm by Leinhar Holle (1482), among others (fig. 2.1). The presence of winds on those published world maps had a triple function: first, to recall the *auctoritas* of the classical geographic culture; second, to orientate the different parts of the *oecumene* in a way that was unknown in the majority of the world maps composed during the Middle Ages, when a "moralized" vision of earthly space was prevailing over the coherence of the spatial order; and third, to suggest and offer visual evidence that the earth is a sphere. This third point seems to be especially important and useful to comprehend the meaning and function of de' Barbari's winds within his *View*.

Like most world maps with winds, those that de' Barbari included surrounding Venice are portrayed in a way that suggests they encircle a curved space. This characteristic is especially evident in the southwestern part of the *View*, where the winds are foreshortened on a curved perspective, so that they give the impression of blowing from below the plan of the city; the

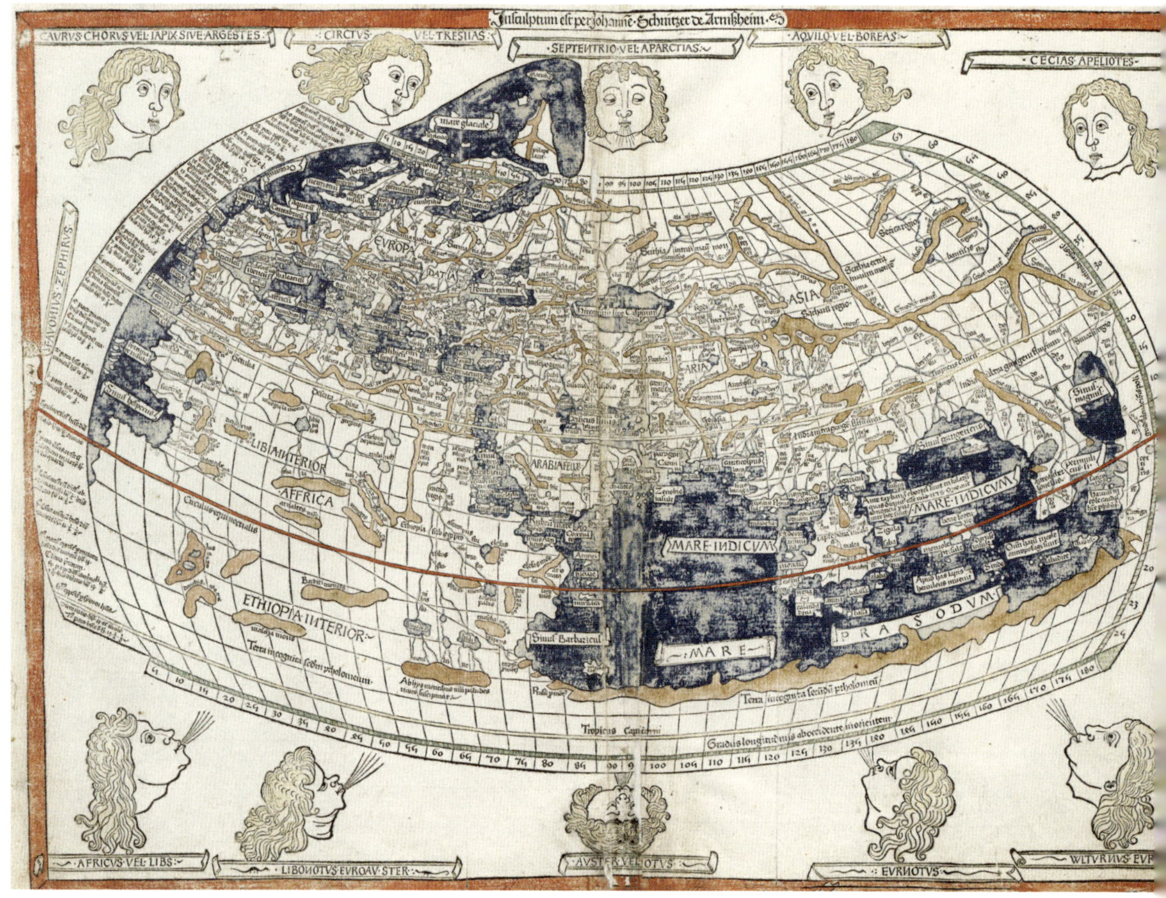

winds blowing from north and south do not follow the same conventions, and their puffs waft from above. It is also important to point out that unlike the heads on Ptolemaic world maps that are portrayed in upside-down positions along the southern edge of the world, on the *View* there is an increasing degree of incline proceeding from the southern wind EVRVS until the western wind FAVONIVS; in fact, his head is turned upside down, and his hair undoubtedly falls due to the effects of gravity. Why this deviation?

A possible response to this question may derive from an interesting experiment carried out on de' Barbari's *View* in 1985. A research team at the CIRCE Laboratory at the University Iuav of Venice superimposed the union grid of the orthophoto of Venice (in 1:500 scale) onto the *View* in an effort to make visible the distortions of parallels and meridians in different areas

44

of the city.[11] The visual result of the experiment is that they appear convex in the western part of Venice and more or less flat in the eastern part.[12] Even though Schulz recognized the convexity in his earlier study, such irregularities have been interpreted as errors introduced during the real process of composition, as discussed above. But they may also represent an attempt to find a solution to the problem of distortion: Given that the urban fabric in the western part of the city is more extended and densely woven in comparison to its eastern part, how is it possible to portray Venice in a manner that respects the framing and the size of the *View*?

The possible solution devised by de' Barbari, together with a team of technical assistants, could have been to project the image of Venice onto a flexible space, a space that has a curved surface similar to the shape of a spoon: to the east, in the narrower part of the city, the projection is flat; to the west, where the urban area is much wider and consequently overcrowded with palaces, churches, houses, canals, bridges, squares, and orchards, the urban fabric is represented as an approximatively convex surface. In sum, the eastern part of Venice would be the join of a spoon's handle, and the western part commensurate with its curvilinear back.

Such a solution could have been deduced by analogy from, or inspired by, Ptolemy's second projection with the presence of the personified winds on the *View* as a deliberate reference to the methods of cartography. The curvature of the space on de' Barbari's representation results from the adoption of a series of different points of view; in this way, the perspective is foreshortened "around" a nonflattened space, so that the depth of the urban fabric on the left side can be contained within the limited size of the image. If this hypothesis were true, the convexity of the *View*'s "parallels" and "meridians" on the western part of Venice would not be an error and/or attributed to the complications that arose during the creation of the overall composition: quite the opposite. It would be the result of an accurate strategy whose aim was to make visible the invisible, albeit with the support of the limited techniques and knowledge available at that time.

The technical features analyzed up to this point suggest that the influence of Ptolemy's *Geography* was not insignificant in the conception of the *View of Venice*. Beyond the issues raised by the question of how it was composed, there is a more general consideration to take into account. One of the most relevant consequences of the invention of the printing press was the wide circulation of a stable image of the world, and that stability centered primarily on the Ptolemaic printed maps of the world published as early as

1477. Before that moment, the shape and size of the world were not really defined, being, in most cases, the medieval mappamundi, which served as an expression of religious ideology rather than a geometrical concept of space. Ptolemy gave to the world a definite shape, a definite extension, and above all a definite *orientation*. The most sophisticated and technically advanced maps produced during the Middle Ages, the portolan charts, are not oriented, because their orientation would be determined according to the ship's route.

The personified winds who determine the *View*'s orientation give it a feature of world maps. Their inclusion seems to impart a suggested message: Venice is a city-world that sums up in itself all the qualities and riches of other cities. It stands at the center along the axis of goodwill that joins the northern peoples with the leading figure of Anton Kolb, the enterprising businessman fundamental in the realization of the *View* and possibly portrayed on its southern edge. In this sense, Jacopo de' Barbari's *View* is not only the celebrated and mysterious masterwork that continues to raise questions and to inspire theories and interpretations. It also can ultimately be considered the first "Ptolemaic perspective map" of a city—yet another innovation for its time.

NOTES

1 Some details of the *View* reproduced with the 1962 edition, and especially the detail of the wind "AVSTER" on the lower part, seem to introduce a variant that can be observed on one of the copies of this work preserved at the British Museum. In 1996, when I was writing the text for a website dedicated to the *View*, Tony Campbell, who at that time was map librarian at the British Library, made possible the understanding that the supposed variant was in fact the result of past restoration work carried out on the print. He wrote to me: "Several sections of the *View* have been filled in with paper and then the restorer has invented the missing outlines in hand-drawn ink. This applies to 'AVSTER.' There is a paper break immediately to the left of the second letter, i.e. removing the initial comma and the A. The old restorer filled in the clouds but didn't know Latin." It is consequently plausible that the 1962 reproduction of the *View* derives from

Piero Falchetta

the copy in London described by Campbell. For the "two short but innovative studies," see Giuseppe Mazzariol and Teresio Pignatti, *La pianta di Jacopo de' Barbari* (Venice: Cassa di Risparmio, 1962); and an enlarged version of Pignatti's essay that was published with the same title two years later in *Bollettino dei Musei Civici Veneziani* 9, nos. 1–2 (1964): 9–49.

2 Juergen Schulz, "Jacopo de' Barbari's View of Venice: Map Making, City Views, and Moralized Geography before the Year 1500," *Art Bulletin* 60, no. 3 (1978): 472; an enlarged Italian version of this study was published later: Juergen Schulz, "La veduta di Venezia di Jacopo de' Barbari: Cartografia, vedute di città e geografia moralizzata nel Medioevo e nel Rinascimento," in *La cartografia tra scienza e arte: Carte e cartografi nel Rinascimento italiano* (Modena: Panini, 1990), 13–63.

3 Schulz, "Jacopo de' Barbari's View of Venice," 439–40.

4 Giorgio Bellavitis, "L'evoluzione della struttura urbana di Venezia attraverso I secoli: I primi documenti cartografici," *Bollettino c.i.s.a.* 18 (1976): 225–39; Giorgio Bellavitis and Giandomenico Romanelli, "La Venezia di Jacopo de' Barbari," in *Venezia* (Rome: Laterza, 1985), 66–76, 247–48; Giandomenico Romanelli, "Venezia 1500," in *A volo d'uccello: Jacopo de' Barbari e le rappresentazioni di città nell'Europa del Rinascimento*, exhib. cat., ed. Giandomenico

Romanelli, Susanna Biadene, and Camillo Tonini (Venice: Arsenale, 1999), 12–18; Juergen Schulz, "La grande veduta 'a volo d'uccello' di Jacopo de' Barbari," in Romanelli, Biadene, and Tonini, *A volo d'uccello*, 58–68; Deborah Howard, "Venice as a Dolphin: Further Investigations into Jacopo de' Barbari's *View*," *Artibus et Historiae* 18, no. 35 (1997): 106.

5 Schulz, "Jacopo de' Barbari's View of Venice," 438.

6 See Piero Falchetta, "La misura dipinta: Rilettura tecnica e semantica della veduta di Venezia di Jacopo de' Barbari," *Ateneo Veneto* 178 (1991): 273–305; Martin Kemp, "Jacopo de' Barbari: *View of Venice*," in *Circa 1492: Art in the Age of Exploration*, exhib. cat, ed. Jay A. Levenson (Washington, DC: National Gallery of Art, 1991), 253–55; and Vanna Bagarolo and Vladimiro Valerio, "Jacopo de' Barbari: Una nuova ipotesi indiziaria sulla genesi prospettica della veduta *Venetie MD*," in *Cartografi veneti: Mappe, uomini e istituzioni per l'immagine e il governo del territorio*, ed. Vladimiro Valerio (Padua: Editoriale Programma, 2007), 118–35.

7 Rejecting the hypothesis that the distortions on the map are errors tout court, Balistreri-Trincanato believes they are "smart amendments" whose aim is to make easier the comprehension of the urban fabric: "Esistono veramente degli 'errori' o in realtà sono intelligenti correzioni adottate dal de' Barbari per ovviare ad 'aberrazioni' prospettiche

che avrebbero disturbato l'occhio di chi osserva la pianta e non avrebbero permesso la lettura di tanta parte della città?" Corrado Balistreri-Trincanato in *Venezia città mirabile: Guida alla veduta prospettica di Jacopo de' Barbari* (Verona: Cierre, 2009), 292. For "analysis that takes its cues from previous investigations," see esp. Andrea Masciantonio, "'Per la materia difficilissima': Spunti per una lettura d'insieme della veduta prospettica di Venezia," in Romanelli, Biadene, and Tonini, *A volo d'uccello*, 76–83; Piero Falchetta, "La veduta prospettica di Venezia tra teoria e pratica di misurazione dello spazio," in Romanelli, Biadene, and Tonini, *A volo d'uccello*, 69–75; Piero Falchetta, "Il putto rovesciato o Venezia nel cucchiaio: Note ultime sulla veduta di Jacopo de' Barbari," in *Venezia e Venezie: Descrizioni, interpretazioni, immagini: Studi in onore di Massimo Gemin*, ed. Fabrizio Borin and Filippo Pedrocco (Padua: il Poligrafo, 2003), 23–28. An intermediate position between the "artistic theory" and the "cartographic theory" has been put forward by Wilson: "Although the role of scientific instrumentation in the production of the de' Barbari woodcut has not been excluded, the extant evidence and topographical complexities suggest the woodcut was a 'studio fabrication' drawn from a recent survey. From 1485 to 1502, in fact, the cityscape was subjected to a thoroughgoing physical inspection, and this may have provided the data for the bird's-eye view." Bronwen Wilson, *The World in Venice: Print, the City, and Early Modern Identity* (Toronto: University of Toronto Press, 2005), 31.

8 Schulz, "Jacopo de' Barbari's View of Venice," 428.

9 Anton Kolb was one of the wealthiest German "businessmen" active in Venice between the end of the fifteenth century and the beginning of the sixteenth; the Venetian authorities also granted him one of the most prestigious rooms at the Fondaco dei Tedeschi at Rialto, next to the room given to a member of the powerful Fugger family, possibly Ulrich Fugger the Elder (1441–1510); see Falchetta, "La misura dipinta."

10 Cesare Ripa, *Iconologia overo Descrittione d'imagini delle virtu', vitii, affetti, passioni humane, corpi celesti, mondo e sue parti* (Padua: Pietro Paolo Tozzi, 1611), 158. I believe the recently expressed interpretation of the north wind must be rejected: "In this [de' Barbari's] case, the North Italian tradition of the North wind as bringer of diseases and spoiler of harvests makes it plausible that the point of the representation is to show a pre-Reformation lack of enlightenment, manners, and civilization." Helena Wangefelt Ström and Federico Barbierato, "'Omne malum ab Aquilone': Images of the Evil North in Early Modern Italy and Their Impact on Cross-Religious Encounters," in *Visions of North in Premodern Europe*, ed. Dolly Jørgensen and Virginia Langum (Turnhout: Brepols, 2018), 268.

11 Francesco Guerra et al., "Informatica e 'infografica' per lo studio della veduta prospettica di Venezia," in Romanelli, Biadene, and Tonini, *A volo d'uccello*, 93–100; and Bagarolo and Valerio, "Jacopo de' Barbari," 124.

12 A similar result was obtained by Schulz, "Jacopo de' Barbari's View of Venice," 438.

Cosimo Monteleone

A Perspectival Investigation of Jacopo de' Barbari's *View of Venice*

3 The *View of Venice* established a turning point in the history of urban mapping. It was an invention, and its exceptional features have led scholars to wonder whether it represents a scientific application of cartography or, rather, a work of art. Until now no documentary sources have emerged to shed light on the production of the *View*, and there is only one record related to its publication. Based on these uncertainties, we can only formulate hypotheses. This essay attempts to indicate new possible paths of interpretation as related to the fifteenth-century study of mathematics, little explored until now. Specifically, it offers new considerations of the *View*, outlining the role of perspective and its discussions within the scientific, cultural, and artistic *milieu* in Venice at the beginning of the sixteenth century—what may have influenced Jacopo de' Barbari's work.

In the Quattrocento, in addition to literary and philosophical works, humanists, including select artists, rediscovered scientific treatises of the Ancients, like Ptolemy's *Geography*, Apollonius's *Conics*, and Proclus's *Comments* in Book I of Euclid's *Elements*. In Venice by the mid-fifteenth century, mathematics incited great curiosity and intellectual interest, indispensable to the Rialto School, where logic and philosophy were taught.[1] Indeed, there was a particular interest in exact sciences due in part to Cardinal Bessarion's prodigious library, which he bequeathed to the Venetian state in 1468; this heritage included many known important mathematical source of the classical world.[2] Among the supporters of this scientific *renovatio* were leading scholars orbiting within Venice (and the Veneto) shortly before the publication of the *View*: Ermolao Barbaro (1410–71), Giorgio Valla (1447–1500), and Luca Pacioli (1445–1517).

The Aristotelian humanist Ermolao Barbaro collected Euclid's works as well as Ptolemy's *Geography* and composed mathematical works, now lost.[3] The other great humanist interested in mathematical writings was Giorgio Valla, whose library was particularly famous in the late fifteenth century because it contained the rare and coveted *Code A* of Archimedes, which had a significant influence on mathematical research of the Cinquecento. The contents of this work, together with those of the rest of Valla's mathematical collection, were included in his *De rebus expedentis at fugiendis*, published in Venice in 1501, a year after the publication of the *View*. Although very different works—one a scientific book and the other an urban view—they both attest to the cultural fervor that Venice experienced at the beginning of the new century. It should also be noted that like the *View*, which constituted a reference point for successive representations of Venice, Valla's treatise was considered an important mathematical encyclopedia for more than forty years following its publication.[4]

Finally, the mathematician Luca Pacioli published two scientific works: *Summa de arithmetica, geometria, proportioni et proportionalità* (Venice, 1494), in which he describes the Albertian *costruzione abbreviata* for the perspectival representation of reality; and *De divina proportione* (Venice, 1509), for which Leonardo da Vinci (1452–1519) illustrated illusionistic Platonic and Archimedean solids.[5] Indeed, a suspended Archimedean polyhedron, in particular a rhombicuboctahedron in a painting attributed to de' Barbari,

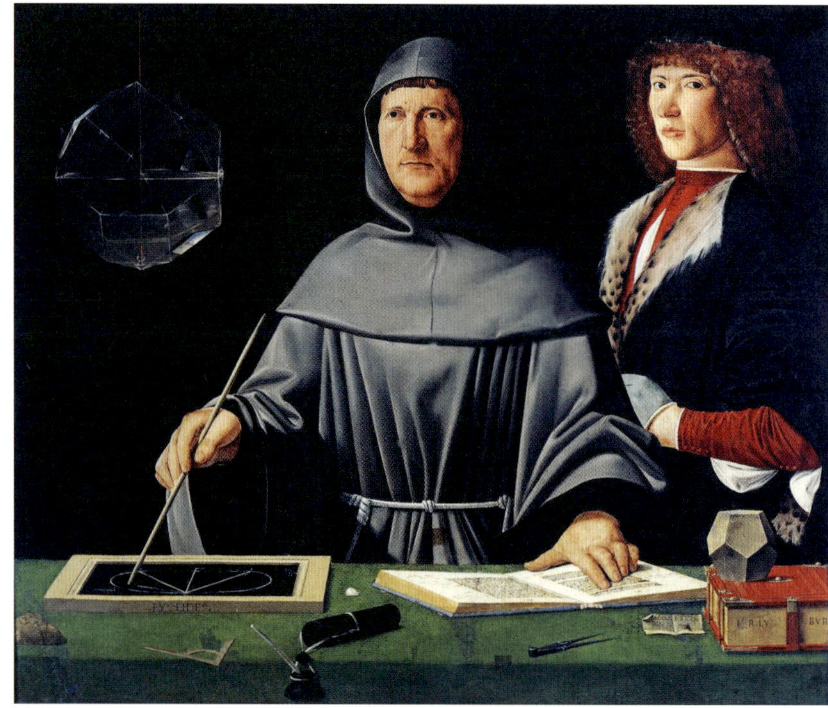

offers an early indication of the possible link between the Venetian artistic culture and its interest in mathematics (fig. 3.1).

This painting, dated 1495 according to the inscribed *cartellino* on the table, depicts Luca Pacioli with a young man at his side, possibly Guidobaldo da Montefeltro, Duke of Urbino (1472–1508).[6] Despite the uncertainty of the attribution to de' Barbari, the painting comes from the Venetian school and shows the mastery of geometric challenges: the *perspectiva artificialis* and the laws of optics.[7] Together with the two depicted men, the painting focuses on a third inanimate protagonist, the crystal rhombicuboctahedron painted in perspective, suspended on a barely perceptible wire in the upper left and partially filled with water. Beyond the difficulty of representing a complex geometric object, the painter was able to render the transparencies exceptionally skillfully, both in the reflection of the transparent surfaces and in the refraction of the water. This solid is one of thirteen Archimedean polyhedrons that, together with the five Platonic solids, symbolized divine perfection and cosmic order.[8] Other elements scattered on the table, like compasses, geometric diagrams, and scientific books, refer to a mathematical conception of the world, pictorially expressed through perspective, that, as a geometric construction, imposes a systematic order on the visual reality from a single point of view.[9]

The definition that Leon Battista Alberti (1404–72) gives of perspective, as a section of the visual pyramid made by a plane, establishes a biunivocal relationship between the points of a real object, for example the square of vertices $ABCD$, and its perspective image, $A'B'C'D'$. Referring the same schema to the *View*, since we have only a perspective image—that is, the bird's-eye view—it is geometrically impossible, with either analog or digital means, to go back to the drawing that de' Barbari portrayed as well as to find the position of his eye (fig. 3.2). These considerations demonstrate the high degree of uncertainty with scholarly attempts at reconstructions to compare the *View* with contemporary maps of today's city by means of computational algorithms or other procedures related to perspectival laws.[10] In all these cases the imprecision of the reconstruction is of the second order of infinity. In enacting these studies, scholars cite the precision of the *View* and the identification of recognizable architectural features (bell towers, noteworthy buildings, the shape of the Venetian *rii* and *calli*) to connect the perspective view with the city of today. But in this way they have taken for granted that the survey, foreshortened by de' Barbari, has been faithful to the contemporary shape of the city. Indeed, all these studies end up highlighting the presence of distortions in the *View*, alternating more or less plausible solutions to explain a phenomenon compromised from the beginning. As Falchetta states: "The 'mistakes' were introduced into the plan not so much when the foreshortening has been carried out, but first, during the measurement and survey phase."[11] In Venice, perspective had been enthusiastically adopted by the main artists practicing there in the fifteenth century. Giovanni Bellini (1433–1516) and Vittore Carpaccio (1465–1525/1526)) had shown great ability in the representation of architecture and space; therefore, the idea to foreshorten Venice could imply that Jacopo de' Barbari had applied this method.

When the *View* was created, the first treatises on linear perspective had not yet been published,[12] except for the brief description of Alberti's *costruzione abbreviata*, which, as mentioned, was also contained in the *Summa* written by Pacioli and published in Venice. However, copies of manuscripts on the subject were circulating in artistic circles and, certainly, the most complete was *De prospectiva pingendi* by Piero della Francesca (1416/1417–92). Piero's work can be considered the first scientific treatise on *perspectiva artificialis*, because it consists of a scrupulous codification of the subject, an

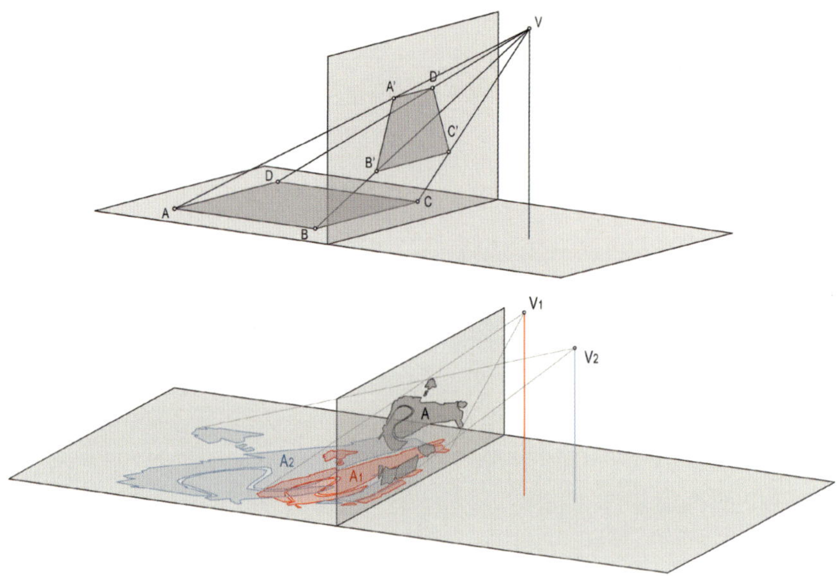

<table>
<tr><td>3.2</td><td>orderly description of rules clarified by examples. Some clues suggest that</td></tr>
</table>

3.2

Leon Battista Alberti's section of the visual pyramid that demonstrates the impossibility of finding the eye of the observer or the shape of the survey of Venice, starting from the perspectival view.

orderly description of rules clarified by examples. Some clues suggest that *De prospectiva pingendi* was available to Venetian artists between the end of the fifteenth century and the beginning of the sixteenth, beyond the fact that manuscripts clearly circulated.[13] The most important indirect evidence is the presence in Venice of Luca Pacioli, friend and pupil of Piero della Francesca. The mathematician refers to his master within his scientific works, encompassing Piero della Francesca's theories and aspects of his treatises. For instance, the formulation of Alberti's *costruzione abbreviata* in the *Summa* is similar to that of Book I in the *De prospectiva pingendi*.[14] Even an Italian translation of Piero's *De quinque corporibus regularibus* is inserted in the *De divina proportione*, which led to the accusation that Pacioli plagiarized.[15] It is therefore legitimate to speculate that the mathematician brought a copy of *De prospectiva pingendi* with him to Venice and that its contents were disseminated to (and discussed within) the scientific and artistic circles of the city, pointing to the recognition of this text through the accusation of plagiarism. To further this claim, it is sufficient to consider *La pratica della perspettiva* (Venice, 1568) by Daniele Barbaro (1514–68), a treatise that clearly owes much to *De prospectiva pingendi*. The book replicates text and figures of *De prospectiva pingendi*, further suggesting that Piero's manuscript circulated

54

in Venice.[16] It is Giovanni Zamberti, the man that Barbaro claimed to be his master, who may have provided a copy of *De prospectiva pingendi* to the scholar; indeed, Zamberti most likely had access to *De prospectiva pingendi* through his brother Bartolomeo (1473–1539), author of a Latin translation of Euclid's *Elements* published in Venice in 1505.[17] We know that Bartolomeo Zamberti was in close contact with Luca Pacioli, who disagreed with some of his positions in the Latin translation, so much so that in 1509 Pacioli decided to publish, also in Venice, a revised version, less humanistic and more mathematical, of Book V of Euclid's *Elements*.[18] While there are no direct links among these figures, it is indisputable that the circles of scholars and artists interested in the theoretical debates of perspective and the larger field of optics would have sought out knowledge and new ideas in an effort to consolidate and strengthen their own published contributions.

Mathematical problems without doubt were the subject of study, lectures, and intellectual conversations in Venice at the beginning of the sixteenth century; indeed, in 1508 Luca Pacioli presented a famous lesson on proportion in San Bartolomeo attended by many exponents of the scientific and artistic community of the city in the Rialto School.[19] This was the environment in which Jacopo de' Barbari was immersed and worked. Some scholars have already amply demonstrated that at the end of the fifteenth century, scientific treatises and measuring instruments were available to carry out the survey of a city.[20] The space could be measured either by direct means, for example annotated strings, or indirect instruments, based on the principles of Euclid's *Optics*, using tools such as the *quadratum geometricum*.

Returning to the *View*, in the petition of Antonio Kolb we read that Venice had been portrayed *iusta et proprimente*, meaning "exactly like it is," suggesting that the artist had first measured (or asked a team of surveyors to measure) the city and later adjusted the survey in order to represent the *forma urbis* in the most optically correct way (see appendix 2). But how could a Renaissance artist have put the plan of a city in perspective from a position he could never have reached in reality? We can find the answer in two treatises: *De prospectiva pingendi* by Piero della Francesca and *De pictura* by Alberti. In Book III, Piero describes the *costruzione legittima* of Filippo Brunelleschi (1377–1426), as applied to shorten complex objects such as the human head.[21] To use this geometric process it is necessary to represent any object of reality in two preparatory drawings (plan and elevation). Then the

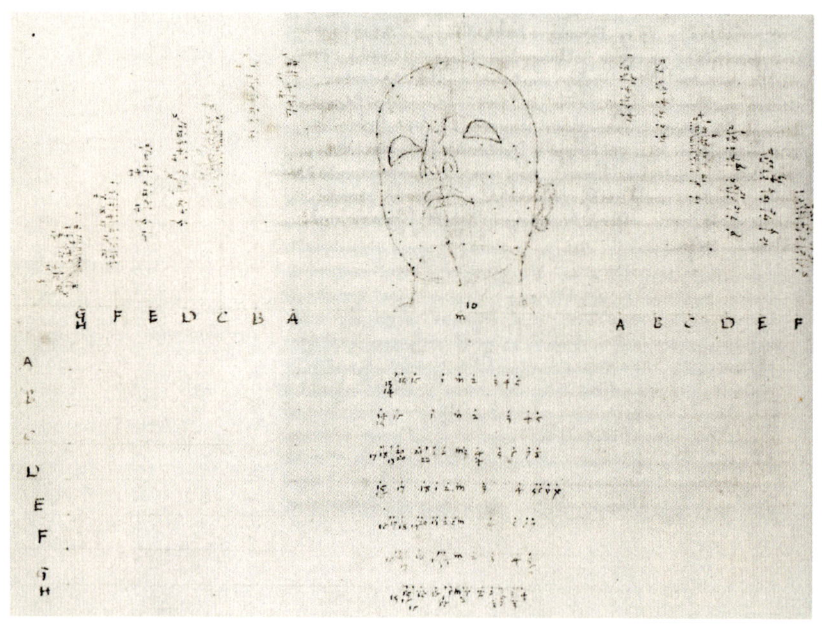
H F E D C B A
A B C D E F
A
B
C
D
E
F
G
H
m

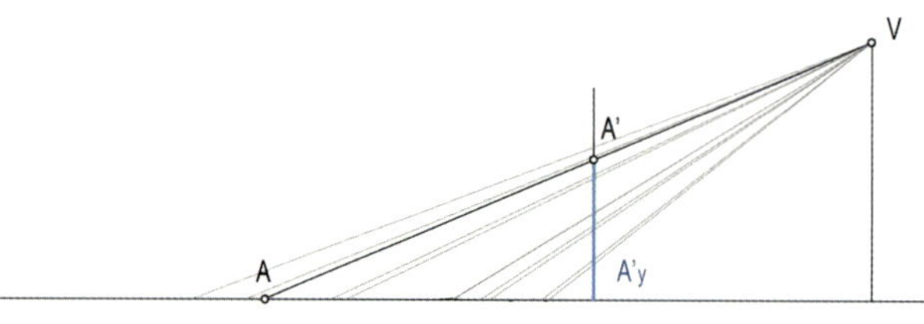
V
A'
A
A'y

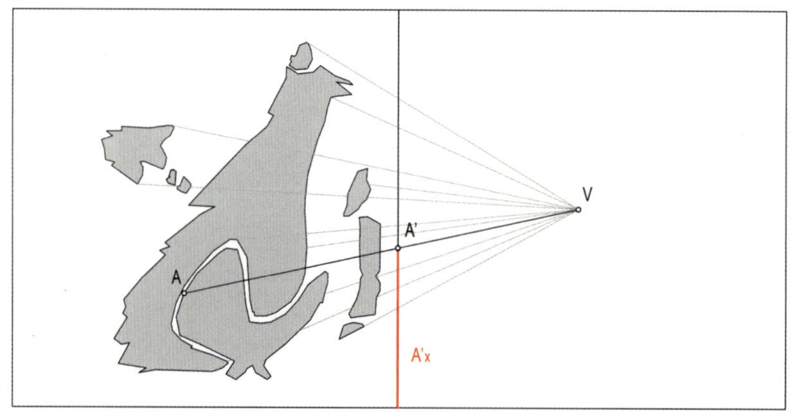
V
A'
A
A'x

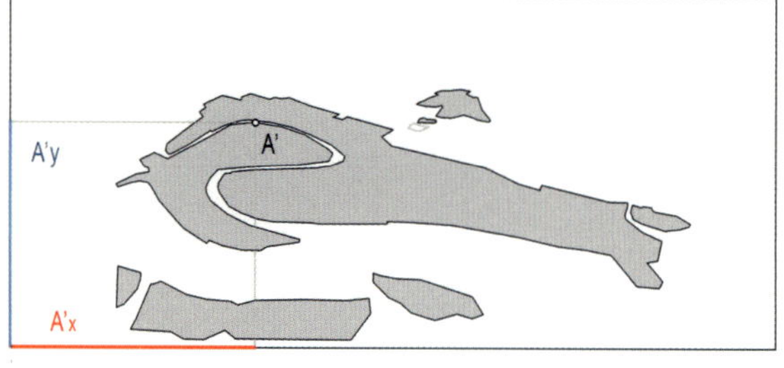
A'y
A'
A'x

draftsman could draw the lines that join selected points of the object to the eye of the observer and identify the intersections that these lines generate with the pictorial plane. The perspectival position of each point is marked on the picture by crossing the distances of the intersections that the draftsman read directly on the preparatory drawings.[22] In the case of the *View*, the application of *costruzione legittima* to the forma urbis is effective because it relates to a map—that is, a drawing in two dimensions—as opposed to a human head, which must be represented in three (fig. 3.3).

A second, more convenient method could have been to place the survey of Venice in front of an Albertian veil to draw directly the perspective appearances of the forma urbis from an established point of view (fig. 3.4).[23] This solution has some practical advantages. In addition to eliminating the lengthy calculation of measurements, the Albertian veil would have been suitable for a subdivision of the drawing adapted to the six wooden blocks necessary for printing. However, with both methods it would have been possible only to shorten the edges of the *View* and, at most, the positions of the most important architectural landmarks drawn in it. The outlines and the details of buildings were probably represented "freely" at a later time, after having enlarged the perspective of the plan that was to be carved into the wooden blocks. The choice to represent the dense urban fabric in axonometry seems, at first glance, linked to a simplification of the drawing. Indeed, viewed in perspective, the edges of the buildings should not have been parallel to each other, as shown in the *View*; rather, they would have converged at the relative vanishing points. This obviously would have complicated the graphic execution considerably. But we cannot exclude that this may have been a specific optical choice, since, given the great distance of the point of view, an axonometric representation of the buildings constitutes a reasonably good approximation of their perspective.

Based on the considerations made in this essay, it is possible to conclude that the *View* is a scientific cartographic representation of Venice, even if its degree of precision is not yet possible to establish. The dissemination of scientific and mathematical treatises, as well as the theories and techniques to survey topographies, make this hypothesis clear. It should be added that in the Renaissance, after its discovery, perspective constituted the privileged means of artists to represent rational, infinite, constant, and homogeneous space. It is therefore reasonable to hypothesize that, to represent Venice from a bird's-eye view, Jacopo de' Barbari translated the measurable shape of his city into an appropriately drawn scale. In this, along with its incredible

Piero della Francesca's perspective of a head (*De prospectiva pingendi*, 91v, mss. Regg. A 41/2, Reggio Emilia, Biblioteca Panizzi) and *costruzione legittima* applied to a survey of Venice to obtain its perspectival view.

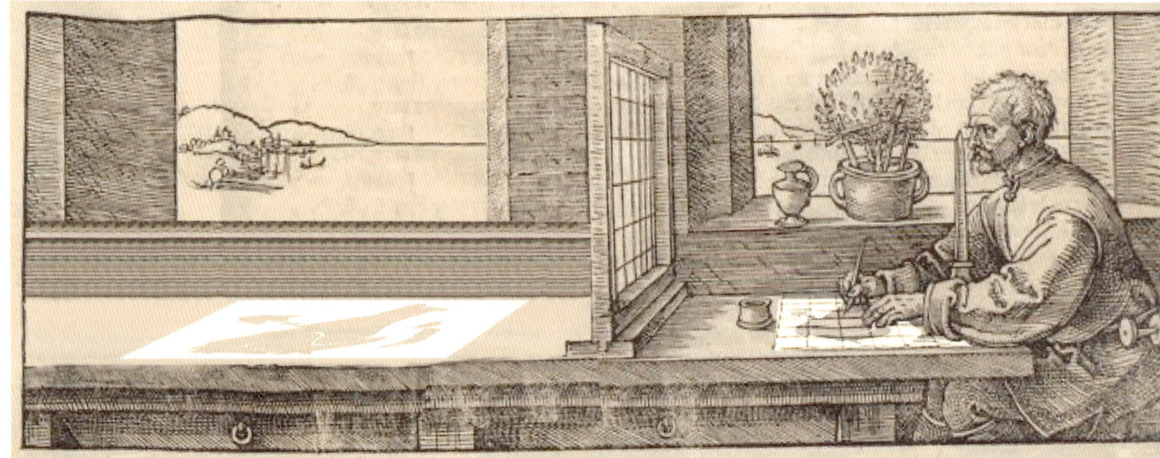

detail, the *View* is also a work of art. The deformations could be explained not only as a compositional invention but also as an adaptation to the limits imposed by the perspective code.[24] It should be recalled that perspective is only an approximation of real vision, which brings the effect of marginal deformations onto perspective images, which artists of the fifteenth century such as Leonardo da Vinci and Piero della Francesca well knew.[25] In most cases, however, artists, in order to avoid marginal deformations and make the perspective image more acceptable, adjusted the final representation, deviating from the scientific rigor of geometric construction.

Although imperfect from a psychophysiological point of view, perspective still allowed for the construction of a figurative space following a geometric model of measurable reality. And for this reason it was held in high regard by the artists of that era. Renaissance artists used perspective to show that there was an effective integration between the figurative world and the exact sciences. These could be the reasons that, since its publication, the *View*'s uncanny correspondence with many aspects of Venice in reality is one of the primary features that continues to fascinate observers today.

1 Bruno Nardi, "La Scuola di Rialto e l'umanesimo veneziano," in *Umanesimo europeo e umanesimo veneziano*, ed. Vittore Branca (Florence: Sansoni, 1963), 93–139.

2 Paul Lawrence Rose, *The Italian Renaissance of Mathematics* (Geneva: Librairie Droz, 1975), 46.

3 Aubrey Diller, "The Library of Francesco and Ermolao Barbaro," *Italia Medioevale e Umanistica* 6 (1963): 254–62; *Quaestiones geometricae* (1490) and *Liber de convenientia astronimiae et medicinae* (1492).

4 Johan Ludvig Heriberg, *Beiträge zur Geschichte Georg Valla und Bibliothek* (Wiesbaden: Harrassowitz, 1968).

5 Luigi Vagnetti, *De naturali et artificiali perspectiva* (Florence: Grafistampa, 1979), 224; Cosimo Monteleone, "I poliedri regolari e semi-regolari tra storia, teorie e nuove frontiere della rappresentazione," in *Territori e frontiere della rappresentazione*, ed. Antonella di Luggo et al. (Rome: Gangemi, 2017), 201–8.

6 Fritz Heinemann, *Giovanni Bellini e i Belliniani* (Venice: Neri Pozza, 1962), 274–75.

7 Cosimo Monteleone, *La prospettiva di Daniele Barbaro: Note critiche e trascrizione del manoscritto It. IV, 39=5446* (Rome: Aracne, 2020), 82–83.

8 Francesca Folicaldi, *Il numero e le sue forme: Storie di poliedri da Platone a Poinsot passando per Luca Pacioli* (Florence: Nardini, 2005).

9 Erwin Panofsky, "Die Perspektive als 'symbolische Form,'" *Vorträge der Bibliothek Warburg* 4 (1927): 258–330; Rudolf Arnheim, *Art and Visual Perception* (Berkeley: University of California Press, 1957).

10 Francesco Guerra et al., "Informatica e 'infografica' per lo studio della veduta prospettica di Venezia," in *A volo d'uccello: Jacopo de' Barbari e la rappresentazione di città nell'Europa del Rinascimento*, exhib. cat., ed. Giandomenico Romanelli, Susanna Biadene, and Camillo Tonini (Venice Mestre: Arsenale, 1999), 92–100; Vanna Bagarolo and Vladimiro Valerio, "Jacopo de' Barbari: Una nuova ipotesi indiziaria sulla genesi prospettica della veduta *Venetie MD*," in *Cartografi veneti: Mappe, uomini e istituzioni per l'immagine e il governo del territorio*, ed. Vladimiro Valerio (Padua: Editoriale Programma, 2007), 119–35.

11 "Gli 'errori' furono introdotti nella pianta non tanto nel momento in cui ne fu effettuato lo scorcio, bensì prima, durante la fase di misurazione e rilevamento." Piero Falchetta, "La misura dipinta: Rilettura tecnica e semantica della veduta di Venezia di Jacopo de' Barbari," *Ateneo Veneto* 178 (1991): 297.

12 Vagnetti, *De naturali et artificiali perspectiva*, 195–280.

13 Margaret Daly Davis, "Carpaccio and the Perspective of Regular Bodies," in *La prospettiva rinascimentale: Codificazioni e trasgressioni*, ed. Marisa Dalai-Emiliani (Florence: Centro Di, 1980), 183–200.

14 Hubert Damisch, *L'origine de la perspective* (Paris: Flammarion, 1987).

15 Margaret Daly Davis, *Piero della Francesca's Mathematical Treatises* (Ravenna: Longo, 1977), 44–63.

16 Cosimo Monteleone, "The Mathematical Space of Daniele Barbaro," in *Nexus Architecture and Mathematics Conference Book*, ed. Kim Williams and Marco Bevilacqua (Pisa: KWB, 2018), 49–54; Monteleone, *La prospettiva di Daniele Barbaro*, 71–77.

17 Bartolomeo Zamberti, *Euclidis megarensis philosophi platonici mathematicarunt disciplinarum janitoris* (Venice: Giovanni Tacuino, 1505).

18 Luca Pacioli, *Euclidis Megarensis philosophi acutissimi mathematicorumque omnium sine controversia principis opera a Campano interprete fidissimo tralata* (Venice: Paganino Paganini, 1509). For the disagreements between Zamberti and Pacioli, see Rose, *The Italian Renaissance of Mathematics*, 52.

19 Erin Mae Black, "La prolusione di Luca Pacioli del 1508 nella chiesa di S. Bartolomeo e il contesto intellettuale veneziano," in *La chiesa di S. Bartolomeo e la comunità tedesca a Venezia*, ed. Natalino Bonazza, Isabella di Leonardo, and Gianmario Guidarelli (Venice: Marcianum, 2013), 87–104.

20 For scientific treatises, see Piero Falchetta, "La veduta prospettica di Venezia tra teoria e pratica di misurazione dello spazio," in Romanelli, Biadene, and Tonini, *A volo d'uccello*, 68–75. For measuring instruments, see Daniela Stroffolino, *La città misurata: Tecniche e strumenti di rilevamento nei trattati a stampa del Cinquecento* (Rome: Salerno, 1999); Daniela Stroffolino, "Tecniche e strumenti per 'misurare con la vista,'" in Romanelli, Biadene, and Tonini, *A volo d'uccello*, 38–51.

21 Massimo Mussini and Luigi Grasselli, *Piero della Francesca: De prospectiva pingendi* (Sansepolcro: Aboca, 2008), 257–61.

22 Giusta Nicco Fasola, *De prospectiva pingendi: Piero della Francesca* (Florence: Sansoni, 1942), 124.

23 Lyle Massey, *Picturing Space, Displacing Bodies: Anamorphosis in Early Modern Theories of Perspective* (University Park: Pennsylvania State University Press, 2003), 104.

24 Juergen Schulz, "La grande veduta a volo d'uccello di Jacopo de' Barbari," in Romanelli, Biadene, and Tonini, *A volo d'uccello*, 58–68.

25 Corrado Maltese, "La prospettiva curva di Leonardo da Vinci e uno strumento di Baldassarre Lanci," in Dalai-Emiliani, *La prospettiva rinascimentale,* 417–25; Vagnetti, *De naturali et artificiali perspectiva,* 212–16.

Giorgio Tagliaferro

An Artist's Address Book

Notes on Venice's Artistic Geography

4 IN OCTOBER 1493 the Marquis of Mantua, Francesco II Gonzaga, commissioned from Gentile Bellini a model of a "portrait" of Venice for a cycle of city views to be frescoed in his palace in Gonzaga.[1] Within a couple of months Bellini sent the marquis a view of St. Mark's Square, along with a retouched drawing of Venice made by his late father, Jacopo, and a sketch of Cairo for the same cycle.[2] When, three years later, Francesco ordered a view of Paris from Giovanni Bellini, the artist spurned the request on the basis that he "had never seen" the city.[3] This might simply be an excuse to decline a commission in which he was not interested. However, his refusal serves to emphasize the difference between depicting an environment one has experienced directly, or even inhabits—as Venice was for Bellini—and

copying it from a model, as Gentile had done when he made a sketch from a "print of Cairo."[4] Had Giovanni accepted the commission, he would have provided a reproductive *View* of Paris. This would not have reflected his own inner *vision* of the city, stemming from an engagement with, or deeper understanding of, its physical and social environment.

This episode highlights, indirectly, the significance of Jacopo de' Barbari's *View of Venice* as the product of an artist who reportedly hailed from, and for some time lived in, the city he portrayed. This aspect has not received particular attention hitherto but may allow us to speculate on this fact: the author has presented us with a view that does not simply register his perceptual experience of Venice but also conveys a vision of his own habitat. In fact, the *View* is not merely a topographical transcription but an evocative representation that elicits an embodied experience. At first glance, Venice appears as a coherent whole, a compact body, so homogeneously structured and firmly situated within its geographical setting that it may seem impenetrable. On closer inspection, however, the viewer is drawn into a detailed depiction of the city's fabric and encouraged to look closely.[5]

The bird's-eye view makes this twofold mode of representation possible: while its synoptic effect leaves the sense of the whole intact, its multifocal structure enables our gaze to freely meander through the web of buildings, streets, squares, and canals. We, as viewers, are urged to move across the surface and navigate these details, thereby performing a virtual itinerary from one *contrada* (neighborhood/parish) to another, each one identified by the name of its corresponding church. However, even while we fix on a spot, our peripheral view anticipates where our eyes will next settle. We are fully immersed in the depths of the city, enjoying its localities, and at the same time we are conscious that these sites form part of an interconnected network in which we are able to orientate ourselves, assisted by the mobile gaze. Each building is meticulously depicted, catching the viewer's attention. Nonetheless, their rendering is summary to some extent, inviting the viewer to observe them over and over again, to explore their shape and positioning in relation to the environment. Simultaneously, the shading system, the swellings of ground, the irregular lines of the chimneys and roof tiles, the wavy surface of the canals, and the suggestively rendered ripples on the lagoon evoke the vibrancy and changing nature of living things. This helps impart the impression of an inhabited city. The fact that a limited number of residents are shown, primarily boatsmen in the waters, leaves us room to fill the empty spaces of the *calli* (streets) and *campi* (squares) with our own virtual presence, to appropriate and inhabit the space of the city through physical and optical movement.

Theoretical Construct of an Artistic Geography

Overall this perceptual engagement communicates—as has been noted— "the temporality and particulars of lived experiences of the city."[6] It may be further argued that the *View*, by inviting us to repeat in our imagination a bodily experience performed through the urban fabric, encapsulates the transitive relation between an inhabitant and the surroundings. Additionally, given that our act of appropriation of the space depicted is set in motion by de' Barbari's own act of appropriation of the real space, it is not secondary that the author was himself a dweller of the city. This fact implies that the representational world of the picture is to the artist what a city is to its citizen. The picture is thereby a mental projection that entails the projection of social practices performed by the artist within the city's environment. It carries not just the view of a distinct urban morphology but also a vision grounded in the artist's ability to make a living place of the clusters of streets, canals, and buildings. The physical structure of Venice is therefore put in relation to its function as a social habitat, experienced concretely from within (by the author) and implicitly from without (by the beholder).

Questions may arise, however, as to how the depiction of Venice's morphology can itself, with the absence of many everyday activities, communicate social meaning to its viewers and how this can transmit a sense of the author's lived experience. In this respect, Henri Lefebvre's theory on the production of space provides us with some useful tools, for it centers the social discourse on the representation of space. According to Lefebvre, space is produced by, and produces, physical, mental, and social practices that reflect respectively the threefold characterization of space as perceived, conceived, and lived. Within this process, the spatial practices that "secrete" the material (i.e., physical, perceived) space of a society are interconnected with two different modes of representation connected respectively with conceived and lived space: "representations of space," which are mental practices conceptualized by planning experts to impose an order based on logic, scientific knowledge, and ideology; and "spaces of representation," which reflect an appropriation of space by its inhabitants and users, most likely including artists, writers, and philosophers, who use images and symbols to impart space with certain meanings.[7]

If we apply Lefebvre's scheme to the *View*, this can be seen as a conceptualized "representation of space" in that it presents Venice as a geographical abstraction, a coherent system of signs informed by scientific knowledge. Moreover, it co-opts established symbols (e.g., Mercury and Neptune) into an ideologized fabrication that conforms to the credo of the ruling (patrician) class, which is precisely what distinguishes this category of Lefebvre's theory. On the other hand, along the lines described above, the bird's-eye view constructs a representational space that, following Lefebvre, can be defined as "directional, situational, or relational, because it is essentially qualitative" and "implies time," thereby prompting the beholder to appropriate that space in a de-ideologized way.[8] The *View* expresses the author's appropriation of the physical space through social practice, inasmuch as it enables the beholder to grasp the lived experience through imagination. In this way it functions as a site for the re-production of space, which receives meaning through consequential acts of appropriation and reappropriation. Through these, the city is reimagined as a place for living, eliciting diverse responses from viewers depending on their familiarity with it.

John Dewey posited that artifacts can be regarded as sediments of lived experience, which set individual and collective subjects (the artist and the audience) in communication with one another.[9] This often happens due to an artwork's power to create a pictorial space that connects the world of the image with the beholder's world, even more so in the case of city views. In particular, Renaissance artists placed the construction of coherent and relatable spatial systems at the heart of their visual communication strategies. Along with these, though, other strategies—of production, labor organization, marketing, self-fashioning, and so on—are brought into play in innumerable situations and combinations throughout the creative process, and function as variables of the social geography of a given context, which the artwork may communicate.

Art historians typically think in terms of a geography of art, where provenance is considered an unconditional source of identity and the focus is on a self-governing subject creator. However, the complexity of the dynamics from which artifacts originate suggests that turning to a consideration of geography, where artistic and social dynamics are intermingled and where the products are better understood as expressions of subjects that are diversified and many-sided, may be more useful. An artistic geography that positions the artist as the catalyst of processes that happen within the structures and contingencies of the lived experience would help unpack the multitude of meanings implicit in a complex and innovative image such as the *View*.

From this perspective, an artist's address book would be even more valuable for us than their identity card. Knowing how networks were formed, organized, and distributed would enable us to explore the spatial practices that, according to Lefebvre, link together "daily reality (daily routine) and urban reality (the routes and networks which link up the places set aside for work, 'private' life, and leisure)."[10] This would provide a basis for further analyzing how artworks reflect, signify, and embody the production, reproduction, and appropriation of social as well as spatial practices, and how these interact with the resources mobilized by artists through creative processes. An understanding of how artists gain useful access to, or fail to integrate in, the social and spatial practices available to them can offer insights into the implementation of artistic strategies as responses to technological advancement, exchanges of information and knowledge, and applied experimentation; or, obversely, as rejections of established behavioral patterns and evidence of socioeconomic struggle.

To this end, the study of social milieus should take into account the interconnections between urban configuration and interpersonal networks, as well as the movement of objects and people. For Venice, an effective methodological approach has been used by scholars dealing with the circulation of information in printed and oral modes, as well as exchanges of professional expertise and technological knowledge within public spaces.[11] Likewise, an analysis of art-making processes may be fruitfully framed within the context of the social transactions instigated by Venice's particular morphology, which facilitated physical proximity and promiscuous public sociability, rendering the city "a space of constant flux" and "a network of networks."[12] An approach that foregrounds the plurality of the social, professional, and material interests linked to the urban economy of Venice may be beneficial in order to emphasize the coexistence of multiple operational modes within the continuities and discontinuities of the city's fabric. This would offset the widespread tendency among art historians to hedge art-making processes as merely aesthetic or technical discourses.

Application of Theoretical Undercurrents

With its unique urban landscape, Venice represents an especially stimulating environment for the study of the aforementioned dynamics. Nonetheless, systematic studies of the city's artistic geography, including synopses of the distribution of artists' workshops and dwellings, are still among the desiderata of Venetian art history. To take one example, the fragmentary nature of the studies that have occasionally explored the market of paintings in sixteenth-century Venice is suddenly revealed when one considers that a local topography of painting practice, which would enable us to weave together the discrete pieces of information about retailing and collecting, is still missing.[13] Interesting results are yielded, though, when we try to locate the figure painters (*figureri*) active in town (fig. 4.1).

 A preliminary survey of the published data concerning the workshops and houses of *figureri* between the 1470s and 1530s indicates a significant concentration in the principal commercial areas of the city, near or around St. Mark's Square and the Rialto. This would facilitate networking with manufacturers and retailers and offer commercial opportunities, especially since the sale of paintings was mostly restricted to painters' workshops, with exceptions for weekly markets (Wednesdays at San Polo, Saturdays at San Marco) and the annual fair of the Ascension (at San Marco).[14] Not only was the Rialto a hub for shops, banks, and warehouses, but it was also the first port of call for people in search of news and information.[15] Unsurprisingly, printing shops and booksellers, which acted as important information centers, also concentrated there.[16] Such a dynamic and multifarious context would further the exchange of knowledge and expertise among different trades and professions. As far as painters are concerned, a possible incentive for networking was the emergence, since the late fifteenth century, of specialized color sellers (*vendecolori*), whose presence created "a nexus for the cross-fertilization among artisan trades using colors."[17] Interestingly, *vendecolori* concentrated their trade between the Rialto, San Bartolomeo, and San Salvador, where a number of painters settled their business.[18] Color selling involved apothecaries, whose outlets were multifunctional centers with additional facilities for gambling, mailing, and printing, serving different trades and social layers and thereby promoting interpersonal networks and information exchange.[19]

 Against this larger background we can set the microhistories of painters who inhabited and acted within the living environment, and ask whether

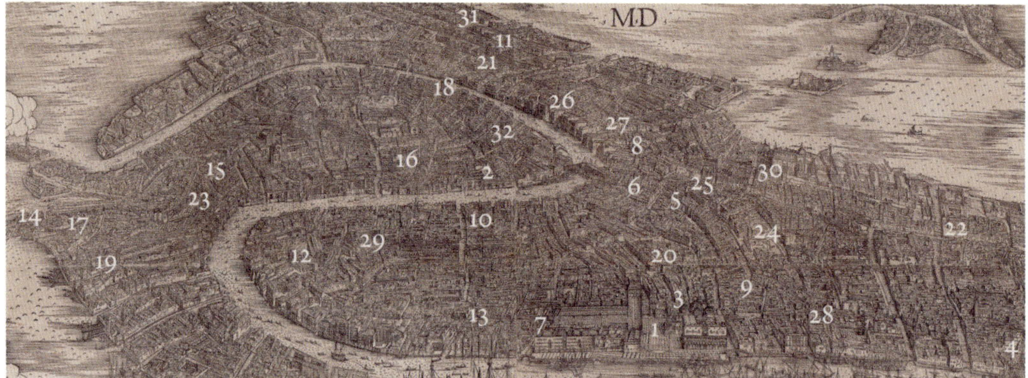

4.1

Detail with select artists' residences ca. 1450–1530 (based on published literature), from Jacopo de' Barbari, *View of Venice*, ca. 1497–1500.

1. *Piazza San Marco:* Alvise Bastiani
2. *Sant' Aponal:* Giovanni Cariani, Girolamo Mocetto
3. *San Basso:* Andrea Bussati, Giovanni Cariani, Jacopo Palma Vecchio
4. *San Giovanni in Bragora:* Jacopo Palma Vecchio
5. *San Lio:* Giovanni da Asola, Marco Bastiani, Alvise Bastiani, Giovanni Bellini, Giovanni Cariani
6. *San Bartolomeo:* Vincenzo Catena
7. *San Geminiano:* Gentile Bellini, Jacopo Bellini
8. *San Giovanni Crisostomo:* Marco Zoppo
9. *San Giovanni Nuovo:* Benedetto Diana, Matteo Duia
10. *San Luca:* Alvise Bastiani, Cima da Conegliano, Leonardo Boldrini
11. *San Marziale:* Francesco Bissolo, Paris Bordon
12. *San Maurizio:* Vittore Carpaccio
13. *San Moisè:* Lazzaro Bastiani, Paris Bordon, Rocco Marconi, Marco Marziale
14. *San Nicolò:* Lazzaro Bastiani
15. *San Pantalon:* Vittore Belliniano
16. *San Polo:* Lazzaro Bastiani, Titian
17. *San Raffaele:* Lazzaro Bastiani
18. *San Stae:* Arrigo Licinio, Bernadino Licinio, Jacopo Palma Vecchio
19. *San Trovaso:* Andrea Bussati, Benedetto Diana
20. *San Zulian:* Paris Bordon, Giovanni Mansueti
21. *Santa Fosca:* Rocco Marconi
22. *Santa Giustina:* Francesco Bissolo
23. *Santa Margherita:* Lazzaro Bastiani
24. *Santa Maria Formosa:* Bartolomeo Vivarini
25. *Santa Marina:* Giovanni Bellini
26. *Santa Sofia:* Giovanni Mansueti
27. *Santi Apostoli:* Giovanni Buonconsiglio
28. *San Provolo:* Sebastiano Zuccato
29. *Sant'Angelo:* Pietro Duia
30. *Santi Giovanni e Paolo:* Giovanni Girolamo Savoldo
31. *Sant'Alvise:* Bonifacio de' Pitati
32. *San Cassian:* Jacopo Tintoretto

and, if so, how their spatial practices are revealed within their art (fig. 4.2). The social networks set up by Vincenzo Catena (ca. 1480–1531), a well-off painter who was contemporaneous with de' Barbari and with whom Giorgione (1473/1474–1510) was apparently associated, suggest possible ways of deepening this approach. Catena lived in the central commercial hub of San Bartolomeo, near the Rialto Bridge. He was connected with noted humanists and collectors and was a member of the wealthy Scuola Grande di San Rocco.[20] In his various wills, he appointed as many as four different *spizieri* (apothecaries) as executors or witnesses.[21] Two of them were based at San Bartolomeo like him, one being the godfather (*compare*) of one of Catena's sons. Catena is also mentioned as an "amiable and dearest brother" in the 1525 will of woodcarver Pietro Scalamanzo (d. 1525), who had his workshop (and home) in the neighboring contrada of San Lio.[22] The painter knew Scalamanzo's property well, for he is recorded there as a legal witness to his woodcarver friend in 1522.[23] Finally, Catena's personal bonds extended into the contrada of Santa Maria Formosa, adjacent to San Lio. Here, the painter Sebastiano del Piombo (ca. 1485–1547) owned a house in which the wedding contract of his sister, Andriana, was drawn up in Catena's presence in 1528.[24]

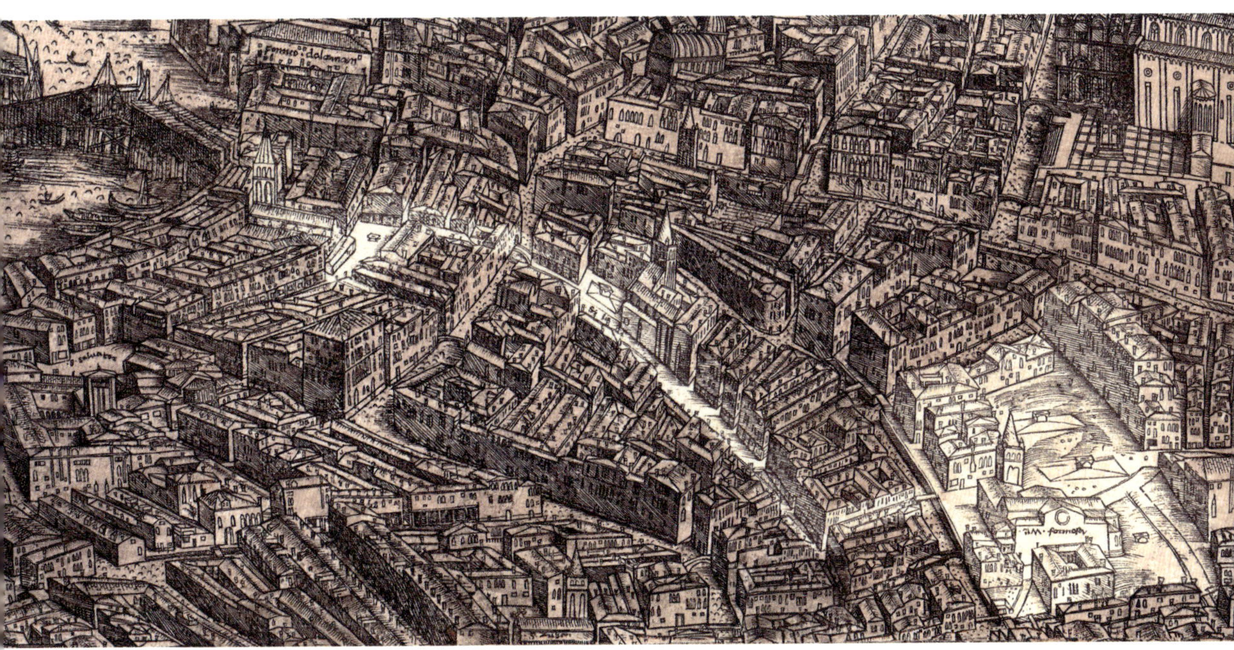

The picture briefly outlined here shows an artist, Catena, who tapped into the city's fabric to cultivate relations through which the professional and personal spheres intertwined. The flurry of economic, financial, and communication transactions that were carried out in and around the artist's contrada exposed him to cross-connections with other trades and diverse social layers, from apothecaries to woodcarvers, not to mention the spectrum of people with different social ranks who would have come to the Rialto for business and trade. His close bond with Scalamanzo may even imply a commercial partnership, as links between painters and woodcarvers were common.[25] This and the relationship with Sebastiano del Piombo's family point to a possible professional network extending throughout the porous confines of Venice's neighborhoods, from San Bartolomeo to the adjoining San Lio, and from there to Santa Maria Formosa. Finally, Catena's membership of the Scuola di San Rocco (on the other side of the Rialto) was another possible means for him to build extra-parochial and socially differentiated connections.

Paintings resulted from creative processes that interlaced with socioeconomic contexts of this kind. Altarpieces, devotional images, and portraits, in which Catena specialized, would have been situated within environments that were experienced at different levels by both artist and audience. They would meet needs and generate conventions that conveyed, embodied, and signified social practices through the painter's craft and lived experiences. Finally, they would represent imagined spaces that overlapped with, complemented, or even redefined the ordinary spaces of everyday practices. The artist's own experience of the physical and social environment may surface in their works and be reframed through their imagination. In the *Virgin and Child with Saint John the Infant* (National Museum of Western Art, Tokyo), Catena reused one of his models for the group of figures and added a portrait of the campo of Santa Maria Formosa as a backdrop (fig. 4.3).[26] The scene is presented as taken from a window with the viewpoint corresponding to an extant building on the north side of the campo. Centered on the main square that gives name to, and identifies, the local contrada, the image produces and reproduces a twofold act of appropriation: the eye appropriates the square perceptually from the same privileged angle of a dweller who, looking out of the window, appropriates the neighborhood socially. This large campo in the *sestiere* of Castello was, and still is, a crucial intersection that many Venetians would cross on regular basis. Catena was certainly familiar with the place, as his attendance to Andriana's wedding contract demonstrates.

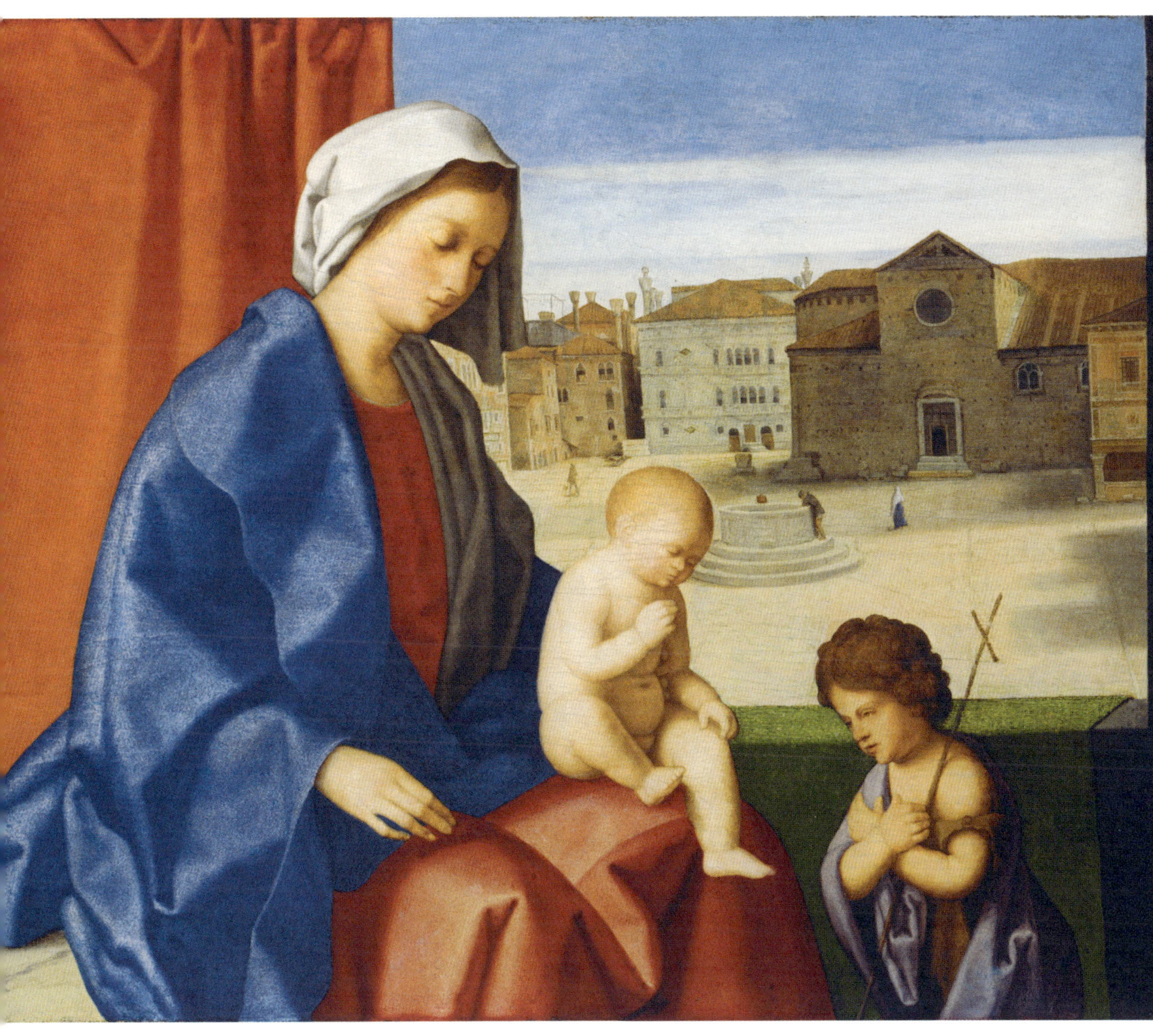

However, whether or not this picture is directly related to that episode is less relevant than the fact that Catena repositioned the actual square within the sphere of devotional practices instigated by the painting, a sphere that has its distinct spatial and temporal dimension and its appropriate functions and meanings. Not only has the artist hypostatized an important nexus of social life, he has also recast it through the vicarious realm of the picture. He has furnished us both with the view of a physical site and with a vision of a lived space alongside its social, economic, political, religious, and cultural functions. De' Barbari has captured this for us on an even grander scale.

I would like to thank Lorenzo Buonanno for reading and sharing his thoughts about this essay, and Julia De Lancey for her comments and suggestions.

Giorgio Tagliaferro

1 Molly Bourne, "Francesco II Gonzaga and Maps as Palace Decoration in Renaissance Mantua," *Imago Mundi* 51 (1999): 54, 70n26, appendix, no. 1.

2 Bourne, "Francesco II Gonzaga," 54–58, appendix, nos. 1–3, 5, 8–12, 22.

3 Bourne, "Francesco II Gonzaga," 59, appendix, no. 36.

4 Bourne, "Francesco II Gonzaga," 70, appendix, nos. 6–7.

5 This double mode of representation has been convincingly described as a combination of geography and choreography by Bronwen Wilson in *The World in Venice: Print, the City, and Early Modern Identity* (Toronto: University of Toronto Press, 2005), 38–42, 47–50.

6 Wilson, *The World in Venice*, 48.

7 Henri Lefebvre, *The Production of Space*, trans. Donald Nicholson-Smith (Oxford: Blackwell, 1991), 33, 36–46. See also Rob Shields, *Lefebvre, Love, and Struggle: Spatial Dialectics* (London: Routledge, 1999), 160–70; Andy Merrifield, *Henri Lefebvre: A Critical Introduction* (New York: Routledge, 2006), 108–11; Christian Schmid, *Stadt, Raum und Gesellschaft: Henri Lefebvre und die Theorie der Produktion des Raumes* (Munich: Franz Steiner, 2005), 191–245; Łukasz Stanek, *Henri Lefebvre on Space: Architecture, Urban Research, and the Production of Theory* (Minneapolis: University of Minnesota Press, 2011), 128–32.

8 Lefebvre, *The Production*, 42. It must be pointed out that this evaluation of the *View* would hardly match Lefebvre's idea of spaces of representation as carriers of "veiled criticism of dominant social orders and … symbolic resistance," like those he identified in the work of Dada and surrealist artists. Shields, *Lefebvre*, 164.

9 John Dewey, *Art as Experience* (New York: Putnam Capricorn, 1934).

10 Lefebvre, *The Production*, 38.

11 The reference here is to the field of studies dealing with the public sphere, a concept first introduced by Jürgen Habermas. For Renaissance and early modern Venice, see, in particular, Filippo de Vivo, *Information and Communication in Venice: Rethinking Early Modern Politics* (Oxford: Oxford University Press, 2007); Rosa Salzberg, *Ephemeral City: Cheap Print and Urban Culture in Renaissance Venice* (Manchester: Manchester University Press, 2014).

12 Salzberg, *Ephemeral City*, 47; Dennis Romano, *Patricians and* Popolani: *The*

Social Foundations of the Venetian Renaissance State (Baltimore, MD: Johns Hopkins University Press, 1987), 10.

13 Isabella Cecchini, "Le figure del commercio: Cenni sul mercato pittorico veneziano nel XVII secolo," in *The Art Market in Italy, 15th–16th Centuries / Il mercato dell'arte in Italia, secc. XV–XVII*, ed. Marcello Fantoni, Louisa C. Matthew, and Sara F. Matthews-Grieco (Modena: Panini, 2003), 389–99; Louisa C. Matthew, "Were There Open Markets for Pictures in Renaissance Venice?," in Fantoni, Matthew, and Matthews-Grieco, *The Art Market in Italy*, 253–61; Enrico Maria Dal Pozzolo, "Cercar quadri e disegni nella Venezia del Cinquecento," in *Tra committenza e collezionismo: Studi sul mercato dell'arte nell'Italia settentrionale durante l'età moderna*, ed. Enrico Maria Dal Pozzolo and Leonida Tedoldi (Vicenza: Terra Ferma, 2003), 49–65; Louisa Matthew, "Painters Marketing Paintings in Fifteenth- and Sixteenth-Century Florence and Venice," in *Mapping Markets for Paintings in Europe, 1450–1750*, ed. Neil De Marchi and Hans J. Van Miegroet (Turnhout: Brepols, 2006), 307–27; James E. Shaw, "Institutional Controls and the Retail of Paintings: The Painters' Guild of Early-Modern Venice," in De Marchi and Van Miegroet, *Mapping Markets for Paintings in Europe*, 107–24.

14 Elena Favaro, *L'arte dei pittori in Venezia e i suoi statuti* (Florence: Olschki, 1975), 73.

15 De Vivo, *Information and Communication*, 86–119.

16 Salzberg, *Ephemeral City*, 47–72.

17 Louisa C. Matthew and Barbara H. Berrie, "'Memoria de colori che bisognino torre a vinetia': Venice as a Centre for the Purchase of Painters' Colours," in *Trade in Artists' Materials: Markets and Commerce in Europe to 1700*, ed. Jo Kirby, Susie Nash, and Joanna Cannon (London: Archetype, 2010), 249.

18 Julia A. DeLancey, "'In the Streets Where They Sell Colors': Placing 'Vendecolori' in the Urban Fabric of Early Modern Venice," *Wallraf-Richartz-Jahrbuch* 72, no. 7 (2011): 193–232. On *vendecolori*, see also Roland Krischel, "The Inventory of the Venetian *Vendecolori* Jacopo de' Benedetti: The Non-pigment Materials," in Kirby, Nash, and Cannon, *Trade in Artists' Materials*, 253–66; Matthew and Berrie, "Memoria," 245–52; Julia A. DeLancey, "Celebrating Citizenship: Alvise della Scala, Titian, and Social Status in Color Sellers in Sixteenth-Century Venice," *Studi Veneziani*, n.s., 76 (2017): 15–60. See also Julia A. DeLancey's essay in this volume.

19 Filippo De Vivo, "Pharmacies as Centres of Communication in Early Modern Venice," *Renaissance Studies* 21, no. 4 (2007): 505–21.

20 For a summary of Catena's life, with bibliography, see Enrico Maria Dal Pozzolo, "Appunti su Catena," *Venezia Cinquecento* 31, no. 16 (2006): 7–8.

21 Gustav Ludwig, "Archivalische Beiträge zur Geschichte der Venezianischen Malerei," *Jahrbuch der Königlich Preussischen Kunstsammlungen* 26, supplement (1905): 83–84, 86–88.

22 Anne Markham Schulz, *Woodcarving and Woodcarvers in Venice, 1350–1550* (Florence: Centro Di, 2011), 171–72, 198–99.

23 Ludwig, "Archivalische Beiträge," 84–85; Markham Schulz, *Woodcarving*, 171.

24 Ludwig, "Archivalische Beiträge," 85.

25 As evidenced by the numerous cases reported in Markham Schulz, *Woodcarving*.

26 Mitsumasa Takanashi, "New Acquisitions," *Annual Bulletin of the National Museum of Western Art* 46 (April 2011–March 2012): 9–13 (with bibliography).

Anna Christine Swartwood House

Beyond Venice

At the Margins of the *View*

SCHOLARSHIP ON JACOPO DE' BARBARI'S woodcut *View of Venice* focuses almost exclusively on its depiction of Venice and its islands.[1] This is likely a by-product of the influential art historical work of Juergen Schulz and Deborah Howard. Schulz brilliantly analyzes the ways the author shaped Venice according to a "moralized geography," while Howard demonstrates how de' Barbari manipulated the appearance of the islands to accord with its delphinic associations of fortune and the sea.[2] To be sure, this has led to a productive discussion about the cartographic and pictorial values of this unprecedented work. Yet it also has had the unforeseen consequence of leaving the "dolphin" at the center as the memory image of de' Barbari's *View* (plate 1). This essay argues that the margins of the *View*, virtually un-

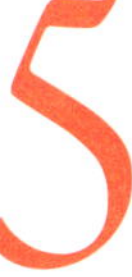

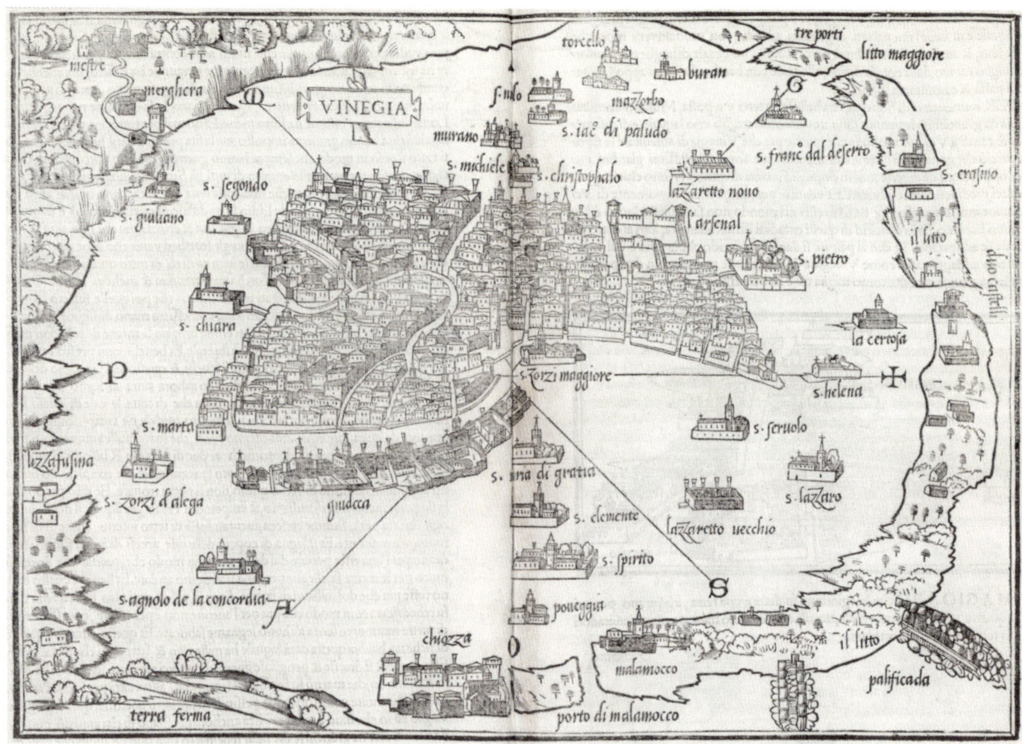

remarked in the scholarship, make valuable claims about Venice and its continuity with the rest of the world. These aquatic and mountain frontiers must be reunited with the center for us to understand the *View*'s pictorial and geographic accomplishments.

In many ways, the margins of the *View* appear different from its center. The regatta entering the scene at the lower right-hand corner introduces an important element of human activity and the dimension of time into a print too easily seen as static and timeless. The curious mainland boundary described along the top three sheets of the work is shown head-on rather than in de' Barbari's celebrated bird's-eye perspective. The orienting features of the margins are the compass winds that derive from the mappamundi tradition. Although Jacopo was not the first to use the winds in a regional rather than a world view, their inclusion shows his ambition, not just in orienting Venice in the grandest possible way but also in showing it as a microcosm of the world.[3] Augmenting the sense of the *View* as a slice of the larger world are what Martin Kemp calls its "dramatically open horizons," wherein the waters continue to the edge of the sheets without decorative framing devices.[4] This openness contrasts with later treatments like the representation of Venice in Benedetto Bordone's *Isolario* (fig. 5.1), in which encircling islands tightly shelter the city proper.

The open aquatic and rural horizons of the *View* also, at first glance, sharply contrast with its meticulously differentiated urban center. This contrast relates to one influential way of envisaging the relationship between a city and its outskirts in the fifteenth century, wherein the periphery conflicts with the center in order to maintain the hierarchy between low and high culture, wild nature and civilized urbanity, that was difficult to live out in the increasingly heterogeneous space of the city but easily maintained in representation. Michael Camille uses a fourteenth-century manuscript, *Life of Saint-Denis*, to exemplify this world view: beggars and rag pickers populate the area outside the city walls of Paris, while the patron saint, Saint Denis, preaches to his congregation at the center.[5] In this case, the artist uses placement rhetorically, literally marginalizing the less desirable elements of the city by pushing them to the edge of the page.

Yet Jacopo de' Barbari's *View* more closely represents a second way of relating city margins and center—a positive, continuous one akin to that outlined in Leonardo Bruni's "Panegyric to the City of Florence," written ca. 1400. In this ode, Bruni fulsomely described the virtues of Florence—magnificence, order, beauty—as reflected in its physical appearance, particularly its architecture, site, and landscape. This beauty-virtue reverberated ever outward, from the well-planned and well-sited Piazza della Signoria and family palaces, out to the city walls, then to the spacious and pleasant country houses that ring the region outside the city, ever farther to the "wooded groves, flowery meadows, pleasant river banks, sparkling fountains, and—best of all—the nature of the place itself fit for delight."[6] In the fourteenth century, Lorenzetti represented a similar idea in his frescoed *Good Government in the City and Countryside*, where the virtues of peace, prosperity, and security reflected in the workings of the city redound to Siena's rural landscape.

The virtues of Venice, as represented by de' Barbari, are largely related to commerce. This is suggested by the fleet of seagoing galleys, responsible for Venice's financial success, as well as the emphasis of the Mercerie, the commercial corridor between the Rialto and Piazza San Marco. And it is stated plainly by the presence of the *View*'s two genii loci, Mercury and Neptune, above and below these sites; the former states, "Mercurius Preceteris Huic Fauste Emporiis Illustro" (I Mercury shine favorably on this above all other emporia); the latter, "Aequora Tuens Portu Resideo Hic Neptunus" (I Neptune reside here, smoothing the waters at this port). Both of these values reverberate outward on the page: Neptune's, horizontally to the vast seas; Mercury's, downward to the Mercerie as well as upward to the mountainous frontier.

The inclusion of this mountainous frontier, which runs continuously across the top three sheets, reminds the viewer of Venice's incursion into the *terraferma*. Venice had its largest-ever holdings on the mainland in 1500, and one recognizes intuitively that the *View*'s frontier represents a continuation of Venice. The cities labeled along the border, all Venetian possessions, include (from left to right) Marghera, Mestre, Treviso, and Serravalle (fig. 5.2). These four have been carefully chosen, as they represent not simply a collection of Venetian sites but also a sequence, one especially familiar to travelers who moved between Venice and Germany. This may represent the city sequence traveled by the German publisher of the *View*, Anton Kolb, who was a resident at the German warehouse and living quarters, the Fondaco dei Tedeschi;[7] Jacopo de' Barbari may also have traced this route as he traveled to Nuremberg to work for the Emperor Maximilian. The

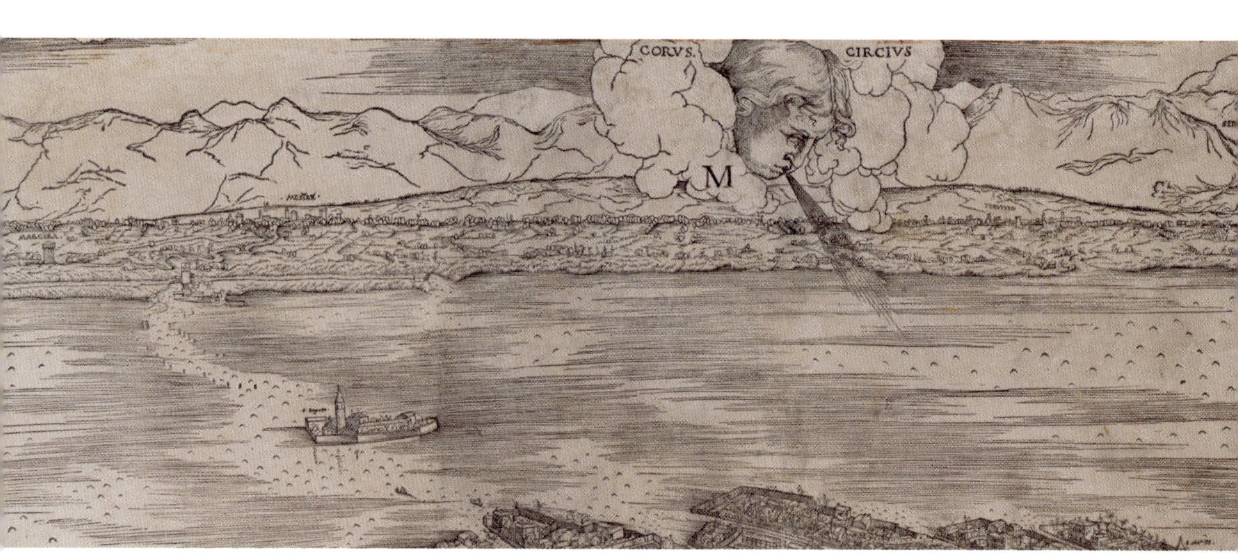

Marghera–Mestre–Treviso–Serravalle route was even likely traversed by copies of the *View* itself, packed into wooden crates and carried over the Brenner Pass to be sold to individual clients or at print fairs.[8]

Numerous sources confirm the popularity of this itinerary. When Count Philipp von Katzenellenbogen went on a pilgrimage to Jerusalem in 1433–34 (Venice was a common stopover for the Jerusalem-bound), he departed from Darmstadt and traveled through Serravalle, Conegliano, Treviso, and Mestre before arriving in Venice.[9] In 1486, Conrad Grunemberg left Constanz with a party of pilgrims and reached Venice via Treviso, Mestre, and Marghera.[10] Treviso and Mestre were common stops for changing or selling horses on this journey—Bordone would also portray Mestre and Marghera in the *Isolario* as gateways to Venice.[11] The Venetian Senate had acted to protect this route in 1375 when it required that German goods travel over Venetian territory, especially Serravalle and Treviso.[12] By 1498, the English author Wynkyn de Worde drew attention to a pilgrimage route from Dover, England, to Jerusalem via Venice through what he called the "Duche Waye": over the Brenner Pass, but bypassing Trent and traveling through the Dolomites. The stops along this "Duche Waye" include Serravalle, Conegliano, Treviso, Mestre, and Venice.[13]

Serravalle, geographically the most distant point from Venice labeled on the map, is the most important destination in this sequence and is evocatively positioned in the valley of the mountain to the left of Mercury. Serravalle had steadily grown as a trading center since the fourteenth century, the opulent Quattrocento and Cinquecento palaces lining its streets a testament to its prosperity. In addition to trading in iron, copper, lead, precious metals, cotton, and wool, by 1500 Serravalle was also Europe's second-largest producer of armor, mostly for Spanish and Portuguese clientele.[14] Although it is positioned at the extremity of the *View*, an observer familiar with the "Duche Waye" would understand Serravalle not as a destination per se but as a node, a center for trading where people and goods traveled to disperse to destinations farther afield. What is more, there is evidence that the nodal space between Venice and its trading partners started to take on its own visual character around 1500.

The permeable frontier between Venice and its trading partners could be a dangerous place. Marin Sanudo, describing a shipment of artillery sent by the Duke of Milan to Genoa during the First Italian War in 1496, reports that it traveled over "that bad and wicked road, that is from Serravalle to Genova by way of the mountains."[15] Paulus Imhoff, from a well-known patrician family of spice importers, died on his journey between Venice and Nuremberg in 1478; his body was not transported to either place but, rather, was buried at Belluno and memorialized with a sculptured relief by the school of Pietro Lombardo at the church of Santa Croce di Lago.[16]

The most famous documentarian of this space between, who treated it as a space of experimentation and possibility, was Albrecht Dürer. Dürer recorded his journey over the Brenner Pass from Nuremberg to Venice in 1494–95 with a series of drawings and watercolors, including the *View of the Arco Valley* (fig. 5.3) that the artist later inscribed "fenedier klawsen," or Venetian outpost. Scholars have long appreciated in these works Dürer's clever combination of pictorial construction with unstudied, plein air im-provisation.[17] However, it is little noted that they, and the territory they described, served as models for the backdrop of the German artist's largest Venetian commission, the *Feast of the Rose Garlands* (fig. 5.4), executed in 1506 for the German confraternity in Venice. This great fictional event is steeped in the real world and its real experience—a *sacra conversazione* made sacred by the presence of the Madonna, Child, Saint Dominic, and musical angels, but otherwise staffed with contemporary figures, from members of the German confraternity to the German emperor Frederick III and the Italian pope Julius II. Dürer also includes a self-portrait before a mountain-ous, populated townscape. This section, still sometimes generically called a "possibly Northern landscape,"[18] in fact combines motifs from several of Dürer's drawings that visually record his journeys between Nuremberg and Venice. The distinctive V-shaped merlons of the fortifications strongly evoke northern Italy and are recorded not only in the watercolor *View of the Arco Valley* but also the ink drawings *Castle of Trent* (British Museum) and *Trent Seen from the North* (until 1945, Bremen, Kunsthalle), all from 1494–95; the stepped and pinnacled building façades and dramatic Alpine profile of the mountains derive from his view of Innsbruck (Vienna, Albertina) of the same year.[19] Trent was a Venetian possession, while Innsbruck was part of the Holy Roman Empire and a favorite city of the Emperor Maximilian.

By intermixing architectural and topographical details, Dürer essen-tially collapses the space between Venice and Nuremberg into one contin-uous horizon. The effect is powerful. The painter had famously complained of Venetian painters' jealous denigration of his painting practice, of his "enemies [who] copy my work in the churches and wherever they can find it," only to "criticize it and claim that it is not done in the antique style."[20] He also regarded the *Feast of the Rose Garlands* as an answer to these criti-

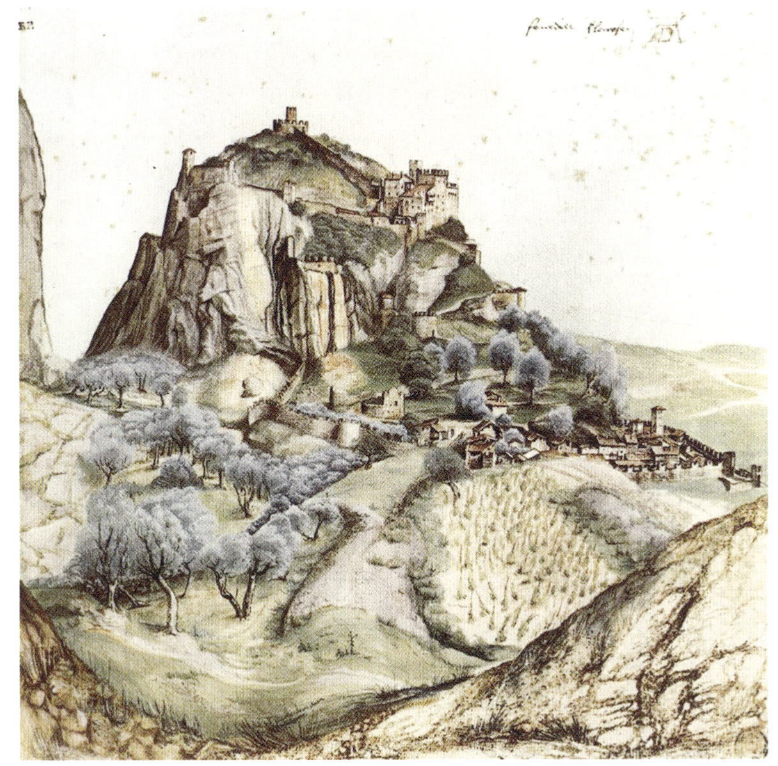

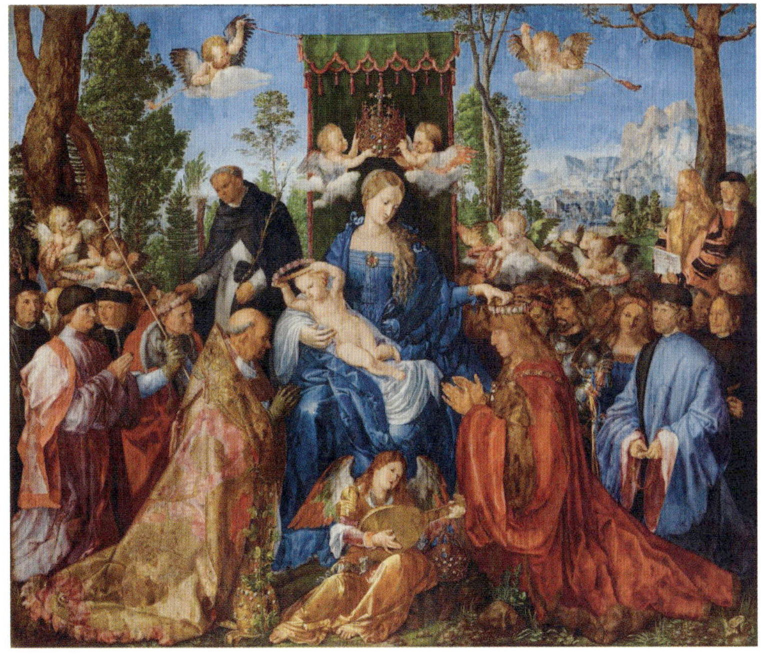

cisms: he boasts to Willibald Pirckheimer that the doge and patriarch have seen his painting; that he has become a Venetian *gentiluomo*; and that he has "shut up all the painters, who used to say that I was good at engraving, but that in painting I didn't know how to handle my colors."[21] These comments give valuable context to Dürer's self-depiction presiding over his decidedly hybrid masterpiece—Venetian in format and coloring, with its Bellini-inspired musical angels, but German in the figure of the Madonna and landscape—while standing at the threshold to the "North."

As has been noted, Jacopo de' Barbari intended that Mercury serve as a form of signature, but it bears underscoring that here he both reigns over Venice and points to its trading partners, particularly Germany, evoked by the mountainous frontier. Interestingly, in the sixteenth century Mercury appeared in emblemata not simply as a god of trade and commerce but also as a god of crossroads. Andrea Alciati's *Emblematum liber*, first published in 1531, contains multiple versions of Mercury before converging paths with the title "wherever the gods call, we must go" and an accompanying epigram referencing a tomb of Mercury where "three ways meet."[22] This epigram concludes, "Oh traveler, hang up garlands to the god so that he may show you the right way. We are all at a crossroads, and in this path of life we err, unless the god himself shows us the way."[23] Versions of Mercury in this guise were published well into the seventeenth century, including prints where Mercury is unnecessarily pointing down a single road. Jacopo de' Barbari's Mercury may also represent an incipient version of this guise, concisely expressing the interrelations of commerce, geography, and the horizon in the sixteenth century. In this too, Mercury's inclusion points to the necessity of merging the center with its margins.

NOTES

---

1 For example, the dedicated volume *A volo d'uccello* (1999) focuses on perspective and the bird's-eye technique as it relates to the depiction of Venice itself, although Susanne Biadene acknowl-edges the presence of "il profilo delle prealpi con SERAVAL a indicare il passo che conduceva al nord"; Giandomenico Romanelli, Susanna Biadene, and Camillo Tonini, eds., *A volo d'uccello: Jacopo*

Anna Christine Swartwood House

de' Barbari e le rappresentazioni di città nell'Europa del Rinascimento, exhib. cat. (Venice: Arsenale, 1999), 137, and with further bibliography.

2 Juergen Schulz, "Jacopo de' Barbari's View of Venice: Map Making, City Views, and Moralized Geography before the Year 1500," *Art Bulletin* 60, no. 3 (1978): 425–74; Deborah Howard, "Venice as a Dolphin: Further Investigations into Jacopo de' Barbari's View," *Artibus et Historiae* 18, no. 35 (1997): 101–11.

3 See Piero Falchetta's essay in this volume.

4 Martin Kemp, "Jacopo de' Barbari: *View of Venice*," in *Circa 1492: Art in the Age of Exploration*, exhib. cat, ed. Jay A. Levenson (Washington, DC: National Gallery of Art, 1991), 255.

5 Michael Camille, *Image on the Edge: The Margins of Medieval Art* (London: Reaktion Books, 1992), 129.

6 Leonardo Bruni, "Panegyric to the City of Florence," trans. Benjamin G. Kohl, in *The Earthly Republic: Italian Humanists on Government and Society*, ed. Benjamin G. Kohl and Ronald G. Witt (Philadelphia: University of Pennsylvania Press, 1978), 141.

7 The copyright petition from Anton Kolb to the Venetian Collegio of October 30, 1500, is extant (see appendix 2): Venice, Archivio di Stato (ASVe), Collegio, Notatorio, registro 15 (anni 1499–1507), fol. 28r; see also Andrew John Martin, "Anton Kolb und Jacopo de' Barbari: Venedig im Jahre 1500," in *Pinxit/sculpsit/fecit, Kunsthistorische Studien: Festschrift für Bruno Bushart*, ed. Bärbel Hamacher and Christi Karnehm (Munich: Deutscher Kunstverlag, 1994), 89.

8 Little is known about the immediate fortunes or collecting history of the *View* in the sixteenth century—as Howard notes, "the international market is confirmed by [Kolb's] request for duty free export," and "opere di Iacomo de Barbarino veneziano, che andò in Alemagna e Borgogna" are listed in Marcantonio Michiel's 1521 inventory of Venetian collections; Howard, "Venice as a Dolphin," 102. For more on the collection and transport of the *View* and Venetian maps, see Lucien Febvre and Henri-Jean Martin, *The Coming of the Book: The Impact of Printing 1450–1800*, trans. David Gerard (London: NLB, 1976), 222–23; Raleigh Ashlin Skelton, *Maps: A Historical Survey of Their Study and Collecting* (Chicago: University of Chicago Press, 1975), 45; and David Landau and Peter Parshall, *The Renaissance Print, 1470–1550* (New Haven, CT: Yale University Press, 1994), 43–44.

9 Henry Simonsfeld, *Der Fondaco dei Tedeschi in Venedig und die Deutsch-Venetianischen Handelsbeziehungen* (Stuttgart: J. G. Gotaa'schen Buchhandlung, 1887), 1:97; Reinhold Rohricht and Heinrich Meisner, *Deutsche Pilgerreisen nach dem Heiligen Lande* (Berlin: Weidmann, 1880), 472. A contemporary descrip-

tion of Philipp's pilgrimage, which includes verses of praise, was discovered in a seventeenth-century copy by J. v. Arnoldi and printed in Arnoldi, "Philipp's, des lezten Grafen zu Katzenelenbogen, Pilgerreise nach Aegypten und Palastina, im Jahr 1433 und 34," in *Die Vorzeit: Ein Taschenbuch* (Marburg: Elwert, 1821), 43–74. For Venice as a common stopover for the Jerusalem-bound, see, for example, the panoramic woodcut view of Venice by Erhard Reuwich in the German pilgrim Bernhard von Breydenbach's *Peregrinatio in Terram Sanctam* (1486), discussed in Elizabeth Ross, *Picturing Experience in the Early Printed Book: Breydenbach's "Peregrinatio" from Venice to Jerusalem* (University Park: Pennsylvania State University Press, 2014), esp. 60–67.

10 "Conrad Grünemberg reitet in Begleitung von Caspar Gaisperg am 22. April 1486 von Constanz aus und gelangt über Trient, Feltre, Treviso, Mestre und Marghero nach Venedig"; Rohricht and Meisner, *Deutsche Pilgerreisen*, 147, citing two handwritten manuscripts describing the pilgrimage, one in the Herzoglichen Bibliothek in Gotha, the other in Karlsruhe.

11 Rohricht and Meisner, *Deutsche Pilgerreisen*, 9, 294.

12 Simonsfeld, *Der Fondaco dei Tedeschi*, 104–5. The Senate injunctions of November 13 and 15, 1375, are found at ASVe, Senato Misti, busta 35, folio 70.

13 The "Informacion peregrinatois ad sanctum sepulcrum by the Duche Waye"

is reproduced in Wynkyn de Worde and E. Gordon Duff, *Information for Pilgrims unto the Holy Land* (London: Lawrence and Bullen, 1893), 37–41.

14 See Rafael M. Girón Pascual, "'Cruzando aceros': El comercio de espadas entre España e Italia en los siglos XVI y XVII," *Gladius* 36 (2016): esp. 171–76.

15 "quella via pessima et cativa, *videlicet* da Seravalle a Zenoa per li monti"; Marino Sanudo, *I diarii di Marino Sanuto (1496–1531)*, ed. Rinaldo Pulin et al. (Venice: F. Visentini, 1902), 1:357.

16 Simonsfeld, *Der Fondaco dei Tedeschi*, 245, describes the tomb monument of Imhoff "at the village church of Santa Croce near Serravalle" (An Dorfkirche von S. Croce bei Serravalle) reading "Paulus Imhoff patritius / Norimbergi. Quod estis / fui. Et quod sum eritis / Migravi die VII men / sis Julii MCCCCLXXVIII." The relief sculpture is still extant and in situ.

17 Felix Thürlemann, "L'aquarelle de Dürer *fenedier klawsen*: La double mimesis dans l'analyse picturale d'un lieu géographique," *Revue de l'art* 137 (2002–3): 9–18.

18 As in Klaus Carl, *Albrecht Dürer*, trans. Marlena Metcalf (New York: Parkstone, 2016), 45.

19 Katherine Crawford Luber also notes the combination of motifs from the Trent and Innsbruck drawings in the *Feast of the Rose Garlands*, though ultimately her

interest lies in how the cityscape reveals a "painterly" rather than "graphic" idea of pictorial space informed by Dürer's sojourn in Venice and study of Venetian paintings; Crawford Luber, *Albrecht Dürer and the Venetian Renaissance* (Cambridge: Cambridge University Press, 2005), 94–104. Dürer had combined these motifs to similar effect in the cityscape background of his drawing *Pupila Augusta* (Windsor Castle), a study for a never-executed print, as well as the engraving of *Saint Anthony* dated 1519. See Christiane Andersson and Larry Silver, "Dürer's Drawings," in *The Essential Dürer*, ed. Larry Silver and Jeffrey Chipps Smith (Philadelphia: University of Pennsylvania Press, 2010), 17–18.

20 Albrecht Dürer, *Records of Journeys to Venice and the Low Countries*, ed. Roger Fry, trans. Rudolf Tombo Jr. (Boston: Merrymount, 1913), 6.

21 Dürer, *Records of Journeys*, 21 ("boasts to Willibald Pirckheimer"), 17 ("Venetian *gentiluomo*"), and 21 ("has 'shut up all the painters'").

22 See Barbara C. Bowen, "Mercury at the Crossroads in Renaissance Emblems," *Journal of the Warburg and Courtauld Institutes* 48 (1985): 222–29.

23 "Suspende viator, serta deo, rectum qui tibi monstrat iter. / Omnes in trivio sumus, atque hoc tramite vitae, / Fallimur ostendat ni deus epse viam." Bowen, "Mercury at the Crossroads," 222; the elegant translation is Bowen's.

Monique O'Connell

Vessels of Political Communication

6 IN HIS 1493 *PRAISE OF THE CITY OF VENICE*, Marino Sanudo (1466–1536) concluded his account of the outstanding characteristics of his home city by pointing to the central role of commerce in the city's development, saying, "Its greatness has grown up only through trade, based on navigation to different parts of the world."[1] The belief that Venetian greatness rested on its unique connection to the sea and that Venetian prosperity came from maritime commerce was a long-standing part of the city's self-definition. A century earlier, the Grand Chancellor and historian Raffaino de Caresini (1314–90) asserted in his *Chronica* that "it is Venice's concern to cultivate the sea, where honor and riches are abundant, and to leave the land alone, which repeatedly has brought her scandal and error."[2] De' Barbari's *View* is a visual counterpart to these ideas, highlighting the city's waterways, commercial prosperity, and military might.

De' Barbari uses composition, text, and image to communicate the essential role of commerce, the divine nature of the Venetian connection to the sea, and the military power that ensured maritime commerce could continue. The commercial axis of Rialto–San Marco in the *View* (plate 5) is framed above and below by the two deities Mercury and Neptune (plate 7). The divine blessing on Venice's commercial pursuits and command of the seas is made even clearer by the accompanying inscriptions: Mercury declares that "I Mercury shine favorably on this above all other emporia," while Neptune says, "I Neptune reside here, smoothing the waters at this port."[3] The protection of the gods over the main institutions of commerce and military communicates the image of a city resting secure in its maritime empire.

The *View* further communicates the impression of maritime prosperity by including more than 500 vessels in the image, including 148 large merchant ships and 85 cargo ships.[4] These represent the backbone of medieval Venetian power; from the fourteenth century on, the Venetian government organized convoys (*mude*) with armed galleys that traveled along predetermined routes to the Black Sea, Cyprus, Alexandria, Beirut, Flanders, southern France, and North Africa.[5] The galleys were built in the state-run Arsenal, and for each voyage individual galleys were auctioned to a group of patrician investors who outfitted the ship and shared the profits and risks of the voyage.[6] There was a wide range of merchandise permitted on the galleys, but merchants tended to transport high-value luxury goods such as spices and Levantine silks, while privately owned round-ships or cogs transported commodities such as grain or oil.[7] In the *View*, all the ships are resting at anchor in the lagoon; none of the larger ships are shown in motion.

There are three main clusters of ships in the lagoon: off the Customs House at the Punto della Dogana, along the Riva between San Marco (fig. 6.1) and the Arsenal (plate 6), and near the mouth of the lagoon next to the now destroyed Ospedale di Messer Gesù Cristo or the Ospedale dei Marinai, in the zone of Sant'Antonio di Castello. The ships are of two principal types: round-ships propelled by sails and galleys powered by both oars and sails. At the end of the fifteenth century, when de' Barbari observed the Venetian fleet, it featured both light galleys primarily designed for battle and great galleys used to carry merchandise on trading voyages.[8] The round-ships, used to transport cargo, grew gradually in size across the course of the fifteenth century: in 1400 the biggest Venetian merchant ship was about four hundred tons, but by 1450 there were six ships of over six hundred tons in the Venetian fleet, and by the end of the century there was one that exceeded a thousand tons.[9] The larger ships were dedicated to long-distance Mediterranean trade, while the smaller vessels were used for interchanges between the city and the mainland as well as shorter voyages in the Adriatic.

The *View* also depicts the institutions that supported, regulated, and controlled trade at the turn of the sixteenth century. Both commercial courts and private banks clustered near the Rialto Bridge, making the piazza in front of San Giacomo the center of credit, marine insurance, and other large-scale financial operations.[10] The Venetian state also had institutions for regulating and controlling foreign merchant communities; at the time of the *View*, the principal example was the Fondaco dei Tedeschi, where from the early thirteenth century, merchants from Germany, Poland, Bohemia, and beyond were all compelled to lodge and to store their goods.[11] Venetian authorities oversaw all business contracted at the Fondaco, appointed its officials, and charged fees for lodging as well as levying taxes; by the late fifteenth century, communal revenues from trade in the Fondaco were 20,000 ducats per year, or 100 ducats per day.[12] In the *View*, the building appears just north of the Rialto Bridge on the San Marco side and is clearly labeled to indicate its central function in this trading zone (plate 4).

The *View* asserts Venetian commercial prosperity overtly, through its placement of Mercury and Neptune and through the banners these classical deities hold. The *View* also presents an implicit argument for prosper-

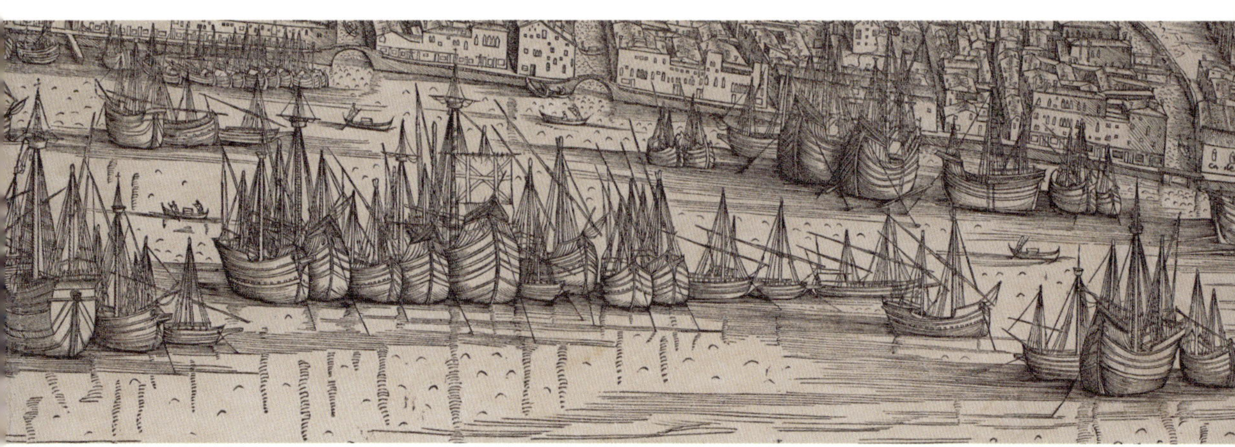

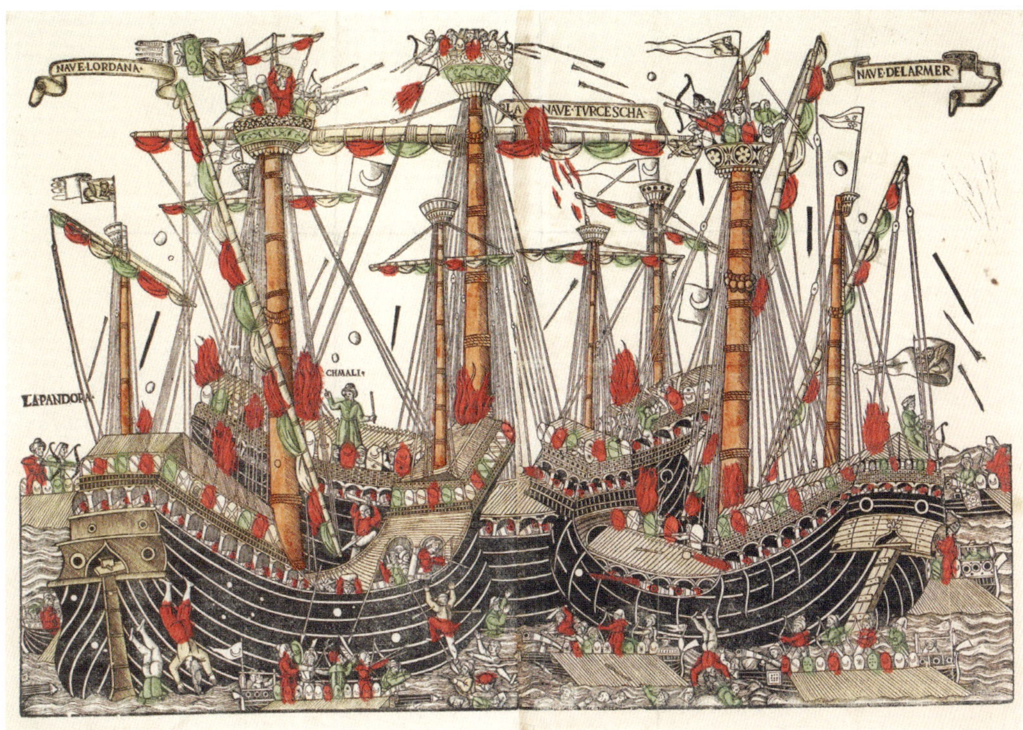

ity by illustrating the instruments of Venetian commerce: the military and merchant fleets that transported luxury goods and commodities between Mediterranean ports and the institutions in the city of Venice that regulated and profited from this commerce. But while some have seen the *View* as a representation of a self-satisfied city at the peak of its prosperity, this contribution argues that it was a product of crisis.

The *View*'s vision of peace and prosperity stands in stark contrast to the tumultuous political and economic events that marked the years necessary to produce the *View*. In 1499, wars on two fronts threatened: in the west, Venice allied with the French against Milan; and in the east, the Venetian loss at the Battle of Zonchio began the second war with the Ottomans.[13] In fact, one of the first prints of an actual naval battle represents a key moment: the Venetian commander Andrea Loredan, on the *Pandora*, the largest of the Venetian round-ships, and another Venetian vessel commanded by Alban D'Armer, attacked the strongest ship in the Ottoman fleet, commanded by Kemal Ali.[14] The woodcut labels the galleys and the Ottoman commander and depicts the most dramatic moment in the battle, when the galleys were

6.2

Battle of Zonchio, 1499–1500. Hand-colored woodcut, 5.7 × 8.25 cm. The British Museum, London.

chained together and the Ottoman powder stores exploded, engulfing all three in flames (fig. 6.2). Unlike the ships in the *View*, these Venetian vessels are depicted in action, actively defending Venetian interests.

Between 1497 and 1500, Venetian merchants were alarmed to learn that the Portuguese had circumnavigated the Cape of Good Hope, threatening Venice's Mediterranean monopoly on the spice trade.[15] The Venetian banker and diarist Girolamo Priuli (1476–1547) famously reported on the news that Portuguese caravels had successfully circumnavigated Africa and returned to Lisbon full of spices, saying, "The city of Venice found itself in great calamity for fear of losing the maritime state, from which proceeded the utility and honor of the Venetian state, because its fame and glory came from the voyages."[16] In the same years, the Venetian economy was rocked by banking failures and structural changes in patrician galley patronage.[17] As Claire Judde de Larivière's detailed analysis of the state-owned galley fleet has demonstrated, there was considerable overlap between the most active investors in public navigation and the political positions they held.[18] She has argued that while public and private interests in navigation were balanced in the fifteenth century, the turn of the sixteenth century saw a progressive concentration of capital invested in the galleys: fewer individuals invested larger amounts of money in the fleet, restricting both the flow of profits from the voyages and the greater public interest in the outcome of those voyages, making maritime commerce the business of a restricted few. While the *View* depicts static galleys, anchored in port without a great deal of surrounding merchant activity, there was in fact a slow, invisible, and long-term change occurring in the financing of those galleys that disrupted the balance between private and public interests.

How does this crisis affect the *View*? In broad terms, the Venetian crisis at the turn of the sixteenth century caused and contributed to major shifts in the city's culture of communication. In the last decade of the fifteenth century, when the *View* was created and Marcantonio Coccio Sabellico (1436–1506) and Sanudo composed their humanist panegyrics praising the glories of the city, Venice's civic culture of memorializing the past and representing the present was shifting to encompass humanist history writing as well as an increasing number of patrician diarists.[19] While humanist history writing had taken hold elsewhere in the Italian peninsula in the first part of the fifteenth century, it was not until the 1480s that humanist history really found its place in Venetian intellectual culture.[20] Bernardo Giustinian (1408–89), among the leading humanists in Venice, composed a work on

Venetian origins that described Venice as Rome's Christian successor and demonstrated a close and critical attention to sources and an elegant Latin style.[21] Sabellico published a history of Venice titled *Rerum venetarum ab urbe condita libri XXXIII* (Venice: Andrea de Torresani da Asola, 1487), a work for which he obtained the first known copyright.[22] These humanist approaches to the Venetian past and classically inspired panegyrics to its present glories complemented the serene and cosmopolitan image of the city presented in the *View*, developing an image of harmony and prosperity. Both print and text worked together to build the myth of Venice, which was flowering in literature, ritual, and historical writing at the turn of the sixteenth century.

At the same time that the official Venetian culture of memorializing events turned to humanist historiography, private historical writing in the form of patrician diaries also flourished, bringing a sense of precise realism to representations of the city. Christiane Neerfeld's analysis connects the work of the patrician diarists Sanudo, Priuli, Pietro Dolfin (1427–1506), and Marcantonio Michiel (1484–1522) to the turbulence of the times they lived through, arguing that their close focus on the political life of the time was a response to the uncertainties and reversals of fortune the city faced.[23] Like medieval chronicles, the diaries offer a roughly chronological account of events, but the authors also express their own interpretations and personal opinions.[24] Each author reflected his own interests—Priuli, a merchant and banker, included more information on prices, taxes, and the vicissitudes of the Venetian fleet; Dolfin was an attentive observer of the conflict with the Ottomans in the eastern Mediterranean; and Michiel focused on artistic and cultural matters.[25] The voluminous diaries of Sanudo shared structural, linguistic, and stylistic features with these other patrician records, but he stands out as the best informed about politics and the most comprehensive chronicler of the specifics of Venetian life.[26] While the humanist histories of Giustinian and Sabellico focused on the large-scale patterns of the Venetian past, the diarists offered a close and detailed focus on particular events. The *View* combines these approaches, offering an overarching vision of the city's appearance as well as a particular focus on individual streets, canals, and buildings.[27]

De' Barbari's *View* is interesting because it has qualities of both modes of representation: not only praise and propaganda but also detailed realism. Neither the humanist histories nor the patrician diarists offer a full picture of Venetian crisis at the turn of the sixteenth century. The humanist historians minimized conflict and change: Giustinian focused on Venetian origins, while Sabellico drew heavily on Venetian chronicles to support his systematic comparison of Venice with ancient Rome. The diaries were much more critical of Venetian politics but generally took a short-term perspective.[28]

In sharp contrast to the diaries, which were not intended for immediate public consumption, print culture offered an avenue for those who wished to produce polemical interpretations of Venetian politics and culture intended to influence public opinion.[29] Recent scholarship on political communication and print culture has pointed to the multiplicity of forms, genres, or technologies used to spread ideas.[30] In the Venetian context, Rosa Salzberg has demonstrated the central role of ephemeral printed materials on communicative culture in the city; she describes a three-way interaction between political and religious authorities, printers and purveyors of print, and people interested in consuming news and information that created a market and a system of information flow in the city.[31] Ephemeral print in particular crossed over into oral culture, as street singers and performers read printed accounts of events in public squares, put them to song and verse, and spread their messages well beyond the initial sphere of print.[32]

The *View* was a part of this communicative culture. The size and cost of the image meant that it was certainly not circulating in the streets, but surviving copies of the work show that the *View* appealed to Venetians as well as to foreigners.[33] It was also produced in a world where people were increasingly accustomed to consuming news, receiving information in polemical form, and seeing and hearing arguments bolstered by combinations of print and image. As de' Barbari walked through Venice studying the city for the *View*, he could not have avoided seeing broadsides sold alongside the carefully produced classical volumes of Aldus Manutius and hearing panicked predictions about the impact of the Portuguese voyages on the Venetian spice trade. Under these circumstances, it is not surprising that his own work functions as a type of political communication as well. In response to the sense of crisis facing the city at the turn of the sixteenth century, the *View* argues in visual terms that Venetian commercial strength would allow the city to persist in the face of adversity.

1 Marino Sanudo, "Praise of the City of Venice," in *Venice: A Documentary History, 1450–1630*, ed. David Chambers and Brian Pullan (1992; repr., Toronto: University of Toronto Press with the Renaissance Society of America, 2004), 4–21; David Chambers, "Bird's Eye View of Venice," in *The Genius of Venice, 1500–1600*, exhib. cat., ed. Jane Martineau and Charles Hope (London: Royal Academy of Arts, 1983), 392–93, suggests a connection with Sabellico's praise of Venice printed in 1490. Deborah Howard, "Venice as a Dolphin: Further Investigations into Jacopo de' Barbari's View," *Artibus et Historiae* 18, no. 35 (1997): 101–11, esp. 103, pairs the view with Sanudo's 1493 panegyric.

2 Raffaele Caresini, *Chronica 1343–1388*, ed. Ester Pastorello, vol. 12, *Rerum Italicarum Scriptores* (Bologna: Zanichelli, 1922), 58.

3 Howard, "Venice as a Dolphin," 104; Juergen Schulz, "Jacopo de' Barbari's View of Venice: Map Making, City Views, and Moralized Geography before the Year 1500," *Art Bulletin* 60, no. 3 (1978): 425–74, esp. 468.

4 Guglielmo Zanelli, *Navi, squeri, traghetti da Jacopo de' Barbari* (Venice: Centro Internazionale della Grafica, 2011), 15.

5 Frederic C. Lane, "Venetian Merchant Galleys, 1300–1334: Private and Communal Operation," *Speculum* 38, no. 2 (1963): 179–205; Bernard Doumerc, "Le galere da mercato," in *Storia di Venezia: Dalle origini alla caduta della serenissima*, vol. 12, *Il Mare*, ed. Alberto Tenenti and Ugo Tucci (Rome: Enciclopedia Italiana, 1991), 357–95.

6 Doris Stöckly, *Le système de l'Incanto des galées du marché à Venise, fin XIIIe–milieu XVe siècle* (Leiden: Brill, 1995).

7 Frederic C. Lane, *Venice: A Maritime Republic* (Baltimore, MD: Johns Hopkins University Press, 1973), 46–48.

8 Frederic C. Lane, *Venetian Ships and Shipbuilders of the Renaissance* (Westport, CT: Greenwood, 1975), 7–26; Dario Zanverdiani, "Navi," in *Venezia città mirabile: Guida alla veduta prospettica di Jacopo de' Barbari*, ed. Corrado Balistreri-Trincanato et al. (Verona: Cierre, 2009), 257–61.

9 Lane, *Venetian Ships and Shipbuilders*, 47.

10 Reinhold C. Mueller, *The Venetian Money Market: Banks, Panics and the Public Debt, 1200–1500* (Baltimore, MD: Johns Hopkins University Press, 1997); James E. Shaw, *The Justice of Venice: Authorities and Liberties in the Urban Economy, 1550–1700* (Oxford: Oxford University Press, 2006), 22–29.

11 The *fondaco* is very well documented; for an introduction and further bibli-

ography, see Olivia Remie Constable, *Housing the Stranger in the Mediterranean World: Lodging, Trade, and Travel in Late Antiquity and the Middle Ages* (Cambridge: Cambridge University Press, 2003), 315–27; Ennio Concina, *Fondaci: Architettura, arte, e mercatura tra Levante, Venezia, e Alemagna* (Venice: Marsilio, 1997), 125–217; Karl-Ernst Lupprian, *Il Fondaco dei Tedeschi e la sua funzione di controllo del commercio tedesco a Venezia* (Venice: Centro Tedesco di Studi Veneziani, 1978).

12 Constable, *Housing the Stranger*, 319.

13 Gaetano Cozzi and Michael Knapton, *La repubblica di Venezia nell'età moderna*, vol. 12, *Storia d'Italia* (Turin: UTET, 1986), 1:82–84.

14 Frederic C. Lane, "Naval Actions and Fleet Organization, 1499–1502," in *Renaissance Venice*, ed. J. R. Hale (London: Faber and Faber, 1973), 146–73, esp. 152.

15 Robert Finlay, "Crisis and Crusade in the Mediterranean: Venice, Portugal, and the Cape Route to India (1498–1509)," *Studi Veneziani* 28 (1994): 45–90.

16 Priuli is quoted in Cozzi and Knapton, *La repubblica di Venezia*, 1:85.

17 Mueller, *The Venetian Money Market*; Bernard Doumerc, "La crise structurelle de la marine vénitienne au XVe siècle: Le problème du retard des mude," *Annales ESC* 40, no. 3 (1985): 605–23.

18 Claire Judde de Larivière, *Naviguer, commercer, gouverner économie maritime et pouvoirs à Venise, XVe–XVIe siècles* (Leiden: Brill, 2008).

19 Eric Cochrane, *Historians and Historiography in the Italian Renaissance* (Chicago: University of Chicago Press, 1981), 77–86, 228–29; Franco Gaeta, "Storiografia, coscienza nazionale e politica culturale nella Venezia del Rinascimento," in *Dal primo quattrocento al concilio di Trento*, vol. 3, *Storia della cultura Veneta* (Vicenza: Neri Pozza, 1980), 1–91; Gaetano Cozzi, "Cultura politica e religione nella 'pubblica storiografia' veneziana del '500," *Bollettino dell'Istituto di Storia I Società dello Stato Veneziano* 5–6 (1963–64): 215–94; Agostino Pertusi, "Gli inizi della storiografia umanistica nel Quattrocento," in *La storiografia veneziana fino al secolo XVI: Aspetti e problemi* (Florence: Olschki, 1970), 269–332.

20 Gaeta, "Storiografia," 27–46; Pertusi, "Gli inizi," 294–305.

21 Patricia Labalme, *Bernardo Giustiniani: A Venetian of the Quattrocento* (Rome: Edizioni di Storia e Letteratura, 1969); Pertusi, "Gli inizi," 306–31; Gaeta, "Storiografia," 49.

22 Ruth Chavasse, "The First Known Author's Copyright, September 1486, in the Context of a Humanist Career," *Bulletin of the John Rylands University Library of Manchester* 69 (1986–87): 11–37.

23 Christiane Neerfeld, *Historia per forma di diaria: La cronachistica veneziana contemporanea a cavallo tra il Quattro e il*

Cinquecento (Venice: Istituto Veneto di Scienze Lettere ed Arti, 2006).

24 Neerfeld, *Historia per forma di diaria*, 175–98.

25 Neerfeld, *Historia per forma di diaria*, 106.

26 For an introduction to the life and works of Sanudo and some excerpts in English translation, see Marino Sanudo, *Venice, Città Excelentissima: Selections from the Renaissance Diaries of Marin Sanudo*, ed. Patricia H. Labalme and Laura Sanguineti White, trans. Linda Carroll (Baltimore, MD: Johns Hopkins University Press, 2008).

27 For the connection of history writing to Venetian visual culture overall, see Patricia Fortini Brown, *Venice and Antiquity: The Venetian Sense of the Past* (New Haven, CT: Yale University Press, 1996).

28 Neerfeld, *Historia per forma di diaria*, 197–98.

29 For Venice, see Filippo de Vivo, *Information and Communication in Venice: Rethinking Early Modern Politics* (Oxford: Oxford University Press, 2007); for Europe more broadly, see Andrew Pettegree, *The Invention of News: How the World Came to Know about Itself* (New Haven, CT: Yale University Press, 2014).

30 Sean E. Roberts, *Printing a Mediterranean World: Florence, Constantinople, and the Renaissance of Geography* (Cambridge, MA: Harvard University Press, 2013); Yoshihisa Hattori, ed., *Political Order and Forms of Communication in Medieval and Early Modern Europe* (Rome: Viella, 2014); Andrea Gamberini and Giuseppe Petralia, eds., *Linguaggi politici nell'Italia del Rinascimento: Atti del Convegno, Pisa, 9–11 novembre 2006* (Rome: Viella, 2007).

31 Rosa Salzberg, *Ephemeral City: Cheap Print and Urban Culture in Renaissance Venice* (Manchester: Manchester University Press, 2014), 7.

32 Rosa Salzberg and Massimo Rospocher, "Street Singers in Italian Renaissance Urban Culture and Communication," *Cultural and Social History* 9, no. 1 (2012): 9–26; Massimo Rospocher and Rosa Salzberg, "'El vulgo zanza': Spazi pubblici, voci a Venezia durante le guerre d'Italia," *Storica* 48, no. 16 (2010): 83–120.

33 Howard, "Venice as a Dolphin," 102.

Bronwen Wilson

Navigating the Business
of Print in Venice
with Jacopo de' Barbari

7 A HEROIC FIGURE OF NEPTUNE appears astride a fantastic sea crea-
ture in the foreground of Jacopo de' Barbari's ambitious woodcut of Venice
(plate 7). His trident, with its tablet and ropes, echoes the riggings of the
galleys adjacent to the Customs House to the left. The angle of the trident
points northwest (toward the wind god Corus), directing us to the Frezzaria,
the artisanal artery that was attracting printers to parishes nearby. The Latin
text on Neptune's tablet informs us he is smoothing the waters, a reference
to his maritime domain but also to printmaking: the block resembles a wood
matrix, its letters carved with a pointed burin and its shape characteristic of
weights used to press paper flat. Neptune looks up toward his lofty collab-
orator Mercury, the messenger god who safeguards trade and shopkeepers

(plate 1). Between these two classical figures lies the Mercerie, the center of commerce, where the publishing industry was flourishing (plate 5).

Scholars have made use of the woodcut's exacting verisimilitude to illustrate locations where printers worked in Venice,[1] but taking my cues from Neptune, Mercury, and the winds, this brief essay proposes that the reason the map's precision enables us to find places associated with print is because it was designed that way—in part purposefully, and in part as a result of the confluence of printmaking, mapmaking, and mobility. Collaboration between de' Barbari, a Venetian artist, and Anton Kolb, the German publisher, was an important factor in this process, as was experimentation with the potential of the medium, the singular cityscape, and uses of instruments for printing, measuring, and traveling. Recall that when Kolb referred to the "new art of printing" in his application to the Collegio for an exemption from duties, he cited the "difficulty of the overall composition" as well as the costs of paper for a "work to be exported and sold in all your lands and cities" (see appendix 2).[2] My proposition, limited to a few but hopefully suggestive details, is that the woodcut functions not only as a topographical map but also as an itinerary that moves viewers from place to place, orienting them to the business of print. That these spaces attracted those involved in the trade after the bird's-eye view was printed offers some retroactive evidence.

When Kolb published the woodcut in 1500, the city was teeming with bookshops, stationers, and street vendors. Around 1473, four years after editions were first published, a scribe grumbled that Venice was "stuffed with books," an efflorescence that Martin Lowry describes as a "sudden explosion in [the city's] vitals."[3] Already twelve printers were operating in the Mercerie, the network of streets that runs from the Clocktower in Piazza San Marco to Rialto. Mostly Germans, they resided around San Paternian (now Campo Manin) and San Zulian. In 1533, there were sixteen booksellers and thirteen printers in the city. When the Sant'Uffizio (Holy Office) made a count in 1567, it reported sixty-four businesses, of which forty-seven had shops, most with street signs. One of those had a stall at Piazza San Marco, and the rest were itinerant sellers found along the Mercerie, at San Salvador, at the portico at Rialto, at the Fondaco dei Tedeschi (the German trading house), and around the church of San Moisè. During feast days and festivals, prints were sold at markets in Campo San Polo and San Marco. All these sites are conspicuous in the woodcut.[4]

In 1500 Venice was a hub and a crossroads for print; the imports and exports from Venice—almost double the volume seen in Paris, then its nearest rival—contributed to its reputation as the largest publishing center in Europe.[5] Its significance was the reason Kolb traveled to Venice, where he was the agent for Anton Koberger, the first printer in Nuremberg. Kolb was carrying copies of the *Nuremberg Chronicle*—Hartmann Schedel's world history, copiously illustrated with 1,809 woodcuts and published by Koberger in 1493.[6] Books were shipped out, for example, by the Gabiano, who sent 1,800 books to correspondents and whose bookshop was at the sign of the Fountain at San Bartolomeo, near the bridge at Rialto.[7] The highly speculative nature of printing—many publishers also traded in textiles, paper, grain, and other merchandise—benefited from transnational networks and flexibility.[8]

Bronwen Wilson

This combination of international investments in print in Venice, and the need to find one's bearings there, resonate with the two different experiences of the city afforded by the de' Barbari woodcut (plate 1). Seen from a distance, and surrounded by personifications of winds, the islands resemble a vast map of the world. The Olympian vantage point presents an idealized, utopian, and timeless image of the city, one that resonates with the government's long history of managing competing interests by integrating individuals into the city as a whole.[9] The forces of the winds also direct us to the historical center, where galleys converge and things move at a pace. On the bottom right, a regatta races back from the Adriatic, its vessels coursing through the waves propelled by the east wind, Subsolanus. The waters calm as the boats approach a tidal marker on the left. A horizon line now organizes the perspective, lowering our point of view. Details of the cityscape and toponyms come into focus and move us purposefully through the city. Façades of buildings are unified into continuous surfaces along canals and streets, their distances measured by bridges that open up alternative routes. Even the paving and arcades in Piazza San Marco guide us through the square, which is populated only by sculptures (plate 2). The absence of human figures in the Piazza and parish campi, importantly, highlights the ubiquity of people on the move; they race toward the center in the regatta, maneuver vessels from the east, and man gondolas in the canals, traveling from place to place throughout the city.

These human figures and their vessels prompt consideration of itineraries: maps that emphasize routes and temporal dimensions of travel. Manuscript itineraries were a mainstay of Venetians, who crisscrossed the Mediterranean for their mercantile activities, chronicled their travels, and reported on their journeys and what could be found there. Cities and landmarks on the mainland were also recorded as a sequence of stopping places. In 1483, the young Marin Sanudo introduces his *Itinerario*, a narrative account of the Venetian *terraferma* that enables readers to follow in his tracks, with verses linking towns, fields, and waterways to Roman gods.[10] The earliest printed examples in Venice, a departure point for journeys to the Holy Land, are pilgrimage guides. Later in the sixteenth century, printed itineraries flourish, especially for travel to Constantinople. Sometimes portable, they provide distances between places, days required to travel, views of ports, and information about merchandise available at stopping points. An itinerary distills a range of choices into a route of recommended sites.[11]

With this kind of map in mind, and recalling that Mercury was tasked with protecting travelers and transporters of goods, consider how the god conducts our navigation by pointing to the southwest of the "illustrious emporium," as Venice is described in the Latin inscription that encircles his torso (plate 1). The lines of the clouds behind his shoulder and the slope of his arm strategically echo the contours of the mountains and the passageway that descends to the left. This was the route through the Alps that Kolb would have taken from Nuremberg. German printers would have continued to Tervixio (Treviso), marked on the mainland to the left, where paper production had been supported by the government since the fourteenth century.[12] Paper was critical to their enterprise, as Kolb's appeal to the Collegio notes, as was access to financial capital for this costly resource.[13] Continuing farther south to Marghera and Mestre, small boats transport goods to and from the islands, where navigable waters are rendered by open space between horizontal lines of black ink.

From the mainland, where toponyms identify cities, stopping points along the southward trajectory are marked by bridges and parishes, their names indicated on the church or the campo.[14] The passageway through Cannaregio opens onto the Grand Canal, from where boats could turn east to the Fondaco dei Tedeschi, or south through Santa Croce, passing Campo Sant'Agostin, where Aldo Manuzio initially established his press, and San Polo, marked by a bridge, where the Ascension Day market was held. Traversing the campo and crossing the Grand Canal again, the itinerary leads south to San Paternian, at the first bridge where German printers resided; to the Frezzaria, at the second bridge; to San Moisè, at the third; and to the Customs House, across the Grand Canal.

This area of the Frezzaria, which sold artisanal goods and arrows (*frezze*), to which Neptune's trident points, became a focus for immigrants and for illustrated books and maps at the beginning of the sixteenth century. Giovanni Andrea Vavassore, for example, a cartographer, publisher, bookseller, engraver, and illustrator of popular themes, and his heirs, were active there from before 1515 to 1585.[15] Around 1522, Giovanni worked with Nicolò Aristotile de' Rossi, known as il Zoppino, and from 1530 he was printing books. In 1537, the Vavassore brothers and Giovanni Andrea, called Guadagnino, could be found at the Ponte di Fuseri, and their heirs had a shop along the Frezzaria, "al segno dell'Ippogrifo" (at the sign of the Hippogriff). Michele and Francesco Tramezzini were drawn to Venice in 1525 by the increasing market for vernacular books.[16] They also produced geographical maps and city views, printed with their trademark, a sibyl. The Bertelli family established its business in Frezzaria in the 1550s. Ferdinando, a publisher, cartographer, and engraver, produced at least two hundred works, selling them at the sign of San Marco.[17] Donato Bertelli was engraving and selling city views and maps from 1558, as were Luca and Pietro Bertelli, who inherited the bookshop.[18] Giacomo Franco, the engraver, etcher, and publisher of maps, costume, festival, and lace books, moved his business and residence from Santa Fosca to Frezzaria at the "Insegna del Sole" (sign of the Sun).[19] By 1592, Cesare Vecellio, the artist, author, and printer, was located nearby in "Frezzaria nelle case de'Preti." Vecellio's address sometimes references the church of the priests, San Moisè, which is where Pietro and Domenico de' Franceschi worked "al segno della Regina" (at the sign of the Queen).[20] Matteo Pagan's shop, "al segno della Fede" (at the sign of the Faith), was a few steps away. Active from 1538 to 1562, he crafted maps and the well-known woodcut of the ducal procession.[21]

Progressing in the other direction, Neptune's upward gaze guides us north toward the Mercerie (plate 5). The first stopping point after the Clocktower is the campo of San Zulian, where the dense cross-hatching of buildings opens up. The church, its name visible on the transept wall, housed the guild of *stracciaruoli* (collectors of rags for paper), and the guild of *cartolai* (paper merchants) was located nearby.[22] The parish attracted German printers prior to 1500, as noted above, and soon also immigrants from the *terraferma*, such as Stefano Scolari from Brescia, a printer and publisher of woodcuts and engravings.[23] Donato Rascicotti, an engraver and printer of views of Venice, could be found at the Ponte de Baretteri, where the *sotoportego*, the passage under the building, leads to San Salvador and where the Manuzio family had bookshops, with signs bearing either the Aldine anchor or Aldo's portrait.[24]

A combination of large and small enterprises was common through the Mercerie to Rialto. The Florentine Giunti set up shop there in 1489, as did the Sessa, whose family publishing business (and trademark cat and mouse) endured for decades. Marcantonio Coccio, known as Sabellico, who received the first copyright in 1486 for his history of Venice, found the bookstalls in the area distracting.[25] He recounts how two friends en route to the Fondaco dei Tedeschi were delayed because they lingered over lists of books for sale posted on shops.[26] Books were sold by peddlers and street vendors, such as Nicolò di Bortolomeo Pierio Toschan from Bergamo, who worked on feast days.[27] The Holy Office made a note that "Zuane de Anzolo, *erbariol* [*erbarolo* = seller of greens] . . . sells books at San Salvador, without a shop."[28] In the 1470s, Johannes de Colonia, who lived at the Fondaco, had one of many bookshops at San Salvador.[29] The caption identifying the parish in the woodcut is printed at an angle, thereby signaling the turn to Rialto, which was also packed with stalls, bookshops, and paper vendors even prior to book printing (upper left, plate 5).

More eye-catching in the woodcut than the bridge are the buildings on either side: the German Fondaco, its name "Fontico dalamani" clearly printed on the white paper ground, and the Palazzo Camerlenghi, where printers applied for trademarks and signs (plate 4). Parishes are identified by toponyms throughout the woodcut, but only a handful of buildings are labeled by name, including the Fondaco, the Customs House, and the Ducal Palace, where the Senate assisted the industry, granting licenses and privileges (copyrights) to protect investments. The Palazzo Camerlenghi, constructed in 1488, housed the Giustizia Vecchia, the magistracy of commerce, which managed printshops and apprentice contracts.[30] The single-story section—likely the "loggia of the Rialto"—in front of the multistoried structure, is rendered parallel to the Fondaco.[31]

The imprint—the stamp and the emblem—was itself a sign of the economic life of the city, as the case of Paolo Forlani exemplifies. An engraver of maps, he worked for several printers in the Mercerie during the 1560s. His designs were published by Giovanni Francesco Camocio, whose shop "Ad signum pyramidis" (at the sign of the pyramid) was at San Lio, just east of Rialto. Forlani also relied on Bolognino Zaltieri, who was nearby "all'insegna di Venetia," and on the Bertelli, who were in Frezzaria, as noted earlier, at the sign of San Marco.[32] Further imprints include "al segno del pozzo," "in merzaria alla libreria della Nave," and "alla libreria della Colonna" (at the well, the ship, and the column, respectively). The latter was Forlani's trademark, and in 1566 he applied to the Giustizia Vecchia for a shop sign to match.[33]

The assortment of printers' marks conjures a vivid picture of the relation between the printed page and the street. Publishers and books were linked to signs of trade more broadly, for which a Spanish dialogue titled *Viaje de Turquía* (*Travel from Turkey*), probably written in 1557 by Cristóbal de Villalón, provides evidence.[34] Pedro, one of the interlocutors, states, "In Florence, as in all the grand cities in France and Italy, those who have a shop, in whatever trade, put on the door a kind of banderole with a sign intended to be easy to recognize and to find again.... So, it suffices to say, Sir, I am in the street of the Swan, or of the Lion, or of the Horse, and so it goes." Juan asks him, "They are like certain figures on the frontispieces of books, such as Fortune, or I don't know what else?" "Exactly," Pedro responds. "That figure is to indicate the sign where the book is sold or where it was printed."[35] For the Spanish traveler, locating oneself in the city resembles the use of imprints to identify a bookshop or printer in the street.

This dynamic, which was surely relevant for the business of print in Venice, resonates with the two kinds of maps in the woodcut—one of the city seen from above, concerned with relations between the parts and the whole, and the other emphasizing mobility and commerce. The former downplays the city's famous landmarks to accentuate Venice as a center—a world unto itself—to which trade is propelled. In contrast, the toponyms of the two itineraries—inscribed in black ink on open expanses of white clouds, mountains, water, walls, and ground—draw us toward the surface of the paper to read them as texts printed on paper. Precluded from seeing the whole, we are incited to follow the canals, noting directions at bridges, and to move through streets, stopping at campi. Not unlike the gods that introduce Sanudo's manuscript *Itinerario* mentioned earlier, Mercury and Neptune, with their caduceus and trident, help us navigate between the view of the whole and its waterways and streets. With the wind gods, they orient us to the practical exigencies of getting from place to place.

Situated at the edges of the representation, the winds mediate between our world and the printed page. Modeled on figures from the *Nuremberg Chronicle*, including the puffed cheeks and Latin nomenclature of its world map, the winds introduce the printer's craft (plate 1).[36] Hair and physiognomies are differentiated from each other, their spiraling locks and styles highlighting the inventive potential of the medium and artistic virtuosity. The inchoate clouds on which the winds float, and the horizontal align-

Bronwen Wilson

ment of their names on the page, showcase the white paper and evoke letterpress printing. The winds, with their fanlike rays, emulate the wind roses that guided mariners on portolans, such as Aquilo, the northeast wind on the upper right, which propels a small boat with its sail. The lines create axes between the winds across the map, with those emanating from Auster and Septentrio on the south and north. Capital letters, such as the pointed *T* (*tramontana*) that marks the North, ensure that we associate the design with compass roses that were being printed on geographical maps.[37] Contributing to this idea of navigation is the geometry of the inscription, mentioned above, that encircles Mercury's body. His right arm reaches out toward the southwest, its sweeping gesture emulating the needle of a compass. An apt image for the god of travelers, Mercury serves as a divine compass: he mediates between the two experiences of the view—the world map, and movement into and through its waterways and streets.

Scholars have speculated about how the design was produced, including the use of government surveys, the creation of a large model, sketches from bell towers, and triangulating distances between towers.[38] The image of a compass—unsurprising in Venice—furthers this story, since the axes of the winds converge at the top of the campanile in Piazza San Marco. At this point in the center, de' Barbari would have surveyed the city as a whole, comparing, aligning, and assembling images measured and sketched from the parish bell towers. Becoming a human compass, and surely using a compass, the artist would have rotated from point to point in the elevated platform. Oriented slightly to the west of magnetic North, and looking out to the horizon, he could plot the journeys of traders—German ones particularly—from the Alps and through the city, providing an itinerary for the business of print. Printers' shops and their signs, as we have seen, would have guided visitors and locals on the ground.

Once we imagine that Mercury is floating in the center of the winds above the campanile, instead of resting at the top of the map, these two points of view converge in the artist's eye and hand. As the messenger between these worlds, Mercury was an apposite alter ego for an artist who translated the city into an image on paper, guiding viewers to its spaces of print like the signs on the streets and the printers' marks on the page. It is especially fitting that de' Barbari, even after he left Venice for Nuremberg, continued to adopt the caduceus as his signature, linking himself with the city and his work of drawing and printing it.[39]

Bronwen Wilson

1 See Rosa Salzberg, "'Per le piaze & sopra il Ponte': Reconstructing the Geography of Popular Print in Sixteenth-Century Venice," in *Geographies of the Book*, ed. Miles Ogborn and Charles W. J. Withers (Farnham, UK: Ashgate, 2010); Natalie Lussey, "Staying Afloat: The Vavassore Workshop and the Role of the Minor Publisher in Sixteenth Century Venice," *Kunsttexte.de* 2 (2017): 1–30.

2 Reprinted in David Chambers and Brian Pullan, eds., *Venice: A Documentary History, 1450–1630* (Oxford: Blackwell, 1992), 373.

3 Martin Lowry, *Nicholas Jenson and the Rise of Venetian Publishing in Renaissance Europe* (Oxford: Blackwell, 1991), 177. For Venice as "stuffed with books," see Martin Lowry, *The World of Aldus Manutius: Business and Scholarship in Renaissance Venice* (Oxford: Blackwell, 1979), 18.

4 Archivio di Stato di Venezia (ASVe), Sant'uffizio, b. 156, unnumbered sheet dated September 13, 1567; cited in Salzberg, "Per le piaze," 121n36.

5 Lowry, *The World of Aldus Manutius*, 19. See also Andrew Pettegree, *The Book in the Renaissance* (New Haven, CT: Yale University Press, 2010), 357.

6 In 1509, thirty-four of Kolb's six hundred copies were still unsold. Pettegree, *The Book in the Renaissance*, 77–78.

7 Angela Nuovo, "Transferring Humanism: The Edition of Vitruvius by Lucimborgo De Gabiano (Lyon, 1523)," in *Lux Librorum: Essays on Books and History for Chris Coppens* (Mechelen: Flanders Book Historical Society, 2018), 21.

8 Nuovo, "Transferring Humanism," 19.

9 Bronwen Wilson, *The World in Venice: Print, the City, and Early Modern Identity* (Toronto: University of Toronto Press, 2005), 25–50.

10 Marin Sanuto, *Itinerario per la terraferma veneziana nell' anno 1483*, ed. Rawdon Brown (Padua: Seminario, 1847), 11–16.

11 Louis Marin, "Establishing a Signification for Social Space: Demonstration, Cortege, Parade, Procession," in *On Representation*, trans. Catherine Porter (Stanford, CA: Stanford University Press, 2001), 38–53.

12 Juraj Kittler, "From Rags to Riches: The Limits of Early Paper Manufacturing and Their Impact on Book Print in Renaissance Venice," *Media History* 21, no. 1 (2015): 14.

13 Kittler, "From Rags to Riches," 10; Lowry, *The World of Aldus Manutius*, 98.

14 For details of the *View*, see DOI: 10.7924/G8MK69TH.

15 On Vavassore, see Lussey, "Staying Afloat."

16 Brian Richardson, *Print Culture in Renaissance Italy: The Editor and the Vernacular Text, 1470–1600* (Cambridge: Cambridge University Press, 1994), 90; Paolo Bellini, "Printmakers and Dealers in Italy during the 16th and 17th Century," *Print Collector* 13 (1975); Giacomo Moro, "Insegne librarie e marche tipografiche in un registro veneziano del '500," *La bibliofilia*, no. 1 (January–April 1989): 76.

17 Bellini, "Printmakers."

18 Fernanda Ascarelli and Marco Menato, *La tipografia del '500 in Italia* (Florence: Leo S. Olschki, 1989), 408–9; Ester Pastorello, *Tipografi, editori, librai a Venezia nel secolo XVI* (Florence: Olschki, 1924), 8.

19 Carlo Pasero, "Giacomo Franco, editore, incisore e calcografo nei secoli xvi e xvii," *La bibliofilia* 37, nos. 8–10 (August–October 1935).

20 Ascarelli and Menato, *La tipografia*, 383; Pastorello, *Tipografi*, n308; Salzberg, "Per le piaze," 118n27.

21 Michael Bury et al., *The Print in Italy, 1550–1620* (London: British Museum Press, 2001), 183–84.

22 Kittler, "From Rags to Riches," 15; Salzberg, "Per le piaze," 117–21.

23 Marino Zorzi, "Stampatori tedeschi a Venezia," in *Venezia e la Germania: Arte, politica, commercio: Due civiltà a confronto* (Milan: Electa, 1986), 122; Cristina Dondi, "Printers and Guilds in Fifteenth-Century Venice," *La bibliofilia* 106 (2004): 229–65.

24 H. George Fletcher III, *New Aldine Studies: Documentary Essays on the Life and Work of Aldus Manutius* (San Francisco: B. M. Rosenthal, 1988), 68–69; cited in Angela Nuovo, *The Book Trade in the Italian Renaissance* (Leiden: Brill, 2013), 132.

25 Marcantonio Coccio Sabellico, *Decades rerum Venetarum* (Venice: Andreas Torresanus, de Asula, 1487). On the privilege, September 1, 1486, see ASVe, Collegio, Notatorio, reg. 11, c. 55r; *Primary Sources on Copyright (1450–1900)*, ed. Lionel Bently and Martin Kretschmer, accessed October 13, 2020, www.copyrighthistory.org.

26 Marcantonio Coccio Sabellico, "De Latinae linguae reparatione," in *Opera omnia*, 4 vols. (Basel: J. Herwagen, 1570), 3:319–35, esp. 322; cited in Nuovo, *Book Trade*, 331.

27 ASVe, Sant'uffizio, b. 156.

28 ASVe, Sant'uffizio, b. 156.

29 Nuovo, *Book Trade*, 22.

30 On the Giustizia Vecchia, see Richard Mackenney, *Tradesmen and Traders: The World of the Guilds in Venice and Europe, c. 1250–c. 1650* (London: Croom Helm, 1987).

31 Paul Hamilton, "The Palazzo dei Camerlenghi in Venice," *Journal of the Society of Architectural Historians* 42, no. 3 (1983): 262.

32 Zaltieri applied to the Giustizia Vecchia on July 10, 1567. Bury et al., *The Print in Italy*, 236.

33 David Woodward, "Paolo Forlani: Compiler, Engraver, Printer, or Publisher?," *Imago Mundi* 44 (1992): 59.

34 Giustizia Vecchia, June 7, 1566; cited in Moro, "Insegne," 64n17.

35 My translation of Giustizia Vecchia, 54n2.

36 For the world map, see "Nuremberg Chronicle World Map," Cornell University Library, accessed October 13, 2020, https://digital.library.cornell.edu/catalog/ss:3293718.

37 On the winds, see Kristin Love Huffman, "Jacopo de' Barbari's *View of Venice* (1500): 'Image Vehicles' and 'Pathways of Culture' Past and Present," *Mediterranea* 4 (2019): 165–214, esp. 169.

38 Juergen Schulz, "Jacopo de' Barbari's View of Venice: Map Making, City Views, and Moralized Geography before the Year 1500," *Art Bulletin* 60, no. 3 (1978): 425–74; Piero Falchetta, "La misura dipinta: Rilettura tecnica e semantica della veduta di Venezia di Jacopo de' Barbari," *Ateneo Veneto* 178 (1991).

39 Wilson, *The World in Venice*, 257.

Valeria Cafà

On the Collection History
of the *View*'s Matrices

THE STORY OF THE SIX WOODEN BLOCKS used to print the *View of Venice* includes only a few certainties prior to their entry into the Museo Civico Correr's "Class XXXIII Collection: Types and Printing in Metal and Wood" (fig. 8.1).[1] Scholarly attention has primarily focused on the prints rather than on the matrices, although their size, which constitutes an overall "monumental" picture of approximately 1,400 by 2,870 millimeters, places them among the largest wooden blocks ever made and among the very few of large format preserved today. Interest in the visual evidence offered by the six wooden blocks is, after all, recent and goes hand in hand with a greater study of the material value of the *View* and in particular, the process of its execution. In 1999, on the occasion of the exhibition *A volo d'uccello: Jacopo de' Barbari and the Representations of Cities in Renaissance Europe*, the matrices underwent a treatment that offered the opportunity to analyze their nature and manufacture and also their state of conservation.[2] In recent years the wooden blocks have been considered a mine of (new) information capable of helping answer questions that are still open, such as the number of woodcutters involved in the stratification of the carvings, not to mention additional data regarding workshop practice.[3] This essay reconstructs known data about the events related to the six blocks before they entered the museum because, although intrinsically linked to the prints, the matrices have had a different life and esteemed value, first among printmakers and later among collectors.

Valeria Cafà

The six wooden blocks were ready for printing as early as October 30, 1500, when the German publisher and merchant Anton Kolb presented an appeal to the Venetian Collegio requesting the privilege of printing and selling the *View of Venice* exclusively and without tax duties (see appendix 2). The extraordinary nature of the work is underlined by Kolb himself, who proves to be its proud commissioner. From his words, which do not explicitly mention the six blocks or who was responsible for them, it can be deduced that the matrices were made in Venice as part of an arduous work period that lasted three years. It can also be deduced that Kolb had already done at least some printing tests, therefore the matrices had already been in use. Exactly how many copies have been printed of the first state from the blocks, is not known, but to date, the twelve known copies testify to the great appreciation and fortune of Kolb's printing enterprise. In subsequent years the matrices underwent some specific changes that resulted in two additional known states of the *View of Venice*.

The first intervention on the six wooden blocks is dated between 1511 and 1514: the small section with the date "MD" disappears, and the conformation of the roof of the bell tower of San Marco is corrected to reflect its completion between 1513 and 1514. Other changes were underway within the urban fabric of Venice, but perhaps that of the bell tower—which, for those unfamiliar with Venice is, together with the square, a point of reference from which to look—was considered the most immediately visible and therefore necessary. It is not possible to confirm that the wooden blocks were still in the hands of Kolb at this date, but there is no reason to believe they were not, given that the merchant from Nuremberg is active and documented in Venice until 1541 (see appendix 3). This first revision of the six wooden blocks, which gave life to the second-state prints, was followed by another

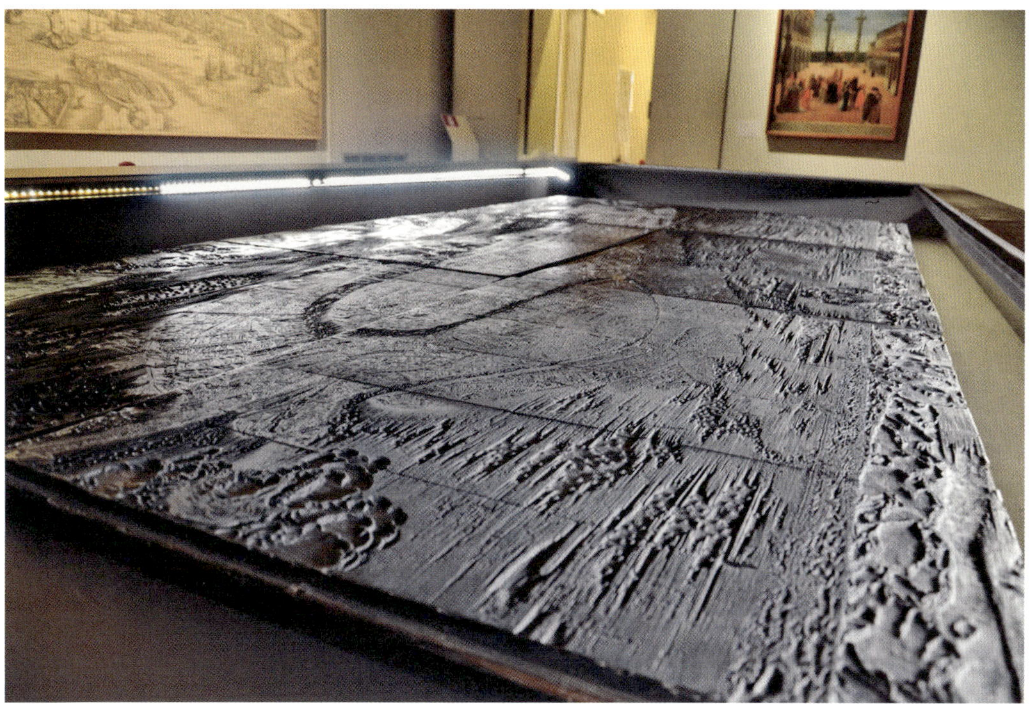

retooling that had the aim of restoring them to their original state and there-fore obtaining prints closer to that of the first. The most credible hypoth-esis is that Venice had changed so much—and especially in key locations, such as the Rialto Bridge, and in the renovated or newly built architecture of its many palaces and churches—that a revision could no longer modify select notable points. All that great work for the survey of the city risked being branded as unreliable because it no longer corresponded to the urban reality. The choice, therefore, was to return to the *View* of 1500, effectively changing the value and purpose of the entire work: no longer a timely docu-mentation of the current state of the city but, rather, its memory at a precise moment—at the turn of a new century. We have no clear dates to propose for this second revision, and it is unknown who was responsible. But on one aspect, all scholars agree: the intervention visible on the four known extant prints is of a lower quality. Regarding the dating of what is therefore called the third (and last) state, scholars are inclined to place it within the sixteenth century, with a propensity toward the second half.[4] The matrices do not seem to have been used for very long for this third-state print run, and the

8.1

Wooden blocks (matrices) of the *View of Ven-ice*. Museo Cor-rer, Venice.

109

production of new impressions was not considered again until the first half of the nineteenth century.[5] But what happened to them in the meantime? If in fact the prints circulated in Venice, throughout Italy, and abroad, the six wooden blocks have seemingly always remained in Venice. For over two centuries, however, their documented presence is lost.

The matrices reappear in the eighteenth century in a short, handwritten note contained in one of the volumes of the *Gradenigo-Dolfin Memorials* maintained in the Library of the Museo Correr (fig. 8.2). The note, datable to the second half of the eighteenth century through systematic analysis of the volume (see below in this chapter), states:

> Print of Venice, six plans engraved by Alberto Duro
>
> 1720. In the House of Barone __________ Tassis, director of the Flanders Post Office in Venice, some precious wood carvings were kept, drawn many years ago by the famous painter Alberto Duro, with which the great city View of Venice was imprinted.[6]

Leaving aside the question of attribution, it should be emphasized, however, that it was most likely this precise reference to the celebrated master Albrecht Dürer as the artist responsible that contributed to the preservation of the six wooden blocks over time.[7]

Within the succinct archival record noted above, it should also be remarked that the space for the first name of Baron Tassis is intentionally left blank. It is possible that there was some uncertainty about the precise identification of the baron at the time the comment was written. Based on an overall analysis of annotations contained within the volume, it was written no later than June 1755. Between 1720 and 1721 there was a generational handover in the Tassis family that occurred between Ferdinando and his son Leopoldo Ottavio (all these names are repeated cyclically in the family tree). The Tassis lived in the district of Cannaregio by the second half of the seventeenth century, in a palace rented from the Morosini family on the Rio di San Canciano. The Tassis (or Tassi or de Tassi) family, of Bergamese origin but with a branch that had held the General Office of the Imperial Post Office in Venice since the mid-fifteenth century, was very well-known in Venice and had extensive and prestigious social connections, both local and international. The family's cachet in the city extends back to 1541, when Holy Roman Emperor Charles V (r. 1519–56) appointed Ruggero Tassis "General of the Imperial Post" of Venice.[8]

154. Angelo Beolco d.° Ruzante, Poeta Padovano, venne non sola
mente grato ad ogni condizione di Persone, per le nobili e
frizzanti facezie, che prontam.te in verso diceva: ma famoso
in tutta l'Italia, per le composizioni poetiche in lingua
Padoana del Contado, dimorò molto tempo nella Villa di
Codivigo presso il Patrizio Luigi Cornaro, ed ivi compose
la maggior parte di tali sue opere, gradite, ed udite
con applauso.

1405. La Terra di Pieve di Sacco custodita da Giacomo del Carico
il Carrarese contro Veneti in modo tale, che scrive il Sardeonio
nunquam aut aliqua spe præmiorum, aut
aut minarum trepidatione induci potuit, ut avey deditionem Venetis faceret; At qui tandem capta Urbe, ipse, ultrò
postea Senatui Veneto se se dedit: a quo / ut par erat / et
laudatus, et honoribus auctus recepit.

1720. Nella Casa del Baron   Tassis Direttore delle Poste di Fiandra in Venezia si conservavano alcuni pregievoli Intagli di
legno, disegnati altre volte dal celebre Pittore Alberto Duro,
co quali s'impresse a stampa la gran Città di Venezia.

1742. Cani chiamati Bomer di lungo pelo, e di più mantelli cioè
noti dalla Germania, Bestie di risoluta guardia si usano
in Venezia nelle Case de Nobili.

.... Laichè, o siano Servidori ad uso di campagna banditi da Venezia per Decreto del Consiglio di Dieci.

1540. Carapetti di lastra di argento, e metalli dorati con pregievole distribuzione di pietre rare, dure, e colorite, inservienti asi
Altari del Tempio della Madonna della Salute.

174. La Città di Costantinopoli, ed il Seraglio del Gran Signore disegnata diligentemente in tre viste, ivi dal Colonello, ed
Ingegniere Veneto Bossini, per farne con dono a S. Antonio
Crizzo qu. Proved.r Gnl.e in Levante.

11

At the time of Ferdinando's death, at the end of 1720, the assets of the Tassis family remained quite solid: debts and credits were basically balanced, despite the countless legal cases in progress; but to these were added real estate properties and assets such as the family's library and noteworthy gallery of painting and art objects. It seems that the art collection was begun

8.2

Commemoriali,
mss. Gradenigo-
Dolfin, n. 200,
tome 11, 11 recto.
Biblioteca del
Museo Correr,
Venice.

at the end of the sixteenth century by an ancestor, also named Ferdinando (1564?–1648), son of Ruggero. Interestingly, the Tassis had ownership of the blocks according to an early eighteenth-century document, but how and exactly when the matrices entered the family's collection remains to be understood.

Valeria Cafà

At the beginning of the seventeenth century, Ferdinando's father, Ottavio Tassis (Venice 1615–ante 1691), and his "famous studio" (in the district of Cannaregio, but at this time in a palace on the Fondamenta of the Madonna dell'Orto) gained extensive mention in Boschini (1660) and, a few years later, in Sansovino-Martinioni (1663).[9] In both illustrious records, however, the matrices are not indicated. In this regard, it is useful to point out Ottavio's interest in artists from the North: Ottavio was responsible for an expansion of the collection with acquisition of works by Hans Holbein, Quentin Metsys, and Anthony van Dyck.[10] Might the long-standing attribution to Dürer, and the family's propensity to collect northern artworks, provide circumstantial evidence for the motivation to acquire the six wooden blocks?

Unfortunately, nothing emerges from Ferdinando's postmortem inventory drawn up on May 6, 1721, currently in the Venetian State Archives.[11] Divided into sections, the inventory is a record of (almost) everything found in the house, from papers and paintings to furniture and linens. The pages dedicated to the paintings contain seventy-two items in which the works are summarily described in terms of subject and location displayed, but unfortunately without hints about the authors or estimated value, which, despite being frustrating for scholars, was not atypical. Assuming that it is not clear how the six wooden blocks of the *View of Venice* were exhibited and/or preserved, among these items there seems to be nothing that could reasonably correspond to them.

Moreover, although the six wooden blocks are not listed in Ferdinando's inventory, they were definitively owned by the Tassis family in the mid-eighteenth century, as attested by yet another handwritten note in the *Gradenigo-Dolfin Memorials*. The information that is invaluable appears in a note in parentheses (fig. 8.3), annotating the transcription of a letter from Francesco Algarotti to Bonomo Algarotti, dated February 10, 1758:

> Opinion on [the] topographical sheet . . . of which it is intended to say that the woods [blocks] are still preserved in Venice (indeed they are but somewhat moth-eaten in the house of Count Baron Leopoldo de Tassis). . . . Here is what needs to be said for now in this regard

8.3

Commemoriali, mss. Gradenigo-Dolfin, n. 200, tome 16, 25 verso. Biblioteca del Museo Correr, Venice.

about a famous map that is very exact; one example of which was in the Sagredo Gallery in Santa Sofia, another in the room of Domenico Pasqualigo in Santa Maria Zobenigo.[12]

This places them, therefore, in the collection of Leopoldo Ottavio, son of the previously mentioned Ferdinando, whose postmortem inventory of 1721 has been referenced above. The remark on the condition of the wooden blocks is also interesting: the matrices had already been heavily attacked by woodworms (reassuringly not moths, as written in the note); years later, at the end of the nineteenth century, the Museo Correr was troubled enough by the six blocks' condition to subject them to a couple of arsenic baths for their preservation.[13]

That "indeed they are but somewhat moth-eaten in the house of Count Baron Leopoldo Tassis" seems to be the result of direct knowledge of the whereabouts of the matrices and the two known prints, adding credibility to the idea that the family had owned them for centuries. The annotation coincides with the reconstruction of the Tassis genealogy in the *Memorials* (the family tree becomes even more complex in this phase),[14] leading to the understanding that the wooden blocks must have passed, together with the title of General of the Imperial Post and the esteemed paintings of the gallery, to Leopoldo Ottavio Tassis of Venice, who died on June 24, 1770. Upon his death, the family's economic situation changed profoundly, and Leopoldo's son Carlo Ferdinando, after receiving the investiture from the emperor as General of the Post Office in 1793, moved to the city of Padua, where he died in 1796. Carlo Ferdinando leaves a compromised patrimonial situation, with a gallery of paintings that is quickly dispersed, indicated in the inventory, which declares: "It should be noted that the Gallery of Paintings existing in the Palazzo di Venezia remains worthless for now, as its value depends more on the price of affection than on the real price."[15]

One wonders what Count Carlo Ferdinando was able to sell of the celebrated works collected by the family and who the interlocutors for the sale were. Among those who benefited from the Tassis family's misfortune was Teodoro Correr, who in those very years had begun his collection of Venetian art and history. Teodoro Correr (1750–1830) belonged to an old Venetian patrician family. From a young age he showed a passion for art and everything that told the long history of Venice, so much so that he became an abbot in 1789 to avoid the traditional political path typical of his rank and also to afford him time to dedicate himself to amassing an expansive collection of the city's memories. No records of his acquisitions have been kept. There are almost no traces of provenance of the works in his collection that he bequeathed to the city of Venice. His collection simply merged into the Museo Civico e Raccolta Correr and forms the nucleus of today's Museo Correr.

Official documentation to establish that the six wooden blocks passed directly from the Tassis family's collection to Teodoro Correr's has not yet come to light.[16] Still to be written is the history of the dispersion of this important Venetian collection. Regarding this crucial passage, Camillo Tonini, the former administrator responsible for the historic collections of the Correr, has put forward a stimulating hypothesis that involves the printing brothers Leone and Angelo Bonvecchiato of the Fratelli Bonvecchiato Library Company.[17] Tonini has suggested that they may have been the interlocutors between the Tassis family and Teodoro Correr. At the moment it is a suggestive theory that takes into account the fact that Correr turned to the Bonvecchiato brothers to find a series of metal plates with Venetian themes; the Museo also turned to them in 1838 when it considered the possibility of reprinting the *View of Venice*, an idea abandoned on careful consideration of the high cost of production with an uncertain outcome.

A final note: Teodoro may have been the first to have displayed the print along with the six wooden blocks in his house museum. An inventory of Teodoro Correr's holdings, compiled in 1831, references the *View* as hung on the wall, "mounted on canvas."[18] In 1847 the art historian Francesco Zanotto described Correr's collection, and in the room dedicated to prints and drawings, the wooden blocks hung on the wall, probably alongside the woodcut, signaling the treasured association between the matrices and the printed *View of Venice*.[19] This same display was replicated in the first room of the Fondaco dei Turchi in 1880 (the present-day Natural History Museum), where the collection was first moved. So, too, today they are displayed together in the Museo Correr in Venice, generating further crossvisual consideration. Their fundamental contribution toward telling the history of Venice, not to mention their exquisite quality—evidence of the very high achievements of graphic arts in the lagoon—were unparalleled. The six wooden blocks of the *View* are not only the heart of the museum but also an invaluable masterpiece, safeguarded and displayed, for all visitors to see.

NOTES

1 "Classe XXXIII—tipi e piastre da stampa in metallo e in legno." A recent overview of Class XXXIII and in particular of the corpus of wooden matrices has been compiled by Ilaria Andreoli, "Il fondo di matrici lignee del Museo Correr:

Una presentazione," *Studi di Memofonte* 17 (2016): 25–57; Elisa Paulin, "Il nucleo di matrici xilografiche a soggetto religioso appartenenti ai legni della collezione Correr: Analisi e prime attribuzioni," *Studi di Memofonte* 17 (2016): 58–80; Luca Canal, "Il progetto di riordino e catalogazione del fondo di matrici lignee del Museo Correr: Primi risultati," *Studi di Memofonte* 17 (2016): 81–85.

2 Giandomenico Romanelli, Susanna Biadene, and Camillo Tonini, eds., *A volo d'uccello: Jacopo de' Barbari e le rappresentazioni di città nell'Europa del Rinascimento*, exhib. cat. (Venice: Arsenale, 1999). For the technical description of the six blocks, in pear wood, see the essay by Stefano Berti, Anna Gambetta, and Simona Lazzeri, "Indagine sulle matrici lignee della veduta di Venezia e prospettive per la conservazione," in Romanelli, Biadene, and Tonini, *A volo d'uccello*, 106–9, with useful notes following the conservative restoration of the late 1990s. The six blocks first received the inventory number cl. XXXIII n. 389 and later n. 1535.

3 For the research work done so far, and for an up-to-date discussion of the *View*, see Kristin Love Huffman, "Jacopo de' Barbari's *View of Venice* (1500): 'Image Vehicles' and 'Pathways of Culture' Past and Present," *Mediterranea* 4 (2019): 165–214.

4 Terisio Pignatti, "La Pianta di Venezia di Jacopo de' Barbari," *Bollettino dei Musei Civici Veneziani* 9, nos. 1–2 (1964): 9–49; Juergen Schulz, "La veduta di Venezia di Jacopo de' Barbari: Cartografia, vedute di città e geografia moralizzata nel Medioevo e nel Rinascimento," in *La cartografia tra scienza e arte: Carte e cartografi nel Rinascimento italiano* (Modena: Panini, 1990), 13–42, appendix.

5 What happened in the mid-nineteenth century is reconstructed by Camillo Tonini, "Una storia in appendice: La ristampa ottocentesca della Veduta prospettica di Venezia," in Romanelli, Biadene, and Tonini, *A volo d'uccello*, 84–91.

6 "Stampa di Venezia, sei piante da Alberto Duro incisa" / "1720. Nella Casa del Barone__________ Tassis direttore delle Poste di Fiandra in Venezia si conservavano alcuni pregievoli Intagli di legno, disegnati altre volte dal celebre Pittore Alberto Duro, co quali s'impresse a stampa la gran Città di Venezia." In the Library of Museo Correr di Venezia (BMCVe), *Commemoriali*, mss. Gradenigo-Dolfin, n. 200, tome 11, c. 11, passage already partially quoted in Tonini, "Una storia in appendice," 91n30; and by Andreoli, "Il fondo di matrici lignee," 29.

7 The earliest documented presence of the *View* is 1627 in the inventory of the assets of Cardinal Francesco Maria del Monte. See Christoph L. Frommel, "Caravaggio's Frühwerk und der Kardinal del Monte," *Storia dell'arte* 9–10 (1971): 35. Schulz further complicates the attribution of woodcut and woodblocks in the

historical overview of attribution, noting Dürer's "fineness of drawing" in the tradition of German woodcutters. See Schulz, "La veduta di Venezia di Jacopo de' Barbari," 425.

8 The profile of the Venetian branch is traced by Bonaventura Foppolo, "La parabola del ramo veneziano dei Tasso da Cornello a Venezia," in *I Tasso e le poste d'Europa: Atti del Convegno Internazionale, Cornello di Tasso 1–3 giugno 2012* (Comune di Camerata Cornello: Museo dei Tasso e della storia postale, 2012), 27–50.

9 See Isabella Cecchini, "Ottavio Tassis," in *Il collezionismo d'arte a Venezia: Il Seicento*, exhib. cat., ed. Linda Borean and Stefania Mason (Venice: Marsilio, 2007), 318–19; Marco Boschini, *La carta del navegar pitoresco* (Venice: Baba, 1660), 319–26; and Francesco Sansovino, *Venetia, città nobilissima et singolare: Con le aggiunte di Giustiniano Martinioni* (1663; repr., Venice: Filippi, 1968), 377; Cecchini, "Ottavio Tassis," 319.

10 Cecchini, "Ottavio Tassis"; Foppolo, "La parabola del ramo veneziano," 32.

11 Mentioned in Foppolo, "La parabola del ramo veneziano," 34. The inventory is kept in Archivio di Stato di Venezia (ASVe), *Giudici di petizion*, inventory dated May 6, 1721, Count Ferdinando Tassis, b. 418, cc. 183ff. See also Cecchini, "Ottavio Tassis," 319, which refers to ASVe, Giudici del Proprio, b. 314, cc. 34ff., dated the day after, May 7, with

estimate of the value made by Agostino Litterini.

12 "Opinione sopra foglio Topografico" "di cui si è inteso dire che in Venezia si conservino tuttavia i legni (*anzi ci sono ma alquanto tarmati in Casa del Conte Baron Leopoldo de Tassis*)....Ecco quanto occorre per ora dire nel proposito riguardo ad una celebre carta esattissima; un esemplare della quale stava nella Galleria di Sagredo da S. Sofia, un'altra nella stanza di Domenico Pasqualigo a S. Maria Zebenigo." BMCVe, *Commemoriali*, mss. Gradenigo-Dolfin, n. 200, tome 16, cc. 25–26, passage already partially quoted in Tonini, "Una storia in appendice," 91n30. The information about the presence of the six wooden blocks in the house of Baron Leopoldo also appears in Luigi Servolini, *Jacopo de' Barbari* (Padua: Le Tre Venezie, 1944), 52, without indicating, however, what the source is: this is noted in Schulz, "La veduta di Venezia di Jacopo de' Barbari," 474.

13 Tonini, "Una storia in appendice," 90n14.

14 Foppolo, "La parabola del ramo veneziano," 34.

15 ASVe, Giudici di Petizion, inventory dated October 29, 1796, Count Ferdinando Tassis, b. 491.

16 In the *Guida artistica e storica di Venezia e delle isole circonvicine* (Venice: Antonelli, 1881), 315, it is recorded that "the said wooden blocks were in Venice in the

house of Barone Tassis in S. Canciano; Correr had them afterwards."

17 Tonini, "Una storia in appendice," 89; hypothesis also discussed by Andreoli, "Il fondo di matrici lignee," 26n6.

18 Memory of the original location in the house-museum of Teodoro Correr is preserved in the drawings by Vincenzo Lazari, third director of the Museo Correr: see BMCVe, Vincenzo Lazari, *Ordinamento primitivo della Raccolta del N. U. Teodoro Correr e disegni vari di oggetti conservati nella stessa*, 1859, ms. 1472. Museo Correr is the only institution to have in its collection printed specimens of the three states.

19 Francesco Zanotto, "Gallerie, Pinacoteche, Raccolte di oggetti d'arte, ecc.," in *Venezia e le sue lagune*, vol. II, part II (Venice: Antonelli, 1847), 470.

Kristin Love Huffman

The Graphic Inventions
of Jacopo de' Barbari

THE GRAPHIC ARTS—woodcuts, engravings, drawings—offered Renaissance artists a medium for creative expression liberated from the constraints
of traditional commissions in typology, content, and site specificity. In the
final decades of the fifteenth century, imaginative painters began to explore
novel subject matter and unprecedented formats. In print, this exploration
lent itself to the creation of multisheet compositions, representing extraordinary subjects in complex ways; the visual novelty presented sophisticated
themes, at times with implied references to other imagery and texts. Printed
sheets—easily circulated and collected—could be held, studied closely,
contemplated. As conversation pieces, they could prompt erudite, variable
considerations of meaning, flexible according to rhetorical emphases (pic-

torial, literary, philosophical, scientific). At the end of the fifteenth century and the beginning of the next, the greatest innovators in print were Andrea Mantegna (ca. 1430/31–1506), Jacopo de' Barbari (ca. 1460/70–1516, *terminus ante quem*), and Albrecht Dürer (1471–1528); all three artists moved in and out of the Veneto. De' Barbari's contributions, while notably inventive, remain less studied.[1]

It is possible, however, to decipher noteworthy clues visually embedded within de' Barbari's early print imagery in an effort to broaden understandings of his inventions. Around the time of his involvement with the ambitiously conceived *View of Venice*, ca. 1497–1500 (plate 1), the artist devised another large-scale, multisheet woodcut set, known as the *Battle of the Satyrs* (fig. 9.1) and *Triumph over the Satyrs* (fig. 9.2), ca. 1496–97.[2] Their significance to his advancement of graphic arts merits further scholarly analysis.[3] Studied together, de' Barbari's woodcuts reveal not only the artist's awareness of humanist themes and his ability to translate them into visual form but also his skill in creating intricate imagery. They represent a moment in time that aligns sophistication of imagery and composition within a medium that, until de' Barbari, had been less exploratory in format and subject matter than its counterpart: engraving.[4]

De' Barbari's woodcuts disclose the artist's fascination with scale and design, companion sets, and thematic connections across imagery. The Satyr narratives represent an early example of pictorial poetry, embraced by artists such as Lorenzo Lotto (ca. 1480–1556/57) and Giorgione (1477/78–1510) in the following decade with small-scale paintings prized by Venetian collectors. Such imagery, inherently multifaceted, has invited viewers, past and present, to uncover layers of interpretative meaning.[5] On investigation, so do de' Barbari's prints. In addition, like the artist's engravings, the Satyr woodcuts embed self-reflexive leitmotifs, namely his identification with Hermes/Mercury and his implied self-recognition as an innovator. Finally, de' Barbari's inventions offer insights into his movement within humanist circles and his invitation to the court of the Holy Roman Emperor in Nuremberg months prior to the official publication of the *View of Venice* in late 1500. This essay's focus on de' Barbari's inventions in the years straddling 1500 presents new considerations of the mysterious artist's early contributions to graphic art—the foundation for his appreciation by prestigious patrons in northern European courts.[6]

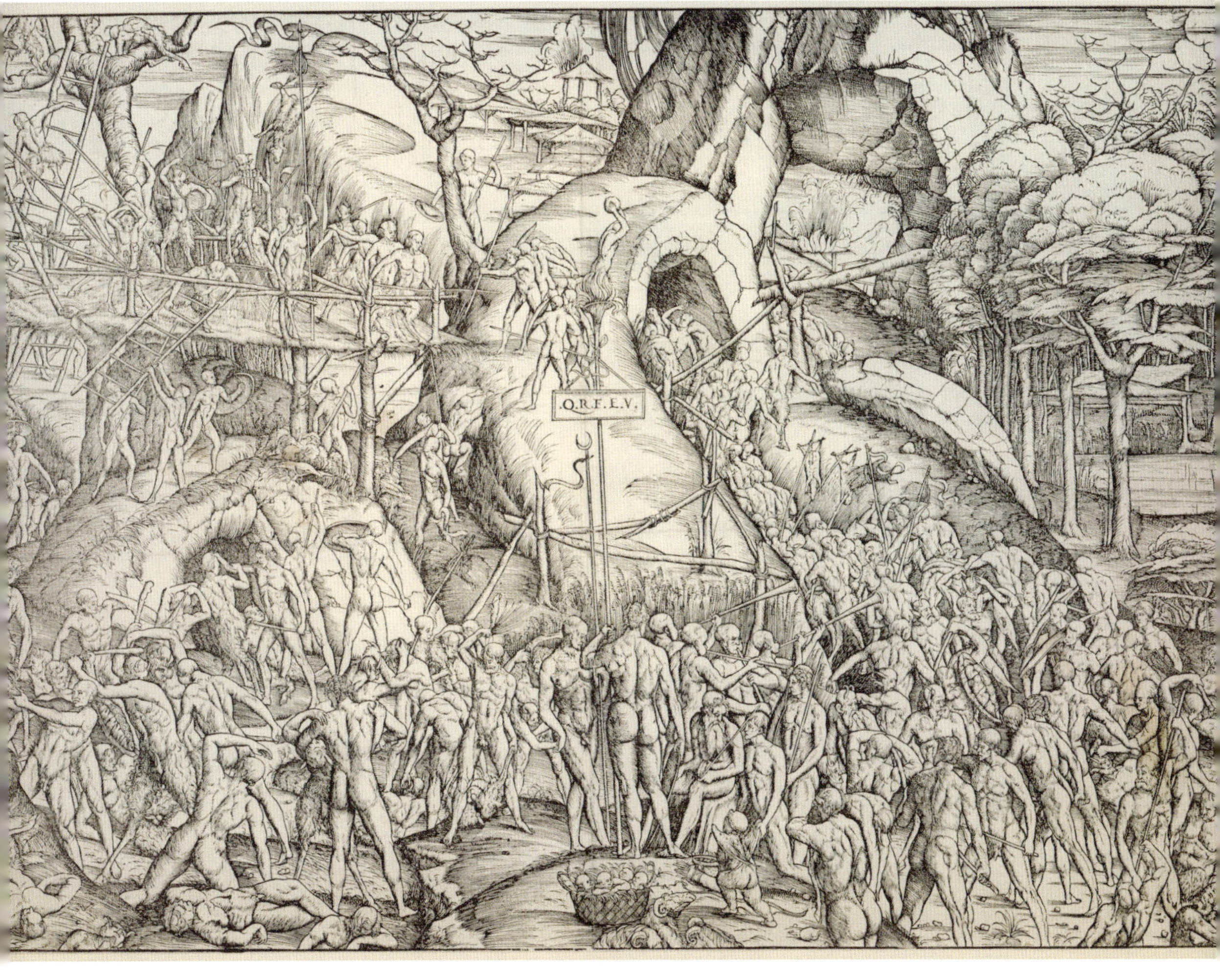

Battle of the Satyrs and Triumph over the Satyrs

The two subjects—the *Battle* (approximately 385 × 495 mm), a single sheet with different dimensions from the three-sheet *Triumph* (approximately 290 × 1270 mm)—nonetheless form a set of two interrelated narratives.[7] Not only do they depict the same cast of characters, but they also present an unfolding narrative intended to be read sequentially. Examined in detail, they reveal de' Barbari's understanding of the current humanist recovery of poetic and philosophical sources; his understanding of figural assemblage (despite the woodcarvers' limited ability to translate his

121

Jacopo de' Barbari, *Triumph over the Satyrs*, ca. 1496–97. Woodcut, 32.8 × 131.2 cm. The Albertina Museum, Vienna.

figure style); his awareness of artistic advancements; and his interest in the natural world.[8] Most relevant to this study, they anticipated the large-scale, multisheet format and complex, highly detailed imagery of the *View of Venice*.[9]

This brief essay considers various humanist underpinnings of these early woodcuts in an effort to decipher the visual, multivalent registers of meaning: allegorical/mythological, literary, political, historical, scientific, and expressly self-referential. The main protagonists who appear in the *Battle* and the subsequent *Triumph* involve the elder leader, his commanding officer, Cupid, men and satyrs, and the basket of satyr babies. The accoutrements in both woodcuts include the tall torch bearing a placard with the inscription QRFEV, batons with waving sheepskins, musical instruments (panpipes, trumpets, and drums), and staffs with fastened tortoise shells. Finally, in the second sheet of the *Triumph*, a pictorial reference paraded through the landscape by picture-bearers as part of the triumphal procession alludes to the *Battle* scene and de' Barbari's print of it.

At a most basic thematic level, the nude males' domination of the satyrs relates allegorically to the triumph of virtue over vice. There is a marked

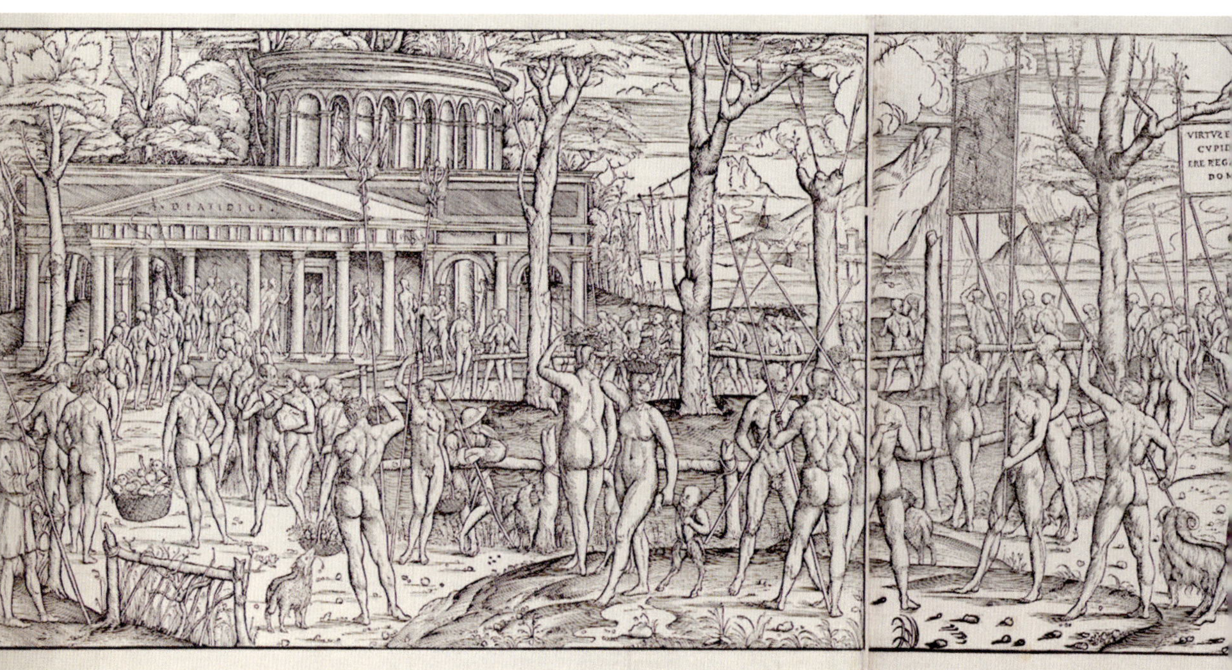

contrast between the chaos of the *Battle* and the progressive rational ordering of men in the *Triumph* from right to left. The procession of men crosses
over from a rustic land to a civilized one, as suggested by the architecture;
the temple in the left sheet and the contemporary walled city featured
in the center one contrast dramatically with the vertical, rocky wilderness
in the *Battle* scene. In the middle sheet there is a banner that bears the Latin
phrase "VIRTUS EXCELSA CUPIDENEM ERE REGNANTEM DOMAT,"
or "Sublime virtue tames ruling cupidity with bronze (or metal)."[10] The
right sheet features a triumphal chariot pulled by fantastical sea creatures.
Seated at the front of the chariot, Cupid, bound and blindfolded, clutches
a bag suggestively filled with metal coins; his quills, used to elicit lust in his
victims, hang inaccessibly appended to the trunk to which he is bound. In
sum, the vices of avarice and lust, attributes of Cupid and the satyrs, have
been tamed by virtue. That this is a civilization with stability and harmony
is highlighted by the left sheet's inclusion of women, one of whom leads a
docile, half-clothed child-satyr along the path toward the temple. This child
and two shepherds who bear witness are the only three figures out of the
throng of many to wear clothes. The child satyrs in the scene, including the

*Graphic
Inventions
of de' Barbari*

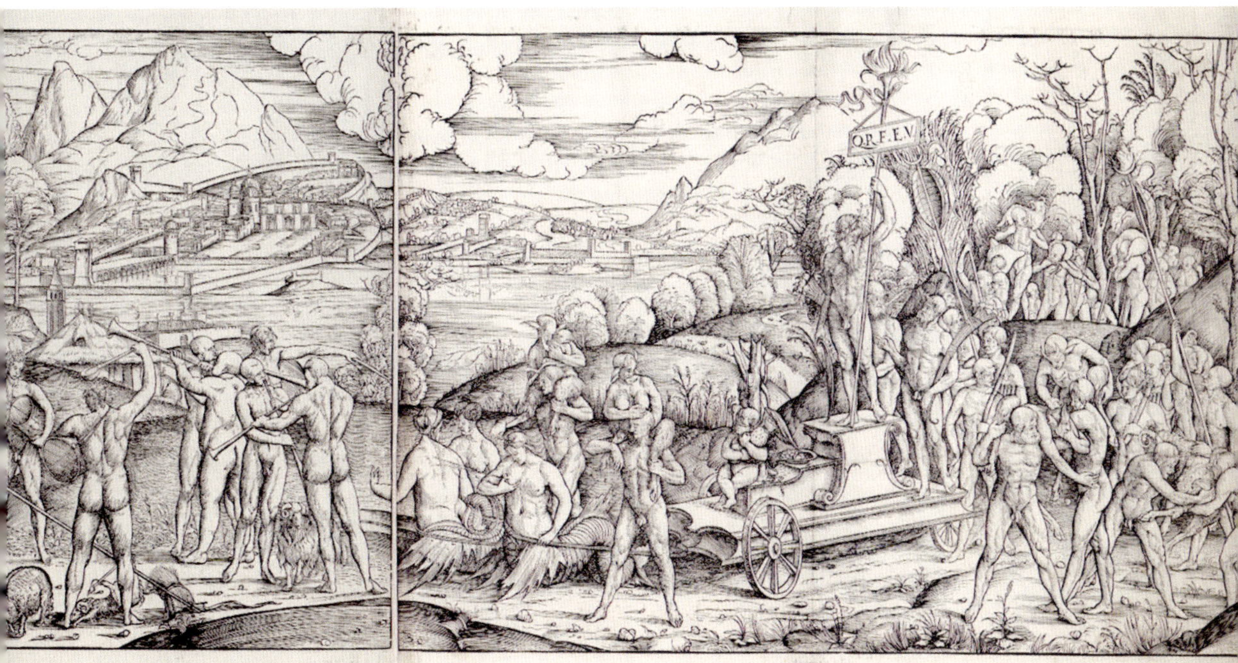

babies carried in a basket toward the Doric temple, imply domestication and the potential for education.

While likely a nod to Sannazaro's *Arcadia* (Naples, 1501), a contemporary bucolic poem circulating at the end of the fifteenth century in manuscript and pirated print editions, de' Barbari's woodcuts also allude to Greek bucolic antecedents, namely Theocritus's *Idylls* (Venice: Aldo Manuzio, 1496) and Virgil's *Eclogues* (Venice: Vindelinus de Spira, 1470).[11] The artist may also have intended a reference to Ovid's *Amores* (Venice: Jacobus Rubeus, 1474), an urbane, three-book collection of poetry that integrated the trope of war and love; the restrained Cupid depicted in de' Barbari's *Battle* and *Triumph* may serve as a pictorial reference to the text. De' Barbari was aware of Ovid's *Amores*, which he excerpted for a signed *cartellino* within his painted *Virgin and Child with Saint John the Baptist and Saint Anthony Abbot*.[12] Finally, there is an implied awareness of Lucretius's *De rerum natura* (Verona: Paulus Fridenberger, 1486; Venice: Theodorus de Ragazonibus, 1495) and the cultural and technological evolution of humankind.[13] While there seems to be no specific text or identifiable passage referenced within the Satyr prints, a general awareness of recently published literature and its broad, interrelating themes inform the pictorial allegory.

In addition to allegorical and literary topoi, the mythological and historical intertwine to celebrate Arcadia as the mythical birthplace of Pan (and the satyrs who resemble him), the son of Hermes. In Greek antiquity, Pan was said to have inhabited the region north of Athens, notable for the mountainous landscape marked with craggy caves near Mount Cyllene. Like the satyrs and shepherds who worshipped him, the god concerned himself with flocks and herds and was often accompanied by goats or rams, animals pictured in the *Battle* and *Triumph*. The mythological allusions within the set, however, extend to include additional deities, namely Hermes (or the Roman Mercury) and Apollo. Credited with the invention of pipes—which Pan, satyrs, and shepherds were all known to play—Hermes also invented the lyre. His first, fashioned from a tortoise shell, captured the attention of Apollo. Hermes gave the instrument to Apollo, who reciprocated by offering Hermes his shepherd's staff with the caduceus, the god's most recognizable attribute.[14] The tortoise shells are raised on staffs, trophies of battle in de' Barbari's image and, therefore, markers of discord that Hermes had refashioned into an instrument of harmony. The inclusion of panpipes and staffs featuring Hermes's caduceus further confirms his relevance; the inscription D. FATIDICE on the façade of the Doric temple, toward which the triumphal procession moves, references Apollo, his oracle, and his divine role as protector of shepherds.

The temple, indicating an archaic, ancient structure rather than a strictly classical one, bridges the precivilized and civilized past, while the city view in the background of the second sheet alludes to the modern present (ca. 1500). This contemporary historical reference, with possible sociopolitical connotations, presents yet another layer of meaning. The architecture and landscape elements of this city clearly situate it in the Veneto. Walls and medieval towers enclose churches and their bell towers, including a Byzantine-inspired, multidomed church, arcaded Renaissance civic structures and/or private buildings, canals—one with boat slips, similar to those found in the Venetian Arsenal—and, finally, the mountains on the horizon that suggest the Alpine foothills and Dolomites. The cityscape's topography may embed messages relevant at the time to the Venetian state and its *terraferma*, or perhaps it offers an undiscovered clue about the mysterious de' Barbari.

Such conjecture is enticing, given that the *Triumph* contains a number of self-referential nods. Like Virgil, who at the end of his *Eclogues* relocates Arcadia to Rome, de' Barbari relocates Arcadia to the Veneto, and, like Virgil and Ovid, he seems to be claiming worldly fame. Just as Hermes was the supposed father of Pan, this image fathered the first known representation of de' Barbari's signature as a caduceus, recognizable with the two staffs carried by men in the left sheet and two more in the center sheet. In addition to the staffs, however, there are further references to the god via the tortoise shells used to fashion his lyre.

In addition to associations with Hermes, another unambiguous self-referential nod comes with the inclusion of the *Battle*, the image processed in a celebratory manner within the *Triumph* itself.[15] It superimposes the victory of de' Barbari's artistic conceit with that of the actual battle. Finally, prominently displayed in the *Battle* and the right sheet of the *Triumph*, a tall blazing torch bears the inscription QRFEV (Quemadmodum Recte Factum Esse Videtur, or "See how all has been well done"); in the *Triumph* this placard initiates the sequential reading of the procession.[16] The proof of what has been accomplished privileges sight: the visual. Like the triumph celebrated within the printed narrative, de' Barbari commemorates his invention, a multisheet woodcut that embeds many possible readings across the pictorial space. These visual connections extend to other independently conceived prints by the artist.

Two of his engravings, *Victory Reclining among Her Trophies*, ca. 1500–

1501, and the *Satyr and His Family*, ca. 1504, continue metonymic references from the Satyr woodcuts. In the *Victory*, a variety of acquisitions that allude to the winged, allegorical figure's triumphal conquests surround her in the foreground; a number of these objects, including two helmets and a shield, display ornamented symbols of Hermes/Mercury. These, along with the caduceus-signature front and center at the top, signal the artist's own victory.[17] De' Barbari's unusual representation of Victory, supine among her trophies, suggests she is momentarily "resting on her laurels" prior to the future replication of her virtuosity with new victories, much like the very print's reproducibility and Jacopo de' Barbari's fame as its maker.

*Kristin Love
Huffman*

The *Satyr and His Family*, with the exception of the caduceus, takes a more understated approach (fig. 9.3). De' Barbari pictures the satyr family as subdued and civilized, much like the implied promise of the satyr youth in the *Triumph*. While satyrs typically play pipes, here de' Barbari's satyr plays a lyre (*lira da braccio*), a contemporary version of Hermes's invention. The multivalent registers of humanist themes could have thus accommodated a variety of learned viewers generating myriad conversations, including recognition of de' Barbari's playful self-recognition as an innovator.

North–South Cultural Exchange

Invention in stand-alone print imagery coincided with the moment when early printed books harnessed the use of illustrations to visualize fantastical literary narratives, such as the exceptional *Hypnerotomachia Poliphili* (Venice: Aldo Manuzio, 1499). The phenomenon also encompassed an interest in presenting traditional material in novel ways, such as the noteworthy inclusion of city views in Hartmann Schedel's *Liber chronicarum* or *Nuremberg Chronicles* (Nuremberg: Anton Koberger, 1493). At the turn of the century, Venice emerged as a leader in the production of printed materials in its sheer volume of publications as well as in innovative form (font, type, imagery, content), with Nuremberg a worthy rival.[18]

A select cast of characters intersecting with the world of printmaking discloses de' Barbari's place within a network of cultural advocates operating in Venice and north of the Alps.[19] The artist's peripatetic northern career, initiated in late 1500, included an intellectual role within the various courts he worked. This is highlighted with a beautiful handwritten letter (ca. 1501) in which he argues for the inclusion of painting as the eighth liberal art.[20]

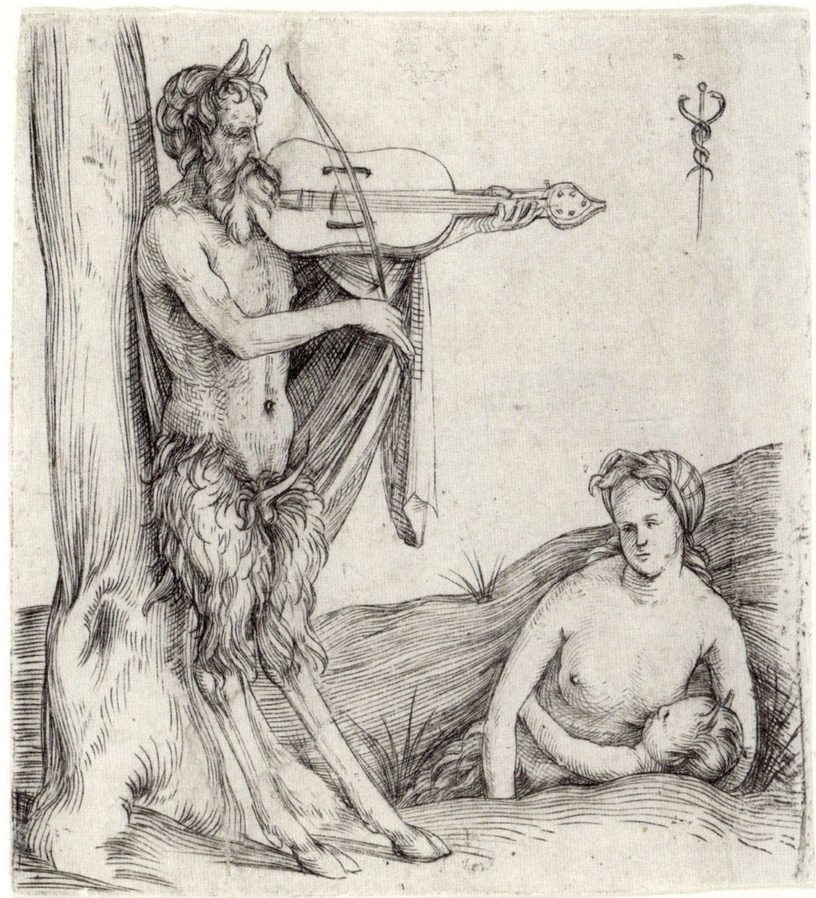

Jacopo de’ Barbari, *Satyr and His Family*, ca. 1503–4. Copperplate engraving on paper, 8.4 × 7.9 cm. Rosenwald Collection, National Gallery of Art, Washington.

It is with these court appointments that documentation concerning the artist has surfaced, facilitating a delineated reconstruction of the esteemed and cultured individuals with whom he shared connections. In 1500 he left Venice to work for the Holy Roman Emperor Maximilian I in Nuremberg; this links the artist with Dürer during the years both were associated with this court, circa fall 1500–winter 1503. A document dated February 29, 1504, from the account books of the Holy Roman Emperor suggests a second possible joint collaboration between de’ Barbari and Anton Kolb;[21] their first had been the extraordinary production of the *View of Venice*. While in the court of Frederick the Wise, Elector of Saxony, de’ Barbari encountered Vincentius Ravennas, who noted the artist's urbanity and deep knowledge of humanism in a 1505 publication.[22] And finally, returning to Dürer, the German artist's letter to Willibald Pirckheimer of February 7, 1506, written

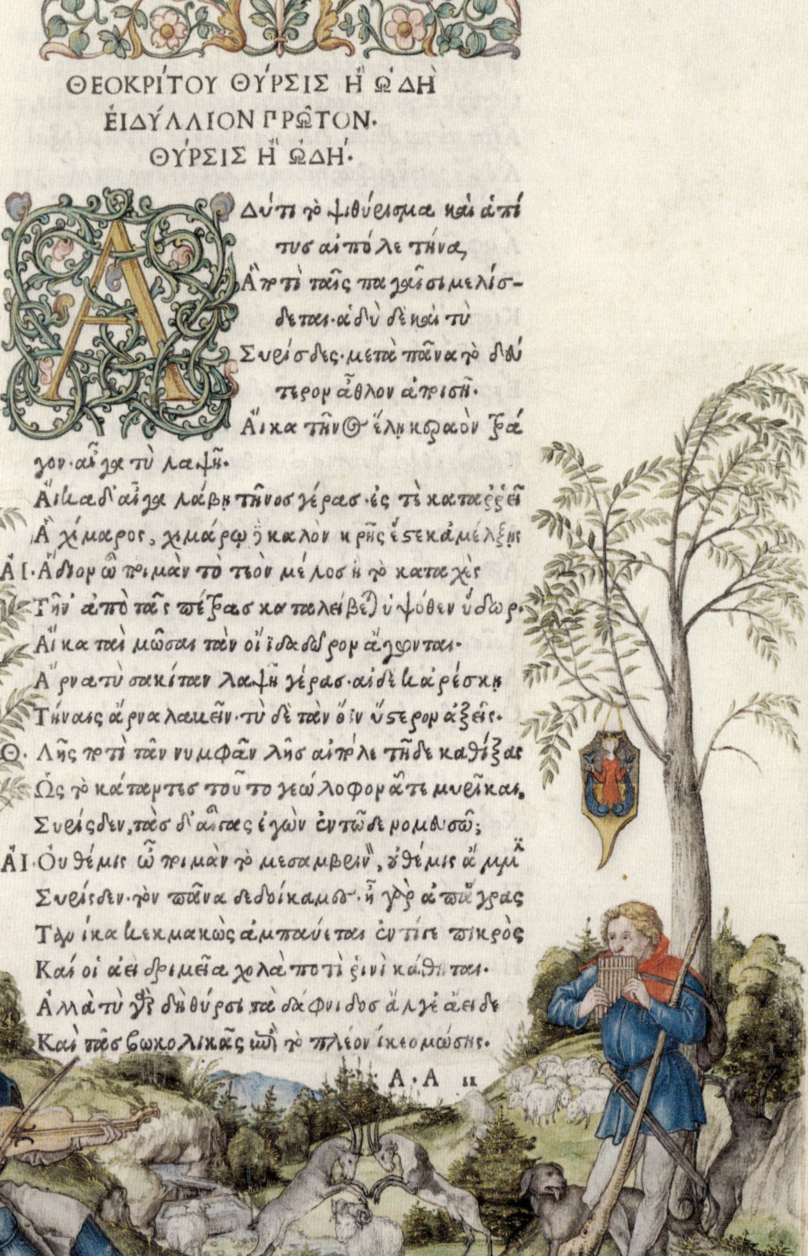

ΘΕΟΚΡΙΤΟΥ ΘΥΡΣΙΣ Ἢ ὨΔῊ
ΕἸΔΎΛΛΙΟΝ ΠΡῶΤΟΝ.
ΘΎΡΣΙΣ Ἢ ὨΔΉ.

Ἁδύ τι τὸ ψιθύρισμα καὶ ἁ πί-
τυς αἰπόλε τήνα,
Ἁ ποτὶ ταῖς παγαῖσι μελίσ-
δεται· ἁδὺ δὲ καὶ τὺ
Συρίσδες· μετὰ Πᾶνα τὸ δεύ-
τερον ἆθλον ἀποισῇ.
Αἴκα τῆνος ἕλῃ κεραὸν τρά-
γον, αἶγα τὺ λαψῇ.
Αἴκα δ' αἶγα λάβῃ τῆνος γέρας· ἐς τὲ καταρρεῖ
Ἁ χίμαρος, χιμάρῳ δὲ καλὸν κρῆς ἔστε κ' ἀμέλξῃς.
ΑΙ. Ἅδιον ὦ ποιμὰν τὸ τεὸν μέλος ἢ τὸ καταχὲς
Τῆν' ἀπὸ τᾶς πέτρας καταλείβεται ὑψόθεν ὕδωρ.
Αἴκα ταὶ Μῶσαι τὰν οἴιδα δῶρον ἄγωνται,
Ἄρνα τὺ σακίταν λαψῇ γέρας· αἰ δέ κ' ἀρέσκῃ
Τήναις ἄρνα λαβεῖν, τὺ δὲ τὰν ὄιν ὕστερον ἀξεῖς.
Θ. Λῇς ποτὶ τᾶν Νυμφᾶν, λῇς αἰπόλε τᾷδε καθίξας,
Ὡς τὸ κάταντες τοῦτο γεώλοφον αἵ τε μυρῖκαι,
Συρίσδεν, τὰς δ' αἶγας ἐγὼν ἐν τῷδε νομευσῶ;
ΑΙ. Οὐ θέμις ὦ ποιμὰν τὸ μεσαμβρινόν, οὐ θέμις ἄμμι
Συρίσδεν· τὸν Πᾶνα δεδοίκαμες· ἦ γὰρ ἀπ' ἄγρας
Τανίκα κεκμακὼς ἀμπαύεται· ἔστι δὲ πικρὸς
Καί οἱ ἀεὶ δριμεῖα χολὰ ποτὶ ῥινὶ κάθηται.
Ἀλλὰ τὺ γὰρ δὴ Θύρσι τὰ Δάφνιδος ἄλγε' ἀείδες
Καὶ τᾶς βουκολικᾶς ἐπὶ τὸ πλέον ἵκεο μοίσας.

Α. Α. ii

during his second stay in Venice, notes Kolb's unwavering esteem for de' Barbari and his assertion that "no better painter lives on earth."[23]

In addition to the personal interactions noted above, printed materials (books, woodcuts, and engravings) reflect refined cultural expressions of this intersecting network. Kolb (and most likely Dürer) distributed copies of Schedel's richly illustrated *Liber chronicarum* in Venice, a straightforward but nonetheless relevant engagement.[24] Schedel pasted six engravings by de' Barbari into his *Liber antiquitatum*, a manuscript that included the German humanist's transcriptions of antique inscriptions copied during his residence in Padua (1463–66). The volume, later bound (December 1504), interspersed a number of graphics to illustrate the earlier text, including not only de' Barbari's engravings but also drawings and woodcut city views from the *Liber chronicarum*.[25]

For his part, Pirckheimer commissioned Dürer to illuminate the opening page of his volume of Theocritus's *Idylls* published by Aldo Manuzio's Venetian press in 1496 (fig. 9.4), noted above in relationship to de' Barbari's pictorial interpretation of bucolic literary motifs.[26] Dürer painted a watercolor over pen and ink, highlighted with gold, of two shepherds shown at leisure in a bucolic setting, each resting against a tree that borders one side of the text. From each tree hangs a coat of arms, that of the Pirckheimer family on the left along with that of Willibald's wife, Margretha Rieterin, on the right. The seated, bearded shepherd on the left, the protagonist Thyrsis, plays a *lira da braccio*; his standing younger counterpart on the right blows into panpipes. In the *bas-de-page*, the shepherds' goats graze or drink water from a trough fed by a stream, while two rams, butting heads above a third, stand out against a rugged, verdant landscape created with washes of color on the paper's bright surface.[27] This scene, brimming with quiet lyricism, sets off the elegant block of Greek text that it frames. Dürer translates the beauty of the Greek text into that of a modern visual pastoral, while his illuminated page of a text printed in Venice illustrates the material expression of another north–south exchange. De' Barbari and Anton Kolb would accomplish yet another north–south graphic feat of skill with the celebrated *View of Venice*.

The *View of Venice* and Invention North of the Alps

While the *Battle* and *Triumph* feature landscapes—one a harsh wilderness, the other a blending of woodlands with architectural and urbanistic forms—

Albrecht Dürer, *Pastoral Landscape with Shepherds Playing a Viola and Panpipes*, ca. 1497. Watercolor and gouache heightened with pen and ink and gold, 31 × 20.3 cm. Widner Collection, National Gallery of Art, Washington.

the *View* is an extraordinary urban panorama. The sheer monumentality of its production, exceptional at the time, included not only the known artist (de' Barbari) and sponsor (Kolb) but also the unknown surveyors, woodcarvers, and printers, not to mention artisans responsible for preparing the sheets of paper and assembling the six pearwood blocks. The printed outcome was six separate sheets, each to be admired for its exquisite detail, and, when placed together, to be telescoped out to form the composite whole—a captivating bird's-eye view.

The sets of early woodcuts are marked as distinctively de' Barbari's work, despite variances in the quality of woodcarving: the interpretation of the natural world (mountains, clouds, vegetation, distinction between land and water); the architecture (namely the churches and bell towers); the representation of the male and female form; and descriptive facial features are all signature. Moreover, the composite format, the complexity of the subjects, and iconographical references are de' Barbari's devices. As one example, de' Barbari's Mercury and his caduceus, above and beyond the inscribed protection of commerce and a figurative stand-in for the artist, could also be said to commemorate his invention—a large-scale, multisheet representation of a unique place, a tangible object that visualized the city's mythical nature, already recounted in contemporary written chronicles.

De' Barbari would go on to devise other inventions within his visibly striking works. Shortly after the production of the *View,* most likely while in residence with Frederick the Wise, the artist reintroduced the genre of still life, a stand-alone subject not seen since antiquity. The *Dead Partridge* (fig. 9.5), ca. 1504, a stunning watercolor on paper of the bird as it would have appeared immediately after the hunt, is yet another "triumph." Like his woodcuts and engravings, this work on paper reflects unprecedented subject matter. And like the *View of Venice,* its mesmerizing detail captures the beholder's eye. As the final two verses of the poem from Ovid's *Amores* 1.15 anticipated (the two previous ones excerpted for the *cartellino* within the artist's aforementioned painting), "Even when the final flame has consumed me, I shall live and a considerable part of me will survive." Indeed, de' Barbari's remarkable oeuvre, its many inventions, and the informed bidirectional north–south exchanges have ensured the artist's ongoing legacy.

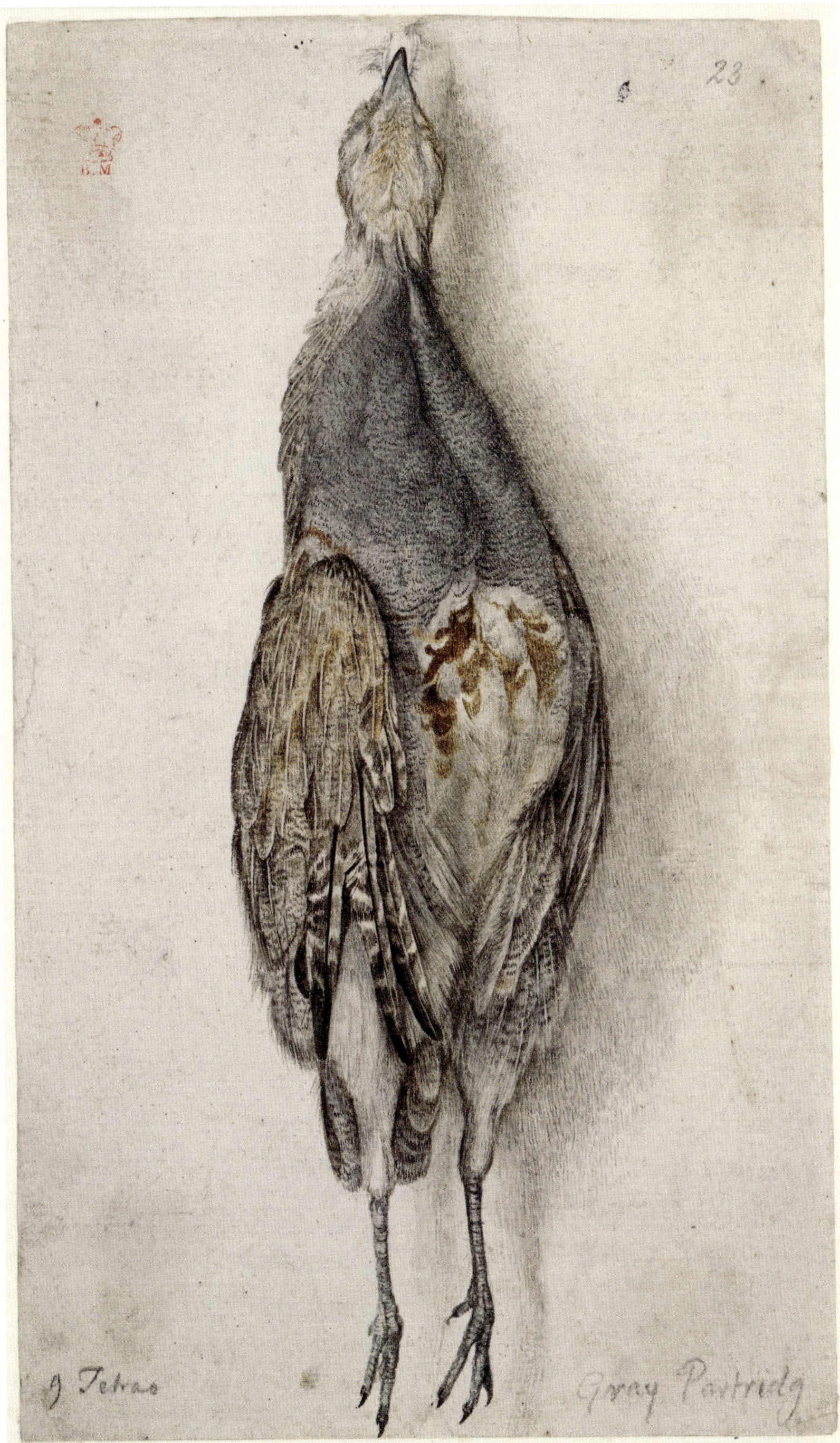
23
J Tetrao
Gray Partridg

This essay has benefited from exchanges with dear colleagues who offered insights and careful readings of the text. I would like to thank in particular Dana Hogan, Holly Hurlburt, Mary Pardo, and Patricia Simons.

Kristin Love Huffman

1 This is due in part to scant archival documentation (none for his Italian career), and in part because de' Barbari's paintings are not on par with Mantegna's, nor Dürer's, nor contemporary Venetian painters, such as the Bellini, Vittore Carpaccio, or Alvise Vivarini with whom he may have trained.

2 See Jay A. Levenson, "Jacopo de' Barbari and Northern Art of the Early Sixteenth Century" (PhD diss., Columbia University, 1978), 266–78; Friedrich von Bartsch, *Die Kupferstichsammlung der K. K. Hofbibliothek in Wien* (Vienna: Braumüller, 1854), 37–38nn366–67. First suggested as a set by Bartsch, Levenson offered the earliest substantial consideration of these prints. This author believes that the woodcuts may have been complete prior to de' Barbari's work on the *View*. Their complexity may have demonstrated his potential to Anton Kolb, were he to be paired with more skilled woodcarvers; there is indeed a progression in the quality of woodcarving from the *Battle*, to the *Triumph*, and then the *View of Venice*. While the artist's intervention may not have been required at the start of the *View* in 1497, most likely Kolb had selected his team of artists and artisans by then.

3 For the most recent considerations, see Simone Ferrari, *Jacopo de' Barbari: Un protagonista del Rinascimento tra Venezia e Dürer* (Milan: Mondadori, 2006), 148–50; and Beate Böckem, *Jacopo de' Barbari: Künstlerschaft und Hofkultur um 1500* (Cologne: Böhlau Verlag, 2016), 52, 428.

4 Mantegna's *Battle of the Sea Gods* introduced a two-sheet format and novel subject matter in engraving. For invention in engraving, see in particular Evelyn Lincoln, *The Invention of the Renaissance Printmaker* (New Haven, CT: Yale University Press, 2000); Konrad Oberhuber, "Mantegna e il ruolo delle stampe: Un prototipo di innovazione artistica in Italia e al Nord," in *Il Rinascimento a Venezia e la pittura del Nord ai tempi di Bellini, Dürer, Tiziano*, ed. Bernard Aikema (Milan: Bompiani, 1999), 144–49; David Landau and Peter Parshall, *The Renaissance Print, 1470–1550* (New Haven, CT: Yale University Press, 1994).

5 For an enlightening introduction to what Giorgione absorbed from late fifteenth-century masters and then extended to become his own inventions, see Wendy Stedman Sheard, "The Widener Orpheus: Attribution, Type, Invention,"

in *Collaboration in Italian Renaissance Art,* ed. Wendy Stedman Sheard and John T. Paoletti (New Haven, CT: Yale University Press, 1978), 189–231. For Giorgione and Renaissance decoding, see Salvatore Settis, *Giorgione's Tempest: Interpreting the Hidden Subject,* trans. Ellen Bianchini (Chicago: University of Chicago Press, 1990). On pastoral iconography, see Robert C. Cafritz, Lawrence Gowing, and David Rosand, eds., *Places of Delight: The Pastoral Landscape* (Washington, DC: Phillips Collection in association with the National Gallery of Art, 1988).

6 See Rangsook Yoon's essay in this volume.

7 The existing versions have slightly different dimensions depending on how they were trimmed and the conservation of the paper.

8 Artistic advancements de' Barbari was probably aware of include Mantegna's achievements in print and painting, along with those of the Bellini workshop, and in my view, the painted cycles being generated in Venice. Regarding de' Barbari's figural groupings, it is tempting to suggest an exchange with Central Italian contemporaries, namely Piero di Cosimo and Luca Signorelli, both of whom took up satyr themes in the 1490s. Closer to home, one thinks of the highly populated scenes created by Vittore Carpaccio, such as the *Martyrdom of Saint Ursula,* ca. 1494, or *Ten Thousand Martyrs,* 1515.

9 I am currently working on a larger study, *The Making and Framing of the View,* that encompasses an analysis of the wooden blocks and prints, along with an understanding of de' Barbari's engagement with artistic theory and practice.

10 Professors Pietro Rossi and Andrea Aldo Robiglio kindly translated the Latin.

11 Levenson, "Jacopo de' Barbari," 269, first noted the shepherds. Eva Allan in her dissertation astutely proposed that their presence alludes to Arcadia, a conclusion I also reached in my study of this set. See Eva D. Allan, "The Triumph Theme and Variations in Long Renaissance Prints" (PhD diss., Yale University, 2014), 121.

12 The passage, from book 1, 15, verses 38–40, refers to the poet who declares that his art will bring him eternal fame. The inscription reads: "*PASCIT[UR] IN VIVIS / LIV[O]R POST / FATA [QU]IESCIT / CUM [S]VVS EX / [MERITO QUEMQUE TUETUR] HONOS* IA. (caduceus) BF." The painting is currently housed in the Louvre, Paris.

13 The Lucretian anthropology also implies that the distant city represents a future world with nomadic shepherds as harbingers of an intermediate stage before urbanization and agriculture.

14 The fourth Homeric Hymn dedicated to Hermes recounts that after giving the lyre to Apollo, Hermes cleverly fashions the pipes.

15 The triumphal images paraded by the picture bearers in Mantegna's *Triumph*

of Caesar, 1484–92, are also depicted at an oblique angle. Vittore Carpaccio referenced his own painting, *Ten Thousand Martyrs*, 1515, in the *Apparition of the Crucifixes of Mount Ararat in Sant'Antonio*. My thanks to Patricia Simons, who noted that, like de' Barbari, Carpaccio simplified the image within an image to highlight landscape.

16 Containing Latin abbreviations and meanings, Marcus Valerius Probis's *Significato litterarum antiquarum* was first edited by Fr. Michael Ferrarinus and published by Boninus de Boninis in Brescia, 1486. Later editions were published in Venice beginning in 1498.

17 Kristin Love Huffman, "Jacopo de' Barbari's *View of Venice* (1500): 'Image Vehicles' and 'Pathways of Culture' Past and Present," *Mediterranea* 4 (2019): 178.

18 See, in particular, Martin Lowry, *The World of Aldus Manutius: Business and Scholarship in Renaissance Venice* (Oxford: Blackwell, 1979); Martin Lowry, *Nicholas Jenson and the Rise of Venetian Publishing in Renaissance Europe* (Oxford: Blackwell, 1991); and Guido Beltramini and Davide Gasparotto, eds., *Aldo Manuzio: Il rinascimento di Venezia* (Venice: Marsilio, 2016).

19 Huffman, "Jacopo de' Barbari's *View of Venice* (1500)," in particular, 172–76.

20 Landesarchiv Thüringen, Hauptstaatsarchiv, Weimar, Ernestinisches Gesamtarchiv, Spalatin Schriften (Papers of Georg Spalatin), reg. O, Signatur 156.

21 February 29, 1504, Augsburg. Österreichisches Staatsarchiv, Vienna, Finanz und Hofkammerarchiv, Alte Hofkammer, Gedenkbücher Epoche Maximilian I (1498–1521), nr. 13, fol. 252.

22 Vincentius Ravennas, *Vicencii Rauennatis Juris vtriusque doctoris floride Academie studii Uuittenburgensis in Jure cesareo ordinarii Oratio publice habita ad felicissimum gloriosissimumque Principem Fredericum Saxonie ducem re* (Wittenberg: Hermann Trebelius, 1505).

23 The letter has gone missing, and scholars rely on Hans Rupprich's transcription in *Albrecht Dürer: Der schriftliche Nachlasse* (Berlin: Deutschen Verein für Kunstwissenschaft, 1956–69), 1:44.

24 See Rangsook Yoon, "Dürer's First Journey to Venice: Revisiting and Reframing the Old Question," in *New Studies on Old Masters: Essays in Renaissance Art in Honour of Colin Eisler*, Essays and Studies 26, ed. John Garton and Diane Wolfthal (Toronto: Center for Reformation and Renaissance Studies, 2011), 69–87.

25 Levenson, "Jacopo de' Barbari," 69–70, for a *terminus ante quem* for de' Barbari's engravings. Hartmann Schedel, n.d., *Liber antiquitatum cum epigrammatibus*, clm. 716, Bayerischen Staatsbibliothek, Munich. For an analysis, see F. J. Worstbrock, "Hartmann Schedels 'Liber Antiquitatum cum epitaphiis et epigrammatibus': Zur Begründung und Erschliessung des historischen Gedächt-

nisses im deutschen Humanismus," in *Franz Josef Worstbrock: Ausgewählte Schriften*, vol. 2, ed. S. Köbele and A. Krass (Stuttgart: Hirzel Verlag, 2005), 311–38.

26 For the most recent publication on this image, see Andrew Robison, "The Drawings of Albrecht Dürer," in *Albrecht Dürer: Master Drawings, Watercolors, and Prints from the Albertina*, exhib. cat. (Washington, DC: National Gallery of Art, 2013), 26–27; Chriscinda Henry, *Playful Pictures: Art, Leisure, and En-tertainment in the Venetian Renaissance Home* (University Park: Pennsylvania State University Press, 2021), 73–76.

27 Friedrich Teja Bach has indicated that Dürer inserts his presence through the ingenious inclusion of his monogram with the compositional arrangement of the rams. See Friedrich Teja Bach, "Albrecht Dürer: Figures of the Marginal," *res: Anthropology and Aesthetics* 36 (1999): 79–99.

Mary Pardo

Revisiting
"lontani et altra fantaxia"

An Eyckian Perspective on
Giovanni Bellini and Jacopo de' Barbari

10 THIS ESSAY REVISITS textual and visual evidence for the art critical connotations of the term *lontani* (distances), which in the years around 1500 was used as a supplement, and sometimes near-synonym, for *paesi* (countrysides)—a term we now translate as "landscapes."[1] In Isabella d'Este's much-cited correspondences with her Venetian agents, lontani were associated with Giovanni Bellini's special gifts as a painter. I will discuss lontani as a specifically "Eyckian" legacy and argue that the term's use correlates with the survival of Jan van Eyck's pictorial strategies and the memory of specific Eyckian novelties into the late fifteenth century. This is attested by works such as Jacopo de' Barbari's dazzling variation on the bird's-eye "city portrait." In this connection, I will interrogate the relationship between

Bellini's approach to lontani and the Eyckian prototypes that are usually cited as sources for Bellini's topographical inventions.

"Lontani": The Critical Frame

Michael Baxandall taught us that the pricing of high-end pictures shifted over the course of the fifteenth century from rewarding displays of quality materials to displays of skill, that is to say, "representational rather than gilt backgrounds … [and] the great master's expensive personal attention."[2] The newly lucrative "representational backgrounds" were the laboratory for a developing catalog of illusionistic landscape effects: "figures, buildings, castles, cities, villas, mountains, hills, plains, water, rocks, costumes, animals, birds and beasts of every kind," as specified in the 1485 contract for Ghirlandaio's Tornabuoni Chapel frescoes in Santa Maria Novella.[3]

Baxandall also demonstrated that the Latinate art critical literature formulated in Italy between 1400 and 1450 was well ahead of the contractual record: court humanists eulogizing the artists favored by their aristocratic patrons, routinely celebrated their skill in depicting "landscape" imagery.[4] In this vein, Bartolommeo Fazio in the mid-1450s declared Jan van Eyck (ca. 1395–1441) "the leading painter of our time" and singled out for praise two paintings we might regard as variations on the theme of "distances": an "orb-like" mappamundi commissioned by Philip the Good of Burgundy (1396–1467); and a picture of a women's bathhouse with nude figures reflected in a mirror, and a plunging outdoor vista (presumably a window view). Both works are lost, but their characteristics may be inferred to some extent by matching the written record to surviving Eyckian paintings.

In the world map's novel depiction of "lands" and "distances," one could "distinguish not only places and the lie of continents, but also, by measurement, the distances between places" (non solum loca situsque regionum, sed etiam locorum distantiam metiendo diagnoscas).[5] Art historian Charles Sterling argued that this Eyckian map "uptilted" a conventional, flat world map centered on the Holy Land and the Mediterranean.[6] The "bird's-eye" projection would allow for a subtle perspectival effect: the continents could have been dotted with an array of topographical features like those in the landscape backgrounds of van Eyck's *Rolin Madonna*, the various *Crucifixions*, or the Antwerp *Saint Barbara*.[7]

If the mappamundi allowed for scaled intervals between depicted localities, the bathhouse picture produced its "distances" by a series of pairings, beginning with the juxtaposition between the intimate interior (duplicated yet miniaturized in the mirror) and the great outdoors peopled with "horses, minute figures of men, mountains, groves, hamlets, and castles, carried out with such skill you would believe one was fifty miles distant from the other."[8] In Fazio's catalog, the jump from horses to men, men to mountains, mountains to groves, and so on, produces a differentiation by scale and category (animal/human, mineral/vegetal, peasant/aristocratic) that transforms "distances" into more than spatial intervals. Twenty years earlier, Fazio's fellow humanist Leon Battista Alberti (1404–72) had identified the sensory/cognitive experience of *comparatione* as the painter's key to representation: "Large and small, long and short, high and low, broad and narrow, bright and dark, luminous and tenebrous, and all [contingent] things . . . are such that they are only known through comparison."[9]

Evidence that Alberti knew about Eyckian paintings' mastery of "large and small, . . . bright and dark, luminous and tenebrous" is compelling, even if indirect: in the early 1430s, before writing *De pictura*, he produced in Rome a set of experimental world landscapes in the form of peep shows displayed in a small box.[10] These *miracoli della pittura*, as Alberti called them, were divided into daytime and nighttime "distances" of land, sea, and sky.[11] Alberti touted their paradoxical impact: through a little hole "you could see enormous mountains and vast countrysides enclosing an immense maritime gulf; then at a view, distant regions so remote that sight failed to penetrate them" (tum e conspectu longe sepositas regiones, usque adeo remotissimas, ut visenti acies deficeret).[12] This calls to mind the backgrounds of the Eyckian *Crucifixions* in New York and Berlin, where minuscule snow-capped Alps dissolve in light at the far horizon under luminescent clouds and a glassy daytime moon.[13] Of his own peep boxes, Alberti declared: "[All the viewers] swore that what they saw were not painted but real things in nature [non pictas, sed veras ipsas res nature]."

By situating his vistas in astronomical space and time, Alberti identified them as parts of a virtual mappamundi: "In the nocturnal [demonstrations], you can see Arcturus, the Pleiades and Orion, and the other glittering constellations, with the moon glowing as it rises over the hillsides and the dawn stars shining from the heights. In the diurnal demonstrations, a widely diffused light irradiates the immense orb of Earth [*irradiat immensum terrarum orbem*], the same [light] that shines after Aurora, as Homer says, ignites the rainbow." Though Alberti did not explain *how* he achieved his effects, it is important that he thought they looked photo-pictorial, literally as if painted by the motions of ambient light: the starry night transitioning to moonrise as morning nears; the global effusion of morning light building to a fiery brilliance. Alberti's *miracoli* were made before 1435–36, and van Eyck's "orbicular" map was nearly contemporaneous. Sterling placed it around 1436, following one of van Eyck's "secret journeys" for Duke Philip. Might Alberti's cosmographic illusions, which were shown at the papal court, have come to van Eyck's notice as he was planning his own world-picture?[14] It is telling that Alberti labeled them demonstrations (*demonstrationes*), a word denoting "argument" or "proof" but also connoting—for their power to deceive eye and mind—something "monstrous."

Alberti's peep box restricted the view to a miniaturized monocular image, which gave him greater control over the simulation of light and shadow, whether painted or contrived with mirrors and lamps. In *De pictura*, the peep hole was formalized (as the apex of the visual pyramid) in a rigorous perspective construction: Alberti offered precise instructions for projecting an accurately scaled view as if "through an open window," but with emphasis on the near and middle distance. He did not return to the cosmographical illusions of his earlier experiments. Even so, Alberti's insight that remote distances could be made present by mimicking the "cosmic paintbrush" of real light had critical relevance. It certainly applies to the remarkable "orbicular" visualization of a three-dimensional Earth suspended between day and night, in a Flemish manuscript from the second half of the fifteenth century (fig. 10.1).[15] This illustration, in a copy of the French translation of Bartholomeus Anglicus's *Of the Properties of Things*, introduces book 9, "On the Movement of the Heavens and Time," which treats the cyclical rotation of stars and planets around the stationary Earth. It is not a proper mappamundi—the image is too small to distinguish landmasses and bodies of water—but the remarkable treatment of light suggests an Eyckian prototype. While it is unlikely that van Eyck's map was modeled to resemble a sphere, it must have been equally sophisticated in suggesting the passage of light over a convex Earth.

The Quattrocento City Portrait and the "Downward View"

The bird's-eye view was not known by that name in the Renaissance. In his treatise on sculpture (1504), the humanist Pomponius Gauricus defined it

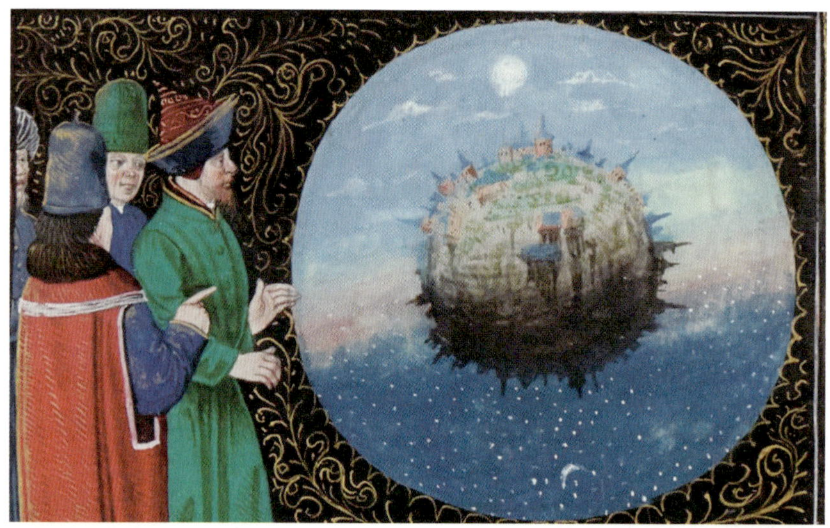

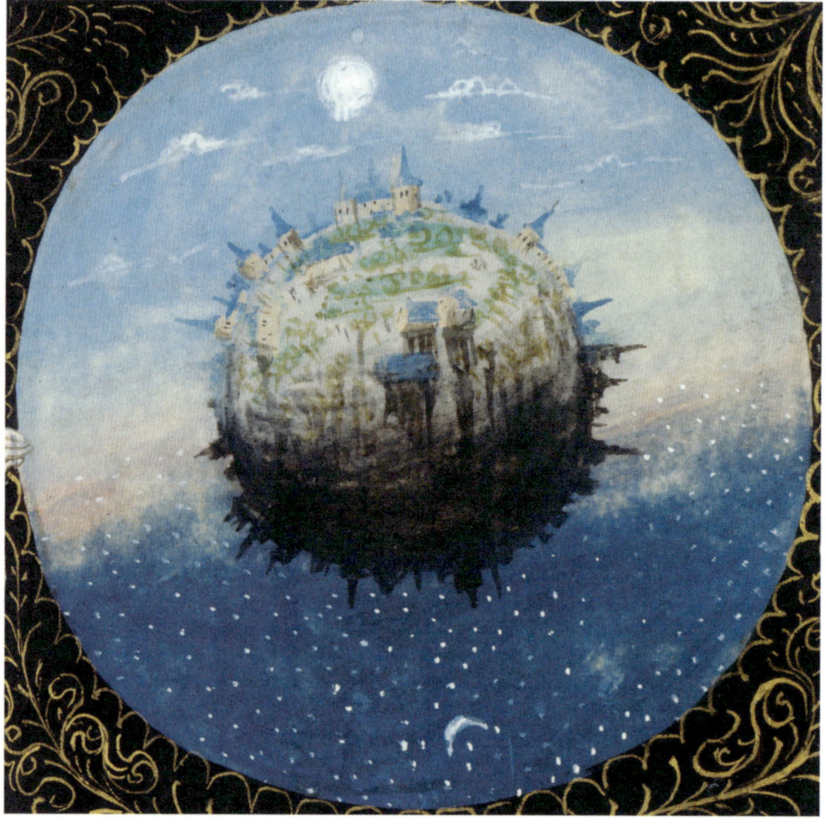

as "this downward-looking method" (*despiciendi hec racio*) and compared it to viewing objects arranged on a desktop.[16] Though not clear on its optics, Gauricus realized that the "downward view" made crowded compositions ("civil disorders, battles, wars, cities, and the like") more legible by minimizing overlap between figures. In fact, the "downward" view was historically tied to the stereometric depiction of landscape forms: it was first perfected in the Trecento, most spectacularly in the rural panorama of the Good Government cycle in Siena; received new currency in the "plateau compositions" favored by Netherlandish painters in the early decades of the fifteenth century; and was repurposed late in the century in the pioneering group of large-scale perspectival "city portraits" that culminate with Jacopo de' Barbari's *View*.[17]

I suspect that de' Barbari's *View* is in conversation with the legacy of the Eyckian mappamundi—particularly if its distinguishing feature was the "uptilting" of a map in order to enable its seeding with stereometric local topographies. For the stereometric "bodying forth" of urban segments in the *View of Venice*, I would also suggest that de' Barbari had the example of Eyckian pictures in the Veneto. The Ca' d'Oro *Crucifixion* (fig. 10.2), already in Padua by 1460, is the close variant of a celebrated Eyckian design considered the prototypical plateau composition.[18] The plateau—the uptilted foreground ridge where the narrative is staged—is the highest point in a topography that slopes into the viewer's space, and backward into a broad valley dominated by a densely built, massively fortified Jerusalem. The onlookers exiting the scene progressively grow tinier on their stepwise descent into the city center far away. Once past the gate, we follow them into a vast, architecturally diversified plaza fitted into a compositional stratum of less than fifteen by twenty centimeters. It is a master class in the illusionistic rendering of a consistently lit urban stereometry. However much de' Barbari may have profited from local topographical resources, the best Quattrocento models available for optically coherent, "portrait-like" urban depictions, achieved with the tools of tonal modeling, were in the panoramic topographies of Eyckian painting, not in surveyors' notations.

Orthogonality

A closer look at the characteristic construction of "distance" in another Eyckian plateau composition documented in Quattrocento Venice may

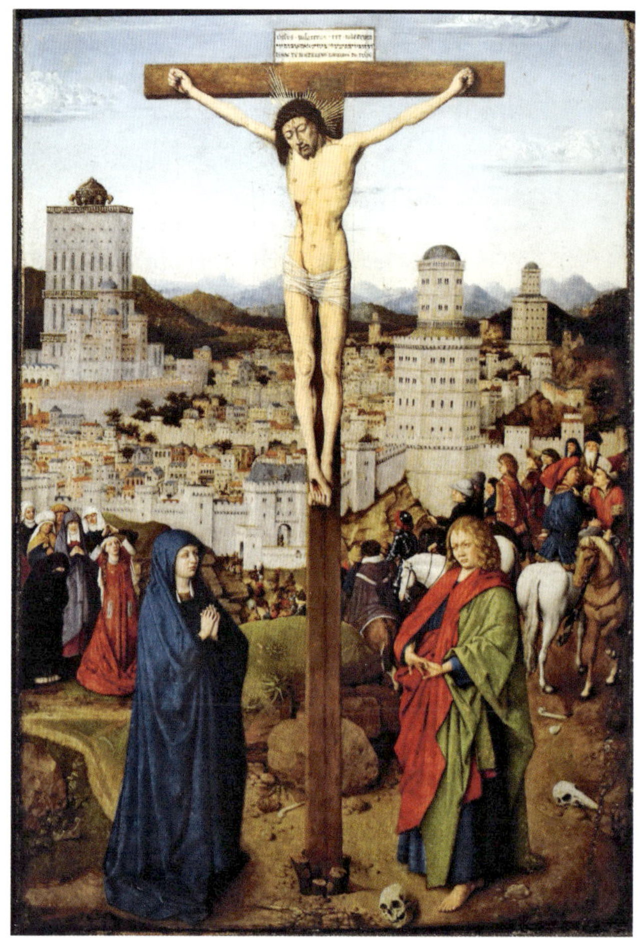

Jan van Eyck (Attributed), *Crucifixion*, 1440s. Oil on panel, 46 × 31 cm. Galleria Franchetti alla Ca' d'Oro, Venice.

provide a bridge to the role of lontani in Giovanni Bellini's art.[19] The Turin *Stigmatization* stages a miraculous—and traumatic—encounter between Saint Francis and a winged apparition, high above a deep landscape, on an uptilted greensward between sedimentary outcrops. Our viewpoint is level with the saint's, as if we were kneeling on the same patch of ground, but our gaze is perpendicular to the event. As in the *Crucifixion*, "distances" are *orthogonal* to the sacred encounter: we note Francis's frozen gesture and the hovering Seraph, but our gaze is sucked into the gap between them, in a heady plunge over the saint's raised hands (right past his wounding) and over forking woodland roads, across a glassy lake, into and over a huge fortification, and onto a vast river valley that spreads below an Alpine range

142

(fig. 10.3). The river sweeps toward the base of a blue mountain shaped to the contour of the Seraph's right wing: But does this assonance bring us back to the foreground, or does it tip the Seraph, like a giant compass needle, into the magnetic pull of the lontano?

Francis plays a double role, as main protagonist and as giant yard-stick for the lontani; his raised hands are colossal when juxtaposed with the diminutive travelers heading into the depths of the hill-scape. And if Francis's hands graze an inaccessible hillside, the tonsured crown of his head, no less colossally, grazes a snowy massif thousands of miles beyond it. In the foreground, Brother Leo's hooded form, folded in on itself, barely registers, as does the brook that spills toward the bottom right edge of the picture from a cleft in the outcrop. But the water's glint introduces a subliminal sense of movement, like water's hypnotic murmur. The Seraph, dripping blood into the space over Leo's head, is both mystical vision

10.3

Detail of Jan van Eyck, *Stigmatization of Saint Francis*, ca. 1428–30. Oil on oak panel, 29.3 × 33.4 cm. Galleria Sabauda, Turin.

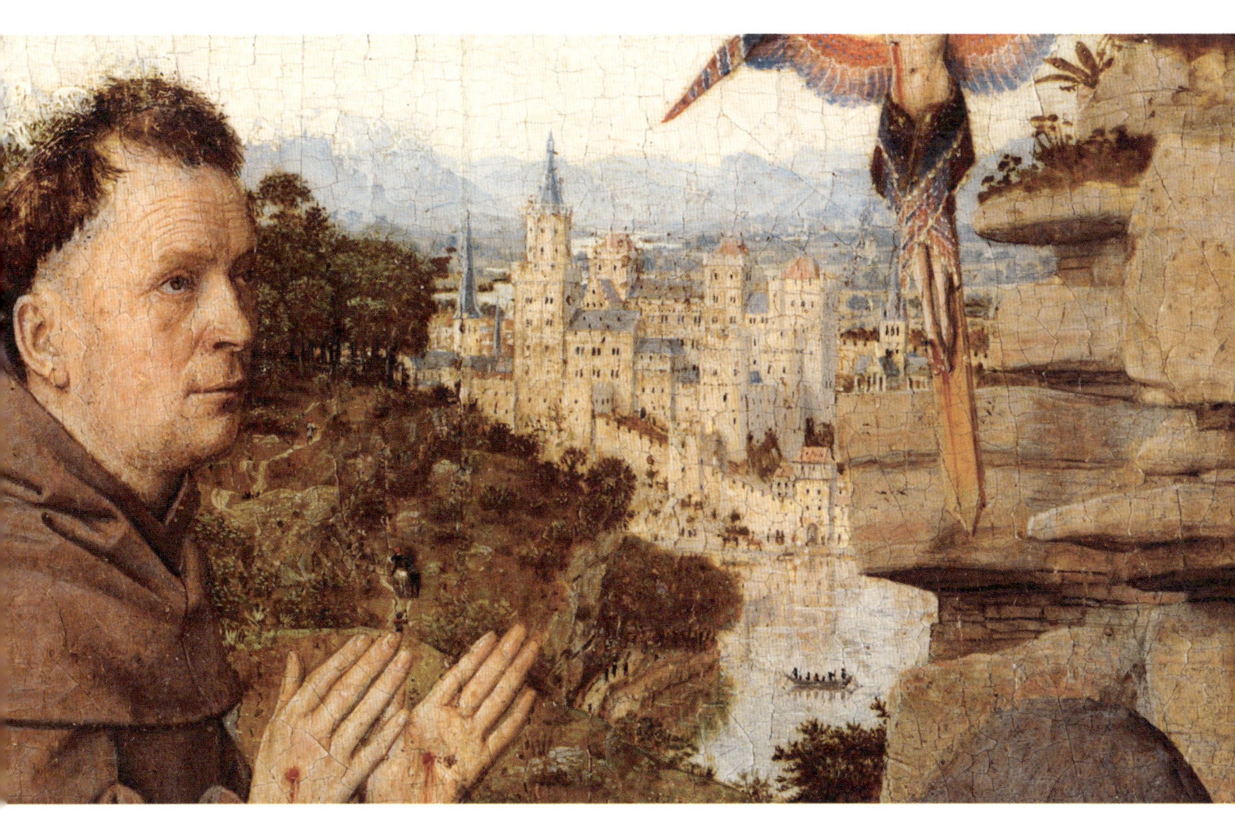

and uncanny dream figure. Eyckian "distance" is a paradoxical device that draws us further and further into what can be *shown,* and also shows that in the incremental surrender of visual acuity to the pull of the faraway, bodies turn into articulated specks and then disappear altogether, huge mountains shrink into the light that flashes off their snowcaps, clouds roll together like molten seed pearls—and waking is not the opposite of dreaming.

Mary Pardo

Bellini's "lontani et altra fantaxia"

In Eyckian pictures, the plateau composition works as a launching platform for "distance," for the activation of an orthogonal journey that sunders foreground from background, story from setting, the palpable from the intangible. In Giovanni Bellini's late-career negotiations with Isabella d'Este, when the artist pragmatically offered to enhance a *sacra conversazione* with lontani, "distances" acquired a different critical inflection. Bellini was familiar with Eyckian painting: the Frick *Saint Francis,* in particular, is frequently cited for its dependence on the Eyckian *Stigmatization* and is certainly an exploration of "plateau composition." But it is also a critique of Eyckian scale and tonal structure.[20]

In Bembo's famous letter of 1506, Bellini is said to experience his own pictorial process in landscape mode. Bembo explains that the "invention" or subject he is to devise for Bellini must be "adapted to the fantasy of him who is to carry it out, whose pleasure it is that not too many fixed boundaries be imposed on his style [or "stylus"], *accustomed—as he says—to always roam at will in his paintings* [emphasis added], so that, as best is in him, they may satisfy whoever gazes upon them."[21] Four years earlier, in lieu of a *Nativity with Saints* requested by Isabella, Michele Vianello quoted Bellini saying that "if it pleased Your Most Illustrious Ladyship, he would make an Our Lady with the Child, as well as the Saint John the Baptist and some distances and [some] other fantasy [*qualche lontani et altra fantaxia*] much more suited to this picture, which would be so much better."[22]

These two letters offer distinct, though related, meanings for the term "fantasy." Vianello's term might be translated as "reverie," or even "whim," suggesting that lontani likewise are unrestricted pictorial accessories. When Isabella was negotiating for an allegory, Bellini consistently tied *fantasia* to his freedom of choice, meaning the picture subject as a whole, not just its background—as in his offer to "make a *fantasia* in his own manner."[23] Isabella tried to pin down this choice: Bellini could follow his own "invention," "so long as he feigns something ancient with a beautiful meaning"—but Bellini resisted.[24]

In Bembo's letter *fantasia* refers to Bellini's "imagination," a psychological faculty possessed by all sentient beings but more highly developed in a "visual specialist" who harnesses the mind's power to reshape what it visualizes. Current scholarship highlights the Christian symbolism in Bellini's landscapes, but if we take Vianello at face value, lontani and altra fantaxia were pictorial features that Bellini regarded as specific to the pleasure (the viewer's and his own) of his art.[25] This is a criterion neglected in our reading of Renaissance art literature. Yet the organs of sense, specialized for the reception of specific perceptual stimuli, are the first threshold for experiential judgments. Pleasure/pain, which trigger attraction/repulsion, are the organic platform for Albertian *comparatione*.[26] By nature sight ingests, and delights in, light and color, to which it is inherently "proportioned." Bellini internalizes his lontani and is pleased to nourish his fantasy by following his paintbrush on an "aimless" journey (*vagare* means "to be a vagrant").

Bellini's *Sacred Allegory* (fig. 10.4), datable to the 1490s, is another version of the plateau composition, and it seems appropriate that it was made around the time of de' Barbari's *View*.[27] It is a decentered image, with a perspectival tiled foreground that yields an elevated viewpoint well to the right of the panel's central axis. In other words, the pavement is a "downward-looking" construction, though its tilt is moderate, as are the "distances" in the background. Rather than an orthogonal rush into deep spaces, it is the horizontal split between measured foreground and fluid middle ground that produces the lontano. The balustraded court encloses a remarkable deconstruction of a centralized *pala* such as the *San Giobbe Altarpiece*, rotated so that the enthroned Virgin at the far left regards her companion saints either at the far right, or outside the enclosure, cross-axially facing the viewer. This allegory is first of all about the structural tension between a proper arrangement *in maestà*, on the one hand, and its dismantling, on the other.

An orthogonal path on the pavement medallion draws the gaze to the cluster of children (one of them the Christ Child) gathering golden fruit at

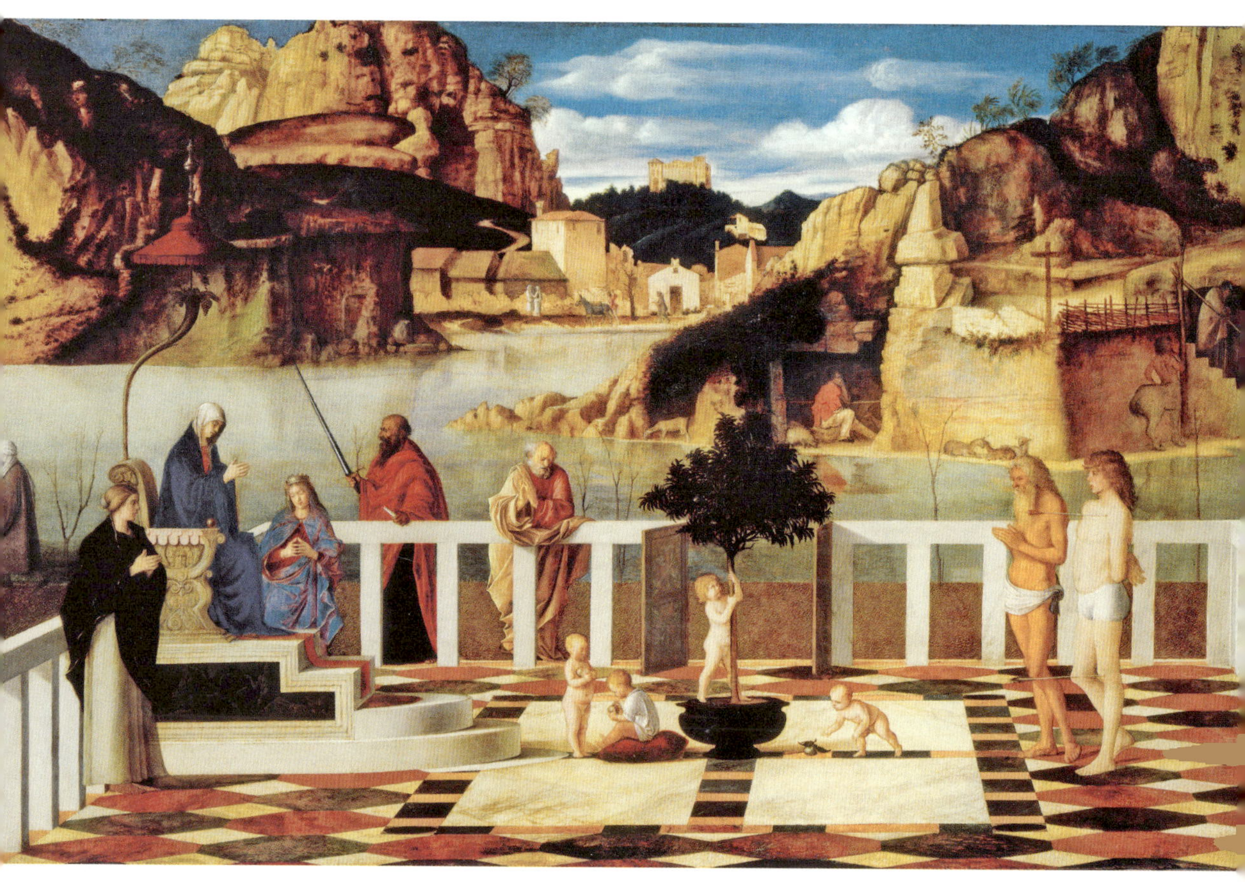

the potted tree. The open gate beckons to an "otherworld" that invites contemplation from the shoreline: the pull of distance is diffused. Between the near and the far shore, the unruffled water gathers light from the sky and gleams with fugitive reflections. Bellini's picture brings together the raking light of the foreground, meteorological light from the sky, and reflected and refracted light in the water, bridging the differences between near and far. The corporeal world itself—its weather, estuaries, rocky outcrops, buildings, bodies—is a natural mirror for the sidereal heavens. Bellini, better than most, grasped that the painting's colored surface is another, artful, mirror among the world's illuminated surfaces.

146

1 See Brigit Blass-Simmen, "'*Qualche lontani*': Distance and Transcendence in the Art of Giovanni Bellini," in *Examining Giovanni Bellini: An Art "More Human and More Divine,"* ed. Carolyn C. Wilson (Turnhout: Brepols, 2015), 77–91.

2 Michael Baxandall, *Painting and Experience in Fifteenth Century Italy* (Oxford: Clarendon, 1972), 23.

3 Baxandall, *Painting and Experience,* 17–18; and Jean K. Cadogan, *Domenico Ghirlandaio, Artist and Artisan* (New Haven, CT: Yale University Press, 2000), 250–51: "et figuras [in the margin: hedifitia, castra, civitates, villas], montes, colles, planities, aquas, lapides, vestes, animalia, aves et bestias quascumque et omnes cuiuscumque generis, aponere, pingere et annotare et ornare . . ."

4 Michael Baxandall, *Giotto and the Orators: Humanist Observers of Painting in Italy and the Discovery of Pictorial Composition, 1350–1450* (Oxford: Oxford University Press, 1971), 78–95.

5 Baxandall, *Giotto,* 106–7, 165–66.

6 Charles Sterling, "Jan van Eyck avant 1432. Appendice IV: La mappemonde de Jan van Eyck," *Revue de l'art* 33 (1976): 69–82; and David Summers, *Vision, Reflection, and Desire in Western Painting* (Chapel Hill: University of North Carolina Press, 2007), 71–83, 93–110. Both scholars envision a "perspectival" variant of the traditional T-O map. The map is rejected by Jacques Paviot, "La mappemonde attribuée à Jan van Eyck par Fàcio: Une pièce à retirer du catalogue de son oeuvre," *Revue des archéologues et historiens d'art de Louvain* 24 (1991): 57–62; but see also Summers, *Vision,* 81–82.

7 See Queen's University and Radbound University, KIK-IRPA, "Closer to van Eyck," accessed October 30, 2020, http://closertovaneyck.kikirpa.be/.

8 Baxandall, *Giotto,* 107, 166: "et item equi hominesque perbrevi statura, montes, nemora, pagi, castella tanto artificio elaborata, ut alia ab aliis quinquaginta milibus passuum distare credas." The humanist "catalog" of landscape features was taken from Pliny the Elder and Vitruvius: see E. H. Gombrich, "The Renaissance Theory of Art and the Rise of Landscape," in *Norm and Form* (London: Phaidon, 1966), 107–21.

9 Leon Battista Alberti, *"On Painting" and "On Sculpture,"* ed. Cecil Grayson (London: Phaidon, 1972), para 18.

10 Summers, *Vision,* 130–35.

11 Anthony Grafton, *Leon Battista Alberti, Master Builder of the Italian Renaissance* (New York: Hill and Wang, 2000), 84–91.

12 Leon Battista Alberti, *Autobiografia e altre opere latine*, ed. Loredana Chines and Andrea Severi (Milan: Rizzoli BUR Classici, 2012), 80–83.

13 See Queen's University, Radbound University, KIK-IRPA, "Closer to van Eyck."

14 Sterling, "Van Eyck avant 1432," 70, proposes that Fazio saw a gift copy of the mappamundi at the Aragonese court in Naples.

15 Barthélemy l'Anglais, *Livre des proprietés des choses*, trans. Jean Corbichon, Paris, Bib. Nat., MS Français 134.

16 Pomponius Gauricus, *De sculptura*, trans. Andre Chastel and Robert Klein (Geneva: Librairie Droz, 1969), 172–74, 184–91. Together with eye-level and worm's-eye views, it constituted one of Gauricus's three standard "perspectives."

17 On plateau compositions, see Millard Meiss, "'Highlands' in the Lowlands: Jan van Eyck, the Master of Flémalle and the Franco-Italian Tradition," *Gazette des beaux-arts* 57, n.s. 6 (1961): 273–314. See also Juergen Schulz, "Jacopo de' Barbari's *View of Venice*: Map Making, City Views, and Moralized Geography before the Year 1500," *Art Bulletin* 60, no. 3 (1978): 425–47.

18 See Meiss, "'Highlands,'" 281–309; and Bernard Aikema and Beverly Louise Brown, "Painting in Fifteenth-Century Venice and the *ars nova* of the Netherlands," in *Renaissance Venice and the North: Crosscurrents in the Time of Bellini, Dürer, and Titian*, ed. Aikema and Brown (New York: Rizzoli, 2000), 176–83, and 202–5 (cat. nos. 10, 11).

19 Mauro Lucco, "Bellini and Flemish Painting," in *The Cambridge Companion to Giovanni Bellini*, ed. Peter Humfrey (Cambridge: Cambridge University Press, 2004), 84–85. Both versions of the *Stigmatization* were owned by Anselme Adornes, who took one on his pilgrimage to the Holy Land and stopped in Venice on his return in 1471.

20 Lucco, "Bellini."

21 "L'invenzione, che mi scrive vostra signoria che io truovi al dissegno, bisognerà che s'accommodi alla fantasia di lui che l'ha a fare, il quale ha piacere che molto signati termini non si diano al suo stile, *uso, come dice, di sempre vagare a sua voglia nelle pitture* [my italics] che, quanto è in lui, possano sodisfare a chi le mira." See Manuela Barause, "Giovanni Bellini: I documenti," in *Giovanni Bellini*, ed. Mauro Lucco and G. C. F. Villa (Milan: Silvana Editoriale, 2008), 352, doc. no. 99.

22 Barause, "Bellini: I documenti," 347–48, doc. no. 77.

23 Barause, "Bellini: I documenti," 345–47 (letters of June 1501, no. 64; August 1501, no. 67; September 1502, no. 73).

24 Barause, "Bellini: I documenti," 345 (letter of June 1501, no. 65).

25 Davide Gasparotto, "Giovanni Bellini and Landscape," in *Giovanni Bellini: Landscapes of Faith in Renaissance Venice* (Los Angeles: J. Paul Getty Museum, 2017), 11–24.

26 See David Summers, *The Judgment of Sense* (Cambridge: Cambridge University Press, 1987), chap. 4.

27 See the entry in Mauro Lucco and G. C. F. Villa, eds., *Giovanni Bellini* (Milan: Silvana, 2008), 236–39. Antonio Mazzotta dates the *Allegory* to 1504, identifying it with the *presepe* ("Nativity") for Isabella d'Este. See Gasparotto, *Giovanni Bellini*, 116–25 (cat. entry #11).

Rangsook Yoon

Jacopo de' Barbari, a Wandering Court Artist in the North

Changing Perspectives on His Role in Northern Renaissance Art

11 AMONG ITALIAN ARTISTS documented to have been active north of the Alps in the late fifteenth and early sixteenth centuries, the most noteworthy is Jacopo de' Barbari (d. 1516). While his role as a cultural mediator who introduced and disseminated Italian Renaissance artistic ideas to Germany is irrefutable, the degree of his critical importance has been diminished in the twentieth century. In a 1920 article concerning Albrecht Dürer's (1471–1528) depictions of Apollo and their connection with de' Barbari, for instance, Erwin Panofsky pointedly wrote, "Certainly de' Barbari was neither great artist nor eminent man."[1] Such a judgment has formed the general outlook of his work and career throughout much of the twentieth century, as echoed in a remark by Jay Levenson in 1978: "A man of some learning,

Barbari was a suitable adornment to any Northern court, regardless of his actual achievements."[2]

In more recent decades, art historian Beate Böckem has attempted to reassess de' Barbari's artistic career, challenging the long-established view of him as a minor artist.[3] Through historiographical examination, she has demonstrated how, in the nineteenth and twentieth centuries, the biographical narratives of de' Barbari, a figure who traversed the Alps, have mainly been constructed along nationalistic lines and used specifically as a credible foil to Dürer.[4] Evaluating the strong influences that Dürer and de' Barbari had on each other has shaped one of the premises of Dürer scholarship since then: their rivaling styles highlight the brilliance of the old-German Dürer who established himself against the achievements of contemporary Italian Renaissance artists.[5]

While considering critical works on the cultural and artistic exchanges between Italy and the North, this essay places de' Barbari's wandering artistic career in the contexts of early modern mobility and the situation of Renaissance court artists. It examines his presence in various northern courts as a fulcrum for spreading Renaissance artistic ideals. In so doing, this essay illustrates de' Barbari's transformative role in conveying the artistic motifs and ideals of the Italian Renaissance to the North. The cultural transfer of Renaissance ideas from Italy to the North was initiated and supported by rulers and their humanist entourages. This cultural movement followed the old mercantile route from Venice in the South to Wittenberg in the North, with the Fondaco dei Tedeschi at its crux. As depicted in the *View of Venice* (1500), the Fondaco dei Tedeschi, a German trading post located at the foot of the Rialto Bridge, was largely dominated by Augsburgers and Nurembergers (plate 4). These merchants brought back home with them not only goods but also the latest news, publications, and even talent.[6] De' Barbari's illustrious yet wandering career—he served at various rulers' courts, from Nuremberg to Wittenberg to Souburg to Mechelen, and instilled Renaissance ideals to the younger artists in these locations—was launched with his involvement in the creation of the *View of Venice* and the recommendation of Anton Kolb, a Nuremberg patrician active in Venice and a friend of both Dürer and Willibald Pirckheimer.

In contrast to Panofsky's censorious judgment of the Venetian artist, numerous written documents indicate that de' Barbari's colleagues in Germany and the Burgundian Netherlands perceived him otherwise. Whether directly or obliquely, these writings testify to his lively intellectual exchanges with notable humanist scholars, his indelible influence on German and Netherlandish innovators like Dürer and Lucas Cranach the Elder (1472–1553) in their formative years, and the high esteem he garnered from many of his contemporaries. Moreover, although many artworks that de' Barbari created are unknown, it is clear that his patrons held in high regard his humanistic knowledge of classical antiquity and fifteenth-century Italian artistic theories. In addition to his benefactors' distinct penchants for humanism and antiquity, discussed further in this essay, a range of written sources demonstrate that de' Barbari was an erudite artist, well versed in classical subjects as well as in contemporary Italian Renaissance ideas derived from ancient sources, qualities that enhanced his social standing and help clarify the reasons why he was invited to various northern royal courts. For instance, as both Levenson and Böckem have thoroughly examined, the Saxon court's account books show that de' Barbari worked at, and frequently traveled between, six different castles in or near Wittenberg, Leipzig, and Weimar, all of which were substantially renovated in the early sixteenth century.[7] The rooms in the Wittenberg castle, for example, are known to have been painted extensively with classical subjects, signaling the type of projects and iconographic programs instituted by de' Barbari during his appointment at the court of Frederick the Wise.[8] Similarly, according to Gerhard Geldenhouwer (1482–1542), secretary of Philip of Burgundy, both de' Barbari and Jan Gossart (1478–1532) were employed to decorate Philip's Souburg residence with mythological scenes.[9] At the Saxon court, de' Barbari also frequently interacted with humanists at the University of Wittenberg, as well as with Cranach the Elder, who became Frederick's official court artist in 1505.[10]

The most coherent and unambiguous evidence conveying de' Barbari's humanistic attainments is his own assertion in a lengthy letter entitled "About the Excellence of Painting," which he composed to seek the patronage of Frederick the Wise.[11] In it, de' Barbari proclaimed that painting should be considered the eighth liberal art—a notion that Italian Renaissance artists and theorists, such as Leon Battista Alberti, had asserted to underscore the nobility of their profession. In this same letter, de' Barbari also commented on the importance of mathematics and geometry for artists, which, he stated, were needed for the proper measurement of proportions.[12] Indeed, his mathematical knowledge, underlining the theoretical discourse about ideal human proportions, was highly appreciated by his patrons in northern courtly circles.

As has been examined by scholars, the most telling evidence of the appreciation for de' Barbari and his consequential influence is found in Dürer's artworks and writings. A series of engravings by Dürer rendering nude figures, created between 1501 and 1504, bear indisputable stylistic similarities and analogous iconographic themes and motifs with de' Barbari's work.[13] Further, textual references to the Venetian artist in Dürer's writings are as numerous and intriguing as his visual references. The most pertinent account appears in two unpublished 1523 drafts composed by Dürer for the dedication text of his *Four Books on Human Proportions*.[14] He wrote:

> When I was "still young," I have found no one who has written about a system of human proportion, except Jacobus, a native of Venice and a lovely painter. He showed me how to construct man and woman based on measurements. When he [first] told of this, I would rather have come into possession of his knowledge than a kingdom.... But Jacobus I noticed did not wish to give me a clear explanation; so I went ahead on my own and read Vitruvius, who describes the proportions of the human body to some extent.[15]

Although Dürer eventually modified his initial great admiration for de' Barbari's commanding knowledge and artistic merit, it is clear that de' Barbari was a critical conduit through whom the Nuremberg artist launched his decades-long investigation into the question of ideal human proportions, a pursuit that began around 1500, when de' Barbari was residing in Nuremberg, and that culminated with Dürer's posthumously published *Four Books on Human Proportion* (1528).[16] Also, in Dürer's so-called *Diary of the Netherlandish Journey* (1520–21), he reported that he had tried to obtain the Venetian's "little book"—de' Barbari's sketchbook or notes on current art theories—while at the court of Archduchess Margaret of Austria.[17]

Certainly, the human figures in de' Barbari's engravings present no apparent systematic measurements that follow the classical proportions devised by other Italian Renaissance artists. Nevertheless, what matters here is contemporary northerners' fascination with de' Barbari's proclamations about rendering the human form *all'antica*—according to classical proportions. For instance, in a 1511 publication, Jan Smerken reported a humorous anecdote that told of de' Barbari making a Hercules snowman with all of its body parts "after measures" outside Philip's residence in Brussels.[18]

The significant intellectual and artistic impact of de' Barbari's presence in the northern courts and the high regard he received in those elite circles cannot be adequately assessed without reevaluating his particular influence on several young but soon-to-be-major northern artists, including Cranach the Elder, Gossart, and Hans Süss von Kulmbach (ca. 1480–1522), as well as Dürer, who grappled throughout his career with ideal human proportions and nude representations.[19] De' Barbari's renderings of nude figures and his studies on the subject of ideal human proportions allegedly derived from the Vitruvian canon, still recondite in the North, acted as a catalyst for shaping these younger artists at the moment that de' Barbari's artistic influence prevailed in the courts that employed them.

Rangsook Yoon

No similar figural proportions can be discerned between the nudes of de' Barbari and Gossart, or between the nudes of de' Barbari and Cranach. This has been used as evidence that de' Barbari did not influence these artists. However, I posit that de' Barbari's atypical methods could have come into play for creating a whole range of northern nude figures with unorthodox human proportions—figures that were not simple transcriptions of the "ideal proportions" promoted by Italian artists.

The panegyrics heaped on de' Barbari by his contemporaries reveal an informed enthusiasm and respect for his erudition. Notably, Vincentius of Ravenna, the Italian humanist who became professor of imperial law at the University of Wittenberg in 1505, praised him as Apelles.[20] Similarly, recounting Philip's humanist study of the ancients, Geldenhouwer lauded Philip's court artists—de' Barbari and Gossart—as painters of the first rank. He called them, respectively, the Zeuxis and Apelles of his age.[21] Nonetheless, reviewing de' Barbari scholarship, it is clear that art historians have critically diminished such encomiums. In fact, nothing demonstrates this prejudice, built on the hierarchical concept of the high aesthetics of Italian Renaissance art, more clearly than comparing scholars' appraisals of the validity of de' Barbari as Zeuxis to the treatments afforded to artists like Dürer, Cranach, and Gossart, each of whom were called the Apelles of their time.[22] It appears that many scholars have been haunted by the seeming contradiction between the high praise that de' Barbari received in his lifetime and what they see in his prints and paintings today. The esteem for de' Barbari by his contemporary patrons, humanists, and colleagues, as well as his overall art historical significance, needs to be reexamined by considering the prestige, artistic assignments, and social position accorded to sixteenth-century court artists, who were often treated as members of a prince's immediate circle and who enjoyed both tangible and intangible benefits. In contrast to the largely dismissive twentieth-century evaluations of the praise ascribed to de' Barbari by his contemporaries, de' Barbari was indeed considered an eminent man—at least in courtly circles in Germany and the Burgundian Netherlands.

In reevaluating de' Barbari's artistic reputation and his somewhat mysterious, wandering northern career, it is useful to consider Martin Warnke's sociocultural study on the history of court artists and the overarching patterns of artistic development from the late medieval era to the nineteenth century.[23] Warnke's broad historical survey demonstrates the prestige of such artists in early modern European aristocratic courts. By the early sixteenth century, the fame of both artist and patron had become so tightly intertwined that the magnanimity of kings and princes was closely identified with their patronage of great artists. As Warnke writes, the courts were critical for shaping self-understanding and encouraging artistic individualism, and it was in the princely courts—not the cities—where Renaissance styles and methods spread.[24] However, Warnke also notes that despite all the gains and benefits that came with a court appointment, such artists were not necessarily always perfectly content. After all, while serving a particular court's secular needs in provisioning luxury befitting a monarch, artists could achieve artistic autonomy no more at court than they could elsewhere.[25] The demands of patrons could prevail over the desires of an artist.

In addition, to reevaluate de' Barbari's wandering career in full, the political and cultural competition among the courts in the Holy Roman Empire and Burgundian Netherlands needs to be considered further, as his role would have been inextricable from the humanist culture that his enlightened patrons aspired to cultivate. In the web of rival aspirations influenced by changing courtly ideals and posthumous fame through artistic patronage, German and Netherlandish monarchs were heavily invested in translating royal power by displaying their humanistic and classical learning and taste and by consciously promulgating such developments.[26] Artists like de' Barbari, who were willing to transplant themselves from Italy, were indispensable for initiating new artistic traditions at princely residences. The employment of de' Barbari at various northern courts, where the taste for antiquity was previously absent or just beginning, seemingly stimulated many northern artists' adoption of Italian Renaissance art theory, subjects, and motifs. Again, it is crucial to consider that the invitation given to de' Barbari to move to Nuremberg was part of an attempt to bring humanistic artistic culture to the Holy Roman Emperor's court.[27] De' Barbari's subsequent moves to other northern courts were also determined by the rising vogue of everything Italian—from classical antiquity to Albertian perspective—as well as due to the princes' own interests in turning their courts into prestigious intellectual and artistic, humanist hubs. For instance, in competition with Maximilian's cultural politics, Frederick the Wise's Saxon court attracted prominent humanist scholars with the founding of the University of Wittenberg in 1502.[28] Likewise, Margaret of Austria, known for her discerning taste and learning, was keen on displaying ancestral portraits of the Habsburg family to celebrate her glorious genealogical line, following in her father's ambitious footsteps.[29]

According to a 1506 letter by Dürer, Venetian painters ridiculed de' Barbari, claiming that a good artist would have never left Venice.[30] Though de' Barbari might not have been esteemed like his contemporaries Giovanni Bellini (1430–1516) or Andrea Mantegna (1431–1506), he was nonetheless an accomplished and erudite artist, willing to cross the Alps to take part in his patrons' ambitions to foster cultural revivals in their courtly settings. It is within this context of aristocratic court culture and patronage that de' Barbari nourished young artists with novel intellectual concepts, such as the claim for the ennoblement of painting as the eighth liberal art. The early 1500s—the particular moment when de' Barbari launched his career north of the Alps—were decisive and fertile years for intercultural and artistic exchanges between Italy and the North. As Michael Baxandall discusses, the explicit differentiation between "Italian" and "German" styles in theoretical discussions can only be discerned from about 1515, even though signs of an earlier emergence of such consciousness are found from the late fifteenth century onward.[31] This was the moment when de' Barbari was recruited by princely courts that eagerly embraced Italian Renaissance courtly culture and art as well as humanism. In them, he was a trailblazer, playing a critical role in crystallizing the artistic thought and principles of what would soon take root and flourish in the North.

Rangsook Yoon

NOTES

1 Erwin Panofsky, "Dürers Darstellungen des Apollo und ihr Verhältnis zu Barbari," *Jahrbuch der Preuszischen Kunstsammlungen* 41 (1920): 359–77, esp. 359.

2 Jay A. Levenson, "Jacopo de' Barbari and Northern Art of the Early Sixteenth Century" (PhD diss., Columbia University, 1978), 39.

3 Beate Böckem, *Jacopo de' Barbari: Künstlerschaft und Hofkultur um 1500* (Cologne: Böhlau Verlag, 2016).

4 See Böckem, *Jacopo de' Barbari*, 13–26; and Beate Böckem, "Die Frage nach Autorschaft—eine Frage der Autorität? Jacopo de' Barbari und die Konstruktion einer Künstlerpersönlichkeit," in *Die Biographie—Mode oder Universalie? Zu Geschichte und Konzept Gattung in der Kunstgeschichte*, ed. Beate Böckem, Olaf Peters, and Barbara Schellewald (Berlin: De Gruyter, 2016), 49–60, esp. 55.

5 Böckem, "Die Frage," 56.

6 Barbara Marx, "Wandering Objects, Migrating Artists: The Appropriation of Italian Renaissance Art by German Courts in the Sixteenth Century," in *Cultural Exchange in Early Modern Europe*, ed. Herman Roodenburg, vol. 4, *Forging European Identities, 1400–1700* (Cambridge: Cambridge University Press, 2006–7), 182.

7 See Levenson, "Jacopo de' Barbari," 11–23; and Böckem, *Jacopo de' Barbari*, 160–76.

8 For descriptions of the castle in a 1508 publication by a Wittenberg city scribe, Andreas Meinhard, see Levenson, "Jacopo de' Barbari," 16–17; Ingetraut Ludolphy, *Friedrich der Weise: Kurfürst von Sachsen, 1463–1525* (Göttingen: Vandenhoeck and Ruprecht, 1984), 121–23. Peter Strieder, however, has argued that Meinhard's accounts are a literary invention. See Peter Strieder, "Ein Traum von Göttern und Heroen: Andreas Meinhardis Dialog über die Schönheit und den Ruhm der hochberühmten Stadt Albioris, gemeinhin Wittenberg gennant," *Anzeiger des germanischen Nationalmuseum* (2005): 25–34.

9 Geldenhouwer does not specify exactly when this occurred.

10 On Cranach the Elder and de' Barbari at the Saxon Court, see Böckem, *Jacopo de' Barbari*, 226–43; and Matthias Müller, "Im Wettstreit mit Apelles: Hofkünstler als Akteure und Rezepteure im Austausch- und Konkurrenzverhältnis europäischer Höfe zu Beginn der Frühen Neuzeit," in *Vorbild, Austausch, Konkurrenz: Höfe und Residenzen in der gegenseitigen Wahrnehmung*, ed. Werner Paravicini and Jörg Wettlaufer (Ostfildern: J. Thorbecke, 2010), 173–91, esp. 185–91.

11 The letter is believed to have been written between November 1500 and August 1501, when Frederick was attending the Nuremberg Reichsregiment. For de' Barbari's text, see Levenson, "Jacopo de' Barbari," 342–45; and Böckem, *Jacopo de' Barbari*, 148–68.

12 Jeffrey Chipps Smith, *Dürer* (London: Phaidon, 2012), 132.

13 See Levenson, "Jacopo de' Barbari," 118–36; Panofsky, "Dürers Darstellungen"; Erwin Panofsky, *The Life and Art of Albrecht Dürer*, 8th ed. (Princeton, NJ: Princeton University Press, 1995), 80–87.

14 Hans Rupprich, ed., *Albrecht Dürer: Der schriftliche Nachlasse*, 3 vols. (Berlin: Deutschen Verein für Kunstwissenschaft, 1956–69), 1:101–4, nr. 45 and nr. 47.

15 Panofsky, *The Life and Art of Albrecht Dürer*, 261; Rupprich, *Albrecht Dürer*, 1:103–4, nr. 47; and William Martin Conway, *The Writings of Albrecht Dürer* (New York: Philosophical Library, 1958), 165.

16 Dürer also adopted de' Barbari's new theoretical stance on painting and his competitive strategies of artistic advancement and self-fashioning. See Ulrich Pfisterer, "The Muses' Grief: Jacopo de' Barbari on Painting, Poetry and Cultural Transfer in the North," in *The Muses and Their Afterlife in Post-classical Europe*, ed. Kathleen W. Christian, Clare E. L. Guest, and Claudia Wedepohl (London: Warburg Institute, 2014), 75–101.

17 In Mechelen, Dürer wrote on August 6, 1521, that Margaret of Austria had promised the *büchlein* to her court painter, Bernard van Orley (ca. 1488–1541). See Rupprich, *Albrecht Dürer*, 1:173; Levenson, "Jacopo de' Barbari," 41; Conway, *The Writings of Albrecht Dürer*, 121; and Smith, *Dürer*, 318.

18 Maryan Ainsworth, "Observations concerning Gossart's Working Methods," in *Man, Myth, and Sensual Pleasures: Jan Gossart's Renaissance. The Complete Works*, exhib. cat., ed. Ainsworth (New York: Metropolitan Museum of Art, 2010), 69–87, esp. 80–81.

19 See Levenson, "Jacopo de' Barbari," 117–67. On de' Barbari's influence on Gossart, see Larry Silver, "'Figure Nude, Historie e Poesie': Jan Gossaert and the Renaissance Nude in the Netherlands," "Renaissance en reformatie en de kunst in de Noordelijke Nederlanden," special issue, *Nederlands Kunsthistorisch Jaarboek (nkj) / Netherlands Yearbook for History of Art* 37 (1986): 1–40, esp. 18, 29; and Stijn Alsteens, "Gossart as a Draftsman," in Ainsworth, *Man, Myth, and Sensual Pleasures*, 89–103, esp. 92. On Kulmbach, see Böckem, "Die Frage," 51; and Levenson, "Jacopo de' Barbari," 42–43. It is noteworthy that, as Koerner mentions in passing, at the time when Hans Baldung Grien entered Dürer's workshop around 1503, he would have observed his master preoccupied with constructing the idealized nude, "copying, abstracting, and perfecting classical prototypes" still heavily under the influence of de' Barbari's nudes. See Joseph L. Koerner, *The Moment of Self-Portraiture in German Renaissance Art* (Chicago: University of Chicago Press, 1993), 253.

20 Beate Böckem, "Jacopo de' Barbari: Ein Apelles am Fürstenhof? Die Allianz von Künstler, Humanist und Herrscher im alten Reich," in *Apelles am Fürstenhof: Facetten der Hofkunst um 1500 im alten*

Reich, exhib. cat., ed. Matthias Müller et al. (Berlin: Lucas Verlag, 2010), 22–33, esp. 27–28.

21 Böckem, "Jacopo de' Barbari," 29. About the significance of humanistic conceits of comparing Renaissance artists with ancient Greeks described by such authors as Pliny the Elder, Plutarch, and Strabo, see Böckem, "Jacopo de' Barbari," 23–27; Müller, "Im Wettstreit"; and Smith, *Dürer*, 80–81.

22 About various praises of Dürer as Apelles by such humanists as Conrad Celtis, Erasmus, and Joachim Camerarius, see Smith, *Dürer*, 164, 227.

23 Martin Warnke, *The Court Artist: On the Ancestry of the Modern Art*, trans. David McLintock (Cambridge: Cambridge University Press, 1993). See also Müller, "Im Wettstreit."

24 Warnke, *The Court Artist*, xiii.

25 Warnke, *The Court Artist*, xvii.

26 See Müller, "Im Wettstreit," 185–91.

27 For more information about Maximilian's wish to assert his imperial genealogy and power above other rulers by deploying printed materials, see Larry Silver, *Marketing Maximilian: The Visual Ideology of a Holy Roman Emperor* (Princeton, NJ: Princeton University Press, 2008). On the humanism and German nationalism influencing the broader visions for Maximilian, see chap. 1, esp. 19–26.

28 Marx, "Wandering Objects," 178–226, esp. 187; Silver, *Marketing Maximilian*, 230–34; and Ludolphy, *Friedrich der Weise*, 137ff. About the competitions between Maximilian and Frederick, see also Larry Silver, "Civic Courtship: Albrecht Dürer, the Saxon Duke, and the Emperor," in *The Essential Dürer*, ed. Silver and Jeffrey Chipps Smith (Philadelphia: University of Pennsylvania Press, 2010), 130–48.

29 Concerning Margaret's courtly patronage, see Dagmar Eichberger and Lisa Beaven, "Family Members and Political Allies: The Portrait Collection of Margaret of Austria," *Art Bulletin* 77, no. 2 (1995): 225–48.

30 Rupprich, *Albrecht Dürer*, 1:43–45, nr. 2; Conway, *The Writings of Albrecht Dürer*, 48–49; and Smith, *Dürer*, 163.

31 Michael Baxandall, *The Limewood Sculptors of Renaissance Germany* (New Haven, CT: Yale University Press, 1980), 135–42.

II

The *View* as a Reflection of Venice and Venetian Life

Richard Goy

Toward the Perfect City

Urban Development in the Quattrocento

JACOPO DE' BARBARI'S *VIEW OF VENICE* represents Venice at the end of a remarkable century of financial and political success, physical growth, urban improvements, and construction activity. In particular, it records the numerous fine new palazzi that epitomize this unique era of wealth and expansion. As the Venetian Republic grew and matured, it gathered around it a collection of Myths (capitalization intentional) to explain the reasons for its legendary peace, stability, and longevity. The Myths reached an "apotheosis" in the sixteenth century, when most of the great events of the annual calendar—Ascension Day, St. Mark's Day, and so on—reached their peak of refinement and expression (and expense). One fundamental strand of these Myths was that of the city's own seemingly miraculous foundation. Legend

12

relates that Mark the Evangelist, sailing in the Adriatic, found himself in the lagoon when a storm arose suddenly, and he was forced to make landfall on one of the islands of the Realtine archipelago. As he landed, he received a vision from an angel, who spoke the equally legendary words prophesying that the site of his safe landing would become a great city: "Pax tibi Marce, evangelista meus . . ."[1]

Richard Goy

The essential point is that the site was divinely chosen, and this divine choice itself gave rise to the city that perforce was to be as unique as its physical context. It was an equally unique practical challenge, but it was ordained by God, and thus the city's establishment and its flourishing development were a direct expression of divine will, as mediated by His Evangelist. This emergent Republic was also to be a true bastion of Christianity, untainted by any classical, pagan associations.[2] This essay considers some of the practical ways in which that vision was fulfilled during the course of the Quattrocento, culminating in Marin Sanudo's written description and de' Barbari's graphic one.

It is clear from the laudations of visitors, such as Petrarch and Philippe de Commynes, as well as natives such as Sanudo, that the entire city was regarded as a single unified entity or organism, an *urbs* that could be perfected in a manner different from any other city in Europe. Although the site had been ordained from above, we should not forget that other cities, too, claimed divine origins, most importantly Rome itself, the *mons vaticanus* being the literal rock on which the Petrine church was to be built.[3] The concept of a perfectible whole derives generally from the Marcian legend and its unique site. More specifically, though, it was also defined and circumscribed by Nature; God and Nature thus acted together to identify one of His most glorious creations. All other cities (so goes the myth) were established and built by humans, and were all notably deficient in this specific deistic creation process.[4]

The earliest surviving illustration of the city is that of the much-traveled Franciscan friar Paolino da Venezia in the little hand-colored plan forming part of his "Compendium," dated 1346, although probably made a little earlier (fig. 12.1).[5] This faded little plan was given new life four centuries later, in 1781, when it was transcribed by Tommaso Temanza, as an illustration to his essay on Paolino.[6] Paolino had claimed that his plan was a copy of a representation of the city as it had appeared in 1150, two centuries earlier. As Temanza himself notes, this was probably true, as the plan depicts several features that were highly anachronistic in 1346. They include the Arsenal,

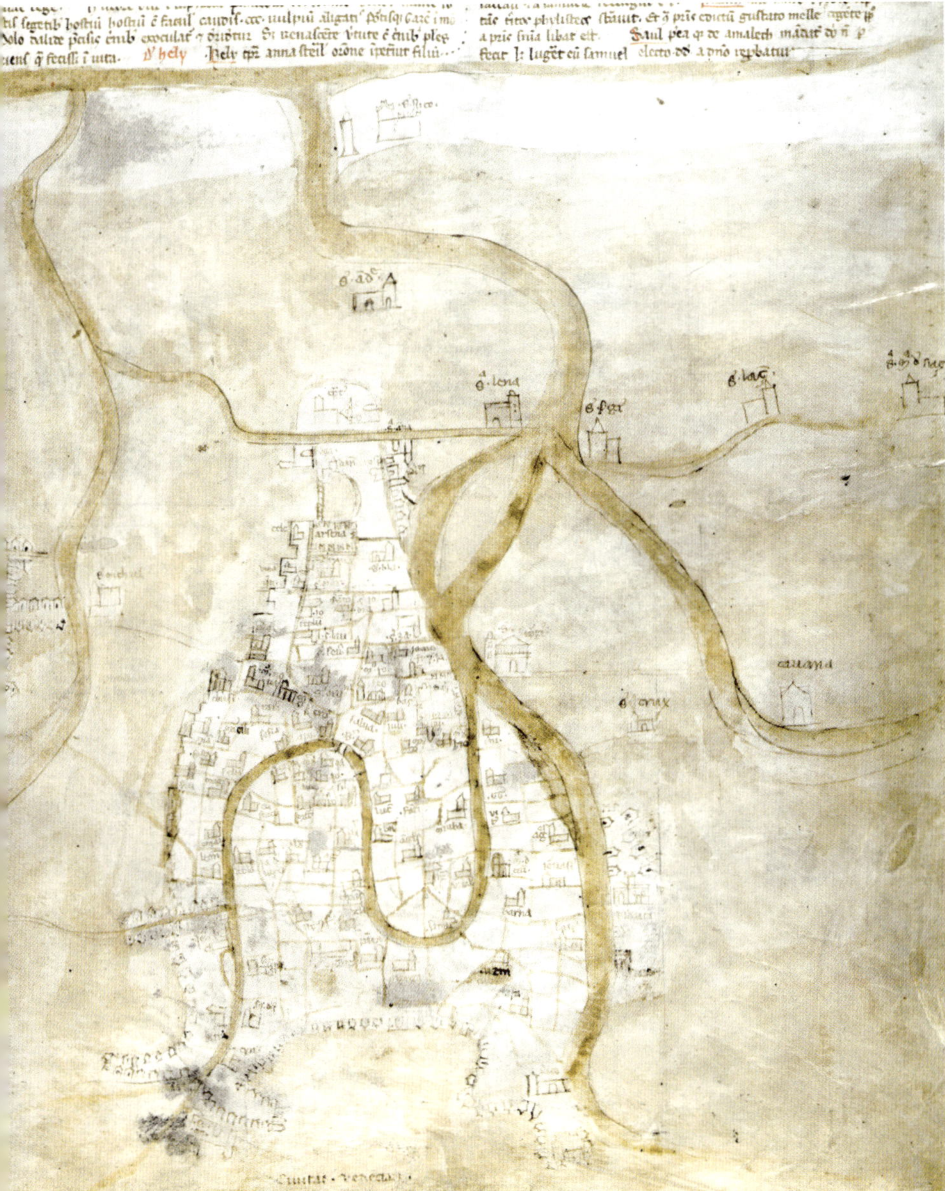

12.1

Fra Paolino da Venezia, *Civitas venetiarum*, ca. 1346. Biblioteca Nazionale Marciana, Venice.

shown solely as the small rectangular fortified basin of the Darsena Vecchia, which had already been substantially increased in size by 1346, as visualized in the *View*; and the enclosure of the Marcian area by crenelated walls, all long gone by 1500. By 1346, the new Molo wing of the Palazzo Ducale was also under construction.

Paolino's plan, however, has a more profound significance that transcends individual details. First, it is a true zenithal plan, rather than the aerial perspectives of de' Barbari and his successors. The city is depicted as a compact, well-defined organism. But the real point is this: Paolino is showing us the city firmly located in its unique context, defined and circumscribed by the lagoon waters, all accentuated with a color wash. He is acutely aware of the importance not just of the surface of those gray-blue waters but also of the deepwater channels beneath them that made the city's site capable of development as a great maritime entrepôt. All the main channels surrounding the city are boldly delineated.

Richard Goy

Despite its significance, however, Paolino's little plan apparently remained sui generis for a century, until the circulation of the two tiny woodcuts of Werner Rolewinck (1479 and 1480–85), and then the much more impressive panorama of Erhard Reuwich, published in Mainz in 1486 (fig. I.2).[7] Their viewpoint (like that of the *View*) is somewhere above the campanile of San Giorgio Maggiore, with a sweeping panorama from Santa Marta in the west to Sant'Antonio in the east. Much of the drawn information is stylized and oversimplified, but again, there is great emphasis on the physical context of the city, with the foreground liberally scattered with vessels of every type and size. Here again, the city's unique context is fully appreciated and expressed.

The perfectible whole was certainly what de' Barbari illustrated shortly after Reuwich's panorama and Sanudo's written laudation (*Laus urbis venetae*, 1493), with the proud, bold title *Venetie MD* at the top.[8] This is the triumphant midmillennial city, frozen, at least for now, in time and space—a model to be appreciated as a whole as well as in its numerous component parts. And to the extent that the city was perceived as perfectible, then each nobleman who built a fine new palazzo on the Grand Canal was taking the city, his city, another step toward this still rather ill-defined condition of urban perfection. We can identify a strong sense of civic and national pride, equally prominent in Sanudo's words. The noble who built one of the many new Gothic palaces of the later Quattrocento was not only glorifying the city of which he was a proud and patriotic citizen but was also maximizing his own investment in very costly real estate: an ideal Venetian combination, therefore, of patriotic pride, practical necessity, and fiscal acumen. And there was indeed a great wave of new palace building, from Ca' Foscari (after 1453), through Palazzo Loredan dell'Ambasciatore (ca. 1461) to Palazzi Giovanelli, Pisani Moretta, and Giustinian (San Moisè), all in the 1470s and 1480s.

Looking more closely at Sanudo's laudation, Venetian palaces, he states, were all built "a modo nostro"—in our own manner, and "not the way they build elsewhere."[9] There is a clear sense of specificity here, of local identity and pride. The unwritten implication is that "we do these things better." Sanudo's *modo nostro* was a direct result of physical necessity in the lagunar context, as he had explained a little earlier. His fine palazzi were built on subterranean forests of timber piles, driven into the stiff *caranto* clay: "et si fa sora palli con gran inzegno le fondamente in acqua" (and the foundations are built with great ingenuity on top of timber piles).[10] His clear message is that the whole city is built by the resourcefulness, determination, and ingenuity of the Venetian people, in a physical environment that most others would consider impossible. Since these foundations are invisible, the palazzi rise, miraculously, straight out of the water. It was almost as if those Venetians were defying the very rules of nature and gravity itself. Let us now review the way in which the city had developed over the century before de' Barbari and Sanudo.

By 1400, the city's form had already reached a fairly advanced stage of maturity. The principal characteristics of development over the Quattrocento were two- or threefold. One was construction on undeveloped or underdeveloped sites, generally to higher densities, three or four stories being the new norm. Another was to increase density by adding further stories onto existing buildings. Two documented examples are Palazzo Sagredo at Santa Sofia and Palazzo Contarini "del Bovolo," both of which had extra stories added.[11] And a third was the intensification of the networks of the city's communications systems, canals, calli, fondamente, and campi. Much of this activity was the result of increased population, as well as wealth. After the final war with Genoa (1379–81), Venice's population was probably around 80,000. Despite setbacks from recurrent plagues and conflicts, it increased steadily to about 102,000 by 1509. This increase (25 percent over the century) is significant when we consider the virtually finite form of the city and its limits.[12]

By 1500, therefore, with the notable exception of the outer fringes (to which I will return), the urban form was nearly fully matured. Almost all the campi shown by de' Barbari have maintained their size and shape down to the present day, the largest single difference being the loss of a number of parish churches, mostly in the post-Napoleonic era.[13] What de' Barbari shows us, therefore, is an almost perfected whole. Future perfectibility was also to take only two or three forms. The first was the question of the perimeter, which basically involved reclamation, thereby increasing the city's physical size and providing new land for development. The second was the further replacement or renovation, over time, of earlier buildings with updated ones, often to even higher densities,[14] and, in the Cinquecento, in a new architectural language. The third, chronologically the last, was the radical modernization programs of the late eighteenth and nineteenth centuries, outside the purview of this study.[15]

Throughout the Quattrocento, much of the city's perimeter was undefined and far from perfect. Although in some zones it terminated with walls and fences, enclosing gardens, orchards, and allotments, elsewhere the city's fringe simply petered out into mudbanks and marshes. There were several such zones, and one of the largest was to the northwest, where the reclamations of the Tereni Nuovi were to take place at the end of the Quattrocento (fig. 12.2).[16] This extensive area of marsh and mudflats extended northward from the backs of the buildings on Rio del Anzolo Rafael (Angelo Raffaele) as far as the back of the monastic house of Santa Croce, and the houses on the south bank of the Grand Canal at San Simon Piccolo. This marsh had formerly extended considerably farther east, too, in the zone once known as the Lago Badoer; but this eastern zone had now long been reclaimed, and the vast Frari church and its extensive monastic buildings occupied much of the site.[17]

Similarly marshy, undefined conditions remained elsewhere, too: between Sant'Anna and Sant'Antonio, for example, in eastern Castello; and along the southern shores of the Giudecca, prominently shown by de' Barbari.[18] These were all the most remote districts from the city center, of course; they thus had the lowest land values and hence generated the least motivation by the Republic or some enterprising private investor to develop. However, the collective impression given by these muddy, undeveloped fringes of this most triumphant city was of a perfectible *urbs*, even if by no means yet perfected. That perfection was arguably to come with two major reclamation programs in the next century: the Tereni Nuovi of Santa Maria Maggiore; and the Fondamente Nove along the north shore, a project with which the doge, Andrea Gritti, was closely associated.[19] The Senate's decision to commence works at the Tereni Nuovi (November 6, 1494) reads in part: "Serà molto utile a questa città, la qual ha bixogno de dar alozamento al populo cresuto in quella et che per gratia del Onipotente Dio cresce et moltiplica per zornata … oltra l'utile.… Serà etiam beleza e ornamento a questa città" (It will be of great use to our city, which has the need to provide housing for the increasing population here, and which by the grace of

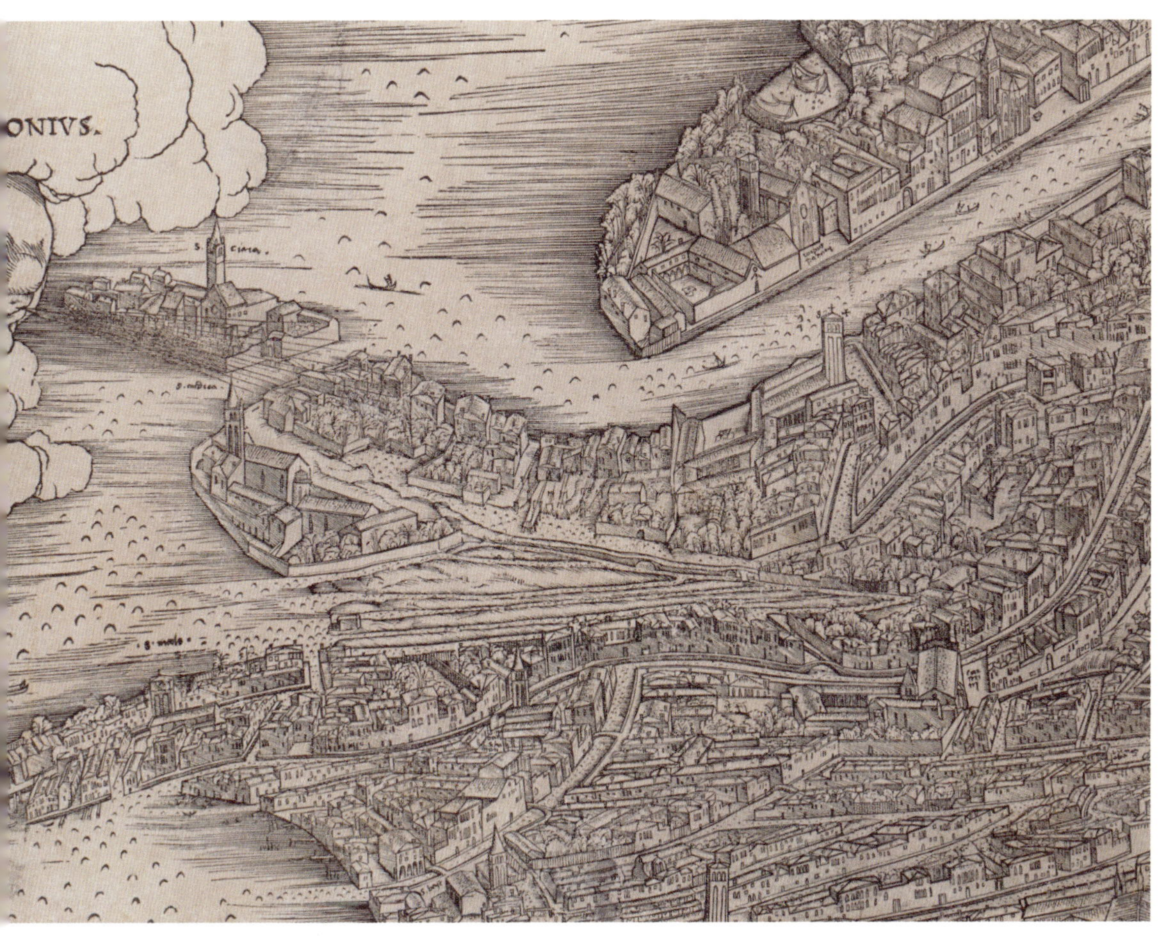

the Omnipotent Lord continues to grow and multiply every day … as well as its practical use.… It will also further beautify and ornament our city).[20]

Practical need was therefore again combined with the desire to enhance and beautify the city. The senators were undoubtedly fully aware that swamps do not present the most favorable first impression to a visitor approaching from the *terraferma* by water. By 1500, the new islands seem to have been at least partially formed out of material excavated from the city's canals, although no housing has yet appeared. The first major new "outpost" was to be Santa Maria Maggiore itself, in 1504.[21]

We can conclude, therefore, that, to the Republic, future perfectibility contained within it two or three major strands. The first was purely practical and pragmatic: reclamation of new land for urban development, a ra-

12.2

Detail of the Tereni Nuovi from Jacopo de' Barbari, *View of Venice*, ca. 1497–1500.

tional, economically driven activity. The second, closely linked, was to ease pressure on the highly congested city center. The new land could either be occupied by the developers themselves or rented to others (mostly the latter). The third strand is more abstract: the very act of reclamation, of redefining the city's perimeter, represented a new stage in the Republic's power over the natural environment. In much the same way that driving timber piles into the clay for a new palazzo represented Venetian ingenuity, resourcefulness, and strength of will, so reclamation reinforced the fact that the Venetians were in overall command and control of their destiny, unconstrained by the accidental vagaries of the natural context. Indeed, some of this command and control was proven before the century's end, by the extensive reclamations along the north shore between La Celestia and Le Vergini to provide new space for a major expansion of the Arsenal, with the great new Darsena Novissima (plate 6). By 1500, it had been enclosed, although it was not to be fully developed for many decades.[22]

Urban improvements during the Quattrocento took several other forms as well. For example, a notorious drought in the winter of 1425–26 resulted in the construction of thirty new public wells to ensure adequate future supplies of potable water.[23] The paving of streets and campi, though, another highly symbolic (and practical) "civilizing" process, was to be an extremely protracted affair, as a glance at de' Barbari's *View* indicates. Even by 1500, some campi were paved only in a small area around the wellhead, while many had no paving at all. Piazza San Marco itself was a rare exception, as, too, was Campo San Polo, also paved in its entirety, mainly because it was the site of a weekly market (fig. 12.3). Another notable early exception to the lack of street paving was the Mercerie (plate 5); a deliberation in the Maggior Consiglio as early as 1271 not only ordered the paving of the whole length of the Mercerie, from the Piazza to Rialto, but also ordered the removal of *tettoie* (awnings or temporary roofs) and the provision of *grondaie* (rainwater gutters and downpipes) to the buildings flanking the street, in an effort to control the discharge of rainwater. This directly reflected an appreciation of the street's critical commercial importance. The whole operation had a budget of 3,000 lire.[24]

Another program of later Quattrocento improvements was the gradual replacement of timber bridges with new ones in brick and stone. A characteristic request by Angelo Trevisan claimed that the proposed rebuilding of his own private bridge at San Stae would nevertheless also be *ad ornamentum civitatis* (for the beautification of the city). And the wealthy and

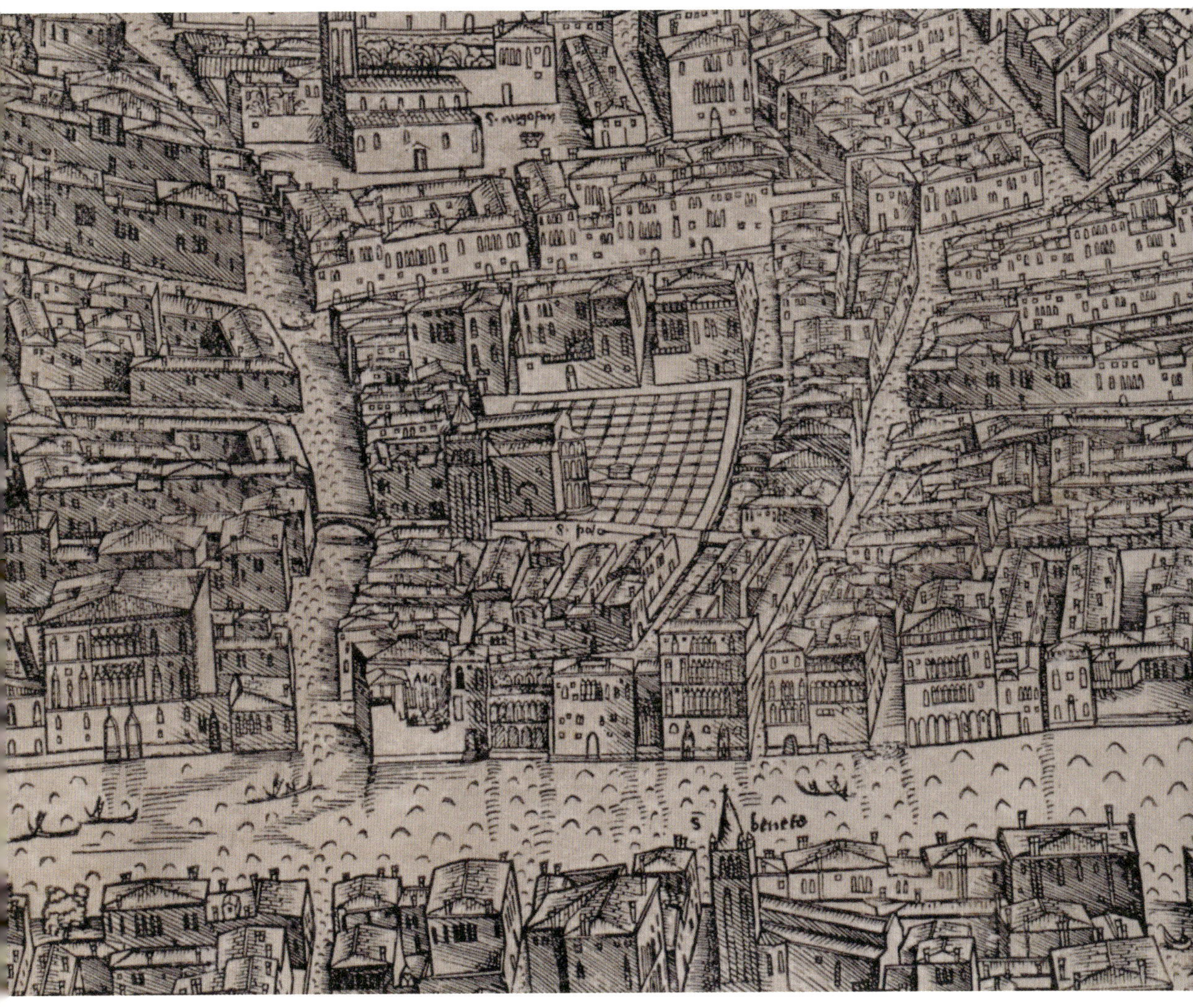

influential Triadan Gritti, who owned the imposing palazzo (today Gritti Badoer) on Campo de la Bragora, requested that all the bridges in Bragora should be refaced. He managed to persuade the Collegio that the cost of this "beautification" should be borne by the parishioners themselves, which probably made him fairly unpopular. In fact, in 1488, the Provveditori di Comun embarked on a much wider program of bridge replacement, paid for from public funds.[25]

To sum up, there was a steady process of urban development, improvement, and "refinement" through much of the Quattrocento, probably reaching a peak, in terms of construction activity at least, in the last two or three decades of the century.[26] It is no coincidence that the Republic was at peace for much of this period; nor is it a coincidence that maritime trade was also flourishing, generating healthy profits for the nobles involved. All of this activity increased the splendor and civilized nature of the metropolis, including its embellishment with grand palaces. This plethora of urban improvement and construction activity is captured comprehensively and in extraordinary detail in de' Barbari's unique record of the "triumphant city." The perfectible *urbs* was indeed a good deal more perfect in 1500, as visualized in the *View*, than it had been in 1400. Already in 1400, Venice was a splendid city, but there was a great deal more marble, Istrian stone, and Verona *broccatello* on the Grand Canal in 1500 than there had been a century earlier. Even greater splendor was to come in the following century.

Richard Goy

NOTES

1 David Rosand, *Myths of Venice: The Figuration of a State* (Chapel Hill: University of North Carolina Press, 2001), 51; Iain Fenlon, *The Ceremonial City: History, Memory and Myth in Renaissance Venice* (New Haven, CT: Yale University Press, 2007), 9–10; Edward Muir, *Civic Ritual in Renaissance Venice* (Princeton, NJ: Princeton University Press, 1981), 79. There is no documentary evidence for this legend, and no evidence in the lagoon for the development of a cult of Saint Mark until several centuries later. The earliest written account seems to be that of Paul the Deacon, ca. 783–86 CE, claiming that Mark founded a Christian church at Aquileia.

2 Rome's own founding myth, in which two brothers were suckled by a she-wolf, and in which one brother later murders the other, was widely invoked in Venice as an unflattering comparison.

3 There is evidence of human settlement on the Palatine and Capitoline Hills from the tenth century BCE; Peter himself is said to have been the first bishop of the city, where he was martyred in ca. 64 CE.

4 Not only were all other cities defined by man, but their urban form was also often "diluted" by considerable development in the *borghi* beyond the walls; see esp. Quattrocento views of Florence, notably the "Berlin" view of around 1470. The view is published in Attilio Mori

and Giuseppe Boffito, eds., *Firenze nelle vedute e piante: Studio storico, topografico e cartografico*, but a fascimile reprint of that of 1926. See also further discussion in Élisabeth Crouzet-Pavan, "Politica e pratiche dell'habitat nell'epoca gotica a Venezia," in *L'architettura gotica veneziana: Atti del Convegno internazionale di studio, Venezia, 27–29 novembre 1996*, ed. Francesco Valcanover and Wolfgang Wolters (Venice: Istituto Veneto di Scienze Lettere ed Arti, 2000), 235–41.

5 Biblioteca Marciana Venezia (BMV), ms. Lat. Zan., 399. Paolino had a remarkably colorful life; for some highlights, see Patricia Fortini Brown, *Venice and Antiquity: The Venetian Sense of the Past* (New Haven, CT: Yale University Press, 1996), 55. Among his eminent friends and colleagues were Petrarch, Boccaccio, and Giotto.

6 Tommaso Temanza, *Antica pianta dell'inclita città di Venezia*, ed. Ugo Stefanutti, facsimile of the 1781 ed. (Bologna: Sala Bolognese, 1977).

7 Giocondo Cassini, *Piante e veduta prospettiche di Venezia, 1479–1855* (Venice: Stamperia di Venezia, 1971), 26, item 2 (Museo Civico Correr, Venezia). For the two tiny woodcuts of Werner Rolewinck, see Cassini, *Piante e veduta*, 25, item 1 (BNM).

8 Cassini, *Piante e veduta*, 30–33, item 5. The bibliography on de' Barbari is now extensive. See esp. the references in Ennio Concina, *Tempo Novo: Vene-*

zia e il quattrocento (Venice: Marsilio, 2006), 205n311. Among the prominent nobles who supported the enterprise were Antonio Tron, deputy responsible for the new Torre dell'Orologio on the Piazza; Pietro Contarini, *provveditore sopra la fabbrica* of the Palazzo Ducale; and Giovanni Morosini, *provveditore* of the Arsenale. All were powerful figures in shaping the *renovatio urbis*. Concina, *Tempo Novo*, 204–5.

9 Marin Sanudo the Younger, *Laus urbis venetae* in *De origine, situ et magistratibus urbis Venetae ovvero la città di Venezia, 1493–1530*, ed. Angela Caracciolo Aricò (Milan: Cisalpino–La Goliardica, 1980), 21.

10 Sanudo, *Laus urbis venetae*, 20.

11 For Palazzo Sagredo, see Jan-Christoph Rössler, *I palazzi veneziani: Storia, architettura, restauri* (Venice: Scripta, 2010), 26, 35n19, 39n93, 62, 95, 128. For Palazzo Contarini, see Rössler, *I palazzi veneziani*, 190–95.

12 Concina, *Tempo Novo*, 122, citing Daniel Herlihy, "The Population of Verona in the First Century of Venetian Rule," in *Renaissance Venice*, ed. John R. Hale (London: Faber and Faber, 1974), 117n9–11. Frederic C. Lane, in *Venice: A Maritime Republic* (Baltimore, MD: Johns Hopkins University Press, 1973), 18–19, states that "in 1348, shortly after Venice and the other largest cities of medieval Europe topped 100,000, they were cut back by the Black Death." At

its peak, the outbreak of 1478 was kill-
ing 240 people a day in the city. Sanudo
claimed that the city's population was
150,000 around the end of the century;
if correct, this represents a very notable
increase indeed.

13 For a full survey, see Elena Bassi,
*Tracce di chiese distrutte: Ricostruzioni
dai disegni di Antonio Visentini* (Venice: Istituto Veneto di Scienze Lettere
ed Arti, 1997). See also Alvise Zorzi,
Venezia scomparsa (Milan: Electa, 1971),
200–263.

14 The pattern of building additional
storeys continued into later centuries.
See, for example, Palazzo Pisani Moretta
and Palazzo Corner Contarini dei Cavalli.

15 See, for example, Zorzi, *Venezia scomparsa*, 35.

16 For a detailed discussion of the highly
protracted process of developing the
Tereni Nuovi, see Giorgio Gianighian
and Paolina Pavanini, *Dietro i palazzi:
Tre secoli di architettura minore a Venezia, 1492–1803* (Venice: Arsenale, 1984),
49–57.

17 Much of this zone is depicted by de'
Barbari in a highly compressed manner,
partly as a result of distortions elsewhere,
for example, eastern Castello, which is
given excessive prominence. However,
this compression may also be the result of the perception that the zone was
peripheral, marshy, and as yet undeveloped—i.e., that hardly anyone lived there

yet. The Lago Badoer was drained after
1234, when the Badoer family donated
the site to the Franciscan Friars Minor.
Their first church was begun in 1250 but
was quickly found to be far too small. The
present, much larger church was begun
in 1323 but was not completed until early
in the following century: see Deborah
Howard and Carlo Corsato, eds., *Santa
Maria Gloriosa dei Frari: Immagini di
Devozione, Spazi della Fede / Devotional
Spaces, Images of Piety* (Padua: Centro
Studi Antoniani, 2015), ix–xi.

18 For the proposed reclamations in
eastern Castello after 1471, adjacent
to Sant'Antonio and San Domenico,
see Concina, *Tempo Novo*, 124–25. For
those at the other end of the city, around
Sant'Andrea della Zirada, see Concina,
Tempo Novo, 125. The Zattere, along the
southern edge of Dorsoduro, were begun
following a decree of February 8, 1520,
and were to extend from Santa Marta to
the Dogana da Mar. A further decree of
the Consiglio dei Dieci (July 23, 1541)
ordered that all timber should hence-
forth be brought ashore here at Santo
Spirito, rather than the north shore, after which date the Zattere acquired its
definitive name (*zattere* means "rafts of
timber"). Giuseppe Tassini, *Curiosità
veneziane*, 4th ed. (1887; repr., Venice:
Filippi, 1964), 704–5.

19 Manfredo Tafuri, *Venice and the Renaissance* (Cambridge, MA: MIT Press,
1989), 184–90. The reclamation of the
Tereni Nuovi was first proposed by the

Savi alle Acque in 1494. Reclamation was to make use of spoil obtained from the dredging of the city's canals. See also Concina, *Tempo Novo*, 125–26, with archive references. See, for example, ASVe, Senato, Terra, reg. 13, cc. 21v–22r, October 20, 1497.

20 Tafuri, *Venice and the Renaissance*, 126; ASVe, Senato, Terra, reg. 12, c. 72r (November 6, 1494), and cc. 84v–86v (February 3, 1495).

21 The reclamations of the Fondamente Nove were rather different in character from the Tereni Nuovi, and a number of influential nobles were involved in promoting the project. See Tafuri, *Venice and the Renaissance*, 184–91.

22 De' Barbari clearly shows the walls of the recently enclosed Darsena Novissima, although it was not yet developed with *tese* (shipbuilding sheds). See Ennio Concina, *L'Arsenale della Repubblica di Venezia* (Milan: Electa, 1984), 74, with archive references.

23 Concina, *Tempo Novo*, 139; see also Marin Sanudo the Younger, *Vite dei dogi*, ed. Giovanni Monticolo (Città di Castello: Stamperia di Scipione Lapi, 1906), 1:53.

24 Cited by Crouzet-Pavan in "Politica e pratiche," 237; from ASVe, Avogadori di Comun, Delib. "Bifrons," 1, c. 38r. However, a later iteration of these same requirements (in 1340) suggests that it was not so easy to enforce these local laws and keep such illegal structures under control. See ASVe, Compilazione Leggi, b. 357, c. 354r and v. Some years after the decree ordering the paving of the Mercerie, a further ordinance of 1287 banned horses from the street on the grounds that it was too congested and potentially dangerous to pedestrians. This may have marked the beginning of the general decline in their use. Other than the Piazza and Campo San Polo, the only other campi paved in whole or in part by 1500 were those of SS Giovanni e Paolo, San Zaccaria, Sant'Angelo, and the Frari. The cost of paving the Mercerie equates to 30,000 ducats, when one ducat per week was the daily wage of a building craftsman.

25 Concina, *Tempo Novo*, 131, with references. See, for example, ASVe, Collegio, Notatorio, 11, c. 119v, October 4, 1472. It seems likely that the program of reconstruction of bridges, often by replacing flat timber ones with arched bridges in brick and stone, was another reason for the slow decline of the use of horses in the later Quattrocento. Donatella Calabi and Paolo Morachiello, *Rialto le fabbriche e il ponte* (Turin: Einaudi, 1997), 186, with references.

26 I am currently engaged in a reevaluation of the later Gothic palazzi, under the working title "Venetian Gothic: Civil Architecture and Identity in a Late Medieval Republic, c. 1380–1500."

Patricia Fortini Brown

The Wellhead as an Amenity
of Venetian Urban Space

13 WHEN WE EXAMINE Jacopo de' Barbari's *View of Venice*, we think of water: a city in the sea, a group of islands, surrounded by water. Yet therein lies a paradox. As the Venetian diarist Marin Sanudo famously wrote, "Venice is in the water and has no water."[1] Before the modern era, the city had no source of fresh water other than the rain from heaven or barges from the mainland. The Venetians learned early on how to capture this precious natural resource by devising an ingenious system of water recovery, with rainwater collected in cisterns hidden beneath almost every campo, cloister, and courtyard in the city. Each was topped by a *vera da pozzo*, or wellhead.[2]

During periods of drought, when insufficient rain fell to meet the city's needs, water workers called *acquaroli* would row large flat-bottomed barges to Lizzafusina, on the mainland at the edge of the lagoon. There they loaded potable water from the Brenta River into their barges by means of a water-wheel. Returning to Venice, the *acquaroli* made their rounds throughout the city and poured river water into the wellheads or sold it directly.[3] The purity of the public cisterns was protected by the authorities. The wells had wooden or metal covers, locked at night and opened every morning by the parish priest or his representative at the ringing of the church bells.[4]

De' Barbari depicts no fewer than fifty-seven wellheads in Venice, the Giudecca, and Murano. Most have been replaced or removed altogether, but twenty still seem to be in place. Campo San Giacomo dall'Orio is a case in point. The two wellheads depicted by de' Barbari, which date from the fourteenth and fifteenth centuries, are still there (figs. 13.1–13.2). A third fourteenth-century wellhead, near the campanile on the opposite side of the church, also remains but is not visible in his print.[5]

A site of encounter, the wellhead was a place not only to fetch water but also to socialize with the neighbors. As such, it was arguably the most important piece of sculpture in the everyday life of Venetians in de' Barbari's Venice. As inscribed on the public wellhead in Campo San Leonardo, it was "for the convenience of the people as well as an ornament of the city."[6] Although no longer in use, wellheads remain distinctively Venetian features of the urban fabric. As we walk through the winding streets of Venice, we still encounter an astonishing variety of wellheads, centerpieces of nearly every public campo and private courtyard. Two hundred fifty-six public wellheads remain in Venice and the other lagoon islands, and roughly another 2,250 in private spaces. During the Renaissance, there were some 7,000 all told.[7]

Since Venice had no stone of its own, all the wellhead material had to be boated in from elsewhere. Venetians were masters at repurposing antique remains, and early on, the archaeological wellhead was made from genuine Roman or Greek *spolia*.[8] The hollowed-out shaft of a Corinthian column, probably brought in from the mainland near Aquileia, once capped a cistern in front of the church of Santa Fosca on Torcello.[9]

The earliest surviving purpose-made wellheads are hollowed-out cubes or cylinders of marble or limestone and date to the eighth to the tenth century, the Carolingian period, when Venice embraced Byzantium.[10] A handsome example, once in Murano, features one of the most common decorative motifs: a large cross flanked by stylized leaves and set beneath an arch, an ensemble called the "life-giving cross" in Byzantine texts. It has been suggested that these crosses were apotropaic, ensuring the purity of the water

Detail of Campo San Giacomo dall'Orio from Jacopo de' Barbari, *View of Venice*, ca. 1497–1500.

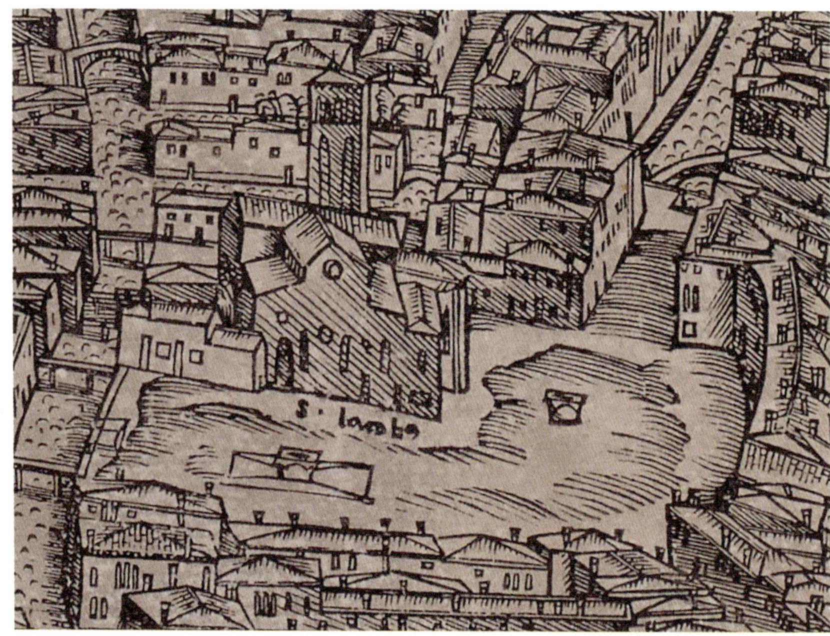

Wellhead, fourteenth century. Pietra d'Istria, 75 × 90 cm. Campo San Giacomo dall'Orio.

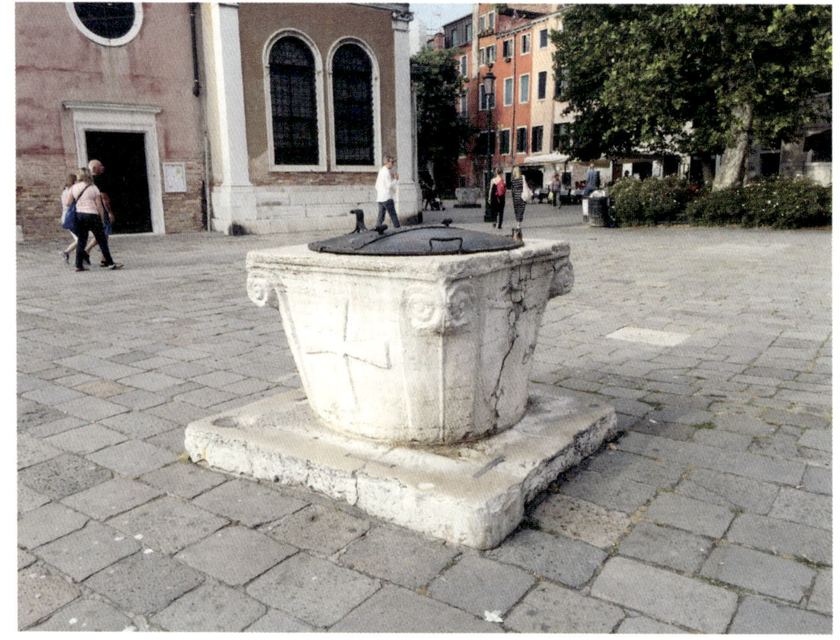

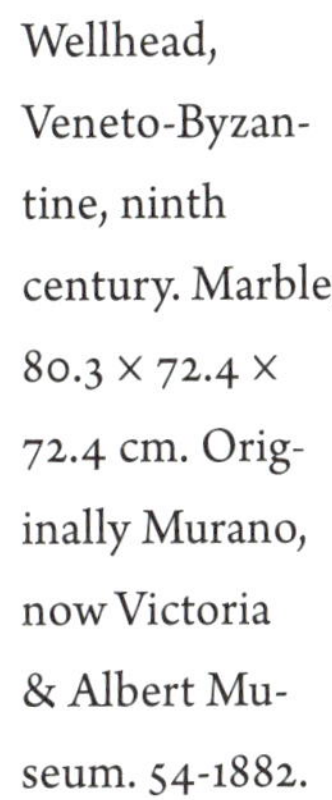

Wellhead, Veneto-Byzantine, ninth century. Marble, 80.3 × 72.4 × 72.4 cm. Originally Murano, now Victoria & Albert Museum. 54-1882.

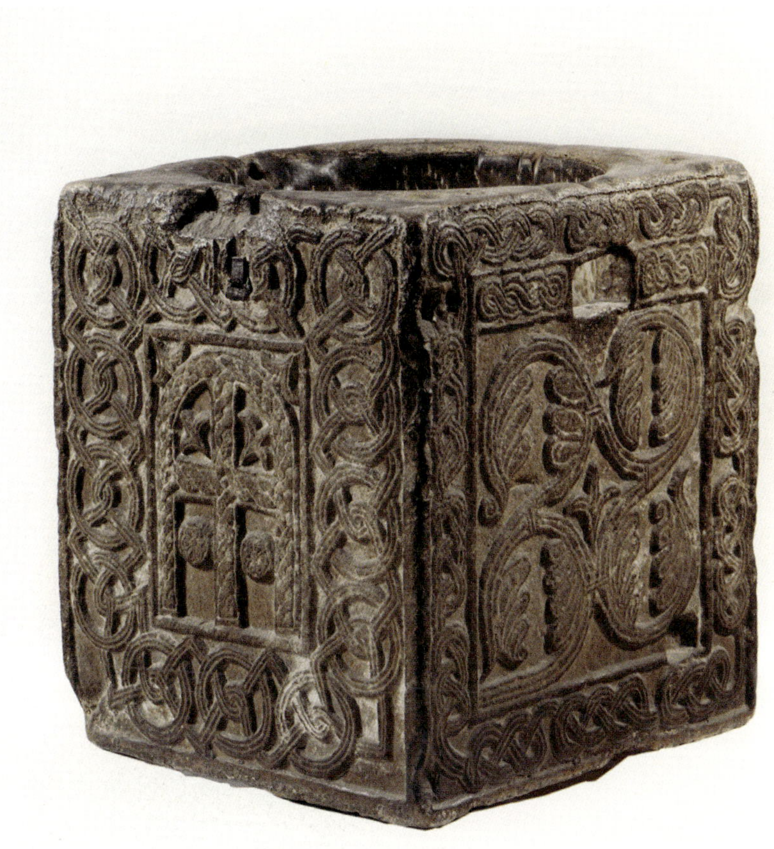

in the cistern and the health of those who drank it. They also had political resonance, linking Venice's salvation to the Byzantine empire (fig. 13.3).[11]

The style and iconography of wellheads mirrored changing tastes in architecture and sculpture in Venice at large. Veneto-Byzantine wellheads of the Romanesque period (eleventh to thirteenth centuries) often combined the cubic and cylindrical shapes of the earlier period with a drum enclosed within a framework of round-headed arches supported by columns. The decorative vocabulary featured an amalgam of Western, Byzantine, and Islamic elements, similar to the *formelle* that one still sees embedded high on the walls of Venetian palaces.[12]

Gothic wellheads inspired by capitals of columns appeared in the fourteenth century, most notably a shape that melded circle and square. Used generically by de' Barbari throughout his *View*, it consists of a slightly tapered

Detail of Campo Do Pozzi, district (*sestiere*) of Castello, from Jacopo de' Barbari, *View of Venice*, ca. 1497–1500.

Wellhead, ca. 1520s–1530s. Pietra d'Istria, 74 × 170 cm. Campo dei Do Pozzi, Castello.

cylindrical drum topped by a squared-off cornice with hanging arches on each side and scooped-out corners (see figs. 13.1 and 13.4). Two such wellheads, still in Corte Nova in Cannaregio where de' Barbari recorded them, may date to 1322, when the city commissioned fifty new public wells.[13] We see the type, often with a variety of subtle differences, in every sestiere in Venice. De' Barbari depicted the Ghetto Nuovo with one of its three wellheads, all dating to the fifteenth century and reworked after 1516 when the Ghetto was established. Each is decorated with a large rosette and a coat of arms emblazoned with three lions rampant, signifying the Lion of Judah.[14] Coats of arms and amphorae were probably the most common decorative motifs on wellheads, whatever their shape, throughout the period.

Wellheads modeled after a classical capital became popular in the late fourteenth century. These might be as simple as the example resembling an Ionic capital in Campo San Giacomo dall'Orio (see fig. 13.2), or as elaborate as Bartolomeo Bon's magnificent piece in red Verona marble inspired by the Corinthian capital in the courtyard of Ca' d'Oro. Dated to 1427–28, it is one of the very few wellheads that can be attributed to a specific sculptor and is recorded as having taken 233 days to carve.[15] Imposing wellheads such as this were usually hidden away in the private courtyards of palaces.

By the late fifteenth and early sixteenth century, wellheads in public squares tended to be simple geometrical shapes—square, round, or hexagonal. They often feature inscriptions and figures of patron saints. In de' Barbari's time, Campo Sant'Angelo once had a basilica and two large wellheads. The church was demolished in the nineteenth century, but the two round wellheads recorded by de' Barbari are still in place. The one on the south side is plain and unadorned, bereft of the Lion of St. Mark that was once carved into its side. But the one on the north side near Ca' Trevisan–Pisani features low reliefs of the Angel Gabriel and the Virgin Annunciate. The iconography relates to the tiny Oratorio dell'Annunziata that remains on the campo.[16]

By contrast, de' Barbari's *View* also depicts the two wellheads that gave Campo dei Do Pozzi in Castello its name, but neither survives. Replaced in the 1520s–1530s by a single round wellhead, both were commemorated by a relief on one of its six panels (figs. 13.4 and 13.5). Two other reliefs opposite one another depict three angels, symbolizing the Holy Trinity, and Saint Martin. These document the division of the campo between the parishes of Santa Ternita (Holy Trinity) and San Martino. The iconography of the new wellhead thus celebrated the square's history and geography.[17]

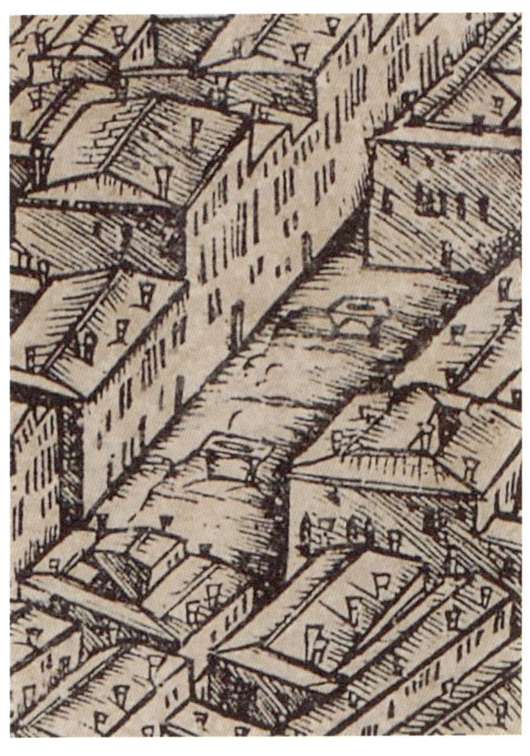

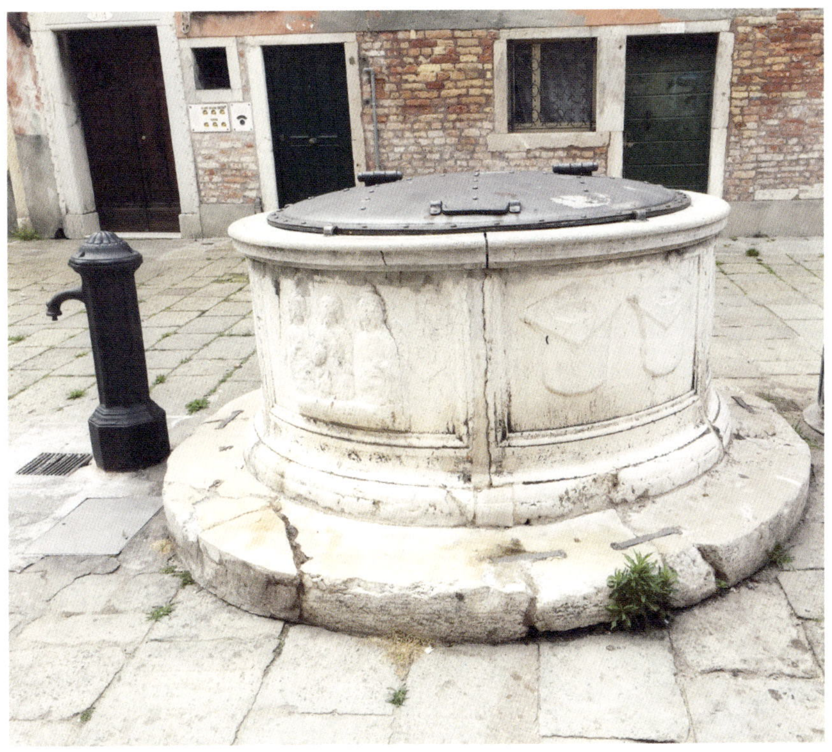

The most impressive wellheads in the city would be installed in the courtyard of the Palazzo Ducale a half century after de' Barbari completed his *View*. Cast in costly bronze to replace earlier ones made of stone, they were meant to impress. Their mannerist decorative vocabulary, often called the Sansovino style, features an exuberant assemblage of grotesque masks, winged cherubs, bare-breasted herms, cartouches, volutes, Moorish strapwork, scrolls, and swags of fruit. It is also found on stucco ceiling decoration, picture frames, book frontispieces, and cannons, but not on other wellheads. Almost as if in competition, each foundry sought to outdo the other by skillfully employing this vocabulary in a distinctly different way.[18] The only bronze wellheads in the city, the pair made an unapologetic statement not only of magnificence but also of civic benevolence, for, like the modest wellhead in Campo San Leonardo, they were intended to be "for the convenience of the people as well as an ornament of the city."

A new shape for wellheads emerged in the seventeenth century. Just as the Gothic and Renaissance masons had been inspired by the capitals of columns, the sculptors of the Baroque period were influenced by the graceful curves of the baluster. The two massive wellheads installed in Campo San Stefano in 1724 are the robust descendants of the balustrade of Palazzo Loredan on the same square. Each displays an empty tondo once sculpted with the Lion of St. Mark "in moleca." These were neatly chiseled off in 1797, mute evidence of the iconoclastic frenzy that swept through the city at the end of the Republic.[19]

A new era was beginning, but water was still being hoisted up in buckets from cisterns beneath the courtyards or brought in by barges. An aqueduct under the lagoon had been proposed in the fifteenth century and again in the sixteenth, seventeenth, and eighteenth, but to no avail.[20] Likewise, repeated attempts had been made to drill artesian wells over the years, without good results. By 1860, eight such wells were in operation, but the water was deemed undrinkable and suitable only for laundry or industrial use.[21] The French medical writer Gabriel Grimaux described the fountain in Campo San Polo. It shot a plume two meters high with perfectly clear water, which contained, however, a large amount of flammable gas. This created "the curious phenomenon of fiery fountains, and can make the fountain a singular, and at the same time very beautiful, candelabrum." Grimaux declared that the water was not potable but suggested that the gas could be used for lighting or heating.[22]

Although such initiatives proved inadequate, a solution was close at hand when a new railway bridge was constructed across the lagoon in 1841–46, linking Venice to the mainland. The engineer Ignazio Michela had proposed at the outset that an aqueduct could be built using the new bridge and culminating in Piazza San Marco with a grandiose fountain crowned by a personification of Venice atop a rocky mountain. "There is," Michela wrote, "no more pleasant spectacle than water gushing in great masses, and such an edifice would join utility to decoration. The ancient and magnificent square in Venice, so rightfully praised everywhere, would acquire a novel and worthy adornment."[23]

A French company finally undertook the project in 1880 and constructed a sixteen-mile-long aqueduct to bring water from the Brenta River into the great Sant'Andrea cistern near Piazzale Roma. The completion of the aqueduct in 1884 was celebrated in a public inauguration by the erection of a fountain in front of San Marco. It was a modest—but, alas, only temporary—version of Michela's project of four decades earlier.[24]

Piping was laid under bridges and pavement, and water eventually flowed out of spigots inside houses and in or near the old wellheads. As the homes of wealthier classes transitioned to running water, many of their elaborate wellheads went into public space to be enjoyed by rich and poor alike.[25] The elegant classicizing wellhead that once adorned the central courtyard in Ca' Corner della Ca' Grande on the Grand Canal was moved, complete with its inscribed base, to Campo Santi Giovanni e Paolo in 1884 and fitted up with a proper water spout. A fifteenth-century wellhead depicted by de' Barbari in the cloister of the monastery of Santa Croce now greets visitors to the city at Piazzale Roma; another situated in his woodcut in the garden of the palace of Matteo Dandolo on the Grand Canal remains in place but is now inside the lobby of the Hotel Monaco & Grand Canal.

Many wellheads became collectors' items, traveling the world. The Austrians led the way, shipping the weighty showpieces to Germany, Austria, Russia, and beyond, but the British were not far behind. The travel writer Augustus Hare lamented that only two thousand wellheads remained in Venice by 1856 of the five thousand there in 1814. "Now [in 1896] only 17 of the earliest or Italo-Byzantine period remain, and nearly half of these are in the hands of antiquity dealers. Venice is always wanting to sell its birthright of art-treasures." This did not stop him from buying two of his own, however, and installing them in his garden back in Sussex. Indeed, Venetian wellheads adorn country estates throughout England. William Waldorf Astor acquired no fewer than nine when he was the American minister to Italy in 1882–85. Becoming a British citizen in 1890, he acquired Hever Castle in Kent in 1903 and installed his trophies there in a new Italian garden.[26] The Victoria & Albert Museum has several superb examples, including one from the house of Jacopo Tintoretto, while the Royal Botanic Gardens in Kew features a fifteenth-century piece in the parterre of the Queen's Garden.[27]

Wellheads were high on the wish list in America's Gilded Age. Some were purchased by private collectors, others by museums. The newspaper magnate William Randolph Hearst purchased a large piece in Verona in 1892 and gave it to his mother, Phoebe Apperson Hearst. She displayed it prominently at the entrance to her Pleasanton country estate, which she named La Hacienda del Pozo de Verona. After Phoebe's death in 1919, the wellhead was moved to the Hearst Castle at San Simeon and placed on the South Terrace, where it was grouped with other wellheads to make an impressive display.[28]

The Metropolitan Museum of Art purchased a handsome late fourteenth- or early fifteenth-century wellhead of Istrian stone from a Munich dealer in 1914.[29] The Minneapolis Institute of Arts was not to be left out. For the tidy sum of $1,500, the museum acquired a fine fifteenth-century example, shaped like a Corinthian capital, for the Gothic Room in its brand-new building that had opened on January 7, 1915.[30] The Cleveland Museum of Art acquired a superb ninth-century piece decorated with a Tree of Life motif the following year.[31] The Toledo Museum of Art came late to the game, acquiring its wellhead only in 1936.[32] Other wellheads found their way to the Musée Jacquemart-Andrés in Paris and to the Museum of Fine Arts in Budapest, where they line the sides of the Renaissance Hall.[33]

Yet some of these wandering wellheads were too good to be true. If originals were not to be had, counterfeiters set out to fill the void. Isabella Stewart Gardner purchased a wellhead for 750 lire in 1899 during one of her last visits to Venice and placed it in the garden of her mansion in Boston. Described as "an old Byzantine wellhead, repaired," it looked to be made of gray limestone and was dated in the museum catalog to the ninth century. It was recently, however, deemed a fake antique and "demoted to the rank of cement moulding."[34] Even Peggy Guggenheim was not immune to the lure of the fake. An impressive wellhead, decorated with Romanesque motifs, in the garden of the Guggenheim Collection in Venice is an artful forgery made in the same period.[35]

Replicas of the finest wellheads wrought by Venetian artisans of an earlier time were also available by mail order from John P. White's factory in Bedford, England. Smaller versions of the massive wellheads in the courtyard of the Palazzo Ducale were on offer in its 1916 catalog, along with a replica of the wellhead from Ca' Corner that had been moved to Campo Santi Giovanni e Paolo. All were available in terra-cotta or, for a price, in marble or Istrian stone.[36]

John Singer Sargent may have included one of these creative anachronisms in his portrait of the architect Richard Morris Hunt. In the 1880s Hunt had designed Biltmore House, a 250-room French Renaissance chateau in the Blue Ridge Mountains, for George Vanderbilt. The two men traveled together throughout Europe and Asia, purchasing paintings, porcelains, bronzes, carpets, tapestries, furniture, and a newly carved(?) Venetian wellhead to furnish the property, reputedly the largest private residence in America.[37] For all that, originals are still to be had. The Metropolitan Museum acquired a very rare, clearly authentic medieval wellhead from a private collector only in 2011.[38] Another fine example sold for little more than $10,000 at a Christie's sale in London in 2012.[39]

The message proclaimed by de' Barbari's Mercury, the God of Trade, would still be relevant four centuries later: "I, Mercury, shine favorably over this above all other emporia." The vast aesthetic reach of the Venetian empire extended not only to trading posts throughout Europe and the Mediterranean but also, eventually, to museums and stately homes throughout Europe and the United States. Venice's political empire and its own Gilded Age may have ended in 1797, but we might conclude that Venice, the city without water, had nonetheless triumphed over adversity and made the entire world its virtual dominion.

NOTES

1 Giorgio Gianighian, "Venice, Italy," in *Management of Historic Centres*, ed. Robert Pickard (London: Taylor & Francis, 2013), 162.

2 Alberto Rizzi, *Vere da pozzo di Venezia: I puteali pubblici di Venezia e della sua laguna / The Well-Heads of Venice: Public Well-Heads in Venice and the Islands of Its Lagoon*, 3rd ed. (Venice: Filippi Editore, 2007), 363–69; Gianighian, "Venice, Italy," 162–63; Donatella Calabi and Ludovica Galeazzo, eds., *Acqua e cibo a Venezia: Storie della laguna e della città*

(Venice: Marsilio, 2015), 257–60. See also an important essay that appeared after this essay went to press: David Gentilcore, "The Cistern-System of Early Modern Venice: Technology, Politics and Culture in a Hydraulic Society," *Water History* 13 (2021): 1–32.

3 Rizzi, *Vere da pozzo*, 336, 354; Calabi and Galeazzo, *Acqua e cibo*, 260–65; Manfredo Tafuri, *Venice and the Renaissance* (Cambridge, MA: MIT Press, 1995), 150–51.

4 Rizzi, *Vere da pozzo*, 11; Norbert Huse and Wolfgang Wolters, *The Art of Renaissance Venice: Architecture, Sculpture, and Painting, 1460–1590* (Chicago: University of Chicago Press, 1990), 8–9.

5 Rizzi, *Vere da pozzo*, 230, 238 (cats. 192–94).

6 "COMMODITATI PVBLICAE / NEC NON VRBIS / ORNAMENTO." Rizzi, *Vere da pozzo*, 23, 163, 178, 423, 427 (cat. 114).

7 Gianighian, "Venice, Italy," 163; Rizzi, *Vere da pozzo*, 7, 9, 11, 337–40, and passim. In 1795, the Magistrato of the Provveditori di Comun listed 157 public wellheads in working order in the city. A survey in 1858 listed 6,046 private wells, 180 public wells, and 556 wells that had been filled in.

8 Rizzi, *Vere da pozzo*, 8, 47, 94, 358, 359, 375, 373–83.

9 Rizzi, *Vere da pozzo*, 284, 286 (cat. 241).

10 Rizzi, *Vere da pozzo*, 10–15, 47, 320, 322–23.

11 Rizzi, *Vere da pozzo*, 15, 16, 17; wellhead, Murano, ninth century, marble, no. 54-1882, Victoria & Albert Museum, London, http://collections.vam.ac.uk/item/O107425/well-head-unknown/; John Osborne, "The 'Cross-under-Arch' Motif in Ninth-Century Venetian Sculpture: An Imperial Reading," *Thesaurismata* 27 (1997): 7–18. Cf. wellhead, Lombardy or Venice, ninth–tenth century, limestone, 66.7 × 77.5 × 79.4 cm, Cleveland Museum of Art, Cleveland, http://www.clevelandart.org/art/1916.1982.

12 Rizzi, *Vere da pozzo*, 47, 52; Anna Tüskés, "Wells in the Medieval Churches of Venice," *Arte cristiana* 104 (2016): 897, 451–60.

13 Rizzi, *Vere da pozzo*, 22, 52, 109, 126, 127 (cats. 56–57).

14 Rizzi, *Vere da pozzo*, 166–67 (cats. 127–29).

15 Rizzi, *Vere da pozzo*, 26–27, 381.

16 Rizzi, *Vere da pozzo*, 74, 77, 80, 92–93, 98 (cats. 25, 37).

17 Rizzi, *Vere da pozzo*, 41, 53, 110, 129 (cat. 61).

18 Victoria Avery, *Vulcan's Forge in Venus' City: The Story of Bronze in Venice, 1350–1650* (Oxford: Published for the British Academy by Oxford University Press, 2011), 103–10, 264–74; Rizzi, *Vere da pozzo*, 48–49.

19 Rizzi, *Vere da pozzo*, 23, 32, 50, 54, 58, 75–76, 95, 271 (cats. 29–30; cf. cat. 224).

20 Nelli-Elena Vanzan Marchini, *Venezia da laguna a città* (Venice: Arsenale, 1985), 125–26; Tafuri, *Venice and the Renaissance*, 150–51.

21 Gabriel Grimaux de Caux, *Venise: Histoire de ses puits artésiens* (Paris: Dunod, 1861), esp. 6, 40–44. See also Vanzan Marchini, *Venezia da laguna a città*, 120, 137n29; "The City of the Sea," *Harper's New Monthly Magazine* 45, no. 268 (September 1872): 488; *Handbook for Travellers in Northern Italy*, 8th ed. (London: John Murray, 1860), 379–80.

22 "le phénomène curieux des fontaines ardentes et peut faire de la fontaine un singulier et en méme temps fort beau candelabra." Grimaux de Caux, *Venise*, 40.

23 Ignazio Michela, *Memoria sull'origine e sullo sviluppo del progetto di condurre acqua potabile dal continente a Venezia* (Turin: Tipografia Zecchi e Bona, 1842), 7–27. The idea of a perpetual fountain in Piazza San Marco had already been proposed in 1596 without results: Elena Svalduz, "In mezzo al'acqua/senza acqua," in *Acqua e cibo a Venezia: Storie della laguna e della città*, ed. Donatella Calabi and Ludovica Galeazzo (Venice: Marsilio, 2015), 248–49.

24 Daniela Mazzotta, "L'acquedotto di Venezia," in *Archeologia industriale nel Veneto*, ed. Franco Mancuso (Milan: Giunta Regionale del Veneto / Silvano Editoriale, 1990), 171.

25 Paolo Gardin, "Dalla trasformazione alla manutenzione e conservazione del patrimonio urbano," *Insula: Un futuro per Venezia*, 55–57, accessed July 26, 2020, http://www.insula.it/images/pdf/resource/quadernipdf/Q04-07.pdf.

26 Anna Tüskés, "Venetian Well-Heads in Nineteenth-Century Taste," *Sculpture Journal* 19, no. 1 (2010): 52–53. Paul Hetherington, "The Venetian Well-Heads at Hever Castle, Kent," *Apollo* 121, no. 277 (1985): 162–67.

27 Tüskés, "Venetian Well-Heads." See also Rizzi, *Vere da pozzo*, 9, 27, 52–53.

28 Ben Procter, *William Randolph Hearst: The Early Years, 1863–1910* (Oxford: Oxford University Press, 1988), 70; John Harris, *Moving Rooms: The Trade in Architectural Salvages* (New Haven, CT: Yale University Press, 2007), 220.

29 It was moved to the Cloisters in 1926. Lisbeth Castelnuovo-Tedesco and Jack Soultanian, eds., *Italian Medieval Sculpture in the Metropolitan Museum of Art and the Cloisters* (New York: Metropolitan Museum of Art, 2010), 220–23.

30 M. T. J. (Margaret T. Jackson), "A Venetian Wellhead," *Bulletin of the Minneapolis Museum of the Arts* 4, no. 7 (July 1915): 74–75.

31 Tüskés, "Venetian Well-Heads," 59; *Handbook of the Cleveland Museum of Art* (Cleveland: Cleveland Museum of Art, 1978), 48.

32 Anita Moskowitz, "A Venetian Well-head in Toledo," *Source: Notes in the History of Art* 14, no. 2 (1995): 1–6.

33 Anna Tüskés, "Vere da pozzo veneziane in Ungheria," *Commentari d'arte* 17, no. 48 (2011): 61–74.

34 Rizzi, *Vere da pozzo*, 459. Cf. Gerd-H. Zuchold, "An Early Venetian Well-Head in the Isabella Stewart Gardner Museum," in *Fenway Court 1988* (Boston: Isabella Stewart Gardner Museum, 1989), 23–31.

35 Rizzi, *Vere da pozzo*, 459.

36 John P. White & Sons, Ltd., *Garden Furniture and Ornament* (Bedford, UK: Pyghtle Works, 1916), 135–40.

37 John Singer Sargent, *Richard Morris Hunt*, 1895, oil on canvas, 254 × 139.7 cm, Biltmore House, Asheville, NC, http://www.jssgallery.org/Paintings/Richard_Morris_Hunt.htm.

38 Wellhead, Venice, eleventh–twelfth century, Istrian stone, 67 × 71.8 × 10.8 cm, no. 2011.245, Metropolitan Museum of Art, New York, https://www.metmuseum.org/art/collection/search/479547.

39 GBP 6,875. North Italian wellhead, Venice, fifteenth–sixteenth century, Istrian marble, 66 × 81.2 cm, lot 169, May 22, 2012, Christie's, London, https://www.christies.com/lotfinder/Lot/a-north-italian-istrian-marble-well-head-5566411-details.aspx.

Jonathan Glixon

Hidden in Plain Sight (and Hearing)

Venetian Bells and Their Towers

I believe the world cannot produce a more surprising, or more beautiful view; a city rising out of the bosom of the waves, crowned with glittering spires.

ANNA MILLER, *Letters from Italy* (1776)

14

As other essays in this volume make clear, Jacopo de' Barbari's *View of Venice* reveals a great deal about Venice at the turn of the sixteenth century. By its very nature as a bird's-eye view, however, it also conceals essential aspects of the city. One of these is purely visual. For anybody viewing Venice at sea level—in 1500; in the 1770s, like Anna Miller; or today—the image of the city is defined by an element that fades into the broader picture of de' Barbari's *View*: the bell towers, about one hundred of which, rising beside the city's churches, dominate the skyline. This vertical element of the city was emphasized (perhaps even overemphasized) in later views of Venice, such as that from the first half of the eighteenth century published by Martin Engelbrecht (fig. 14.1).

The Bell Towers

Jonathan Glixon

Everywhere in Europe, bells were hung in towers that were integral to the architecture of the church. In Italy, however, independent, often freestanding towers were the norm. Most medieval Italian bell towers fit Ann Priester's description of those in Rome: "They consist of a series of superimposed, roughly cube-shaped stories, resting on a tall base. The divisions of the stories are marked by cornices, and the stories themselves are pierced with arched openings of one, two or three lights."[1] Although mostly freestanding, the campanili of Venice, as clearly documented in the *View*, are in many ways distinct from those elsewhere in Italy. Common to just about all Venetian towers are two basic architectural elements: first, a brick shaft, almost always a single, tall unit, without openings; and second, an architecturally distinct belfry. Some belfries have a base, and many are topped by a spire often standing on a drum or attic, although sometimes they spring directly from the belfry itself. Venetian builders seem to have combined these elements in almost every possible configuration, as can be seen in the *View* (see "Church Bell Towers" in appendix 1).[2]

Counting features of the *View* has often been a pastime, and bell towers are no exception. Various numbers have been proposed, notably by Onofri, as discussed below, but my count is as follows. There should be 121 churches, but only 116 are visible. Three on the Giudecca are hidden by clouds or out of view to the west; San Basso is hidden by San Marco; and San Silvestro is mysteriously hidden. In addition, only the façade of Sant'Elena is visible at the extreme right of the image. Of the 116 fully visible churches, 94 possess freestanding campanili, to which we can add the 12 campanili *a vela* (a small structure on the edge of the roof of the church or a nearby building pierced by arches), for a total, in the city itself, of 106. In addition, de' Barbari depicts 22 more on islands of the lagoon (there are three additional churches with no tower visible), for a grand total of 128.

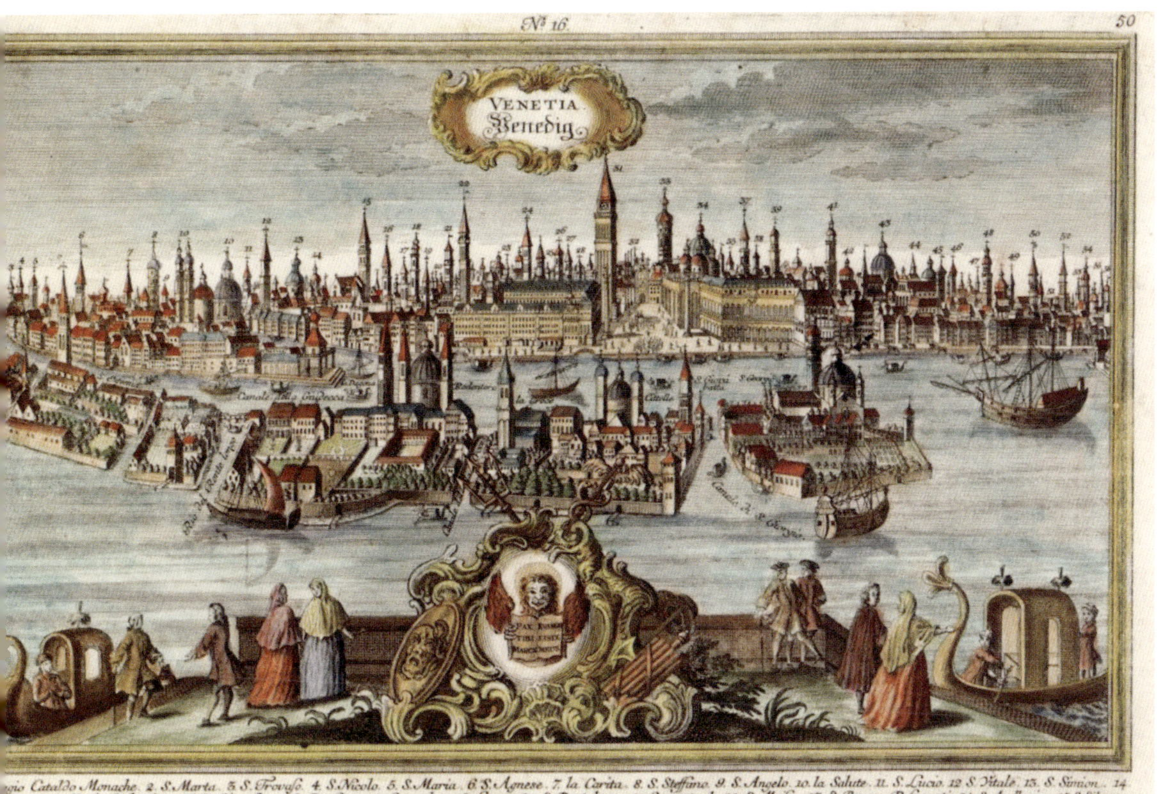

Bells and Bell Ringing

Bringing the bell towers back into focus also makes us aware of another way that a bird's-eye view such as de' Barbari's obscures reality. From the vantage point of the *View*, Venice appears quiet and serene, but at ground level, it was not only occupied by over 100,000 busy people but also filled with sounds, none of them louder or more ubiquitous than those produced by the three hundred or so bells that rang out from all those bell towers.

By 1500, Venice had a long tradition of bell making. As Victoria Avery has recounted, there were active foundries in the city by 1128, at the latest.[3] The foundries were concentrated in the area between Piazza San Marco and San Luca, most importantly near each of the three bridges on

14.1

Johan Georg Ringlin after Friedrich Bernhard Werner, *Venetia/Venedig*, ca. 1725–50. Published by Martin Engelbrecht in Augsburg, Germany.

191

Jonathan Glixon

the Calle dei Fabbri. Documents about bells in Venetian churches before the fifteenth century are rare, but it seems clear that by the time of the *View*, most churches possessed a set of three bells in their campanile, usually designated simply as the *piccola, mezana,* and *grande* (small, midsized, and large). Some of the larger monasteries and parish churches (San Stefano, San Francesco della Vigna, the Frari, San Nicolò dei Mendicoli, and San Cassiano, for example) had four bells, or even five (e.g., San Marco), and a few of smallest nunneries and parish churches had only one or two. In addition, most owned a small bell (*sonello*) to be rung inside the church at the Elevation during Mass. Various attempts have been made to count the bells, most notably by Fedele Onofri in 1666.[4] Adding up all his numbers, and estimating from the churches he omits, one can reach a total of well over four hundred, but this probably includes the *sonelli* and not just tower bells, as Onofri often counts four bells in churches for which clear documentation indicates a ring of three. A more likely total, therefore, would be a little more than three hundred.

The bells themselves, of course, varied greatly in size (and therefore pitch and volume). While bells were often recast out of necessity, those for any given church appear to have remained pretty much the same size over the centuries.[5] While I have located documentation, sometimes quite extensive, of bells for many Venetian churches, it is mostly from 1650 and later, and therefore, beyond de' Barbari's time. Nevertheless, the general stability of bell sizes enables an understanding of the earlier situation. For many churches, the largest bell would have weighed something approaching 1,000 Venetian *libbre*, quite close to the modern pound. Some of the smallest nunneries and parish churches, such as Sant'Anna and San Benetto, had bells in the range of only 400 pounds.[6] The largest documented nunnery bell, at San Daniele, weighed in at about 1,500, and the largest parish church bell, at Santa Maria Formosa, at just over 2,000.[7] The Augustinian friary of San Stefano possessed a bell of nearly 3,500 pounds.[8] On a different scale entirely were the bells of San Marco, which topped out at over 7,000 pounds. That was matched by at least one other bell (perhaps also one bell at two other churches, although documents are lacking) at San Francesco della Vigna that served as an official echo of San Marco's Marangona for calling into session the Maggior Consiglio (discussed below).[9]

While most churches in the modern world ring their bells once or twice a day, or perhaps only on Sundays and holidays, in Renaissance Venice things were very different. Every one of the hundred-plus churches would

192

have sounded their bells at least three or four times every day, and sometimes much more.[10] Nunnery and monastic churches rang for the Divine Hours—since some were combined and the tower bells were probably not rung during the night for Matins, this would mean perhaps five services—and a daily morning mass. Parish churches, on ordinary days, rang for Mass and sometimes Vespers, and for the Ave Maria morning, noon, and night. For all these churches, nonfestival ringing was usually one to three peals of a single bell. Documentation for the length of a peal is nearly absent, likely because it was taken for granted, but it seems to have been what was described as "lo spazio d'un Miserere," the time it would take to recite Psalm 51—that is, about three minutes (although this was quite different at San Marco, as discussed below). Unlike Florence, where the ringing of church bells seems to have been coordinated directly with the ringing of civic bells, Venetian churches seem to have been allowed to arrange their own schedules (although, for convenience, some relied on San Marco's timing).[11]

Festival ringing—with each church observing at least thirty festivals a year in addition to Sundays—was more elaborate. Three peals was standard for each service, and not with just one bell but with all three (the technique referred to in the documents as *suonare doppio*). In addition, churches seem to have had an additional, special ring for the feasts of their patron saints. This was the *campanò*, ringing *a martello*, in which, rather than swinging the bell so that the clapper hit at a regular pace, the clapper itself was swung by hand, hitting the bell much more frequently. According to the documents, this ringing (later banned in many churches because of its tendency to damage the bells) would continue for either the entire day before the festival or the entire morning of the festival, or both (whether that means without pause is unclear).

Dominating this soundscape was the ringing of the campanile of San Marco. This tower had four large bells (plus a fifth used only for executions), named, in descending order of size, the Marangona (so called because one of its functions was to call to work the carpenters of the Arsenal), Nona (for the ninth hour, noon), Trottiera (explained below), and Mezza-terza (for the time of day).[12] The basic ringing schedule served several principal functions: to mark the religious services of San Marco, to indicate important moments in the workday, and to mark the times in the evening and night that, for reasons of safety, outdoor activities were limited. Each bell and the way it was rung was distinct, and the various sounds would have been understood by all. Guides for the *campanaro*, the man in charge of ringing the bells, described the ringing using two formulas: a specific number of individual strikes; or a length of time for continuous ringing, which for the latter employed sandglasses.[13]

The ringing began at dawn with 16–18 strikes of the Mezza-terza, followed a half hour later (except on Sundays and festivals) by 16–18 strikes of the Marangona to mark the beginning of the workday. After another half hour, the Mezza-terza sounded for a full half hour (marking the opening of the state attorneys' office and the beginning of the religious day at San Marco with the first mass starting at the end of the half hour), by which point any Arsenal worker not inside the gates would be marked as late, followed at Terce itself by 15–16 strikes of the Marangona (the moment for courts to announce their decisions). At noon, the Nona struck 16–18 times (the beginning of the lunch break for workers, in the Arsenal and elsewhere), followed thirty minutes later (except on Sundays and festivals) by a half-hour continuous ringing of the Trottiera, the end of which indicated the return to work. An hour after that was time for the Ave Maria (marking obligatory prayers for all citizens), indicated by the Nona, this time with three sets of 9–10 strikes each. Vespers was marked by 15–16 strikes of the Marangona, except on festivals, when all four bells were struck 18–20 times each. The day finished with another series of rings: at sunset, the Marangona for 15–16 strikes (the end of the workday), one hour later the Mezza-terza for twelve minutes (calling the guards to their nighttime posts), followed, after a break of twelve minutes, by the same span of the Nona (when official documents to be sent out of the city were to brought to Rialto to the courier's office). Two hours after nightfall, the Marangona rang for twelve minutes, alerting the guards to begin their rounds, and the day ended with 16–18 strokes of the Nona at midnight. In all, this adds up to, on an ordinary day, more than one and a half hours of continuous ringing plus about 135 individual strikes (on Sundays and festivals, less continuous ringing, but more strikes).

On top of all of this, the bells of San Marco also served to announce the meetings of the Senate and the Great Council. The Senate met, usually, in the early afternoon on weekdays (although not every day). The senators were called to the Doge's Palace by, first, twelve minutes of the Trottiera, followed immediately by one half-hour continuous ringing of the Mezza-terza. The Great Council met instead on Sundays, although special meetings could be called on other days. In the summer, when the council would meet in the morning to avoid the heat, the bells rang in warning on the evening before with twelve minutes of the Trottiera just after sundown. In the winter, when the council met in the afternoon, this announcement happened that morning. One hour before the meeting was scheduled to begin, the Marangona began to sound: four sets of 50 strikes, followed by five sets of 25, for a total of 325, lasting an hour. Then, as the meeting began, the Trottiera rang for one continuous hour (one half hour during the shorter winter days)—the members had this time to "trot" to the Palace to avoid the consequences of being considered late.[14] To be sure that all the patricians from across the city would be able to hear the announcement of the Great Council meetings, the Marangona rings were duplicated by large bells at San Francesco della Vigna to the east, the Frari to the west, and San Geremia to the north. So, on a Sunday when the Great Council met, the bells of San Marco rang for just over two hours continuously plus nearly 600 individual strikes!

In addition to the bells of San Marco, two additional bells rang for civic purposes: in the tower of the church of San Giovanni Elemosinario, at the Rialto, there was the Realtina, which sounded to announce the end of the workday for all the apprentices and workers in that busy commercial district; at the entrance of the Arsenal hung a bell that was rung to mark the beginning and end of the workday there, and also the hours for the midday meal break (in coordination, apparently, with the bells of San Marco) and, in the longer summer days, for the supper interval.

All the bells discussed so far rang on schedules determined in large part by the length of the day, serving the needs of both the churches and the labor force. But there were also bells that rang the hours: those on public clocks. It is unclear how many public clocks there were in Venice in 1500. The count of twenty-seven by Schott in his 1601 *Itinerarium*, however, seems unlikely.[15] The only clock visible in the *View* is the one, just recently completed at the time, in Piazza San Marco. That replaced one without a dial over the Sant'Alipio doorway of San Marco (the northernmost entry on the front façade). San Giacomo di Rialto possessed a clock with a dial as early as 1410, and others were added in the sixteenth century (in the courtyard of the Doge's Palace and perhaps on the gate of the Arsenal) and later.

In addition to the predictable bells on solar or hourly schedules, others might disrupt the daily routine, often not in a welcome way. In the case of fire, the church bells of the affected parish would be rung *a martello* (i.e., with the clapper swung by hand), and the word passed to the church of Sant'Antonino, in the eastern district of Castello, whose bell was then rung (presumably in a recognizable way) to call the workers of the nearby Arsenal, who served as the city's fire brigade. In the event of the death of an important figure, such as the doge, patriarch, pope, ambassador, or certain other high-ranking figures, the bells of San Marco would toll, followed by those around the city; the number of peals and number of days this ringing was repeated would vary based on the rank of the deceased. Equally, the election of such a figure would be marked by very different ringing: all the churches sounding their bells *a martello*. Something similar announced a military victory or peace treaty or welcomed a distinguished foreign figure to the city. Processions, both regular and special, were also marked by bell ringing: during official events in St. Mark's Square (of which there were more than a dozen annually at the time of de' Barbari), all the bells of San Marco would ring from the moment the doge exited the Ducal Palace until he circled the square and eventually entered St. Mark's church. When processions, celebratory or funereal, would go through the city, the bells of each parish church would ring while the participants were within the parish boundaries.

Of course, bells were not the only sounds of Renaissance Venice, but even considered by themselves, it becomes clear that while Venice might have been the Most Serene Republic, peaceful and majestic as depicted by de' Barbari, it was anything but quiet, being filled with a complicated but well-understood series of sounds defining the religious and civic lives of Venetians.

A visitor arriving in Venice for the first time, or a resident returning home from abroad, would have been welcomed by the sight of the more than one hundred bell towers of the city, de-emphasized by the very nature of de' Barbari's *View*. Similarly, anyone in or near Venice, at almost any time of day, would hear the sounds of the city's many bells. Looking at the *View* with this in mind, we can almost hear them ourselves.

Epigraph: Anna Miller, *Letters from Italy, Describing the Manners, Customs, Antiquities, Paintings, &c. of that Country* (London: Edward and Charles Dilly, 1776), 3:243.

1 Ann E. Priester, "The Belltowers of Medieval Rome and the Architecture of *Renovatio*" (PhD diss., Princeton University, 1996), 10.

2 For more on the history of bell towers, on the general characteristics of Italian towers, and on Venetian towers in detail, see appendix 1.

3 Victoria Avery, *Vulcan's Forge in Venus' City: The Story of Bronze in Venice, 1350–1650* (Oxford: Published for the British Academy by Oxford University Press, 2011), esp. chap. 7. See also Marialuisa Bottazzi, "Fonditori di campanie: Dalla bottega medievale alla produzione industriale nell'ambiente artistico del Rinascimento veneziano," in *L'industria artistica del bronzo del Rinascimento a Venezia e nell'Italia settentrionale: Atti del convegno internazionale di studi, Venezia, Fondazione Giorgio Cini, 23–24 ottobre 2007,* ed. Matteo Ceriana and Victoria Avery (Verona: Scripta, 2008), 363–74; and Marialuisa Bottazzi, "Artigiani? Venezia: l'arte di fondere: Dalla documentazione d'archivio e dalle scritture incise (secc. XIII–XVI)," in *Formazione della ricchezza e strutture produttive a Venezia e nell'area alpino-adriatica fra Due e Cinquecento: Tre saggi,* ed. Paolo Cammarosano, *Bullettino dell'Istituto storico italiano per il Medio Evo* 111 (2009): 319–42.

4 Fedele Onofri, *Cronologia veneta: Nella quale fedelmente, e con brevita' si descrivono le cose piu' notabili di questa famosissima citta' di Venetia fino all' anno 1666* (Venice: Ginammi, 1666).

5 An excellent source for information on the bells currently hanging in Venetian campanili that also contains a considerable amount of historical data is the CD-ROM *Venice Bells* produced by the bell enthusiast Mario Pannizut, available at https://www.venicebells.net/.

6 Archivio di Stato di Venezia (ASVe), Sant'Anna b. 21, April 22, 1716; Archivio storico del Patriarcato di Venezia (ASPVe), Parrocchia di San Benetto, reg. di cassa 2, fol. 52, September 3, 1608.

7 ASVe, San Daniele, b. 27, filza cassa, n. 100, May 6, 1737; ASPVe, Parrocchia di Santa Maria Formosa, Amministrazione, b. 2, n. 6, fasc. 1, n. 1, May 18, 1752.

8 ASVe, Santo Stefano, b. 24, proc. 365, November 16, 1585.

9 ASVe, Inquisitori di Stato 710, Avvisi, September 6, 1727.

10 The most useful sources for Venetian church bell ringing are ASPVe, Par-

rocchia San Fosca, b. 196, Catastico 1, Consuetudini 1521; Archivi Storici della Chiesa di Venezie, Parrocchia di San Silvestro, Parrocchia di San Giovanni Elemosinario, Ceremoniale; ASVe, San Salvador b. 98, filza sacrestia 1782–86; ASVe, Sant'Eufemia di Mazzorbo, b. 5; Biblioteca del Museo Correr (BMCVe), ms. Cicogna 562 (rules for nuns of Santa Teresa, 1737).

11 Niall Atkinson, *The Noisy Renaissance: Sound, Architecture, and Florentine Urban Life* (University Park: Pennsylvania State University Press, 2017), esp. chaps. 1 and 2. ASPVe, Parrocchia Santa Maria Formosa, Capitolo, Verbali e parti 2, fol. 20, June 11, 1665.

12 Venice operated under two systems of time. The twenty-four hours of civil time were counted from sunset. See Michael Talbot, "*Ore italiane*: The Reckoning of the Time of Day in Pre-Napoleonic Italy," *Italian Studies* 40, no. 1 (1985): 51–62. Church hours (Prime, Terce, Sext, and Nones), on the other hand, began at dawn. While Nones, the ninth hour, was originally in the midafternoon, by the later middle ages, it had shifted several hours earlier to midday, hence the designation of the midday bell as the Nona (this is also the origin of the English term "noon").

13 See Gregorio Gattinoni (Rosolino), *Il campanile di San Marco: Monografia storica* (Venice: Giovanni Fabbris, 1910), 194–201; Giuseppe Filosi, *Narrazione istorica del campanile di San Marco in Venezia* (Venice: Recurti, 1745), 25–28; and Venice, BMCVe, cod. PD 258b.

14 The exact consequences are unclear but seem to have included, in addition to missing important votes, not being considered for election to a desired post or election to an onerous and undesired one.

15 Franz Schott, *Andreae Schotti: Itinerarium Italiae* (Wesel: Typis Andreae ab Hoogenhuysen, 1655), 55.

Jonathan Glixon

Saundra Weddle

Santa Lucia and Corpus Domini at the Turn of the Sixteenth Century

The *View* and Urban Patterns

IN HIS HISTORY OF VENETIAN CHURCHES, Flaminio Corner describes a conflict that occurred in 1461 after a new Augustinian convent, known initially as Santissima Annunziata and later as Santa Lucia, was founded near the Dominican nuns' complex of Corpus Domini.[1] These uneasy neighbors were at odds over a number of matters, but in this particular case Corpus Domini tried to force the relocation of the new religious community by appealing to a historic rule issued by the Dominican Order, which limited the proximity of other monastic houses: simply put, Corpus Domini told Church authorities that the new convent was too close and would disrupt its devotional life (fig. 15.1).[2] The patriarch of Venice rejected this claim and the explanation of his decision tells us much about attitudes

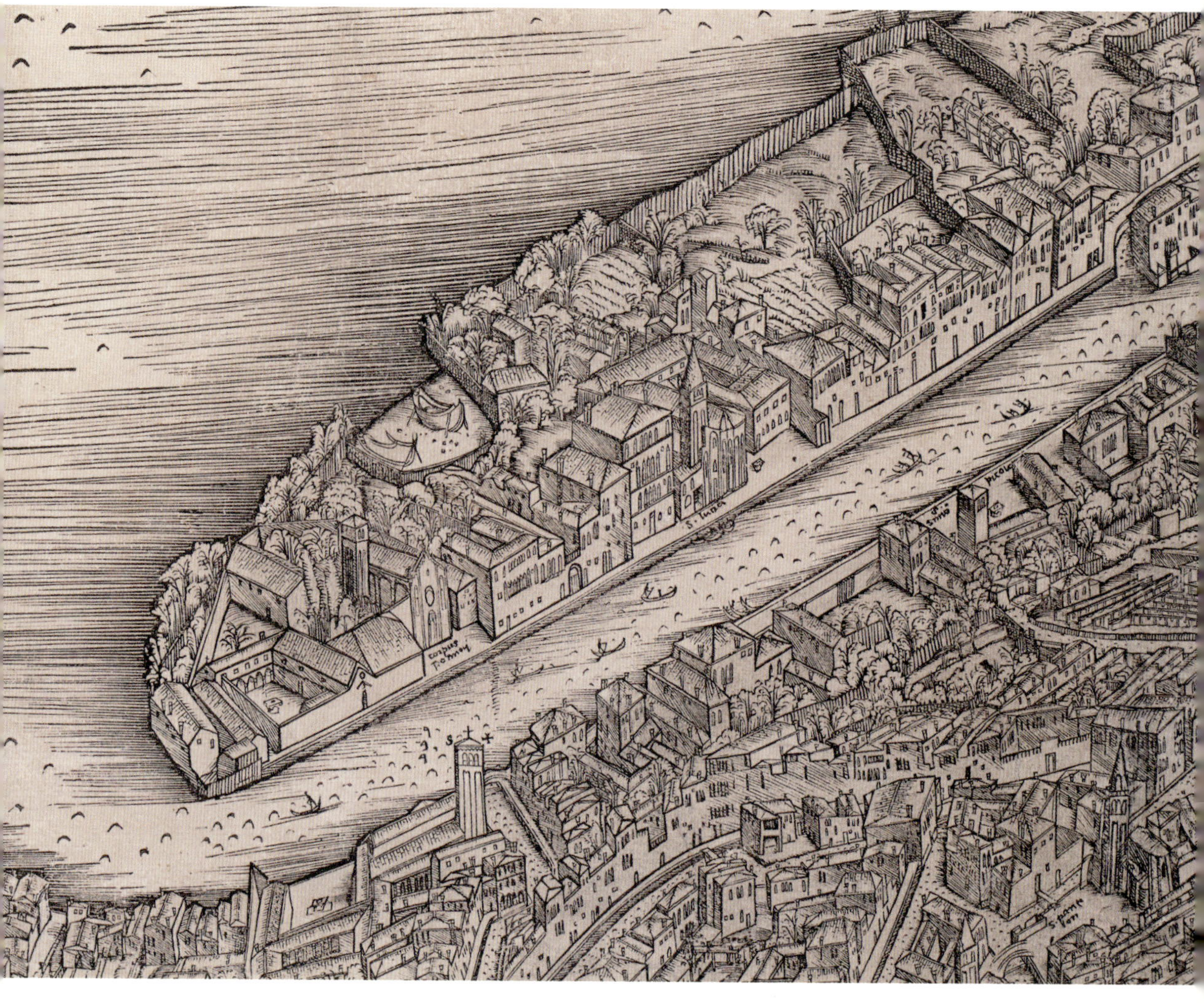

toward building and urban development in Venice.[3] According to Corner, the patriarch said he would overlook the Dominican rule because of "the great difficulty involved in building in this city, and the ample number of people who live there."[4] This pragmatic attitude foregrounds the signal importance of geography as a determinant not only of Venice's urban form but also of its culture. The privileging of practicality is borne out by processes of urban development, patterns of convent foundation, and architectural and spatial adjacencies that meaningfully affected neighborhood relationships.

De' Barbari produced a visual rhetoric that reinforces the sense of the city as La Serenissima: a fixed and stable entity, a coherent whole, disguising the fact that Venetian urban fabric and convent architecture were products of dynamic, accretive processes. The city's assembled quality is not denied completely by the *View*, but many islands and their aqueous interstices are difficult to read. The viewpoints are not high enough to show every calle, fondamenta, or *rio*, and surfaces and textures are difficult to distinguish without the advantages of digital enlargement or highlighting. De' Barbari's representational mode and the timing of the *View*'s production make it difficult to discern how geography once supported the goals of monastic enclosure by literally isolating convents, naturally reinforcing their segregating features.

Historically, convents served as urbanistic anchors and imposed a formal hierarchy on an island—not just because of their scale but also because of their chronological position. For example, the first houses for religious women—the ninth-century Benedictine convents of San Zaccaria and San Lorenzo—were established on some of the lagoon's earliest-inhabited islands, in the sestiere of Castello (fig. 15.2).[5] Wladimiro Dorigo's informative if imperfect reconstructions show that before 1300 these sites were relatively disconnected from their urban surroundings, but by 1360 Castello had become much more developed, and the convents' isolation was already beginning to be compromised.[6] Convent sites came to be stitched into the urban fabric through networks of calli, campi, and bridges, and surrounding buildings ultimately encroached on the borders of monastic complexes, obscuring their secluded origins. By around the mid-fourteenth century, convents began to occupy sites on the city's less developed outer shores, where they could construct spacious complexes and support the imperative of separation from the profane realm.

Convents were fundamentally unlike almost every other segregating site in Venice in the sense that their enclosures were intended to be absolute and permanent; relegation to the city's margins must have been meant to deter breaches.[7] But even these site conditions, which initially supported the ideal of absolute and permanent enclosure, were eventually made less potent by urban infill. The de' Barbari *View* shows that by 1500 the city had filled in, often with residential or mixed-use structures that brought secular life to the convents' doorstep, occasionally at the convents' instigation

Detail of Corpus Domini (*upper left*) and Santa Lucia (*upper center*), from Jacopo de' Barbari, *View of Venice*, ca. 1497–1500.

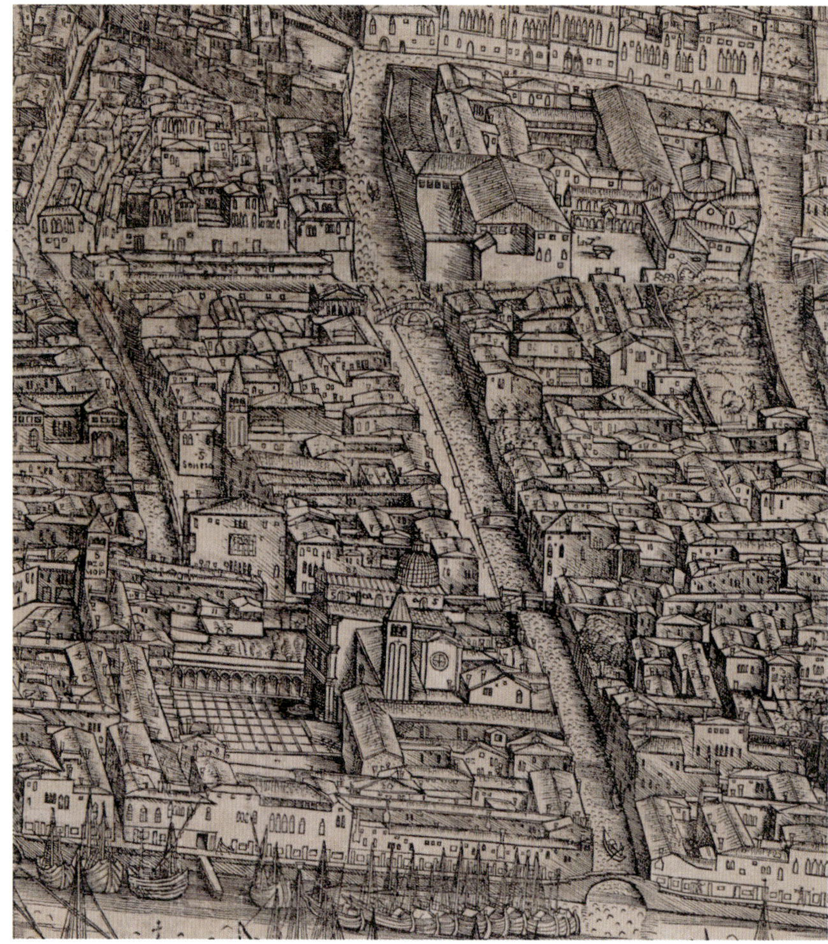

Detail of convents of San Zaccaria (*lower left*) and San Lorenzo (*upper right*), from Jacopo de' Barbari, *View of Venice*, ca. 1497–1500.

when adjacent properties were purchased to generate revenue.[8] De' Barbari's depiction of monastic complexes on the Giudecca islands offers a sense of what convent site conditions were like before urban densification made such a significant impact.

The pattern of convent development—isolation followed by embeddedness—held true for the majority of convents, which were built *ex novo*. Some convents founded in the fifteenth and sixteenth centuries took a different approach, settling within already-dense sites, where the challenge of expansion required the acquisition of neighboring properties, allowing convents to grow in a piecemeal fashion over time. Hence, while the transition from isolated to embedded site was certainly the norm, some convents developed differently, inserting themselves into a more densely developed urban condition.

The *View*—a static representation of the limited time span during which the city was surveyed—elides these dynamic processes. A telling case can be found with the two neighboring convents mentioned above—the Dominican house of Corpus Domini and the Augustinian convent of Santa Lucia. The first was inserted into an undeveloped site, and the second was founded later on a denser site; their relationship was conditioned by their urban context.

Corpus Domini

Building chronology provides needed context for de' Barbari's representation of Corpus Domini. Its site, the spit of land at Venice's northwestern edge, was the product of land reclamation projects undertaken sometime before the early 1100s.[9] The area remained sparsely developed even in the mid-1300s, when Corpus Domini was founded: according to the convent's chronicle, the community's first buildings were modest wooden structures; by 1394, however, its complex had grown significantly to accommodate the rising number of women living there.[10] The convent also established a lay confraternity that tied it to Venice's ritual topography through processions of a cherished relic of the holy sacrament, raising the community's profile.[11] But there were also setbacks. A storm that occurred in 1409 caused the bell tower and at least one chimney to fall, crashing through the dormitory roof; the laundry room and the vineyard's enclosing wall (said to have been connected to the parlor) were also damaged.[12] A major building campaign followed with the purchase of neighboring land parcels and buildings, and construction continued into the 1440s with the addition of an infirmary and a new church, whose estimated total cost was 4,000 ducats.[13] Around this time, the nuns of Corpus Domini were granted custodianship of the relics of Saint Lucy, housed at the nearby parish church of Santa Lucia; this likely enhanced the nuns' income, since the relics probably attracted many pilgrims, along with their alms, perhaps contributing to the cost of their own construction projects.[14] No known records of additional building projects predate 1500. De' Barbari's representation, therefore, can be assumed to reflect the results of this mid-fifteenth-century construction project.

Saundra Weddle

The *View* represents the transitional nature of the city's far reaches, with open and undeveloped *barene* exposed to winds blowing in from the west and the expanse of water just beyond. By contrast, we can appreciate the value of real estate facing the Grand Canal as buildings concentrate at the waterway's edge, heightening awareness of the importance of Corpus Domini's frontage. In the *View*, we see two entries into the Corpus Domini complex—one from the campo and one from the fondamenta. From the campo, one could enter into what was then the fairly recently reconstructed church, which rejects the preferred and prescribed east–west orientation in favor of a monumental façade facing the Grand Canal. This increased its public presence and created space for public gatherings, perhaps in relation to the ritual procession associated with the associated confraternity: an example where an architectural ideal—east–west orientation—was compromised for pragmatic and rhetorical reasons.[15]

We can only speculate about the locations of different functions within the convent complex. The *View* shows a second door giving onto the fondamenta. Perhaps it gave onto storage spaces with a kitchen beyond, because deliveries were likely made by water; if so, these might be connected to the refectory, because adjacency to the kitchen was a common practice for monastic dining halls. De' Barbari's depiction of a cross at the end of the building volume at the rear wing of the cloister suggests the location of the infirmary or a dormitory, because chapels were a common feature in or near both infirmaries and dormitories.

A 1595 plan of the site from the Venice State Archive builds on information depicted in the *View* (fig. 15.3). It confirms that the volume facing the campo from the west, whose façade is not visible in the *View*, had two doors (at least eventually)—perhaps leading to the parlor, which had to be located near the public way. On the complex's eastern side, this plan also shows the presence of a calle that separates the church from another volume of convent spaces, connected at the end of the alley by a gateway.[16] From this calle there are two lateral entrances into the church, a strange and inhospitable configuration given the privacy of that narrow and dark space, a hidden venue that would have been ideal for nefarious activities. The convent's connection to the volume to the east of the calle is indiscernible in de' Barbari's *View*, although the opening from the fondamenta to the calle is indicated.

The de' Barbari *View* suggests some of the ways that Corpus Domini's architecture exemplified the model of the convent founded on an isolated

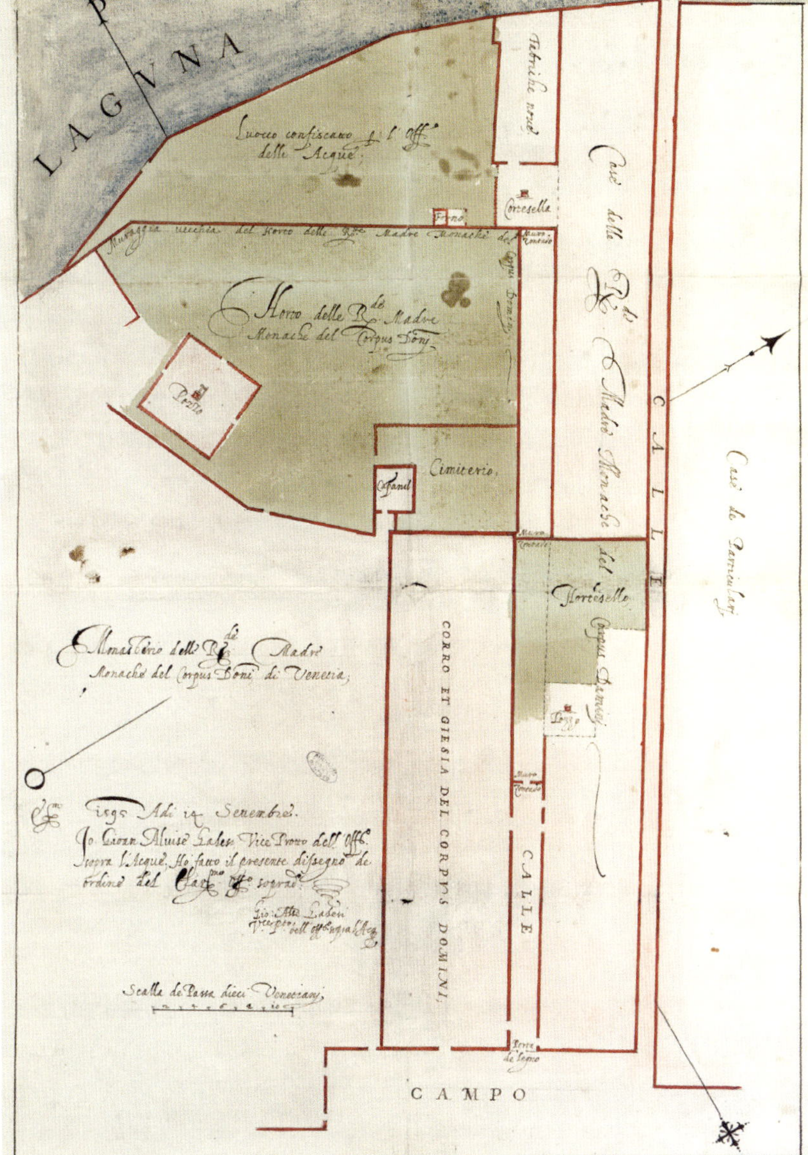

Plan, Corpus Domini, Venice. Archivio di Stato di Venezia, Corpus Domini, b. 1.

site, eventually bordered by built fabric. The convent seems to have benefited initially from its remote location by expanding in response to changing needs and circumstances. This sprawling complex developed to the west in an ad hoc, additive way, with irregular building volumes of varied scale and orientation. These contrasted the earlier building volumes just to the east, which were more orderly and coherent. Where the convent ends and the neighboring secular structures begin is difficult to confirm with the *View* alone.

Santa Lucia

Saundra Weddle

The impact of these urban processes and conditions on neighborhood relationships is better understood through a study of Corpus Domini's neighboring convent. In the mid-fifteenth century, a group of tertiaries (lay women associated with a religious order) established a residence in a house near the parish church of Santa Lucia and took on a dedication to the Annunciation, recalling the alternative name sometimes associated with the church of Santa Lucia. Around 1459 this group of women began purchasing adjacent buildings and connecting them to their original house, forming a cloister.[17] In 1461, they professed solemn vows and accepted the Augustinian Rule, thereby formalizing their conversion to a legitimate convent; they then began to pursue the construction of their own church with a bell tower and cemetery—no small challenge, because, as already mentioned, the Dominicans at Corpus Domini protested the community's very existence. But this fledgling community also lacked funding. Although church authorities had rebuffed Corpus Domini's objections and approved this new convent, only in 1476 did the Augustinians find a resourceful solution to their desire for their own church—they appealed to Pope Sixtus IV, successfully, to take possession of the parish church of Santa Lucia, just across the calle from their convent, and along with it, its famous relics. Naturally, this further incensed the nuns of Corpus Domini, who had previously been granted custodianship of the church and its relics. Their response was to steal the relics, causing a great scandal, but again, to no avail, and the transfer of Santa Lucia (both church and relics) to the new convent was finalized in 1477, with the Augustinians changing their dedication from the Annunciation to Santa Lucia.[18] After they built a connection from their complex to the parish church of Santa Lucia, the only known major building projects before 1500 include the addition of an infirmary and a kitchen.[19]

Santa Lucia is more difficult to read in the *View*, perhaps because it exemplifies a different development model from that seen at Corpus Domini. Of course, the church itself predated even the convent of Corpus Domini, but the convent of Santa Lucia was inserted into a fairly dense site, with its neighbors along the Grand Canal coming right up to its sides. The compactness of its convent complex made it that much more difficult for de' Barbari to represent; from a higher perspective, the different building volumes and roof heights would have been legible, but instead the complex appears to curl like a spiral, with five wings that produce a courtyard, and with no apparent gardens or outbuildings. De' Barbari shows a row of chimneys at the back of the complex, perhaps corresponding to a dormitory or cells. Beyond, there are vineyards, gardens, or perhaps orchards, with no indication of which, if any, buildings they belong to, although they were probably not associated with the convent, since it is impossible to trace a consistent garden enclosure that connects to the convent complex itself.

The age of the church, the oldest in the neighborhood, is reflected in de' Barbari's *View*. The building maintains its original east–west orientation, turning its flank toward the canal. It had a Gothic-style apse with tall arches and windows at its east end.[20] The church's scale allowed it to make a dominant, monumental impression along the waterfront, and it is the most clearly represented (and likely, to de' Barbari, the most visible) part of the convent. In the *View* there is an entry into the church's flank from the fondamenta, but the likely original entrance would have given the faithful an axial connection to the main altar; that point of entry was, by 1500, accessible from a narrow calle—in a condition not unlike the alleyway that bordered the flank of Corpus Domini's church, practically hidden by the buildings to the west, which were allowed to crowd the church as development progressed.

De' Barbari provides important context for neighborhood disputes, such as Corpus Domini's original argument—that the convent of Santa Lucia was too close and would disrupt its devotional life. It seems unlikely that Santa Lucia's nuns could have been heard all the way over at Corpus Domini; the combination of distance and the secular buildings in between the two convents would have overwhelmed any noise made by the nuns, and other neighbors—especially the *squero*, located between and behind the two houses, and its construction and reparations of boats—would have made a greater sonic impact than Santa Lucia's nuns.

Instead, Corpus Domini's concerns related, at least in part, to the sounds of bells, which the nuns claimed would create "disorder."[21] This dispute started before the new convent took over the church of Santa Lucia, when it proposed building its own church and bell tower, not an unusual request given that convents used bells as internal and external communication systems, signaling the canonical hours and other community events. But the urban context and the proximity of these religious institutions posed a problem. The bell tower associated with the parish church of Santa Lucia, the first in the neighborhood, was tall and massive; its voice communicated the church's status within the area and likely had precedence over the bells of Corpus Domini, which would probably have rung only after an interval of time passed after the first tones were sounded by Santa Lucia's bells.[22] It is easy to imagine the confusing cacophony that would have ensued with the addition of a third campanile. The hierarchy of bell ringing conveyed status and power, and Corpus Domini likely feared a demotion in neighborhood standing because the sound of its bells would be lost.[23] These concerns were dispelled when the Augustinians gained control of Santa Lucia, but others remained.

Saundra Weddle

Another possible threat to Corpus Domini's status was related to the Saint Lucy relics. De' Barbari showed that the convent was actually some distance away from Santa Lucia, and its administrative connection to the noteworthy remains would never have been urbanistically obvious. It is therefore possible that Corpus Domini worried that the new convent, at first just across the calle from the relics, would siphon off financial support by virtue of its proximity to them. Once it took over the parish church, the convent of Santa Lucia was ordered to make an annual payment of fifty ducats to Corpus Domini to compensate for the loss of alms, suggesting that this was, after all, one (and perhaps the most important) of the underlying concerns, not the potential disturbance caused by another convent or its bell tower.

These examples demonstrate that the de' Barbari *View*'s extraordinary details can help decode urban histories and the effects of urban change at a moment of particular importance for Venetian convents. The year of publication, 1500, marks a point just before church and civic authorities got serious about advancing an organized program of convent reform in which architecture played a significant role, particularly with regard to enclosure.[24] Interestingly, these reforms focused almost exclusively on controlling and renovating convent architecture; they seldom proposed alterations to secular buildings that encroached on convents, which, as these case studies have shown, could create particular kinds of pressures in the neighborhood context. The *View* offers an opportunity to consider convent architecture before the most dramatic of these reform measures were instituted, documenting a time period when convent complexes were ultimately less conditioned by idealizing and self-referential logics, like monastic rules and reforming decrees, and more by their natural and built urban contexts and the demands of practicality.

NOTES

1 Flaminio Corner, *Notizie storiche delle chiese e monasteri di Venezia* (Venice: A. Forni, 1758), 253.

2 Archivio di Stato di Venezia (ASVe), Santa Lucia b. 3, 19v–20r, relating to these events, references a rule issued by Pope Urban V stipulating a distance of at least ninety *cane* between houses, and concerns about "losing order, the noise of bells, and the clamor of the people."

3 Corner, *Notizie storiche*, 253. The patriarch was Andrea Bondimerio.

4 Corner, *Notizie storiche*, 253.

5 San Zaccaria was located on the island named Ombriola, and San Lorenzo was located on one of the Gemelle.

6 Wladimiro Dorigo, *Venezia romanica: La formazione della città medievale fino all'età gotica* (Verona: Cierre, 2003), 846–48.

7 Other segregating sites, like the Jewish ghetto, the municipal brothel, and the *fondachi* for German and, later, Turkish merchants, were porous enclosures that controlled and limited movement beyond their walls. Their sites were from their inception more integrated into the heart of the city. The Lazzaretto Vecchio is the one enclosure that functioned like convents in its permanence, since plague victims who went there usually died at the hospital. Its site near the Lido reinforced the absolute nature of confinement there.

8 Ludovica Galeazzo, "Entrepreneurship beyond Convent Walls: The Augustinian Nuns of S. Caterina dei Sacchi in Venice," in *Convent Networks in Early Modern Italy*, ed. Marilyn Dunn and Saundra Weddle (Turnhout: Brepols, 2020), 193–229.

9 Dorigo, *Venezia romanica*, table 15A, 834, 846–48.

10 Bartolomea Riccoboni, *Life and Death in a Venetian Convent*, ed. Daniel Bornstein (Chicago: University of Chicago Press, 2000), 3–9.

11 Edward Muir, *Civic Ritual in Renaissance Venice* (Princeton, NJ: Princeton University Press, 1981), 223–30. ASVe, Corpus Domini, b. 19, unpaginated, in-

cludes a sixteenth-century document describing a dispute between the convent and its neighbors, identifying a site just east of the convent church that belonged to the confraternity.

12 Riccoboni, *Life and Death in a Venetian Convent*, 44. There is some confusion about the date of this storm. See, for example, Trevor Dean, "Storm, Suicide and Miracle: Venice 1342," in *Venice and the Veneto during the Renaissance: The Legacy of Benjamin Kohl*, ed. Michael Knapton, John E. Law, and Alison A. Smith (Florence: Firenze University Press, 2014), 315.

13 These parcels were purchased from the Diedo family in 1436; Riccoboni, *Life and Death in a Venetian Convent*, 38–39. Dorigo, *Venezia romanica*, 847–48, does not list any property owned by the Diedo family before 1360, so the exact sites cannot be identified. On the infirmary, built by Tommaso Tommasini, see Corner, *Notizie storiche*, 319.

14 Corner, *Notizie storiche*, 319, states that the convent was granted custodianship in 1444.

15 Wladimiro Dorigo, *Venezia: Origini, ipotesi, metodi* (Milan: Electa, 1983), 463–77, discusses the orientation of Venice's oldest churches.

16 ASVe, Corpus Domini, b. 19, reveals that the convent's converse (lay servants) were housed in one of the structures in this area.

17 ASVe, S. Lucia, b. 3, 18r, describes houses purchased from the Pisanelli, Brochetta, and Dandolo families. None of these names are mentioned by Dorigo, suggesting that the sellers acquired their property after 1360. It is interesting to note, however, that Pope Eugenius IV, who originally approved of the convent, was a Condulmer, and Dorigo notes that the Condulmers owned property in this area, although this may refer to a different branch of the family. Dorigo, *Venezia romanica*, 846–48.

18 Corner, *Notizie storiche*, 256. For a description of the site, see ASVe, S. Lucia, b. 3, 18r–21r.

19 ASVe, S. Lucia, b. 3, 18r–21r. Around this time, some sepulchers were also built in the church.

20 These are not unlike those seen at the Frari, begun around 1340.

21 ASVe, S. Lucia, b. 3, 19v–20r.

22 The number of bells in these bell towers at the time of this dispute is not known. Corpus Domini's nineteenth-century inventory notes that there were three bells in its campanile when the convent was suppressed. ASVe, Demanio, b. 10.

23 For example, this hierarchy and ringing order was the source of disputes between the Florentine convents of Sant'Ambrogio and Le Murate. Sister Giustina Niccolini, *The Chronicle of Le*

Murate, ed. Saundra Weddle (Toronto: CRRS, 2011), chap. 4. See also Niall Atkinson, *The Noisy Renaissance: Sound, Architecture, and Florentine Urban Life* (University Park: Pennsylvania State University Press, 2017), 141.

24 In 1521, the patriarch sought to convert lax conventual communities into strict observant ones, and after 1563, Tridentine decrees imposed even more restrictive practices.

Ludovica Galeazzo

Monastic and Convent Life as a City Phenomenon

16

There is not a more august or holy building in a city than a church…used for the gathering and practice of human company.
BERNARDO GIUSTINIAN, *Historia di m. Bernardo Giustiniano gentilhuomo vinitiano dell'origine di Vinegia* (1545)

Venice has always identified itself with the religious buildings that marked its legendary foundation. From San Giacomo di Rialto, allegedly the city's oldest church, to St. Mark, the shrine rebuilt to house the body of its patron saint, from the patriarchal seat in San Pietro di Castello to the dozens of churches speckled throughout the city, the image of the "church" worked as a forceful reminder of Venetian *christiana religio*.[1] Yet it embodied the distinctive civic identity of a capital that promoted itself as *altera Roma*.[2] A long line of official historiographers celebrated the providential plan behind the miraculous origin of the lagoon city and, consequently, its mythical liberty. Historians such as Lorenzo de' Monacis (ca. 1351–1428) and Lauro Quirini (ca. 1420–72/81) emphasized Venice as the true descendant of ancient Rome, as well as its role as keeper of piety and Catholic faith.[3] Moreover, the fall of Constantinople in 1453 triggered a new wave of outward faith that stirred the city for almost a century. Venice established itself as the natural heir and defender of Byzantium's holy legacy endangered by the iconoclastic impiety of the Ottomans. This spiritual turmoil provided the backdrop to a wide range of social, artistic, and intellectual activities related to spiritual houses, which characterized the final decades of the century. Over time, these cultural maneuvers were sustained and aggrandized by literature, imagery, and cartography, arts that were called on to reinforce the *imago urbis*: solid, self-sufficient, and, above all, pious.

A Sacred Geography: Religious Buildings and the Urban Fabric

Churches, convents, and monasteries became the most visible evidence of public religion in literary and iconographic descriptions of Venice. But fifteenth-century guidebooks, foreigners' chronicles, pilgrims' diaries, and historiographical writings also depicted them as landmarks of the city's topography. In particular, in Marin Sanudo's *De origine, situ et magistratibus urbis Venetae* (1483–93) and Marcantonio Sabellico's *De situ urbis venetae* (1491–92), parish churches and monastic complexes symbolized many reference points for celebratory itineraries across the city related not only to spiritual activities but also, foremost, to political, cultural, and ceremonial events.[4]

In those same years, the image of the city was enriched by a series of iconographic representations, including Jacopo de' Barbari's *View*.[5] In the unmatched portrait of Venice, the artist depicted a city that was not simply the image of an ideal capital. Rather, the urban fabric was visualized as a dynamic and organic phenomenon, its identity shaped by environmental and artificial layers of intervention. Sacred houses are no exception to that. Churches and monasteries are not formulaic visual images of spiritual refugees. On the contrary, de' Barbari lingered on their architectural details and features, as well as on the labeling of their toponymy. In the *View*, the panorama of religious buildings is updated to include the most recent urban and architectural interventions, as well as the most striking novelties of early Renaissance architecture within the city.[6] Interestingly, intentional distortions and large-scale shifts emerge to signal the architecture's language, which was slowly appearing within the lagoon's contours. One example of many is the highly visible depiction of Santa Maria dei Miracoli, whose refined marble encasement seems to overshadow the surrounding medieval urban fabric.[7] Despite inaccuracies and discrepancies repeatedly pointed out by scholars over time, the abundance of architectural details for religious complexes is extraordinary.[8] Likewise, the artist paid special attention to their surroundings and to those spaces that, although belonging to ecclesiastical communities, were intimately bound to the city. Nearly spying beyond the forbidding walls, the enclosed world of convents and monasteries opens up to onlookers as visual testimony of their integration with the socioeconomic and cultural life of Venice. Orderly orchards, vegetable gardens, rows of vineyards, facilities, and commodities mark the adjacent open spaces of almost every sacred complex, thereby rejecting the topos of religious life as a spiritual and secluded world. This engrossment in detail conveys a remarkable sensitivity to the specificity of each site, in addition to a clear recognition of the clergy's involvement in the city's everyday life activities.

The attention paid to greenery and rural areas deserves consideration. Given the now well-established allegorical interpretation of the *View*, the importance attributed to nature in a city almost deprived of any horticultural territory is perhaps not accidental. Forty years after the *View*'s production, Alvise Cornaro celebrated the Venetian art of agriculture, which he interpreted as both an ethical and political instrument related to the military security of the Serenissima. For the intellectual patrician, self-sufficiency and control over nature were building blocks for a peaceful state.[9] By lingering on green areas, de' Barbari might have—intentionally or not—highlighted a fundamental element in reciprocal economic relations between monasteries and the city center.

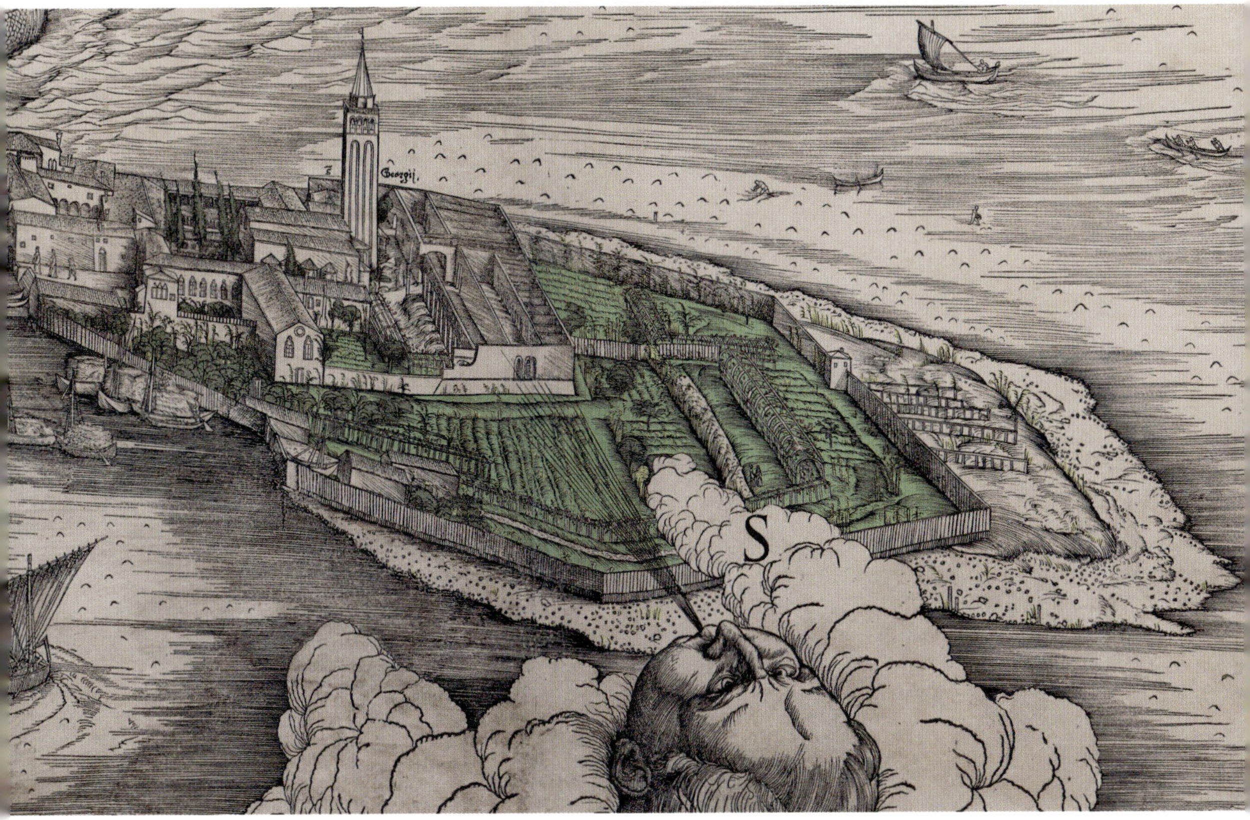

Nestling in Greenery: Orchards, Vegetable Gardens, and Intellectual Spaces within Monastic Walls

The complex of San Giorgio Maggiore rises majestically in the woodcut print, with its imposing buildings and luxuriant garden (fig. 16.1). The observer's eye captures the abundance and extension of green areas surrounding the Benedictine monastery. Francesco Sansovino recalled that the religious complex originally hosted a vineyard, a small woods, and a two-wheel mill that "served the Ducal Palace." Then, right after the construction of the new church (thirteenth century), "the island was entirely covered by delicate gardens and charming orchards," including "laurel oaks and bushes," which adorned the main cloister.[10] All these elements are insightfully described in the *View* and allow us to retrieve visually the life of the sixteenth-century community.

The woods, donated to the monks as early as the end of the tenth century by Doge Tribuno Memmo, are visible on the left side of the area, in the corner facing the canal of San Giorgio.[11] To its right, vegetable gardens and a vineyard, whose trellis once extended all along the southern area of the island, provided sustainable resources for the complex. Wooden pergolas, intersecting each other and stretching to reach the lagoon, occupied most of the remaining space and were used for the cultivation of roses. These plants were renowned not only for their horticultural beauty but also for their medicinal and culinary use.[12] Sixteenth-century tenant farmers' contracts confirm the extensive production of rose petals within Venetian monastic complexes, destined to be sold outside their precincts.[13]

Looking closer at the island, a series of religious figures appears to animate the stage and enjoy the pleasantness of the idyllic landscape. Given the seemingly calculated placement of people within the *View*, this might be interpreted as reflecting a deliberate choice to emphasize the social role of San Giorgio Maggiore in early modern Venice.[14] Like the monastery, the garden was a center of the most contemporary spiritual and intellectual culture and, in the first half of the sixteenth century, the main catalyst for the reform movement in Venice.[15] It is precisely in this agreeable oasis that the Florentine Antonio Brucioli set one of his dialogues on moral philosophy (1537). He depicted Reginald Pole—the English cardinal in exile in the Veneto—strolling through the garden and the small woods and discussing virtue with Gregorio Cortese, the abbot of the monastery.[16] No longer simply an undefined background, the religious landscape assumes the value of a historical source.[17]

Not far from San Giorgio, on the large strip of land projecting over the south contour of the Arsenal, another green space offered its horticultural products to the city. A fine watercolor on parchment predates the woodcut by forty years and, for the sake of its north–south orientation, allows us to penetrate edges that are not visible in the *View* (fig. 16.2). The anonymous drawing minutely represents the site extending between the demolished monasteries of San Domenico and Sant'Antonio di Castello and the island of San Servolo.[18] Aside from being an extraordinary source for interpreting buildings that no longer exist, this view constitutes another remarkable document for understanding the organization and typical schema of Venetian monastic green spaces. It shows the monastery of San Domenico arranged around two large cloisters: the first one, squared, hosted a monumental well; the second, with a slightly longer shape, was embellished by

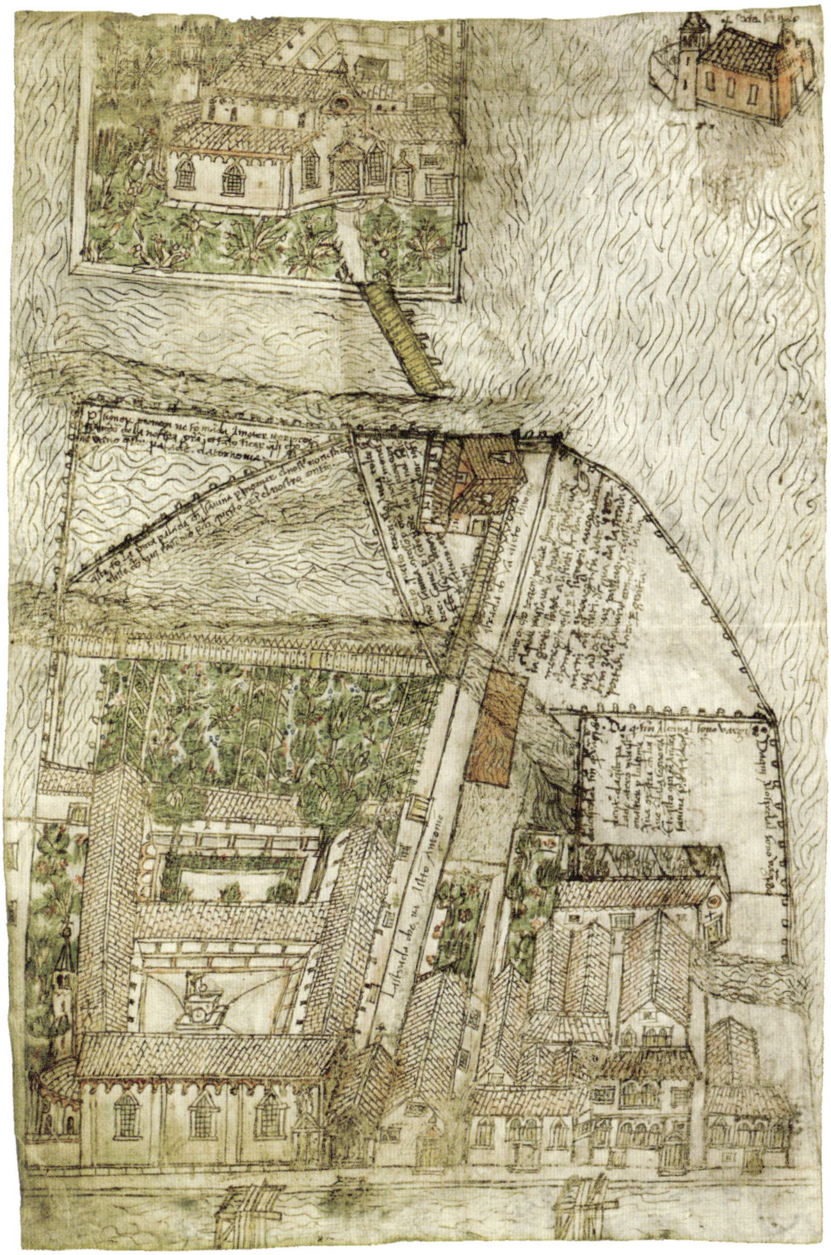

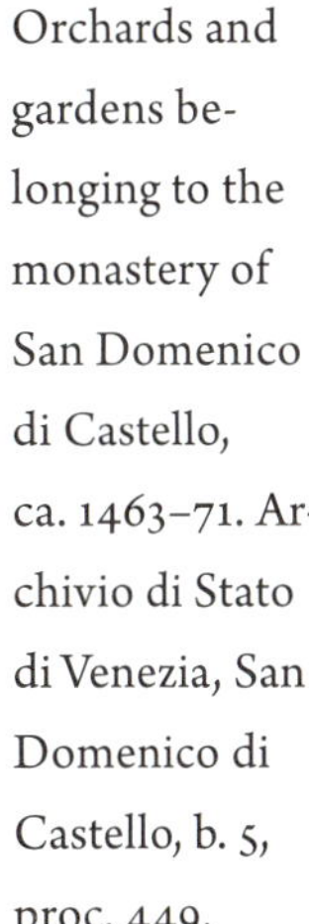

16.2

Orchards and gardens belonging to the monastery of San Domenico di Castello, ca. 1463–71. Archivio di Stato di Venezia, San Domenico di Castello, b. 5, proc. 449.

flowerbeds. Just beyond these places, a large and colorful space devoted to both garden and orchard extended to the canal. Archival sources use the Latin term *viridarium*—the garden of Roman houses.[19] This was an elaborated location in which high-growing plants, fruit trees, and flowerbeds were finely divided by orderly walkways that ran in line with the fencings. A barrel-vaulted trellis—also prominent in the *View*—marked the principal axis of the garden, while two wooden flat-roofed tunnels along both sides of the garden allowed the growth of the roses and vines.[20] Here as in several other monasteries and convents, this series of spaces was instrumental in securing the financial independence of its community, while also contributing to the city's general food supply.[21]

Ludovica Galeazzo

Economic and Cloistered Life

The interlocking exchange between religious institutions and Venice did not concern food alone. As widely demonstrated, nunneries and monasteries were an integral part of Venetian social and cultural life, as well as the urban and economic essence of the everyday city. Again, San Giorgio held a special place in notions of both monastic hospitality and economy. Within its walls, a lavish guesthouse lodged foreign ambassadors and dignitaries before their meeting with the doge,[22] while at the far southwestern tip of the island two *cavane* (roofed boat slips) offered shelter to sailors, fishermen, and merchants. Other facilities arranged in the complex included warehouses, storages, and staff houses that served both the monastic populace and the larger Venetian community.[23] Finally, along the southern side of the area, the waning seashore equipped with docks had been arranged for merchant ships carrying hay or straw.

If the lagoon's ecclesiastical complexes, because of their location and condition of insularity, were naturally inclined to house manufacturing activities, similarly monastic institutions located at the edges of the city offered patches of land for the production of goods. A singular case is that of Santi Giovanni e Paolo. Located on the northern rim of the city, the Dominican monastery—one of the main humanistic centers of Venice—played a significant role in commercial operations related to timber.[24] As the print elucidates, the area around the complex was devoted to wood manufacture and was filled with timber yards and storage facilities for the crafting of lumber. The monastery itself had extensive possessions, warehouses, and shops that were rented to private citizens at high prices.[25] However, according to the 1564 tax record, the friars also rented internal areas of their monastery for various activities. For instance, the old Dominican refectory was lent to

Zamaria di Formenti for storing oil, while the chapter house was leased by Vincenzo Valgrisio for keeping his books.[26] Sacred and secular coexisted within these religious complexes, contributing to the territory's social and economic life.

Yet monastic communities were not the only religious groups that actively engaged in commercial activities. Select parish churches owned large territories around their walls and used them for both residential and economic activities. One well-known case is that of the church of San Pantalon, which, since the fourteenth century, had claimed property rights on the area known as the *chiovere*.[27] These were open spaces assigned for drying dyed cloths and, in particular, sails. Situated directly behind the complex of San Rocco, this place is portrayed in the *View* as a vast terrain dotted with racks that also includes a two-story wooden shed (fig. 16.3). These structures, along with facilities in the *chiovere* of San Girolamo and Santa Croce, had a primary importance in the flourishing Venetian textile market.[28]

Manufacturing beyond religious walls could sometimes take the form of proto-industrial activities. In describing the Augustinian monastery located in the now demolished island of San Cristoforo, the canon and pilgrim Pietro Casola (1427–1507) lingered on the wax-bleaching processes that took place in the garden in such a great quantity that, he said, "it seemed to me it ought to suffice for all the world."[29] Another outstanding case was the famous pastry-making laboratory inside the nunnery of Santa Croce on the Giudecca. A rare fifteenth-century document shows the complex articulation of inner spaces fitted for the intensive rearing of hens: a space (*albergo*) in which to make eggs, a room for the chickens' coop, a courtyard and portico for feeding them, and a granary to store their grain (fig. 16.4). There was a big oven for the extensive production of cakes, using those very eggs, to delight the palates of inhabitants.[30]

Monastic Complexes and the City's Urbanization

Principally arranged as a ring along the contours of the city, in settlements physically on the verge of land and water, many Venetian ecclesiastical institutions vigorously contributed to the spatial maturation process that led to the physical creation of new areas of the city. Since the early thirteenth century, religious communities had initiated land reclamation operations, at

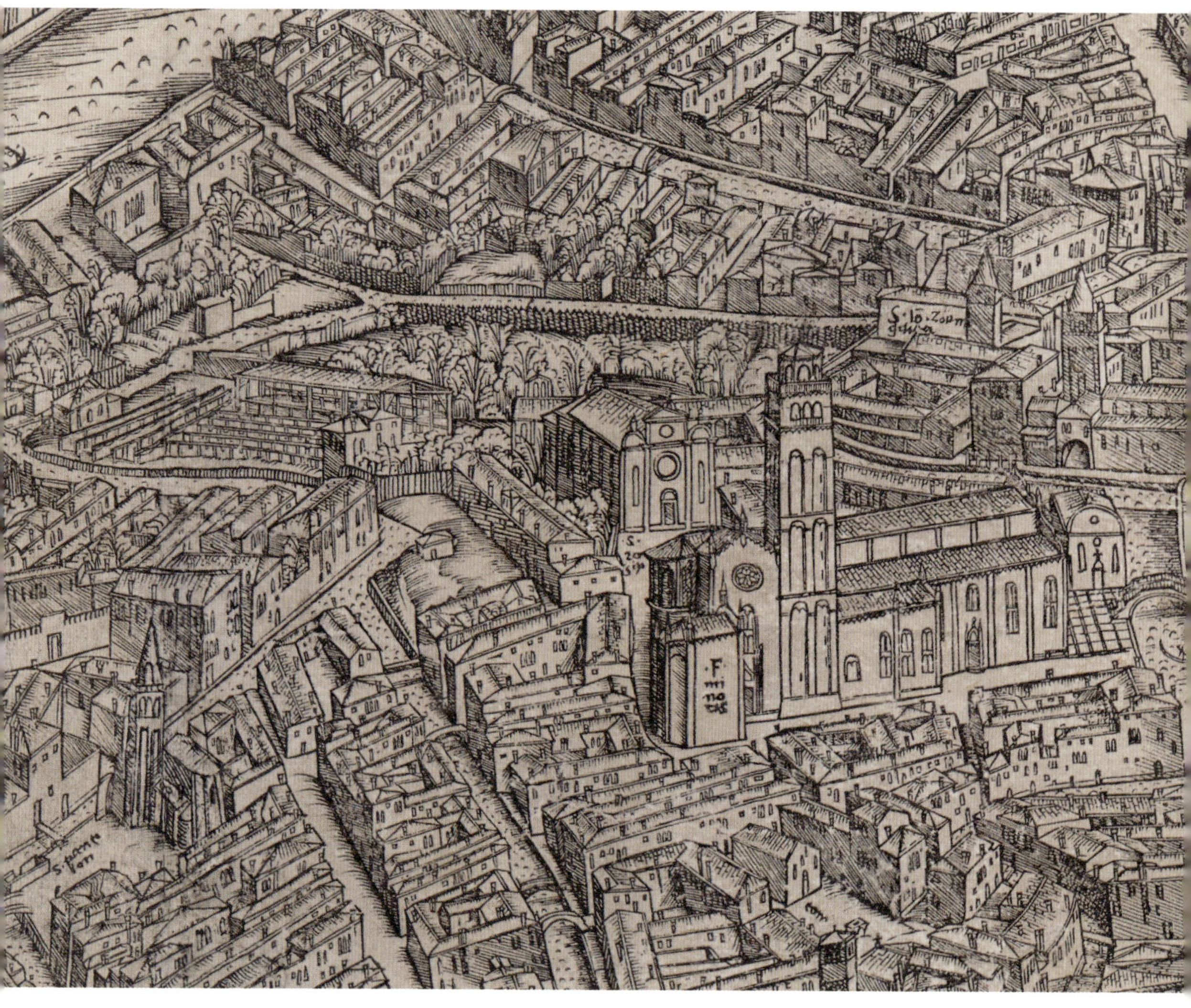

16.3

Detail of the *chiovere* of San Pantalon from Jacopo de' Barbari, *View of Venice*, ca. 1497–1500.

times on the scale of entire neighborhoods.[31] These pioneering campaigns sought to rectify Venice's frayed and irregular borders and to enhance urban areas still dominated by swamps and marshes. These programmatic efforts intensified in the sixteenth century, when the explosion in population and the necessity of draining mud from the excavations of canals, as well as the government's need to create a regular and permanent boundary for the urban settlement, drove new efforts to expand.

Hundreds of landfill interventions were carried out by the state, private citizens, and the foremost religious complexes. The strips of poor bear-

220

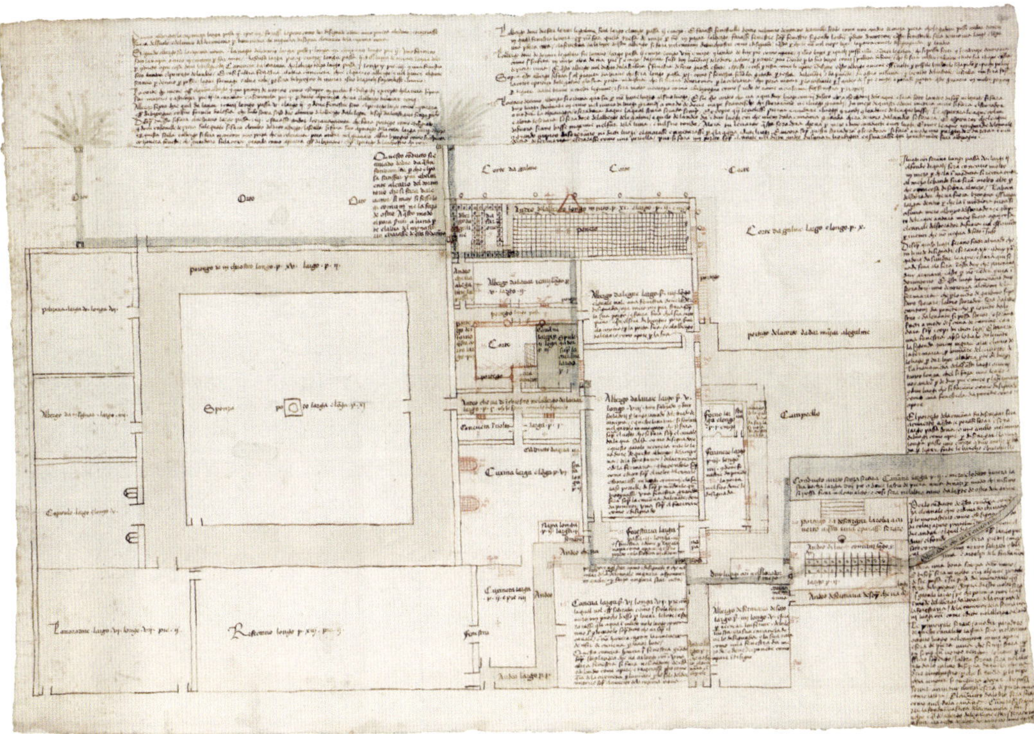

ing subsoil and wooden pilings appearing in the *View* around the sacred precincts disclose the efforts made by ecclesiastical communities to move the civic borders farther out into the lagoon. Clearly visible on the western tip of the *View*, the urban development behind the complexes of San Domenico and Sant'Antonio di Castello was extended during de' Barbari's time (fig. 16.5). A series of swamps and branches of canals leading into unsolidified soil is evidence of recent intervention, while a row of pilings on the right most likely reveals an alignment for more new land to be filled in. This activity had started decades before, around 1463, when the Dominican monks began drainage interventions along the margins of their monastery.[32] Due to this process of land reclamation carried on by the ecclesiastical community, the area slowly neared completion, so much so that the Senate decided to build a *cohopertum* (a covered structure) for beggars and old sailors—then known as the hospital of Messer Gesù Cristo (1474)—and, a few decades later, the church of San Nicolò (1490–1503).[33]

This form of dynamism has been meticulously recounted by both the Giudici del Piovego and—from the beginning of the sixteenth century—

16.4

Map of the convent of Santa Croce in the Giudecca with places for rearing hens, sixteenth century. Archivio di Stato di Venezia, Santa Croce alla Giudecca, b. 4, disegno 3.

the new government office of the Savi ed Esecutori alle Acque. Their technical reports trace the empirical and fragmentary logic of the interventions. However, their visual memory is mostly entrusted to schematic sketches that show plans of reclaimed areas.[34] For this reason, once more, de' Barbari's *View* represents an incredible iconographic source, not only because it captures the exigencies of the city's physical growth but also because it shapes, in a sort of *descriptio aedificandi*, the undergoing process.

Powerful, operational, and shaped by human activities: the image of the church in the *View* is the portrait of a singular microcosm. It is not a representation of a "sacred topography" but, rather, the transliteration of a heightened awareness of Venetian churches. Religious houses represented connective hubs within a network of supply, organization, and distribution of resources. Their role in supporting the economy of the city as well as in determining the final shape of its contours constituted an integral part of the prosperity and grandeur of Venice.

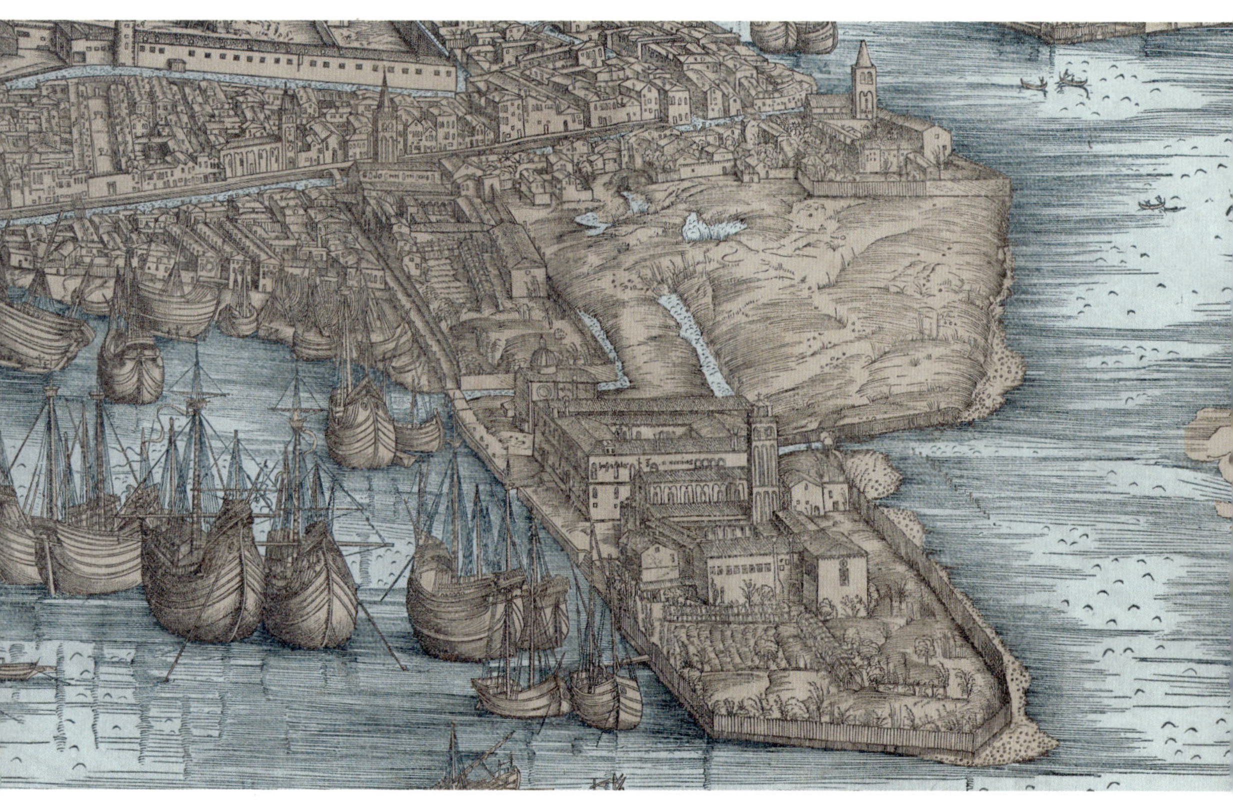

1 On the relationship between Venice and its sacred buildings, see Ennio Concina, *Venezia: Le chiese e le arti*, 2 vols. (Udine: Magnus, 1995); and Ennio Concina, *Tempo Novo: Venezia e il quattrocento* (Venice: Marsilio, 2006), 177–90.

2 Manfredo Tafuri, *Venezia e il Rinascimento: Religione, scienza, architettura* (Turin: Einaudi, 1985), 24–27.

3 On the fifteenth-century encomiastic literature about Venice, see Franco Gaeta, "L'idea di Venezia," in *Dal primo Quattrocento al Concilio di Trento*, vol. 3, *Storia della cultura veneta*, ed. Girolamo Arnaldi and Manlio Pastore Stocchi (Vicenza: Neri Pozza, 1981), 565–98.

4 It must be noted that Sabellico almost completely ignored the private palaces in favor of a systematic analysis of all the religious complexes. See Paola Modesti, "Quasi come in un dipinto: La città e l'architettura nel 'De situ urbis Venetae' di Marcantonio Sabellico," *Arte Veneta: Rivista di storia dell'arte* 66 (2010): 19.

5 On the fifteenth-century image of Venice, see Giorgio Bellavitis and Giandomenico Romanelli, *Venezia* (Rome: Laterza, 1985), 68–69.

6 Giandomenico Romanelli, "Venezia 1500," in *A volo d'uccello: Jacopo de' Barbari e le rappresentazioni di città nell'Europa del Rinascimento*, exhib. cat., ed. Giandomenico Romanelli, Susanna Biadene, and Camillo Tonini (Venice: Arsenale, 1999), 12–18.

7 This sketches another close correspondence with Sabellico's work in which Santa Maria dei Miracoli is described as "magnifica" and ranked next to the "golden temple" of St. Mark. Marcantonio Sabellico, *Del sito di Venezia città* (1502), ed. Giancarlo Meneghetti (Venice: Libreria Filippi, 1985), 23.

8 For one article pointing out inaccuracies and discrepancies, see Juergen Schulz, "Jacopo de' Barbari's View of Venice: Map Making, City Views, and Moralized Geography before the Year 1500," *Art Bulletin* 60, no. 3 (1978): 439.

9 Marco Cornaro and Cristoforo Sabbadino, *Scritture sopra la laguna* (Modena: Ferrari, 1941), 10. See also Manfredo Tafuri, "Sapienza di Stato e atti mancati: Architettura e tecnica urbana nella Venezia del 500," in *Architettura e utopia nella Venezia del Cinquecento*, exhib. cat., ed. Lionello Puppi et al. (Milan: Electa, 1980), 33.

10 Francesco Sansovino, *Venetia, città nobilissima et singolare […]* (Venice: appresso Iacomo Sansovino, 1581), 81v–82r.

11 For the Doge Tribuno Memmo's donation of the woods, see Gino Damerini, *L'isola e il cenobio di San Giorgio*

Maggiore (Venice: Fondazione Giorgio Cini, 1956), 8–13.

12 On the use of distilled rosewater, see Carla Coco, *Venezia in cucina* (Rome: Laterza, 2011). See also chap. 23, dedicated to rose gardens, by the Paduan botanist Africo Clemente in the *Trattato dell'agricoltura di m. Africo Clemente Padovano* [...] (Venice: ad instantia di M. Africo Clemente Padoano, 1572), 220–22.

13 See, for example, Archivio di Stato di Venezia (ASVe), Santa Maria degli Angeli di Murano, b. 9, July 15, 1564.

14 It should be noted that the city's principal sites, St. Mark's Square and the Rialto, appear completely empty in the *View*. By contrast, the contours of the urban fabric are filled with dozens of characters involved in everyday life actions: sailors, fishermen, carpenters, water carriers, and clam diggers, as well as monks and nuns.

15 On San Giorgio Maggiore as a cradle for the *spirituali*, see Damerini, *L'isola e il cenobio di San Giorgio Maggiore*, 109–25; and Stephen D. Bowd, *Reform before the Reformation: Vicenzo Querini and the Religious Renaissance in Italy* (Leiden: Brill, 2002), 210–12.

16 Antonio Brucioli, *Dialogi di Antonio Brucioli* (Venice: per Gregorio de Gregori, 1526), dialogue 11, 82v.

17 On landscape in Renaissance art, see Alessandra Pattanaro, "Il paesaggio dipinto fra Quattrocento e Cinquecento: Storia dell'arte e memoria del territorio," in *Il paesaggio costruito, il paesaggio nell'arte*, ed. Gianmario Guidarelli and Elena Svalduz (Padua: Padova University Press, 2017), 91–103.

18 The drawing is in ASVe, San Domenico di Castello, b. 5, proc. 449. Although not dated, the watercolor was almost certainly made between 1463 (a date annotated on the drawing) and 1471. See Ludovica Galeazzo, "Orti e giardini di proprietà del monastero di San Domenico di Castello," in *Acqua e cibo a Venezia: Storie della laguna e della città*, ed. Donatella Calabi and Ludovica Galeazzo (Venice: Marsilio, 2015), 229.

19 ASVe, San Domenico di Castello, b. 5, August 13, 1569.

20 Natsumi Nonaka, *Renaissance Porticoes and Painted Pergolas: Nature and Culture in Early Modern Italy* (London: Routledge, 2017).

21 Fabien Faugeron, *Nourrir la ville: Ravitaillement, marchés et métiers de l'alimentation à Venise dans les derniers siècles du Moyen âge* (Rome: École Française de Rome, 2014).

22 Stefanie Cossalter, "Dai porti alle isole: Cerimoniali di accoglienza nella Serenissima," in *Spazi veneziani: Topografie culturali di una città*, ed. Sabine Meine (Rome: Viella Libreria, 2014), 125–48.

23 The 1564 tax record of the monastery lists a series of houses inhabited by farmers, a baker, and a tailor working in the

monastery. ASVe, Sopraintendenti alle decime del clero, b. 32, fasc. 82.

24 Silvia Moretti, "I Domenicani dei Santi Giovanni e Paolo a Venezia nel XVI secolo: Contraddizioni di un margine urbano," *Mélanges de l'École Française de Rome* 116, no. 2 (2005): 641–63.

25 An example concerns the timber merchants Francesco and Alessandro de Lazzari, who rented a timber workshop for 100 ducats per year. ASVe, Sopraintendenti alle decime del clero, b. 33, fasc. 142, fol. 2r (1564).

26 The rent was twenty-two and twelve ducats, respectively.

27 Lucia Nadin Bassani, *Migrazioni e integrazione: Il caso degli albanesi a Venezia, 1479–1552* (Rome: Bulzoni, 2008), 117–18.

28 Ennio Concina, *Venezia nell'età moderna: Struttura e funzioni* (Venice: Marsilio, 1989), 66–67.

29 Pietro Casola, *Viaggio di Pietro Casola a Gerusalemme*, ed. Anna Paoletti (Alessandria: Edizioni dell'Orso, 2001), 92.

30 The drawing is in ASVe, Santa Croce alla Giudecca, b. 4, dis. 3 (sixteenth century). See Michela Dal Borgo, *L'arte dei gallineri e la cucina dei volatili nella Repubblica di Venezia* (Venice: Archivio di Stato, 2009), docs. 3–4.

31 See Élisabeth Crouzet-Pavan, "La conquista e l'organizzazione dello spazio," in *L'età del Comune*, vol. 2 of *Storia di Venezia dalle origini alla caduta della Serenissima*, ed. Gherardo Ortalli and Giorgio Cracco (Rome: Istituto della Enciclopedia Italiana, 1996), 549–76.

32 Paola Pavanini, "Venezia verso la pianificazione? Bonifiche urbane nel XVI secolo a Venezia," in *D'une ville à l'autre*, ed. Jean-Claude Marie Vigeuer (Rome: Ecole Française de Rome, 1989), 494–506.

33 See Odilla Battiston, ed., *Chiese e monasteri distrutti a Castello dopo il 1807: S. Domenico, S. Nicolò di Bari, Ospedale di Messer Gesù Cristo, Seminario ducale, Convento delle Cappuccine, S. Antonio* (Venice: Filippi, 1992), 9–40.

34 Elena Svalduz, "Al servizio del magistrato: I proti alle acque nel corso del primo secolo d'attività," in *Architetto sia l'ingegniero che discorre*, ed. Giuliana Mazzi and Stefano Zaggia (Venice: Marsilio, 2004), 233–68.

Holly Hurlburt

Gendered Space(s) and the *View*

ON FIRST GLANCE, Jacopo de' Barbari's Venice seems to confirm the city's masculine and patriarchal ideology. The eight winds that border the scene are male. A bristling and brawny Neptune astride a fish (dolphin) guards the city's sacred and most ceremonial center, while an equally muscular Mercury looks down from above (plate 7). An inscription praising Venice as a mercantile entrepôt accompanies each god.[1] There is an eerie lack of human forms of either gender occupying the city's usually bustling religious, commercial, and political centers, but dozens if not hundreds of boatmen ply the waters of the Grand Canal and the Arsenal and move around the city. Although de' Barbari did not devote much detail to these figures, we must generally assume them to be male.[2] The only hint of Venice as a city of women in the *View* comes with the names of female saints scrawled on the religious institutions that bear their names. One could be forgiven for concluding, along with Scottish seventeenth-century traveler Fynes Moryson, that the women of Venice lived quasi-cloistered lives, "locked up at home, as if in prison," and thus rarely if ever entered the public spaces as showcased in de' Barbari's plan.[3]

This essay challenges that familiar assumption, demonstrating that elite and common women, both foreign and Venetian, recurrently engaged in civic ritual and politics in the spaces rendered void of men and women by de' Barbari, while their bodies, clad in Venetian traded and manufactured wares such as damask and pearls, formed a living tableau of Venetian commercial dominance. As Deborah Howard and others have demonstrated, de' Barbari deviated from his overall bird's-eye perspective to foreground both the city's religious and political hub, the Piazzetta in front of the Doge's Palace and San Marco, and its triumphant approach, the Grand Canal.[4] His emphasis on these spaces accentuated their ritual potential. Like the *View*, ceremony in fifteenth-century Venice served to inform and engage citizens and foreigners alike in Venetian power, wealth, and beauty. Venetians participated in a full calendar of religious rituals, which featured the doge, magistrates, and members of confraternities processing by land, and in fleets of boats and floats moving down the Grand Canal. Ritual time and space became more congested in the last third of the fifteenth century: in addition to a crowded calendar of religious feasts, Venice elected eight doges whose inaugurations ran days or weeks and featured pageants winding across land and water before arriving at San Marco. And during and after the long reign of Doge Francesco Foscari (1423–57), official welcomes for international visitors of worth to the city became ever more frequent, elaborate, and expensive, featuring choreographed entrances, departures, entertainments, and visits to the city's most important sites: the Treasury of San Marco, the Mercerie, and the Arsenal.[5]

In the long process of study and preparatory drawing that preceded the creation of his masterpiece, de' Barbari most likely would have observed such rituals in the spaces he would depict. He would have witnessed the personnel and apparatus of the state (doge, ambassadors, chancellor, secretaries, senators), which in many ways embodied the entirety of the Venetian sociopolitical hierarchy. Also present at such events were confraternity members, guild workers who built and manned the floats, and every kind of boat and boatman. On certain occasions an equally socially diverse group greeted Italian, European, and Mediterranean rulers, their families and entourages creating a visual juxtaposition of republican and monarchical governing systems.

At these events de' Barbari and thousands of Venetians and visitors would also have seen women. As a republic, the Venetian state was gendered emphatically masculine. However, Venetian symbolism and ritual highlighted allegories of women, the ideal woman, and real women. The sea, gendered female, featured prominently in many Venetian rituals—none more so than the annual festival of the Sensa (Venetian dialect for Ascension), a religious event marked by the doge's Marriage of the Sea. After Mass in San Marco, the doge and magistrates boarded the ceremonial barge or Bucintoro, sitting at rest at the Arsenal in the *View*, another reminder of ceremonial potential. Accompanied by other vessels, they rowed out into the lagoon, where the doge dropped a ring into the waters, asserting patriarchal authority over the feminine sea by saying, "We espouse you, O sea, as a sign of true and perpetual dominion."[6] With a little help from Neptune, who in the *View* holds his delphinic mount firmly by a chain and claims to "smooth the waters at this port," Venetians imagined they controlled the sea's tempestuous body and thus guaranteed the continued prosperity of their maritime trade and Mediterranean ascendancy. Venetians also anthropomorphized their city as a woman. "Venetia" appeared on the Doge's Palace (plate 2) in the fourteenth century and thereafter in countless painted political allegories within its walls as well as at other sites. Her iconography drew variously from the Virgin Mary, embodiments of Justice, and even the Roman goddess Venus—herself born (like the Venetian economy) from the sea.[7] However, although Venetia herself was powerful, she was not a sign of female empowerment: patriarchy, in the form of the male republic, created Venetia and controlled her even as it did the feminine sea.

Although women—allegorical or real—are absent from de' Barbari's ritual spaces, they did observe and participate in ceremonies. For example, dozens of women appear as spectators in Gentile Bellini's *Miracle of the Cross at the Bridge of San Lorenzo*, ca. 1500 (fig. 17.1). Created at approximately the same time as the *View*, Bellini's scene is filled with throngs of participants and spectators, including the queen of Cyprus, Caterina Corner (1454–1510), and eight of her ladies. In addition, dozens of other women, of all ages and in both secular and religious garb, populate the crowds of observers—on the bridge, in the crowd, and even in a boat beneath the Bridge of San Lorenzo.

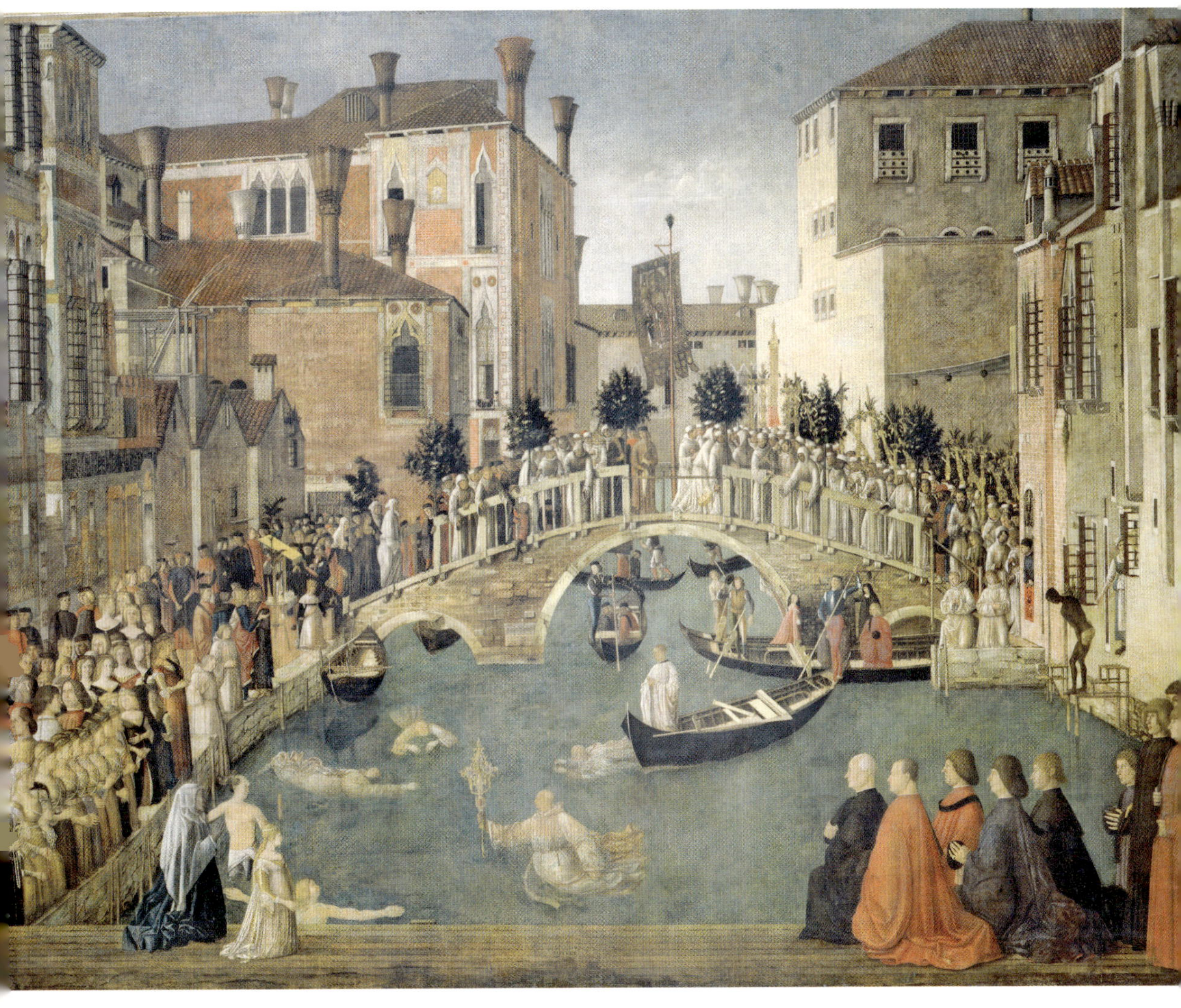

In the era that de' Barbari and Bellini depicted Venice, women had become more than ritual bystanders, increasingly taking center stage in civic ceremonies. Since at least the thirteenth century, the doge's wife, or dogaressa, had her own ritual entrance into the Doge's Palace as part of the celebrations marking her husband's election. The fifteenth century witnessed up to ten such entries, during which the dogaressa, family members, servants, and an honor court of patrician ladies traveled the Grand Canal and filled the piazza along with celebrating guilds and local and foreign spectators. Its reputation in the fifteenth century and elaboration and recording in books of ceremony in the sixteenth century normalized this female-focused civic ritual. What's more, many of the aforementioned foreign dignitaries who toured Venice were women—traveling with their husbands, as in the case of Leonor of Portugal (1434–67), the wife of Holy Roman Emperor Frederick III (r. 1452–93), who came in 1452, or on their own, such as Maria of Aragon, en route to marry Marquis Lionello d'Este (r. 1441–50) in Ferrara in 1444.[8] De' Barbari may have witnessed the pageantry accompanying the visit of mother and daughter Eleonora d'Este (1450–93) and Beatrice Sforza (1475–97), who visited in 1493 on behalf of their husbands—the Duke of Ferrara and future Duke of Milan, respectively—to mark the conclusion of a political alliance. On these diplomatic occasions, scores of women occupied the ritual stage: the Este/Sforza retinue totaled in the hundreds, and typical diplomatic greetings featured the wife or daughter of the doge and an honor guard of elaborately clad Venetian patrician women.[9]

The presence of so many women at these ritual events accentuated their own generative potential: after all, the state may have been republican, male, and guarded by male deities, but it was the wives of Venice that bore and nurtured every future senator, sea captain, and citizen, as the thirteenth-century Porta Sant'Alipio mosaic on the façade of San Marco, with its clusters of women and children framing and witnessing the Translation of the relics of the church's name saint, suggests (fig. 17.2).[10] The fundamental necessity of marriage and procreation to the Venetian sociopolitical system was especially evident in elaborate wedding rituals that, with increasing pomp and frequency, wound their way from palace to canal to piazza and back again. In his voluminous diaries, contemporaneous with the *View*, Marin Sanudo recorded dozens of nuptial ceremonies that included banquets, dancing and other performances, and processions featuring hundreds of elaborately clad men and women, of whom Sanudo often took particular note. Describing the particularly elaborate wedding of Doge Andrea Gritti's granddaughter in 1525, Sanudo waxed rhapsodic on the clothes and jewels of the bride and the ninety-five women who accompanied her, "all of whom were wearing heavy gold chains and lots of pearls." "After Mass, the women followed the newly-wed bride out of the church [of San Marco]. One by one they processed across the piazza.... I note that among them there were six women of the people, whom the doge specially invited, and one foreigner. And there were many people in the piazza. It was a fine sight to see these women walking by."[11]

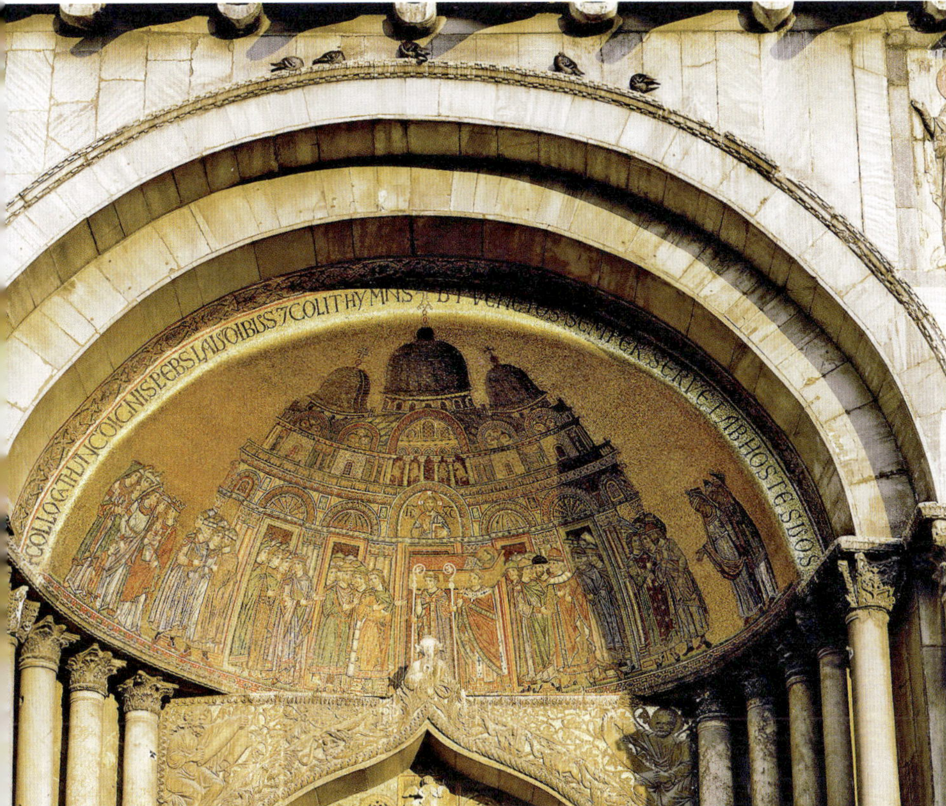

Sanudo understood that female display at these events served multiple purposes. Whether matronly or nubile, elite women were the connective tissue for the political and commercial ties that knitted the state together. Their dowries moved funds between families—funds that might be invested in Venetian commerce, architecture, or luxury goods. With suspension or lax enforcement of sumptuary laws on such occasions, female bodies, like those described by Sanudo, formed a montage, displaying for all to see the wealth generated by merchant families: by Venetian textile manufacture in damask, silk, and cloth of gold, and by Venetian trade in goods such as gemstones and pearls that adorned these women's figures.

In de' Barbari's lifetime, ceremonies also marked the commencement and conclusion of a most unusual marriage: that of Venetian noblewoman Caterina Corner (seen with her court in the left foreground, fig. 17.1). Caterina's father and uncle, prominent Venetian patricians with business interests in Cyprus, arranged her marriage to King Jacques II Lusignan in 1468. Lusignan was reluctant to marry a woman without a title, and because Cyprus was so crucial to Venetian Mediterranean interests, the state took the unprecedented step of adding a woman to its number. Enfolding Caterina and her spouse neatly into its patriarchal embrace, the Senate adopted Caterina as "daughter of the republic" before she departed for Cyprus in 1472. There she reigned as sole monarch after the deaths of her spouse in 1473 and newborn son in 1474. An attempted coup demonstrated her vulnerability and encouraged the Venetian Senate to take an ever-heavier hand in "parenting" the young queen. When it seemed she might marry an heir of the king of Naples in 1488, Venice forced her to relinquish her crown, adding Cyprus to its *stato da mar* (overseas empire). Caterina's reentry to the city of her birth in June 1489 was not just another ruling consort's visit. She traveled by Bucintoro, with a coterie of ladies, the doge, the Senate, and musicians, from San Nicolò on the Lido down the length of the Grand Canal to the Duke of Ferrara's palace, "something which had never before happened to any Venetian lady," according to Pietro Bembo.[12] The following day, this group retraced its steps to San Marco, where Caterina met Doge Agostino Barbarigo and "made a free gift of the realm of Cyprus to the republic," a scene depicted on the Great Council Hall in the Doge's Palace, on the monument honoring Caterina in San Salvador (ca. 1580), and in several panels decorating Corner family palaces and chapels in Venice.[13]

These and other rituals that permeated the ceremonial spaces laid out in de' Barbari's *View* became perhaps the most significant means of projecting to residents and visitors alike an idealized Venetian state.[14] A myriad of processions, consisting of monarchical, aristocratic, and popular elements, displayed Venice's "perfect" government celebrated in Gasparo Contarini's *De magistratibus et republic Venetorum* (*The Commonwealth and Government of Venice*, 1543). Visits by foreign dignitaries reflected the successes of Venetian diplomacy, called to mind Venice's resistance to foreign invasion, and underlined her unique status as a republic surrounded by dynasts. Although many have deemed these spaces masculine (as mentioned above), large numbers of women participated in and witnessed civic rituals. These events encapsulated women in their ideal roles as the wives and mothers of the city's governors, bureaucrats, and merchants and literally adorned in the city's astonishing wealth, as we can see in the Porta Sant'Alipio mosaic (fig. 17.2) and Bellini's *Miracle at the Bridge of San Lorenzo* (fig. 17.1). Even ceremonies that, like the Sensa and Caterina Corner's return, featured real or allegorical women, visually underscored the economic and political triumphs of the *stato da mar*, precisely at its moment of greatest strength and influence.

These civic rituals that filled de' Barbari's ceremonial spaces masked a political reality that was much more chaotic and a political space that extended from the Doge's Palace out into the Piazzetta, the site of the *broglio*, where patricians gossiped, debated, and on occasion sought to fix votes. However, in reality it was the totality of de' Barbari's city that made up what Filippo de Vivo has rightly called "Venice's political arena," where patricians, foreigners, merchants, barbers, printers, tavern keepers, apothecaries, and even brothel matrons and other women became conduits of news and thus crucial, if informal, cogs in governance and commerce.[15] Such sites were not the only centers for unofficial politicking in de' Barbari's Venice. The *View* illustrates the growing number of elaborate patrician palaces along the Grand Canal and elsewhere in the city.

If palace, garden, and villa walls could talk, they would tell tales of patrician plotting with kinsmen and allies for political advantage. Politicking mixed easily with *feste* and weddings and also blended easily with the discourses at Venetian *ridotti*, intellectual or entertainment gatherings similar to French salons; during these occasions, women also played an important political role.[16] After her return from Cyprus, Caterina Corner divided her time between the hill town of Asolo, her hunting lodge near there, and the family palace at San Cassian, where she hosted weddings for family members and her ladies-in-waiting. Such events allowed her to collect information about both Cypriot and Venetian politics, which she likely shared with her brother, Zorzi, a senator.[17] Caterina's status as a queen and "daughter of the republic" may have afforded her a unique ability to participate in Venice's political arena. But she was not alone, which should come as no surprise, since patrician palaces were multifunctional and far more than walled-off private realms. In 1472, the Council of Ten revealed that the widow Elisabetta Barbo Zen—niece of Pope Eugenius IV (1431–47), sister of recently deceased Pope Paul II (1464–71), and mother of Cardinal Gianbattista Zen—had hosted a *ridotto* popular with patrician governors. While senators chatted about the news of the day, two secretaries secretly collected their words and dispatched them to her cardinal son in Rome. Elisabetta and several male kinsmen were imprisoned and later exiled for convicted state treason. With regard to this case, nineteenth-century Venetian historian Pompeo Molmenti concluded that Elisabetta was "a solitary exception to the rule that women never stepped outside their natural sphere."[18]

He was wrong. Mattea Collalto was detained by the Council of Ten fifteen years later for a similar crime of sharing with the enemies of Venice information obtained from senators hosted at one of her "parties."[19] Women not only bore and raised the politicians of Venice and knit together kinships groups, as Stanley Chojnacki has shown; they also could and did act as conduits of political information. Because of the very nature of the home as, at least in theory, private, evidence for this kind of female political engagement is less common but can be found, as these examples show, in the records of the Ten, in Inquisition files, and even in the pages of Sanudo's diary. Arriving in the Piazza San Marco one morning in 1498, he found "our [Chancellery] secretary Antonio de Landi, aged about 70, hanging between the two columns." The crime, Sanudo revealed, had taken place in the house of Landi's "kept woman" Laura Troylo, where Landi met regularly with his friend Zuan Battista Trevisan, then in the employ of the Marquis of Mantua. Troylo's associate Hironimo "hid behind the bed and heard these two discussing matters of the state and secrets of the Senate."[20] Hironimo made an accusation, but it was Laura who earned twenty-five ducats from the Venetian state, a payment that tacitly acknowledged the value of women as information brokers.

In blended private and public spaces—behind palace walls, in taverns, at weddings, in civic processions, as allegorical representations—women of all classes and ages contributed to the makeup of Venice's urban fabric, as Gentile Bellini's *Miracle* image suggests. Scholars such as Monica Chojnacka and Paula Clarke, among others, have complicated Fynes Moryson's notion that the city was neatly segregated into public/political and private/domestic spheres, showing the range of spaces occupied by working-class women, from the contrada to churches to shops and taverns.[21] In so doing they have populated with women the ceremonial and commercial centers of Venice that de' Barbari left vacant. This short examination achieves the same for elite women who could and did perform in civic rituals along with elaborate wedding rituals that imitated them in both their pomp and processional routes. In rituals, both real women (like Caterina Corner) and allegorical women (like Venetia) embodied the patriarchal state and its goals. Behind the scenes, however, the very connections that women created through marriage and procreation, which in essence sustained the state, also allowed them access to information that they occasionally used to shape and/or subvert it. Women likewise interacted with, influenced, or at times subverted the state in more private spaces. All of Venice was thus

Holly Hurlburt

a stage, much like Jacopo de' Barbari portrays in his *View*, with all its men and women players in the constant unfolding of great ritual and political drama.

NOTES

1 Juergen Schulz translates the inscriptions in "Jacopo de' Barbari's *View of Venice*: Map Making, City Views, and Moralized Geography before the Year 1500," *Art Bulletin* 60, no. 3 (1978): 468.

2 The only figure depicted by de' Barbari that might indicate a female appears in a group of three figures embarking into gondolas at the monastery of San Giorgio Maggiore, though this viewer finds the garb and demeanor of these figures to be too ambiguous to definitively indicate gender.

3 Fynes Moryson, *An Itinerary written by Fynes Moryson [...] containing his ten yeeres travel through the twelve dominions* (London: Ioan Beale, 1617), 1:70, as quoted in Monica Chojnacka, *Working Women of Early Modern Venice* (Baltimore, MD: Johns Hopkins University Press, 2001), 103. Scholars have largely supported this notion: see Robert C. Davis, "The Geography of Gender in the Renaissance," in *Gender and Society in Renaissance Italy*, ed. Judith Brown and Davis (London: Longman, 1998), 19–38; and Dennis Romano, "Gender and the Urban Geography of Renaissance Venice," *Journal of Social History* 23 (1989): 339–53.

4 Deborah Howard, "Venice as a Dolphin: Further Investigations into Jacopo de' Barbari's View," *Artibus et Historiae* 18, no. 35 (1997): 104–5.

5 Edward Muir, *Civic Ritual in Renaissance Venice* (Princeton, NJ: Princeton University Press, 1981), 185–250; on Foscari, see Dennis Romano, *The Likeness of Venice: A Life of Doge Francesco Foscari, 1373–1457* (New Haven, CT: Yale University Press, 2007). On entrances generally, see also Patricia Fortini Brown, "Measured Friendship and Calculated Pomp: The Ceremonial Welcomes of the Venetian Republic," in *Triumphal Celebrations and the Ritual of Statecraft*, vol. 1 of *"All the World's a Stage": Art and Pageantry in Renaissance and Baroque Europe*, ed. Barbara Wisch and Susan Munshower (University Park: Pennsylvania State University Press, 1990).

6 Muir, *Civic Ritual*, 122.

7 David Rosand, *"Venetia Figurata*: The Iconography of a Myth," in *Interpretazioni veneziane: Studi di storia dell'arte in onore di Michelangelo Muraro* (Venice: Arsenale, 1984), 177–96; and Jutta Sperling, *Convents and the Body Politics in Late Renaissance Venice* (Chicago: University of Chicago Press, 1999), 72–96. Howard concluded that Barbari adjusted the proportions of his map to suggest a dolphin, an avatar for the goddess Venus. Howard, "Venice as a Dolphin," 106–7. It is especially interesting to note that Neptune, in Barbari's image, rides a dolphin whose harness is a chain.

8 Holly Hurlburt, *The Dogaressa of Venice, 1200–1500: Wife and Icon* (New York: Palgrave Macmillan, 2006), 44–74 (dogaressa's entrance), 96–105 (foreign visitors).

9 Beatrice d'Este described the pageantry of her visit in a letter to her husband Ludovico Sforza, as published in Pompeo Molmenti, *Venice: Its Individual Growth from the Earliest Beginnings to the Fall of the Republic*, trans. Horatio Brown (London: John Murray, 1907), 2:267–69.

10 Hurlburt, *The Dogaressa of Venice*, 88.

11 As quoted in Patricia Labalme, Laura Sanguineti White, and Linda Carroll, "How to (and How Not to) Get Married in Sixteenth-Century Venice (Selections from the Diaries of Marin Sanudo," *Renaissance Quarterly* 52, no. 1 (1999): 56–57.

12 Pietro Bembo, *History of Venice*, trans. Robert Ulery (Cambridge, MA: I Tatti Renaissance Library, Harvard University Press, 2007), 1:49.

13 Antonio Colbertaldo, *Storia di Caterina Corner Regina di Cipro: La prima biografia*, ed. Daria Pedrocco (Padua: Poligrafo, 2012), 132. On the repetition of Caterina's abdication scene, see Holly Hurlburt, *Daughter of Venice: Caterina Corner, Queen of Cyprus and Woman of the Renaissance* (New Haven, CT: Yale University Press, 2016), 229–35.

14 Schulz refers to the physical features in Barbari's plan as "material manifestations of the state." Schulz, "Jacopo de' Barbari's View of Venice," 468.

15 Filippo de Vivo, *Information and Communication in Venice: Rethinking Early Modern Politics* (Oxford: Oxford University Press, 2007), 46–48 and (on women and movement of information) 112–19. On non-elite women's commercial activities and informal exchange of information, see also Chojnacka, *Working Women*; and Paula Clarke, "The Business of Prostitution in Early Renaissance Venice," *Renaissance Quarterly* 58, no. 2 (2015): 419–64.

16 De Vivo, *Information and Communication*, 47–48.

17 Caterina used her awareness of current events to her advantage in lobbying for her nephew to become Grand Commander of Cyprus; Hurlburt, *Daughter of Venice*, 187–89.

18 Molmenti, *Venice*, 2:170. For the details of the February 1472 case, see Archivio di Stato di Venezia, Consiglio dei Dieci, Deliberazioni miste, reg. 17, fols. 147v–150r.

19 Christine Shaw, *The Politics of Exile in Renaissance Italy* (Cambridge: Cambridge University Press, 2000), 100–101.

20 Marino Sanudo, *Venice: Città Excelentissima: Selections from the Renaissance Diaries of Marin Sanudo*, ed. Patricia H. Labalme and Laura Sanguineti White, trans. Linda Carroll (Baltimore, MD: Johns Hopkins University Press, 2008), 121.

21 Chojnacka, *Working Women*; Clarke, "The Business of Prostitution."

Stanley Chojnacki

Wifely Mobility
in Renaissance Venice

18 Residential Variety among Patrician Families

IN HIS 1859 CLASSIC *The Civilization of the Renaissance in Italy*, Jacob Burckhardt famously contrasted Renaissance Venice with Florence: while the latter was lively, "the city of incessant movement," Venice was placid and stable, "the city of apparent stagnation."[1] To be sure, Quattrocento Florence underwent notable political vicissitudes, although one of them, the toppling of the Albizzi regime in 1434, ushered in six decades of fairly secure Medici domination, which ended only with foreign invasion. Venice experienced no such changes of regime, although, as Dennis Romano and others have revealed, tensions roiled under the apparently unchanging surface, leading most dramatically to the forced abdication of Doge Francesco Foscari in 1458.[2]

This essay, however, deals with movement and stability on another register, that of families and individuals around the city. Jacopo de' Barbari's *View of Venice* from 1500 enables us to track patricians, parish by parish, over the course of their lives, and in particular to observe differences in residential mobility among them. This essay follows a variety of Venetians related by blood or marriage over decades of experience to illustrate and explain some of those differences. In her comprehensive examination of space and its significances in late medieval Venice, Élisabeth Crouzet-Pavan noted how, despite dispersion of their individual members throughout the city, patrician lineages tended to cluster in particular parishes (contrade).[3] Indeed, some families inhabited certain neighborhoods for decades, even centuries. One of the best-known examples is the Dandolo family: the Dandolos established themselves in the parish of San Luca by the early twelfth century, or possibly the late eleventh, and were still present there in large numbers in the sixteenth century and beyond.[4] Another family, not residentially documented as early as the Dandolos but still well entrenched in their parish over several generations, were the Veniers of San Moisè (fig. 18.1).

In the fiscal census (*estimo*) of 1379, compiled while a Genoese fleet besieged Venice, six Veniers were documented as owning property in the parish of San Moisè, in the sestiere of San Marco.[5] One of these, Andrea, had a son named Nicolò, whose own son, Antonio, drafted a will in 1403 in which he identified himself as a resident of San Moisè, as did his widow, Margherita Signolo, in her will of 1405.[6] The residence in San Moisè of this branch of the Veniers continued into the next generation. One of Antonio and Margherita's sons, Benedetto, noted in his will in 1433 that he dwelled there, as did another of their sons, Biagio, who was identified as residing in San Moisè in notarized business transactions in 1422 and 1437.[7] By the time of the 1437 transaction, however, Biagio was preparing to advance the fortunes of the next generation of San Moisè Veniers. On March 4, 1438, he pledged to underwrite the dowry restitution of the newly married wife of his son Moisè, also "de confinio Sancti Moisi."[8] Over the following decade this Moisè traveled to oversee his family's possessions on Crete and the neighboring island of Kythira (Cerigo). Nevertheless, in his deathbed will of 1448 he still identified himself as a resident of San Moisè.[9] His three sons kept the family's multigenerational San Moisè tradition alive through the fifteenth century. Indeed, they enhanced it in the 1490s by purchasing

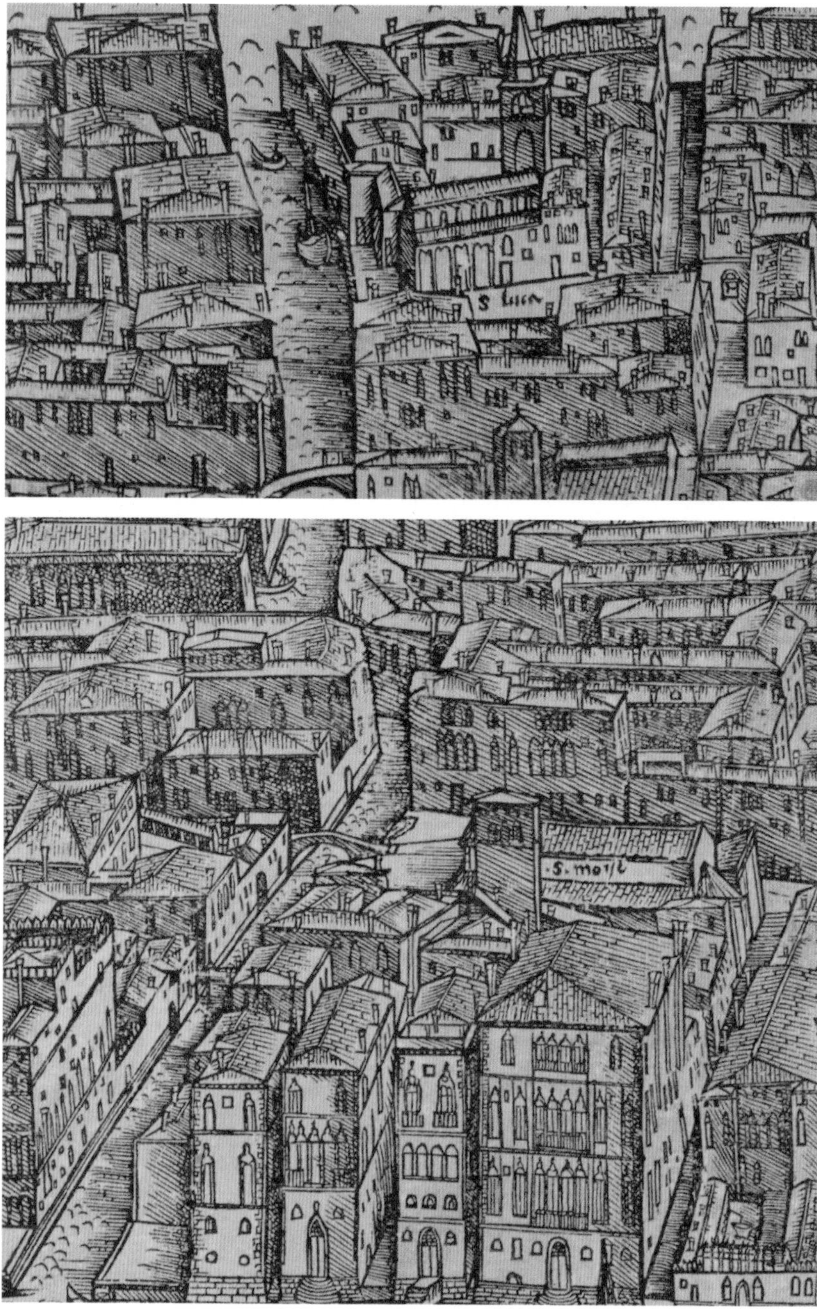
S. luca
.S. mo᷈l

rental property neighboring their main "caxa granda al ponte di fuxeri."[10] And when the second of the three brothers, Girolamo, dictated his will in 1501, he was still describing himself as residing in San Moisè.[11]

The multigenerational stability of the line of Andrea Venier in San Moisè contrasts with the restless record of another noble, Lorenzo di Nicolò Vitturi (fig. 18.2). In his will of 1407, he declared that he was an inhabitant of the parish of San Giacomo dall'Orio, in the sestiere of Santa Croce. But when his wife, Orsa, testated six years later, she stated that she was living in Santa Margherita, in the sestiere of Dorsoduro. Lorenzo must have been living with her there, since Orsa identified herself as his wife and appointed him an executor of her will.[12] But neither San Giacomo nor Santa Margherita would become Lorenzo's permanent address. In 1438, at the marriage of his daughter Cateruzza, her bridegroom acknowledged receipt of her dowry from her father, Lorenzo Vitturi, "de confinio Sancti Thome" in the sestiere of San Polo.[13] But San Tomà did not become Lorenzo's stable residence either. In 1460, when Cateruzza, now widowed and remarried, summoned a notary to draw up a *procura* authorizing her new husband to see to the sale of a slave, she did it "in the contrada of Santa Ternita in the residence of Lorenzo Vitturi," her father.[14] Since Santa Ternita was in the sestiere of Castello, Lorenzo's residence there makes it the fourth of Venice's six sestieri in which he made his home. Lorenzo's peripatetic residential life contrasts sharply with the Venier generations that spanned the fifteenth century, from Antonio to Biagio to Moisè to Moisè's three sons, all of whom were solidly rooted in San Moisè. So it comes as no surprise that, unlike those Veniers, Lorenzo Vitturi's sons continued the family's itinerary of Venice's sestieri. Arsenio made his home in a fifth sestiere, Cannaregio, where he was a parishioner of San Felice when he filed a claim to his share of his mother's estate in 1457.[15] And Nicolò di Lorenzo rounded out the family's itinerancy when he wrote his will a year later while living in San Samuele, in the sixth sestiere, San Marco.[16]

There are many explanations for the intergenerational endurance in one contrada of some families and the relocations around the city of other families, and of individuals such as Lorenzo Vitturi and his sons. An example of tension between the two tendencies is the lawsuit filed in 1462 by two Dandolo brothers to reclaim, in exchange for cash, a part of their family compound in San Luca that had been awarded to the widow of a Dandolo cousin as partial restitution of her dowry.[17] In another such case, in 1375 three Morosini brothers, similarly eager to maintain the integrity of their

241

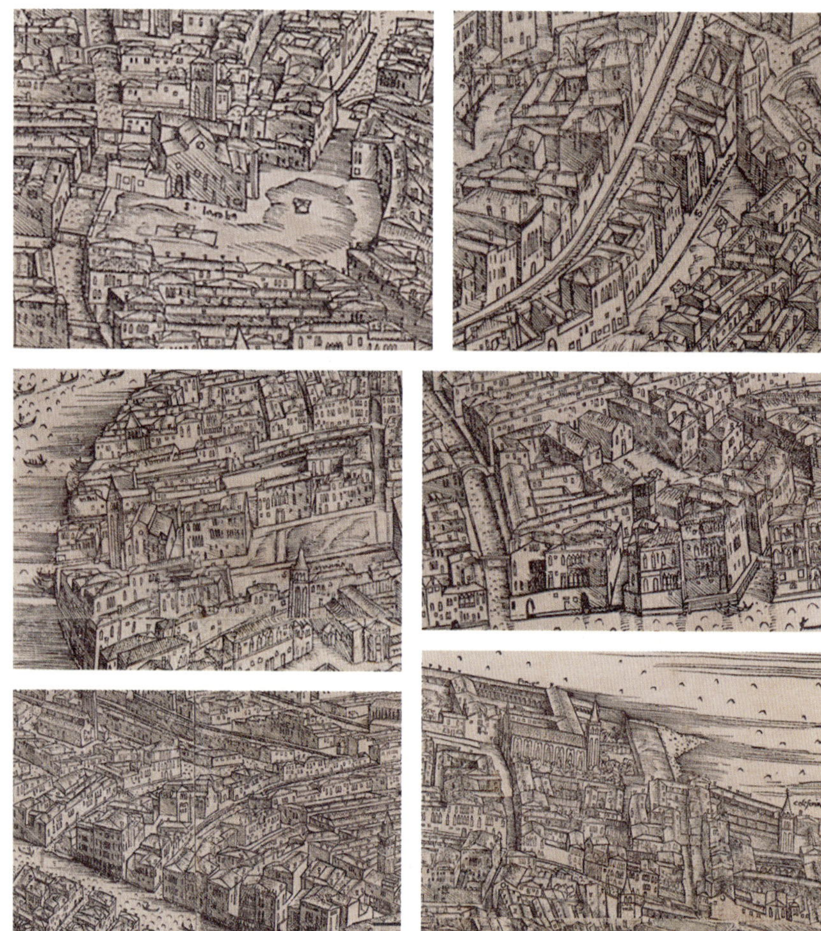

family residence, pooled 2,000 lire to purchase the family's *domus magna* at Santa Maria Formosa from their widowed mother, to whom it had been awarded in restitution of her dowry.[18]

Despite the efforts of the Dandolo and Morosini brothers and the success of the San Moisè Veniers in keeping their lineage property, it was not easy to prevent alienation of family dwellings. As their examples show, a chief reason was marriage, specifically dowries. Because patrician dowries rose relentlessly during the fourteenth through sixteenth centuries, cash-poor fathers arranging marriages for their daughters were obliged to woo potential sons-in-law with real estate, breaking up families' residential complexes, as did the father of Vittoria Vitturi, whose husband, Valerio Zeno, noted in his will of 1445 that he had received from Vittoria a dowry of 2,400 ducats, "of which 1,000 are secured over my possessions in San Giacomo dall'Orio, which I had from her as part of my dowry." He now bequeathed the properties back to Vittoria.[19] (We will see more of Vittoria further along.) A marriage contract of January 1527 illustrates both how dowry requirements could lead male patricians to alienate their lineage property, and also why an individual male noble might, like Lorenzo Vitturi, change his place of residence. In the contract between Francesco Zane and Nicolò Gradenigo, acting for his daughter Maria, Gradenigo agreed not only to give Zane a dowry of 2,500 ducats but also to take his prospective son-in-law into his home and to live with him "for their mutual benefit as a good father and a good son, since [Nicolò] had no other children besides Maria." The contract was subscribed by Nicolò Gradenigo's brother, Piero, who promised Maria, his niece, "my portion of our house of residence in return for 500 ducats." Thus, the potential offspring of Francesco and Maria, members of the Zane line, would gain possession of the Gradenigo family palazzo now voluntarily yielded by the two brothers, acting exactly the opposite of the Dandolos of San Luca.[20] One final transaction illustrates how other motives, also arising from real property in a dowry, could prompt a husband to exchange an old home for a new one. In the absence of brothers, Suordamor Zeno and her sister had inherited their father's palazzo on the Grand Canal at Santa Sofia. That inheritance figured in Suordamor's dowry when she married Marino Contarini. Taking advantage of the favorable site of the ex-Zeno property, Contarini promptly left his previous dwelling, tore down his wife's dowry property, and in its place commenced building the palazzo that would come to be known as Ca' d'Oro (see fig. A1.2).[21]

The Residential Vicissitudes of Patrician Wives

Valerio Zeno, Francesco Zane, and Marino Contarini changed their residences thanks to new property they received in their dowries. Lorenzo Vitturi's itinerary around Venice's sestieri remains unexplained, although at least one of his moves might likewise have been to property obtained as part of his wife's dowry, or to a dwelling in her possession.[22] Whatever the circumstances, the likelihood—and in Marino Contarini's case the certainty—is that these men made a conscious choice to relocate to their new residence, just as the Veniers of San Moisè, the Dandolos of San Luca, and the Morosinis of Santa Maria Formosa chose instead to preserve their family homes. The possibility of choice was less likely in the case of women—girls, really—who, except for unusual cases like that of Maria Gradenigo, took up residence in their husbands' dwellings upon marriage, especially brides marrying for the first time. A girl who married in her mid-teens was normally thrust into her husband's, or his father's, home with little or no voice in the matter, unless her mother's contribution to the dowry enabled her to support a daughter's preference.[23] Moreover, although many husbands provided in their wills for their prospective widows' habitation and living expenses, even those women depended on the men's goodwill.

Stanley Chojnacki

The incidents of the uxorial cycle regularly saw women moving around Venice as their status evolved from bride to wife to widow. But the case of Cateruzza Vitturi shows those incidents multiplying in a way that made Cateruzza unusually peripatetic. Cateruzza, the daughter of the residentially mobile Lorenzo Vitturi, was the wife whom Moisè di Biagio Venier, of the San Moisè Veniers, married in 1438. In the course of a venturesome married life that only began with her marriage to Moisè, Cateruzza, like her father, dwelled in several different contrade. But in the end the nature of her marriage to Moisè called her back to the enduring Venier property in San Moisè where she had begun her married life. Her story, traced in rapid outline here, shows that unpredictable events and circumstances made Venice, for some patrician women and men, though in different ways, a "city of incessant movement," not at all the stagnant place Burckhardt described (fig. 18.3).

At the time of Cateruzza's first wedding in 1438, her father, Lorenzo, was residing in San Tomà when his son-in-law, Moisè Venier, acknowledged to him the receipt of Cateruzza's dowry. Though Cateruzza may have spent her early years with her parents in Santa Margherita or San Tomà or some other contrada that they inhabited, upon marrying she settled in her husband's parish of San Moisè, as attested by the notary to whom, while pregnant, she dictated a will in 1440.[24] She was still there when Moisè dictated his deathbed will in 1448. But the following years swiftly brought changes. The most dramatic was her seemingly hasty remarriage in 1449 or 1450 to Nicolò di Andrea Vitturi, from a different branch of her natal clan.[25] This second marriage occasioned Cateruzza's move from San Moisè across the Grand Canal to her new husband's home in the contrada of Sant'Agnese. As described by neighbors in San Moisè, testifying in court in support of Cateruzza's claim to her dowry after Nicolò's death in 1469, transporting Cateruzza's personal effects by boat from San Moisè to Sant'Agnese was itself an adventure. The goods required several boats (*plui barche*), one of

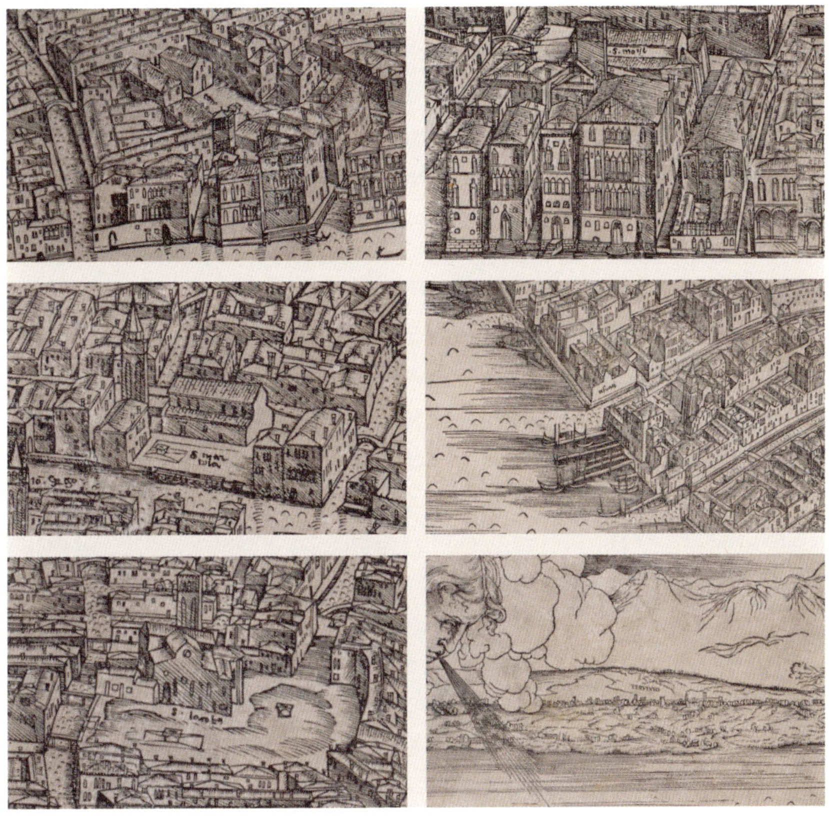

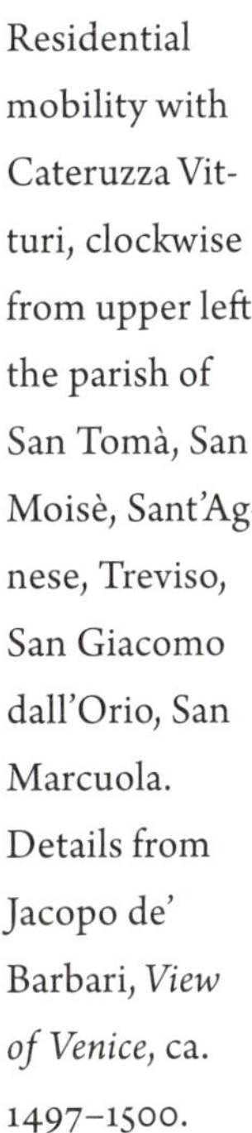

Residential mobility with Cateruzza Vitturi, clockwise from upper left: the parish of San Tomà, San Moisè, Sant'Agnese, Treviso, San Giacomo dall'Orio, San Marcuola. Details from Jacopo de' Barbari, *View of Venice*, ca. 1497–1500.

which capsized with all its contents.[26] (The cases and chests thrown into the water were, however, recovered.)[27]

Cateruzza remained with Nicolò in Sant'Agnese at least until September 1456, when she wrote her second will. But the will itself hints at trouble on the horizon, for she mentioned Nicolò as neither executor, nor beneficiary, nor caretaker of her three sons from her marriage to Moisè Venier; rather, she assigned those benefits and responsibilities to her mother, one of her brothers, and a sister and the latter's husband. In fact, she neglected to mention Nicolò at all. Instead, she left the bulk of her estate to her three sons and requested burial in the tomb of her first husband, Moisè.[28] The suggestion of difficulty in her marriage to Nicolò burst open three years later, in 1459, in a complaint filed by Nicolò in the civil court of the Giudici del Procurator.[29] In it, he declared that he had provided for Cateruzza and her three sons since their wedding, and now, having been elected a Venetian official in nearby Treviso, he wanted Cateruzza to accompany him there—

245

but without her sons. Not only did she refuse, but she also wanted Nicolò to provide living expenses for her, and presumably her sons, in Venice. Thus began six years of tension and conflict, and more mobility.

It is difficult to trace with precision Cateruzza's whereabouts in the period following Nicolò's suit, but one thing emerges clearly. The turbulent vicissitudes of their marriage led to several changes of residence for Cateruzza, displaying the unstable situations of wives in marriages that went wrong. The first hint of a reaction by her to the tension evident in Nicolò's suit demanding that she accompany him to Treviso is the procura, mentioned earlier, that she had drawn up in 1460 commissioning Nicolò to arrange the sale of a slave for her. We noted that the transaction took place in the home of her father, the much-traveled Lorenzo Vitturi, in the contrada of Santa Ternita. It is probable that the antagonism between the two spouses led to Cateruzza's abandoning Nicolò's residence in Sant'Agnese—or being expelled from it—and finding refuge with her father.

Her mobility, however, continued. According to witnesses deposed in 1465 in support of a separation (*divortium*) suit she brought before the court of the patriarch of Venice, Cateruzza did dwell for a time with Nicolò after their marriage, both in Treviso and in Nicolò's villa outside that city. But Nicolò's cavorting with a mistress there drove Cateruzza back to Venice, where she took refuge with Nicolò's sister Vittoria, whom we met earlier as the wife of Valerio Zeno and who now, after Valerio's death, was married to Lorenzo Contarini, of the contrada of San Giacomo dall'Orio, where she comforted her distressed sister-in-law.[30] But in 1463, two years before initiating the separation suit, Cateruzza had petitioned the patriarch's court to declare her marriage to Nicolò valid. This step was likely to ensure that when she subsequently filed for the separation she would get her dowry back. In any case, the record of that validation request reveals that she was then living in still another location, the parish of San Marcuola in the sestiere of Cannaregio.[31]

Cateruzza prevailed in both suits, receiving the patriarch's validation of her marriage in 1463 and the ecclesiastical decree of divortium in 1465. Where she dwelled after her separation from Nicolò is unknown, but eventually, or perhaps sooner, she returned to her original marital home, the Venier property in San Moisè. Her sons were living there in the 1470s; we noted earlier that in the 1490s they expanded their holdings in the contrada. And Cateruzza herself was identified as a resident there when she dictated her last will, in 1497.[32] But that embrace of the setting of her first marriage, to Moisè Venier, did not exclude enduring traces of her second, to Nicolò Vitturi. When Cateruzza filed for the restitution of her dowry, estimated at 780 ducats, from Nicolò's estate, the judges awarded her four rental properties inhabited by tenants in Sant'Agnese.[33] It seems fitting that even in her last years, the much-traveled Cateruzza retained a presence in two parishes, each associated with one of her marriages.[34]

NOTES

1 Jakob Burckhardt, *The Civilization of the Renaissance in Italy*, Modern Library ed. (New York: Random House, 1954), 51.

2 Dennis Romano, *The Likeness of Venice: A Life of Doge Francesco Foscari, 1373–1457* (New Haven, CT: Yale University Press, 2007), esp. 254–331.

3 Élisabeth Crouzet-Pavan, *"Sopra le acque salse": Espaces, pouvoir et société à Venise à la fin du Moyen Age*, 2 vols. (Rome: École française de Rome, 1992), 1:383–92.

4 Juergen Schulz, "The Houses of the Dandolo: A Family Compound in Medieval Venice," *Journal of the Society of Architectural Historians* 52, no. 4 (1993): 391–415.

5 Gino Luzzatto, ed., *I prestiti della Repubblica di Venezia, Sec. XIII–XV*, vol. 1, *Documenti finanziari della Repubblica di Venezia* (Padua: A. Draghi, 1929), 152–53. San Marco was one of Venice's six districts, called *sestieri*; see below for other sestieri.

6 Antonio: Archivio di Stato di Venezia (ASVe), Notarile Testamenti, b. 364, Darvasio, prot., no. 72. Margherita: Notarile Testamenti, b. 895, Ravagnan, no. 491. In 1416 corrections were inserted in Margherita's original text of 1405.

7 Benedetto's will is in ASVe, Notarile Testamenti, b. 1156, Croci, no 613. Biagio's business commission to a Ferrarese named Bartolomeo del Brunio in 1422 is in ASVe, Notarile Testamenti b. 1157, Croci, prot. I, fol. 24v. His 1437 commission from Maffeo da Molin is in ASVe, Cancelleria Inferiore, notai, b. 122, Tebaldo de Manfredis, paper register "1436–1437," fol. 97r.

8 ASVe, Cancelleria Inferiore, notai, b. 213, Odorico Tabarino, "fasc. 1438," fols. 8v–9r.

9 "ego Moise Venerio qd domini Blaxii de confinio sancti Moixi." ASVe, Notarile

Testamenti, b. 985, Francesco Rogeri, no. 39.

10   ASVe, Procuratori di San Marco, Commissarie Miste, b. 3, file of Girolamo qd. Moisè 1 Venier, account book "1487–1501," fol. 4v. The Ponte dei Fuseri connects the street called the Frezzaria in the parish of San Moisè with the parish of San Luca.

11   ASVe, Procuratori di San Marco, Commissarie Miste, b. 3, file of Girolamo qd. Moisè 1 Venier, loose parchment dated November 22, 1501.

12   Margherita: ASVe, Notarile Testamenti, b. 1254, Pietro Zane, no. 8, September 3, 1413. Lorenzo: ASVe, Notarile Testamenti, b. 1254, Pietro Zane, no. 99, July 24, 1407.

13   ASVe, Cancelleria Inferiore, notai, b. 213, Odorico Tabarino, "fasc. 1438," fols. 8v–9r, March 6, 1438.

14   "in contracta Sancte Ternite in domo habitationis spectabilis viri domini Laurentii Victuri." ASVe, Procuratori di San Marco, Commissarie Ultra, b. 307, Nicolò Vitturi, fasc. 1, loose parchment dated July 11, 1460.

15   "vir nobilis Arsenius Victuri filius Laurentii Victuri de confinio Sancti Felicis." ASVe, Giudici del Proprio, Lezze e Giudice Delegato, reg. 6, fol. 39v, July 11, 1457.

16   "mi Nicolò Vituri de miser Lorenzo de la contra de san Samuel." ASVe, Procuratori di San Marco, Commissarie Miste, b. 3, file of Girolamo Venier quondam Moisè 1, parchment dated July 7, 1458.

17   ASVe, Giudici del Proprio, Lezze e Giudice delegato, reg. 7, fol. 2r.

18   ASVe, Cancelleria Inferiore, notai, b. 115, Marino S. Tomà, prot. 1374–77, no. 144.

19   ASVe, Notarile Testamenti, b. 558, Gambaro, no. 124.

20   ASVe, Avogaria di Comun, Contratti di Nozze, reg. 142/3, fols. 87r–88r.

21   Richard J. Goy, *The House of Gold: Building a Palace in Medieval Venice* (Cambridge: Cambridge University Press, 1992), 29–31.

22   An example of a husband residing in a house belonging to his wife is Sebastiano Priuli, whose wife, Lucia, noted in her will of 1502–3 that "misser Sebastian vene a star in chaxa mia al mio maridar." ASVe, Notarile Testamenti, b. 66, Piero Busenello, no. 246, January 18, 1502–3.

23   On mothers' participation in their daughters' marriage arrangements, see Stanley Chojnacki, "'The Most Serious Duty': Motherhood, Gender, and Patrician Culture," in *Women and Men in Renaissance Venice* (Baltimore, MD: Johns Hopkins University Press, 2000), 169–82, esp. 178–79.

24   ASVe, Notarile Testamenti, b. 560, Francesco Gritti, no. 314, June 29, 1440.

Cateruzza noted that she was "pregnans" at the time.

25 The exact date of this second marriage is uncertain. According to the sixteenth-century genealogist Marco Barbaro, it took place in 1454. Marco Barbaro, "Libro di nozze patrizie," Biblioteca Nazionale Marciana, mss. Italiani, classe VII, no. 156 (8492), fol. 432r. However, references within the text of Cateruzza's claim for restitution of her dowry after Nicolò's death make it clear that the two were married by 1450. ASVe, Procuratori di San Marco, Commissarie Miste, b. 3, fasc. Girolamo Venier, parchment dated January 27, 1469–70.

26 "una dele ditte barche se rovesso cum tute le robe dentro. In la qual barcha rovesa era confani e casse." Testimony of Franceschina, wife of Jacopo, a *calafato* (caulker) at the Arsenale, Venice's shipyard. ASVe, Procuratori di San Marco, Commissarie Miste, b. 3, fasc. Venier Girolamo, parchment dated January 27, 1469–70.

27 "vidit coffanos et capsas que fuerunt extracte ex aqua." Testimony of Perina, wife of Jacopo, a carpenter. ASVe, Procuratori di San Marco, Commissarie Miste, b. 3, fasc. Venier Girolamo, parchment dated January 27, 1469–70.

28 ASVe, Notarile Testamenti, b. 985, Rogeri, no. 235, September 20, 1456.

29 ASVe, Procuratori di San Marco, Commissarie Ultra, b. 307, fasc. Nicolò Vitturi I, parchment dated September 4, 1459.

30 Archivio storico del Patriarcato di Venezia (ASPVe), sezione antica, Liber Testificationum, 1464–66 (no foliation); testimony of Nicolò's sister Vittoria, January 31, 1465. Another witness, Maria Vitturi—apparently, despite her surname, a non-noble unrelated to either Nicolò or Cateruzza—testified on the same day that it had been ten years previously that Cateruzza lived in Treviso with Nicolò. The separation case will be treated more fully elsewhere.

31 ASPVe, sezione antica, Liber Actorum 1463, fol. 63r.

32 For a property division between the three brothers in 1477, ASVe, Giudici del Proprio, Lezze e Giudice Delegato, reg. 9, fol. 26r–v, June 4, 1477. For Cateruzza's 1497 will, see ASVe, Notarile Testamenti, b. 1227, Cristoforo Rizzo no. 100.

33 ASVe, Procuratori di San Marco, Commissarie Miste, b. 3, Girolamo qd. Moisè 1, parchment dated February 16, 1469–70.

34 On the back of Cateruzza's last will, dated November 15, 1497, the notary wrote, "Obiit die Sabbati septimo mensis Aprilis 1498."

Giada Damen

Two Palaces, a Chapel, and an Art Collection on the Grand Canal

The World of Domenico di Piero in Jacopo de' Barbari's *View of Venice*

19 DOMENICO DI PIERO (1406–97) was a merchant of jewels and antiquities active in Venice in the fifteenth century.[1] He was a wealthy *cittadino*, or citizen, who had a long life and a successful career, dying at the very end of the century at the age of ninety-one. His name often appears both in past literature and in contemporary scholarship, yet many details about his life are still obscure. Through a close review of written sources and careful study of Jacopo de' Barbari's *View of Venice*, this essay sheds light on new aspects of the jeweler's life in the lagoon and, most importantly, identifies his residence on the Grand Canal.

In the documents concerning his business dealings, Domenico is mentioned with various epithets, such as "merchatande in Venetia" (merchant in Venice), "spectabile viro" (respectable man), "magister gemmarum" (expert in the art of gems), "zogielier e antiquario singular" (jeweler and exceptional antiquarian), "Domenego dalle zoglie" (Domenego of the jewels), or simply "il zoielier" (the jeweler), all of which attest to his importance and reputation. From his will of 1496 we know that by the end of his life, Domenico had amassed a huge fortune in cash, precious objects, and real estate holdings.[2] Numerous archival records shed light on his business transactions and reveal that he served a wide network of clients throughout Europe, among whom were the most prestigious collectors of the fifteenth century.[3] The merchant's wealthy clientele included, for example, Lorenzo de' Medici (1449–92) in Florence. It was to Lorenzo that, in the fall of 1487, Domenico sold the highly prized *Sigillo di Nerone*, a Roman carnelian carved with the images of Apollo, Marsyas, and Olympos that came to be the most famous and copied antique gem in the Renaissance.[4] The archives of the papal court contain numerous bills of payments to Domenico di Piero for jewels and objects mounted with precious stones selected especially for Pius II (1458–64), Paul II (1464–71), and Innocent VIII (1484–92). The expenditures amount to many thousands of ducats for gem-encrusted objects acquired by the popes over several decades from 1459 to 1486.[5]

In addition to the Medici family in Florence and the popes in Rome, the Este in Ferrara were also among the jeweler's most assiduous customers.[6] Over the years Domenico sold pearls, rings, diamonds, and gold antique coins to the dukes, and in 1465 he procured for Borso d'Este (1431–71) some rare Persian leopards trained to hunt.[7] King Matthias Corvinus (1443–90) of Hungary and his wife, Beatrice d'Este (1457–1508), together with Ferrante d'Aragona (1423–94) and Giovanni Sforza (1466–1510), all owed Domenico money when the jeweler died.[8]

When on February 6, 1486, Galeazzo Trotti, the Este representative in Venice, visited Domenico's home in the lagoon, he described in a letter to Ercole d'Este (1431–1505) the "infinite number of wonderful things" the merchant had to offer for sale.[9] Among these objects, he singled out ancient bronze statuettes, antique cameos, engraved gems, porphyry and chalcedony vases, damascene incense burners, and a multitude of ivory objects. From Trotti's description, it appears that Domenico's home also doubled as a display gallery for the jeweler's precious inventory of expensive items. A considerable percentage of the objects for sale was supplied directly from the eastern Mediterranean. It in fact appears that Domenico's nephew, Domenico di Giorgio, had been placed in charge of part of the business in

Damascus.[10] From Venice, Domenico's merchandise was then delivered to his many clients either by the jeweler himself or through intermediaries.

If letters, account books, and other archival documents help us reconstruct Domenico's business activities, Jacopo de' Barbari's *View of Venice*, produced during the jeweler's lifetime, illustrates aspects of Domenico's world in the lagoon. He was a member of the Scuola Grande di San Marco, where he held the prestigious elected position of Guardian Grande for multiple years: in 1473, 1482, 1487, and again in 1496.[11] This lay confraternity, one of six in the city, was perhaps its most esteemed, as Saint Mark was the principal patron saint of Venice. Domenico's commitment to the confraternity is also seen in his own testament, in which he left 300 ducats to be used to provide dowries for indigent girls.

Giada Damen

Yet Domenico's importance in shaping the life of the Scuola is mainly connected with the reconstruction of its marble-encrusted façade during the last decades of the century. After a catastrophic fire destroyed the confraternity's headquarters on the evening of March 31, 1485, Domenico, together with four other members, was nominated to oversee the reconstruction as *provveditore sopra la fabbrica*.[12] The jeweler held the post for life, supervising the building campaign from 1485 until his death in 1496, when the façade was largely completed by the premier architect-sculptors working in Venice at the time. Pietro Lombardo (1435–1515) and Giovanni Buora (1450–1513) were involved in the construction initially, while starting in 1490 the architect Mauro Codussi (1440–1504) took charge of the project as *proto*.

The *View* offers a panoramic representation of the Scuola Grande di San Marco with its newly rebuilt façade, admired by locals and visitors alike (fig. 19.1). Already in 1494, the pilgrim Pietro Casola described the building as "very beautiful and richly adorned with marbles and gold."[13] Domenico's influence on the appearance of the sumptuous façade, encrusted with marbles, rare stones, and a rich apparatus of sculpted details, has been elaborated on by several scholars.[14] As *guardian grande* in 1487, the highest-ranking officer of the confraternity, he held the power to decide the scale of the reconstruction project that consisted both in the rebuilding of the structure and in the refurbishing of the façade facing the Campo Santi Giovanni e Paolo (fig. 19.2). The taste for the lavish display of many varieties of polychrome stones on the new façade most likely reflects Domenico's personal taste for luxury and expensive materials. This can be inferred by comparing it with the jeweler's own private commissions undertaken in those same years.

Between 1488 and 1494, Domenico di Piero had commissioned a pri-

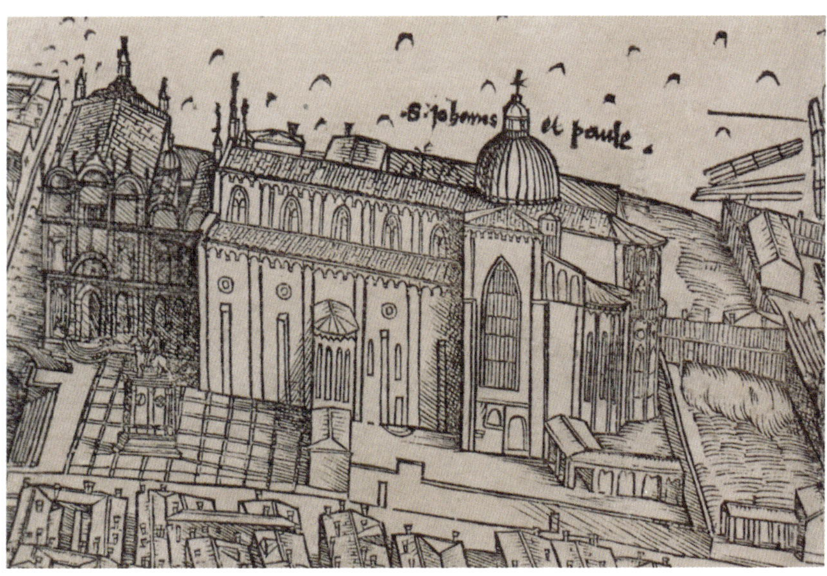

Scuola Grande di San Marco from Jacopo de' Barbari, *View of Venice*, ca. 1497–1500.

19.2

Façade of the Scuola Grande di San Marco, Venice.

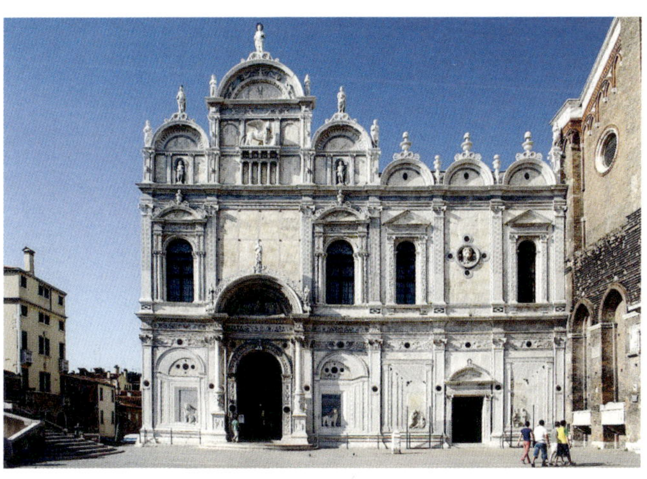

vate funerary chapel to be built and embellished within the church of Santa Maria della Carità.[15] The chapel dedicated to Christ the Saviour no longer exists, as it was demolished in 1807. Yet its lavish appearance can be inferred by the frequent mention of it by contemporary sources that singled out the monument as one of the most notable sites in Venice.[16] The abundance of precious materials ornamenting it was noted with particular emphasis. Marcantonio Michiel mentions the chapel as "ornatissima de pietre" (highly decorated with stones), and Francesco Sansovino describes it as "notabilissima fra tutte quelle della città, edificata da Domenico di Pietro gioielliero ricchissimo, e antiquario, con marmi, con porfidi, e con serpentini molto alla grande" (most notable among those in the city, built by Domenico di Piero, extremely wealthy jeweler and antiquarian, with marbles, porphyries, and serpentines in a grand manner).[17] In a later document of 1548 the chapel is mentioned simply as "la Ricca" (the Rich).[18]

Significantly, the architect and historian Tommaso Temanza (1705–89), while discussing the architect responsible for the reconstruction of the Scuola Grande di San Marco, mentions Domenico's chapel in Santa Maria della Carità, noting the affinity of stylistic language between the two commissions. Temanza suggested: "And why can we not ascribe to him also the Chapel of the Savior in the Church of the Carità, which in Sansovino's time was called the Jeweler's Chapel richly encrusted with marbles, porphyries, and serpentines as it was fashionable at that time?"[19]

It was precisely around the church of the Carità that Domenico's daily life presumably unfolded. He had owned an important palace on the Grand Canal near the church of San Giacomo dall'Orio. At some point, however, the building, described by Marin Sanudo as "una casa … bellissima" (a house … most beautiful), was acquired from the jeweler by the Signoria, a branch of government, for the exorbitant sum of 10,000 ducats. In 1483 the Republic presented the palace as a gift, along with the castle of Cittadella and the castle of Montorio, to the military commander Roberto da Sanseverino (1418–87) to compensate him for his services.[20] The expensive *casa* has never been identified, but it was probably one of the few buildings indicated in Jacopo de' Barbari's *View* facing the Grand Canal in the parish of San Giacomo dall'Orio, not far from the Fondaco dei Turchi, which at the time was a palace owned by the Duke of Ferrara. Unfortunately, the *View* does not depict the existing structures in detail due to their positioning on the south side of the Grand Canal. According to Sanudo, on receiving the valuable and high-profile real estate gift, Roberto da Sanseverino had his coat of arms exhibited on the palace's façade and established one of his representatives in the residence. It is unclear, however, how often Roberto himself really enjoyed this Venetian property over the years.

By 1483, therefore, Domenico di Piero was certainly residing somewhere else in Venice, but his new palace has never been identified. In 1496, when he drafted his will, he was living in the "parish of Sant'Agnese," and there he died a year later. The Italian historian Giuseppe Tassini specifies that the jeweler's *casa* "alla Carità in Sant'Agnese" was on the Grand

Canal—a prominent location that was perfectly fitting, given the merchant's affluence.[21] Until now, no research has been done on Domenico's palace. But we can infer that the building was a new construction from the *registri* of the Procuratori di San Marco (account books of the state procuracy), which shows a payment by Domenico to the procurators in 1489 for twenty-five slabs of marble to be employed in the construction of the façade of his house: "al fabricar de la sua caxa mese in la faca de quela" (to build his house, placed on its façade).[22] Unsurprisingly the jeweler's palace, like his chapel in Santa Maria della Carità and the façade of the Scuola Grande di San Marco that he had commissioned, was encrusted with slabs of expensive marble.

Jacopo de' Barbari's *View* shows the area of the parish of Sant'Agnese, next to the church of Santa Maria della Carità, when it was still an *isola* surrounded by canals that would be filled in later to create pedestrian thoroughfares. Only a few buildings existed on the small portion of waterfront facing the Grand Canal, and among these was the palace known today as the Palazzo Contarini Polignac (fig. 19.3).[23] In de' Barbari's *View* the palace stands at the corner of the Grand Canal and the Rio di Sant'Agnese—a canal reclaimed in the nineteenth century—with a garden facing the Rio and enclosed by a wooden fence (fig. 19.4). While little is known of the origins, construction, and first ownership of the Palazzo Contarini Polignac, architectural historians have long agreed that it should date to the second half of the fifteenth century. The hypothesis that the first owner of the palace was Pietro di Angarano, a professor of law at the University of Padua in the mid-fifteenth century, was short lived; and the story of the palace's ownership is usually told by starting in the sixteenth century, when the branch of the Contarini family known as Contarini dal Zaffo is documented as owning the building and restoring it in the 1560s–1580s.[24]

The decoration of the façade, with a profusion of marble details and inserts of colored stone, together with its dating to the end of the fifteenth century, makes the palace a very likely candidate to be identified as Domenico di Piero's commission. Paolo Paoletti compared certain architectural decorations on the palace façade with ornamental details at the Scuola Grande di San Marco and suggested that this revealed the architectural intervention of Giovanni Buora, the very same master involved in those years in the reconstruction of the Scuola's façade.[25]

Although no documentary evidence so far has been brought to light to prove that Palazzo Contarini was previously indeed Domenico's residence,

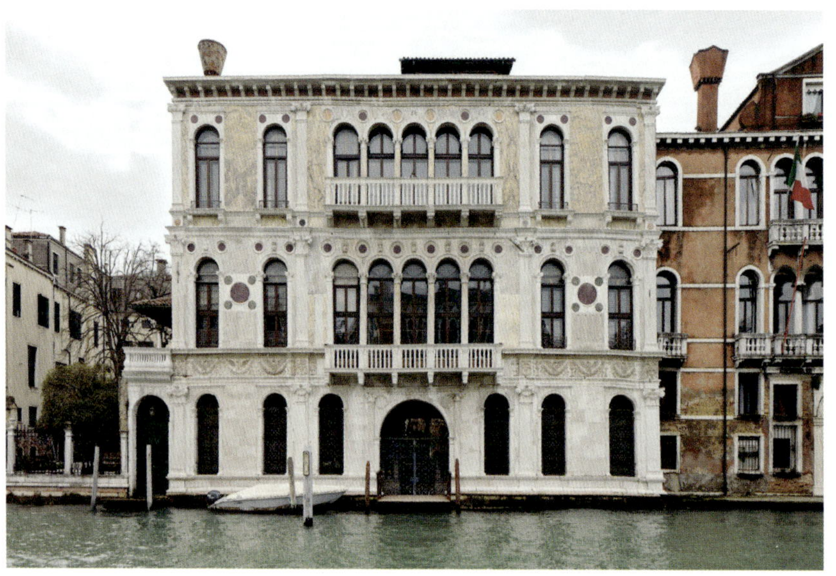

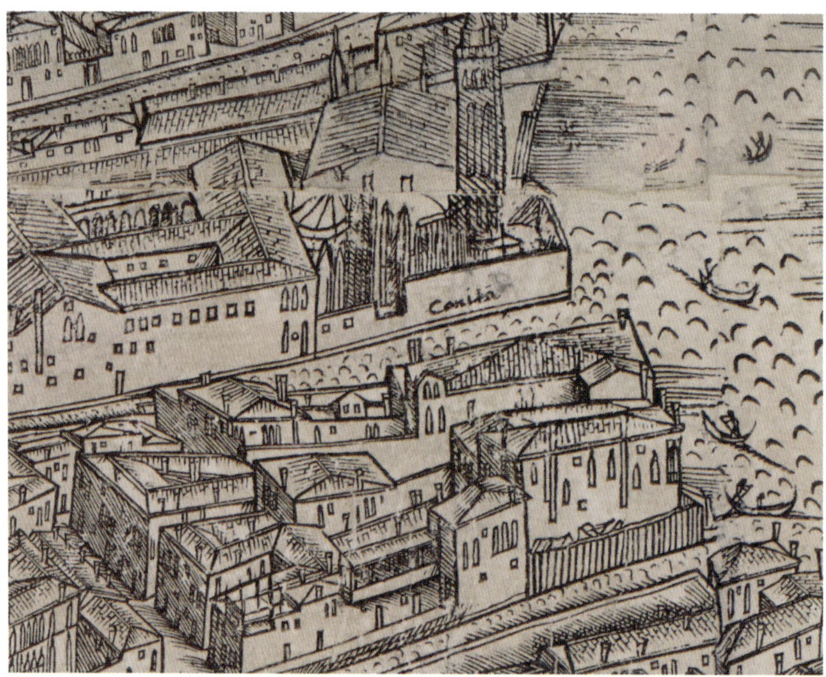
Carità

it is certainly plausible that the wealthy merchant—with his income from a prosperous business, his reputation as a jeweler to the most prestigious men in modern-day Italy, and the high purchase price paid for his property near San Giacomo dall'Orio—could have afforded to commission such an important, highly visible new home nearby the entry into the Grand Canal.[26] The building was just steps away from the church of the Carità, where Domenico was establishing his funerary chapel, similarly decorated with colorful marbles and sculpted details. It is not difficult to imagine that this beautiful palace on the Grand Canal had been built for the jeweler—a jewel box of its own—to house and display the many magnificent objects he had accumulated for business and for his private collection.

NOTES

1 For a brief biography of Domenico di Piero, see Rosella Lauber, "Domenico di Piero," in *Il collezionismo d'arte a Venezia: Dalle origini al Cinquecento*, ed. Linda Borean et al. (Venice: Marsilio, 2008), 269–70.

2 For the archival location of Domenico's will and its numerous later revisions and additions, see Lauber, "Domenico di Piero," 270. The will is partially transcribed in Paolo Paoletti, *L'architettura e la scultura del Rinascimento a Venezia: Ricerche storico-artistiche* (Venice: Ongania-Naya, 1893–97), vol. 2, doc. 204.

3 A useful summary of the documents regarding Domenico's activities as a dealer is in Laurie S. Fusco and Gino Corti, *Lorenzo de' Medici: Collector and Antiquarian* (Cambridge: Cambridge University Press, 2006), 300.

4 See Melissa Meriam Bullard and Nicolai Rubinstein, "Lorenzo de' Medici's Acquisition of the Sigillo di Nerone," *Journal of the Warburg and Courtauld Institutes* 62 (1999): 283–86.

5 Archival references to these expenses were first published in Eugène Müntz, *Les arts à la cour des papes pendant le XV et le XVI siècle: Recueil de documents inédits tirés des archives et des bibliothèques romaines*, 3 vols. (Paris: E. Thorin, 1878–82).

6 Many references to payments to Domenico di Piero are in Adolfo Venturi, "L'arte a Ferrara nel periodo di Borso d'Este," *Rivista storica italiana* 2 (1885):

Façade of Palazzo Contarini Polignac, Venice.

Detail of the zone around the Carità from Jacopo de' Barbari, *View of Venice*, ca. 1497–1500.

687–749; Adolfo Venturi, "L'arte ferrarese nel periodo d'Ercole I d'Este," *Atti e memorie della R. Deputazione di Storia Patria per le provincie di Romagna* 6 (Modena: G. T. Vincenzi e nipoti, 1888), 91–119.

7   Conte Gandini, "The Court of Ferrara in the Fifteenth Century," *Scottish Review* 25 (1895): 83.

8   They are all listed as Domenico's debtors in the jeweler's will; see Paoletti, *L'architettura e la scultura*, vol. 2, doc. 204.

9   Archivio di Stato di Modena, *Ambasciatori Venezia: Dispacci, Galeazzo Trotti*, 1486, I–II, letter of January 18, 1486.

10   References to Domenico di Giorgio in Damascus appear in Domenico di Piero's will.

11   Philip Sohm, *The Scuola Grande di San Marco, 1437–1550: The Architecture of a Venetian Lay Confraternity* (New York: Garland, 1982), 18n18.

12   Matteo Ceriana, "'Si fabricha di nuovo bellissima': La facciata della Scuola Grande di San Marco a Venezia," in *La Scuola Grande di San Marco a Venezia*, ed. Gherardo Ortalli and Savatore Settis (Modena: Franco Cosimo Panini, 2017), 67–98.

13   Pietro Casola, *Canon Pietro Casola's Pilgrimage to Jerusalem in the Year 1494*, ed. and trans. M. Margaret Newett (Manchester: Manchester University Press, 1907), 138.

14   Sohm, *The Scuola Grande di San Marco*, 118–22; Ceriana, "'Si fabricha di nuovo bellissima,'" 70–71.

15   For the dates of the construction of the chapel, see Rosella Lauber, "'Ornamento lodevole' e 'ornatissima di pietre': Marcantonio Michiel nella Chiesa veneziana di Santa Maria della Carità," *Arte veneta* 55 (1999): 144–50.

16   A bronze statue of a *Resurrected Christ* in Milan at the Museo Poldi Pezzoli has been identified as the only surviving piece from Domenico's chapel, see Paoletti, *L'architettura e la scultura*, 183. On the bronze statue, see also Alexander Nagel and Christopher S. Wood, "Interventions: Toward a New Model of Renaissance Anachronism," *Art Bulletin* 87, no. 3 (2005): 403–15.

17   Marcantonio Michiel, *Notizia d'opere di disegno, pubblicata e illustrata da D. Jacopo Morelli: Seconda edizione riveduta ed aumentata per cura di G. Frizzoni* (Bologna: Nicola Zanichelli, 1884), 86; and Francesco Sansovino, *Venetia, città nobilissima et singolare: Con aggiunta di tutte le cose notabili della stessa città fatte e occorse dall'anno 1580 fino al presente 1663 da D. Giustiniano Martinoni* (Venice: Stefano Curti, 1663), 267.

18   See Lauber, "Domenico di Piero," 269.

19   Tommaso Temanza, *Vite dei piu' celebri architetti e scultori veneziani che fiorirono nel secolo decimo sesto* (Venice: C. Palese, 1778), 1:96: "E perché non

Giada Damen

gli si può attribuire anche la Cappella del Salvatore nella Chiesa della Carità, la quale ai tempi del Sansovino chiamavasi la Cappella del Giojelliero ricca di marmi, porfidi, e serpentini come di quei tempi era l'uso?"

20 Marin Sanudo il Giovane, *Le vite dei dogi, 1474–1494*, ed. Angela Caracciolo Aricò (Padua: Antenore, 1989–2001), 412–13.

21 Giuseppe Tassini, *Cittadini veneziani*, Venice, Biblioteca del Museo Correr, Provenienze Diverse, ms. P.D. c. 4, pp. 83–84. Tassini mistakenly writes, however, that it was the house in Sant'Agnese that was given to Roberto da Sanseverino, not the one in San Giacomo dall'Orio, as reported by Sanudo.

22 Archivio di Stato di Venezia (ASVe), Procuratori di San Marco de Supra, Registri per conto Chiesa, Giornali Cassier, b. 1, 1486–1492, c. 78v, July 17, 1489. The record is published in Paoletti, *L'architettura e la scultura*, 118.

23 Because of its long history, the palace has been known over time with many different names: Contarini dal Zaffo, Ruzzini, Manzoni, Angaran, Montecuccoli, and Polignac-Decazes. See Elena Bassi, *Palazzi di Venezia: Admiranda Urbis Venetae* (Venice: La Stamperia di Venezia, 1976), 94–97.

24 Giuseppe Tassini, *Alcuni palazzi ed antichi edifici di Venezia* (Venice: M. Fontana, 1879), 209–11; Loredana Olivato Puppi and Leonello Puppi, *Mauro Codussi* (Milan: Electa, 1977), 236–38.

25 Paoletti, *L'architettura e la scultura*, 256.

26 While noting that many decorative details on the palace façade recall Florentine practices, Elena Bassi mentions Michelozzo Michelozzi's sojourn in Venice when—according to Vasari—he worked at the service of many gentlemen and friends of Cosimo de' Medici. Bassi's suggestion that one of these friends could have been the original owner of the palace would fit with Domenico de' Piero, who, as we have seen, was in tight business connections with the Medici in Florence.

Blake de Maria

Luxury Goods in Jacopo de' Barbari's Venice

20 JACOPO DE' BARBARI'S *VIEW OF VENICE* is rightfully lauded as one of the most, if not *the* most, comprehensive representations of an early modern European city. But the *View*'s fame stems from far more than its painstakingly detailed depiction of Venice's dense urban fabric: the monumental woodcut also celebrates the inseparable bonds between the lagoon city and mercantile enterprise. From the placement of Mercury, the god of commerce, hovering over the city to the emphasis on the thriving Rialto Bridge and the adjacent market area, the *View* offers viewers a vivid celebration of Venice's commercial dominance in the early sixteenth century.

The *View* must be understood as more than a tool used by merchants to gain information about a city famed for commercial enterprises, however, for the *View* itself was a luxury good in its own right. Using it as a starting point, this essay examines Venetian participation in the luxury goods market during a pivotal era in global trade: from approximately 1480 to 1550. The import and export of luxury objects ranging from gemstones, tooled leather wall hangings, and sumptuous fabrics to maps and printed books served as the lifeblood of the Venetian economy. To understand better this market phenomenon, a brief overview of what constituted a luxury good in sixteenth-century Venice—and the problems inherent in the notion of luxury/*luxuria*—proves instructive.

A universal definition of luxury is remarkably difficult to find, with many attempts recalling Justice Potter Stewart's definition of pornography: in essence, "I cannot describe it, but I know it when I see it."[1] In its most basic, standard understanding, luxury encompasses those items that qualify as something more than necessary for subsistence. This "something more" may be found in the rarity of the materials (e.g., ivory, gemstones, gold) or the purported singularity of an item (e.g., a unicorn horn)—or even the brand name of the manufacturer. In Renaissance Venice, a creation by Titian enjoyed a level of renown and exclusivity that today might be bestowed on a bespoke Dolce & Gabbana gown.[2] These are but a few items that satisfy a psychological desire and need that exist well beyond the fundamental bodily necessities of food, clothing, and shelter.[3]

Even within this most basic and decidedly broad definition, slippage occurs—in both time and place—as to what constitutes a luxury good.[4] Such is the case for those middling objects that improve quality of life but may not have the same social prestige as a finely carved ebony casket. Soap offers just one example of a commodity that in most twenty-first-century cosmopolitan centers is considered a necessity rather than an extravagance. However, Renaissance Venice had a reputation as an international urban metropolis, and for Venetians, soap enjoyed an elevated market position. The Vendramin family, whose fortune stemmed from soap manufacture, counted among Venice's cultural elite. Brothers Andrea and Gabriele Vendramin owned a sumptuous palace in Cannaregio, which housed one of the Republic's most notable art collections, boasting ancient and modern masterpieces, including Giorgione's famed *Tempesta* (fig. 20.1).[5]

For an engaged intellectual such as Gabriele Vendramin, the concept of luxury extended well beyond the confines of material culture. Rather, broader theoretical issues, specifically social dictates on the vice *luxuria*, loomed large. Debates concerning the propriety of expenditure on those el-

Giorgione, *The Tempest*, ca. 1507–8. Oil on canvas, 83 × 73 cm. Gallerie dell'Accademia, Venice.

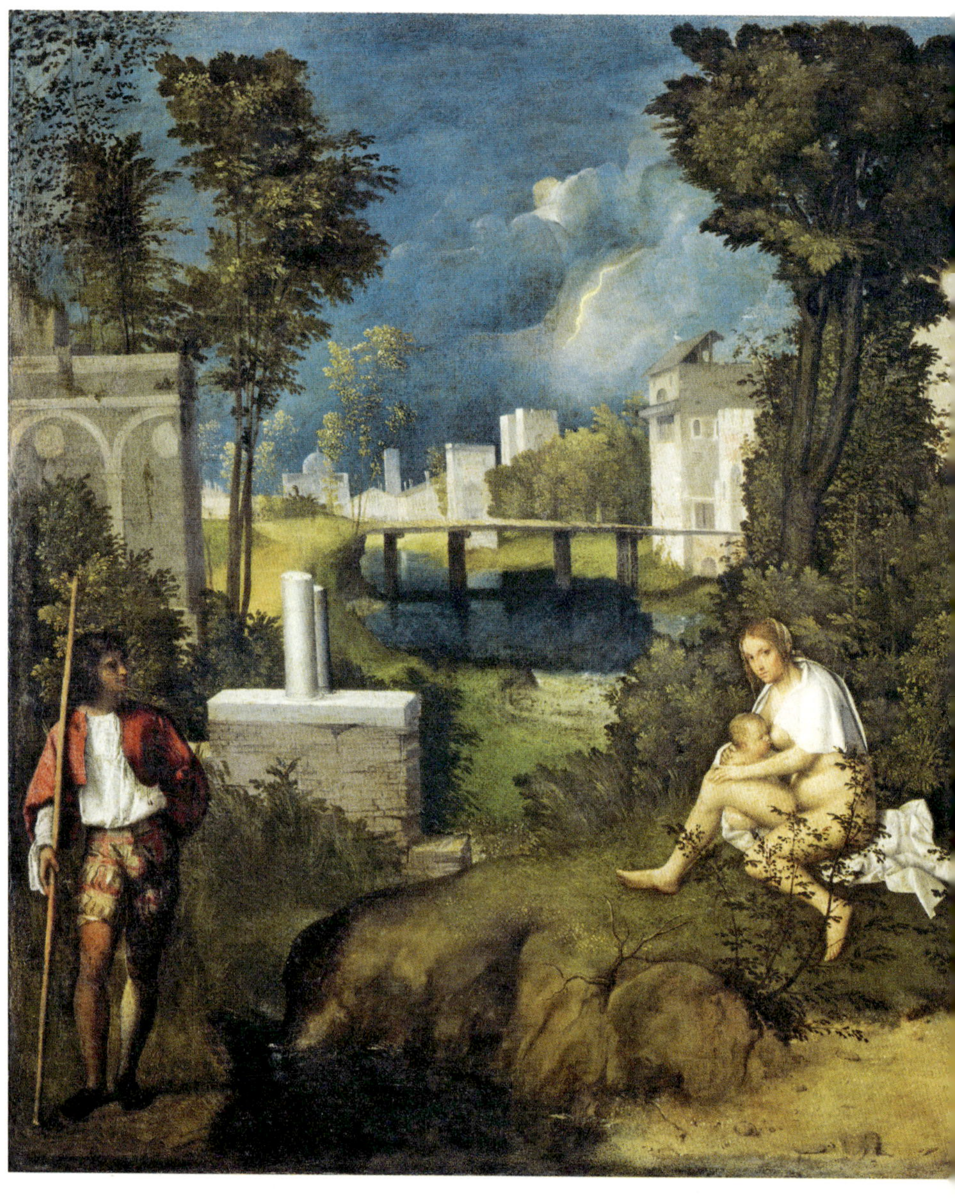

ements beyond necessity appear in numerous classical treatises.[6] However, Aristotle's *Nicomachean Ethics* offered Renaissance consumers their most potent justification for conspicuous consumption.[7] For Aristotle, luxury objects served as "expressions of dignity befitting the great."[8] But a classical pedigree did not completely erase social concerns about the conspicuous

262

display of wealth. In many ways, this trend manifested itself most visibly in the accumulation of luxury goods, for one man's luxury could be viewed as another man's *luxuria*. The notion of indulgence and excess inherent in *luxuria* was, in turn, linked to illicit sexuality, a notion exemplified by the Berlin *Portrait of a Man*, a representation sometimes attributed to none other than Jacopo de' Barbari (fig. 20.2).[9]

This enigmatic two-sided portrait offers viewers tantalizing glimpses of just some of the luxury goods that a visitor to de' Barbari's Venice—such as the anonymous merchant represented on the front of the panel—might find in Venice.[10] Glassware of all kinds, including mirrors, counted among Venetian market mainstays in the early modern period. Yet these products offered just one category of goods that attracted consumers and merchants to the city. The Republic's long-standing trade agreements allowed Venetian merchants to reside in the likes of Alexandria, Istanbul, Aleppo, and Basrah. Such residencies ensured a constant supply of items from the East available for purchase in the lagoon city. The "luxury" designation of these foreign objects stemmed not only from the value of the materials used in their creation but also from their place of origin. In the Renaissance period, material culture from distant lands became associated with the notion of the exotic, which elevated the status of many a necessity into a luxury good.[11]

Most early modern visitors to the city arrived in the northwestern area, traveling across the lagoon past the island of San Secondo, and their first point of entry to the city proper was the Cannaregio canal (fig. 20.3). Whether one looks at this section of the *View* or the entire woodcut, de' Barbari records what seems to be—and in certain cases is—a confusing, dense city without any discernible organization. The city's aqueous setting combined with the lack of an orderly Roman foundation grid resulted in an urban environment that seemingly developed in a haphazard fashion.

Within this urban chaos, however, there was an order. As was the case with so many other aspects of early modern Venice, that order stemmed from mercantile concerns. The processing of commodities into luxury goods often took place in peripheral areas of the city. Certainly, this decision satisfied practical concerns. Such locations offered ease for product movement, as goods could be transported around the open waterways surrounding the city rather than through the smaller and more crowded canals cutting through it. In addition, many of the workers who transformed raw materials, such as textiles, into the fine-hewn fabric bolts available for purchase in

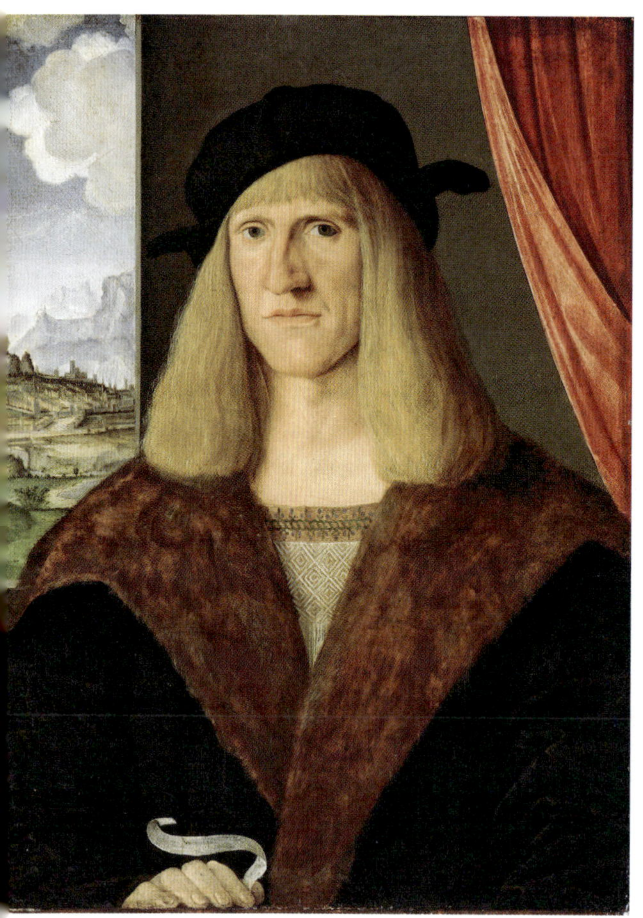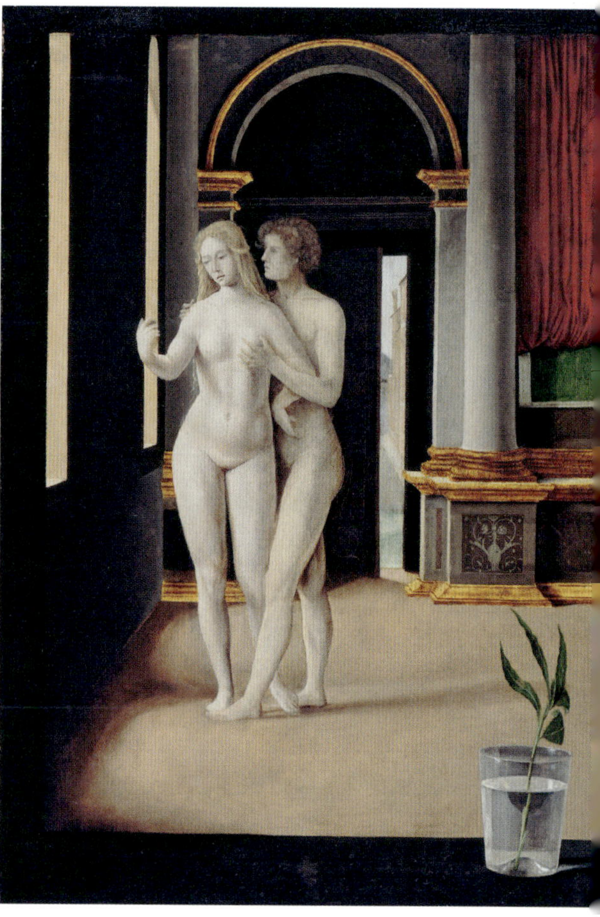

Jacopo de' Barbari (Attributed), *Portrait of a Man* (obverse), *Couple* (reverse), ca. 1500. Oil on poplar panel, 61 × 46 cm. Staatliche Museen, Berlin.

many a Venetian *bottega* lived in row housing built in these outlying areas. Since dyeing, spinning, and weaving often took place in the home, many of these workers were women. In addition, in the decades that followed the printing of the *View*, land reclamation projects expanded the city's perimeter. These ventures enabled some of the great merchant families, such as the d'Anna and the di Mutti, to construct row housing and rental units in Santa Maria Maggiore and San Girolamo, respectively.[12] These structures helped with the perennial problem of affordable houses for workers while simultaneously allowing the d'Anna and the di Mutti families to expand their commercial enterprises from cloth production to real estate development. Odorous activities likewise took place on the edge of city.[13] For example, close to the Cannaregio canal, in the parish of San Giobbe, documents tell

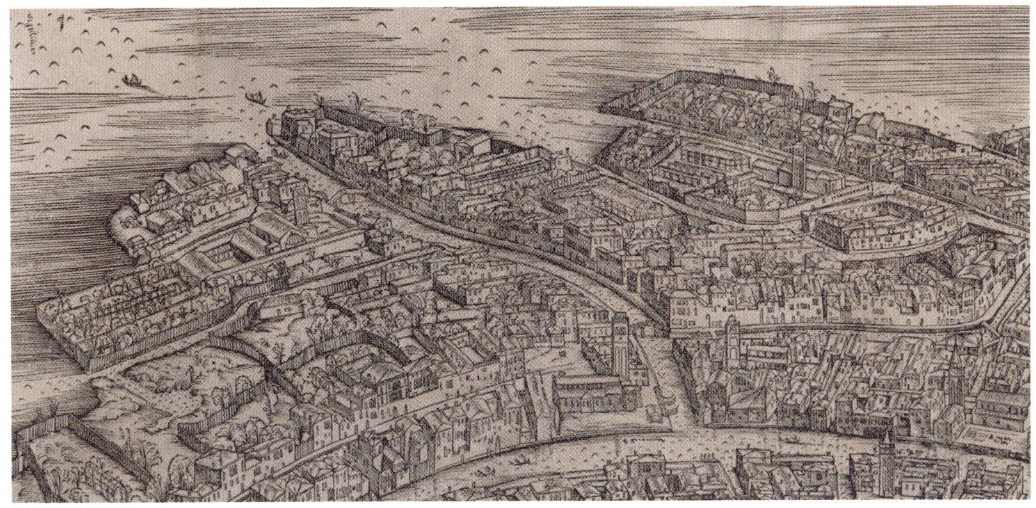

of a slaughterhouse, tannery, and rendering plant (see fig. 20.3).[14] This waterside location aided in the presumably challenging transport of cattle from the mainland across the lagoon to Venice proper.

The raw materials inherent in commodities such as cattle were in turn fashioned into a variety of products ranging from necessities, such as basic foodstuffs, to luxury goods, such as tooled leather hangings destined for the wall of a Grand Canal palace or carving roasts to be served at a princely banquet. Finally, it is worth noting that glassware—one of Venice's most important luxury industries, and one of the few whose manufacture took place almost in its entirety in the lagoon—had been transferred from the city proper to the outlying island of Murano in the late thirteenth century. The government forced the relocation of the furnaces due to understandable concerns over fires.

But to acquire the truly newest, finest, or most unusual object, a luxury goods enthusiast would make their way to the Rialto market area (plate 4). After strolling through the Rialto in 1494—just a few years before de' Barbari completed the *View*—Canon Pietro Casola recorded his oft-quoted description of that district:

> Something may be said about the quantity of merchandise in said city, although not nearly the whole truth, because it is inestimable. Indeed it seems as if all the world flocks there, and that human beings have

20.3

Detail of Cannaregio from Jacopo de' Barbari, *View of Venice*, ca. 1497–1500.

concentrated there all their force for trading. ... And who could count
so many shops so well furnished that they seem [to be] warehouses,
with so many cloths of every make—tapestry, brocades, and hangings
of every sort, camlets of every color and texture, silks of every kind,
and so many warehouses full of spices and groceries and drugs, and
so much beautiful white wax! These things stupefy the beholder, and
cannot be fully described to those who have not seen them.[15]

Blake de Maria

In many ways, the barrage of information included in the *View* parallels
Casola's observations concerning the abundance of luxury goods to be
viewed and/or acquired in the Rialto market area. It occupies the upper
middle sheet of the woodcut, and de' Barbari includes several visual cues
to emphasize this area's importance. Both Mercury's right hand and Neptune's left hand—as well as the trident he holds within that hand—lead the
viewer's eye directly to the sole object that linked the *de ultra* and *de citra*
sides of the early modern city: the Rialto Bridge.

On closer inspection, de' Barbari's representation offers an invaluable
record of this international mercantile entrepôt at its zenith, just fifteen
years before fire decimated the area, including the only extant record of the
now-destroyed Loggia dei Mercanti (visualized in plate 4). In the early sixteenth century, textile merchants displayed their wares on tables situated underneath this architectural overhang. Here customers interested in the finest
textiles for a luxury gown would likely do their shopping on a day established
as *da paragon*—usually Wednesdays—days when the finest textile samples
were placed on display side by side to allow for comparison shopping.[16]

San Giacomo di Rialto sat directly behind the Loggia. The thirteenth-century church once bore an exterior inscription with a potent
reminder for buyers and sellers alike: "Round about this church may the
law-merchant be equitable, the weights just, and may no fraudulent contract
be negotiated."[17] That this admonition concerning equity, weights, and fraud
overlooked the Ruga dei Oresi, a primary location for the sale and acquisition of precious stones and jewelry, should come as little surprise. Certainly,
gemstones qualify as luxury goods, and their fungibility further increased
their value. Venice was geologically incapable of producing gems (although
Venetians were notorious jewel forgers, which makes sense given the city's
glassmaking facilities).[18] Thus, like the majority of luxury goods sold in the
city, the gems had to be imported. A 1526 inventory of the jeweler Giurato
Bonarrigo's shop confirms the international scope of the Venetian gem

market. According to this legal document, a consumer who entered Bonar-rigo's bottega on the Ruga dei Oresi would have access to a wide spectrum of gems for purchase, including ballas, sapphires, diamonds (both raw and rough cut), rubies, and pearls.[19] In the sixteenth century, the stones would have been mined in India (diamonds), Sri Lanka (sapphires), or Myanmar (both rubies and ballas—a less valuable member of the corundum family), then exported to Venice.

For those who could not afford to purchase gemstones, sumptuous textiles, or gilt picture frames at retail price, numerous alternative possibilities for acquisition existed, including public auctions. These events attracted a lively crowd. Whether curious to see items confiscated from fugitives and debtors, or merely there in search of a bargain, auction-goers were treated to a panoply of luxury objects at these events, including paintings, clothing, furniture, and jewelry.[20] Venice likewise enjoyed a thriving secondhand market in luxury goods; almost every object commonly found in the home or worn on the body could be rented, for just a weekend or for years on end.[21]

While the Rialto may have been the first stop for the acquisition of luxury goods, it was certainly not the only point of consumer interest. The Mercerie, the city's most important commercial thoroughfare, linked the marketplace to the city's political and ritual center at Piazza San Marco (plate 5). Boutiques such as those described by Pietro Casola lined the entirety of this high street. Some stores specialized in a specific category, such as gold or antiquities, while others carried a full array of luxury items. The latter was certainly the case for the two most famous shops located on the Mercerie: La Luna and Dal Calice. The Bontempelli family, members of Venice's citizen caste, owned both entities and earned a vast fortune from their trade activities.[22] The family's account books and personal correspondence confirm that a constant supply of pearls, furniture, carpets, and other valuables were to be found within the shops. In the course of the sixteenth century, La Luna and Dal Calice became a preferred shopping venue for European royalty.[23]

The short walk down the Mercerie concluded at none other than the Piazza San Marco (plate 2). Once a year this space transformed from the political center of the Republic to the locus of one of Europe's most famous luxury fairs. Held each spring in conjunction with the Feast of the Ascension (the Sensa), the event served as yet another quintessentially Venetian fusion of custom and commerce.[24] The Ascension held a special place in the Venetian ritual calendar, for on this day the doge would marry the sea, a ritual consummated when the political leader of the Republic threw a gold ring into the Adriatic. In the two weeks following the symbolic nuptials, stalls and booths were erected in the Piazza. These ephemeral botteghe functioned in a manner akin to contemporary pop-up shops.

In addition to the commercial opportunities available in and around the Piazza San Marco, the Venetian Customs House (Dogana del Mar) likewise played an important role in the Venetian luxury goods market. Situated directly across the Bacino from Piazza San Marco, this location receives pride of place in the *View* (plate 3). If the Cannaregio canal may be identified as the primary entry point for consumers to the city, then the Dogana may be identified as the primary entry for the luxury objects they hoped to purchase. In the *View*, de' Barbari depicts two types of commercial vessels adjacent to the Dogana. Here, at the Customs House, leaders of the merchant fleets would officially register their cargo and, in return, receive permission to unload their cargo within the city limits.[25] In the years following de' Barbari's depiction, this area would be further developed in order to bolster Venetian trade supremacy.

Yet this architectural embellishment hid a startling new reality: fundamental trade-related shifts had already begun. By 1500, when the *View* was published, the Portuguese had navigated the Cape of Good Hope, and Columbus had returned from his third voyage to the Americas. Thus, on completion of the *View*, the ramifications of these events were just being recognized. Tantalizing hints of globalism began to appear in the early modern world, with few, if any, as telling as a recently discovered detail at the Vatican. At the behest of Pope Alexander VI, Pinturicchio frescoed a series of biblical narratives in the papal apartments, including the *Resurrection* (fig. 20.4). The image, which dates to 1494–95, has long been studied as a statement of papal piety, but a recent restoration highlights its function as a symbol of global papal power. In the deep background of the painting, specifically at the vanishing point, Pinturicchio has included the earliest known European representation of Indigenous people of the Americas (fig. 20.5).[26] This compositional strategy, commonly employed in central Italian painting, utilizes pictorial depth for symbolic purpose. Pinturicchio's Indigenous people occupy the same place traditionally reserved for Roman soldiers and other pagan persons, visually equating the Indigenous figures with the ancient nonbelievers.

However, for early modern Venetians, the implications of expanding global travels had a profound impact on their present and future, specifically their long-held commercial dominance. Throughout the sixteenth

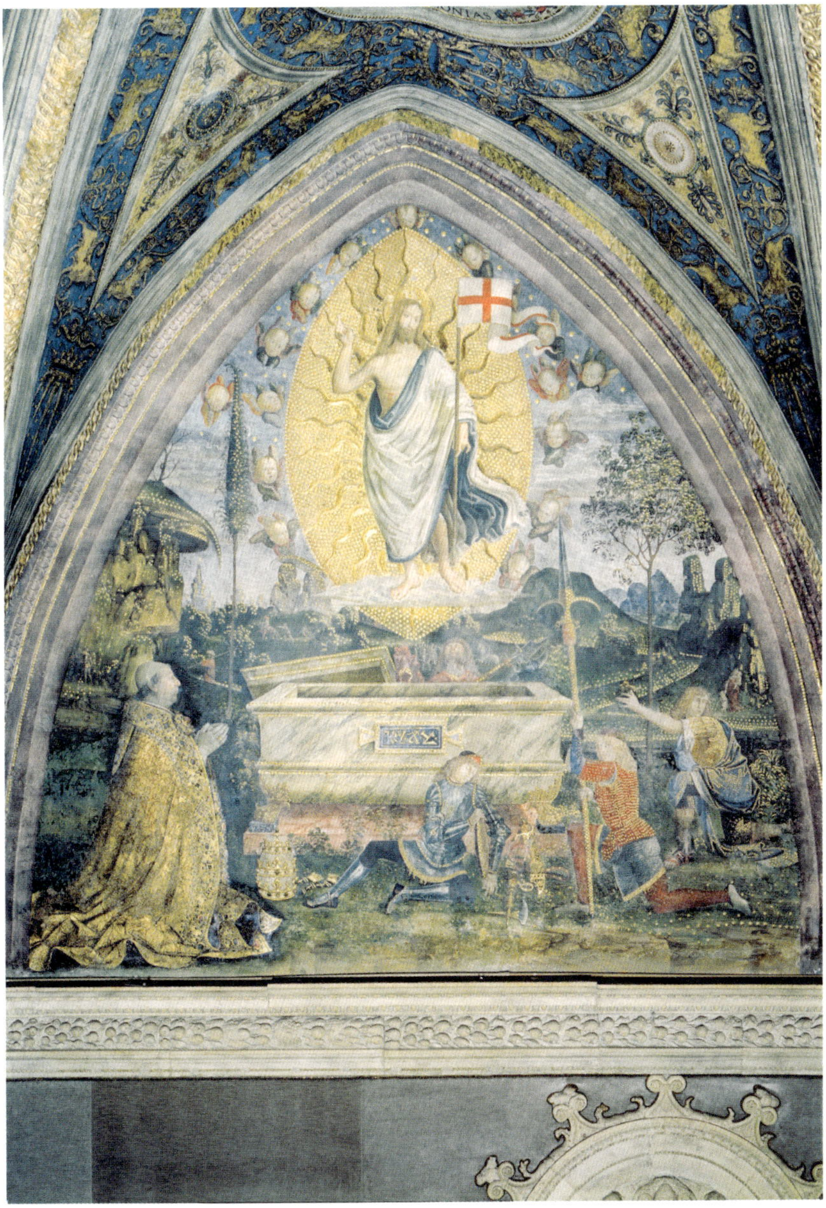

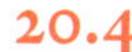

Pinturicchio, *Resurrection with Alexander VI*, ca. 1492–94. Fresco. Hall of Faith in Borgia Apartments, Vatican Museums, Vatican.

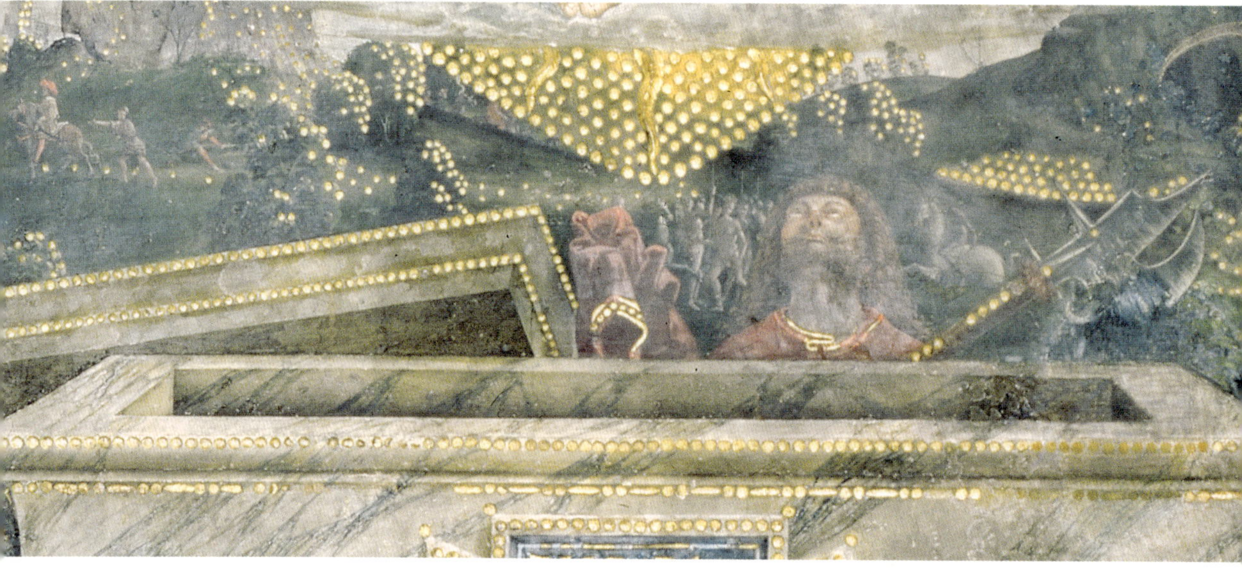

century, luxury goods from the Americas, including gold, cochineal, and emeralds, made their way into the Venetian marketplace. Thus, in a strange twist of fate, despite the expansion of the luxury goods market and the development of global trade, Venice would no longer enjoy the primacy of place of the wealthy mercantile entrepôt memorialized in Jacopo de' Barbari's *View*.

NOTES

1 Paul Gerwitz, "On 'I Know It When I See It,'" *Yale Law Journal* 105, no. 4 (January 1996), 1023–24.

2 See, for example, the 2018 blockbuster exhibition at the Metropolitan Museum of Art in New York. Andrew Bolton, ed., *Heavenly Bodies: Fashion and the Catholic Imagination*, exhib. cat. (New York: Metropolitan Museum of Art, 2018), 10–17.

3 Christopher J. Berry, *The Idea of Luxury: A Conceptual and Historical Investigation* (Cambridge: Cambridge University Press, 1994), 8–11.

4 Berry, *The Idea of Luxury*, 177–95; and Peter McNeil and Giorgio Riello, *Luxury: A Rich History* (Oxford: Oxford University Press, 2016), 4–6.

5 On the family and their noble status, see Patricia Fortini Brown, *Private Lives in Renaissance Venice* (New Haven, CT: Yale University Press, 2004), esp. 225–29; for their collections, see Jaynie Anderson, "A Further Inventory of Gabriele Vendramin's Collection," *Burlington Magazine* 121, no. 919 (1979): 639–48; and Salvatore Settis, *Giorgione's Tempest: Interpreting the Hidden Subject*, trans. Ellen Bianchini (Chicago: University of Chicago Press, 1990).

6 Grant Parker, "*Ex Oriente Luxuria*: Indian Commodities and Roman Experience," *Journal of Economic and Social History of the Orient* 45, no. 1 (2002): 55–58.

7 A. D. Fraser Jenkins, "Cosimo de' Medici's Patronage of Architecture and the Theory of Magnificence," *Journal of the Warburg and Courtauld Institutes* 33 (1970): esp. 166–67; for a broader history, see also David Thomson, *Renaissance Architecture: Critics, Patrons, Luxury* (Manchester: Manchester University Press, 1993).

8 Marina Belozerskaya, *Luxury Arts of the Renaissance* (Los Angeles: J. Paul Getty Museum, 2005), 2.

9 Bernard Aikema and Beverly Louise Brown, "Painting in Fifteenth-Century Venice and the *ars nova* of the Netherlands," in *Renaissance Venice and the North: Crosscurrents in the Time of Bellini, Dürer, and Titian*, ed. Aikema and Brown (Venice: Bompiani, 1999), 234–35; Brown, *Private Lives*, 167–70. For the link between *luxuria* and illicit sexuality, see Patricia Allerston, "Consuming Problems: Worldly Goods in Renaissance Venice," in *The Material Renaissance*, ed. Michelle O'Malley (Manchester: Manchester University Press, 2010), 22.

10 Two-sided panel paintings, as well as portraits with painted covers, were extremely popular at the turn of the century, as evidenced by Carpaccio's *Two Venetian Women on a Terrace / Letter Rack* (Venice, Museo Correr) and Lorenzo Lotto's *Allegory of Chastity* (Washington, DC, National Gallery of Art) to name but a few.

11 McNeil and Riello, *Luxury*, 79–115; see also Benjamin Schmidt, *Inventing Exoticism: Geography, Globalism and Europe's Early Modern World* (Philadelphia: University of Pennsylvania Press, 2015).

12 Blake de Maria, *Becoming Venetian: Immigrants and the Arts in Early Modern Venice* (New Haven, CT: Yale University Press, 2010), 116–21.

13 Spatial designations such as this were not uncommon in the medieval period, a point perhaps best illustrated by the city plan of Baghdad. Jacob Lassner, *The Topography of Baghdad in the Middle Ages* (Detroit: Wayne State University Press, 1970).

14 Ennio Concina, *Structure urbaine et fonctions des bâtiments du XVIe au XIXe siècle* (Venice: UNESCO / Save Venice, 1982), esp. 50–69.

15 Pietro Casola, *Canon Pietro Casola's Pilgrimage to Jerusalem in the Year 1494*, ed. and trans. M. Margaret Newett (Manchester: Manchester University Publications, 1907), 128–29.

16 Luca Molà, *The Silk Industry of Renaissance Venice* (Baltimore, MD: Johns Hopkins University, 2000), 97–103; Evelyn Welch, *Shopping in the Renaissance: Consumer Cultures in Italy, 1400–1600* (New Haven, CT: Yale University Press, 2005), 123.

17 Reinhold C. Mueller, *The Venetian Money Market: Banks, Panics and the Public Debt, 1200–1500* (Baltimore, MD: Johns Hopkins University Press, 1997), 36.

18 Blake de Maria, "Multifaceted Endeavors: Considerations on Gems and Jewelry in Early Modern Venice," in *Reflections on Renaissance Venice*, ed. de Maria and Mary Frank (Milan: Five Continent/Abrams, 2013), 128.

19 Archivio di Stato di Venezia (ASVe), Miscellanea Notai Diversi, b. 37, doc. 63, "Zoglie stimato […] in Ruga in Rialto et fu del 1526."

20 For example, see ASVe, Notarile Atti, Catti, b. 3549, 8r. See also Welch, *Shopping*, 191–200.

21 Patricia Allerston, "The Market in Second Clothes and Furnishings in Venice, circa 1500–1650" (PhD diss., European University, Florence, 1996).

22 Stefania Mason, "A l'enseigne du calice et de la lune: Les Bontempelli, marchands, commanditaires et collectioneurs," *Revue de l'art* 160, no. 2 (2008): 35–44.

23 Giada Damen, "Shopping for *Cose Antiche* in Late Sixteenth-Century Venice," in de Maria and Frank, *Reflections on Renaissance Venice*, 133.

24 Welch, *Shopping*, 177–84.

25 Frederic C. Lane, *Venice: A Maritime Republic* (Baltimore, MD: Johns Hopkins University Press, 1973), 13.

26 Sylvia Poggioli, "Long Hidden, Vatican Painting Linked to Native Americans," *The Two-Way*, National Public Radio, May 5, 2013, https://www.npr.org/sectionsIo-way/2013/05/05/180860991/long-hidden-vatican-painting-linked-to-native-americans.

Julia A. DeLancey

"Both by Sea and Land"

Venetian Trade and Retail in the *View*

SOLD AT THE RELATIVELY PRINCELY SUM of three florins, Jacopo de' Barbari's *View of Venice* proved popular among members of the Serenissima, as attested by the eight versions that still reside in the city.[1] In addition to its cost, the large size would have necessitated space for storage and viewing. It is tempting to imagine the *View* taking up residence in Venice, perhaps even somewhere in the *porteghi*, ample quasi-public spheres of the city's grand palazzi.[2] Much of Venice's success relied on her prosperous merchant class, some of whom were involved in its pigment trade. With both the means to afford the *View* and a vested interest in the civic pride it embodies, merchants represent an interesting audience from which to consider the *View*'s creation. Members of these prosperous families could cast their eyes

21

across the print and place a finger on their own palaces as well as along the Grand Canal and other prominent areas of Venice. For example, shortly after the *View*'s publication, the construction of the Ca' Cuccina on the Grand Canal announced the success of the naturalized *cittadino* merchant Alvise Cuccina—whose wife's family, the di Mutti, made their fortune in part on the new, less expensive, and more abundant supply of the red pigment, cochineal, coming in from the Americas—as would the home on the Canale di Cannaregio of Alvise della Scala, key color seller for lead white pigment.[3]

What might merchants like Alvise Cuccina have thought of de' Barbari's image? The associations brought about by the *View* would likely have been rich and many: the winds that allowed their ships to move around seas such as the Mediterranean and Adriatic and across the Atlantic; the ships and boats that ferried their goods around the world and across the city; and the buildings that housed spaces for import and export, manufacture, storage, and sale—as well as the exchange of ideas. Their viewing experience would have also likely been animated by an awareness of the closeness of spaces to those of other merchants working in the same trades and the ways in which that proximity reinforced ties of kinship.[4] Building on Michael Baxandall's observations from decades ago about how mercantile activities may have determined what merchants saw in visual works, there is also something in de' Barbari's mark-making throughout the *View*—a regularity, consistency, and measured quality—that may have resonated with merchants for whom measuring, weighing, and evaluating the world around them played a central role.[5] After all, at the heart of the genesis of the project lay the mercantile aims of the German Anton Kolb and the Italian de' Barbari (likely Venetian, although he also worked in Germany for some time). The interest in trade courses throughout the *View* in many rich and varied ways. Naturally, the image embodies much more than trade, manufacture, and retail, yet those ties remain at the heart of Venetian identity.

This essay examines the *View of Venice* from the perspective of Venetian mercantile activities and the movement of goods around, throughout, and within the city. It takes as a case study merchants dealing in coloring materials (*vendecolori*). Venetian merchants traded a staggering array of goods, but *vendecolori* make a particularly good case study. As we understand it now, they were particular to Venice at least around the time of the *View*'s publication in 1500; they stood to make vast sums of money from their work; and their goods were used in a wide array of the kinds of materials for which Venice was so justly known: paintings, glass, and textiles.[6] What

*Julia A.
DeLancey*

might such a Venetian merchant have seen when he (they were generally male) looked at this monumental representation of Venice? What might he have discussed with his fellow merchants—partners in trade and possible kin as well—when handling and looking at the *View*?[7]

Ships, Boats, and Wayfinding

The built fabric, surrounding water, and figurative compass winds dominate the *View* and have received a great deal of attention. Second only to those key elements, though, are the hundreds of ships and boats of all kinds that move through and rest in the waters around Venice. Enumerated at more than five hundred, the types of water vessels range from the largest caravels or round-ships immediately to the south of the Arsenal, to the smallest gondolas that travel everywhere from narrow canals to the wide-open spaces north of the Fondamente Nove.[8] In the *View*, oarsmen row gondolas and galleys through the lagoon (most notably in the massive—and labeled—regatta in the lower right sheet); sailors struggle to command the sails of a *tartana* in rough water; and a whole array of galleys and cogs await either departure or repairs near the Arsenal (indeed, at least five *arsenalotti* work on two round-ships in the waters just south of the Arsenal).[9] In addition, countless passengers ride throughout the city, some protected by *felze* and others enjoying the sea breezes. Small details also suggest the dynamic movement of boats around the city. For example, just northwest of San Moisè, a gondola turns from the Rio de' Barcaroli into the Rio delle Veste, the front *ferro di prua* obscured by its movement to the west. These details animate the city and make clear the ways in which people and goods would have moved about.

The ships that dominate the *View* make possible mercantile activity in the lagoon city and embody Venice's central role in international import and export as well as manufacturing and sales (retail and wholesale).[10] The presence of round-ships—so important for long-haul trade—near the Customs House (Dogana) and the Arsenal highlight Venice's key role in international trade and also in shipbuilding, maintenance, and repair (plates 3 and 6); in the same way, the galleys, fewer in number and huddled near the southernmost tail of Castello, signal Venice's military prowess.[11] The proximity of small ships such as *bregantin* immediately next to round-ships moored by the Customs House remind us of the importance of customs and duties in overall trade.[12] A midsized, masted ship in the Grand Canal immediately

275

northwest of the church of the Trinity in Dorsoduro would have moved larger cargos from the Bacino up to the Rialto market area.[13] Two further examples are the boats loaded with wood and the tugboat pulling a larger ship up the Grand Canal.[14]

Routes and Movement of Goods

Julia A.
DeLancey

Venice acted as a true entrepôt. During the early modern period, her trade network extended from the eastern coast of the Atlantic to the western coast of the Black Sea and beyond. Venetian merchants traded in everything from goods completed elsewhere, such as carpets, to raw materials that would be imported into Venice, processed, and then either used in the city or exported elsewhere.[15] And along the way, of course, countless individuals would be involved, including local workmen at docks, Venetian-born merchants who might live their whole working lives in a city other than Venice, and those from outside Venice who might become naturalized citizens.

Through the winds, the suggestions of the larger lagoon, and the distant landscape at the top of the print, de' Barbari's *View* hints at this larger world of trade. However, the *View* by its nature emphasizes the movement of goods within Venice herself, particularly as the larger ships that would have been involved in that trade, rest moored in the Bacino. The presence of the vessels would have certainly helped the merchant viewers of the *View* to recall the essential steps whereby goods would be handed over from long-distance trade to the vast Venetian networks for manufacturing, retail, and wholesale.[16] The mooring of *burchi*, communal transport ships, near (for example) the Magazzini del Sal di San Gregorio make clear the transfer of goods around and throughout the city.[17]

In addition to the ships suggesting movement, the *View*'s very layout emphasizes the waterways by which goods would have made this journey. The increasing narrowness of Venetian waterways—from basin and lagoon to the Grand, Giudecca, and Cannaregio canals, to the smaller *rii*— necessitated a change in conveyance. In addition, essential bridges that allowed intersections between foot- and waterways limited the height of boats as well. Of course, the main and widest route to the Rialto market area was the Grand Canal, impeded in 1500 only by the Rialto Bridge. Although narrower and shallower, other pathways to the Rialto provided shorter, more direct access. The *View* emphasizes most clearly passages from the north and the south, the areas where larger cargos were most likely delivered.[18] The route that wove from the Rio del Palazzo to the Rio di San Zulian to the Rio della Fava to the Rio Fondaco dei Tedeschi could deposit boats directly at the Rialto. Vessels could also continue on the Rio della Fava to any number of connections leading to the Fondamente Nove (fig. 21.1). The Ponte della Paglia, which allows pedestrians on the Riva degli Schiavoni to cross the opening of the aforementioned route, would have also meant that lower, narrower boats would need to be used. The *View* also makes clear the opening of the Rio dei Mendicanti, alongside the Scuola Grande di San Marco and Santi Giovanni e Paolo, and the Rio dei Gesuati, both of which gave ready access to the Rialto from the north. Of the many canals shown in the view, the Rio dei Mendicanti and the Rio del Palazzo are among the rare ones of which we are given an unimpeded view. In addition, viewers are given an uninterrupted image of the palazzi that line the Rio dei Gesuati. Farther along the Riva, the openings to the Rio dei Greci and Rio de la Pietà and the (again) open views emphasize routes direct from the Bacino to the northern lagoon.

To get a sense of what this movement of goods might look like beyond the *View*, we might take, as a case study, one of the coloring materials: white lead (also known as *cerussa*, *biacca*, or *biacca di Venezia*).[19] While we think of lead white as a pigment, it would have also been of use in glazes and as a flux in both ceramics and glassmaking industries in Venice.[20] During the early modern period, Venetians not only produced the highest-quality lead white pigments in western Europe, they also developed the production of lead white on a large scale and, as a result, dominated the market in that material.[21] As practiced today, the beginning of the production of white lead would be the mining of lead ore (perhaps in the form of galena—lead sulfide). Even in ancient Rome, mines existed all over Italy as well as western Europe, and it is likely that the ore would have traveled to the lagoon city from a mine, perhaps in the Italian Alps visible at the top of the *View*, or from farther afield, in England.[22] Through smelting, the lead itself would have been separated from the ore (a process that has also remained largely unchanged since ancient times) and then cast into the necessary form.[23] The process for creating *biacca* from lead was well-known, refined by the Venetians for large-scale production, and reported widely.[24] Philiberto Vernatti describes the process used for bigger production (generally known as the stack or Dutch process) in which lead bars are suspended over vinegar in pots. Those pots can then be sealed, sometimes surrounded by dung (to generate heat), and stacked one on top of the other.[25] The heat and vinegar

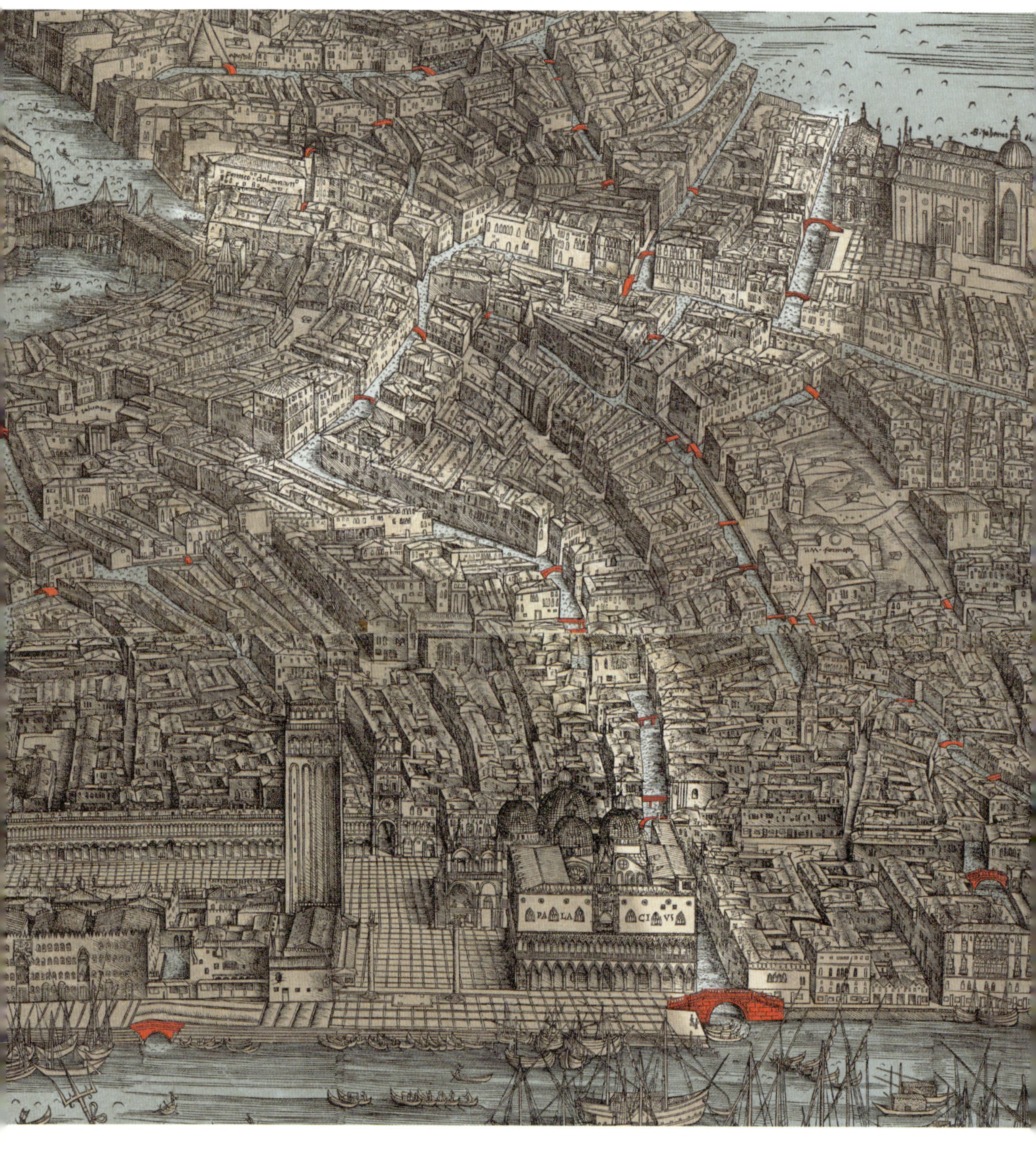

Fontico dalamani
PALACIVS
S. Iohannes

produce a white precipitate on the surface of the lead, which can then be scraped off and ground to make the pigment. Barbara Berrie and Louisa Matthew have found inventories of Venetian concerns that processed lead white. These spaces included benches for pounding lead; areas and basins for washing lead white; molds for forming the lead into loaves, cakes, or strips; and grinders and mills.[26] Partnerships were even formed for "lead white man-ufactor[ies]" near the Rialto.[27] In addition to this large-scale production, Ve-netian color sellers also imported and sold significant quantities of lead white pigments.[28] For example, a shipment from 1561 on the *Alexandrina* contained a hundred barrels of lead white, and merchants such as Alvise Gradignan della Scala (whose portrait Titian likely painted in 1561) stored large amounts in dedicated spaces (*magazen*) in hopes of making significant profits.[29]

Traces of that particular business example appear in de' Barbari's *View*. The botteghe and *magazzini* of Venice appear in the Rialto area and beyond. For our merchant viewer who knew the built fabric of the city, traces of mer-cantile activity appear in the manufacture of various goods, such as fabrics and bricks.[30] Viewers would have recognized a typical format for a bottega, with one main door and an opening on one or both sides of the door for the display of goods.[31] For example, blocks of botteghe lie in Santa Croce near the Campo dei Tedeschi and also along the Riva del Vin in the Rialto.[32] And very clear views of botteghe appear near the Ponte della Paglia, and along the Campo San Bartolomeo (fig. 21.2); by the early fourteenth century, at least one *magazzino* or similar storage facility existed there.[33] Indeed, that area lay not only in the heart of the Rialto market district but also at the center of one of Venice's main industries: the trade, production, and sale of coloring materials such as pigments and dyes.

When we think of the lived lives, the human experiences implied in everything above, the *View* conceals as much as it reveals. We do not see transactions, interiors, the fruits of the trade, or the costs. We do not see the 10,000-ducat dowry that one of Alvise Gradignan della Scala's neph-ews gave to his daughter, raised at least in part through profitable business transactions in white lead, nor the diseases, suffering, and death caused by working so closely and consistently with this substance.[34] We smell neither the lead nor the mines nor the sea breezes alluded to in the movement of boats and water. And yet despite those lacunae, the *View* still presents a re-markably vivid and thorough image of the various ways in which trade and mercantile activity enlivened La Serenissima both to our merchant viewer from the past but also to us today.

Detail of the passageways into Venice from the Bacino up to the Rialto, then up to the Fon-damente Nove, from Jacopo de' Barbari, *View of Venice*, ca. 1497–1500.

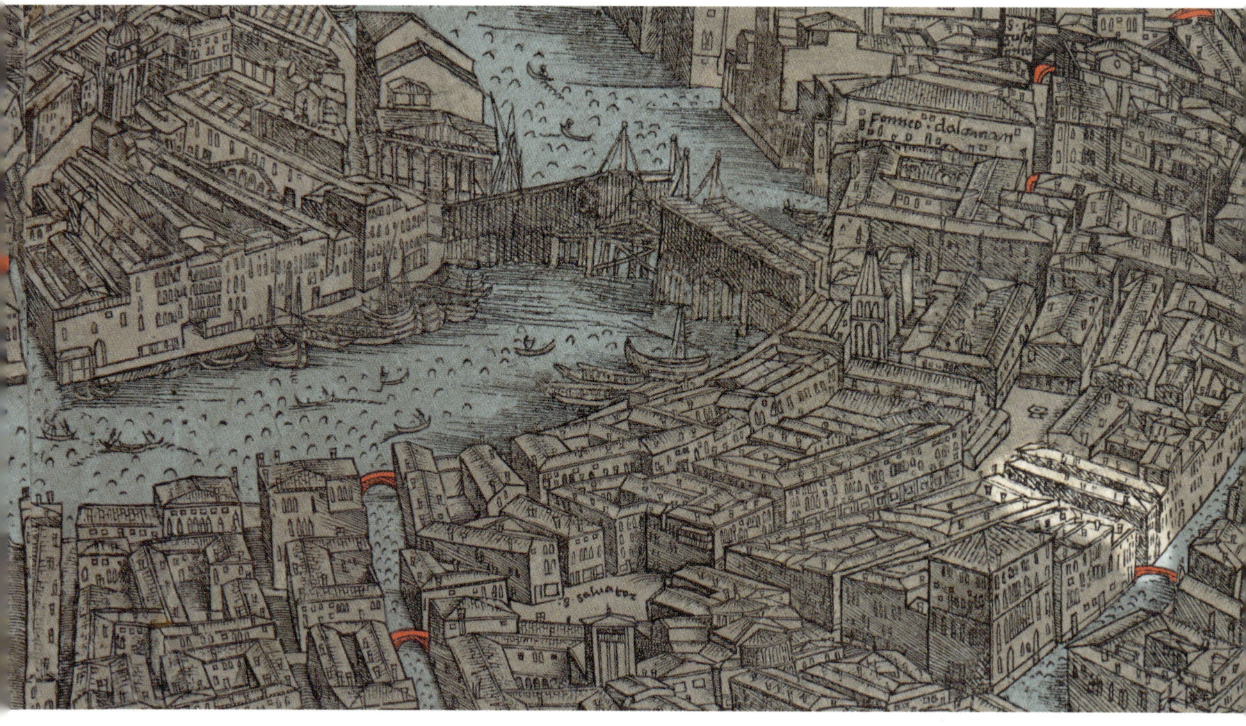

NOTES

This essay has benefited greatly from the interventions of Kristin Huffman and John Garton; of course, all errors remain my own.

1 For the surviving versions, see Teresio Pignatti, "La Pianta di Venezia di Jacopo de' Barbari," *Bollettino dei Musei Civici Veneziani* 9, nos. 1–2 (1964): 40–44; and Juergen Schulz, "Jacopo de' Barbari's View of Venice: Map Making, City Views, and Moralized Geography before the Year 1500," *Art Bulletin* 60, no. 3 (1978): 474, for additional versions. On three florins being the amount earned in a month by an average skilled worker in Venice, see Kristin Love Huffman, "Jacopo de' Barbari's *View of Venice* (1500): 'Image Vehicles' and 'Pathways of Culture' Past and Present," *Mediterranea* 4 (2019): 165–214.

2 Kristin Huffman is working on a forthcoming article on visual strategies and display in relation to the Barbari *View*.

3 Blake de Maria, *Becoming Venetian: Immigrants and the Arts in Early Modern Venice* (New Haven, CT: Yale Univer-

sity Press, 2010), 45–47, 157–59; Julia A. DeLancey, "Celebrating Citizenship: Alvise della Scala, Titian, and Social Status in Color Sellers in Sixteenth-Century Venice," *Studi Veneziani*, n.s., 76 (2017): 15–60.

4 Julia A. DeLancey, "'In the Streets Where They Sell Colors': Placing 'Vendecolori' in the Urban Fabric of Early Modern Venice," *Walraf-Richartz-Jahrbuch* 72, no. 7 (2011): 193–232.

5 Michael Baxandall, *Painting and Experience in Fifteenth Century Italy: A Primer in the Social History of Pictorial Style*, 2nd ed. (Oxford: Oxford University Press, 1988), 86–102.

6 See, for example, Louisa C. Matthew, "'Vendecolori a Venezia': The Reconstruction of a Profession," *Burlington Magazine* 144, no. 1196 (2002): 680–86. See also three articles by Roland Krischel: "Zur geschichte des Venezianischen pigmenthandels: Das sortiment des Jacobus de Benedictis à coloribus," *Wallraf-Richartz-Jahrbuch* 63 (2002): 93–158; "The Inventory of the Venetian *Vendecolori* Jacopo de' Benedetti: The Non-pigment Materials," in *Trade in Artists' Materials: Markets and Commerce in Europe to 1700*, ed. Jo Kirby, Susie Nash, and Joanna Cannon (London: Archetype, 2010), 253–66; and "The Venetian Pigment Trade in the Sixteenth Century," in *Colors between Two Worlds: The Florentine Codex of Bernardino de Sahagún*, ed. Gerhard Wold and Joseph Connors with

Louis A. Waldman (Cambridge, MA: Villa I Tatti in association with Harvard University Press, 2011), 317–32. See also DeLancey, "Celebrating Citizenship."

7 Deborah Howard, "Venice as a Dolphin: Further Investigations into Jacopo de' Barbari's View," *Artibus et Historiae* 18, no. 35 (1997): 102–3.

8 For the numbers of vessels present in the *View*, see, for example, Guglielmo Zanelli, *Navi, squeri, traghetti da Jacopo de' Barbari* (Venice: Centro Internazionale Della Grafica, 2011), 15. On Venetian vessels in general, see Lilian Ray Martin, *The Art and Archaeology of Venetian Ships and Boats* (College Station: Texas A&M University Press, 2001). One of the best sources for identification of particular vessels is Corrado Balistreri-Trincanato et al., eds., *Venezia città mirabile: Guida alla veduta prospettica di Jacopo de' Barbari* (Verona: Cierre, 2009).

9 On the galleys, in particular, see Lucien Basch, "Les galères de la 'Vue de Venise' de Jacopo de Barberi [*sic*] (1500)," in *Boats, Ships and Shipyards: Proceedings of the Ninth International Symposium on Boat and Ship Archaeology*, ed. Carlo Beltrame (Oxford: Oxbow, 2003), 233–40.

10 I am very grateful to Mauro Bandioli and especially to Katarina Batur for their generous bibliographic suggestions.

11 According to Zanverdiani, large round-ships could carry 2,500 *botti* of cargo, roughly equivalent to 1,500 cubic

tons. See Dario Zanverdiani, "Navi," in Balistreri-Trincanato et al., *Venezia citta' mirabile*, 259.

12 See Zanverdiani, "Navi," 257–58.

13 "Gilberto Penzo—Barche e Navi Veneziane," Venice Boats, accessed July 9, 2018, http://www.veniceboats.com/index.htm.

14 Zanverdiani, "Navi," 260.

15 See, for example, Giovanni Curatola, "Venice's Textile and Carpet Trade: The Role of Jewish Merchants," in *Venice and the Islamic World, 818–1797*, ed. Stefano Carboni (New Haven, CT: Yale University Press, 2007), 204–11.

16 Irena Radić Rossi, Mariangela Nicolardi, and Katarina Batur, "The Gnalić Shipwreck: Microcosm of the Late Renaissance World," in *Croatia at the Crossroads: A Consideration of Archaeological and Historical Connectivity* (Oxford: Archaeopress, 2016), 223–48. On moving throughout the city, see Corrado Balistreri-Trincanato, "Canali, fondmente, calli, salizzade, sottoportici," in Balistreri-Trincanato et al., *Venezia citta' mirabile*, 93–110.

17 Balistreri-Trincanato et al., *Venezia citta' mirabile*, 77–78.

18 To facilitate connections between the Venice of the de' Barbari *View* and the present-day city, the following descriptions use contemporary names for waterways.

19 Kirby, Nash, and Cannon, *Trade in Artists' Materials*, 454. See also William Henry Pulsifer, *Notes for a History of Lead and an Inquiry into the Development of the Manufacture of White Lead and Lead Oxides* (New York: D. Van Nostrand, 1888).

20 Barbara Berrie and Louisa C. Matthew, "Lead White from Venice: A Whiter Shade of Pale?," in *Studying Old Master Paintings: Technology and Practice*, ed. Marika Spring with Helen Howard (London: Archtype, 2011), 296. I am grateful to Wynne Wilbur for sharing with me her expertise on lead as a flux in ceramics.

21 See, for example, Daniel Fabian and Giuseppino Fortunato, "Tracing White: A Study of Lead White Pigments Found in Seventeenth-Century Paintings Using High Precision Lead Isotope Abundance Ratios," in Kirby, Nash, and Cannon, *Trade in Artists' Materials*, 428; Berrie and Matthew, "Lead White from Venice," 295; and D. J. Rowe, *Lead Manufacturing in Britain: A History* (Abingdon, UK: Routledge, 1983).

22 Agricola writes in particular of the lead found in the Goslar mines in the Harz Mountains of central Germany, worked since at least the tenth century (Georgius Agricola, *De re metallica*, trans. Herbert Clark Hoover and Lou Henry Hoover [New York: Dover, 1950], 5, 5n11, 37n19). Ian Blanchard, *International Lead Production and Trade in the "Age of the Saigerprozess," 1460–1560* (Stuttgart: Franz Steiner Verlag, 1995),

222–26, identifies lead mines in the Vicentine Alps near the Posina, Leogra, and Agno Rivers. I am grateful to Blake de Maria for the suggestion of the role English lead mines may have played in Venetian industry.

23 Fabian and Fortunato, "Tracing White," 427.

24 Spike Bucklow, "Lead White's Mysteries," in *The Matter of Art: Materials, Practices, Cultural Logics, c. 1250–1750*, ed. Christy Anderson, Anne Dunlop, and Pamela H. Smith (Manchester: Manchester University Press, 2015), 142–43; and Fabian and Fortunato, "Tracing White," 427.

25 Philiberto Vernatti, "A Relation of the Making of Ceruss, by Sir Philiberto Vernatti," *Philosophical Transactions, 1665–1678* 12 (1677): 935–36. Bucklow states that Vernatti is describing the process as done in Venice.

26 Berrie and Matthew, "Lead White from Venice," 296. On the shipping of colors, see, for example, Julia A. DeLancey, "Shipping Colour: *Valute*, Pigments, Trade, and Francesco di Marco Datini," in Kirby, Nash, and Cannon, *Trade in Artists' Materials*, 74–85.

27 Berrie and Matthew, "Lead White from Venice," 297.

28 See Berrie and Matthew, "Lead White from Venice"; and DeLancey, "Celebrating Citizenship."

29 See Berrie and Matthew, "Lead White from Venice," 297; DeLancey, "Celebrating Citizenship"; and DeLancey, "'In the Streets.'"

30 See Dario Zanverdiani, "Manifatture," in Balistreri-Trincanato et al., *Venezia citta' mirabile*, 229–31.

31 Evelyn Welch, *Shopping in the Renaissance: Consumer Cultures in Italy, 1400–1600* (New Haven, CT: Yale University Press, 2005), 123–64.

32 For the identification of these buildings, see Corrado Balistreri-Trincanato, "Case fondaco, fondaci, botteghe," in Balistreri-Trincanato et al., *Venezia citta' mirabile*, 126–29.

33 Wladimiro Dorigo, *Venezia: Origini, ipotesi, metodi* (Milan: Electa, 1983), 2:747.

34 See DeLancey, "Celebrating Citizenship"; and Vernatti, "A Relation of the Making of Ceruss," which describes in detail some of the symptoms of those working in the lead mines and with lead.

Maartje van Gelder *and* Claire Judde de Larivière

Imagining Social and Political Relations in the *View*

From Piazza San Marco to Murano

22 APPROXIMATELY 120,000 PEOPLE lived in Venice around the time of the *View*'s publication in 1500.[1] The city was brimming with men and women, citizens born in the lagoon and immigrants from faraway lands, world travelers and people who never left their parishes. Inhabitants included patricians, *cittadini* (members of the citizen class), and a general populace of artisans and shopkeepers, workers, servants and enslaved people, boatmen, porters, innkeepers, booksellers, midwives, and prostitutes, among others. The list of occupations and activities was extensive: as one of the largest and most populated Renaissance cities in the Mediterranean and Europe, Venice was a vibrant and cosmopolitan community.[2]

Not many inhabitants, however, can be seen in Jacopo de' Barbari's *View of Venice*. Apart from a few exceptions—boatmen on the water or workers in the Arsenal—almost no one is represented. The city appears empty; only by using our imagination can we envision the many residents necessary to maintain Venice as a dynamic political, economic, and cultural center. The campi and the streets, the canals and the port area, the Arsenal in the east, the quays of Cannaregio in the north, the markets around Rialto at its core, and the Customs House at the entry to the Grand Canal, not to mention Piazza San Marco, were all spaces that would have been bustling with activity. But de' Barbari chose to leave them largely empty, focusing his representation on the built environment.[3]

One way of understanding the image, however, is to consider buildings and spaces as embodiments of the population. The *View* offers a lens through which to understand Venetian society around 1500. By closely examining the built environment, it is possible to reconstruct the social fabric, and despite the invisibility of inhabitants, the many social and economic interactions as well as the political relations and tensions that formed the Venetian state, known as La Serenissima (the most serene Republic), can be perceived. The *View* highlights many spaces of political practice where patricians and non-elite Venetians met, socialized, and negotiated power. Specific sites and their buildings expressed and shaped these power relations. Moving from the San Marco area in the south to the island of Murano in the north, this essay traces how the city's inhabitants would have filled the *View*'s otherwise empty spaces and thus how Venetian society functioned.

Piazza San Marco, the Venetian State, and Social Hierarchy

The San Marco area (plate 2) was one of the major spaces for Venetian social life, a place for multiple activities where inhabitants crossed paths and interacted.[4] The comings and goings formed an integral aspect of Venetian urban life.[5] At the quays, Venetians and foreigners disembarked from the docked ships and went about their various activities. Others worked in the area or passed through, generating a daily hustle and bustle of activity and movement. The Piazza itself was the theater of religious and political rituals that brought together patricians, *cittadini*, and *popolani*, men and women, government officials and subjects: spectators often filled not just the square but also the balconies and even the rooftops.[6] Most processions started or ended at St. Mark's church, and it was on the Piazza that newly elected doges and military commanders were celebrated, festivities documented with imagery represented routinely by Venice-based engravers. The enactment of justice, too, was often a public spectacle. Authorities used exemplar punishments, especially executions, to impress upon their subjects the need to comply with the law. The symbolic space between the two large columns on the Piazzetta—bearing representations of the city's two patron saints, Mark and Theodore—was the site for rituals of punishment. Evenhanded and impartial justice was a fundamental element of the Venetian self-image, even though the notion of justice was in practice a complex matter.[7] All these various spectacles heightened the symbolic meaning of the space.[8] Witnessed by a cross-section of the urban population, they expressed cohesion and harmony—a process cleverly designed by those in power to reinforce the myth of the Serenissima.[9]

In daily life, the Piazza also formed an arena for the exchange of information.[10] People spoke about news and repeated gossip as they went to mass or crossed the Piazza en route to transact business. Street singers recited poems from small wooden platforms.[11] Standing atop the Pietra del Bando, the stump of a porphyry column in front of St. Mark's church (fig. 23.2), town criers made announcements, informing passersby of new laws to control plague epidemics, restrictions on upcoming Carnival celebrations, and sumptuary laws to control noblewomen's fashion, or calling on witnesses to denounce thieves and vandals.[12]

The area was also an animated economic hub. The numerous ships depicted by de' Barbari represent the commercial exchange that connected the lagoon to the Adriatic, the larger Mediterranean, northern Europe, and—by way of the Levantine ports—the caravan routes coming from East Asia. This area was not just the center of long-distance trade; it also hosted everyday urban commerce. The Piazzetta was the location of a regular food market, centered around the Beccaria (Butchers' Hall), on its southwestern part (the present-day location of the Marciana Library). Bakers sold bread next to the bell tower, traders sold fruit and vegetables from temporary stalls, salami and cheese sellers occupied the quay in front of the Mint, and that same quay was also the location of a fish market. Shoppers and retailers talked and negotiated inside the Beccaria, while butchers chopped meat.

The figure of Neptune, positioned within the Bacino of St. Mark's, holds a trident directing the viewers' gaze to the line of buildings, including the Beccaria, that extend over to the Terranova area, facing the basin (plate 1). The site had previously housed the communal shipyard (predecessor to the Arsenal) as well as wooden cages with lions and leopards, diplomatic gifts offered to the Venetian state, according to Francesco Sansovino's sixteenth-century guidebook.[13] During the first half of the fourteenth century, the old shipyard was demolished (the lions and leopards long gone) and, after a devastating famine, the state granaries—the Granai di Terranova—were constructed. The enormous Granai formed part of the government's infrastructure of provisioning, which, among others, also included a warehouse for flour at the Rialto. They consisted of four linked buildings, the largest in Venice, which dwarfed their surroundings. The structure housed the state's grain stocks and the offices of various administrators involved in maintaining the provisioning structure. It was also a location of trade, because it was here that the government concluded its deals with grain sellers.[14] Shortly after the fall of the Republic to Napoleon in 1797, this interconnected administrative, commercial, and storage structure was razed and replaced by the Giardini Reali.

In the *View*, the Granai buildings are part of the representation of Venetian good government.[15] Their monumental façade, with the Lion of St. Mark at the top of the main entrance, expressed order and Venetian power, both mercantile and political: behind the brick walls lay an abundance of grain and flour for the urban population, imported on Venetian ships from as far as the Black Sea and Egypt.[16] The imposing brick façade was four stories high, with crenellations along the top; the many windows kept the building airy in order to preserve the quality of the grain stored inside the deposits. With these buildings, representing sufficient food for its large population even in times of hunger, the Venetian government broadcast its self-representation as a politically and socially stable society, the so-called myth of Venice.

Given that bread dominated the diet of ordinary city dwellers—and thus the majority of inhabitants—urban governments feared the threat of upheaval caused by famine. In Venice as elsewhere, the ruling elite was acutely aware of the risk of bread riots. Stocking grain was one way to mitigate this risk, especially in periods that experienced cyclical harvest failures due to climatic conditions, with public stores to be sold below market prices when famine hit.[17] The Venetian government provided a provisioning infrastructure through various state warehouses, public bakeries, and controlled bread prices in an effort to maintain social harmony.[18] Signaling the importance of food supplies, the Council of Ten, responsible for state security, had control over this element of urban governance, including the warehouse.

The Granai, along with other state warehouses and public bakeries, formed a focal point in the life of poorer Venetians. During famines, these were the places where they lined up to receive allotted portions of bread or flour. Yet even with this distribution system in place, social control was never complete and satisfaction never guaranteed. Bread and flour shortages caused riots and upheaval, even in Venice. During a famine in 1569, for example, more than four hundred poor Venetians roamed the city, searching for food at the empty bread shops. When the Council of Ten ordered state flour to be distributed through the warehouses, crowds gathered at the Granai, causing the authorities to order the doors be kept closed once the daily stocks had run out. People were crushed to death; others resorted to plundering.[19]

De' Barbari's *View* idealizes the San Marco area as it existed before the sixteenth-century renovation projects removed much of the food market and temporary stalls in an effort to emphasize it as a monumental governmental space.[20] Government sources cite aesthetic reasons for the renewal of this area: this marked the location to which travelers arrived by ship, stepping onto the quay at the Piazzetta and venturing into the city. Many of the money-changing booths, bakers' shops, vegetable stalls, and cheese sellers in huts had to be eliminated, as did the meat market.[21] In the sixteenth century, unsightly latrines around the columns and next to the entrance of the Ducal Palace were also removed.[22] These works were carried out to enhance the significance of the piazza as the political heart of the Republic, which was already represented by the many political symbols carefully reproduced by de' Barbari: these include the winged lions of St. Mark on the façade of the Ducal Palace, on the Granai, atop one of the two columns at the entry, and on the Clocktower.

Officially, politics had to be conducted exclusively inside the Ducal Palace, the center of power and the location of the doge's residence. Yet certain public places, particularly those around the Ducal Palace and St. Mark's church, were locations for electioneering (the *broglio*).[23] Patricians strolled and congregated while exchanging information and canvassing for votes prior to entering the Ducal Palace, which housed a large internal court with various rooms wrapping around its periphery. St. Mark's church flanked the outside of the court on the north side. The eastern part of the building was reserved for the various branches of government. The southern and western façades, with loggias at multiple levels, opened out onto the Piazzetta and the Bacino di San Marco, linking exterior and interior spaces.

Inside the Ducal Palace, patricians kept busy with political and administrative tasks, exchanges occurring informally in the stairs and corridors, and more formally in committee rooms or the large room of the Great Council. Their secretaries of the citizen class (*cittadini originari*) took notes and copied decisions, assisting with the urban administration, and ensuring that the Venetian state operated with efficiency. In the corridors and on the backstairs, servants, doorkeepers, and janitors maintained the palace's organization and cleanliness. The palace's internal courtyard contained a large staircase that led up into the council chambers. Though that staircase is not visible in the *View*, it held great symbolic power: after election, each doge was crowned at the top of the stairs, signifying the start of his ducal tenure. Crowds would watch from the Piazza, looking through the Porta della Carta. Yet it was also on these stairs that soldiers, galley rowers, and Arsenal workers would protest against low salaries and bad working conditions. At times, crowds of protesters gathered in the Piazza, and people shouted their political opinions while patricians hid behind the palace's locked doors.[24]

By contrast to this public engagement and the many bustling activities in this political and economic hub of the city, de' Barbari's *View* is strikingly empty and devoid of people. This visual effect is enhanced by the sheer size of the square delineated by architecture that served the state: St. Mark's church, the Granai, and the Ducal Palace, among other political buildings. Highlighting the most important place of patricians' political authority, de' Barbari inscribed PA-LA-CI-US on the palace's south façade, insisting on the edifice's—and indeed the entire area's—political importance. This cue, coupled with the absence of the city's inhabitants, served to underscore the image of Venice as La Serenissima.

Murano: Independence and Interdependence in the Lagoon

Like Piazza San Marco, Murano is highly visible in de' Barbari's *View* (plate 1). On that island, however, a different kind of social and political setting existed, reminiscent of the numerous parishes—small islets—that initially composed Venice (fig. 22.1). Closer examination permits an understanding

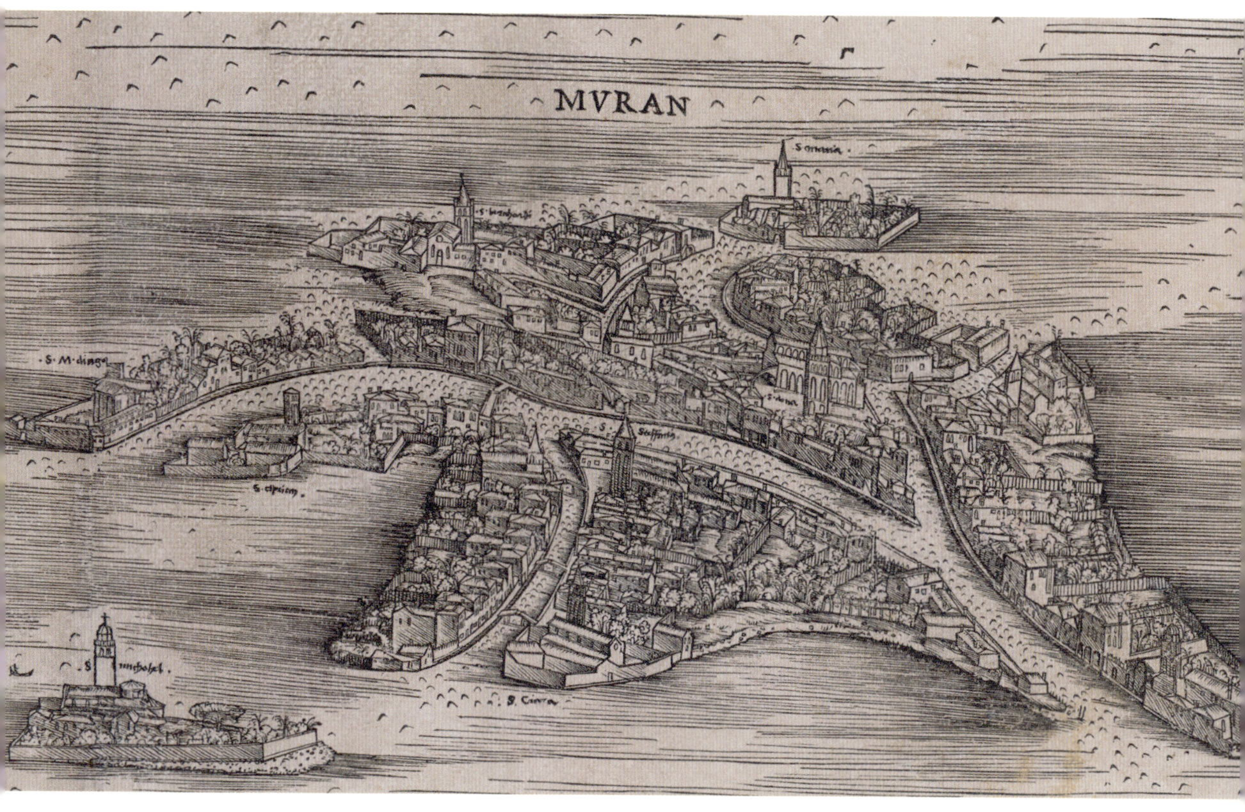

of the life of local communities. As part of the Venetian dominion, Murano fell under the state's political guidance, with its own institutions under the rule of a Venetian patrician, the podestà.[25] This elected official governed the community and local institutions, overseeing its inhabitants and ensuring that legislation was respected.

The numerous archival documents produced by the community testify to the complexity of political interactions between the inhabitants of the island. For example, in January 1511, the Muranese community vehemently expressed its disapproval of the Venetian podestà Vidal Vitturi at the end of his mandate. He fled under a storm of protests (including snowballs), departing hastily from the island and precipitously taken back to Venice proper by his gondolier. Although this kind of event was rare in the lagoon, political conflicts did happen. In fact, inhabitants expressed their agreement and disagreement with patricians and in this way exercised their voice.[26]

De' Barbari clearly delineates the social and political spaces that organized Murano: the island's two main parts were divided by its own Grand Canal, running from west to east. The north of the island was populated by peasants and fishermen who resided in straw houses, worked their gardens, and dried their nets along the quays. The southern part of the island was the location of the famous glass furnaces and other trades contributing to the distinctive life of the community. The only way to cross Murano's Grand Canal was the Ponte Lungo (Long Bridge), visible in the *View*, a strategic point of passage between the two parts of the islands and, as such, a place of regular conflicts and brawls between the peasants of the north and the artisans of the south.

The northern part was also the center of power, represented by the church of Santi Maria e Donato and the Palazzo del Podestà, where the state-appointed leader lived and where the local councils met. On Murano as well, this space, where church and political power shared the same square, was the main site for collective and ritual activities: here the regular ritual of transfer of power between one podestà and another took place; during Carnival, this was the place where the podestà organized a ball for the island's inhabitants. The southern part of the island was structured along the Rio dei Vetrai, a small but busy canal that ran north to south. The canal, crossed by three bridges, formed the heart of economic life, with shops and workshops where glass objects were produced and sold. The whole area bustled with the comings and goings of narrow boats, which brought ashes and wood for the furnaces and left with precious glassware. Economic and social interactions happened along the two long quays, and this was where Murano inhabitants met and discussed life, did business, and shopped.

If, on the one hand, Murano life revolved around the glass industry, on the other hand it was also a destination for patricians and visitors looking for entertainment and pleasant surroundings. The consistent flow of air along the Rio dei Vetrai was said to keep the island cool and the air clean. Patricians and other rich Venetians used the island as a place of *villegiatura*, or countryside escape. De' Barbari represents their sumptuous palaces on the island, with their gardens that contained palms and other exotic species. Chroniclers and poets narrated stories of private festivities and balls that were organized on the island, especially during Carnival, when patricians partied all night before leaving in the morning, while ordinary inhabitants resumed their daily work activity.[27]

Conclusion

In the Venetian lagoon, spaces had a strong political significance. Even if in the *View* they are represented as relatively devoid of inhabitants, one can reconstruct how the unique morphology of Venice and its architecture embodied the complex social and political hierarchies and economic infrastructure that ordered, formed, and informed the community. While these spaces were mostly peaceful, they could also become the object and location of tense negotiation and power struggles. Conflicts and political tensions have been generally obfuscated by chroniclers and rulers. The same intention seems at play in de' Barbari's *View*, with its empty streets and squares and the absence of inhabitants, reflecting civic concordance. As such, the *View* is an ideological representation, idealizing Venetian society by highlighting the state's mythologized sociopolitical serenity.[28] Perhaps even more than state-produced texts and archives, this visualization has shaped the public image of Venice. It is up to modern viewers to reconstitute the narrative and repopulate, even imaginatively, the *View*. Because, ultimately, all the people invisible in de' Barbari's representation formed the Republic: their institutional and public work embodied the collective and collegial authority of the Venetian state.

NOTES

1 Daniele Beltrami, *Storia della popolazione di Venezia dalla fine del secolo XVI alla caduta della Repubblica* (Padua: Cedam, 1954), 59.

2 Giuseppe Trebbi, "La società veneziana," in *Dal Rinascimento al Barocco*, vol. 6 of *Storia di Venezia: Dalle origini alla caduta della Serenissima*, ed. Gaetano Cozzi and Paolo Prodi (Rome: Istituto della Enciclopedia Italiana, 1994), 129–213; Andrea Zannini, *Venezia città aperta: Gli stranieri e la Serenissima XIV–XVIII sec.* (Venice, Marcianum, 2009).

3 Juergen Schulz, "Jacopo de' Barbari's View of Venice: Map Making, City Views, and Moralized Geography before the Year 1500," *Art Bulletin* 60, no. 3 (1978): 425–74.

4 Manuela Morresi, *Piazza San Marco: Istituzioni, poteri e architettura a Venezia*

nel primo Cinquecento (Milan: Electa, 1999).

5 Iain Fenlon, *Piazza San Marco* (Cambridge, MA: Harvard University Press, 2009); Rosa Salzberg, *Ephemeral City: Cheap Print and Urban Culture in Renaissance Venice* (Manchester: Manchester University Press, 2014).

6 See, for example, Edward Muir, *Civic Ritual in Renaissance Venice* (Princeton, NJ: Princeton University Press, 1981); Élisabeth Crouzet-Pavan, *Venice Triumphant: The Horizons of a Myth* (Baltimore, MD: Johns Hopkins University Press, 2002); Fenlon, *Piazza San Marco*.

7 Gaetano Cozzi, "Authority and the Law in Renaissance Venice," in *Renaissance Venice*, ed. John R. Hale (London: Faber, 1974), 293–345.

8 Patricia Fortini Brown, *Venetian Narrative Painting in the Age of Carpaccio* (New Haven, CT: Yale University Press, 1988).

9 Muir, *Civic Ritual*.

10 Crouzet-Pavan, *Venice Triumphant*, see especially the chapter "Scenes from Daily Life"; Filippo de Vivo, *Information and Communication in Venice: Rethinking Early Modern Politics* (Oxford: Oxford University Press, 2007).

11 Massimo Rospocher and Rosa Salzberg, "An Evanescent Public Sphere: Voices, Spaces, and Publics in Venice during the Italian Wars," in *Beyond the Public Sphere: Opinions, Publics, Spaces in Early Modern Europe (XVI–XVIII)*, ed. Massimo Rospocher (Bologna: Il Mulino/Duncker & Humblot, 2012), 93–114.

12 Claire Judde de Larivière, "Voicing Popular Politics: The *Comandatore* of the Community of Murano in the Sixteenth Century," in *Voices and Texts in Early Modern Italian Society*, ed. Stefano Dall'Aglio et al. (London: Routledge, 2016), 37–51.

13 Francesco Sansovino, *Venetia, città nobilissima et singolare: Con aggiunta di tutte le cose notabili della stessa città fatte e occorse dall'anno 1580 fino al presente 1663 da D. Giustiniano Martinoni* (Venice: Steffano Curti, 1663), 316.

14 Giulia Vertecchi, *Il "masser ai formenti in Terra Nova": Il ruolo delle scorte granarie a Venezia nel XVIII secolo* (Rome: Croma, 2009).

15 Ennio Concina, *Storia dell'architettura di Venezia dal VII al XX secolo* (Milan: Electa, 2003), 89.

16 Domenico Malipiero, *Annali Veneti dell'anno 1457 al 1500 con aggiuntovi i dispacci al Senato Veneto* (Florence: Vieusseux, 1844), 2:690.

17 Ennio Concina, *Venezia nell'età moderna: Struttura e funzioni* (Venice: Marsilio, 1989); Richard J. Goy, *Building Renaissance Venice: Patrons, Architects and Builders, c. 1430–1500* (New Haven, CT: Yale University Press, 2006), 12.

18 Brian Pullan, *Rich and Poor in Renaissance Venice: The Social Institutions of a Catholic State, to 1620* (Oxford: Blackwell, 1971).

19 Sixteenth-century chronicle cited in David Chambers and Brian Pullan, eds., *Venice: A Documentary History, 1450–1630* (Oxford: Blackwell, 1992), 108–9.

20 Manfredo Tafuri, ed., *Renovatio urbis: Venezia nell'età di Andrea Gritti, 1523–1538* (Rome: Officina, 1984).

21 Deborah Howard, *Jacopo Sansovino: Architecture and Patronage in Renaissance Venice* (New Haven, CT: Yale University Press, 1975).

22 Morresi, *Piazza San Marco*, 47.

23 De Vivo, *Information and Communication*, 47–48.

24 Maartje van Gelder, "The People's Prince: Popular Politics in Early Modern Venice," *Journal of Modern History* 90, no. 2 (2018): 249–91.

25 Claire Judde de Larivière, *The Revolt of Snowballs: Murano Confronts Venice, 1511*, trans. Thomas V. Cohen (London: Routledge, 2018).

26 Maartje van Gelder and Claire Judde de Larivière, eds., *Popular Politics in an Aristocratic Republic: Political Conflict and Social Contestation in Late Medieval and Early Modern Venice (Venice, 13th–18th Century)* (London: Routledge, 2020).

27 Marin Sanudo, *I diarii di Marin Sanuto*, ed. Rinaldo Fulin et al. (Venice: Visentini, 1879–1903), vol. XIII, column 483 (1512).

28 Schulz, "Jacopo de' Barbari's View of Venice."

Martina Massaro

Cosmopolitanism in Venice and State Strategies

FOR CENTURIES ST. MARK'S SQUARE had been the gateway to Venice (Porta da Mar), a space that overlooked the sea and the city's dominions, part of a commercial corridor with market exchanges that extended out into the Mediterranean Sea (plate 2). The Customs House in St. Mark's basin, as portrayed in Jacopo de' Barbari's *View of Venice*, constituted the main Venetian port and highlighted the city's commercial activity (plate 3). Crowded and bustling in 1500 with ships docked or raising anchor, today this port is a distant memory. The transformation began in the nineteenth century, when the city was joined to the *terraferma* through the railway bridge crossing the lagoon, and finalized at the beginning of the twentieth century, when the port was officially moved to the mainland.[1]

23

From its origins, the square's art and architecture played a sociopolitical and symbolic role. Until the sixteenth century, it also served a highly commercial one. This essay proposes that the relationship between the sixteenth-century architectural transformations at Piazza San Marco, along with urban interventions such as those at the Rialto and the Ghetto, were related to the cosmopolitan Venetian identity and the city's changing needs.[2] Ultimately, what had been the international hub of Venice at Piazza San Marco at the time of de' Barbari's *View* shifted when new architectural projects and renovations emphasized a triumphant Venice. As a result, the Rialto became the city's principal economic center as well as site of cosmopolitan exchange, and new locations emerged within Venice to house the growing number of international residents.

Venice was one of the most multicultural cities of the early modern period. Identified as Civitas Mercatorum, it was an emporium of trade with transcultural connections out into the eastern Mediterranean and up through northern Europe. The city was also part of the pilgrimage route to the Holy Land for reverent wayfarers, amplifying the number of foreign visitors. At the beginning of sixteenth century, the city strategically positioned itself to serve a network of worldwide trade, welcoming foreign merchants.

De' Barbari's *View* preserves the symbolic and economic function of the city prior to a number of interventions that reconfigured St. Mark's Square as a sociopolitical stage and de-emphasized its economic role in the sixteenth century. The strong link between St. Mark's Square and the Rialto and their economic functions is readable in the *View*, highlighted by the Mercerie, the principal commercial thoroughfare that connects them (plate 5). Hundreds of different shops faced this street, offering for sale an extravagant variety of wares. As Marin Sanudo wrote, "Here is all the merchandise you can think of, and whatever you ask for is there."[3] While the enlargement of the Piazza took place in the twelfth century, and its general shape was already in place at the time of the *View*, the sixteenth-century renovation of extant buildings, along with the erection of new structures, proved highly significant for the transformation of the space.[4] With respect to the square in the late fifteenth century, paintings contemporaneous to de' Barbari's *View*, such as Gentile Bellini's *Procession in St. Mark's Square*, ca. 1496 (fig. 23.1) and Lazzaro Bastiani's *Piazzetta of St. Mark's Square*, ca. 1487 (fig. 23.2), offer a sense of the shape of the buildings encircling it. Following the *View*'s publication, a series

296

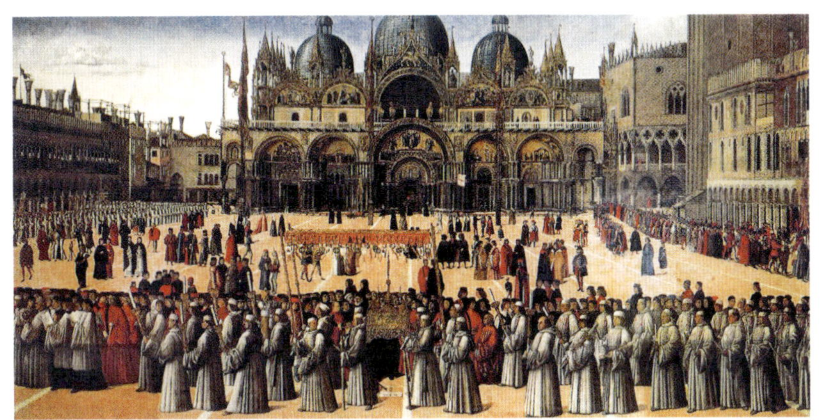

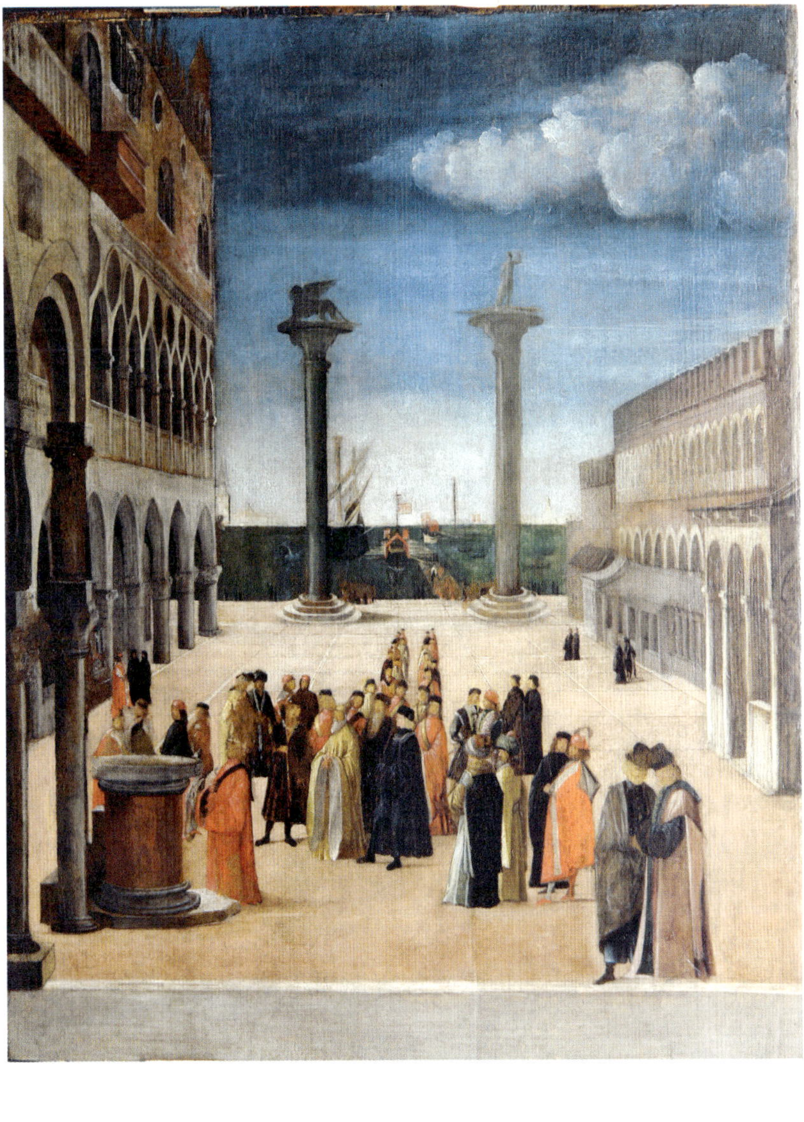

of urban and architectural transformations occurred, beginning in 1513 with Pietro Bon, and then, in 1529, with Jacopo Sansovino, both of whom had been appointed *proti* (state architects) by the procurators of Saint Mark, the second most powerful office of the Venetian state, with the doge at its head.

Undoubtedly, the *View* is one of the most important visual sources for Venice's urban history. This representation of the city was intended not only for Venetians but also for non-Venetians. Indeed, the publication of the *View* coincided with the initiation of a new government strategy for welcoming immigrants. Thus, within this portrait of the city, certain areas have been emphasized, namely, sites devoted to market exchanges: the harbor, St. Mark's Square, and the Rialto (plate 4), along with the Fondaco dei Tedeschi, the residential and commercial hub of the German community, and the nearby Fondaco dei Persiani on the corner of Rio della Fava near San Giovanni Crisostomo.[5]

Two fires—one that occurred in 1512 and destroyed the northern side of St. Mark's Square, and another in 1514 that burned the Rialto—generated a need to redesign and rebuild these two main districts, not to mention extended an opportunity to rethink their functions. The importance of these two urban sites to the Venetian state was underscored by the extraordinarily rapid restoration and prioritization of the projects in comparison to other contemporary public works.[6] However, the removal of commercial activities from St. Mark's Square to its immediate surroundings took more time than the procurators wanted, and despite several warnings issued between 1537 and 1578, the process was never fully realized according to initial expectations.[7] As architectural historian Manuela Morresi has stressed, the apartments on the north side of the square (namely the Procuratie Vecchie) rented by wealthy foreign merchants residing in the city, together with the shops on both sides of the Piazza and the buildings for the *osterie* (taverns and hostelries), had been the main source of income for the Procuratia since the thirteenth century.[8] The *osterie*, used for short-term occupancy by those who came temporarily to Venice for business transactions, were located in the Piazzetta del Molo, facing St. Mark's basin. The small inns were located in the building, with an underlying portico facing the Ducal Palace, as seen in the *View*.[9] Starting from 1529, most of the *osterie* (the Luna, the Rizza, the Cavalletto, the Leon Bianco) were relocated outside the square after

the state commissioned Sansovino for the library.[10] By contrast, even after
the Procuratie Vecchie on the north side were converted into apartments
for the procurators, all the shops on the first floor remained. In addition to
these permanent shops, shacks and food stalls (although fewer than before)
temporarily set up shop in St. Mark's, with vendors selling various foods,
including a bakery that provided bread to foreigners still residing in the area.
Indeed, almost until the nineteenth century, the area clearly visible in de'
Barbari's *View* between the Terranova warehouse and the walkway in front of
the Bacino maintained an economic function, even if the zone's commercial
role diminished overall with the sixteenth-century renewal.

The diminishment of commercial activity at St. Mark's, however,
served to emphasize it as the site of political authority and social display,
one steadily destined to highlight the oligarchic system of the Venetian state
and proclaim a Venice Triumphant. Its reorganization was crucial for the
development of the city's other principal site devoted to market and trade
activity: the zone around the Rialto. During the first half of the sixteenth
century, the Venetian state transferred most commercial activities that had
been located at St. Mark's to the Rialto, making it the primary locus for Venetian market activity and international exchange.[11]

At the very moment that the economic core shifted to concentrate at
the Rialto, Venice reconsidered its policy management about the various
foreign communities residing in the city. Political acts issued by the Great
Council, the largest governing body within the state, established that the
various foreign communities must be given separate areas in which to live.
Quite often, these sites coincided with the places where foreign groups
already conducted their business. Armenians, Germans, Lucchesi (from
Lucca), and Turks were offered facilities to store goods and reside; the
government received a steady tax revenue in exchange.[12] These decisions
led to the birth of new residential spaces devoted specifically to foreigners
who, while maintaining a consistent yet transitory presence within the city,
became permanent or semipermanent residents.

In sum, the relocation of numerous national communities was part
of a general "zoning" operation through which the Republic rationalized
its urban structure. To this extent, it is relevant to highlight the influence
of the Venetian government on the building programs.[13] On the one hand,
the state's interventions resulted in highly specialized but limited architectural interventions, which stressed technical reliability, such as in the Old
Procuracies, in the Fabbriche Nuove by Sansovino at the Rialto, or in the

German warehouse.[14] On the other hand, the influence of the government—although involved not as the patron but as the agency of control—most likely generated a necessary strategic connection between different areas of building interventions. This also reaffirms the proposed hypothesis of the relationship between the architectural transformations at Piazza San Marco, along with other contemporaneous urban interventions, as connected to the international presence in Venice.

Martina Massaro

While some foreigners, such as the Germans, were moved into *fondaci* (warehouses), the Jews were the first to obtain a permanent, unified, and clearly demarcated area within the city through the establishment of the Ghetto in 1516. By controlling the sites, either as buildings or isolated campi, the state welcomed numerous non-Venetian communities while simultaneously monitoring their presence. Even if the establishment of the Jewish district does not immediately appear linked to the early sixteenth-century urban transformations at St. Mark's Square, the simultaneity of these events and the underlying strategy of the Republic bears underscoring. Certainly, the relocation of non-Venetian inhabitants from Piazza San Marco set into motion a series of state-regulated decisions regarding the economic complexities of Venetian cosmopolitanism. Even before the creation of the Ghetto, the Jewish presence in Venice was regulated by *condotte*.[15] These rules, issued by the Great Council, contained several prohibitions addressed specifically to the Jews. In particular, the *condotta* of 1385 prohibited them from coming and working in Venice.[16] In 1396 the Republic allowed stays of up to fifteen days per year in the city. Thus, until the opening of the Ghetto in 1516, wealthy Jewish merchants would have spent short periods of time in Venice, working next to the market area in the Rialto and staying in guesthouses near St. Mark's Square.

Studies on the Jewish presence in Venice have clearly established the link between the social, economic, and urban history of the city and the emergence of the Ghetto.[17] The establishment of a Jewish quarter as a permanent area of residence initiated a new Venetian strategy of welcoming immigrants by offering them guarantees, such as the ability to retain their cultural traditions, even if subject to segregation.[18] While vigilant surveillance was exercised over all the foreign and religious communities, the Jews, like other minorities, were precious for the state due to their economic activity; in particular they were moneylenders and creditors in the market exchanges. Indeed, the Venetian market was dependent on the wealth and occupations of its foreigners. To be successful, however, the cosmopolitan economy required that foreigners enjoy legal rights comparable to (although never equal to) Venetians. For example, the Republic offered Jews the guarantees to practice Judaism and build their own synagogues that accommodated different rituals for the national communities present in the Ghetto; they were also allocated a permanent residence regulated by state law (Ius casaca' more Hebreorum), which, while excluding them from owning property, permitted a lifetime rental agreement. In return, the Jews paid heavy taxes, were obligated to lend money, and, most important, had to ensure the indispensable credit of the Venetian market for the circulation and the exchange of goods around the world.[19]

Archival documents have made it possible to shed light on the Jewish presence in Venice as well as on the Venetian state's strategy regarding the city's immigrants. Documents reveal that, from the Ghetto's establishment in 1516, the Republic wanted the Jews, and especially their financial capital, to stay in the city.[20] Even if different political factions clashed over the decision of establishing, and later enlarging, the Jewish quarter in the sixteenth and seventeenth centuries, documentary evidence proves that the Republic was interested not only in confirming the important presence of Jews but also in increasing their population. Political debates focused on the way to attract wealthy Jewish merchants; their residence in the city was perceived as a means to secure new trade opportunities for the local market. It bears stating, however, that Venice, with its xenophobic and anti-Semitic tendencies, always maintained a protectionist stance.

The growth of the Venetian Ghetto encompassed three different phases that indicate the state's desire to facilitate an increased population of Jews: 1516 (Ghetto Nuovo), 1541 (Ghetto Vecchio), and 1630 (Ghetto Nuovissimo). The last enlargement coincided with a specific offer made by the Venetian Republic to Jewish merchants from around the world. This series of interventions resulted in three interconnected spaces, corresponding to the area between the Rio de San Girolamo and the Canale di Cannaregio on de' Barbari's *View*; each of these ghettos housed different Jewish communities. The zone became its own cosmopolitan microcosm: a place where one could hear a host of languages and witness different clothing styles. It should be noted, however, that the process of extending the space of the Jewish quarter never led to a complete assimilation among the different Jewish groups, reflecting within this cosmopolitan microcosm the overriding spirit of "other," a sentiment pervasive within the Venetian state. The Jewish quarter was in itself a cosmopolitan microcosm within a cosmopolitan city.

The enlargement of the third area, the Ghetto Nuovissimo, bears particular consideration. A decree of February 1630 states that the intention of the Senate was "for the convenience of the Jewish merchants who at that time found themselves in this city and lived in cramped accommodation, as well as for those who ... would come with substantial belongings and capital to this city, that they should be allowed to expand in the enclosure of the ghetto with new dwellings."[21] The initiative was addressed to those who already lived in the city and to those who, for business reasons, might move there. The documentary importance of this text is that it expresses the many interests at play, including the state's intention to continue channeling new economic forces and guarantee favorable conditions in an effort to encourage new Jewish merchants to relocate to Venice; the influx of new residents would continue to benefit the economy and the state.

Not all were in favor of the state's initiative. In particular, the greatest opposition arose from Venetian, non-Jewish owners of dwellings in the Ghetto Nuovo and Vecchio (Minotto, Querini, and Parisan families), along with Jewish families who had invested in building restorations (although without owning the property). Two drawings housed in the Venetian State Archives portray this area of expansion (the Ghetto Nuovissimo), similar to that outlined in the Senate resolutions of February 1630.[22] This document marks the first construction phase of the third zone designated for the Jews, implemented three years later, in 1633.[23] The two drawings enable verification of crucial passages in the establishment of the Ghetto Nuovissimo.[24] Many merchants who possessed houses in the Ghetto Vecchio relocated their residences to the Nuovissimo, further underscoring the social hierarchy prevalent throughout the state and the notion of a cosmopolitan microcosm within Venice. The general growth and surge in residents during this period caused the verticality that defined Ghetto urbanism (with its buildings rising up nine stories).

The city's multicultural identity has been rooted in its past. This can be demonstrated by the eventual repopulation of the Jews at St. Mark's Square following the opening of the Ghetto in 1797. My research on the link between Jewish patronage, business, and cosmopolitanism in Venice has demonstrated that some families, once they obtained civil rights such as the ability to acquire property, invested in prestigious real estate. Some of them concentrated investments in the zone around St. Mark's, which became the city's premier financial district in the nineteenth century.[25] By purchasing property in the Procuratie Vecchie, which, as noted earlier,

Martina Massaro

served as apartments for foreigners, the Jews reappropriated a historically cosmopolitan site, which later became the Venetian headquarters of a powerful Italian insurance company: the Generali. This most emblematic case well describes the centuries-long exchange and synergy between Venice and Jewish merchants, who over the centuries chose to settle in Venice and conduct business and benefit from the trade that animated the city's market, a mutually reciprocated investment that served the state well around the time of Jacopo de' Barbari's *View*.

NOTES

1 For the nineteenth century, see Adolfo Bernardello, *La prima ferrovia fra Venezia e Milano: Storia della imperial-regia privilegiata strada ferrata Ferdinandea Lombardo-Veneta, 1835–1852* (Venice: Istituto Veneto di Scienze Lettere ed Arti, 1994); for the twentieth, see Enrico Coen Cagli, ed., *Porto Marghera: Conferenza tenuta alla R. Scuola d'Ingegneria di Padova in Occasione dell'VIII Fiera Campionaria il 17 giugno 1926: Estratto dagli Annuali della R. Scuola d'Ingegneria di Padova, Anno II* (Padua: Società Tipografica, 1927).

2 Manuela Morresi, *Piazza San Marco: Istituzioni, poteri e architettura a Venezia nel primo Cinquecento* (Milan: Electa, 1999), and *Jacopo Sansovino* (Milan: Electa, 2000).

3 Marino Sanudo il Giovane, *De origine, situ et magistratibus urbis Venetae ovvero la città di Venezia, 1493–1530*, ed. Angela Caracciolo Aricò (Milan: Cisalpino-La Goliardica, 1980), 25.

4 This process started back in the twelfth century, when the longitudinal size of the square was smaller. In fact, the space extending just behind the bell tower was limited by the Batario canal. See Michela Agazzi, *Platea Sancti Marci: I luoghi maarcini dall'XI al XIII secolo e la formazione della Piazza* (Venice: Comune di Venezia, Assessorato agli affair istituzionali, Assessorato alla cultura, 1991).

5 Regarding the Fontego dei Persiani, see Alethea Wiel, "The Demolition of the Warehouse of the Persians in Venice," *Burlington Magazine* 13 (1908): 221–22.

6 See Donatella Calabi, *Foreigners and the City: An Historiographical Exploration for the Early Modern Period*, Working Papers 111 (Milan: Fondazione Eni Enrico Mattei, 2006), 13.

7 Deborah Howard, *Jacopo Sansovino: Architecture and Patronage in Renaissance Venice* (1975; repr., New Haven, CT: Yale University Press, 1987), 10–28.

8 Morresi, *Piazza San Marco*; Morresi, *Jacopo Sansovino*, 16. For the apartment rentals by wealthy foreign merchants, see Agazzi, *Platea Sancti Marci*, 93–120, 133–34; and Juergen Schulz, "La Piazza di San Marco," *Annalo di Architettura* 4–5 (1992–93): 134–56.

9 Martin da Canal, *Les estoires de Venise: Cronaca veneziana in lingua francese dalle origini al 1275*, vol. 7 of *Civiltà veneziana, fonti e testi*, ed. Alberto Limentani (Florence: Olschki, 1972).

10 Donatella Calabi, *Il mercato e la città: Piazze, strade, architetture d'Europa in età moderna* (Venice: Marsilio, 1993), 65–66n7.

11 Donatella Calabi and Paolo Morachiello, *Rialto le fabbriche e il ponte* (Turin: Einaudi, 1997). For the transfer of commercial activities from St. Mark's to the Rialto, see Donatella Calabi, "Le due piazze di San Marco e di Rialto: Tra eredità medievali e volontà di rinnovo," *Annali di architettura* 4–5 (1993): 190–201.

12 Calabi, *Foreigners and the City*, 1–41; Donatella Calabi and Stephen Turk Christensen, eds., *Cities and Cultural Exchange in Europe, 1400–1700* (Cambridge: Cambridge University Press, 2007).

13 Ennio Concina, *Venezia nell'età moderna: Struttura e funzioni* (Venice:

Marsilio, 1989); Hellmut Lorenz, "Überlegungen zum venezianischen Palastbau der Renaissance," *Zeitschrift für Kunstgeschichte* 43 (1980): 33–53; Paolo Maretto, *La casa veneziana nella storia della città dalle origini all'ottocento* (Venice: Marsilio, 1986); Manfredo Tafuri, *Venezia e il Rinascimento: Religione, scienza, architettura* (Turin: Einaudi, 1985); André Wirobisz, "L'attività edilizia nel XIV e XV secolo," *Studi veneziani* 7 (1965): 307–43.

14 Manfredo Tafuri, "Il pubblico e il privato: Architettura e committenza a Venezia," in *Dal Rinascimento al Barocco*, vol. 6 of *Storia di Venezia dalle origini alla caduta della Serenissima*, ed. Gaetano Cozzi and Paolo Prodi (Rome: Istituto della Enciclopedia Italiana, 1994), http://treccani .it/enciclopedia/il-pubblico-e-il-privato -architettura-e-committenza-a-venezia _%28Storia-di-Venezia%29/.

15 See Reinhold C. Mueller, "Les prêteurs juifs de Venise au Moyen Âge," *Annales Histoire, Sciences Sociales* 30, no. 6 (1975): 1277–302.

16 Archivio di Stato di Venezia (ASVe), *Sopraconsoli dei mercanti*, b. 1, reg. 1, Capitolare, fols. 66v–67v, November 24, 1385. Cited in Renata Segre, "Before the Ghetto," in *Venice, the Jews, and Europe, 1516–2016*, exhib. cat., ed. Donatela Calabi (Venice: Marsilio, 2016), 89n8.

17 Donatella Calabi, Ugo Camerino, and Ennio Concina, eds., *La città degli ebrei: Il Ghetto di Venezia architettura e urbanistica* (Venice: Albrizzi, 1991).

Martina Massaro

18 The scholar Cecil Roth was the first, in 1920s, to frame the Ghetto area not only as a place of segregation but also as a culturally blooming site due to the dynamic relationships between the Jewish minority and the Serenissima. Cecil Roth, *Venice* (Philadelphia: Jewish Publication Society of America, 1930). See also Riccardo Calimani, *Storia del Ghetto di Venezia* (Milan: Mondadori, 1995); Gaetano Cozzi, ed., *Gli ebrei a Venezia: Secoli XIV–XVIII: Atti del convegno internazionale organizzato dall'Istituto di Storia della Societa e dello Stato Veneziano della Fondazione Giorgio Cini, Venezia, Isola di San Giorgio Maggiore, 5–10 giugno 1983* (Milan: Edizioni Comunità, 1987); Robert C. Davis and Benjamin Ravid, eds., *The Jews of Early Modern Venice* (Baltimore, MD: Johns Hopkins University Press, 2001); Uwe Israel, Robert Jütte, and Reinhold C. Mueller, eds., *"Interstizi": Culture ebraico-cristiane a Venezia e nei suoi domini dal medioevo all'età moderna* (Rome: Edizioni di Storia e Letteratura, 2010); Donatella Calabi, *Venezia e il Ghetto* (Milan: Bollati, 2016).

19 See Francesca Trivellato, *The Familiarity of Strangers: The Sephardic Diaspora: Livorno and Cross-Cultural Trade in the Early Modern Period* (New Haven, CT: Yale University Press, 2009); and Francesca Trivellato, "Jews and Credit in Early Modern Europe and the Mediterranean: From Usury to International Trade," in Calabi, *Venice, the Jews, and Europe*, 364–67.

20 Martina Massaro, "The Trade in Seventeenth and Eighteenth Centuries," in Calabi, *Venice, the Jews, and Europe*, 318–23.

21 ASVe, Senato, Deliberazioni, Terra, filza 347, February 15, 1630.

22 ASVe, Senato, Deliberazioni, Terra, reg. 398, cc. 173r–v, May 18, 1780; Ludovica Galeazzo and Martina Massaro, "Le Digital Humanities per i cinquecento anni del Ghetto di Venezia," in *La città multietnica nel mondo mediterraneo: Porti, cantieri, minoranze*, Proceedings of the International Conference of AISU (Genoa, June 4–5, 2018), ed. Alireza Naser Eslami and Marco Folin (Milan: Bruno Mondadori, 2019), 182–87.

23 Ivi, reg. 109, cc. 6v–7r, March 3, 1633.

24 ASVe, Scuola Grande della Misericordia, Commissaria Marcello, b. 37. (dis. 1, 2).

25 Martina Massaro, "Gli investimenti ebraici a Venezia al principio del XIX secolo: Il ruolo dei Treves e l'acquisto della procuratia a San Marco," *Venetica* 3, no. 2 (2016): 7–28.

Tracy E. Cooper

Epilogue

Venice Lost, and Found

Architectural historians have found old city plans of the greatest usefulness, as documents of the histories of individual buildings and urban planning schemes.
JUERGEN SCHULZ, "The Printed Plans and Panoramic Views of Venice" (1970)

LOOKING AT JACOPO DE' BARBARI'S *View of Venice* as a whole has long provided us with a sort of cartographic surrogate for a historical time and place, even to the particular technologies employed in its creation— literally in its points of view. The image compels us to see in it a kind of "way-back machine" through which the past reality of the city seems as if it can be comprehended, reconstructed, and experienced. It is this very authority and persistence of the *View* that simultaneously obstructs, however, as its viewpoints, in bird's-eye or diagonal and perspective views, are necessarily selective and so obscure parts of the urban fabric. Thus, as the perspectives privilege some areas and not others, a visual neglect and loss of information that necessarily influenced subsequent visual and even scholarly attention fruitfully provokes further exploration. The utility of de' Barbari's *View* that Juergen Schulz described in the epigraph quotation is a testament to the convincing amount of urban detail that can be independently verified which also contributes to its homogeneity and, ultimately, its meta-identity as a representation of Venice.[1] Yet this scholar's own subsequent deeper study of the *View* led him to reverse his own earlier thinking about its instrumental veracity.[2] Schulz's shift in focus from the *View*'s accuracies to its idealizing function has been noted by other scholars, such as Bronwen Wilson, who drew attention as to how the manipulation of the medium promoted graphic uniformity in rendering details; these extend evenly throughout, from the edges through the center, and they are reinforced with regularized hatching. She proposed that a republican *civitas* was evoked through the strategic repetition of forms given local tags, with emphasis on the whole strengthened further by the marginalization of the *isole* and periphery.[3]

The current volume and its accompanying digital humanities project present digital technology as a palimpsest laid over those technologies in use at the opening of the sixteenth century in printmaking, cartography, and image-making (see the prologue and introduction of this volume). This iteration has opened new avenues of research, extending the original graphic systems and information into a digital dimension, and simultaneously recapturing the *View*'s very essence as artifact, by revealing the insistent three-dimensionality of the printed woodcut image. The result is an increased appreciation for the alluring tactility of the image-as-object, a sensuous appeal that further incites a phenomenological reaction—a place-making tactic that we register with our bodies as our eyes try to orient us in space.[4] These digital technological advances have enabled new insights on the process of the *View*'s creation. The merger of systems of cartographic and pictorial representation in the *View* resist disentanglement. Compare Leonardo da Vinci's *Plan and Elevation of Milan* of about the same date for an idea of the diverse perspectives to be brought together, a conceptual process of mating a calculated space with a sense of place.[5] Cosimo Monteleone has found elements within de' Barbari's image that shed light on the mathematical means and the required contemporary knowledge to achieve the appearance of such a seamless transformation of perspectives (see Monteleone).

Invoking a sensation of mobility vis-à-vis details (as subtle as the strokes indicating wavelets, winds) and cartographic methods (such as the planimetric curved surface of world-map construction; see Falchetta), reflecting the necessity of traversing aqueous versus pedestrian modes in surveying, have suggested a familiarity that has pointed to the artist as being Venetian (see Tagliaferro), just as the authorial bird's-eye view has been associated with the artist's self.[6] The intimacy of a personal itinerary is reinforced by the place-names tagged on buildings within the dense urban setting rather than having to make a mental link from individual sites to a separate key.[7] These "locational attributes," as Denis Cosgrove described them, are among the various rhetorics deployed to "command trust."[8]

Such "phenomenological descriptiveness," as Wilson has put it, is integral to forming the composite body of the city fabric in the *View*.[9] One of the earliest published computer projects to employ de' Barbari's *View* leveraged this power of the detail; the results appear in Corrado Balistreri-Trincanato and Dario Zanverdiani's *Jacopo de' Barbari: Il racconto di una città* (2000).[10] The authors reproduced abundant thumbnails of individual details to illustrate diverse elements of the fabric of the city and of the iconographical elements of the *View*. These were organized in fifty categories, from "Abbaini" (dormer or attic windows) through "Zattere" (literally "rafts," but used for fondamente or waterfront quays). This minute observation of the city is illustrated with 890 images, the majority from the *View*, others as *comparanda*, including many drawings made by the eminent architect historian who revolutionized the study of Venetian vernacular, Egle Renata Trincanato (*Venezia minore*, 1948).[11] It is worth realizing the contribution of this Y2K scholarly enterprise for its attention to the quotidian aspects as being equal to the notable monuments, thereby reproducing Jacopo de' Barbari's own strategy in which the sense of veracity is enlivened by the ordinary and the ubiquitous.

Another advance in the close study of the *View* that is made by the *Portrait of Venice* project comes from the microexamination afforded by the new ultra-high-resolution scanning of the original, as well as the digital displays accompanying the Nasher exhibition highlighting urban systems.[12] As many of the essays here demonstrate, this enhanced vision has allowed more exactitude in identifying different aspects in the *View*. These range from close observation, such as locating the critical networks of wells that fed water to the city and realizing a more thorough detailed accounting (see Brown), to recognizing obstacles in the way of seeing elements, such as campanile being obscured by the diagonal perspective, to mobilizing in order to reverse the erasure and invisibility of subversive populations (see Massaro, Weddle).[13]

Such detail constantly evokes multiple sensory dimensions: the sound of bells that called the faithful to church are suggested by the presence of so many campanili (see Glixon), just as one can imagine the seabirds and sounds of water and people moving along on their daily business, all of which simultaneously contributes to the lifelikeness/ liveliness of the urban portrait. The *View* repeatedly invites numeration, and the powers in such suggestive quantities has a symbolic dimension, as with the strength intimated in the numerous ships depicted, both military might (see O'Connell) and trading power (see de Maria, Swartwood House). Such tactics were an appeal to knowledge systems of the period and their translation into visual skills, the "period eye" informed by commercial trade practices and knowledge as theorized by Michael Baxandall (see DeLancey).[14] From its inception, then, the *View* exerted an authority due to its exceptional level of detail and precision of execution, whose "locational imagery" seemed to be verifiable with observed experience of the topography, so much so that it would serve as the basis for subsequent cartographic renderings of Venice well into the seventeenth century.[15] Other current digital research projects tend to map this emulation, or else source the *View*, as Alvise Zorzi did for evidence of a "lost Venice" in his project *Venezia scomparsa*.[16]

Venezia scomparsa is the title of an essential book chronicling the transformation of the urban fabric—its monuments, systems of circulation and transportation, even daily life. Written by scholar and public intellectual Alvise Zorzi (1922–2014), the book went through eighteen editions between its initial publication in 1971 and 1977, and multiple reprints since.[17] Turning its pages confirms the foundational status of Jacopo de' Barbari's *View of Venice* for our visual knowledge of the lagoon city circa 1500: its woodcut details often appear as evidence of the only remaining sign of a vanished place or of the original setting for those areas that still exist or came later.

Historians of the Renaissance have routinely consulted *Venezia scomparsa* for its compilation of visual and textual evidence of vanished or mutilated buildings and their contents and decorative programs—lost, sold, transferred, but at least in some cases recorded by Venice's dedicated antiquarians.[18] Closer examination of the book reveals that details from the *View* were used selectively. Its first appearance is in a detail showing the

zone of the Arsenal, contrasting the image to the text account of its despo-
liation.[19] In particular, Zorzi employed the details from de' Barbari to convey the sense of a larger set of spatial and social past relationships in those
areas of Venice almost totally unrecognizable in today's urban reality, such
as the Napoleonic Giardini or the industrial train station at Santa Lucia.[20]
The approach Zorzi used in assembling all types of available visual information in conjunction with archival and textual information constituted a
historical methodology, instructive and influential, that equated the *View*
with the truth of a vanished—or lost—Venice.

It does not seem accidental that the sharp contrasts invoked in *Venezia scomparsa* convey the message of post-Republic desecration similar to
that voiced by cultural historian Pompeo Molmenti (1852–1928) in a di-
atribe/lament published in *Art Journal* in 1900. Opening with a popular
quotation from Shakespeare—"Venetia, Venetia. Chi non ti vede, non ti
pretia" (*Love's Labour's Lost*, 4.2.94)—Molmenti followed a long tradition
of signaling Venice's visual impact as evidence of its singularity.[21] The article
used photographs to represent "as it is" and early engravings and paintings
to show "as it was," setting up a comparative model thoroughly Venetian
in prizing "com'era." He argued that the everyday Venice was as worthy of
preservation as that of its famous monuments—republican values we have
seen conveyed in the *View*'s urban fabric. "It is said that the present-day
demolitions destroy the ugliness of Venice, but that they respect the monuments. But the ugliness, as it appears to the minds of the promoters of
these demolitions, precisely consists of certain roads, bridges, and streams
which constitute the inexpressible poetry of Venice. Indeed, it is not only
the monuments sacred to the study of artists and poets, but Venice herself
in her own wonderfully original dress, which we cannot appreciate, unless
we have also seen her in her frank singularity."[22] Venetian exceptionalism,
aligned with republicanism and longevity, had long been a favorite topos,
one inevitably associated with its appearance, itemized and catalogued, as
with the portraits of people and things that comprised the whole of Francesco Sansovino's *Venetia, città nobilissima et singolare* (Venice, 1581). Denis Cosgrove has referred to "cartography's insistent ethical dimension."[23]
Perhaps it is the power of Jacopo de' Barbari's own fashioning of a vision
of Venice as remarkable not only in its aqueous singularity but also in its
performance as a lively and successful entrepôt, a cartographical "myth
of Venice," that appeals in its ideology as it is continued in perpetuity
in the *View*.

Tracy E. Cooper

My warmest thanks to Kristin Huffman for the invitation to speak at the opening of the conference "Stories about Venice and de' Barbari's Marvelous View of 1500" at the Nasher Museum of Art, Duke University, in October 2017. Those remarks form the basis for this essay.

1 Juergen Schulz, "The Printed Plans and Panoramic Views of Venice (1486–1797)," *Saggi e memorie di storia dell'arte* 7 (1970): 9.

2 Juergen Schulz, "Jacopo de' Barbari's View of Venice: Map Making, City Views, and Moralized Geography before the Year 1500," *Art Bulletin* 60, no. 3 (1978): 439, such as missing seven "districts," too few houses on four campi, continuing roof lines creating blocks rather than individual buildings in five locations.

3 Bronwen Wilson, *The World in Venice: Print, the City, and Early Modern Identity* (Toronto: University of Toronto Press, 2005), 30–31nn24–26, 34.

4 Tracy E. Cooper, "On the Sensuous: Recent Counter-Reformation Research," in *The Sensuous in the Counter-Reformation Church*, ed. Marcia B. Hall and Tracy E. Cooper (New York: Cambridge University Press, 2013), 25.

5 Leonardo da Vinci, *Plan and Elevation of Milan* (Milan, Biblioteca Ambrosiana, Codex Atlanticus), fol. 73v-a (fol. 199v), https://www.ambrosiana .it/en/opere/atlantic-codex-codex-atlan ticus-f-199-verso/; David Buisseret, *The Mapmakers' Quest: Depicting New Worlds in Renaissance Europe* (Oxford: Oxford University Press, 2003), 36 and fig. 16; Constance Moffatt, "Leonardo's Maps," in *Illuminating Leonardo: A Festschrift for Carlo Pedretti Celebrating His 70 Years of Scholarship (1944–2014)*, *Leonardo Studies*, ed. Sara Taglialagamba, Constance J. Moffatt, and Carlo Pedretti (Boston: Brill, 2016), 348 and fig. 24.4, discusses a dating between 1490 and 1510, http:// search.ebscohost.com.libproxy.temple .edu/login.aspx?direct=true&db=e000 xna&AN=1160169&site=ehost-live &scope=site.

6 Moffatt, "Leonardo's Maps," 355; Wilson, *The World in Venice*, 49.

7 Schulz, "Jacopo de' Barbari's View of Venice," 473–74, appendix.

8 Denis Cosgrove, "Cultural Cartography: Maps and Mapping in Cultural Geography," *Annales de géographie* 660–61, no. 2 (2008): 165.

9 Wilson, *The World in Venice*, 50.

10 Corrado Balistreri-Trincanato and Dario Zanverdiani, *Jacopo de' Barbari: Il racconto di una città* (Venice: Iuav, 2000). The authors identify their 1989 computer as an Amiga 2000, used for

scanning and computer-aided design
(1:4).

11 Egle Renata Trincanato, *Venezia minore* (Milan: Edizioni del Milione, 1948), published in forty editions between 1948 and 2010 in three languages.

12 See Kristin Love Huffman, "Jacopo de' Barbari's *View of Venice* (1500): 'Image Vehicles' and 'Pathways of Culture' Past and Present," *Mediterranea* 4 (2019): 165–214; and Huffman, introduction to this volume.

13 Saundra Weddle, "Technologies of Segregation in Early Modern Venice," WUSTL Digital Gateway Image Collections & Exhibitions, accessed August 12, 2020, http://omeka.wustl.edu/omeka/exhibits/show/technologies-of-segregation/views-of-venice/jacopo-de—bar bari-s-view-of-v. The campanili have also attracted other digital investigations: on GigaPan by Jonathan Gross, "Help Find All 103 Bell Towers in This 500-Year-Old Map of Venice, Italy," 2014, accessed August 12, 2020, http://gigapan.com/gigapans/166926; and Nick Colucci et al., "Bells and Towers," Worcester Polytechnic Institute, Venice Project Center, 2018, accessed August 12, 2020, http://www.veniceprojectcenter.org/vpc/project/bells-and-towers. And a detailed accounting of the network of wells was also the subject of an earlier "Visualizing Venice" summer program at Venice International University: Giorgio Gianighian, "The Waters of Venice: Visu-

alizing the Cistern Network," June 4–16, 2012.

14 Michael Baxandall, *Painting and Experience in Fifteenth Century Italy: A Primer in the Social History of Pictorial Style*, 2nd ed. (Oxford: Oxford University Press, 1988), 101.

15 Schulz, "The Printed Plans and Panoramic Views of Venice," catalog and bibliography; Wilson, *The World in Venice*, 34, notes that later iterations often show the detail sacrificed in the general fabric and replaced with highlights within recognizable frame; this is the famous fish shape, after Deborah Howard, "Venice as a Dolphin: Further Investigations into Jacopo de' Barbari's View," *Artibus et Historiae* 18, no. 35 (1997): 101–11; for a side-by-side digital exploration of the visual continuities and discontinuities in the 1676 Giovanni Merlo *View*, see Lia Markey, *Merlo's Map: The Religious Geography of Venice*, Newberry Library, 2017, virtual exhibition, accessed August 12, 2020, https://publications.newberry.org/venice/; and James R. Akerman, "Jacopo de' Barbari, 1500," under "Cartographic Context," in Markey, *Merlo's Map*. For "locational imagery," see Buisseret, *The Mapmakers' Quest*, 36 and 36n23.

16 "De' Barbari," Venice Project Center, Worcester Polytechnic Institute, accessed August 12, 2020, http://www.veniceprojectcenter.org/vpc/application/de-barbari; "Mapping the Art and Architecture of Renaissance Venice," Media Cen-

ter for Art History, Columbia University, 2002–5, accessed August 12, 2020, http://projects.mcah.columbia.edu/venice/index.html. For the problems inherent in using georeferencing to align with the *View*, see Ertan Kazikli, "Art Mapping Venice: Progress and Implementation Choices," last modified November 25, 2013, https://artmappingvenice.wordpress.com/2013/11/25/art-mapping-venice-progress-and-implementation-choices/. For a digital research project that maps this emulation of the *View*, see "The Venice Atlas: A Digital Humanities Atlas Project by DH101 EPFL Students," Ecole Polytechnique Fédérale de Lausanne, 2016, accessed August 12, 2020, http://veniceatlas.epfl.ch/mapping-venice-1500-searching-the-de-barbari-map-final-report/, a searchable map with a spatially linked historical database.

17 The edition cited here is Alvise Zorzi, *Venezia scomparsa* (Milan: Mondadori, 2001).

18 Originally published in two volumes: vol. 1, "Storia di una secolare degradazione"; vol. 2, "Repertorio degli edifici veneziani distrutti, alterati o manomessi." Zorzi drew on a wide array of images and descriptions, from historical planimetric maps, to drawn, painted, and engraved views, and to early photographs, as his project encompassed the large-scale de-struction of Venetian patrimony after the fall of the Republic in 1797 and on through the Industrial Revolution to twentieth-century modernization. It was a political project for the author, drawing on his ingrained knowledge of the city, grounded in visual culture and histori-cal research. He called out the massive campaigns of destruction of successive political regimes, from the French to the Austrians to industry and progress, by evocatively restoring a memory city through marshaling evidence of what had been lost. It is fitting to find that *Venezia scomparsa* is catalogued by the Library of Congress under the headings "Conserva-tion and Restoration" and "Mutilation, Defacement, Etc."

19 Zorzi, *Venezia scomparsa*, 44 and fig. 23.

20 Zorzi, *Venezia scomparsa*, 65 and fig. 41, 111 and fig. 87.

21 Pompeo Molmenti, "Venice, Italy," *Art Journal* 1839–1912 (March 1900): 83, http://libproxy.temple.edu/login?url=https://search-proquest-com.libproxy.temple.edu/docview/7084636?accountid=14270.

22 Molmenti, "Venice, Italy," 88–89.

23 Cosgrove, "Cultural Cartography," 160.

Kristin Love Huffman

The *View* and Its Relevance Today

Venice Then and Now

When standing high up in the bell tower of San Giorgio Maggiore (fig. 16.1) to look out and take in Venice's curvilinear urban form, the present-day city appears not unlike Jacopo de' Barbari's portrait of it in 1500 (plate 1). The city and its infrastructure—built during the Middle Ages to peak at the turn of a demi-millennium and the year of the *View*'s printing—has been a metaphorical bridge across space and time. Venice is certainly unique, composed of more than one hundred interconnected islands situated within a brackish lagoon. Spanning its legendary history of more than 1,500 years, the city has continually shown a resilient fluidity, ebbing and flowing in adaptive ways to ensure its own survival. Its perseverance over environmental and human disturbances has called on modern-day feats of engineering and the reappropriation of its architecture and spatial fabric for evolving purposes. This appendix helps travelers and readers bridge the past and present. It includes brief catalog-like entries on the spaces and architecture of significance within de' Barbari's woodcut print that have remained important today. In this, these entries anchor Tracy Cooper's preceding epilogue, which evinces the *View*'s relevance in scholarly study, especially noteworthy today with advanced digital technologies and methods. Interestingly, none of the scholars who have written entries for this appendix was born in the city, yet each has adopted it as the site of their ongoing life work.

     Whether as a destination for pilgrims en route to the Holy Land in the Renaissance or travelers on an eighteenth-century European Grand Tour, Venice as a man-made spectacle has continued to inspire wonder. And despite Lord Byron's assessment in the nineteenth century that Venice was in decay and imminent ruin, the city has continued not only to endure but also to display remarkable splendor. This appendix features the three centers still most visited by tourists today: Piazza San Marco, the Rialto, and the Arsenal. In addition, it considers the buildings of significance—the spaces of premodern governance and industry; the palaces that line the Grand Canal; and the many churches and their bell towers, evidence of the city's wealth. Finally, it ends with a consideration of the Venetians who have long inhabited the lagoon; in relation to the architecture of Venice's past and present, they have been somewhat marginalized, but the city's very survival has rested on their shoulders.

Venice has cultivated and maintained an independent spirit and steadfast celebration of its exceptionality. Over the centuries, this has presented challenging philosophical and ethical concerns regarding the (literal and figurative) costs of the state's economic and political ambitions. Let us peruse the *View* together in a manner that permits comparison between Renaissance Venice and its treasures with those of its modern-day descendants. With such close observation, we can visually read the similarities and differences between then and now, including the significant urban renewal that occurred in the sixteenth century after the *View*'s publication. This section prompts present-day visitors to the city and readers of this volume to ponder the following questions while considering the remarkable value of Venice's principal sites, architectural innovations and idiosyncrasies, and changes to the urban fabric: How do we as visitors take in the wonders of Venice that have affected and inspired travelers over the centuries? What is our collective responsibility to protect Venice, an invaluable artifact of the past that continues to have global resonances today? And, finally, what does the future hold for such an invaluable repository of cultural heritage?

Piazza San Marco

Kristin Love Huffman

Piazza San Marco (St. Mark's Square) has long been regarded as the crown jewel of Venice (plate 2). Either standing in the center of the square facing east toward the Byzantine-inspired church that contains the precious relic of Saint Mark, or arriving by boat via the Bacino to transition from the water to the square, visitors immediately recognize that Piazza San Marco reigns supreme as the most architecturally splendid and bustling site within the city. This brief entry outlines the architectural features that define the late fifteenth- and early sixteenth-century space as pictured within the *View*. In considering the buildings that form the square's perimeter, interventions of sixteenth- and seventeenth-century urban renewal along with reconfigurations of the early nineteenth century will be identified. The Piazza seems remarkably intransient, but early modern changes to the square underscored a message of Venice Triumphant despite the state's waning power and, later, after the fall of the Republic in 1797, revealed Napoleonic ambitions.

Regardless of subsequent interventions, the overall grandeur of the extant architecture highlights the distinctiveness of a city regarded for centuries as a world apart. And despite architectural modifications, Piazza San Marco's outward continuity makes the task of identifying past interventions a challenge for today's visitor. At the time of the *View*, the square was the vibrant epicenter of a geopolitically expansive early modern Republic, and the buildings and their decorative detail communicated messages about Venice's power and wealth. The state encompassed significant landholdings on the mainland, including western Italy over to just east of Milan and north from Venice along the coastline, dropping south into present-day Croatia to frame and control the Adriatic. It also extended into the eastern Mediterranean to manage strategically positioned islands, such as Crete and Cyprus. In celebrating the vast Venetian state, the square remained the principal site of ritual processions that reinscribed into the physical space the visible presence of order and control. This furthered the impression of the state's wealth and power, not only for the city proper and its vast and expansive Republic but also for other foreign states.

If arriving by water like celebrated state dignitaries, visitors would have disembarked near the paired columns at the edge of the Piazzetta. Venice's patron saints stand atop, facing inward toward the square to protect the city. Saint Theodore, an Eastern saint (on the left when one faces into the square), highlighted the city's association with Byzantium. Saint Mark, one of the four Evangelists, represented as a lion, eventually overshadowed Theodore when merchants brought his body back to Venice from Alexandria, Egypt, in 828. Part of Venice's legendary history, the saint had purportedly foretold his future resting place when shipwrecked in the lagoon in the first century. The church of St. Mark became a sacred reliquary to house his body along with other precious relics and treasures; mosaics on the front, western façade narrate stories associated with the saint's return. On the church's south façade, another legend is alluded to with the relief sculpture visualized in the *View*, and therefore imagery that, like the two patron saints, immediately greeted the visitor arriving by water. The two figures represent the Annunciation of the Virgin Mary by the Archangel Gabriel: the March 25 foretelling of the birth of Christ in December. The city's own birth was considered to be March 25, 421, the liturgical date of this momentous event in Christianity. The city continues to celebrate this anniversary date today.

St. Mark's church also functioned as the chapel of the doge, the head of the Venetian Republic, who resided in the adjacent Ducal Palace (Palazzo Ducale). Seen in the *View* and identified with an inscription, the Ducal Palace was also the principal seat of government. At the time it also housed the prisons, which in the later sixteenth century were moved across the canal in a separate autonomous building that can be visited today via the Ponte dei Sospiri (Bridge of Sighs). The architecture of the Ducal Palace remains as distinctive as the flanking church. Its open, two-story Gothic arcades support a solid third floor punctuated with pointed windows and topped with an Eastern-inspired flame-like pattern that stands out from the roofline. The central, ornate window corresponds to the large meeting room that extends across most of the expanse of the Ducal Palace itself—the Sala del Maggior Consiglio, where all adult male patricians would convene to determine matters of state. Within this window's ornate decoration appears the doge kneeling before the Lion of St. Mark. Over and above the roofline, de' Barbari has allowed us to glimpse into the palace's interior courtyard. The solid architectural elements wrap around the periphery of this open space with rooms dedicated to routine and diplomatic affairs, law, and apartments for the doge.

Allowing the eye to move past the roofline of the Ducal Palace, through its courtyard and beyond the domes of St. Mark's, it fixes on the Clocktower rising on the north side of the piazza. The Clocktower's imagery comprehensively announces divine protection over the wealth, power, and wisdom of the Venetian state. The façade's bottommost register forms a triumphal arch that frames the entryway into the Mercerie, the economic corridor that extends from Piazza San Marco to the Rialto Bridge (plate 5). The tier above the clock features the divine protection of the Virgin and Child, while above on the third level, the doge kneels before the Lion of St. Mark as at the Ducal Palace. The topmost register has two bronze shepherds, symbolic of Arcadia and humanist learning and knowledge, who ring the bell to announce the hour. It should be noted that until the 1990s a family appointed by the Venetian state, the Peratoner, resided in the tower and managed the clock's intricate features and remarkable precision for centuries.

Flanking the left of the Clocktower and spanning the northern expanse of the piazza were the procurators' and other state-managed residences. Turning the corner, they reach the church of San Geminiano, shown in its Gothic form on the western flank of the piazza. It is here that changes to the Piazza become recognizable as part of the sixteenth-century urban renewal program of Doge Andrea Gritti (1523–34), a campaign led by the state architect, Jacopo Sansovino, to reassert Venetian authority and wealth following the humiliating defeats and economic losses incurred in battles initiated by the League of Cambrai. Suffice it to say that this ambitious program, one that continued into the seventeenth century, forever changed the shape of the piazza and its architecture as captured by de' Barbari in the *View*. The church of San Geminiano was renovated midcentury by Sansovino, and new procurators' residences were later added under the direction of Vincenzo Scamozzi and Baldassare Longhena.

Returning to the *View*, the Butchery flanks the bell tower of St. Mark's on the southwest corner of the Piazzetta. It should be noted that the building is an eyesore, highlighted by de' Barbari with its large hole and emanating cracks—not the noble architecture one would expect. Adjacent to the Butchery is the old Mint, where coins would be made, with shops on the exterior. To the left of the Mint, spanning the remaining southern expanse of the piazza, stood the state warehouses, a superstructure of administrative buildings and granary to store food in times of shortage. This entire section was transformed, including the demolition of the Butchery. In the sixteenth century, responding to Doge Gritti's prompt, Sansovino built a library (long considered overdue to house a precious collection of Greek and Latin manuscripts bequeathed to the state in 1486 by Cardinal Bessarion), a new Mint, and a loggia to frame the entrance into the bell tower—what one sees today when visiting the piazza. In the nineteenth century, Napoleon demolished the warehouses to create a private garden. He also demolished the church of San Geminiano to make way for a ballroom; today this nineteenth-century intervention gives the western flank of the piazza the appearance of a uniform structure across the expanse of original procurators' residences. In thinking about these transformations to the space, the *View* serves as a visual document for the appearance of the Piazza prior to renovations and renewal. These architectural and decorative interventions added new layers of Roman mythological associations atop the Christian ones. Of course, there are other noteworthy changes as well, prompting the contemporary visitor to continue making discoveries and visual distinctions between past and present, between the imagery featured in the *View* and the architecture experienced today.

Rialto

Ludovica Galeazzo

According to medieval chronicles, Rivoaltus, or Rialto, is the legendary island that offered shelter to a group of people from the Veneto region escaping repeated waves of barbarian invasions (plate 4). Here, on March 25, 421, they purportedly founded the first sacred building of the city that marked the official birth of Venice, the church of San Giacomo (affectionately called San Giacometto), dedicated to the apostle Saint James. Although this event is regarded today as part of the great myth of the city, for centuries, Rialto, along with Piazza San Marco, represented one of the two main stages of the Venetian state, a Republic where political, socioeconomic, religious, architectural, and urban interests converged. Located in the center of the *View* to connect the two sides of the Grand Canal, the Rialto and its bridge functioned as one of two foci for the administrative apparatus of the Republic as well as the site of flourishing commercial activity. Straddling the city's main waterway, both banks were lined with government buildings, seats of various local offices related to justice, trade guilds, and food and merchandise control. Moreover, this zone housed financial and tax offices related to state capital, including the Palazzo dei Camerlenghi, headquarters of the Venetian Treasury, a building still standing today.

Thanks to its position, easily accessible via waterways and the Mercerie, the thoroughfare that still connects it to Piazza San Marco (plate 5), the zone around Rialto also functioned as a primary locus for international trade, cosmopolitan exchange, and mercantile transactions and negotiations. Over the centuries it systematically developed and became equipped to host a variety of specialized markets that persevered despite unfortunate events and subsequent urban transformations. De' Barbari has portrayed its appearance immediately before the great fire that nearly destroyed the entire area during a cold and windy night in January 1514, opening the possibility for an architectural and functional renovation. Quays on both sides of the Grand Canal welcomed goods from around the Mediterranean world. On the east side, near the German church of San Bartolomeo, spices from the eastern trade routes would have presented visual and olfactory experiences. Farther down the bank, coal and iron were unloaded daily, resources for the basic maintenance of the city. Across the bridge, stalls for the sale of meat, fish, bread, fruit, and vegetables as well as wine, oil, and flour, dotted the curved contours of the canal. The wooden bridge itself, located in the center of Venice to join the two parts of the city, contained shops that functioned as part of the market (fig. A1.1). These two rows of stores sold a variety of luxury goods: books, musical instruments, shoes, fabric, perfumes, paintings, leather products, and furs. A mechanical marvel, the central opening of the bridge consisted of two retractable footbridges that slid back on wooden wheels. This permitted larger mercantile or ceremonial boats to continue along the canal, including the ceremonial barge of the doge, known as the Bucintoro.

At the foot of the bridge on the western side, a long portico of the Ruga dei Oresi was crowded with jewelers and goldsmiths, as well as drapers, tailors, and haberdashers. On the other side of the portico, Campo San Giacomo served as the heart of finance and business. Across from the church stood a *pietra del bando*, known as "Gobbo di Rialto" due to the peculiar form of the statue, a bearded and naked hunchback bearing a stone podium and flanking a porphyry column (the present-day version in place by 1541). It embodied the highest symbol of Venetian justice and authority.

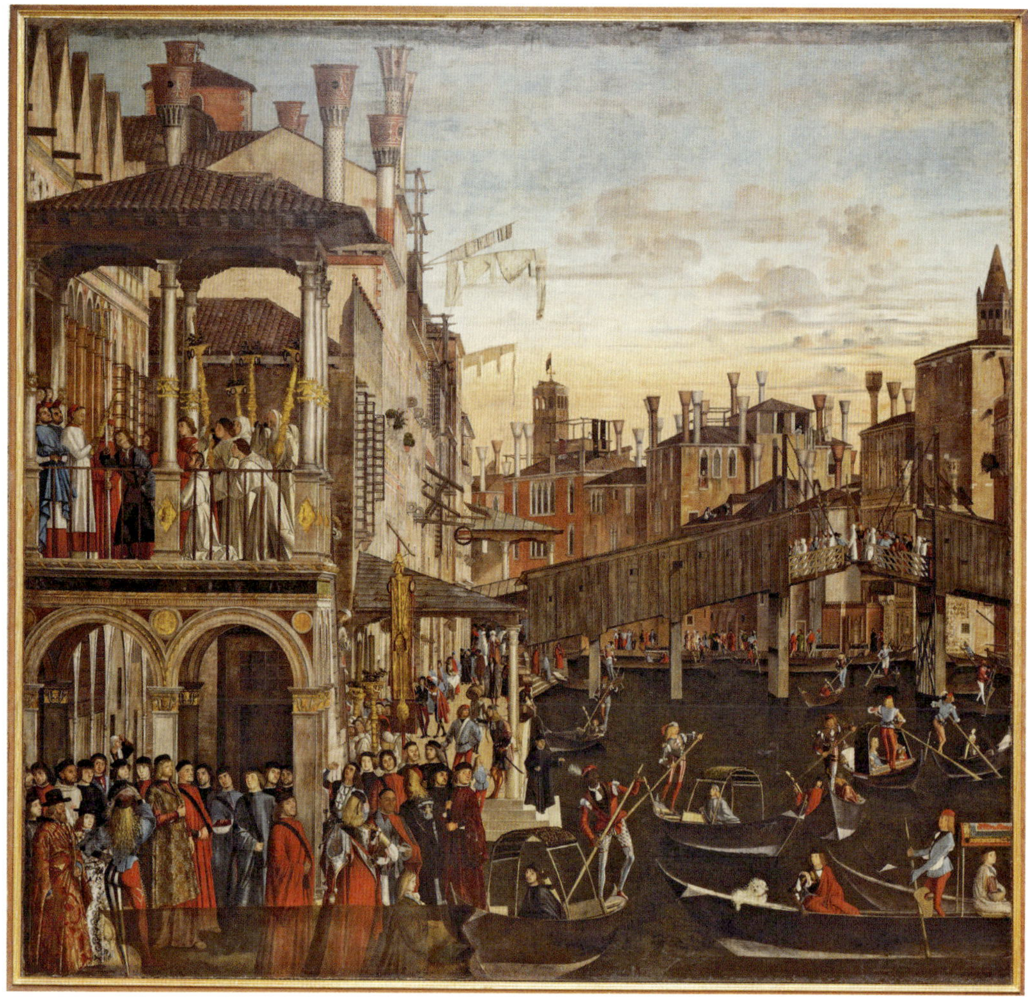

Standing in front of this statue, Venetian officials read announcements and issued public proclamations, ranging from the sentencing of civil criminals to broadcasting breaking news from around the world.

The cosmopolitan nature of Rialto, however, extended beyond its main core. In the old neighborhood parish of San Matteo to the north, twelve popular taverns and inns offered temporary accommodations to a multitude of foreign visitors among poor houses and warehouses squeezed into dark and ill-reputed streets. Wealthier hostelries, such as the famous Sturion, were instead located along the Grand Canal. Controlled by the Great Council and under the supervision of the Giustizia Vecchia, these spaces for hospitality were an important aspect of the welcome *and* control policies of Venice.

While commensurate with trades of merchants, travelers, and foreign ambassadors, the hostelries also ensured the Republic's strict surveillance of their activities. As a place of state supervisory action as well as the free initiative of individuals and international exchange, the Rialto embodied the idea of the transcultural practices and relationships that the Venetian state built with the rest of the world over the centuries.

The Arsenal

Maartje van Gelder

In the *View*, the Arsenal, or state shipyard, dominates the city's eastern district (plate 6). Funded and controlled by the state, the Arsenal was the foundation of Venice's maritime power. A naval-industrial complex with the largest workforce in premodern Europe, it consisted of several shipyards, covered docks, timberyards, storehouses, and an armory as well as rope and sail factories, all surrounded by defensive walls. The Arsenal constructed and maintained both the Venetian military fleet and ships for commercial convoys that connected the Levant to western Europe.

Modeled on older Byzantine examples, the name of the Arsenal stemmed from the Arabic *dār al-ṣināʻah* (house of manufacture). Initially located in the San Marco area, by the twelfth century the yard had moved to the eastern district of Castello. By the early fourteenth century, the Arsenal had quadrupled in size, mirroring the growth of Venetian maritime ambitions. When the Ottomans started building their own large shipyard in Istanbul after capturing the city in 1453, the Venetians again expanded their Arsenal. Around 1500, the diarist and historian Marino Sanudo described the shipyard as "truly one of the finest sights imaginable.... Here every skill in building galleys and other craft is practiced.... It is the most beautiful and marvelous thing to see our Arsenal so well provisioned."[1]

De' Barbari gives us a snapshot of the fifteenth-century expansion project. The large upper dock, the Newest Arsenal (Darsena Novissima), remains unfinished and not yet in use. The new Porta Magna, the monumental gate completed in 1460, can be seen next to the drawbridge water entrance. It was one of the first Renaissance-style structures in Venice, modeled after a Roman triumphal arch. The gate, with a winged lion on top to reference the city's patron saint of Saint Mark, again testifies to Venice's naval ambitions.

Vittore Carpaccio, *Miracle of the Relic of the Holy Cross at the Rialto Bridge*, ca. 1496. Tempera on canvas, 371 × 392 cm. Gallerie dell'Accademia, Venice.

Next to the gate stand the three houses—Hell, Purgatory, and Paradise—where the Patroni, or Lords of the Arsenal, the three patricians governing the yard, resided during their time in office.

In the sixteenth century, the Arsenal employed roughly 1,000–2,500 people, most of them members of three major guilds: the *marangoni* (carpenters), *calafati* (caulkers), and *remeri* (oar makers). The Arsenal also employed numerous others connected either to shipbuilding (female sailmakers, foundry workers, supply masters) or to state officials of bureaucracy and control (guards, customs officials, bookkeepers, bell ringers). Production followed a high degree of division of labor, like a modern assembly line process, with the Marangona, the largest bell of St. Mark's campanile, signaling the start of the workday, the workers' lunch break, and end of the day. In the yard, the ships' hulls were first constructed and then towed to different locations for caulking and outfitting of masts, weapons, ropes, oars, sails, and anchors. The Venetian government was wary of industrial and military espionage but did allow important guests to visit the site, aiming to impress them with the Arsenal's productivity. When Henri III of France visited in 1574, the state arranged for a galley to be built within an hour while the king ate his dinner.

De' Barbari has depicted ships in different stages of construction, reflecting the Arsenal's efficiency. One ship lies on its side, ready to be caulked. Outside the Arsenal, in the water, workers are also caulking a tilted roundship. To the right of the tilted ship in the Arsenal, workers can be seen working on either a mast or oar. The long buildings containing the ropeworks, the Corderie della Tana (from *corda*, rope), catch the eye. Immediately to the left of the drawbridge, squads of female sailmakers worked in the two-story building. In the oldest part of the Arsenal, the Darsena Vecchia, directly accessible by water through the drawbridge, de' Barbari has portrayed the Bucintoro, the doge's gilded ceremonial barge. The Arsenal workers maintained the Bucintoro, manning its oars on ceremonial occasions when the barge was decked out in crimson satin. This vessel thus represents the link between the Venetian head of state and the Arsenal's workers.

Today, the Arsenal still covers roughly one-tenth of Venice's historic center. The industrial complex has nonetheless undergone many transformations since de' Barbari's *View*. The end of the Republic, French and Austrian occupations of Venice, and the subsequent unification of Italy as well as the transition from sail to steam and from wood to metal all made significant impacts on the shipyard, which continued to thrive, especially in the late nineteenth century. After World War II, the Arsenal went into a drawn-out decline, the yard being too small for modern shipbuilding. Echoes of the Arsenal's past still prevail though: almost half of the Arsenal area is controlled by the Italian navy and closed off to civilians. The other half, however, has become one of the most visited sights of the city: since the 1990s, the Biennale di Venezia has occupied some of the Arsenal's most imposing buildings, such as the Corderie, for its art and architecture exhibitions, presenting one of the more striking examples of urban redevelopment in modern-day Venice.

The Grand Canal and Palatial Splendor

Kristin Love Huffman

Until the nineteenth century, Venice, as a city built on water, could be reached from the mainland only via water, and its network of canals facilitated ease of circulation—people *and* goods—to interstitial locations deep within its dense urban fabric. In the early modern period, movement on water was an experience many visitors described poetically, as the city seemed to unfold in magical ways depending on the season, weather, and time of day. Modern-day mariners have said that Venetians knew how to calculate the time necessary to move from one site to another, calibrated with precision according to the tides, winds, and lunar cycles. While there are many canals interconnecting the city, the most grandiose was the Grand Canal. This stately aqueous boulevard, which had ceremonial and serviceable functions, confirms its named designation and status as Venice's most important thoroughfare. Notably, palaces face the canal to receive residents and guests, and their many balconies invite seeing and being seen. Today it is possible to miss the waterborne experience, as navigating via streets, causeways, and narrow passageways presents the visitor with another option; there are presently four bridges crossing the expanse of the Grand Canal. As pictured in the *View*, the only crossing in 1500 was the wooden bridge at Rialto (plate 4).

The palaces that lined the Grand Canal projected an image of wealth and majesty. The appellation *case* (or houses, shortened in Venetian dialect to Ca') distinguished them from *the* palace in Venice, the Palazzo Ducale, or residence of the doge and seat of government in Piazza San Marco (plate 2).

Given the prime value of real estate fronting the Grand Canal, most palaces followed variations on a general formulaic design, understood when looking at the façade, which, while often narrow, hid its depth. These included a ground floor for storage of goods and generally not inhabited. The second and third floors, often replicated in design, had suites of windows for fresh air and light. These windows corresponded to the large central hall, known as a *portego*, and these large spaces—long, open rooms that often extended the width and/or length of the palace—could be reconfigured for varying purposes, including banquets and parties. Some palaces were quite grand and belonged to the wealthiest Venetian residents. One such late medieval palace featured prominently in the *View* and that can be visited today as a museum, the Gallerie Franchetti, is the Ca' d'Oro, or House of Gold (fig. A1.2), built and resided in for centuries by the patrician Contarini family. De' Barbari captures decorative features and exquisite detail not only for this palace but also for others. Not an uncommon practice for palace façades

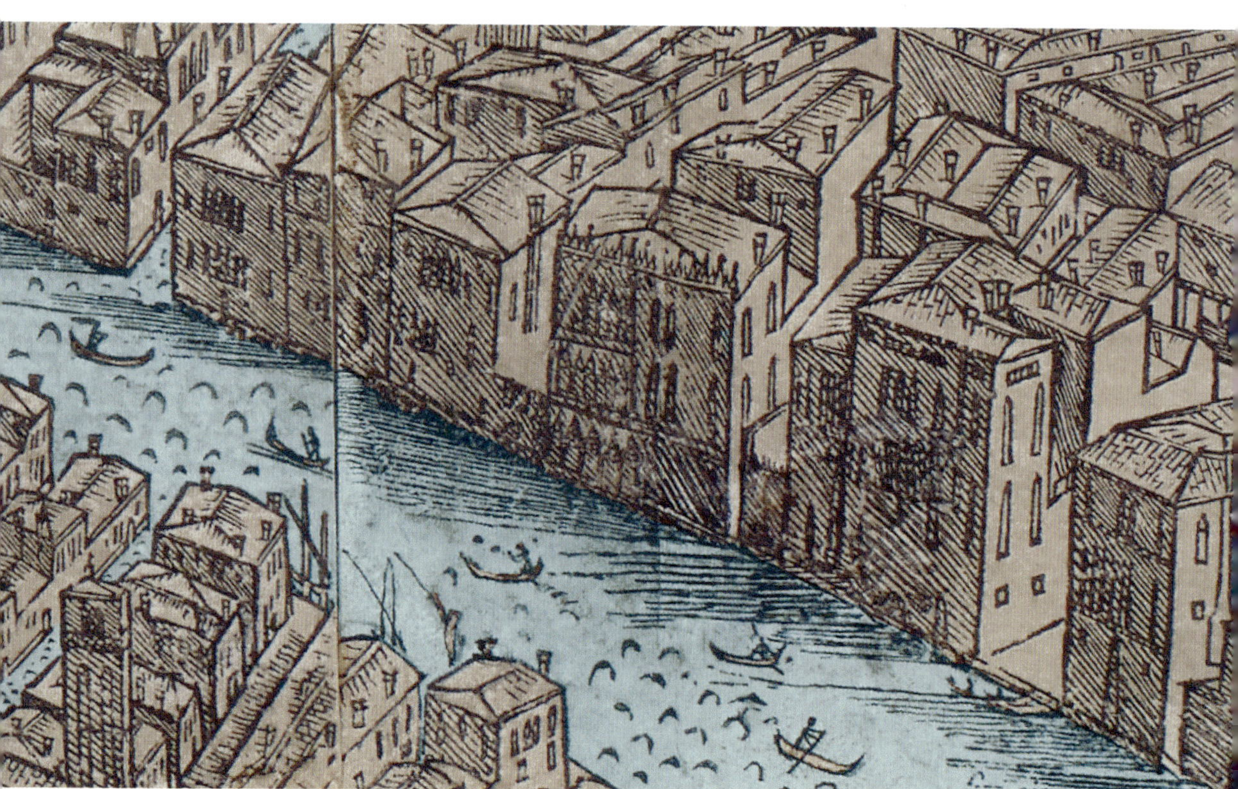

in the Renaissance, yet largely lost today, were painted decorative frescoes. The distinctive chimney pots, designed to keep cinders (and fires) at bay, still punctuate the skyline of Venice (see fig. A1.1).

Finally, it should be noted that palaces are not the only type of building lining the Grand Canal. The city's status as an international entrepôt is marked with administrative buildings such as the Customs House at the opening of the Grand Canal (plate 3). On the *View*, one can see larger boats moored at this site to unload goods and pay necessary taxes, prior to moving up the Grand Canal toward the Rialto and its Palazzo dei Camerlenghi, offices for the state treasury (plate 4). Near the only bridge in this zone is the German Warehouse—the Fondaco dei Tedeschi, as labeled in the woodcut—a commercial and residential building occupied by the German foreign community. And, as we shall see, churches, although at times oriented differently in 1500, also lined the Grand Canal and fronted important waterways.

Venice's Churches

Kristin Love Huffman

A noteworthy change from past to present was that most of the churches pictured in the *View* were oriented according to traditional ecclesiastical expectations, that is, east to west. It is only with subsequent renovations, many of which occurred in the sixteenth and seventeenth centuries, that architects sidestepped this convention to realize the full visual splendor of an orientation toward water. One such church is Santa Lucia (fig. 15.1). Until the nineteenth century, and the need to make space for the train station, the conventual complex at the northern end of the Grand Canal had been reoriented in the sixteenth-century reconstruction to face the waterway, visible in painted and engraved representations. This type of façade orientation can be experienced today in full force with the grandiose façades of Andrea Palladio's San Giorgio Maggiore and il Redentore, not to mention Longhena's Santa Maria della Salute; the latter includes an elegant staircase that makes a majestic transition from the Grand Canal and its fronting campo up to the church and its entryway.

The churches are the only uniformly labeled feature within the *View of Venice*. In the city today, their presence is nearly impossible *not* to notice given the veritable, variable soundscape generated by numerous tolling bells that reverberate across the waterways. That the *View* initiated a cartographic trend wherein subsequent representations of Venice prioritized an inclusion of labeled churches, often later identified within a key or legend, was not arbitrary. Such a prioritization of the churches fit with the self-constructed identity and image of the city—that it had a pure birth (a virginal conception), and that its piety was unlike any other state in the world (include Papal Rome). As the site of departure for pilgrimage trips to the Holy Lands and a location that contained many holy relics of saints within its churches, Venice was able to make assertive claims about its interwoven piety and origins for centuries.

In general, Venetian monastic and conventual churches, those that were associated with a particular religious order, were located on the fringes of the city, forming an outer ring that extended to satellite islands. This was because, in general, the larger grounds and more expansive property of their complexes, often including gardens, helped the religious communities maintain independence and self-sustainability; they also generated revenue by provisioning food and services to the city's population. One such large-scale mendicant church notable in the *View* is the church of San Giorgio Maggiore, on the eponymous island in the lower center of the woodcut (fig. 16.1); it too happened to be oriented east–west prior to its renovation in the sixteenth century. This Benedictine complex had expansive gardens and accommodated guests on its grounds. Two additional noteworthy religious complexes in Venice include Santa Maria Gloriosa dei Frari (fig. A1.3), built in the thirteenth century in the Venetian district of San Polo (the district on the northern side of the Rialto Bridge) by the Franciscans, and the complex of Santi Giovanni e Paolo in the district of Castello (fig. 19.2), a worthy rival constructed by the Dominicans along the northern rim of the city. The latter church became the burial site of many doges throughout the centuries and, therefore, a site of regular ducal processions.

In addition to these monastic sites, there were also conventual complexes that remained historically tied to the building history of Venice. One of the most notable was San Zaccaria, located just east beyond Piazza San Marco and identifiable in the *View* by its open, paved square (fig. 15.2). The Benedictine convent had bequeathed to the Venetian state orchards on precious land that abutted St. Mark's. This bequest permitted this vital square's expansion, and in honor of the generous gift, the doge promised a ducal procession to the church from St. Mark's each Easter Sunday, linking the two sites ritually in perpetuum. The rebuilt Renaissance church of San

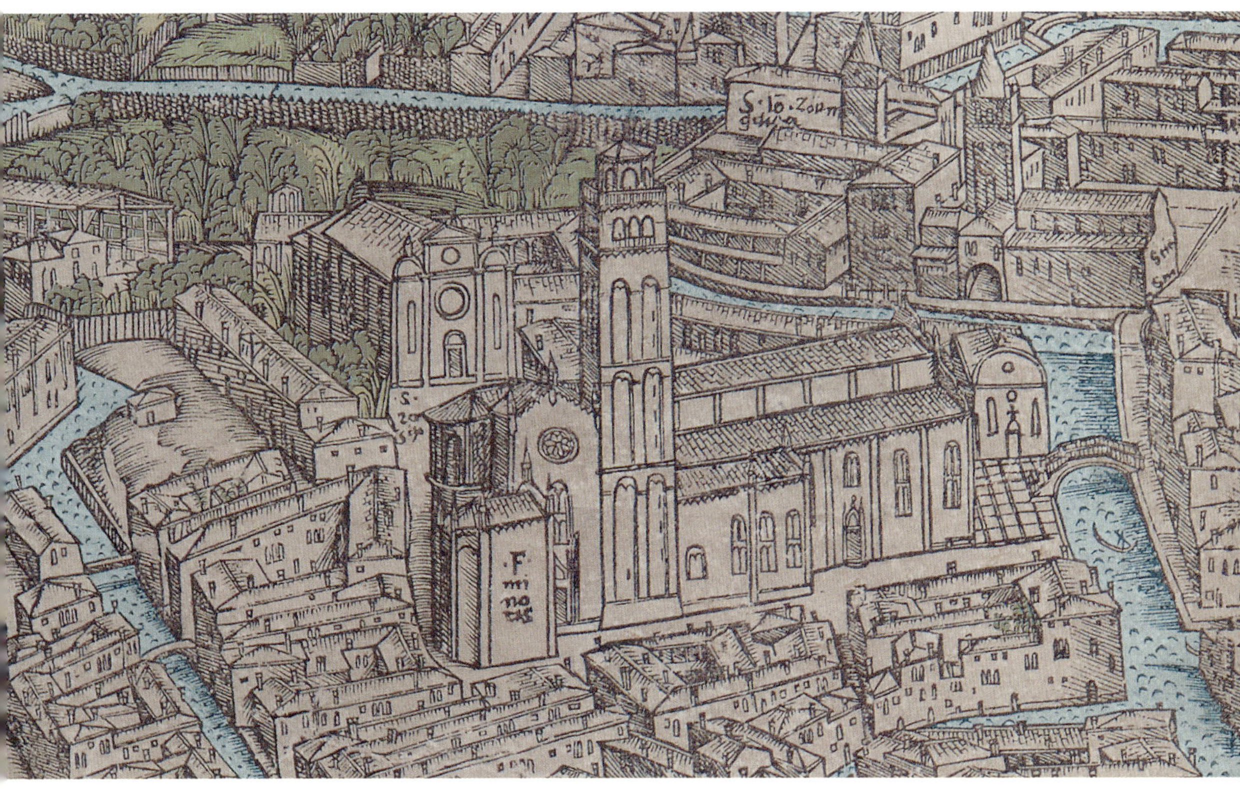

Zaccaria, still visible today, contains an ambulatory or pathway that enables visitors to walk (amble) behind the high altar to follow the curved apse of its eastern end—a rare feature in Venetian church construction.

At the eastern edge of the city stands the church of San Pietro di Castello (fig. A1.4) on its own island. Like St. Mark's, this church served a unique function. San Pietro was the seat of the patriarch, the highest religious official in the city, and therefore the site of the bishopric. While several churches today bear the "basilica" or cathedral label, including San Marco and San Giorgio, that of San Pietro di Castello was the only official one in the premodern era, as was common practice in each major city-state. While the patriarch had overall religious jurisdiction, the doge managed seven different churches within the city of Venice. This included not only San Marco as the official state church but also the parish church of San Giacomo di Rialto, at the foot of the Rialto Bridge. This church, known affectionately as San Giacometto (Little Saint James), was the site of Venice's foundational

A1.3

Detail of Santa Maria Gloriosa dei Frari, with colorization, from Jacopo de' Barbari, *View of Venice*, ca. 1497–1500.

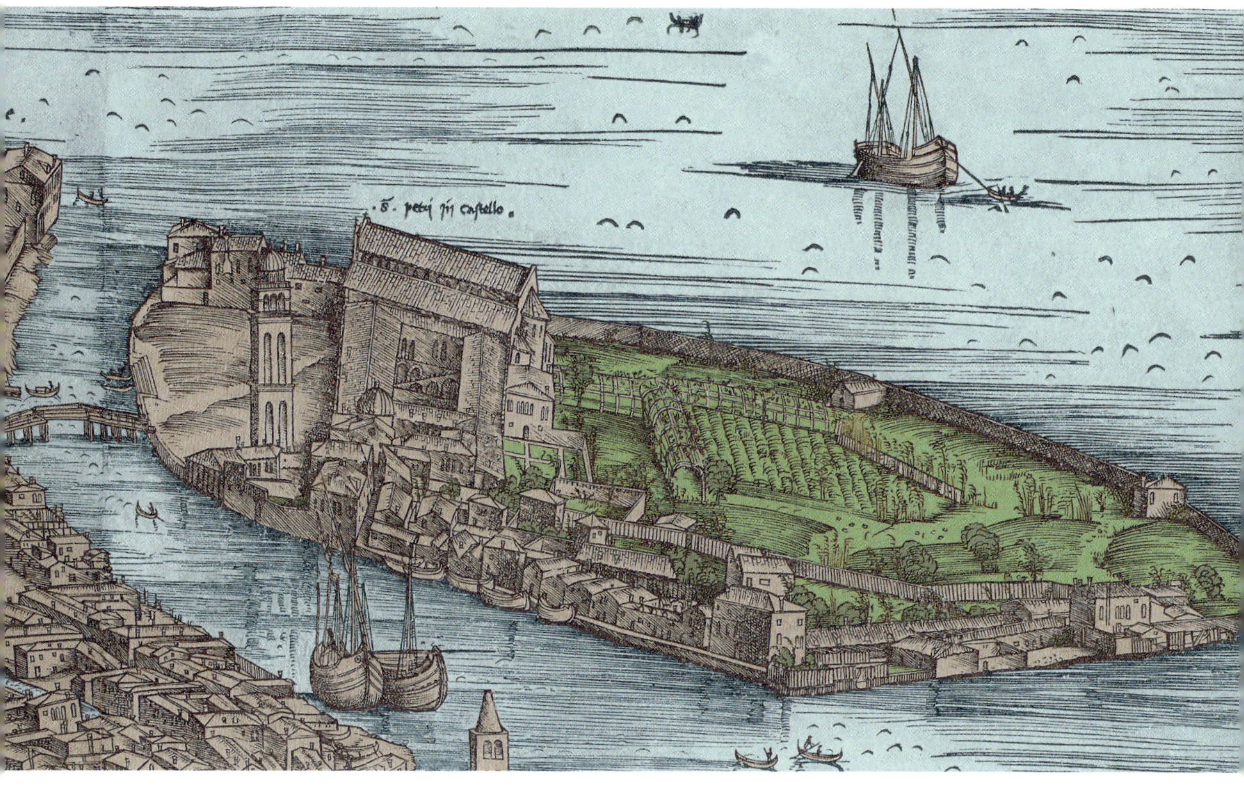

A1.4

Detail of the island of San Pietro di Castello, with colorization, from Jacopo de' Barbari, *View of Venice*, ca. 1497–1500.

history. As noted in the entry related to St. Mark's Square and the Rialto, the city's origins extend back to March 25, 421, according to Venice's self-constructed myth.

Regardless of any such significance, San Giacomo was one of many parish churches scattered throughout the interstices of Venice and identified in the *View of Venice*. These most numerous of the Venetian churches functioned, like the name suggests, as a neighborhood's sacred space. It was here that the cyclical elements of life and religious rites occurred and were mostly recorded—births, baptisms, marriages, deaths, and burials. Following Napoleon's occupation of the city at the end of the eighteenth century, civil codes changed, and these spaces and their functions were forever altered. The great cemetery of San Michele was built as one result of the efforts toward new sanitation practices under altered code. This period also marked a moment when select sacred spaces were either reconfigured or demolished, such as the church of San Geminiano, which had faced the church of San

330

Marco in St. Mark's Square; a ballroom was built in its stead. Although many of these transformations are nearly imperceptible today, the *View of Venice* visually documents the appearance of this thriving metropolis, including the majesty and suggested function of ecclesiastical buildings and their spatial configurations. While perhaps less well-known to a contemporary visitor, many discussed in this entry were on an early modern visitation circuit due to their religious and historic value, visibly noted in the *View*.

Church Bell Towers

Jonathan Glixon

The bell towers (campanili) of Venice's churches today, although somewhat fewer in number than in 1500, continue to dominate the city's skyline. The predominance of campanili and elements of their uniqueness as visual markers of Venetian piety can be seen in the *View*, making a reading of their visible presence and architecture important. Only a small minority of the extant towers resemble their original form. Many have been restored or replaced over the years, often along with their churches. In many cases, the churches themselves, along with their campanili, were demolished, mostly following early nineteenth-century suppressions. This brief study assists in understanding their prevalence throughout the city and their unique architectural features, especially in relationship to their containment of bells, the subject of my essay within this volume.

Apart from Italy, medieval bell towers were elements almost exclusively integrated within a church's architecture. In Italy, most campanili were independent structures—sometimes adjoining the church, sometimes detached—rather than components integral to the structure and its aesthetics. The campanili of Venice are distinguished from those elsewhere in Italy in other ways as well. Common to almost all are two basic architectural elements: a brick shaft, almost always a single, tall unit; and an architecturally distinct belfry, the topmost structure supporting the bells. Some have a base, and many are capped with a spire, often standing on a drum or an attic that served as a visual transition and structural support, although at times the spires sprang directly from the belfry itself. Venetian builders seem to have assembled these architectural elements in almost every possible combination.

The position of a tower with respect to its church also varied, some-times due to constraints of the site. Most often they abutted the church it-self. These were usually accessible through a door inside the church. Some notable campanili were completely detached from their church, including San Pietro di Castello (fig. A1.4) and, of course, San Marco (plate 2). In these examples, a door would be built into the base or bottom of the shaft. The shafts of Venetian campanili were not marked by architectural openings, apart from small windows to provide illumination for the interior passage-way to the top. De' Barbari shows these windows in several campanili, in-

cluding Santa Maria Gloriosa dei Frari (the Frari, fig. A1.3) and San Marco. This does not mean, however, that the shafts were devoid of design elements. While a few were plain brick walls (as at San Samuele), most featured tall arches created by pilasters built in brick, like the rest of the structure.

The junction between the shaft and the belfry is clearly articulated, although the scale of the campanili in the *View* does not always make the nature of the articulation clear. For the campanile of San Pietro di Castello (fig. A1.4), completed in the 1480s, and one of the newest bell towers fea-tured in the woodcut print, the architect Mauro Codussi employed large Renaissance cornices at the juncture of the shaft and belfry as well as an ar-ticulation midshaft. In the medieval example of the Frari, decorative brick-work is visible. For most others, de' Barbari simply draws a straight line.

The belfries of Venetian campanili are roughly cubic structures, pierced on all sides by arched openings usually springing directly from the top of the brickwork or cornice to separate them from the shafts. The vast majority have two or three openings, but a few have only one, and others, notably San Giorgio Maggiore and San Marco, have four. Quite common are the four corners topped by a pinnacle (San Stin, at the right of fig. A1.3; this is typical of the façades of Venetian Gothic churches). Also frequent was a balustrade of white Istrian stone to top the belfry (an element that con-tinued to be used in later Venetian campanili), as in San Pietro di Castello. Most Venetian towers, as shown clearly in the *View* (but more dramatically in the later Engelbrecht engraving featured in my essay), went beyond the essential elements of shaft and belfry and also had some sort of spire, as noted above. Among the most common shapes for the spires themselves is the cone (San Stin), although pyramids, either four-sided or octagonal, are also common. There are a few domes (San Pietro di Castello) and hipped roofs (Santa Fosca). In select instances, the spire, even if planned, was never built, and the belfry or attic is simply covered by a roof (Frari). De' Barbari at times shows the material covering the spire, such as textured tiles on the cone of Santa Croce on the Giudecca.

Those campanili shown in the *View* that are extant today demonstrate, in most cases, the remarkable detail of de' Barbari's depictions. Two free-standing campanili (since demolished) are also worthy of note. Uniquely among those of the lagoon, the tower of San Paternian in the district of San Marco was hexagonal in plan; moreover, the hexagon appears to be irregular. Also unique was the cylindrical campanile of San Secondo, a nonextant church on an island northwest of Venice proper. While it is impossible to determine with any accuracy the heights of the towers shown in the *View*, there are enough extant to provide indications. Most are roughly 100 feet tall, although they range from the 46 feet of Santa Maria della Misericordia to the 226 of the Frari. The rebuilt campanile of San Marco now stands at 321 feet, but it can be estimated that at the time of the *View* in 1500, it was about 215 feet. All but the shortest of these structures would have towered above the rest of the city, rivaled only by a few domes of the churches, such as that of Santi Giovanni e Paolo (fig. 19.2).

While the large majority of Venetian campanili are independent structures, de' Barbari depicts one additional type, known generally as *alla romana*, but in Venice called *a vela* (an apropos designation meaning "like a sail"). This is a small structure with arches which is located on the edge of the roof of its church or nearby building and from which the bells are directly hung (San Nicolò della Latuga, left rear of fig. A1.3). De' Barbari depicts several churches with seemingly no bell tower of any kind. In some instances, this is because the campanile *a vela* is on the north side of the church and too low to emerge visibly above the roofline (such as that at Santa Maria dei Servi). Others were built later than the *View*, like Santa Giustina, while some, like that at San Gregorio, lack documentation to confirm the physical presence (or absence) of a tower.

The campanili of Venice—in both their prominence and their distinctiveness—provided Venetians of both de' Barbari's time and our own with anchors for their community. These could be localized, such as for monastic communities or parishes, or noteworthy for the entire city, such as that of San Marco. Notably, these campanili were visual markers, as portrayed in the *View*, as well as aural via their bells, a significance largely hidden from us. This audible nature in Venice was vital in the structuring of life for Venetians of de' Barbari's era, an acoustic landscape element lost on visitors today with the passage of time despite the continued reverberations of the towers' bells.

Venetians: Visible and Invisible Inhabitants

Kristin Love Huffman

The *View*—*the* quintessential representation of Venice—like the city it portrays, elicits pride and wonder in natives and visitors alike, then and now. This final entry is dedicated to the people who gave life to Venice—building, maintaining, and animating its legacy. Scholars have grappled with the general absence of people in the *View of Venice*, especially given that in 1500, approximately 120,000 people inhabited the city; by contrast, estimates of Venice's population in 2022 put it just below 50,000. As a portrait of Venice, it should be noted that de' Barbari's representational objective was to present the urban fabric, its noteworthy architecture, and idiosyncratic details. Human figures scattered across open spaces, such as Piazza San Marco or the Rialto, would have interrupted the eye's movement across topographical details and from site to site.

On closer examination, however, one discovers a fair number of people in select locations. Many perform tasks, such as preparing or maintaining ships in the Arsenal, to highlight the industriousness and technical skills required for a city built on water. Most show that passage within the city required movement on water within gondolas, often manned by lone standing oarsmen. The most discernible location—along the Grand Canal, the aqueous boulevard that winds throughout the city and divides it in two—has many such boatsmen, some ferrying passengers. Randomly the eye catches select gondolas with a *felza*, or framed apparatus for luxurious coverings to maintain privacy for its travelers when enclosed—the opportunity to see without being seen, a Venetian pastime. Occasionally in the channels, slightly larger boats appear with sails or pulling larger ships intended for deeper waters. On closer examination of larger vessels in proximity to the Arsenal, men work high up in the masts or sit across the boom pulling up ropes or folding up sails. Near to and within the Arsenal's walls, men stand on platforms secured to tipped boats, repairing, caulking, or varnishing the large hulls. Back over to the island of San Giorgio, across from Piazza San Marco, two men stand knee deep in water, fishing at low tide. On the island proper, within the monastery's enclosed gardens, Benedictines make exchanges, one under a trellis that bears roses. The flowers suggest that the weather is seasonably warm, further encouraging productivity among inhabitants.

As noted, the majority of figures represented in the *View* highlight men related to waterborne services. But there were many more people residing in the city and managing its operations, including foreigners and women. For example, women, invisible in the *View*, were integral to the state, often expressed through civic ritual and honorary processions winding throughout the city as living pageantry of Venice's wealth, including the dogaressa, the consort of the doge, who headed the Venetian state. Jewish residents formed the first permanent foreign community in 1516, with other neighborhood pockets of non-Venetians, like the Greeks, Armenians, and Dalmatians, soon to follow. A series of mandates established by the state around the time of the *View* led to the relocation of non-Venetians from temporary locations and guesthouses near Piazza San Marco to other places in Venice; the concomitant shift of economic activity to center predominantly at the Rialto facilitated state control over foreign communities and provided steady sources of tax revenue to the city.

The View and Its Relevance Today

Today, even though on most days people occupying the city are transitory visitors as part of the tourist industry, there remain long-standing Venetian families living and working in neighborhoods that thrive and pulsate with everyday life. These include the parish of San Giacomo dell'Orio, the Jewish Ghetto, and the zone around San Francesco della Vigna (to name a few), zones where the visibility of Venetian life actively persists—children going to school in the morning and later playing soccer in the squares, laundry hanging out to dry on lines outside residences, and people bustling to make purchases at the food stalls clustered around the Rialto and Campo Santa Margherita. That the city continues to negotiate its waterborne status is visibly evident with the many boats that transport mail, goods, and a public, still navigated today by the city's savvy mariners, men as well as women. The inhabitants of Venice, past and present, have given the city its life. And like their presence in the *View*, though largely hidden, continue to form the very backbone of the city's survival.

NOTE

---

1 David Chambers and Brian Pullan, eds., *Venice: A Documentary History,* *1450–1630* (Oxford: Blackwell, 1992), 18.

Anton Kolb's Copyright Permission and
Export License Request for the *View of Venice*

A2.1

Request by Anton Kolb to the Collegio, October 1500. Archivio di Stato di Venezia, Collegio Notatorio, reg. 15, fol. 28r.

This document records Anton Kolb's request in October 1500 for a copyright and free export license for the *View of Venice*, intended at the time to be sold at a cost of three florins. It is worth noting that Kolb's original appeal to the Collegio, the executive body of the Venetian state, seems to have gone missing. A referenced copy, currently maintained in the Venetian State Archives (ASVe, Collegio, Notatorio, Registro 15 [anni 1499–1507], fol. 28r.), includes the German merchant's petition amalgamated with the Collegio's response. The state maintained such official documents as evidence of requests and subsequent decisions. Given the varying modern transcriptions of this document since the nineteenth century, not to mention its perplexing juxtaposition of clauses, the original is included here

M·ccccc———ᵐⁱ

Serenissimo principo et Exᵐ Signoria. Antonio cholb marchadante todescho
supplica ala gᵃ vra. Cum sit et lui principalmente ad fima de questa
exᵃ cita de venetia quella habia fadto justa et propriamente retrare
et stampare. laqual opera hora de poy lo tempo di tre anni formita: et po
esse in molte cosse ale altre opere se fimo asei eptradto. si p la materia
dificilissima et in credibele poterne fre vero desegno si p la grandeza
sua et dela carta et mni simele non fo fadta. Si anchora p la noua
arte de stampar forme di tal grandeza: et p la dificulta dele coposio
tute in seme le qual cosse fusse non essendo p suo valor stimate dale
zente: nela smilleza del intellecto le forme stampando possmo suplir
et p mancho de cerchas a tre fiorini una opera se posse revedere p
tanto universalmente non spiera rechaварne la messa faculta, supplica
rdoncha ala subᵗ vra et in ora li sia conceduto et dicta opera senza
danno et senza impedimento in tuti li luogi et da tute terre vre pormi tute
et vendere possa

Die xxx octᵇ 1500.

Infrascripti tui consiliarii terminauerunt et deliberauerunt et cocessent
supscripto supplicanti. et aliquis non possit facere amodo ad annos quatuor
in simili forma et h possit esphere opus predidum pro omnibus locis
soluendo dritta consueta: et fiant ei tre patentes in ampla forma. /

Consiliarii
p Aloysius mudatio
p Joannes mauroceno
p petrus Comureno
p Antonius trono ./

for readers to peruse and interpret themselves. As with many Venetian
state chronicles, Venetian dialect appears alongside what will later become
standardized Italian.

Will of Anton Kolb, October 12, 1541

ASVe, Notarile Testamenti, b. 128 (notary Francesco Bianco), no. 157, fols. 67ᵛ–68ʳ

In nomine Dei eterni amen: Anno ab incarnatione domini nostri Iesu Christi millesimo quingentesimo quadragesimo primo / die duodecimo mensis octobris Indictione quintadecima: Rivoalti: Cum uite Sue terminum vnusquisque prorsus ignoret et nil certius morte. nichil autem incertius eius hora in hoc seculo habeamus / Ideo Vnicuique Inminet precauendum ne incautus occumbat· Et sua bona Indisposita derelinquat: Quapropter Ego Antonius Kolb q. D. Stephani / de Nierembergo / ad presens habitator Venetiis. in fonticu allemanorum sannus mente / & Corpore ualde infirmus /

Set uolens de bonis meis ordinare / Vocaui et venire feci ad me presbyterum
Franciscum blanchum Venetiarum notarium / quem Rogaui ut hoc meum
ultimum scriberet testamentum / Vulgari Sermone Iuxta leges Venetiarum
In quo in primis recommittens animam meam suo Creatori / Volgio che
Sia mio Solo & unico commissario / El magnifico Et honorando misier
Antonio focher. mio honorando patron & signor / Lasso a germano mio
fiol natural Carissimo El priuilegio, et la autorita che Io ho, per lo inzegno /
che ho fatto de cauar Canali alla Illustrissima Signoria de Venetia / Et de
far li Instrumenti de dicta Cauation. Come in dicto priuilegio Se contiene.
Ancora li lasso al dicto germano mio fiol natural Tuto el mio Credito che
Io ho da hauer dalla dicta Illustrissima Signoria de Venetia per ogni Causa /
Item lasso a Iordano / laltro mio fiol natural· ducati Cinquanta in segno de
amor / Domandado de alijs locis piis. Et Interrogandis· Respondo che Io
non ho che lassare in hospedali / ne de quelli uolgio altro ordenar· del presente mio testamento Sia fatto far Vno particular Inuentario per manno del
nodaro infrascripto / Et quello Sia dato· al soprascripto magnifico misier
Antonio focher· mio Sollo commissario accio· Se uedi quello che se trouera
del mio / alla mia morte / Lasso Tuti li mej beni che me aspetta· stabili, o
possession per rason paterna o materna· & non altramente / a Tuti li mej
piuj propinqui parenti / li quali beni Io li renuntio per non li hauer havuti
Lasso alli doi hospedali de Nierembergo ducatos diese per cadauno per lan-
ima mia: El RESiduo ueramente de Tuti li altri | (fo. 68ᵛ) mei beni mobili &
stabili· presenti & futuri / Caduchi desordenadi· & prononscripti Et Tuto
quello che me potesse aspetare per lo aduegnir· Tuto lasso a misier Antonio
focher mio Commissario soprascripto per le molte grande obligatione che
Io ho cum luj / El qual misier Antonio Io instituisco mio herede uniuersal /
Et questo uoio che sia el mio ultimo testamento / el qual uolgio che ualgi
in cada uno loco / Et Si per via de testamento Come per via de donatione
o uero per via de Codicillo / uero per ogni altro mior [sic] modo derason /
Lasso a misier mathio ortel / Et a misier christopholo Muoelich Et a misier
Rigo Vaiblingner / Vno liuto de li miei per Cadauno / in segno de amor:
Lasso a misier Zuan baptista de pauia medico Vna figura de Cerere & bacho /
depenta a guazo / in segno de amor: Item Io ricomando li Soprascripti mei
fioli / al Sopradicto misier Antonio focher mio commissario & patron:
Si come so certo fara: preterea· plenissimam uirtutem & potestatem do
Tribuo & Confero Suprascripto meo Sollo [sic for soli] commissario pre-
sentem meam commissariam Intromitendi adminstrandi &c ut in forma
Consueta &c

Io xforro Muelich da augusta fui testimonio pregato et Jurato

Io Mathio hortel da augusta fui testimonio pregato et Jurato

Io arigo Waiblinger de augusta fui Testimonio pregato et Jurato

[sign] Ego presbyter Franciscus Blanchus venetiarum notarius Compleui
Et Roboraui

	D. Christophorus muelich de Augusta	omnes allemani et
[Testes]	D. Matheus ortel de Augusta	mercatores in fonticu
	D. Enricus Vaiblingner de Augusta	allemanorum

Obijt suprascriptus Testator die 4 mensis nouembris 1541 / Et presens
testamentum fuit per me notarium publicum publicatum die quinta dicti
mensis nouembris / 1541

BIBLIOGRAPHY

Archival Primary Sources

ARCHIVIO DI STATO DI MODENA, MODENA

Ambasciatori Venezia: Dispacci, Galeazzo Trotti, 1486, I–II

ARCHIVIO DI STATO DI VENEZIA, VENICE

Avogaria di Comun, Contratti di Nozze, registri 142, 143

Avogaria di Comun, Deliberazioni del Maggior Consiglio, Bifrons 1

Cancelleria Inferiore, Miscellanea Notai Diversi, buste 37, 115, 122, 213

Collegio, Notatorio, registri 11, 14, 15

Compilazione Leggi, busta 357

Consiglio dei Dieci, Deliberazioni miste, registri 15, 17

Corpus Domini, busta 19

Demanio, busta 10

Giudici del Proprio, Lezze e Giudice Delegato, registri 6, 7, 9, 314

Giudici di Petizion, buste 418, 491

Inquisitori di Stato, Avvisi

Notarile Atti, busta 3549

Notarile Testamenti, buste 41, 66, 68, 364, 558, 560, 573, 574, 575, 595, 752, 895, 922, 985, 1062, 1156, 1227, 1254

Procuratori di San Marco, Commissarie Miste, buste 3, 307

Procuratori di San Marco, Commissarie Ultra, busta 307

Procuratori di San Marco de Supra, Registri per conto Chiesa, Giornali Cassier, busta 1

Provveditori alle fortezze

San Daniele, busta 27

San Domenico di Castello, busta 5

San Salvador, busta 98

Santa Croce alla Giudecca, busta 4

Santa Lucia, busta 3

Santa Maria degli Angeli di Murano,
busta 9

Sant' Anna, busta 21

Sant' Eufemia di Mazzorbo, busta 5

Santo Stefano, busta 24

Sant'Uffizio, busta 156

Scuola Grande della Misericordia, Commissaria Marcello, busta 37

Senato, Terra, Deliberazioni, registri 3,
12, 13, 109, 398

Senato Misti, busta 35

Sopraconsoli dei Mercanti, busta 1

Sopraintendenti alle decime del clero,
buste 32, 33

ARCHIVIO STORICO DEL PATRIAR-
CATO DI VENEZIA, VENICE

Parrocchia di San Benetto, registro di
cassa 2

Parrocchia San Fosca, busta 196

Parrocchia Santa Maria Formosa, Amministrazione, busta 2

Parrocchia Santa Maria Formosa, Capitolo, Verbali e parti 2

Sezione Antica, Liber Actorum, 1463

Sezione Antica, Liber Testificationum,
1464–66

ARCHIVI STORICI DELLA CHIESA
DI VENEZIE, ECCLESIAE VENETAE,
VENICE

Parrocchia di San Giovanni Elemosinario,
Ceremoniale

Parrocchia di San Silvestro

BAYERISCHEN STAATSBIBLIOTHEK,
MUNICH

Schedel, Hartmann. n.d. Liber antiquitatum cum epigrammatibus, clm.
716

BIBLIOTECA DEL MUSEO CORRER,
VENICE

Cicogna 562

Codice PD 258b

Commemoriali, MSS Gradenigo-Dolfin
200, tomes 11, 16

Lazari, Vincenzo. *Ordinamento primitivo
della Raccolta del N. U. Teodoro Correr e disegni vari di oggetti conservati
nella stessa*, 1859, ms. 1472

Tassini, Giuseppe. *Cittadini Veneziani*,
Venice, Provenienze Diverse, MS.
P.D. C. 4

BIBLIOTECA NAZIONALE MARCI-
ANA, VENICE

Barbaro, Marco. "Libro di nozze patrizie."
MSS Italiani, classe 7, 156 (8492)

Brown, Horatio. "Schedario di Horatio F. Brown." MSS Italiani, classe 7
(2500-12077)

Fondo Antico Latino Zanetti, MSS 399

BIBLIOTHÈQUE NATIONALE DE
FRANCE, PARIS

Collection de 500 Colbert, inv. no. 128

L'Anglais, Barthélemy. *Livre des proprietés des choses*. Translated from Latin
by Jean Corbichon. Ms., Français
134, bk 9

LANDESARCHIV THÜRINGEN,
HAUPTSTAATSARCHIV, WEIMAR

Ernestinisches Gesamtarchiv, reg. Bb,
    Signatur 4180, 4183, 4185, 4188 &
    reg. O, Spalatin Schriften, Signatur 156.

ÖSTERREICHISCHES STAATSARCHIV,
VIENNA

Finanz und Hofkammerarchiv, Alte
    Hofkammer, Gedenkbücher, Epoche Maximilian I (1498–1521)

Printed Primary Sources

Agricola, Georgius. *De re metallica* (1556).
    Translated by Herbert Clark Hoover
    and Lou Henry Hoover. New York:
    Dover, 1950.

Alberti, Leon Battista. *Autobiografia e
    altre opere latine.* Edited by Loredana
    Chines and Andrea Severi. Milan:
    Rizzoli BUR Classici, 2012.

Alberti, Leon Battista. *"On Painting"
    and "On Sculpture."* Edited by Cecil
    Grayson. London: Phaidon, 1972.

Algarotti, Francesco. *Opere del Conte
    Algarotti.* Cremona: Manini, 1781.

Arnoldi, J. v. "Philipp's des lezten Grafen
    zu Katzenelnbogen, Pilgerreise nach
    Aegypten und Palastina; im Jahr
    1433 und 34 [1658]." In *Die Vorzeit:
    Ein Taschenbuch,* 43–75. Marburg:
    Elwert, 1821.

Bartoli, Cosimo. *Del modo di misurare.*
    Venice, 1564.

Bembo, Pietro. *History of Venice.* Translated by Robert Ulery. Vol. 1. Cambridge, MA: I Tatti Renaissance
    Library, Harvard University Press,
    2007.

Boschini, Marco. *La carta del navegar
    pitoresco.* Venice: Baba, 1660.

Brucioli, Antonio. *Dialogi di Antonio
    Brucioli.* Venice: per Gregorio de
    Gregori, 1526.

Bruni, Leonardo. "Panegyric to the City
    of Florence." Translated by Benjamin
    G. Kohl. In *The Earthly Republic:
    Italian Humanists on Government
    and Society,* edited by Benjamin G.
    Kohl and Ronald G. Witt, 135–75.
    Philadelphia: University of Pennsylvania Press, 1978.

Caresini, Raffaele. *Chronica 1343–1388.*
    Edited by Ester Pastorello. Vol. 12 of
    Rerum italicarum scriptores. Bologna:
    Zanichelli, 1922.

Casola, Pietro. *Canon Pietro Casola's Pilgrimage to Jerusalem in the Year 1494.*
    Edited and translated by M. Margaret Newett. Manchester: Manchester
    University Press, 1907.

Casola, Pietro. *Viaggio di Pietro Casola
    a Gerusalemme.* Edited by Anna
    Paoletti. Alessandria: Edizioni
    dell'Orso, 2001.

"The City of the Sea." *Harper's New
    Monthly Magazine* 45, no. 268 (September 1872): 481–501.

Clementi, Africo. *Trattato dell'agricoltura
    di m. Africo Clemente Padovano [...].*
    Venice: ad instantia di M. Africo
    Clemente Padoano, 1572.

Colbertaldo, Antonio. *Storia di Caterina*

Corner Regina di Cipro: La prima biografia. Edited by Daria Pedrocco. Padua: Poligrafo, 2012.

Corner, Flaminio. Notizie storiche delle chiese e monasteri di Venezia. Venice: A. Forni, 1758.

Da Canal, Martin. Les estoires de Venise: Cronaca veneziana in lingua francese dalle origini al 1275. Vol. 7 of Civiltà veneziana, fonti e testi, edited by Alberto Limentani. Florence: Olschki, 1972.

Dal Borgo, Michela. L'arte dei gallineri e la cucina dei volatili nella Repubblica di Venezia. Venice: Archivio di Stato, 2009.

Dandolo, Andrea. Chronicon venetum (r. 1343–54). 2 vols. Venice: Filippi, 1968.

Dandolo, Andrea. Chronicon venetum (r. 1343–54). Reprinted in Francesco Sansovino, Venetia, città nobilissima et singolare: Con aggiunta di tutte le cose notabili della stessa città fatte e occorse dall'anno 1580 fino al presente 1663 da D. Giustiniano Martinoni. Venice: Stefano Curti, 1663.

de Worde, Wynkyn, and E. Gordon Duff. Information for Pilgrims unto the Holy Land (1498). London: Lawrence and Bullen, 1893.

Dürer, Albrecht. Records of Journeys to Venice and the Low Countries. Edited by Roger Fry and translated by Rudolf Tombo Jr. Boston: Merrymount, 1913.

Filosi, Giuseppe. Narrazione istorica del campanile di San Marco in Venezia. Venice: Recurti, 1745.

Filosi, Giuseppe. Narrazione istorica del campanile di San Marco in Venezia. Venice: Appresso Bortolo Occhi, 1757.

Finot, Jules. Inventaire sommaire des archives départementales antérieures à 1790. Série B, vol. 8: Chambre des comptes de Lille, nos. 3390 à 3665. Lille: I. Danel, 1895.

Gauricus, Pomponius. De sculptura. Translated by Andre Chastel and Robert Klein. Geneva: Librairie Droz, 1969.

Grimaux de Caux, Gabriel. Venise: Histoire de ses puits artésiens. Paris: Dunod, 1861.

Handbook for Travellers in Northern Italy. 8th ed. London: John Murray, 1860.

Hypnerotomachia poliphili. Venice: Aldine, 1499.

John P. White and Sons, Ltd. Garden Furniture and Ornament. London: Pyghtle Works, 1916.

Lotto, Lorenzo. Il libro di spese diverse (1538–56). Edited by Francesco De Carolis. Trieste: EUT, 2017.

Lotto, Lorenzo. Il "libro di spese diverse" con aggiunta di lettere e d'altri documenti (1538–1556). Edited by Pietro Zampetti. Venice: Istituto per la Collaborazione Culturale, 1969.

Malipiero, Domenico. Annali Veneti dell'anno 1457 al 1500 con aggiuntovi i dispacci al Senato Veneto. Florence: Vieusseux, 1844.

Michelant, Henri. "Inventaire des vaisselles, joyaux, tapisseries, peintures, manuscrits, etc. de Marguerite d'Autriche, régente et gouvernante des Pays-Bas, dressé en son palais de Malines, le 9 juillet 1523." *Compte-rendu des séances de la commission royale d'histoire*, deuxième série, tome 12 (1871): 33–78, 83–136.

Miller, Anna. *Letters from Italy, Describing the Manners, Customs, Antiquities, Paintings, &c. of that Country.* Vol. 3. London: Edward and Charles Dilly, 1776.

Moryson, Fynes. *An Itinerary written by Fynes Moryson [. . .] containing his ten yeeres travel through the twelve dominions.* London: Ioan Beale, 1617.

Niccolini, Sister Giustina. *The Chronicle of Le Murate* (1598). Edited by Saundra Weddle. Toronto: Centre for Reformation and Renaissance Studies, 2011.

Onofri, Fedele. *Cronologia veneta: Nella quale fedelmente, e con brevita "si descrivono le cose piu" notabili di questa famosissima citta' di Venetia fino all' anno 1666.* Venice: Ginammi, 1666.

Pacioli, Luca. *Euclidis Megarensis philosophi acutissimi mathematicorumque omnium sine controversia principis opera a Campano interprete fidissimo tralata.* Venice: Paganino Paganini, 1509.

Probis, Marcus Valerius. *Significato litterarum antiquarum.* Edited by Fr. Michael Ferrarinus. Brescia: Boninus de Boninis, 1486.

Ravennas, Vincentius. *Vicencii Rauennatis Juris vtriusque doctoris floride*

Academie studii Uuittenburgensis in Jure cesareo ordinarii Oratio publice habita ad felicissimum gloriosissimumque Principem Fredericum Saxonie ducem re. Wittenberg: Hermann Trebelius, 1505.

Riccoboni, Bartolomea. *Life and Death in a Venetian Convent.* Edited by Daniel Bornstein. Chicago: University of Chicago Press, 2000.

Ripa, Cesare. *Iconologia overo Descrittione d'imagini delle virtu', vitii, affetti, passioni humane, corpi celesti, mondo e sue parti.* Padua: Pietro Paolo Tozzi, 1611.

Sabellico, Marcantonio. *Decades rerum venetarum.* Venice: Andreas Torresanus de Asula, 1487.

Sabellico, Marcantonio. *Del sito di Venezia città* (1502). Edited by Giancarlo Meneghetti. Venice: Libreria Filippi, 1985.

Sabellico, Marcantonio. *Opera omnia.* 4 vols. Basel: J. Herwagen, 1570.

Sansovino, Francesco. *Venetia, città nobilissima et singolare [. . .].* Venice: appresso Iacomo Sansovino, 1581.

Sansovino, Francesco. *Venetia, città nobilissima et singolare: Con aggiunta di tutte le cose notabili della stessa città fatte e occorse dall'anno 1580 fino al presente 1663 da D. Giustiniano Martinoni.* Venice: Steffano Curti, 1663.

Sansovino, Francesco. *Venetia, città nobilissima et singolare: Con le aggiunte di Giustiniano Martinioni* (1581). Venice: Filippi, 1968.

Sanudo, Marino. *De origine, situ et magistratibus urbis Venetae ovvero la città di Venezia, 1493–1530*. Edited by Angela Caracciolo Aricò. Milan: Cisalpino-La Goliardica, 1980.

Sanudo, Marino. *I diarii di Marino Sanuto, 1496–1531*. Edited by Rinaldo Pulin, Federico Stefani, Nicolò Barozzi, Guglielmo Berchet, and Marco Allegri. Venice: F. Visentini, 1902.

Sanudo, Marino. *Itinerario per la terraferma Veneziana nell'anno 1483*. Edited by Rawdon Brown. Padua: Seminario, 1847.

Sanudo, Marino. "Praise of the City of Venice." In *Venice: A Documentary History, 1450–1630*, edited by David Chambers and Brian Pullan, 4–21. Oxford: Blackwell, 1992.

Sanudo, Marino. *Venice, Città Excelentissima: Selections from the Renaissance Diaries of Marin Sanudo*. Edited by Patricia H. Labalme and Laura Sanguineti White. Translated by Linda Carroll. Baltimore, MD: Johns Hopkins University Press, 2008.

Sanudo, Marino. *Vite dei dogi*. Edited by Giovanni Monticolo. Vol. 1. Città di Castello: Stamperia di Scipione Lapi, 1906.

Sanudo, Marino. *Le vite dei dogi, 1474–1494*. Edited by Angela Caracciolo Aricò. Padua: Antenore, 1989–2001.

Schedel, Hartmann, Michael Wolgemut, and Wilhelm Pleydenwurff. *Weltchronik*. Nuremberg: Anton Koberger, 1493.

Schott, Franz. *Andreae Schotti: Itinerarium italiae*. Wesel: Typis Andreae ab Hoogenhuysen, 1655.

Temanza, Tommaso. *Antica pianta dell'inclita città di Venezia* (1781). Edited by Ugo Stefanutti. Bologna: Sala Bolognese, 1977.

Temanza, Tommaso. *Vite dei piu' celebri architetti e scultori veneziani che fiorirono nel secolo decimo sesto*. Vol. 1. Venice: C. Palese, 1778.

Vernatti, Philiberto. "A Relation of the Making of Ceruss, by Sir Philiberto Vernatti." *Philosophical Transactions, 1665–1678* 12 (1677): 935–36.

Zamberti, Bartolomeo. *Euclidis megarensis philosophi platonici mathematicarunt disciplinarum janitoris*. Venice: Giovanni Tacuino, 1505.

Secondary Sources

Agazzi, Michela. *Platea Sancti Marci: I luoghi marciani dall'XI al XIII secolo e la formazione della Piazza*. Venice: Comune di Venezia, Assessorato agli affair istituzionali, Assessorato alla cultura, 1991.

Aikema, Bernard, and Beverly Louise Brown. "Painting in Fifteenth-Century Venice and the *ars nova* of the Netherlands." In *Renaissance Venice and the North: Crosscurrents in the Time of Bellini, Dürer, and Titian*, edited by Aikema and Brown, 176–239. Venice: Bompiani, 1999; New York: Rizzoli, 2000.

Ainsworth, Maryan, ed. *Man, Myth, and Sensual Pleasures: Jan Gossart's Re-*

naissance. The Complete Works. New York: Metropolitan Museum of Art, 2010. Exhibition catalog.

Ainsworth, Maryan. "Observations concerning Gossart's Working Methods." In Ainsworth, *Man, Myth, and Sensual Pleasures,* 69–87.

Akerman, James R. "Jacopo de' Barbari, 1500." Under "Cartographic Context" in *Merlo's Map: The Religious Geography of Venice,* edited by Lia Markey, virtual exhibition, Newberry Library, 2017. Accessed August 12, 2020. https://publications .newberry.org/venice/.

Akerman, James R. "The Structuring of Political Territory in Early Printed Atlases." *Imago Mundi* 47 (1995): 138–54.

Allan, Eva D. "The Triumph Theme and Variations in Long Renaissance Prints." PhD diss., Yale University, 2014.

Allerston, Patricia. "Consuming Problems: Worldly Goods in Renaissance Venice." In *The Material Renaissance,* edited by Michelle O'Malley, 11–46. Manchester: Manchester University Press, 2010.

Allerston, Patricia. "The Market in Second Clothes and Furnishings in Venice, circa 1500–1650." PhD diss., European University, Florence, 1996.

Almagià, Roberto. *Monumenta Italiae cartographica, riproduzioni di carte generali e regionali d'Italia dal secolo XIV al XVII.* Florence: Istituto Geografico Militare, 1929.

Almagià, Roberto. "On the Cartographic Work of Francesco Rosselli." *Imago Mundi* 8, no. 1 (1951): 27–34.

Alpers, Svetlana. *The Art of Describing.* Chicago: University of Chicago Press, 1983.

Alsteens, Stijn. "Gossart as a Draftsman." In Ainsworth, *Man, Myth, and Sensual Pleasures,* 89–103.

Anderson, Jaynie. "A Further Inventory of Gabriele Vendramin's Collection." *Burlington Magazine* 121, no. 919 (1979): 639–48.

Andersson, Christiane, and Larry Silver. "Dürer's Drawings." In *The Essential Dürer,* edited by Larry Silver and Jeffrey Chipps Smith, 12–34. Philadelphia: University of Pennsylvania Press, 2010.

Andreoli, Ilaria. "Il fondo di matrici lignee del Museo Correr: Una presentazione." *Studi di Memofonte* 17 (2016): 25–57.

Arnaldi, Girolamo, and Manlio Pastore Stocchi, eds. *Dal primo quattrocento al concilio di trento III.* Vol. 3 of *Storia della cultura veneta.* Vicenza: Neri Pozza, 1981.

Arnheim, Rudolf. *Art and Visual Perception.* Berkeley: University of California Press, 1957.

Ascarelli, Fernanda, and Marco Menato. *La tipografia del '500 in Italia.* Florence: Leo S. Olschki, 1989.

Ashcroft, Jeffrey. *Albrecht Dürer: Documentary Biography.* 2 vols. New Haven, CT: Yale University Press, 2017.

Atkinson, Niall. *The Noisy Renaissance:*

Sound, Architecture, and Florentine Urban Life. University Park: Pennsylvania State University Press, 2017.

Avery, Victoria. *Vulcan's Forge in Venus' City: The Story of Bronze in Venice, 1350–1650*. Oxford: Published for the British Academy by Oxford University Press, 2011.

Bach, Friedrich Teja. "Albrecht Dürer: Figures of the Marginal." *res: Anthropology and Aesthetics* 36 (1999): 79–99.

Bagarolo, Vanna, and Vladimiro Valerio. "Jacopo de' Barbari: Una nuova ipotesi indiziaria sulla genesi prospettica della veduta *Venetie MD*." In *Cartografi veneti: Mappe, uomini e istituzioni per l'immagine e il governio del territorio*, edited by Vladimiro Valerio, 118–35. Padua: Editoriale Programma, 2007.

Balistreri-Trincanato, Corrado. "Canali, fondmente, calli, salizzade, sottoportici." In Balistreri-Trincanato et al., *Venezia città mirabile*, 93–110.

Balistreri-Trincanato, Corrado. "Case fondaco, fondaci, botteghe." In Balistreri-Trincanato et al., *Venezia città mirabile*, 126–29.

Balistreri-Trincanato, Corrado, Emiliano Balistreri, Anna Maria Ghion, and Dario Zanverdiani, eds. *Venezia città mirabile: Guida alla veduta prospettica di Jacopo de' Barbari*. Verona: Cierre, 2009.

Balistreri-Trincanato, Corrado, and Dario Zanverdiani. *Jacopo de' Barbari: Il*

racconto di una città, 2 vols. Venice: Iuav, 2000.

Barause, Manuela. "Giovanni Bellini: I documenti." In *Giovanni Bellini*, edited by Mauro Lucco and G. C. F. Villa, 327–61. Milan: Silvana, 2008.

Barbon, Ferdy Hermes. *I segni mercanti al Fondaco dei Tedeschi*. Treviso: Antiga, 2005.

Bartsch, Adam von. *Le peintre graveur*. Vol. 8. Vienna: Degen, 1808.

Bartsch, Friedrich von. *Die Kupferstichsammlung der K. K. Hofbibliothek in Wien*. Vienna: Braumüller, 1854.

Barzman, Karen-edis. "Cartographic Line and the Paper Management of the Early Modern State: A Case Study of Venetian Dalmatia." *Mapline* 122 (2014): 1–15.

Barzman, Karen-edis. *The Limits of Identity: Early Modern Venice, Dalmatia, and the Representation of Difference*. Leiden: Brill, 2017.

Barzman, Kristijan Juran, and Josip Faričić. "Cartography in the Service of the Venetian State: An Early Sixteenth-Century Map of Central and Northern Dalmatia by an Unknown Draftsman." *Geoadria* 24, no. 2 (2019): 93–139.

Basch, Lucien. "Les galères de la *Vue de Venise* de Jacopo de' Barberi [sic] (1500)." In *Boats, Ships and Shipyards: Proceedings of the Ninth International Symposium on Boat and Ship Archaeology*, edited by Carlo Beltrame, 233–40. Oxford: Oxbow, 2003.

Bassi, Elena. *Palazzi di Venezia: Admi-*

randa Urbis Venetae. Venice: La Stamperia di Venezia, 1976.

Bassi, Elena. *Tracce di chiese distrutte: Ricostruzioni dai disegni di Antonio Visentini*. Venice: Istituto Veneto di Scienze Lettere ed Arti, 1997.

Battiston, Odilla, ed. *Chiese e monasteri distrutti a Castello dopo il 1807: S. Domenico, S. Nicolò di Bari, Ospedale di Messer Gesù Cristo, Seminario ducale, Convento delle Cappuccine, S. Antonio*. Venice: Filippi, 1992.

Baxandall, Michael. *Giotto and the Orators: Humanist Observers of Painting in Italy and the Discovery of Pictorial Composition, 1350–1450*. Oxford: Oxford University Press, 1971.

Baxandall, Michael. *The Limewood Sculptors of Renaissance Germany*. New Haven, CT: Yale University Press, 1980.

Baxandall, Michael. *Painting and Experience in Fifteenth Century Italy: A Primer in the Social History of Pictorial Style*. 2nd ed. Oxford: Oxford University Press, 1988.

Bellavitis, Giorgio. "L'evoluzione della struttura urbana di Venezia attraverso i secoli: I primi documenti cartografici." *Bollettino c.i.s.a.* 18 (1976): 225–23.

Bellavitis, Giorgio, and Giandomenico Romanelli. *Venezia*. Rome: Laterza, 1985.

Bellavitis, Giorgio, and Giandomenico Romanelli. "La Venezia di Jacopo de' Barbari." In Bellavitis and Romanelli, *Venezia*, 66–76.

Bellini, Paolo. "Printmakers and Dealers in Italy during the 16th and 17th Century." *Print Collector* 13 (1975): 17–45.

Bellini, Paolo. "Stampatori e mercanti di stampe in Italia nei secoli XVI e XVII." *I quaderni del conoscitore di stampe* 26 (1975): 19–34.

Belozerskaya, Marina. *Luxury Arts of the Renaissance*. Los Angeles: J. Paul Getty Museum, 2005.

Beltrami, Daniele. *Storia della popolazione di Venezia dalla fine del secolo XVI alla caduta della Repubblica*. Padua: Cedam, 1954.

Beltramini, Guido, and Davide Gasparotto, eds. *Aldo Manuzio: Il rinascimento di Venezia*. Venice: Marsilio, 2016.

Bently, Lionel, and Martin Kretschmer, eds. "Primary Sources on Copyright (1450–1900)." Accessed October 13, 2020. www.copyrighthistory.org.

Bernardello, Adolfo. *La prima ferrovia fra Venezia e Milano: Storia della imperial-regia privilegiata strada ferrata Ferdinandea Lombardo-Veneta, 1835–1852*. Venice: Istituto Veneto di Scienze Lettere ed Arti, 1994.

Berrie, Barbara H., and Louisa C. Matthew. "Lead White from Venice: A Whiter Shade of Pale?" In *Studying Old Master Paintings: Technology and Practice*, edited by Marika Spring with Helen Howard, 295–301. London: Archtype, 2011.

Berry, Christopher J. *The Idea of Luxury: A Conceptual and Historical Investigation*. Cambridge: Cambridge University Press, 1994.

Berti, Stefano, Anna Gambetta, and Simona Lazzeri. "Indagine sulle matrici lignee della veduta di Venezia e prospettive per la conservazione." In Romanelli, Biadene, and Tonini, *A volo d'uccello*, 106–9.

Black, Erin Mae. "La prolusione di Luca Pacioli del 1508 nella chiesa di S. Bartolomeo e il contesto intellettuale veneziano." In Bonazza, di Lenardo, and Guidarelli, *La chiesa di S. Bartolomeo e la comunità tedesca a Venezia*, 87–104.

Blanchard, Ian. *International Lead Production and Trade in the "Age of the Saigerprozess," 1460–1560.* Stuttgart: Franz Steiner Verlag, 1995.

Blass-Simmen, Brigit. "'Qualche lontani': Distance and Transcendence in the Art of Giovanni Bellini." In *Examining Giovanni Bellini: An Art "More Human and More Divine,"* edited by Carolyn C. Wilson, 77–91. Turnhout: Brepols, 2015.

Böckem, Beate. "'Contrafeter und Illuminist': Jacopo de' Barbari im Dienst Maximilians I." In *Kulturtransfer am Fürstenhof: Höfische Austauschprozesse und ihre Medien im Zeitalter Kaiser Maximilians I,* edited by Matthias Müller, Karl-Heinz Spiess, and Udo Friedrich, 218–42. Berlin: Lucas Verlag, 2013.

Böckem, Beate. "Die Frage nach Autorschaft—eine Frage der Autorität? Jacopo de' Barbari und die Konstruktion einer Künstlerpersönlichkeit." In *Die Biographie—Mode oder Universalie? Zu Geschichte und Konzept Gattung in der Kunstgeschichte,* edited by Beate Böckem, Olaf Peters, and Barbara Schellewald, 49–60. Berlin: De Gruyter, 2016.

Böckem, Beate. "Jacopo de' Barbari: Ein Apelles am Fürstenhof? Die Allianz von Künstler, Humanist und Herrscher im alten Reich." In *Apelles am Fürstenhof: Facetten der Hofkunst um 1500 im alten Reich,* edited by Matthias Müller, Klaus Weschenfelder, Beate Böckem, and Ruth Hansmann, 22–33. Berlin: Lucas Verlag, 2010. Exhibition catalog.

Böckem, Beate. *Jacopo de' Barbari: Künstlerschaft und Hofkultur um 1500.* Cologne: Böhlau Verlag, 2016.

Bolton, Andrew, ed. *Heavenly Bodies: Fashion and the Catholic Imagination.* New York: Metropolitan Museum of Art, 2018. Exhibition catalog.

Bonazza, Natalino, Isabella di Lenardo, and Gianmario Guidarelli, eds. *La chiesa di S. Bartolomeo e la comunità tedesca a Venezia.* Venice: Marcianum, 2013.

Bonucci, Anicio. *Opere volgari di Leon Battista Alberti.* Vol. 1. Florence: Tipografia Galileiana, 1843.

Boorsch, Suzanne. "The Case for Francesco Rosselli as the Engraver of Berlinghieri's Geographia." *Imago Mundi* 56, no. 2 (2004): 152–69.

Bottazzi, Marialuisa. "Artigiani? Venezia: L'arte di fondere: Dalla documentazione d'archivio e dalle scritture incise, secc. XIII–XVI." In *Formazione*

Bibliography

della ricchezza e strutture produttive a Venezia e nell'area alpino-adriatica fra Due e Cinquecento: Tre saggi, edited by Paolo Cammarosano. *Bullettino dell'Istituto storico italiano per il Medio Evo* 111 (2009): 319–42.

Bottazzi, Marialuisa. "Fonditori di campanie: Dalla bottega medievale alla produzione industriale nell'ambiente artistico del Rinascimento veneziano." In *L'industria artistica del bronzo del Rinascimento a Venezia e nell'Italia settentrionale: Atti del convegno internazionale di studi, Venezia, Fondazione Giorgio Cini, 23–24 ottobre 2007,* edited by Matteo Ceriana and Victoria Avery, 363–74. Verona: Scripta, 2008.

Bourne, Molly. "Francesco II Gonzaga and Maps as Palace Decoration in Renaissance Mantua." *Imago Mundi* 51 (1999): 51–82.

Bove, Christopher, Kristin Gallagher, Meghan Hickey, and James Honicker. "Preserving Venice's Bells and Their Towers." Undergraduate research report produced for Worcester Polytechnic Institute, 2015. Accessed July 26, 2020. https://web.wpi.edu /Pubs/E-project/Available/E-proj ect-121815-055420/unrestricted /VE15-Bells_Final_Report.doc.pdf.

Bowd, Stephen D. *Reform before the Reformation: Vicenzo Querini and the Religious Renaissance in Italy.* Leiden: Brill, 2002.

Bowen, Barbara C. "Mercury at the Crossroads in Renaissance Emblems." *Jour-nal of the Warburg and Courtauld Institutes* 48 (1985): 222–29.

Bratti, Daniele Ricciotti. "La pianta prospettica di Venezia dell'anno 1500: Cenni storici." *Rivista mensile della città di Venezia* 6 (1927): 43–54.

Brown, Horatio. *The Venetian Printing Press: An Historical Study.* London: J. C. Nimmo, 1891.

Brown, Patricia Fortini. "Measured Friendship and Calculated Pomp: The Ceremonial Welcomes of the Venetian Republic." In *Triumphal Celebrations and the Ritual of State-craft,* vol. 1 of *"All the World's a Stage": Art and Pageantry in Renaissance and Baroque Europe,* edited by Barbara Wisch and Susan Munshower, 136–86. University Park: Pennsylvania State University Press, 1990.

Brown, Patricia Fortini. *Private Lives in Renaissance Venice.* New Haven, CT: Yale University Press, 2004.

Brown, Patricia Fortini. *Venetian Narrative Painting in the Age of Carpaccio.* New Haven, CT: Yale University Press, 1988.

Brown, Patricia Fortini. *Venice and Antiquity: The Venetian Sense of the Past.* New Haven, CT: Yale University Press, 1996.

Bucklow, Spike. "Lead White's Mysteries." In *The Matter of Art: Materials, Practices, Cultural Logics, c. 1250–1750,* edited by Christy Anderson, Anne Dunlop, and Pamela H. Smith, 141–59. Manchester: Manchester University Press, 2015.

Buisseret, David. *The Mapmakers' Quest: Depicting New Worlds in Renaissance Europe*. Oxford: Oxford University Press, 2003.

Burckhardt, Jakob. *The Civilization of the Renaissance in Italy*. Modern Library ed. New York: Random House, 1954.

Bury, Michael. *The Print in Italy, 1550–1620*. London: British Museum, 2001.

Cadogan, Jean K. *Domenico Ghirlandaio: Artist and Artisan*. New Haven, CT: Yale University Press, 2000.

Cafritz, Robert C., Lawrence Gowing, and David Rosand, eds. *Places of Delight: The Pastoral Landscape*. Washington, DC: Phillips Collection in association with the National Gallery of Art, 1988.

Calabi, Donatella. "Le due piazze di San Marco e di Rialto: Tra eredità medievali e volontà di rinnovo." *Annali di architettura* 4–5 (1993): 190–201.

Calabi, Donatella. *Foreigners and the City: An Historiographical Exploration for the Early Modern Period*. Working Papers 111. Milan: Fondazione Enrico Mattei, 2006.

Calabi, Donatella. *Il mercato e la città: Piazze, strade, architetture d'Europa in età moderna*. Venice: Marsilio, 1993.

Calabi, Donatella. *Venezia e il Ghetto*. Milan: Bollati, 2016.

Calabi, Donatella, ed. *Venice, the Jews, and Europe, 1516–2016*. English ed. Venice: Marsilio Editori, 2016. Exhibition catalog.

Calabi, Donatella, Ugo Camerino, and Ennio Concina, eds. *La città degli ebrei: Il Ghetto di Venezia architettura e urbanistica*. Venice: Albrizzi, 1991.

Calabi, Donatella, and Stephen Turk Christensen, eds. *Cities and Cultural Exchange in Europe, 1400–1700*. Cambridge: Cambridge University Press, 2007.

Calabi, Donatella, and Ludovica Galeazzo, eds. *Acqua e cibo a Venezia: Storie della laguna e della città*. Venice: Marsilio, 2015.

Calabi, Donatella, and Paolo Morachiello. *Rialto le fabbriche e il ponte*. Turin: Einaudi, 1997.

Calimani, Riccardo. *Storia del Ghetto di Venezia*. Milan: Mondadori, 1995.

Camille, Michael. *Image on the Edge: The Margins of Medieval Art*. London: Reaktion Books, 1992.

Canal, Luca. "Il progetto di riordino e catalogazione del fondo di matrici lignee del Museo Correr: Primi risultati." *Studi di Memofonte* 17 (2016): 81–85.

Caniato, Giovanni. "La strada dei burchieri: Navigazione, porti e commerci lungo il Sile." In *Il Sile*, edited by Aldino Bondesan, Giovanni Caniato, Francesco Vallerani, and Michele Zanetti, 206–23. Sommacampagna: Cierre, 1998.

Carl, Klaus. *Albrecht Dürer*. Translated by Marlena Metcalf. New York: Parkstone, 2016.

Carnelos, Laura. "Words on the Street: Selling Small Printed 'Things' in Sixteenth- and Seventeenth-Century Venice." In *News Networks in Early

Modern Europe, edited by Joel Raymond and Noah Moxham, 739–55. Leiden: Brill, 2016.

Cassini, Giocondo. *Piante e vedute prospettiche di Venezia, 1479–1855.* Venice: Stamperia di Venezia, 1971.

Castelnuovo-Tedesco, Lisbeth, and Jack Soultanian, eds. *Italian Medieval Sculpture in the Metropolitan Museum of Art and the Cloisters.* New York: Metropolitan Museum of Art, 2010.

Casti, Emanuela. "State, Cartography, and Territory in Renaissance Veneto and Lombardy." In *Cartography in the European Renaissance*, vol. 3 of *The History of Cartography*, edited by David Woodward, 874–908. Chicago: University of Chicago Press, 1987.

Cecchini, Isabella. "Le figure del commercio: Cenni sul mercato pittorico veneziano nel XVII secolo." In Fantoni, Matthew, and Matthews-Grieco, *The Art Market in Italy*, 389–99.

Cecchini, Isabella. "Ottavio Tassis." In *Il collezionismo d'arte a Venezia: Il Seicento*, edited by Linda Borean and Stefania Mason, 318–19. Venice: Marsilio Editore, 2007. Exhibition catalog.

Cerasuolo, Angela, Patrizia Piscitello, and Marina Santucci. "Scheda." In *La citta ideale: L'utopia del Rinascimento a Urbino tra Piero della Francesca e Raffaello*, edited by Alessandro Marchi and Maria Rosaria Valazzi, 238–40. Milan: Electa, 2012. Exhibition catalog.

Ceriana, Matteo. "'Si fabricha di nuovo bellissima': La facciata della Scuola Grande di San Marco a Venezia." In *La Scuola Grande di San Marco a Venezia*, edited by Gherardo Ortalli and Savatore Settis, 67–98. Modena: Franco Cosimo Panini, 2017.

Chambers, David. "Bird's Eye View of Venice." In Martineau and Hope, *The Genius of Venice*, 392–93.

Chambers, David, and Brian Pullan, eds. *Venice: A Documentary History, 1450–1630.* Oxford: Blackwell, 1992.

Chavasse, Ruth. "The First Known Author's Copyright, September 1486, in the Context of a Humanist Career." *Bulletin of the John Rylands University Library of Manchester* 69 (1986–87): 11–37.

Chipps Smith, Jeffrey. *Dürer.* London: Phaidon, 2012.

Chojnacka, Monica. *Working Women of Early Modern Venice.* Baltimore, MD: Johns Hopkins University Press, 2001.

Chojnacki, Stanley. "Measuring Adulthood: Adolescence and Gender." In Chojnacki, *Women and Men in Renaissance Venice*, 185–205.

Chojnacki, Stanley. "'The Most Serious Duty': Motherhood, Gender, and Patrician Culture." In Chojnacki, *Women and Men in Renaissance Venice*, 169–82.

Chojnacki, Stanley, ed. *Women and Men in Renaissance Venice: Twelve Essays on Patrician Society.* Baltimore, MD: Johns Hopkins University Press, 2000.

Christie, Neil. "On Bells and Bell-Towers: Origins and Evolutions in Italy and Britain, AD 700–1200." *Church Archaeology* 5–6 (2004): 13–30.

Cicogna, Emmanuele Antonio. *Delle iscrizioni veneziani.* Venice: Orlandelli, 1834.

Clarke, Paula. "The Business of Prostitution in Early Renaissance Venice." *Renaissance Quarterly* 58, no. 2 (2015): 419–64.

Cochrane, Eric. *Historians and Historiography in the Italian Renaissance.* Chicago: University of Chicago Press, 1981.

Coco, Carla. *Venezia in cucina.* Rome: Laterza, 2011.

Coen Cagli, Enrico, ed. *Porto Marghera: Conferenza tenuta alla R. Scuola d'Ingegneria di Padova in Occasione dell'VIII Fiera Campionaria il 17 giugno 1926: Estratto dagli Annuali della R. Scuola d'Ingegneria di Padova, Anno II.* Padua: Società Tipografica, 1927.

Colucci, Nick, Candan Iuliano, Fivos Kavassalis, Philippe Lessard, and Bill Michalson. "Bells and Towers." Worcester Polytechnic Institute, Venice Project Center, 2018. Accessed August 12, 2020. http://www.veniceprojectcenter.org/vpc/project/bells-and-towers.

Concina, Ennio. "Alpi e Rinascimento." In *Titianus Cadorinus: Celebrazioni in onore di Tiziano,* edited by Ugo Fasolo, 61–78. Vicenza: Cassa di risparmio di Verona Vicenza e Belluno, 1982.

Concina, Ennio. *L'Arsenale della Repubblica di Venezia.* Milan: Electa, 1984.

Concina, Ennio. *Fondaci: Architettura, arte, e mercatura tra Levante, Venezia, e Alemagna.* Venice: Marsilio, 1997.

Concina, Ennio. *Storia dell'architettura di Venezia dal VII al XX secolo.* Milan: Electa, 2003.

Concina, Ennio. *Structure urbaine et fonctions des bâtiments du XVIᵉ au XIXᵉ siècle.* Venice: UNESCO / Save Venice, 1982.

Concina, Ennio. *Tempo Novo: Venezia e il quattrocento.* Venice: Marsilio, 2006.

Concina, Ennio. *Venezia: Le chiese e le arti.* 2 vols. Udine: Magnus, 1995.

Concina, Ennio. *Venezia nell'età moderna: Struttura e funzioni.* Venice: Marsilio, 1989.

Constable, Olivia Remie. *Housing the Stranger in the Mediterranean World: Lodging, Trade, and Travel in Late Antiquity and the Middle Ages.* Cambridge: Cambridge University Press, 2003.

Conway, William Martin. *The Writings of Albrecht Dürer.* Introduction by Alfred Werner. New York: Philosophical Library, 1958.

Cooper, Tracy E. "On the Sensuous: Recent Counter-Reformation Research." In *The Sensuous in the Counter-Reformation Church,* edited by Marcia B. Hall and Tracy E. Cooper, 21–27. New York: Cambridge University Press, 2013.

Cornaro, Marco, and Cristoforo Sabbadino. *Scritture sopra la laguna.* Modena: Ferrari, 1941.

Cornell University Library. "Nuremberg Chronicle World Map." Accessed October 13, 2020. https://digital.library .cornell.edu/catalog/ss:3293718.

Cosgrove, Denis. "Cultural Cartography: Maps and Mapping in Cultural Geography." *Annales de géographie* 660–61, no. 2 (2008): 159–78.

Cossalter, Stefanie. "Dai porti alle isole: Cerimoniali di accoglienza nella Serenissima." In *Spazi veneziani: Topografie culturali di una città*, edited by Sabine Meine, 125–48. Rome: Viella Libreria Editrice, 2014.

Cozzi, Gaetano. "Authority and the Law in Renaissance Venice." In *Renaissance Venice*, edited by John R. Hale, 293–345. London: Faber, 1974.

Cozzi, Gaetano. "Cultura politica e religione nella 'pubblica storiografia' veneziana del '500." *Bollettino dell'Istituto di Storia I Società dello Stato Veneziano* 5–6 (1963–64): 215–94.

Cozzi, Gaetano, ed. *Gli ebrei a Venezia: Secoli XIV–XVIII: Atti del convegno internazionale organizzato dall'Istituto di Storia della Societa e dello Stato Veneziano della Fondazione Giorgio Cini, Venezia, Isola di San Giorgio Maggiore, 5–10 giugno 1983.* Milan: Edizioni Comunità, 1987.

Cozzi, Gaetano, and Michael Knapton. *La repubblica di Venezia nell'età moderna.* Vol. 12 of *Storia d'Italia.* Turin: UTET, 1986.

Crouzet-Pavan, Élisabeth. "La conquista e l'organizzazione dello spazio." In *L'età del Comune*, vol. 2 of *Storia di Venezia dalle origini alla caduta della Serenissima*, edited by Gherardo Ortalli and Giorgio Cracco, 549–76. Rome: Istituto della Enciclopedia Italiana, 1996.

Crouzet-Pavan, Élisabeth. "Politica e pratiche dell'habitat nell'epoca gotica a Venezia." In *L'architettura gotica veneziana: Atti del Convegno internazionale di studio, Venezia, 27–29 novembre 1996*, edited by Francesco Valcanover and Wolfgang Wolters, 235–41. Venice: Istituto Veneto di Scienze Lettere ed Arti, 2000.

Crouzet-Pavan, Élisabeth. *"Sopra le acque salse": Espaces, pouvoir et société à Venise à la fin du Moyen Age.* Vol. 1. Rome: École française de Rome, 1992.

Crouzet-Pavan, Élisabeth. *Venice Triumphant: The Horizons of a Myth.* Baltimore, MD: Johns Hopkins University Press, 2002.

Curatola, Giovanni. "Venice's Textile and Carpet Trade: The Role of Jewish Merchants." In *Venice and the Islamic World, 818–1797*, edited by Stefano Carboni, 204–11. New Haven, CT: Yale University Press, 2007.

Dalché, Patrick Gautier. "The Reception of Ptolemy's *Geography* (End of the Fourteenth to Beginning of the Sixteenth Century)." In *Cartography in the European Renaissance*, vol. 3 of *History of Cartography*, edited by David Woodward, 285–364. Chicago: University of Chicago Press, 1987.

Dal Pozzolo, Enrico Maria. "Appunti su Catena." *Venezia Cinquecento* 31, no. 16 (2006): 7–8.

Dal Pozzolo, Enrico Maria. "Cercar quadri e disegni nella Venezia del Cinquecento." In *Tra committenza e collezionismo: Studi sul mercato dell'arte nell'Italia settentrionale durante l'età moderna*, edited by Enrico Maria Dal Pozzolo and Leonida Tedoldi, 49–65. Vicenza: Terra Ferma, 2003.

Daly Davis, Margaret. "Carpaccio and the Perspective of Regular Bodies." In *La prospettiva rinascimentale: Codificazioni e trasgressioni*, edited by Marisa Dalai-Emiliani, 183–200. Florence: Centro Di, 1980.

Daly Davis, Margaret. *Piero della Francesca's Mathematical Treatises*. Ravenna: Longo, 1977.

Damen, Giada. "Shopping for *Cose Antiche* in Late Sixteenth-Century Venice." In de Maria and Frank, *Reflections on Renaissance Venice*, 132–41.

Damerini, Gino. *L'isola e il cenobio di San Giorgio Maggiore*. Venice: Fondazione Giorgio Cini, 1956.

Damisch, Hubert. *L'origine de la perspective*. Paris: Flammarion, 1987.

Davis, Robert C. "The Geography of Gender in the Renaissance." In *Gender and Society in Renaissance Italy*, edited by Judith Brown and Robert C. Davis, 19–38. London: Longman, 1998.

Davis, Robert C. *Shipbuilders of the Venetian Arsenal: Workers and Workplace in the Preindustrial City*. Baltimore, MD: Johns Hopkins University Press, 1991.

Davis, Robert C., and Benjamin Ravid, eds. *The Jews of Early Modern Venice*. Baltimore, MD: Johns Hopkins University Press, 2001.

Dean, Trevor. "Storm, Suicide and Miracle: Venice 1342." In *Venice and the Veneto during the Renaissance: The Legacy of Benjamin Kohl*, edited by Michael Knapton, John E. Law, and Alison A. Smith, 309–22. Florence: Firenze University Press, 2014.

de Hevesy, André. *Jacopo de Barbari: Le maitre au caducée*. Paris: Librairie Nationale d'Art et d'Histoire, 1925.

DeLancey, Julia A. "Celebrating Citizenship: Alvise della Scala, Titian, and Social Status in Color Sellers in Sixteenth-Century Venice." *Studi Veneziani*, n.s., 76 (2017): 15–60.

DeLancey, Julia A. "'In the Streets Where They Sell Colors': Placing 'Vendecolori' in the Urban Fabric of Early Modern Venice." *Walraf-Richartz-Jahrbuch* 72, no. 7 (2011): 193–232.

DeLancey, Julia A. "Shipping Colour: *Valute*, Pigments, Trade, and Francesco di Marco Datini." In Kirby, Nash, and Cannon, *Trade in Artists' Materials*, 74–85.

De Marchi, Neil, and Hans J. Van Miegroet, eds. *Mapping Markets for Paintings in Europe 1450–1750*. Turnhout: Brepols, 2006.

de Maria, Blake. *Becoming Venetian: Immigrants and the Arts in Early Modern Venice*. New Haven, CT: Yale University Press, 2010.

de Maria, Blake. "Multifaceted Endeavors: Considerations on Gems and Jewelry in Early Modern Venice." In de Maria and Frank, *Reflections on Renaissance Venice*, 118–31.

de Maria, Blake, and Mary Frank, eds. *Reflections on Renaissance Venice: A Celebration of Patricia Fortini Brown*. Milan: Five Continents / Abrams, 2013.

de Vivo, Filippo. *Information and Communication in Venice: Rethinking Early Modern Politics*. Oxford: Oxford University Press, 2007.

de Vivo, Filippo. "Pharmacies as Centres of Communication in Early Modern Venice." *Renaissance Studies* 21, no. 4 (September 2007): 505–21.

Dewey, John. *Art as Experience*. 1934. Reprint, New York: Perigee Books, 2005.

Dilke, O. A. W. "Roman Large-Scale Mapping in the Early Empire." In *Cartography in Prehistoric, Ancient, and Medieval Europe and the Mediterranean*, vol. 1 of *The History of Cartography*, edited by J. B. Harley and David Woodward, 212–33. Chicago: University of Chicago Press, 1987.

Diller, Aubrey. "The Library of Francesco and Ermolao Barbaro." *Italia medioevale e umanistica* 6 (1963): 254–62.

Dondi, Cristina. "Printers and Guilds in Fifteenth-Century Venice." *La bibliofilía* 106 (2004): 229–65.

Dorigo, Wladimiro. *Venezia: Origini, ipotesi, metodi*. 2 vols. Milan: Electa, 1983.

Dorigo, Wladimiro. *Venezia romanica: La formazione della città medievale fino all'età gotica*. Venice: Cierre, 2003.

Doumerc, Bernard. "La crise structurelle de la marine vénitienne au XVe siècle: Le problème du retard des mude." *Annales ESC* 40, no. 3 (1985): 605–23.

Doumerc, Bernard. "Le galere da mercato." In *Storia di Venezia: Dalle origini alla caduta della Serenissima*, vol. 12 of *Il mare*, edited by Alberto Tenenti and Ugo Tucci, 357–95. Rome: Enciclopedia Italiana, 1991.

Dueck, Daniela. "The Geographical Narrative of Strabo of Amasia." In *Geography and Ethnography: Perceptions of the World in Pre-modern Societies*, edited by Kurt A. Raaflaub and Richard J. A. Talbert, 236–51. Oxford: Wiley-Blackwell, 2010.

Ecole Polytechnique Fédérale de Lausanne. "The Venice Atlas: A Digital Humanities Atlas Project by DH101 EPFL Students." 2016. Accessed August 12, 2020. http://veniceatlas.epfl.ch/mapping-venice-1500-searching-the-de-barbari-map-final-report/.

Edgerton, Samuel. *The Renaissance Rediscovery of Linear Perspective*. New York: Harper and Row, 1976.

Eichberger, Dagmar. "Margaret of Austria and the Documentation of Her Collection in Mechelen." In *The Inventories of Charles V and the Imperial*

Family, vol. 3, edited by Fernando Checa Cremades, 2351–63. Madrid: Fernando Villaverde, 2010.

Eichberger, Dagmar, and Lisa Beaven. "Family Members and Political Allies: The Portrait Collection of Margaret of Austria." *Art Bulletin* 77, no. 2 (1995): 225–48.

Eser, Thomas. "'In onore della città e dei suoi mercanti': Presenza e rappresentazione della città di Norimberga a San Bartolomeo nell'età di Dürer." In Bonazza, di Leonardo, and Guidarelli, *La chiesa di S. Bartolomeo e la comunità tedesca a Venezia*, 68–70.

Fabian, Daniel, and Giuseppino Fortunato. "Tracing White: A Study of Lead White Pigments Found in Seventeenth-Century Paintings Using High Precision Lead Isotope Abundance Ratios." In Kirby, Nash, and Cannon, *Trade in Artists' Materials*, 426–43.

Falchetta, Piero. *Fra Mauro's World Map with a Commentary and Translations of the Inscriptions*. Turnhout: Brepols, 2006.

Falchetta, Piero. *Jacopo de Barbari e le Vedute di Venezia: Una guida multimediale*. Venice: Marsilio/Tridente, 1997.

Falchetta, Piero. "La misura dipinta: Rilettura tecnica e semantica della veduta di Venezia di Jacopo de' Barbari." *Ateneo veneto* 178 (1991): 273–305.

Falchetta, Piero. "Il putto rovesciato o Venezia nel cucchiaio: Note ultime sulla veduta di Jacopo de' Barbari." In *Venezia e Venezie: Descrizioni, interpretazioni, immagini. Studi in onore di Massimo Gemin*, edited by Fabrizio Borin and Filippo Pedrocco, 23–28. Padua: il Poligrafo, 2003.

Falchetta, Piero. "La veduta prospettica di Venezia tra teoria e pratica di misurazione dello spazio." In Romanelli, Biadene, and Tonini, *A volo d'uccello*, 68–75.

Fantoni, Marcello, Louisa C. Matthew, and Sara F. Matthews-Grieco, eds. *The Art Market in Italy, 15th–16th Centuries / Il mercato dell'arte in Italia, secc. XV–XVII*. Modena: Panini, 2003.

Faugeron, Fabien. *Nourrir la ville: Ravitaillement, marchés et métiers de l'alimentation à Venise dans les derniers siècles du Moyen âge*. Rome: École Française de Rome, 2014.

Favaro, Elena. *L'arte dei pittori in Venezia e i suoi statute*. Florence: Olschki, 1975.

Febvre, Lucien, and Henri-Jean Martin. *The Coming of the Book: The Impact of Printing, 1450–1800*. Translated by David Gerard. London: NLB, 1976.

Fenlon, Iain. *The Ceremonial City: History, Memory and Myth in Renaissance Venice*. New Haven, CT: Yale University Press, 2007.

Fenlon, Iain. *Piazza San Marco*. Cambridge, MA: Harvard University Press, 2009.

Ferrari, Simone. *Jacopo de' Barbari: Un protagonista del Rinascimento tra Venezia e Dürer*. Milan: Mondadori, 2006.

Finlay, Robert. "Crisis and Crusade in the Mediterranean: Venice, Portugal, and the Cape Route to India (1498–1509)." *Studi Veneziani* 28 (1994): 45–90.

Fiorani, Francesca. "Cycles of Painted Maps in the Renaissance." In *Cartography in the European Renaissance*, vol. 3 of *The History of Cartography*, edited by David Woodward, 804–30. Chicago: University of Chicago Press, 1987.

Fletcher, H. George, III. *New Aldine Studies: Documentary Essays on the Life and Work of Aldus Manutius*. San Francisco: B. M. Rosenthal, 1988.

Fletcher, Jennifer M. "Bellini's Social World." In Humfrey, *The Cambridge Companion to Bellini*, 13–47.

Fletcher, Jennifer M. "Isabella d'Este and Giovanni Bellini's 'Presepio.'" *Burlington Magazine* 113, no. 825 (1971): 703–11.

Folicaldi, Francesca. *Il numero e le sue forme: Storie di poliedri da Platone a Poinsot passando per Luca Pacioli*. Florence: Nardini, 2005.

Foppolo, Bonaventura. "La parabola del ramo veneziano dei Tasso da Cornello a Venezia." In *I Tasso e le poste d'Europa: Atti del Convegno Internazionale, Cornello di Tasso 1–3 giugno 2012*, 27–50. Comune di Camerata Cornello: Museo dei Tasso e della storia postale, 2012.

Fraser Jenkins, A. D. "Cosimo de' Medici's Patronage of Architecture and the Theory of Magnificence." *Journal of the Warburg and Courtauld Institutes* 33 (1970): 162–70.

Friedman, David. "'Fiorenza': Geography and Representation in the Fifteenth Century City View." *Zeitschrift für Kunstgeschichte* 64 (2001): 56–77.

Frommel, Christoph L. "Caravaggio's Frühwerk und der Kardinal del Monte." *Storia dell'arte* 9–10 (1971): 5–52.

Fusco, Laurie S., and Gino Corti. *Lorenzo de' Medici: Collector and Antiquarian*. Cambridge: Cambridge University Press, 2006.

Gaeta, Franco. "L'idea di Venezia." In Arnaldi and Stocchi, *Dal primo quattrocento al concilio di trento III*, 565–98.

Gaeta, Franco. "Storiografia, coscienza nazionale e politica culturale nella Venezia del Rinascimento." In Arnaldi and Stocchi, *Dal primo quattrocento al concilio di trento III*, 1–91.

Galeazzo, Ludovica. "Entrepreneurship beyond Convent Walls: The Augustinian Nuns of S. Caterina dei Sacchi in Venice." In *Convent Networks in Early Modern Italy*, edited by Marilyn Dunn and Saundra Weddle. Turnhout: Brepols, 2020.

Galeazzo, Ludovica. "Orti e giardini di proprietà del monastero di San Domenico di Castello." In Calabi and Galeazzo, *Acqua e cibo a Venezia*, 229.

Galeazzo, Ludovica. *Venezia e i margini urbani: L'insula dei Gesuiti in età mod-*

erna. Venice: Istituto Veneto di Scienze Lettere ed Arti, 2018.

Galeazzo, Ludovica, and Martina Massaro. "Le Digital Humanities per i cinquecento anni del Ghetto di Venezia." In *La città multietnica nel mondo mediterraneo: Porti, cantieri, minoranze*, Proceedings of the International Conference of AISU (Genoa, June 4–5, 2018), edited by Alireza Naser Eslami and Marco Folin, 181–92. Milan: Bruno Mondadori, 2019.

Gamberini, Andrea, and Giuseppe Petralia, eds. *Linguaggi politici nell'Italia del Rinascimento: Atti del Convegno, Pisa, 9–11 novembre 2006*. Rome: Viella, 2007.

Gandini, Conte. "The Court of Ferrara in the Fifteenth Century." *Scottish Review* 25 (1895): 70–90.

Gardin, Paolo. "Dalla trasformazione alla manutenzione e conservazione del patrimonio urbano." *Insula: Un futuro per Venezia*. Accessed July 26, 2020. http://www.insula.it/images/pdf/resource/quadernipdf/Q04-07.pdf.

Gasparotto, Davide. "Giovanni Bellini and Landscape." In *Giovanni Bellini: Landscapes of Faith in Renaissance Venice*, 11–24. Los Angeles: J. Paul Getty Museum, 2017.

Gattinoni (Rosolino), Gregorio. *Il campanile di San Marco in Venezia: Monografia storica*. Venice: Giovanni Fabbris, 1910; Emiliani, 1912.

Gaudio, Michael. "Matthew Paris and the Cartography of the Margins." *Gesta* 39, no. 1 (2000): 50–57.

Gentilcore, David. "The Cistern-System of Early Modern Venice: Technology, Politics and Culture in a Hydraulic Society." *Water History* 13 (2021): 1–32.

Germanisches National Museum. "Dürers Personen-Netzwerk." Last modified 2012. http://duererforschung.gnm.de/index.php.?id=430&show_id=749.

Gerwitz, Paul. "On 'I Know It When I See It.'" *Yale Law Journal* 105, no. 4 (January 1996): 1023–47.

Gianighian, Giorgio. "Venice, Italy." In *Management of Historic Centres*, edited by Robert Pickard, 162–86. London: Taylor and Francis, 2013.

Gianighian, Giorgio, and Paolina Pavanini. *Dietro i palazzi: Tre secoli di architettura minore a Venezia, 1492–1803*. Venice: Arsenale, 1984.

Gilbert, Creighton. "When Did a Man in the Renaissance Grow?" *Studies in the Renaissance* 14 (1967): 7–32.

Girón Pascual, Rafael M. "'Cruzando aceros': El comercio de espadas entre España e Italia en los siglos XVI y XVII." *Gladius* 36 (2016): 161–79.

Gombrich, Ernst H. *Norm and Form*. London: Phaidon, 1966.

Goy, Richard J. *Building Renaissance Venice: Patrons, Architects and Builders, c. 1430–1500*. New Haven, CT: Yale University Press, 2006.

Goy, Richard J. *The House of Gold: Building a Palace in Medieval Venice*. Cambridge: Cambridge University Press, 1992.

Grafton, Anthony. *Leon Battista Alberti: Master Builder of the Italian Renaissance.* New York: Hill and Wang, 2000.

Gross, Jonathan. "Help Find All 103 Bell Towers in This 500-Year-Old Map of Venice, Italy." 2014. Accessed August 12, 2020. http://gigapan.com/gigapans/166926.

Guerra, Francesco, Caterina Balletti, Carlo Monti, Evangelos Livieratos, and Chryssoula Boutoura. "Informatica e 'infografica' per lo studio della veduta prospettica di Venezia." In Romanelli, Biadene, and Tonini, *A volo d'uccello*, 92–100.

Gurney, Tessa C. "Echoes of Wartime in Late Sixteenth Century Italian Comedy." *Journal of Iberian and Latin American Studies* 24, no. 1 (2018): 155–74.

Hale, John R., ed. *Renaissance Venice.* London: Faber and Faber, 1974.

Haller von Hallerstein, Helmut Freiherr. "Grösse und Quellen des Vermögens von hundert Nürnberger Bürgern um 1500." In *Beiträge zur Wirtschaftsgeschichte Nürnbergs*, vol. 1, 117–76. Nuremberg: Selbstverl. des Stadtrats, 1967.

Hamilton, Paul. "The Palazzo dei Camerlenghi in Venice." *Journal of the Society of Architectural Historians* 42, no. 3 (1983): 258–71.

Handbook of the Cleveland Museum of Art. Cleveland: Cleveland Museum of Art, 1978.

Haraway, Donna. "Situated Knowledges: The Science Question in Feminism and the Privilege of Partial Perspective." *Feminist Studies* 14, no. 3 (1988): 575–99.

Harris, John. *Moving Rooms: The Trade in Architectural Salvages.* New Haven, CT: Yale University Press, 2007.

Harvey, P. D. A. *The History of Topographical Maps: Symbols, Pictures and Surveys.* London: Thames and Hudson, 1980.

Harzen, Ernst. "Jacob de Barbary, der Meister mit dem Schlangenstabe." *Archiv für die zeichnenden Künste* 1 (1855): 210–20.

Hattori, Yoshihisa, ed. *Political Order and Forms of Communication in Medieval and Early Modern Europe.* Rome: Viella, 2014.

Heinemann, Fritz. *Giovanni Bellini e i Belliniani.* Venice: Neri Pozza, 1962.

Henry, Chriscinda. *Playful Pictures: Art, Leisure, and Entertainment in the Venetian Renaissance Home.* University Park: Pennsylvania State University Press, 2021.

Heriberg, Johan Ludvig. *Beiträge zur Geschichte Georg Valla und Bibliothek.* Wiesbaden: Harrassowitz, 1968.

Herlihy, David. "The Population of Verona in the First Century of Venetian Rule." In Hale, *Renaissance Venice*, 91–120.

Hess, Daniel, and Thomas Eser, eds. *The Early Dürer.* London: Thames and Hudson, 2012. Exhibition catalog.

Hetherington, Paul. "The Venetian Well-

Heads at Hever Castle, Kent." *Apollo* 121, no. 277 (1985): 162–67.

Hind, Arthur M. *Early Italian Engraving: A Critical Catalogue with Complete Reproduction of All the Prints Described.* 7 vols. London: B. Quaritch, 1938–48.

Howard, Deborah. *Jacopo Sansovino: Architecture and Patronage in Renaissance Venice.* 1975. Reprint, New Haven, CT: Yale University Press, 1987.

Howard, Deborah. *Venice and the East: The Impact of the Islamic World on Venetian Architecture, 1100–1500.* New Haven, CT: Yale University Press, 2006.

Howard, Deborah. "Venice as a Dolphin: Further Investigations into Jacopo de' Barbari's View." *Artibus et Historiae* 18, no. 35 (1997): 101–11.

Howard, Deborah, and Carlo Corsato, eds. *Santa Maria Gloriosa dei Frari: Immagini di devozione, spazi della fede / Devotional Spaces, Images of Piety.* Padua: Centro Studi Antoniani, 2015.

Huffman, Kristin Love. "Jacopo de' Barbari's *View of Venice* (1500): 'Image Vehicles' and 'Pathways of Culture' Past and Present." *Mediterranea* 4 (2019): 165–214.

Humfrey, Peter, ed. *The Cambridge Companion to Giovanni Bellini.* Cambridge: Cambridge University Press, 2004.

Hurlburt, Holly. *Daughter of Venice: Caterina Corner, Queen of Cyprus and Woman of the Renaissance.* New Haven, CT: Yale University Press, 2016.

Hurlburt, Holly. *The Dogaressa of Venice, 1200–1500: Wife and Icon.* New York: Palgrave Macmillan, 2006.

Huse, Norbert, and Wolfgang Wolters. *The Art of Renaissance Venice: Architecture, Sculpture, and Painting, 1460–1590.* Chicago: University of Chicago Press, 1990.

Israel, Uwe, Robert Jütte, and Reinhold C. Mueller, eds. *"Interstizi": Culture ebraico-cristiane a Venezia e nei suoi domini dal medioevo all'età moderna.* Rome: Edizioni di Storia e Letteratura, 2010.

Jackson, Margaret T. "A Venetian Wellhead." *Bulletin of the Minneapolis Museum of the Arts* 4, no. 7 (July 1915): 74–75.

Jacoby, Joachim. "Arbeitsunfall eines Malers im Jahr 1500: Überlegungen zu Jacopo de Barbari." *Dresdener Kunstblätter* 46, no. 1 (2002): 24–28.

Judde de Larivière, Claire. *Naviguer, commercer, gouverner économie maritime et pouvoirs à Venise: XVe–XVIe siècles.* Leiden: Brill, 2008.

Judde de Larivière, Claire. *The Revolt of Snowballs: Murano Confronts Venice, 1511.* Translated by Thomas V. Cohen. London: Routledge, 2018.

Judde de Larivière, Claire. "Voicing Popular Politics: The *Comandatore* of the Community of Murano in the Sixteenth Century." In *Voices and Texts in Early Modern Italian Society*, edited by Stefano Dall'Aglio et al., 37–51. London: Routledge, 2016.

Kazikli, Ertan. "Art Mapping Venice: Progress and Implementation

Choices." Last modified November 25, 2013. https://artmappingvenice .wordpress.com/2013/11/25/art -mapping-venice-progress-and -implementation-choices/.

Kemp, Martin. "Jacopo de' Barbari: *View of Venice*." In *Circa 1492: Art in the Age of Exploration*, edited by Jay A. Levenson, 253–55. Washington, DC: National Gallery of Art, 1991. Exhibition catalog.

King, Margaret. "An Inconsolable Father and His Humanist Consolers: Jacopo Antonio Marcello, Venetian Nobleman, Patron and Man of Letters." In *Supplementum Festivum: Studies in Honor of Paul Oskar Kristeller*, edited by James Hankins, 221–46. Binghamton, NY: Binghamton University Press, 1987.

Kirby, Jo, Susie Nash, and Joanna Cannon, eds. *Trade in Artists' Materials: Markets and Commerce in Europe to 1700*. London: Archetype, 2010.

Kittler, Juraj. "From Rags to Riches: The Limits of Early Paper Manufacturing and Their Impact on Book Print in Renaissance Venice." *Media History* 21, no. 1 (2015): 8–22.

Klein, Holger A. "Refashioning Byzantium in Venice, ca. 1200–1400." In *San Marco, Byzantium and the Myths of Venice*, edited by Henry Maguire and Robert S. Nelson, 193–226. Washington, DC: Dumbarton Oaks Research Library and Collection, 2010.

Koerner, Joseph L. *The Moment of Self-Portraiture in German Renaissance Art*. Chicago: University of Chicago Press, 1993.

Krischel, Roland. "The Inventory of the Venetian *Vendecolori* Jacopo de' Benedetti: The Non-pigment Materials." In Kirby, Nash, and Cannon, *Trade in Artists' Materials*, 253–66.

Krischel, Roland. "The Venetian Pigment Trade in the Sixteenth Century." In *Colors between Two Worlds: The Florentine Codex of Bernardino de Sahagún*, edited by Gerhard Wold and Joseph Connors with Louis A. Waldman, 317–32. Cambridge, MA: Villa I Tatti in association with Harvard University Press, 2011.

Krischel, Roland. "Zur Geschichte des venezianischen Pigmenthandels: Das Sortiment des Jacobus de Benedictis à Coloribus." *Wallraf-Richartz-Jahrbuch* 63 (2002): 93–158.

Kristeller, Paul. *L'oeuvre de Jacopo de' Barbari*. Paris: Sociéte Internat. Chalcographique, 1896.

Labalme, Patricia. *Bernardo Giustiniani: A Venetian of the Quattrocento*. Rome: Edizioni di Storia e Letteratura, 1969.

Labalme, Patricia, Laura Sanguineti White, and Linda Carroll. "How to (and How Not to) Get Married in Sixteenth-Century Venice (Selections from the Diaries of Marin Sanudo)." *Renaissance Quarterly* 52, no. 1 (1999): 43–72.

Lambert, Giselle. *Les premières gravures italienne: Quattrocento du cinquecento. Inventaire de la collection du Dépar-*

tement des Estampes et de la Photographie. Paris: Bibliotèque nationale de France, 1999.

Landau, David. "Printmaking in Venice and the Veneto." In Martineau and Hope, *The Genius of Venice*, 303–54.

Landau, David, and Peter Parshall. *The Renaissance Print, 1470–1550*. New Haven, CT: Yale University Press, 1994.

Lane, Frederic C. "Naval Actions and Fleet Organization, 1499–1502." In Hale, *Renaissance Venice*, 146–73.

Lane, Frederic C. "Venetian Merchant Galleys, 1300–1334: Private and Communal Operation." *Speculum* 38, no. 2 (1963): 179–205.

Lane, Frederic C. *Venetian Ships and Shipbuilders of the Renaissance*. Westport, CT: Greenwood, 1975.

Lane, Frederic C. *Venice: A Maritime Republic*. Baltimore, MD: Johns Hopkins University Press, 1973.

Larner, John. "The Church and the Quattrocento Renaissance in Geography." *Renaissance Studies* 12, no. 1 (1998): 26–39.

Lassner, Jacob. *The Topography of Baghdad in the Middle Ages*. Detroit: Wayne State University Press, 1970.

Lauber, Rosella. "Domenico di Piero." In *Il collezionismo d'arte a Venezia: Dalle origini al Cinquecento*, edited by Linda Borean, Michel Hochmann, Rosella Lauber, and Stefania Mason Rinaldi, 269–70. Venice: Marsilio, 2008.

Lauber, Rosella. "'Ornamento lodevole' e 'ornatissima di pietre': Marcantonio Michiel nella Chiesa veneziana di Santa Maria della Carità." *Arte veneta* 55 (1999): 144–50.

Lazari, Vincenzo. *Notizia delle opere d'arte e d'antichità della Raccolta Correr di Venezia*. Venice: Tip. del Commercio, 1859.

Lefebvre, Henri. *The Production of Space*. Translated by Donald Nicholson-Smith. Oxford: Blackwell, 1991.

L'Eremita Venezia. *Dissertazione sui campanili di Venezia: Con un appendice sopra i comignoli ed alture*. Venice: Tip. Ex Cordella, 1891.

Lestringant, Frank. *Le Livre des Isles: Atlas et récits insulaires de la genèse à Jules Verne*. Geneva: Droz, 2002.

Levenson, Jay A. "Jacopo de' Barbari and Northern Art of the Early Sixteenth Century." PhD diss., Columbia University, 1978.

Levi, Cesare Augusto. *I campanili di Venezia: Notizie storiche*. Venice: Ongania, 1890.

Lincoln, Evelyn. *The Invention of the Renaissance Printmaker*. New Haven, CT: Yale University Press, 2000.

Lorenz, Hellmut. "Überlegungen zum venezianischen Palastbau der Renaissance." *Zeitschrift für Kunstgeschichte* 43, no. 1 (1980): 33–53.

Lorenzi, Giambattista. *Monumenti per servire alla storia del Palazzo Ducale di Venezia: Serie di atti pubblici dal 1253 al 1797*. Venice: Marco Visentini, 1868.

Lowry, Martin. *Nicholas Jenson and the*

Bibliography

Rise of Venetian Publishing in Renaissance Europe. Oxford: Blackwell, 1991.

Lowry, Martin. *The World of Aldus Manutius: Business and Scholarship in Renaissance Venice.* Oxford: Basil Blackwell, 1979.

Luber, Katherine Crawford. *Albrecht Dürer and the Venetian Renaissance.* Cambridge: Cambridge University Press, 2005.

Lucco, Mauro. "Bellini and Flemish Painting." In Humfrey, *The Cambridge Companion to Giovanni Bellini,* 75–94.

Lucco, Mauro, and G. C. F. Villa, eds. *Giovanni Bellini.* Milan: Silvana, 2008.

Ludolphy, Ingetraut. *Friedrich der Weise: Kurfürst von Sachsen, 1463–1525.* Göttingen: Vandenhoeck and Ruprecht, 1984.

Ludwig, Gustav. "Archivalische Beiträge zur Geschichte der Venezianischen Malerei." *Jahrbuch der Königlich Preussischen Kunstsammlungen* 26, supplement (1905): 83–88.

Lupprian, Karl-Ernst. *Il Fondaco dei Tedeschi e la sua funzione di controllo del commercio tedesco a Venezia.* Venice: Centro Tedesco di Studi Veneziani, 1978.

Lussey, Natalie. "Staying Afloat: The Vavassore Workshop and the Role of the Minor Publisher in Sixteenth Century Venice." *Kunsttexte.de* 2 (2017): 1–30.

Luzio, Alessandro. "Disegni topografici e pitture dei Bellini." *Archivio storico dell'arte* 1 (1888): 276–78.

Luzzatto, Gino, ed. *I prestiti della Repubblica di Venezia, Sec. XIII–XV.* Vol. 1 of *Documenti finanziari della Repubblica di Venezia.* Padua: A. Draghi, 1929.

Mackenney, Richard. *Tradesmen and Traders: The World of the Guilds in Venice and Europe, c. 1250–1650.* Edited by Anonymous. London: Croom Helm, 1987.

Maier, Jessica. "Francesco Rosselli's Lost View of Rome: An Urban Icon and Its Progeny." *Art Bulletin* 94, no. 3 (2012): 395–411.

Mallett, Michael. *The Military Organization of a Renaissance State: Venice, 1400–1617.* Cambridge: Cambridge University Press, 1984.

Maltese, Corrado. "La prospettiva curva di Leonardo da Vinci e uno strumento di Baldassarre Lanci." In *La prospettiva rinascimentale: Codificazioni e trasgressioni,* vol. 1, edited by Marisa Dalai-Emiliani, 417–25. Florence: Centro Di, 1980.

Maretto, Paolo. *La casa veneziana nella storia della città dalle origini all'ottocento.* Venice: Marsilio, 1986.

Marin, Louis. "Establishing a Signification for Social Space: Demonstration, Cortege, Parade, Procession." In *On Representation,* translated by Catherine Porter, 38–53. Stanford, CA: Stanford University Press, 2001.

Marino, John. "Administrative Mapping

in the Italian States." In *Monarchs, Ministers, and Maps: The Emergence of Cartography as a Tool of Government in Early Modern Europe*, edited by David Buisseret, 5–25. Chicago: Newberry Library, 1992.

Markey, Lia. *Merlo's Map: The Religious Geography of Venice*. Virtual exhibition, Newberry Library, 2017. Accessed August 12, 2020. https://publications.newberry.org/venice/.

Markham Schulz, Anne. *Woodcarving and Woodcarvers in Venice, 1350–1550*. Florence: Centro Di, 2011.

Martin, Andrew John. "Anton Kolb und Jacopo de' Barbari: Venedig im Jahre 1500." In *Pinxit/sculpsit/fecit, Kunsthistorische Studien: Festschrift für Bruno Bushart*, edited by Bärbel Hamacher and Christi Karnehm, 84–94. Munich: Deutscher Kunstverlag, 1994.

Martin, Lilian Ray. *The Art and Archaeology of Venetian Ships and Boats*. College Station: Texas A&M University Press, 2001.

Martineau, Jane, and Charles Hope, eds. *The Genius of Venice, 1500–1600*. London: Royal Academy of Arts, 1983. Exhibition catalog.

Marx, Barbara. "Wandering Objects, Migrating Artists: The Appropriation of Italian Renaissance Art by German Courts in the Sixteenth Century." In *Forging European Identities, 1400–1700*, vol. 4 of *Cultural Exchange in Early Modern Europe*, edited by Herman Roodenburg, 178–226.

Cambridge: Cambridge University Press, 2006–7.

Masciantonio, Andrea. "'Per la materia difficilissima': Spunti per una lettura d'insieme della veduta prospettica di Venezia." In Romanelli, Biadene, and Tonini, *A volo d'uccello*, 76–83.

Mason, Stefania. "À l'enseigne du calice et de la lune: Les Bontempelli, marchands, commanditaires et collectionneurs." *Revue de l'art* 160, no. 2 (2008): 35–44.

Massaro, Martina. "Gli investimenti ebraici a Venezia al principio del XIX secolo: Il ruolo dei Treves e l'acquisto della procuratia a San Marco." *Venetica* 3, no. 2 (2016): 7–28.

Massaro, Martina. "The Trade in Seventeenth and Eighteenth Centuries." In Calabi, *Venice, the Jews, and Europe*, 318–23.

Massey, Lyle. *Picturing Space, Displacing Bodies: Anamorphosis in Early Modern Theories of Perspective*. University Park: Pennsylvania State University Press, 2003.

Matthew, Louisa C. "Painters Marketing Paintings in Fifteenth and Sixteenth-Century Florence and Venice." In De Marchi and Van Miegroet, *Mapping Markets for Paintings in Europe 1450–1750*, 307–27.

Matthew, Louisa C. "'Vendecolori a Venezia': The Reconstruction of a Profession." *Burlington Magazine* 144, no. 1196 (2002): 680–86.

Matthew, Louisa C. "Were There Open Markets for Pictures in Renaissance

Bibliography

Venice?" In Fantoni, Matthew, and Matthews-Grieco, *The Art Market in Italy*, 253–61.

Matthew, Louisa C., and Barbara H. Berrie. "'Memoria de colori che bisognino torre a vinetia': Venice as a Centre for the Purchase of Painters' Colours." In Kirby, Nash, and Cannon, *Trade in Artists' Materials*, 245–52.

Mazzariol, Giuseppe, and Terisio Pignatti. *La pianta di Jacopo de' Barbari.* Venice: Cassa di Risparmio, 1962.

Mazzotta, Daniela. "L'acquedotto di Venezia." In *Archeologia industriale nel Veneto*, edited by Franco Mancuso, 171–72. Milan: Giunta Regionale del Veneto / Silvano Editoriale, 1990.

McAndrew, John. *Venetian Architecture of the Early Renaissance.* Cambridge, MA: MIT Press, 1981.

McNeil, Peter, and Giorgio Riello. *Luxury: A Rich History.* Oxford: Oxford University Press, 2016.

Media Center for Art History, Columbia University. "Mapping the Art and Architecture of Renaissance Venice." 2002–5. Accessed August 12, 2020. http://projects.mcah.columbia.edu /venice/index.html.

Meiss, Millard. "'Highlands' in the Lowlands: Jan van Eyck, the Master of Flémalle and the Franco-Italian Tradition." *Gazette des beaux-arts* 57, n.s. 6 (1961): 273–314.

Meiss, Millard. "Strabo's Geography in Albi." In *Andrea Mantegna as Illumi-*

nator. New York: Columbia University Press, 1957.

Meriam Bullard, Melissa, and Nicolai Rubinstein. "Lorenzo de' Medici's Acquisition of the Sigillo di Nerone." *Journal of the Warburg and Courtauld Institutes* 62 (1999): 283–86.

Merrifield, Andy. *Henri Lefebvre: A Critical Introduction.* New York: Routledge, 2006.

Michela, Ignazio. *Memoria sull'origine e sullo sviluppo del progetto di condurre acqua potabile dal continente a Venezia.* Turin: Tipografia Zecchi e Bona, 1842.

Michiel, Marcantonio. *Notizia d'opere di disegno, pubblicata e illustrata da D. Jacopo Morelli: Seconda edizione riveduta ed aumentata per cura di G. Frizzoni.* Bologna: Nicola Zanichelli, 1884.

Modesti, Paola. "Quasi come in un dipinto: La città e l'architettura nel De situ urbis Venetae di Marcantonio Sabellico." *Arte Veneta: Rivista di storia dell'arte* 66 (2010): 17–35.

Moffatt, Constance. "Leonardo's Maps." In *Illuminating Leonardo: A Festschrift for Carlo Pedretti Celebrating His 70 Years of Scholarship (1944–2014),* edited by Sara Taglialagamba, Constance J. Moffatt, and Carlo Pedretti, 342–58. Boston: Brill, 2016.

Molà, Luca. *The Silk Industry of Renaissance Venice.* Baltimore, MD: Johns Hopkins University Press, 2000.

Molmenti, Pompeo. "Venice, Italy." *Art Journal* 1839–1912 (March 1900).

Molmenti, Pompeo. *Venice: Its Individual Growth from the Earliest Beginnings to the Fall of the Republic.* Translated by Horatio Brown. Vol. 2. London: John Murray, 1907.

Monteleone, Cosimo. "The Mathematical Space of Daniele Barbaro." In *Nexus Architecture and Mathematics Conference Book,* edited by Kim Williams and Marco Bevilacqua, 49–54. Pisa: KWB, 2018.

Monteleone, Cosimo. "I poliedri regolari e semi-regolari tra storia, teorie e nuove frontiere della rappresentazione." In *Territori e frontiere della rappresentazione: Atti del 39° Convegno internazionale dei docenti delle discipline della rappresentazione, Napoli, 14–15–16 settembre 2017,* edited by Antonella di Luggo, 201–8. Rome: Gangemi, 2017.

Monteleone, Cosimo. *La prospettiva di Daniele Barbaro: Note critiche e trascrizione del manoscritto It. IV, 39=5446.* Rome: Aracne, 2020.

Moretti, Silvia. "I Domenicani dei Santi Giovanni e Paolo a Venezia nel XVI secolo: Contraddizioni di un margine urbano." *Mélanges de l'École Française de Rome: Italie et Méditerranée* 116, no. 2 (2005): 641–63.

Mori, Attilio, and Giuseppe Boffito, eds. *Firenze nelle vedute e piante: Studio storico, topografico e cartografico.* Florence: Giunta, 1926.

Moro, Giacomo. "Insegne librarie e marche tipografiche in un registro veneziano del '500." *La bibliofilia,* no. 1 (January–April 1989): 51–80.

Morresi, Manuela. *Jacopo Sansovino.* Milan: Electa, 2000.

Morresi, Manuela. *Piazza San Marco: Istituzioni, poteri e architettura a Venezia nel primo Cinquecento.* Milan: Electa, 1999.

Moskowitz, Anita. "A Venetian Wellhead in Toledo." *Source: Notes in the History of Art* 14, no. 2 (1995): 1–6.

Mueller, Reinhold C. "Les prêteurs juifs de Venise au Moyen Âge." *Annales. Histoire, Sciences Sociales* 30, no. 6 (1975): 1277–302.

Mueller, Reinhold C. *The Venetian Money Market: Banks, Panics and the Public Debt, 1200–1500.* Baltimore, MD: Johns Hopkins University Press, 1997.

Muir, Edward. *Civic Ritual in Renaissance Venice.* 1981. Reprint, Princeton, NJ: Princeton University Press, 1986.

Müller, Matthias. "Im Wettstreit mit Apelles: Hofkünstler als Akteure und Rezepteure im Austausch- und Konkurrenzverhältnis europäischer Höfe zu Beginn der Frühen Neuzeit." In *Vorbild, Austausch, Konkurrenz: Höfe und Residenzen in der gegenseitigen Wahrnehmung,* edited by Werner Paravicini and Jörg Wettlaufer, 173–91. Ostfildern: J. Thorbecke, 2010.

Müntz, Eugène. *Les arts à la cour des papes pendant le XV et le XVI siècle: Recueil de documents inédits tirés des archives et des bibliothèques romaines.* 3 vols. Paris: E. Thorin, 1878–82.

Mussini, Massimo, and Luigi Grasselli.

Piero della Francesca: De prospectiva pingendi. Sansepolcro: Aboca, 2008.

Nadin Bassani, Lucia. *Migrazioni e integrazione: Il caso degli albanesi a Venezia, 1479–1552*. Rome: Bulzoni, 2008.

Nagel, Alexander, and Christopher S. Wood. "Interventions: Toward a New Model of Renaissance Anachronism." *Art Bulletin* 87, no. 3 (2005): 403–15.

Nardi, Bruno. "La Scuola di Rialto e l'umanesimo veneziano." In *Umanesimo europeo e umanesimo veneziano*, edited by Vittore Branca, 93–139. Florence: Sansoni, 1963.

Neerfeld, Christiane. *Historia per forma di diaria: La cronachistica veneziana contemporanea a cavallo tra il Quattro e il Cinquecento*. Venice: Istituto Veneto di Scienze Lettere ed Arti, 2006.

Nicco Fasola, Giusta. *De prospectiva pingendi: Piero della Francesca*. Florence: Sansoni, 1942.

Nonaka, Natsumi. *Renaissance Porticoes and Painted Pergolas: Nature and Culture in Early Modern Italy*. London: Routledge, 2017.

Nuovo, Angela. *The Book Trade in the Italian Renaissance*. Leiden: Brill, 2013.

Nuovo, Angela. "Transferring Humanism: The Edition of Vitruvius by Lucimborgo De Gabiano (Lyon, 1523)." In *Lux Librorum: Essays on Books and History for Chris Coppens*, 17–37. Mechelen: Flanders Book Historical Society, 2018.

Nuovo, Angela, and Christian Coppens. *I Giolito e la stampa nell'Italia del XVI secolo*. Geneva: Droz, 2005.

Nuti, Lucia. "The Perspective Plan in the Sixteenth Century: The Invention of a Representational Language." *Art Bulletin* 76, no. 1 (1994): 105–28.

Oberhuber, Konrad. "Mantegna e il ruolo delle stampe: Un prototipo di innovazione artistica in Italia e al Nord." In *Il Rinascimento a Venezia e la pittura del Nord ai tempi di Bellini, Dürer, Tiziano*, edited by Bernard Aikema, 144–49. Milan: Bompiani, 1999.

Onda, Sebatiano. *La chiesa di San Francesco della Vigna: Guida artistica*. Venice: Parrocchia di San Francesco della Vigna, 2003.

Osborne, John. "The 'Cross-under-Arch' Motif in Ninth-Century Venetian Sculpture: An Imperial Reading." *Thesaurismata* 27 (1997): 7–18.

Padrón, Ricardo. *The Spacious Word: Cartography, Literature, and Empire in Early Modern Spain*. Chicago: University of Chicago Press, 2004.

Pannizut, Mario. *Venice Bells*. 2018. CD-ROM. https://www.venicebells.net/.

Panofsky, Erwin. "Dürers Darstellungen des Apollo und ihr Verhältnis zu Barbari." *Jahrbuch der Preuszischen Kunstsammlungen* 41 (1920): 359–77.

Panofsky, Erwin. *The Life and Art of Albrecht Dürer*. 8th ed. Princeton, NJ: Princeton University Press, 1995.

Panofsky, Erwin. "Die Perspektive als 'symbolische Form.'" *Vorträge der Bibliothek Warburg* 4 (1927): 258–330.

Paoletti, Paolo. *L'architettura e la scultura del Rinascimento a Venezia: Ricerche storico-artistiche.* Vol. 2. Venice: Ongania-Naya, 1893–97.

Parker, Grant. "*Ex Oriente Luxuria*: Indian Commodities and Roman Experience." *Journal of Economic and Social History of the Orient* 45, no. 1 (2002): 40–95.

 Pasero, Carlo. "Giacomo Franco, editore, incisore e calcografo nei secoli XVI e XVII." *La bibliofilia* 37, nos. 8–10 (August–October 1935): 332–56.

Pastorello, Ester. *Tipografi, editori, librai a Venezia nel secolo XVI.* Florence: Olschki, 1924.

Pattanaro, Alessandra. "Il paesaggio dipinto fra Quattrocento e Cinquecento: Storia dell'arte e memoria del territorio." In *Il paesaggio costruito, il paesaggio nell'arte*, edited by Gianmario Guidarelli and Elena Svalduz, 91–103. Padua: Padova University Press, 2017.

Paulin, Elisa. "Il nucleo di matrici xilografiche a soggetto religioso appartenenti ai legni della collezione Correr: Analisi e prime attribuzioni." *Studi di Memofonte* 17 (2016): 58–80.

Pavanini, Paola. "Venezia verso la pianificazione? Bonifiche urbane nel XVI secolo a Venezia." In *D'une ville à l'autre*, edited by Jean-Claude Marie Vigeuer, 485–507. Rome: Ecole Française de Rome, 1989.

Paviot, Jacques. "La mappemonde attribuée à Jan van Eyck par Fàcio: Une pièce à retirer du catalogue de son oeuvre." *Revue des archéologues et historiens d'art de Louvain* 24 (1991): 57–62.

Pertusi, Agostino. "Gli inizi della storiografia umanistica nel Quattrocento." In *La storiografia veneziana fino al secolo XVI: Aspetti e problemi*, edited by Agostino Pertusi, 269–332. Florence: Olschki, 1970.

Pesenti, Giuliano. "Libri censurati a Venezia nei secoli XVI–XVII." *Bibliofilia* 58 (1956): 15–30.

Pettegree, Andrew. *The Book in the Renaissance.* New Haven, CT: Yale University Press, 2010.

Pettegree, Andrew. *The Invention of News: How the World Came to Know about Itself.* New Haven, CT: Yale University Press, 2014.

Pfisterer, Ulrich. "The Muses' Grief: Jacopo de' Barbari on Painting, Poetry and Cultural Transfer in the North." In *The Muses and Their Afterlife in Post-classical Europe*, edited by Kathleen W. Christian, Clare E. L. Guest, and Claudia Wedepohl, 75–101. London: Warburg Institute, 2014.

Pignatti, Terisio. "La Pianta di Venezia di Jacopo de' Barbari." *Bollettino dei Musei Civici Veneziani* 9, nos. 1–2 (1964): 9–49.

Pinto, John. "Origins and Development of the Ichnographic City Plan." *Journal of the Society of Architectural Historians* 35, no. 1 (1976): 35–50.

Poggioli, Sylvia. "Long Hidden, Vatican Painting Linked to Native Americans." *The Two-Way*, National Pub-

lic Radio, May 5, 2013. https://
www.npr.org/sections/thetwo
-way/2013/05/05/180860991/long
-hidden-vatican-painting-linked
-to-native-americans.

Priester, Ann E. "The Belltowers of Medieval Rome and the Architecture
of *Renovatio*." PhD diss., Princeton
University, 1996.

Priester, Ann E. "The Italian Campanile:
Where Did It Come From?" In *Pra-
tum Romanum: Festschrift Richard
Krautheimer*, edited by Renate L.
Colella and Meredith J. Gill, 259–75.
Wiesbaden: Ludwig Reichert Ver-
lag, 1997.

Procter, Ben. *William Randolph Hearst:
The Early Years, 1863–1910*. Oxford:
Oxford University Press, 1988.

Pullan, Brian. *Rich and Poor in Renaissance Venice: The Social Institutions
of a Catholic State, to 1620*. Oxford:
Blackwell, 1971.

Pulsifer, William Henry. *Notes for a His-
tory of Lead and an Inquiry into the
Development of the Manufacture of
White Lead and Lead Oxides*. New
York: D. Van Nostrand, 1888.

Puppi, Loredana Olivato, and Leonello
Puppi. *Mauro Codussi*. Milan: Electa,
1977.

Queen's University and Radbound University, KIK-IRPA. "Closer to van
Eyck." Accessed October 30, 2020.
http://closertovaneyck.kikirpa.be/.

Rebel, Ernst. *Albrecht Dürer: Maler und
Humanist*. Munich: Orbis Verlag,
1996.

Resini, Daniele. *Venice from the Bell Towers*. London: Merrell, 2002.

Reske, Christoph. *Produktion der sche-
delschen Weltchronik*. Wiesbaden:
Harrassowitz, 2000.

Reynolds, David West. "*Forma urbis romae*: The Severan Marble Plan and
the Urban Form of Ancient Rome."
PhD diss., University of Michigan,
1996.

Richardson, Brian. *Print Culture in Renaissance Italy: The Editor and the Vernacular Text, 1470–1600*. Cambridge:
Cambridge University Press, 1994.

Rizzi, Alberto. *Vere da pozzo di Venezia: I
puteali pubblici di Venezia e della sua
laguna / The Well-Heads of Venice:
Public Well-Heads in Venice and the
Islands of Its Lagoon*. 3rd ed. Venice:
Filippi Editore, 2007.

Roberts, Sean E. *Printing a Mediterranean
World: Florence, Constantinople, and
the Renaissance of Geography*. Cambridge, MA: Harvard University
Press, 2013.

Robison, Andrew. *Albrecht Dürer: Master Drawings, Watercolors, and Prints
from the Albertina*. Washington, DC:
National Gallery of Art, 2013. Exhibition catalog.

Rohricht, Reinhold, and Heinrich Meisner. *Deutsche Pilgerreisen nach dem
Heiligen Lande*. Berlin: Weidmann,
1880.

Romanelli, Giandomenico. "Venezia
1500." In Romanelli, Biadene, and
Tonini, *A volo d'uccello*, 12–18.

Romanelli, Giandomenico, Susanna Biadene, and Camillo Tonini, eds. *A volo d'uccello: Jacopo de' Barbari e le rappresentazioni di città nell'Europa del Rinascimento*. Venice: Arsenale, 1999. Exhibition catalog.

Romanelli, Rita. "'Cose lunghe come campanili': Fortuna e carattere delle torri medievali di Ravenna." *Arte medievale* 2nd ser., nos. 12–13 (2000): 49–64.

Romano, Dennis. "Gender and the Urban Geography of Renaissance Venice." *Journal of Social History* 23, no. 2 (1989): 339–53.

Romano, Dennis. *The Likeness of Venice: A Life of Doge Francesco Foscari, 1373–1457*. New Haven, CT: Yale University Press, 2007.

Romano, Dennis. *Patricians and Popolani: The Social Foundations of the Venetian Renaissance State*. Baltimore, MD: Johns Hopkins University Press, 1987.

Rosand, David. *Myths of Venice: The Figuration of a State*. Chapel Hill: University of North Carolina Press, 2001.

Rosand, David. *"Venetia Figurata: The Iconography of a Myth." In Interpretazioni veneziane: Studi di storia dell'arte in onore di Michelangelo Muraro*, 177–96. Venice: Arsenale, 1984.

Rose, Paul Lawrence. *The Italian Renaissance of Mathematics*. Geneva: Droz, 1975.

Rospocher, Massimo. "'In Vituperium Status Veneti': The Case of Niccolò Zoppino." *The Italianist* 34, no. 4 (2014): 349–61.

Rospocher, Massimo, and Rosa Salzberg. "An Evanescent Public Sphere: Voices, Spaces, and Publics in Venice during the Italian Wars." In *Beyond the Public Sphere: Opinions, Publics, Spaces in Early Modern Europe. XVI–XVIII*, edited by Massimo Rospocher, 93–114. Bologna: Il Mulino / Duncker & Humblot, 2012.

Rospocher, Massimo, and Rosa Salzberg. "'El vulgo zanza': Spazi pubblici, voci a Venezia durante le guerre d'Italia." *Storica* 48, no. XVI (2010): 83–120.

Ross, Elizabeth. *Picturing Experience in the Early Printed Book: Breydenbach's "Peregrinatio" from Venice to Jerusalem*. University Park: Pennsylvania State University Press, 2014.

Rossi, Irena Radić, Mariangela Nicolardi, and Katarina Batur. "The Gnalić Shipwreck: Microcosm of the Late Renaissance World." In *Croatia at the Crossroads: A Consideration of Archaeological and Historical Connectivity*, edited by David Davison, Vincent L. Gaffney, Preston T. Miracle, and Joanna R. Sofaer, 223–48. Oxford: Archaeopress, 2016.

Rössler, Jan-Christoph. *I palazzi veneziani: Storia, architettura, restauri*. Venice: Scripta, 2010.

Roth, Cecil. *Venice*. Philadelphia: Jewish Publication Society of America, 1930.

Rowe, D. J. *Lead Manufacturing in Britain: A History*. Abingdon, UK: Routledge, 1983.

Rozzo, Ugo. *Linee per una storia dell'edi-*

toria religiosa in Italia (1465–1600). Udine: Arti Grafiche Friulane, 1993.

Rupprich, Hans, ed. *Albrecht Dürer: Der schriftliche Nachlasse*. Vol. 1. Berlin: Deutschen Verein für Kunstwissenschaft, 1956–69.

Salzberg, Rosa. *Ephemeral City: Cheap Print and Urban Culture in Renaissance Venice*. Manchester: Manchester University Press, 2014.

Salzberg, Rosa. "'Per le piaze & sopra il Ponte': Reconstructing the Geography of Popular Print in Sixteenth-Century Venice." In *Geographies of the Book*, edited by Miles Ogborn and Charles W. J. Withers, 111–32. Farnham, UK: Ashgate, 2010.

Salzberg, Rosa. "'Selling Stories and Many Other Things in and through the City': Peddling Print in Renaissance Florence and Venice." *Sixteenth Century Journal* 42, no. 3 (2011): 737–59.

Salzberg, Rosa, and Massimo Rospocher. "Street Singers in Italian Renaissance Urban Culture and Communication." *Cultural and Social History* 9, no. 1 (2012): 9–26.

Schmid, Christian. *Stadt, Raum und Gesellschaft: Henri Lefebvre und die Theorie der Produktion des Raumes*. Munich: Franz Steiner, 2005.

Schmidt, Benjamin. *Inventing Exoticism: Geography, Globalism and Europe's Early Modern World*. Philadelphia: University of Pennsylvania Press, 2015.

Schulz, Juergen. "La grande veduta a volo d'uccello di Jacopo de' Barbari." In Romanelli, Biadene, and Tonini, *A volo d'uccello*, 58–68.

Schulz, Juergen. "The Houses of the Dandolo: A Family Compound in Medieval Venice." *Journal of the Society of Architectural Historians* 52, no. 4 (1993): 391–415.

Schulz, Juergen. "Jacopo de' Barbari's View of Venice: Map Making, City Views, and Moralized Geography before the Year 1500." *Art Bulletin* 60, no. 3 (1978): 425–74.

Schulz, Juergen. "La piazza medievale di San Marco." *Annali di Architettura* 4–5 (1992–93): 134–56.

Schulz, Juergen. "Pinturicchio and the Revival of Antiquity." *Journal of the Warburg and Courtauld Institutes* 25 (1962): 35–55.

Schulz, Juergen. "The Printed Plans and Panoramic Views of Venice (1486–1797)." *Saggi e memorie di storia dell'arte* 7 (1970): 5–182.

Schulz, Juergen. "La veduta di Venezia di Jacopo de' Barbari: Cartografia, vedute di città e geografia moralizzata nel Medioevo e nel Rinascimento." In *La cartografia tra scienza e arte: Carte e cartografi nel Rinascimento italiano*, 13–42. Modena: Panini, 1990.

Segre, Renata. "Before the Ghetto." In Calabi, *Venice, the Jews, and Europe*, 82–89.

Servolini, Luigi. *Jacopo de' Barbari*. Padua: Le Tre Venezie, 1944.

Settis, Salvatore. *Giorgione's Tempest: Interpreting the Hidden Subject*. Translated by Ellen Bianchini. Chicago: University of Chicago Press, 1990.

Shaw, Christine. *The Politics of Exile in Renaissance Italy*. Cambridge: Cambridge University Press, 2000.

Shaw, James E. "Institutional Controls and the Retail of Paintings: The Painters' Guild of Early-Modern Venice." In De Marchi and Van Miegroet, *Mapping Markets for Paintings in Europe 1450–1750*, 107–24.

Shaw, James E. *The Justice of Venice: Authorities and Liberties in the Urban Economy, 1550–1700*. Oxford: Oxford University Press, 2006.

Sheard, Wendy Stedman. "The Widener Orpheus: Attribution, Type, Invention." In *Collaboration in Italian Renaissance Art*, edited by Wendy Stedman Sheard and John T. Paoletti, 189–231. New Haven, CT: Yale University Press, 1978.

Shields, Rob. *Lefebvre, Love, and Struggle: Spatial Dialectics*. London: Routledge, 1999.

Silver, Larry. "Civic Courtship: Albrecht Dürer, the Saxon Duke, and the Emperor." In *The Essential Dürer*, edited by Larry Silver and Jeffrey Chipps Smith, 130–48. Philadelphia: University of Pennsylvania Press, 2010.

Silver, Larry. "'Figure Nude, Historie e Poesie': Jan Gossaert and the Renaissance Nude in the Netherlands." In "Renaissance en reformatie en de kunst in de Noordelijke Nederlanden," special issue, *Nederlands Kunsthistorisch Jaarboek (NKJ) / Netherlands Yearbook for History of Art* 37 (1986): 1–40.

Silver, Larry. *Marketing Maximilian: The Visual Ideology of a Holy Roman Emperor*. Princeton, NJ: Princeton University Press, 2008.

Simonsfeld, Henry. *Der Fondaco dei Tedeschi in Venedig und die Deutsch-Venetianischen Handelsbeziehungen*. Vol. 1. Stuttgart: J. G. Gotaa'schen Buchhandlung, 1887.

Skelton, Raleigh Ashlin. *Maps: A Historical Survey of Their Study and Collecting*. Chicago: University of Chicago Press, 1975.

Smith, Norris Kelly. "The Lost Tavolette." In *Here I Stand: Perspective from Another Point of View*. New York: Columbia University Press, 1994.

Sohm, Philip. *The Scuola Grande di San Marco, 1437–1550: The Architecture of a Venetian Lay Confraternity*. New York: Garland, 1982.

Sperling, Jutta. *Convents and the Body Politics in Late Renaissance Venice*. Chicago: University of Chicago Press, 1999.

Stanek, Łukasz. *Henri Lefebvre on Space: Architecture, Urban Research, and the Production of Theory*. Minneapolis: University of Minnesota Press, 2011.

Stanford University. "Digital Forma Urbis Romae Project." Accessed June 23, 2020. https://formaurbis.stanford.edu.

Stenhouse, William. "The *Forma urbis romae* before Nolli: Antiquarian

Scholarship in the Sixteenth and Seventeenth Centuries." In *Giambattista Nolli and Rome: Mapping the City before and after the Pianta Grande*, edited by Ian Verstegen and Allan Ceen, 15–26. Rome: Studium Urbis, 2013.

Sterling, Charles. "Jan van Eyck avant 1432. Appendice IV: La mappemonde de Jan van Eyck." *Revue de l'art* 33 (1976): 69–82.

Stöckly, Doris. *Le système de l'Incanto des galées du marché à Venise: Fin 13ᵉ–milieu 15ᵉ siècle*. Leiden: Brill, 1995.

Stoichita, Victor. *L'instauration du tableau: Métapeinture à l'aube des temps moderne*. 2nd ed. Geneva: Librairie Droz, 2017.

Strieder, Peter. "Ein Traum von Göttern und Heroen: Andreas Meinhardis Dialog über die Schönheit und den Ruhm der hochberühmten Stadt Albioris, gemeinhin Wittenberg gennant." *Anzeiger des germanischen Nationalmuseum* (2005): 25–34.

Stroffolino, Daniela. *La città misurata: Tecniche e strumenti di rilevamento nei trattati a stampa del Cinquecento*. Roma: Salerno, 1999.

Stroffolino, Daniela. "Tecniche e strumenti per 'misurare con la vista.'" In Romanelli, Biadene, and Tonini, *A volo d'uccello*, 38–51.

Summers, David. *The Judgment of Sense*. Cambridge: Cambridge University Press, 1987.

Summers, David. *Vision, Reflection, and Desire in Western Painting*. Chapel Hill: University of North Carolina Press, 2007.

Svalduz, Elena. "Al servizio del magistrato: I proti alle acque nel corso del primo secolo d'attività." In *Architetto sia l'ingegniero che discorre*, edited by Giuliana Mazzi and Stefano Zaggia, 233–68. Venice: Marsilio, 2004.

Svalduz, Elena. "In mezzo al'acqua / senza acqua." In Calabi and Galeazzo, *Acqua e cibo a Venezia*, 248–49.

Szépe, Helena K. "Artistic Identity in the Dream of Poliphilo." *Papers of the Bibliographical Society of Canada* 35, no. 1 (1997): 39–77.

Tafuri, Manfredo. "Il pubblico e il privato: Architettura e committenza a Venezia." In *Dal Rinascimento al Barocco*, vol. 6 of *Storia di Venezia dalle origini alla caduta della Serenissima*, edited by Gaetano Cozzi and Paolo Prodi. Rome: Istituto della Enciclopedia Italiana, 1994. Accessed July 26, 2020. http://treccani.it/enciclopedia/il-pubblico-e-il-privato-architettura-e-committenza-a-venezia_%28Storia-di-Venezia%29/.

Tafuri, Manfredo, ed. *Renovatio urbis: Venezia nell'età di Andrea Gritti, 1523–1538*. Rome: Officina, 1984.

Tafuri, Manfredo. "Sapienza di Stato e atti mancati: Architettura e tecnica urbana nella Venezia del 500." In *Architettura e utopia nella Venezia del Cinquecento*, edited by Lionello Puppi, Giulio Carlo Argan, Manfredo Tafuro, and Staale Sinding-Larsen,

16–39. Milan: Electa, 1980. Exhibition catalog.

Tafuri, Manfredo. *Venezia e il Rinascimento: Religione, scienza, architettura.* Turin: Einaudi, 1985.

Tafuri, Manfredo. *Venice and the Renaissance.* Cambridge, MA: MIT Press, 1989. Reprint, Cambridge, MA: MIT Press, 1995.

Takanashi, Mitsumasa. "New Acquisitions." *Annual Bulletin of the National Museum of Western Art* 46 (April 2011–March 2012): 9–13.

Talbot, Michael. "*Ore italiane:* The Reckoning of the Time of Day in Pre-Napoleonic Italy." *Italian Studies* 40, no. 1 (1985): 51–62.

Tassini, Giuseppe. *Alcuni palazzi ed antichi edifici di Venezia.* Venice: M. Fontana, 1879.

Tassini, Giuseppe. *Curiosità veneziane.* 4th ed. 1887. Reprint, Venice: Filippi, 1964.

Thomson, David. *Renaissance Architecture: Critics, Patrons, Luxury.* Manchester: Manchester University Press, 1993.

Thürlemann, Felix. "L'aquarelle de Dürer *fenedier klawsen:* La double mimesis dans l'analyse picturale d'un lieu géographique." *Revue de l'art* 137 (2002–3): 9–18.

Tonini, Camillo. "Una storia in appendice: La ristampa ottocentesca della Veduta prospettica di Venezia." In Romanelli, Biadene, and Tonini, *A volo d'uccello,* 84–91.

Tracy, David. "The Catholic Imagination: The Example of Michelangelo." In *Heavenly Bodies: Fashion and the Catholic Imagination,* edited by Andrew Bolton, 10–17. New York: Metropolitan Museum of Art, 2018. Exhibition catalog.

Trebbi, Giuseppe. "La società veneziana." In *Storia di Venezia: Dalle origini alla caduta della Serenissima,* vol. 6, *Dal Rinascimento al Barocco,* edited by Gaetano Cozzi and Paolo Prodi, 129–213. Rome: Istituto della Enciclopedia Italiana, 1994.

Trincanato, Egle Renata. *Venezia minore.* Milan: Edizioni del Milione, 1948.

Trivellato, Francesca. *The Familiarity of Strangers: The Sephardic Diaspora. Livorno and Cross-Cultural Trade in the Early Modern Period.* New Haven, CT: Yale University Press, 2009.

Trivellato, Francesca. "Jews and Credit in Early Modern Europe and the Mediterranean: From Usury to International Trade." In Calabi, *Venice, the Jews, and Europe,* 364–67.

Tüskés, Anna. "Venetian Well-Heads in Nineteenth-Century Taste." *Sculpture Journal* 19, no. 1 (2010): 49–61.

Tüskés, Anna. "Vere da pozzo veneziane in Ungheria." *Commentari d'arte* 17, no. 48 (2011): 61–74.

Tüskés, Anna. "Wells in the Medieval Churches of Venice." *Arte cristiana* 104, no. 897 (2016): 451–60.

Vagnetti, Luigi. *De naturali et artificiali perspectiva.* Florence: Grafistampa, 1979.

van der Sman, Gert Jan. "De eeuw van

Titiaan: Venetiaanse prenten uit de Renaissance." In *Le siècle de Titien: Gravures vénitiennes de la Renaissance*, 40–41. Zwolle: Waanders Uitgevers, 2003.

van Gelder, Maartje. "The People's Prince: Popular Politics in Early Modern Venice." *Journal of Modern History* 90, no. 2 (2018): 249–91.

van Gelder, Maartje, and Claire Judde de Larivière, eds. *Popular Politics in an Aristocratic Republic: Political Conflict and Social Contestation in Late Medieval and Early Modern Venice (Venice, 13th–18th Century)*. London: Routledge, 2020.

Vanzan Marchini, Nelli-Elena. *Venezia da laguna a città*. Venice: Arsenale, 1985.

Vasari, Giorgio. *Le vite de' più eccellenti pittori, scultori ed architettori*. Edited by Gaetano Milanesi. Florence: Sansoni, 1878–85.

Venice Boats. "Gilberto Penzo—Barche e Navi Veneziane." Accessed July 9, 2018. http://www.veniceboats.com/index.htm.

Venice Project Center. "Bells." Accessed July 26, 2020. http://bells.veniceprojectcenter.org/#/map.

Venice Project Center. "De' Barbari." Accessed August 12, 2020. http://www.veniceprojectcenter.org/vpc/application/de-barbari.

Venturi, Adolfo. "L'arte a Ferrara nel periodo di Borso d'Este." *Rivista storica italiana* 2 (1885): 687–749.

Venturi, Adolfo. "L'arte ferrarese nel periodo d'Ercole I d'Este." *Atti e memorie della Regia Deputazione di Storia Patria per le Provincie di Romagna* 6, 91–119. Modena: G. T. Vincenzi e nipoti, 1888.

Vertecchi, Giulia. *"Il masser ai formenti in Terra Nova": Il ruolo delle scorte granarie a Venezia nel XVIII secolo.* Rome: Croma, 2009.

Wangefelt Ström, Helena, and Federico Barbierato. "'Omne malum ab Aquilone': Images of the Evil North in Early Modern Italy and Their Impact on Cross-Religious Encounters." In *Visions of North in Premodern Europe*, edited by Dolly Jørgensen and Virginia Langum, 265–86. Turnhout: Brepols, 2018.

Warnke, Martin. *The Court Artist: On the Ancestry of the Modern Art*. Translated by David McLintock. Cambridge: Cambridge University Press, 1993.

Weddle, Saundra. "Technologies of Segregation in Early Modern Venice." WUSTL Digital Gateway Image Collections and Exhibitions. Accessed August 12, 2020. http://omeka.wustl.edu/omeka/exhibits/show/technologies-of-segregation/views-of-venice/jacopo-de—barbari-s-view-of-v.

Welch, Evelyn. *Shopping in the Renaissance: Consumer Cultures in Italy, 1400–1600*. New Haven, CT: Yale University Press, 2005.

Wiel, Alethea. "The Demolition of the Warehouse of the Persians in Venice." *Burlington Magazine* 13 (1908): 221–22.

Wilson, Bronwen. "Afterword: Ornament and the Fabrication of Early Modern Worlds." In *Bodies and Maps*, edited by Louisa Arizzoli and Maryanne Horowitz, 376–401. Leiden: Brill, 2020.

Wilson, Bronwen. "Venice, Print, and the Early Modern Icon." *Urban History* 33 (2006): 39–64.

Wilson, Bronwen. *The World in Venice: Print, the City, and Early Modern Identity.* Toronto: University of Toronto Press, 2005.

Wirobisz, André. "L'attività edilizia nel XIV e XV secolo." *Studi Veneziani* 7 (1965): 307–43.

Witcombe, Christopher L. C. E. *Copyright in the Renaissance: Prints and the "Privilegio" in Sixteenth-Century Venice and Rome.* Studies in Medieval and Reformation Thought, vol. 100. Leiden: Brill, 2004.

Woodward, David. "Paolo Forlani: Compiler, Engraver, Printer, or Publisher?" *Imago Mundi* 44 (1992): 45–64.

Worstbrock, F. J. "Hartmann Schedels 'Liber Antiquitatum cum epitaphiis et epigrammatibus': Zur Begründung und Erschliessung des historischen Gedächtnisses im deutschen Humanismus." In *Franz Josef Worstbrock: Ausgewählte Schriften*, vol. 2, edited by S. Köbele and A. Krass, 311–38. Stuttgart: Hirzel Verlag, 2005.

Yoon, Rangsook. "Dürer's First Journey to Venice: Revisiting and Reframing the Old Question." In *New Studies on Old Masters: Essays in Renaissance Art in Honour of Colin Eisler*, Essays and Studies 26, edited by John Garton and Diane Wolfthal, 69–87. Toronto: Center for Reformation and Renaissance Studies, 2011.

Zanelli, Guglielmo. *Navi, squeri, traghetti da Jacopo de' Barbari.* Venice: Centro Internazionale Della Grafica, 2011.

Zannini, Andrea. *Venezia città aperta: Gli stranieri e la Serenissima XIV–XVIII sec.* Venice: Marcianum, 2009.

Zanotto, Francesco. "Gallerie, Pinacoteche, Raccolte di oggetti d'arte, ecc." In *Venezia e le sue lagune*, vol. 2, part 2, 467–82. Venice: Antonelli, 1847.

Zanverdiani, Dario. "Manifatture." In Balistreri-Trincanato et al., *Venezia città mirabile*, 229–31.

Zanverdiani, Dario. "Navi." In Balistreri-Trincanato et al., *Venezia città mirabile*, 257–61.

Zimerman, Heinrich, and Franz Kreyczi. "Urkunden und Regesten aus dem K u K. Reichs-Finanz-Archiv." *Jahrbuch der Kunsthistorischen Sammlungen des allerhochsten Kaiserhauses* 3, no. 2 (1885): 1–81.

Zorzi, Alvise. *Venezia scomparsa.* Milan: Electa, 1971. Reprint, Milan: Mondadori, 2001.

Zorzi, Marino. "Stampa, illustrazione libraria e le origini dell'incisione figurative a Venezia." In *Il Quattrocento*, vol. 2 of *La pittura nel Veneto*, edited by Mauro Lucco, 686–702. Milan: Electa, 1990.

Zorzi, Marino. "Stampatori tedeschi a Venezia." In *Venezia e la Germania: Arte, politica, commercio: Due civiltà a confronto*, 115–40. Milan: Electa, 1986.

Zuchold, Gerd-H. "An Early Venetian Well-Head in the Isabella Stewart Gardner Museum." *Fenway Court 1988*, 23–31. Boston: Isabella Stewart Gardner Museum, 1989.

Zucker, Mark, ed. *The Illustrated Bartsch 24 Commentary: Early Italian Masters*. New York: Abaris, 1999.

Zupko, Ronald Edward. *Italian Weights and Measures from the Middle Ages to the Nineteenth Century*. Philadelphia: American Philosophical Society, 1981.

Bibliography

CONTRIBUTORS

KAREN-EDIS BARZMAN is a Scholar in Residence at the Newberry Library. She has published on a range of topics, including monographs on the Florentine Accademia del Disegno (2000) and tropes of dismemberment and decapitation in Venetian cultural production defining identity at the edges of Venetian rule (2017). Over the past fifteen years her research has shifted to practices of mapping. Her current book project focuses on the first analog geographic information system (GIS): an early modern collection of works on paper that made knowledge of place shareable at a glance, at multiple scales, and in portable formats. *Government Mapping in Early Modern Venice* documents how the Venetian state established this precedent in information technology by calling for visualizations of accurate quantitative and qualitative geospatial data in "nested" layers with directional indicators and metadata in text, to aid in the management of its sprawling empire.

ANDREA BELLIENI, an architect and presently director of the Correr Museum and Library and Venice Clocktower, began his early career with the restoration of historical buildings. His work in museums started when he won the public competition for conservator of the Civic Museums of Treviso in 2003, contributing to the opening and installation of the Museum of Santa Caterina. In 2008 he began working in the Civic Museums of Venice, where he has curated and hosted a range of exhibitions. He is currently coordinating the long-term, critical reorganization and display of the Correr Museum's permanent collections, including the restoration of the Galleria Napoleonica and the Royal Apartments, among others. His scholarly contributions include numerous articles and publications on art, architecture, and the decorative arts; the recovery and cataloging of the collection of ceramics (thirteenth through nineteenth centuries) of the Civic Museums of Treviso; and the rediscovery and reconstruction of the thirteenth-century portal of the Cathedral of Treviso.

PATRICIA FORTINI BROWN is professor emerita at Princeton University, where she taught in the Department of Art and Archaeology (1983–2010) and served as chair (1999–2005). Brown was Slade Professor of Fine Arts at the University of Cambridge and served as president of the Renaissance Society of America. A recipient of the British Academy Serena Medal in Italian Studies and the Paul Oscar Kristeller Lifetime Achievement Award from the Renaissance Society of America, she is a trustee of Save Venice and has held prestigious fellowships, including a Guggenheim Fellowship and the Rome Prize. Brown's award-winning books include *Venetian Narrative Painting in the Age of Carpaccio* (1988); *Venice and Antiquity: The Venetian Sense of the Past* (1996); *Art and Life in Renaissance Venice* (1997); *Private Lives in Renaissance Venice: Art, Architecture, and the Family* (2004); and *The Venetian Bride: Bloodlines and Blood Feuds in Venice and Its Empire* (2021).

VALERIA CAFÀ is a historian of architecture, with a specialization in prints and drawings and the rediscovery of antiquity. She is presently curator at the Correr Museum, Fondazione Musei Civici di Venezia, a position she has held since 2014. In 2010–12, she was the recipient of an Andrew W. Mellon Postdoctoral Curatorial Fellowship in the role of research assistant at the Metropolitan Museum of Art, New York, where she cocurated an exhibition on Fabergé and collaborated with the team of conservators and scholars involved in the restoration of *Adam* by Tullio Lombardo. In 2006, she won the James Ackerman Award in the History of Architecture with her doctoral dissertation (published 2007) on the Palazzo Massimo alle Colonne by Baldassarre Peruzzi. She has collaborated with Cisa Palladio of Vicenza in the production of exhibitions and publications, and she continues to research drawings reflecting Antiquity as well as modern and contemporary sculpture.

STANLEY CHOJNACKI received his PhD from the University of California, Berkeley, where he studied under Gene Brucker and William Bouwsma. From 1967 to 1994, he taught at Michigan State University before moving to the University of North Carolina at Chapel Hill, where he taught until his retirement as professor emeritus in 2005. Supported by grants from the National Endowment for the Humanities, the John Simon Guggenheim Foundation, the Institute for Advanced Study, and the National Humanities Center, his research has focused on Venetian patrician society in the fourteenth through sixteenth centuries, with a special focus on the family and the role of women. His essays have appeared in many publications, and twelve of them are collected in the volume *Women and Men in Renaissance Venice* (2000).

TRACY E. COOPER is professor of art history at the Tyler School of Art and Architecture, Temple University. She is a member of the board of directors of Save Venice, Inc., the leading American nonprofit organization dedicated to preserving the artistic heritage of Venice, for which she is director of the research track of the Women Artists in Venice (WAV) program. Tracy's current project, "The Subversive Arts of Arachne: *Tele e Merletto*," was recently presented to the European Seminar at the Renaissance Center of Newberry Library in Chicago. She is best-known for *Palladio's Venice: Architecture and Society in a Renaissance Republic* (2006), which won the Phyllis Goodhart Gordan Prize from the Renaissance Society of America. She is editing a forthcoming volume of contributed essays, *Women Artists and Artisans in Venice and the Veneto, 1400–1750: Uncovering the Female Presence.*

GIADA DAMEN completed her PhD in art history at Princeton University under the guidance of Patricia Fortini Brown, where her research culminated in a dissertation titled *The Trade in Antiquities between Italy and the Eastern Mediterranean ca. 1400–1600*. After working for six years at the Morgan Library & Museum in New York, Giada joined Christie's in 2020, where she is associate specialist in the Department of Old Master Drawings. She has published both in English and Italian on a variety of topics dealing with early modern Italian art and collecting. She has been the recipient of international grants and fellowships from the Gladys Krieble Delmas Foundation, the Metropolitan Museum of Art, the Renaissance Society of America, and the Francis Haskell Memorial Fund.

JULIA A. DELANCEY is professor of art history at the University of Mary Washington. Her archival scholarship has dealt with artists' coloring materials and with the individuals who imported, exported, manufactured, bought, and sold those same materials. Her research on the specialist Venetian *vendecolori* (color sellers) has examined their place in the city's urban fabric and the impact their trade had on issues of social status. More recent projects explore the history of disabilities in early modern Venice, focusing especially on mental health and blindness. Her research has been supported by organizations such as the National Endowment for the Humanities, the Renaissance Society of America, Istituto Nazionale di Studi sul Rinascimento, and the Gladys Krieble Delmas Foundation.

PIERO FALCHETTA worked at the Marciana National Library in Venice as head of the map department until June 2015. He is a historian of cartography and has written books and articles on Fra Mauro's world map, Jacopo de' Barbari's *View of Venice*, medieval nautical cartography, Bartolomeo da li Sonetti, Battista Agnese, and the cartography of the Arabian peninsula, among other topics. He has also written about navigation, including Benedetto Cotrugli's treatise *De navigatione* and Michele da Rodi's nautical manuscript, as well as on voyages like Nicolò Manuzzi's *Storia do Mogor*. He is a member of the Deputazione Veneta di Storia Patria and of the Ateneo Veneto (historical scholarly institutions) and serves as a referee for the journal *e-Perimetron* and as a columnist for the collector's journal *Charta*.

LUDOVICA GALEAZZO is associate professor of architectural history in the Department of Cultural Heritage at the University of Padua. Her research focuses on Venetian architecture in the early modern period, with a special interest in using new technologies to demonstrate a city's change over time. She received her PhD from the Graduate School Ca' Foscari-Iuav in Venice and was later a Research Fellow at Iuav University

(2013–16), a Postdoctoral Associate at Duke University (2016–17), and a Digital Humanities Research Associate at I Tatti, the Harvard University Center for Italian Renaissance Studies (2019–22). She is a member of the international project *Visualizing Venice / Visualizing Cities* and serves on the editorial board of the *Architectural Histories* journal (EAHN). She is the author of *Venezia e i margini urbani: L'insula dei Gesuiti in età moderna* (2018) and is currently the principal investigator of the European Research Council–awarded project *Venice's Nissology: Reframing the Lagoon City as an Archipelago* (VeNiss).

JONATHAN GLIXON is professor emeritus of musicology, and formerly University Research Professor, and Provost's Distinguished Service Professor at the University of Kentucky. He has received grants from the National Endowment for the Humanities (Fellowships in 1997–98 and 2004–5), the Gladys Krieble Delmas Foundation (most recently for 2018–19), the American Council of Learned Societies, and the American Philosophical Society. He has presented papers at numerous conferences, including several in Italy, England, and Canada, and has published the results of his work in such journals as the *Journal of the American Musicological Society*, the *Journal of Musicology*, and *Music and Letters*, and in other English, Italian, and Australian publications. He has published three books: *Honoring God and the*

City: Music at the Venetian Confraternities, 1260–1807 (2003); *Inventing the Business of Opera: The Impresario and His World in Seventeenth-Century Venice* (coauthored with Beth Glixon, 2005); and *Mirrors of Heaven or Worldly Theaters? Venetian Nunneries and Their Music* (2017).

RICHARD GOY has been a practicing architect in London for over forty years, until his recent retirement. Much of his work has been in the field of conservation and restoration. More recently he has served as a consultant for the master planning of a number of large acute hospitals in the United Kingdom. Parallel to this professional career, Richard has also pursued an academic path and, following several years of research, was awarded a doctorate at University College London. He has written and lectured extensively on the urban history and architecture of Venice and its lagoon, particularly the city's "minor architecture" and that of the early Renaissance, and has written a monograph on the Ca' d'Oro. He has also published architectural guides to both Venice and Florence. He is currently working on a similar guide to Sicily and is also engaged in a major reevaluation of later Venetian Gothic palazzi.

ANNA CHRISTINE SWARTWOOD HOUSE is associate professor of art history and director of undergraduate studies in the School of Visual Art and Design at the University of South Carolina. Her research focuses on Re-naissance cross-culturalisms, artists' biographies, and the reception of art. Her book *Antonello da Messina and the History of Art*, which was supported by a Samuel H. Kress Fellowship in Art History from the Renaissance Society of America, is forthcoming. Research for her second book, on the frescoed façade in Cinquecento Venice and the Veneto, is supported by the Gladys Krieble Delmas Foundation, which awarded her the Henry A. Millon Award in Art and Architectural History. She serves on the executive board of the NEH-sponsored *Digital Piranesi*, an enhanced digital edition and translation of Giovanni Battista Piranesi's *Opere*. She received her PhD in art history from Princeton University.

KRISTIN LOVE HUFFMAN is an art and architectural historian of the early modern world. Her scholarship focuses primarily on the material and visual culture of Renaissance Venice, and she is known for her work on architectural spaces and urban systems, printed bird's-eye and cartographic representations of Venice, transcultural exchanges of visual knowledge, and digital art history. She has curated interactive exhibitions that include *A Portrait of Venice: Jacopo de' Barbari's View of 1500* (2017) and *Senses of Venice* (2019). Her scholarship has been awarded grants and fellowships by the National Endowment for the Humanities, the Samuel H. Kress Foundation, the Gladys Krieble Delmas Foundation, the Furthermore Foundation, and the

Center for the Advanced Study of Visual Arts. Select publications feature her methods of combining traditional art history (archival work and on-site visual analyses) with digital tools that enhance critical looking and discovery, and her most recent work evaluates spatial systems of Renaissance Venice and intended yet often lost meanings.

HOLLY HURLBURT is the author of two books on women, gender, politics, and the state in late medieval and early modern Venice and the Mediterranean: *Daughter of Venice: Caterina Corner, Queen of Cyprus and Woman of the Renaissance* (2006) and *The Dogaressa of Venice, 1200–1500: Wife and Icon* (2015). She has received grants and fellowships from the American Historical Association; the Gladys Krieble Delmas Foundation; Villa I Tatti, the Harvard University Center for Italian Renaissance Studies; the Renaissance Society of America; and the Newberry Library. Her current work focuses on notions of exile in the wider Mediterranean. She is currently professor of history and assistant dean and executive director of Academic Enrichment Programming in University College at NC State University.

CLAIRE JUDDE DE LARIVIÈRE is professor of medieval history at the University of Toulouse. She studies the history of late medieval and early modern Venice, especially the social and politi-

cal life of the Venetian *popolo*. She has published several articles and books on the topic, among them *The Revolt of Snowballs: Murano Confronts Venice, 1511* (2018) and *L'ordinaire des savoirs: Une histoire pragmatique de la société vénitienne (XVᵉ–XVIᵉ siècle)* (2023). She has recently coedited, with Maartje van Gelder, *Popular Politics in an Aristocratic Republic: Political Conflict and Social Contestation in Late Medieval and Early Modern Venice (Venice, 13th–18th Century)* (2020) and is currently embarking on a new research project on waste management and pollution in Renaissance Venice.

BLAKE DE MARIA received her undergraduate degree from UCLA, where she specialized in Islamic art, and then earned her PhD from Princeton University. She holds the Harold and Edythe Toso Chair at Santa Clara University, where she teaches a wide variety of courses on early modern Mediterranean visual culture. Her publications include *Becoming Venetian: Immigrants and the Arts in Early Modern Venice* (2010) and *Reflections on Renaissance Venice: Essays in Honor of Patricia Fortini Brown*; the latter received the Gladys Krieble Delmas Award from the Renaissance Society of America. She has also published essays on the Oracles of Leo the Wise and the material culture of dining in early modern Venice. A forthcoming publication includes her two-volume reference guide *All Things Renaissance*.

MARTINA MASSARO is an art and architectural historian. Following the completion of her PhD in 2015 in Venice, she served as a Research Fellow at the University Iuav of Venice until 2016; since 2017 she has been a Research Fellow at the ICEA Department (Civil, Environmental and Architectural Engineering) at the University of Padua. She has continued her active involvement in *Visualizing Venice / Visualizing Cities* since 2013. Her research interests include the study of patrons and collectors during the eighteenth and nineteenth centuries, with a particular interest in Jewish patronage and its significance to Venetian social and economic history, and she has published extensively in journals and books and presented her work at international conferences in the fields of art, architectural, and urban history. She served as assistant curator of *Venice, the Jews, and Europe: 1516–2016*, hosted in the Ducal Palace of Venice (June–November 2016) and dedicated to the five hundredth anniversary of the Ghetto's foundation.

COSIMO MONTELEONE is associate professor of descriptive geometry and the digital representation of architecture at the Università degli Studi di Padova in Italy. In 2003 he obtained his degree in architecture at the University Iuav of Venice, where he also earned his PhD in 2010 with his study on the Guggenheim Museum by Frank Lloyd Wright, later published as a book: *Frank Lloyd Wright: Geometria e astrazione nel Guggenheim Museum* (2013). His current research focuses on architectural, urban, and landscape survey; 3D modeling of architecture and urban environments; augmented and virtual reality; gnomonics; science and technique applied to art and architecture; and the history of representation. He has directed digital installations for national and international exhibitions, and his most recent books include a monograph on the polymath Daniele Barbaro and his treatise: *Daniele Barbaro's Perspective of 1568* (2021) and *La prospettiva di Daniele Barbaro: Note critiche e trascrizione del manoscritto It. IV, 36=5446* (2020).

MONIQUE O'CONNELL is professor of history and chair of the History Department at Wake Forest University, where she holds the James P. Barefield Endowed Faculty Fellowship. Her scholarly work focuses on the history of Renaissance Venice and its empire, a topic that has taken her into the details of economic exchange, early print culture, political communication, classicizing rhetoric, clerical conspiracies, and the history of botany. Her first book, *Men of Empire: Power and Negotiation in Venice's Maritime State* (2009), placed Venice's overseas holdings into the larger debate on early modern empires and state formation, offering a new reading of how Venice successfully administered a wide swath of diverse territory for hundreds of years. Her second book, coauthored with Eric Dursteler, is titled *The Mediterranean World: From the Fall of Rome to the Rise of Napoleon* (2016). She is currently the project editor of Rulers of Venice (rulersofvenice.org).

MARY PARDO, former faculty of the Department of Art and Art History at the University of North Carolina in Chapel Hill, earned her doctorate at the University of Pittsburgh with a concentration on art criticism and theory of the Italian Renaissance. Throughout her career, she has been intrigued by word and image relationships, a theme that has influenced many of her academic projects. Her current research continues to focus on vernacular art writing's engagement with classical literary theory and on art that redefined the boundary between the tangible and the intangible. In her publications, she has explored facets of Venetian art and culture and has made scholarly contributions related to the artistic contributions of Giotto, Leonardo da Vinci, Giovanni Bellini, Savoldo, and Titian.

GIORGIO TAGLIAFERRO (PhD Venice, Ca' Foscari) is associate professor in Renaissance art at the University of Warwick. He specializes in Renaissance and early modern European art, with a focus on Venice. His research areas include visual arts and the display of power; painting and representation; drawing and the creative process; art-

ists' workshops; and the art market. He is principal author of the book *Le botteghe di Tiziano* (Alinari, 2009), which stemmed from a research project funded by the Fondazione Centro Studi Tiziano e Cadore (2004–9), and was a coeditor of the volume *Jacopo Tintoretto: Identity, Practice, Meaning* (Viella, 2022). He has been a scholar in residence at the Getty Research Institute (2012) and has received a British Academy Small Grant (2015–16) and a Leverhulme Research Fellowship (2016–17). He is currently working on a monograph related to the sixteenth-century pictorial cycles in the Doge's Palace, Venice.

MAARTJE VAN GELDER is associate professor of early modern history at the University of Amsterdam. She is interested in early modern politics, urban revolts, and the politics of collective forgetting. She has held research fellowships at the Institute for Advanced Study in Princeton (2019), the Netherlands Institute for Advanced Study (2018), and the Italian Academy for Advanced Study in New York (2013) and visiting appointments at Columbia University (2013) and Birkbeck (2011). Her book *Trading Places* (2009) examines how Dutch merchants connected the Mediterranean and Atlantic commercial worlds, thereby permanently changing the Venetian economy. She coedited a volume on Venetian popular politics with Claire Judde de Larivière and is currently working on a book arguing that collective contestation formed a fundamental dimension of Venetian politics, a fact that was systematically erased from state archives and thus from history. Parts of the project have appeared as articles in the *Journal of Modern History* and *Past and Present*.

SAUNDRA WEDDLE is professor of architectural and urban history and theory at the Hammons School of Architecture at Drury University. Her scholarship focuses on gender and architecture in early modern Italian cities. She has published widely on convents in Florence and Venice, including the edited and annotated translation of the *Chronicle of Le Murate* (2011) and the coedited volume *Convent Networks in Early Modern Italy* (2020). Her current research uses mapping to analyze the sex trade's place-based social and commercial networks, deepening understandings of how the city's built fabric framed the experiences and interactions of urban dwellers. Research for the book has been supported by the National Humanities Center, the Clark Art Institute, the National Endowment for the Humanities, the Gladys Krieble Delmas Foundation, the Samuel H. Kress Foundation, and an Andrew Mellon Foundation–Divided Cities grant from Washington University in Saint Louis.

BRONWEN WILSON is professor of early modern art history, Edward W. Carter Chair in European Art, and director of the Center for 17th- and 18th-Century Studies at UCLA. She has published on print, cartography, costume, and portraiture and coedited several volumes. She writes on the history of Venetian art, the subject of her book *The World in Venice: Print, the City, and Early Modern Identity* (winner of the Roland H. Bainton Prize for Art History in 2006), and has published several articles on European images of Ottoman Turks and Turkish costume. A recently completed book, *The Face of Uncertainty*, turns to increasing doubt about the trustworthiness of the human face and accompanying artistic experimentation with physiognomy, animals, and sensation in northern Italy. She also coedited, with Angela Vanhaelen, *Making Worlds: Global Invention in the Early Modern Period*, essays from the Clark Library series of conferences (2022).

RANGSOOK YOON is an art historian and curator. A native Korean, she earned her PhD in art history from the Institute of Fine Arts, New York University, specializing in Renaissance and Baroque art. Her scholarly publications on the work of Albrecht Dürer include "Dürer's First Journey to Venice: Revisiting and Reframing the Old Question," in *New Studies on Old Masters* (2011), and "Dürer's *Unterweysung der Messung* and the Geometric Construction of Alphabets," in *Visual Culture and Mathematics in the Early Modern Period* (2017). She has contributed numerous essays to exhibition and collection catalogs and scholarly lexica and has curated over thirty exhibitions, such as *Allure of Ancient Rome* (2014) and *Fashionable Portraits in Europe* (2015). One of the ten international curators selected by the Association of Art Museum Curators for its 2021–22 Mentorship program, she is currently senior curator at the Sarasota Art Museum in Florida.

INDEX

devotional images and practices, 14–15, 70–71, 199–200, 207–8

Dewey, John, 65

Diana, Benedetto, *68*

diary writing, 91–92. *See also individual diarists*

digital humanities, xxiv, 19–20, 308, 310

di Mutti family, 264, 274

distortions, 27n7, 42, 44–45, 47n7, 58, 174n17. *See also* perspective

district (*sestiere*). *See* Cannaregio (district of); Castello (district of); Dorsoduro (district of); San Marco (district of); San Polo (district of); Santa Croce (district of)

doge: bucintoro of, 228, 232, 321, 324; ceremony and, 196, 218, 227, 230, 267, 286, 289; churches and, 228, 318; dogaressa as wife of, 229–30, 335; as head of Republic, 82, 298; representations of, 318–19. *See also* Ducal Palace (Palazzo Ducale, Doge's Palace); Republic (Venetian state)

Dolfin, Pietro, 91

Dolomites, 79, 125. *See also* mountains

Domenico di Piero, 17, 250–57

Dominicans, 14, 199–200, 203, 206, 218, 221. *See also* convents; Corpus Domini; monasteries and monastic life; Santi Giovanni e Paolo

Dorigo, Wladimiro, 201

Dorsoduro (district of), 174n18, 241, 276

Dover, 79

dowries, 231, 239, 241–44, 246–47, 252, 279. *See also* marriage; women

drawings: by Dürer, 80, 84n19; as graphic art, 119, 129, 153–54; maps, 29, 31–32, 34, 35, 41–42, 118n19; of religious complexes, 204, *205*, 216, 217, 219, 221; of Venice, 41–42, 55–57, 62, 302, 309

Ducal Palace (Palazzo Ducale, Doge's Palace): representation in the *View of Venice*, 2–3; seat of government and doge's residence, 31–32, 101, 165, 196, 215, 288–89, 318–19; staircase (Scala dei Giganti), 239; wellheads, 182, 185. *See also* St. Mark's Square

Duia, Matteo, *68*

Duia, Pietro, *68*

Dürer, Albrecht: Apollo (depictions of), 150; attribution to the *View of Venice*, 110; de' Barbari and, 11, 127, 151, 153; human proportion and, 153–54; illustrations by, 127–29; influences on, 152; letters by, 127–29, 156; nude figures of, 153–54, 158n19; on painting, 158n16; perspective (use of), 6–7, 58; pictorial space, 80–82; print culture and, 120; self-portrait of, 82; writings by, 153
—works: *Feast of the Rose Garlands*, 80, *81*, 82, 84n19; *Pastoral Landscape with Shepherds Playing a Viola and Panpipes*, 128; *View of the Arco Valley*, 80, *81*

ebony, 261

Eclogues (Virgil), 124–25

economics, 66–67, 89–90, 218–19, 239, 260–61, 265–66, 286, 300–302. *See also* banks; commerce; cosmopolitanism; globalism

Eleonora of Naples, 15

Emblematum liber (Alciati), 82

Engelbrecht, Martin, 190, *191*

Euclid, 51, 55

Eugenius IV, 210n17

Fabbriche Nuove, 299. *See also* Rialto

façades, 98; of churches, 190, 204, 230, 327; of palaces, 23, 254–55, 256, 259n26, 326–27; Scuola Grande di San Marco, 252, *253*; in St. Mark's Square, 18, 287–89, 318–19

Falchetta, Piero: chapter by, 40–49; referenced, 6, 53

invisibility and visibility, 14, 167, 178, 189, 229, 279, 285, 334–35. *See also* cistern network; women

islands, 25, 98–99, 169, 177, 315, 328; Murano, 18, 265, 289–91, *290*; Rivoaltus, 320; San Giorgio Maggiore, 15, 166, 215–16, 235n2, 315, 327–28, 332; in the *View of Venice*, 75, 176, 201–2. *See also* archipelago; Crete; Cyprus; Giudecca; Venice: *forma urbis*

Isolario (Bordone), 76, 77

itineraries: of families, 241, 309; parishes and, 63; of printing, 96–103; of Venetian territories, 78–79; of wives, 243–47

ivory, 251, 261

Jerusalem, 5, 19, 78–79, 84n9, 316, 328

jewelry, 17, 250–52, 254–55, 257, 266–67. *See also* gemstones

Jewish people, 19, 209n7, 300–303. *See also* Ghetto

Judde de Larivière, Claire: chapter by (with Maartje van Gelder), 284–94; referenced, 18, 90

Julius II, 80

Katzenellenbogen, Count Philipp von, 79

Kemp, Martin, 42

Koberger, Anton. See *Nuremberg Chronicle* (*Liber chronicarum*)

Kolb, Anton: biographic details, 43, 78, 98–99; collaboration with de' Barbari, 2, 97, 127, 129–30, 152, 274; copyright privilege, 2, 28, 36, 83n7, 108, 336–37; as financier of the *View of Venice*, 9, 48n9, 108; on measurement, 55; print materials distributed by, 98, 129; protections for the *View of Venice*, 28; will of, 338–40; in the *View of Venice*, 42–43. *See also* Fondaco dei Tedeschi

Kythira (Cerigo), 239

labor, 9, 65, 195, 284, 324

Lago Badoer, 168, 174n17

Landi, Antonio de, 234

land reclamation, 13, 31, 167–70, 203, 219–21, 264. *See also* urbanization

Lapis, Domenico de, 43

Lazari, Vincenzo, 115

leather, 261, 265, 321

Lefebvre, Henri, 64–66

Leipzig, 152

Leonardo da Vinci, 51, 58, 308

Leonor of Portugal, 230

Levenson, Jay, 132n2, 150–52

Liber chronicarum (Schedel). See *Nuremberg Chronicle* (*Liber chronicarum*)

libraries, 15, 51, 110–11

Library of St. Mark (Marciana), 51, 286, 299, 320. *See also* Bessarion, Cardinal

Licino, Arrigo, *68*

Licino, Bernardino, *68*

Lisbon, 90

Lizzafusina, 177

Loggia dei Mercanti, 101, 266

Lombardo, Pietro, 80, 252

Longhena, Baldassare, 319

lontani (distances), 136–46

Loredan, Andrea, 89

Lorenzetti, Ambrogio, 77

Lorenzo de' Monacis, 213

Lotto, Lorenzo, 120

Lowry, Martin, 97

Lucchesi, 299

Lucretius, *De rerum natura*, 124

Lusignan, Jacques, II, 232

luxury goods, 7, 16–17, 87, 231, 260–70, 321. *See also* commerce

Magazzini del Sal di San Gregorio, 276

Mansueti, Giovanni, *68*

Mantegna, Andrea, 10, 120, 132n4, 133n8, 133n15, 156

IMAGE CREDITS

Plates

1 Jacopo de' Barbari, *View of Venice.* Image courtesy of Duke Digital Repository: 10.7924/G8MK69TH.

2 Detail of Piazza San Marco from *View of Venice.* Image courtesy of Duke Digital Repository: 10.7924/G8MK69TH.

3 Detail of the Customs House from *View of Venice.* Image courtesy of Duke Digital Repository: 10.7924/G8MK69TH.

4 Detail of the Rialto from *View of Venice.* Image courtesy of Duke Digital Repository: 10.7924/G8MK69TH.

5 Detail of the Mercerie from *View of Venice.* Image courtesy of Duke Digital Repository: 10.7924/G8MK69TH.

6 Detail of the Arsenal from *View of Venice.* Image courtesy of Duke Digital Repository: 10.7924/G8MK69TH.

7 Details of Mercury (*above*) and Neptune (*below*) from *View of Venice.* Image courtesy of Duke Digital Repository: 10.7924/G8MK69TH.

8 Detail of the Winds from *View of Venice.* Image courtesy of Duke Digital Repository: 10.7924/G8MK69TH.

Figures

I.1 Venice, page from the *Nuremberg Chronicle* or *Liber chronicarum.* Image courtesy of the Library of Congress, Rare Book and Special Collections Division.

I.2 Erhard Reuwich, *Civitas veneciarum,*

from *Peregrinatio in Terram Sanctam.* Image courtesy of the Library of Congress, Rare Book and Special Collections Division.

1.1 Map of the northern part of Venetian Dalmatia, including the coastal city of Zara, capital of the province, and Novigrad, the easternmost Venetian fortress near the meandering border with Ottoman Bosnia. By permission of the Archivio di Stato di Venezia.

1.2 *Appearance of the Fortress of Novigrad* (*Aspetto della fortez[z]a di Novegradi*), site drawing with unframed legend, enclosed with a dispatch dated June 5, 1620. By permission of the Archivio di Stato di Venezia.

1.3 Map of Novigrad and the arable land, hills, and waterways in its jurisdiction, enclosed with a dispatch dated October 10, 1605. By permission of the Archivio di Stato di Venezia.

2.1 Johann Schnitzner, *Ptolemaic Map.* Image courtesy of the Norman B. Leventhal Map & Education Center at the Boston Public Library.

3.1 Jacopo de' Barbari (Attributed), *Portrait of Luca Pacioli.* Photo: Scala / Ministero per i Beni e le Attività culturali / Art Resource, NY.

3.2 Leon Battista Alberti's section of the visual pyramid that demonstrates the impossibility of finding the eye of the observer or the shape of the survey of Venice, starting from the perspectival view. Image: Cosimo Monteleone.

3.3 Piero della Francesca's perspective of a head (*De prospectiva pingendi,* 91v, mss. Regg. A 41/2, Reggio Emilia [IT], Biblioteca Panizzi) and *costruzione legittima* applied to a survey of Venice to obtain its perspectival view. Image: Cosimo Monteleone.

3.4 Adaptation of Albrecht Dürer's engraving of Alberti's veil (ca. 1525) applied to a survey of Venice to obtain its perspectival view. Image: Cosimo Monteleone.

4.1 Detail with select artists' residences ca. 1450–1530, from the *View of Venice.* Image: Hannah Jacobs.

4.2 Detail of the interconnected spaces related to Vincenzo Catena, from the *View of Venice*: from left to right, Campo San Bartolomeo, Campo San Lio, and Campo Santa Maria Formosa. Image: Hannah Jacobs.

4.3 Vincenzo Catena, *Virgin and Child with Saint John the Baptist.* By permission of the National Museum of Western Art, Tokyo, Japan. Photo: NMWA/DNPartcom.

5.1 Venice, from Benedetto Bordone, *Isolario di Benedetto Bordone* (Venice: Nicolo d'Aristotile, 1534), 2:XXX. Image courtesy of David Rumsey Map Center at Stanford University.

5.2 Detail of cities along the mountainous border from the *View of Venice.* Image courtesy of Duke Digital Repository: 10.7924/G8MK69TH.

13.1 Detail of Campo San Giacomo dall'Orio from the *View of Venice*. Image courtesy of Duke Digital Repository: 10.7924/G8MK69TH.

13.2 Wellhead, fourteenth century, in Campo San Giacomo dall'Orio. Photo: Patricia Fortini Brown.

13.3 Wellhead, Veneto-Byzantine, ninth century, originally in Murano. By permission of © Victoria & Albert Museum, London.

13.4 Detail of Campo Do Pozzi, district (*sestiere*) of Castello, from the *View of Venice*. Image courtesy of Duke Digital Repository: 10.7924/G8MK69TH.

13.5 Wellhead in Campo dei Do Pozzi, Castello. Photo: Patricia Fortini Brown.

14.1 Johan Georg Ringlin after Friedrich Bernhard Werner, *Venetia/Venedig*. Image courtesy of Geographicus Rare Antique Maps.

15.1 Detail of Corpus Domini (*upper left*) and Santa Lucia (*upper center*) from the *View of Venice*. Image courtesy of Duke Digital Repository: 10.7924/G8MK 69TH.

15.2 Detail of the convents of San Zaccaria (*lower left*) and San Lorenzo (*upper right*) from the *View of Venice*. Image courtesy of Duke Digital Repository: 10.7924/G8MK69TH.

15.3 Plan, Corpus Domini, Venice. By permission of the Archivio di Stato di Venezia.

16.1 Detail of the island of San Giorgio Maggiore, with colorization of the gardens, from the *View of Venice*. Image: Hannah Jacobs.

16.2 Orchards and gardens belonging to the monastery of San Domenico di Castello. By permission of the Archivio di Stato di Venezia.

16.3 Detail of the *chiovere* of San Pantalon from the *View of Venice*. Image courtesy of Duke Digital Repository: 10.7924/G8MK69TH.

16.4 Map of the convent of Santa Croce in the Giudecca with places for rearing hens. By permission of the Archivio di Stato di Venezia.

16.5 Detail of the area between San Domenico and Sant'Antonio di Castello, with colorization of the lagoon, from the *View of Venice*. Image: Hannah Jacobs.

17.1 Gentile Bellini, *Miracle of the Cross at the Bridge of San Lorenzo*. By permission of © Gallerie dell'Accademia di Venezia / su concessione del Ministro della Cultura. Photo: Scala / Ministero per i Beni Culturali e Attività culturali / Art Resource, NY.

17.2 *Translatio of the Body of Saint Mark*, Porta Sant'Alipio, Church of San Marco, Venice. Photo: Erich Lessing / Art Resource, NY.

18.1 Residential stability among families: details from the *View of Venice*. Image: Kristin Love Huffman.

18.2 Residential mobility with the Vitturi family: details from the *View of Venice*. Image: Kristin Love Huffman.

18.3 Residential mobility with Cateruzza Vitturi: details from the *View of Venice*. Image: Hannah Jacobs.

19.1 Scuola Grande di San Marco from the *View of Venice*. Image courtesy of Duke Digital Repository: 10.7924/G8MK69TH.

19.2 Façade of the Scuola Grande di San Marco, Venice. Photo: Giada Damen.

19.3 Façade of Palazzo Contarini Polignac, Venice. Photo: Giada Damen.

19.4 Detail of the zone around the Carità from the *View of Venice*. Image courtesy of Duke Digital Repository: 10.7924/G8MK69TH.

20.1 Giorgione, *The Tempest*. By permission of © Gallerie dell'Accademia di Venezia / su concessione del Ministro della Cultura. Photo: Scala / Ministero per i Beni Culturali e Attività culturali / Art Resource, NY.

20.2 Jacopo de' Barbari (Attributed), *Portrait of a Man* (obverse), *Couple* (reverse). Photo: bpk Bildagentur / Gemäldegalerie, Staatliche Museen, Berlin / Joerg P. Anders / Art Resource, NY.

20.3 Detail of Cannaregio from the *View of Venice*. Image courtesy of Duke Digital Repository: 10.7924/G8MK69TH.

20.4 Pinturicchio, *Resurrection with Alexander VI*. Photo: Scala / Art Resource, NY.

20.5 Detail of Indigenous people from Pinturicchio, *Resurrection with Alexander VI*. Photo: Scala / Art Resource, NY.

21.1 Detail of the passageways into Venice from the Bacino up to the Rialto, then up to the Fondamente Nove, from the *View of Venice*. Image: Hannah Jacobs.

21.2 Detail of Campo San Bartolomeo with the color sellers' shops highlighted, from the *View of Venice*. Image: Hannah Jacobs.

22.1 Detail of Murano from the *View of Venice*. Image courtesy of Duke Digital Repository: 10.7924/G8MK69TH.

23.1 Gentile Bellini, *Procession in St. Mark's Square*. By permission of © Gallerie dell'Accademia di Venezia / su concessione del Ministro della Cultura.

23.2 Lazzaro Bastiani, *The Piazzetta of St. Mark's Square*. By permission of Museo Correr, Venice.

A1.1 Vittore Carpaccio, *Miracle of the Relic of the Holy Cross at the Rialto Bridge*. By permission of © Gallerie dell'Accademia di Venezia / su concessione del Ministro della Cultura.

A1.2 Detail of the Ca' d'Oro, with colorization, from the *View of Venice*. Image: Hannah Jacobs.

A1.3 Detail of Santa Maria Gloriosa dei Frari, with colorization, from the *View of Venice*. Image: Hannah Jacobs.

Image Credits

414